Historical and Contemporary Issues of Democracy, Person and Human Rights

Ius, Lex et Res Publica
Studies in Law, Philosophy and Political Cultures

Edited by Barbara Janusz-Pohl

Volume 41

Ewa Dawidziuk / Anna Tarwacka / Sławomir Kursa (eds.)

Historical and Contemporary Issues of Democracy, Person and Human Rights

PETER LANG

Berlin · Bruxelles · Chennai · Lausanne · New York · Oxford

Bibliographic Information published by the Deutsche Nationalbibliothek
The Deutsche Nationalbibliothek lists this publication in the Deutsche Nationalbibliografie; detailed bibliographic data is available online at
http://dnb.d-nb.de.

Library of Congress Cataloging-in-Publication Data
Names: Dawidziuk, Ewa, editor. | Kursa, Slawomir editor. | Tarwacka, Anna editor. | Lazaro Guillamon, Carmen editor. | Montanana Casani, Amparo editor.
Title: Historical and contemporary issues of democracy, person, and human rights / editors, Ewa Dawidziuk, Slawomir Kursa, Anna Tarwacka, Carmen Lazaro Guillamon, Amparo Montanana Casani.
Description: New York : Peter Lang, 2025. |
Series: Ius, lex et res publica, 2191-3250 ; 41 |
Includes bibliographical references.
Identifiers: LCCN 2025020141 (print) | LCCN 2025020142 (ebook) | ISBN 9783631928349 (hardback) | ISBN 9783631928356 (pdf) | ISBN 9783631940631 (epub)
Subjects: LCSH: Rule of law. | Civil rights. | Persons (Law) | Democracy. | Freedom of information.
Classification: LCC K3171 .H57 2025 (print) | LCC K3171 (ebook) | DDC 340/.11--dc23/eng/20250424
LC record available at https://lccn.loc.gov/2025020141
LC ebook record available at https://lccn.loc.gov/2025020142

Cover illustration: Courtesy of Benjamin Ben Chaim.

This publication was financially supported by the Faculty of Law of the SWPS University as well as by the Cardinal Stefan Wyszynski University in Warsaw.

SWPS University

ISSN 2191-3250
ISBN 978-3-631-92834-9 (Print)
E-ISBN 978-3-631-92835-6 (E-PDF)
E-ISBN 978-3-631-94063-1 (E-PUB)
DOI 10.3726/b23045

Published by Peter Lang GmbH, Berlin (Germany)
info@peterlang.com

This publication has been peer reviewed.

www.peterlang.com

Table of Contents

Chapter IV. Human rights in a democratic state

Chapter V. Access to information in a democratic state

Chapter I.
Democracy in Ancient Rome

Anna Tarwacka[1]

The missing pieces. Elements of control in the puzzle of the Roman Republic*

Abstract: This article deals with the policy of the Roman Republic, and in particular with the elements of control that were supposed to guarantee stability. One such element was the office of the plebeian tribune, whose powers were of a blocking nature: he had veto power over the decisions of other officials, the popular assemblies and the senate. The office of censor was the second element of control. These magistrates could influence the composition of the assemblies, the senate and the army, as well as the political careers of individuals. The most important instrument of control was the censorial mark, which was a means of social degradation and loss of good name.

Keywords: Roman Republic, censorship, *nota censoria*, censorial mark, plebeian tribune

The Republican system in ancient Rome was an extremely precise mechanism. Elements worked perfectly together but could also inhibit each other. Its analysis is not an easy task. We owe the classical theory of political systems to Aristotle,[2] who in the *Politics* divided them according to two criteria: the number of people in power (one person, a small group or a large group) and in whose interest power was exercised. In the latter case, he distinguished between correct and deviant constitutions. Among the former, he listed monarchy (rule by an individual), aristocracy (rule by a minority) and polity (rule by the majority), while the latter included tyranny, oligarchy and democracy respectively. The difference between the two was to be determined by whose interest the power was exercised: if it was in the interest of the general public, it was a correct constitution, and if it was in the interest of the ruler, it was a deviant one. According to this classification, the system of Republican Rome is of a mixed nature, somewhat similar to that of Sparta described by Aristotle.

---

1 Cardinal Stefan Wyszynski University in Warsaw, ORCID: 0000-0002-6171-4117.

* The article is a result of the project 2018/29/B/HS5/00949 financed by the National Science Centre, Poland.

2 Arist., *Polit.* 3,1279a-b. Cf. K. Inamura, *Justice and Reciprocity in Aristotle's Political Philosophy*, Cambridge 2015, p. 48 ff.

The analysis of the Republican system was carried out by Polybius, the historian and author of the *Histories*, who was a hostage in Rome and knew it from the inside. At the same time, as an outsider, he had an interesting point of view, because the way the Republic worked did not seem natural to him, and this makes his analysis an invaluable source of knowledge for us.

According to Polybius,[3] the entire Republican system consisted of three elements: the monarchical, represented by the power of the consuls; the oligarchical, represented by the power of the senate; and the democratic, represented by the power of the people. These elements worked together supporting, controlling and inhibiting each other, ensuring that none could take the upper hand over the others. It was the balance that was to constitute the superiority of this form of system over the others.

In describing the tasks of the consuls, Polybius made a clear distinction between their powers in the city and those in warfare.[4] In Rome, almost all the officials were subordinate to the consuls; only the plebeian tribunes could veto their decisions. In the senate, it was the consuls who brought important matters for debate and then dealt with the execution of resolutions. The same was true in the assemblies. In wartime, on the other hand, the consuls were in charge of recruiting the army, and could demand troops from the allies. They were allowed to apply all kinds of punishments to soldiers, without any possibility of appeal, i.e. *provocatio*. The claim by Polybius that a consul could take any sums from the treasury through a quaestor is highly questionable in interpretation. Polybius seems to have heard of such a case during the consulship of Scipio Africanus and regarded it as a rule.[5]

In discussing the powers of the senate, Polybius mentioned the management of the state treasury and the direction of foreign policy, in particular the reception and sending of envoys. This last function caused many foreigners to regard Rome as an aristocratic state, as they had to deal only with the senate and its legates. It is worth mentioning here a story from 168 BC, whose protagonist was C. Popillius Laenas sent to Egypt as legate on behalf of the senate.[6] The reason for his mission

---

3 Polyb. 6,11. Cf. A. Lintott, *The Constitution of the Roman Republic*, Oxford 1999, pp. 16-26; J.A. North, *The Constitution of the Roman Republic*, [in:] *A Companion to the Roman Republic*, eds. N. Rosenstein, R. Morstein-Marx, Malden (USA) 2006, pp. 269-270.

4 Cf. H. Beck, *Consular power and the Roman constitution: the case of 'imperium' reconsidered*, [in:] *Consuls and Res Publica. Holding High Office in the Roman Republic*, eds. H. Beck, A. Duplá, M. Jehne, F. Pina Polo, Cambridge 2011, pp. 78 ff.

5 Polyb. 6,12,8; cf. A. Lintott, *The Constitution...*, p. 17.

6 Cf. T.R.S. Broughton, *The Magistrates of the Roman Republic*, vol. I, Atlanta 1951 (reprint 1986), p. 430.

was the invasion of the Ptolemaic kingdom by Antiochus IV Epiphanes, ruler of the Seleucid empire. This episode was described by Valerius Maximus,[7] a fan of anecdotes. Popillius, having met Antiochus, did not accept his outstretched hand, but handed him a tablet bearing a resolution of the senate ordering his army to withdraw from Egypt. When the king expressed his wish to consult his friends, Popillius drew a circle on the ground around Antiochus and said that he would only be allowed to leave it when he had given his answer to the senate. Only when Antiochus declared that he would withdraw from Egypt did Popillius shake his hand as an ally of the Roman people. According to Valerius Maximus, the legate in this case epitomised the curia of the senate itself. He was dignified, resolute and - even though he was talking to the king - put himself in the position of a sovereign who could not tolerate opposition. This anecdote perfectly illustrates the tendency of foreigners to view Rome through the prism of the power of the senate and its legates.

The people, according to Polybius' account, decided rewards and punishments: they could pass death sentences, try former officials and elect to office. Besides, it was the assemblies that passed laws, decided on war and peace and ratified alliances. In conclusion, the author stated that the success of the Republic as a political form was determined primarily by the balance between its components.

Analysing the rules of the Roman Republic is not an easy research problem. The formation of these rules took place in the first decades of the Republic, after the expulsion of the last of the kings, Tarquin the Proud. This period was also the time of the plebeians' struggle for equality with the patricians in political rights, which had a great impact on the future shape of the system. It was eventually established, as Polybius wrote, that power in Rome was held by officials, the senate and the popular assemblies. Rules related to running for office, or *cursus honorum* - the path of honours - were regulated in detail. These rules, initially customary

---

7 Val. Max. 6,4,3: *C. vero Popillius a senatu legatus ad Antiochum missus, ut bello se quo Ptolomaeum lacessebat, abstineret, cum ad eum venisset atque is prompto animo et amicissimo vultu dexteram ei porrexisset, invicem illi suam porrigere noluit, sed tabellas senatus consultum continentis tradidit. quas ut legit Antiochus, dixit se cum amicis conlocuturum. indignatus Popillius, quod aliquam moram interposuisset, virga solum, quo insistebat, denotavit et 'prius' inquit 'quam hoc circulo excedas da responsum, quod senatui referam'. non legatum locutum, sed ipsam curiam ante oculos positam crederes: continuo enim rex adfirmavit fore ne amplius de se Ptolomaeus quereretur, ac tum demum Popillius manum eius tamquam socii adprehendit. quam efficax est animi sermonisque abscisa gravitas! eodem momento Syriae regnum terruit, Aegypti texit.* Cf. also Cic., *Phil.* 8,8,23; Polyb. 29,27; Vell. Pat. 1,10,1-2; Liv. 45,12.

and then subject to statutory regulation with the enactment of the *lex Villia*, dealt with the order in which to apply for offices and the age required to hold them. The principles of holding office, such as collegiality, tenure, incompatibility and gratuitousness, were also observed, and restrictions were placed on the possibility of being re-elected to the same office (*iteratio*) and the obligation to take a break of at least one year after the expiry of the term before running again (*vacatio*). The senate was composed of former officials appointed by the censors entitled to perform the *lectio senatus* by virtue of *lex Ovinia*. The assemblies (*comitia centuriata, tributa* and *curiata*) were open to all citizens. The right to convene them was vested in officials endowed with the *ius agendi cum populo*. All three components of government had a great influence on each other.[8] Thus, for example: the officials were elected by the assemblies, but they in turn had the exclusive right to convene them and put legislation before them.

The picture drawn by Polybius thus consists of three essential elements which together formed the Republican system: the consuls and other magistrates, the senate and the assemblies. Power was concentrated in these three centres, which remained interdependent. This arrangement could be likened to a system of checks and balances.

However, two key elements still do not seem to have been sufficiently emphasised in Polybius' account. The period of the formation of the Republican system was determined by the struggle of the plebeians to gain political rights. The plebeians succeeded early on (494 BC after the first secession of the plebs) in establishing the office of plebeian tribune,[9] and in time also plebeian assemblies, whose powers included the passing of plebiscites. The tribunes' task was initially mainly to protect the interests of the plebeians against the abuses of patrician magistrates, but later to protect the interests of all citizens. The tribunes were given quite strong instruments for this purpose: they were inviolable (*sacrosanctitas*) and had the right to block (*ius intercedendi*) the decisions of other state bodies: magistrates except the dictator, popular assemblies, and the senate. In addition to these powers of a negative nature, they also had the ability to convene plebeian assemblies and to bring plebiscite motions,[10] which gave them the

---

8 Cf. P.A. Brunt, *The Fall of the Roman Republic*, [in] *The Fall of the Roman Republic and Related Essays*, Oxford 1998, pp. 12-23.

9 Cf. W. Kunkel, R. Wittmann, *Staatsordnung und Staatspraxis der römischen Republik. Zweiter Abschnitt. Die Magistratur*, München 1995, p. 554 ff.

10 On plebiscites cf. J. Zabłocki, *'Leges votatae' nelle assemblee popolari*, "Diritto@Storia" 10-11/2011-2012, http://www.dirittoestoria.it/10/Tradizione-Romana/Zablocki-Leges-voto-assemblee-popolari.htm.

ability to create laws. Their functions were therefore of a controlling nature, but not only. A large percentage of late-Republican legislation consisted precisely of plebiscites, which leads us to believe that the role of the tribunes was increasingly important systemically.

The other piece of this puzzle overlooked by Polybius was the office of censor.[11] This magistracy was also created in the course of the struggle of orders. The plebeians, who were initially marginalised, were already so close to gaining access to the office of consul that the patricians decided to salvage what they could. The tactic they used was to set up new offices, taking over some of the powers of the highest magistracy. The task of the censors was to take a census. According to Livy's account,[12] their role was initially rather insignificant; only later, with the acquisition of the power to control citizens' observance of ancestral customs (*mores maiorum*) and to punish with a censorial mark, did they acquire a higher rank. This opinion, however, is not convincing. The conduct of the census was also associated with the performance of a purification of the state - a sacred rite called *lustrum condere*, which ensured the Republic's prosperity for the next five years.[13] It was this honour that the patricians were by no means willing to pass on. It can therefore be thought that censorship was a dignity of great importance from its inception. The competence of the censors also points to their colossal importance for the shape of the polity. Census and the censorial mark were tools for controlling the social structure of the state. Officials could move an individual up the hierarchy, thus influencing, for example, the composition of the army, the assemblies, the senate or an individual's political career.

At the time of the census, citizens were enlisted according to property classes, centuries and *tribus*.[14] The influence of the censors on the composition of the two types of popular assemblies, the *comitia centuriata* and the *comitia tributa*, as well as the plebeian assemblies, the *concilia plebis*, which were also *tributa*,[15] was therefore undeniable. The censors reviewed the equestrian centuries as well – *recognitio equitum*. In addition, since the enactment of the *plebiscitum Ovinium*, their duties also included compiling the list of senators - *lectio senatus*.[16]

---

11 Cf. W. Kunkel, R. Wittmann, *op. cit*. pp. 391 ff.; A. Tarwacka, *Prawne aspekty urzędu cenzora w starożytnym Rzymie*, Warszawa 2012, passim.

12 Liv. 4,8.

13 Val. Max. 4,1,10.

14 Cf. Cic., *De leg*. 3,7; 3,11; 3,44.

15 Cf. J. Zablocki, *'Leges votatae'*..., pp. 40-41.

16 Cf. Fest. 290 L., s.v. *praeteriti senatores*.

Alongside these powers, a complementary competence of the censors developed, called *regimen morum*, i.e. the supervision of morality to as *mores maiorum*. The term *mores maiorum* basically means "customs of the ancestors", but a simple translation does not convey the depth of its meaning: it is not just about moral norms, but rather a whole complex of rules regulating the functioning of the state in its various aspects. Particular attention should be paid here to the fact that the Republican system was not, as a rule, regulated in written law.[17] Certain institutions were indeed specified in statutes over time, but many others remained in the realm of *mores*. For example, the *cursus honorum* was initially customary and was later consolidated in the *lex Villia* of 180 BC, but the rules for the conduct of the senate were not regulated by statute. Many Republican jurists produced works on the system, explaining these unwritten rules. We can mention, for example, Gracchanus' treatise *De potestatibus* or Tuditanus' work *Libri magistratuum*. Varro's *Antiquitates rerum humanarum et divinarum* also contained a wealth of information.

One can therefore conclude that the sphere of competence of the censors covered not only the private life of citizens, but also the political life of the state. Executing the *regimen morum*, these officials could punish a citizen with a censorial mark, degrading him socially and depriving him of his good name. The mark could result in the removal of a senator from the senate or the omission of a candidate meeting the criteria of the *lex Ovinia*, the removal of an equestrian from the horsemen's century, as well as the transfer to the *aerarii, the* lowest census group, and a change of *tribus*, which entailed a restriction of political rights.[18]

The surviving source texts make it possible to see the control activities of the censors in several spheres of political life: abuses of officials, irregularities in command posts in the army, dishonouring of office through improper behaviour.[19]

Abuses of office generally had to do with exceeding powers or failing to respect the limits of authority. A case in point is the violation of the principle of collegiality of offices by failing to take into account the *intercessio* of a colleague. The following case (based on fact) was to be argued by the young Marcus Aurelius at the request of his teacher Fronto: the tribune Marcus Lucilius imprisoned a Roman

17 Cf. J.A. North, *The Constitution…*, pp. 256 ff.

18 Cf. in more detail A. Tarwacka, *Adoption under the scrutiny of the censors in Republican Rome*, [in:] *Family, Law, and Society: from Roman Law to the Present Day*, red. E. Dawidziuk, P. Panero, A. Tarwacka, Berlin-Lausanne-Bruxelles-Chennai-New York-Oxford 2023, pp. 77 ff.

19 Cf. more extensively A. Tarwacka, *Censors as Guardians of Family and Public Life in Republican Rome*, London-New York 2025, pp. 176 ff.

citizen against the opposition of the other tribunes, for which he was punished by the censors.[20] Lucilius exercised his *ius prendendi*, but in view of the *intercessio* he should have released the citizen. The intervention of the other tribunes can be seen as a grant of *auxilium* to the citizen, which leads to the conclusion that Lucilius additionally violated one of the citizens' rights (*ius auxilii*), which led to the censorial mark.[21] Another rule that the censors guarded was the principle of tenure: censorial interventions could, for example, concern situations where an official left the post entrusted to him too early: such an accusation was made against Gaius Gracchus, who returned from the province assigned to him during the quaestorship before the governor had left.[22]

Officials had the right to use coercive measures, the extent of which correlated with their powers. The case of L. Quinctius Flaminius, who exceeded his powers by executing a convict at a banquet, which was a violation of the dignity of the office and was therefore sanctioned by a censorial mark, is very interesting in this context.[23]

The censors also paid attention to sacred issues, the most significant of which seems to be the power of magistrates to carry out auspices. Abuses in this area could also have formed the basis for the application of the *nota*.[24]

The deliberations of the senate were also controlled, and censorial sanctions were threatened against an official who allowed a resolution to pass before sunrise or after sunset.

All this leads to the recognition of the censor's powers as very broad. An additional rationale may be provided by the concept of an ideal system created by

---

20 Fronto, *Ad M. Caes.* 5,42: *M. Lucilius tribunus pl(ebis) hominem liberum, civem Romanum, cum collegae mitti iuberent, adversus eorum sententiam ipsius vi in carcerem compegit. Ob eam rem a censoribus notatur.*

21 Cf. F.X. Ryan, *The Censorship of Acilius*, [in:] *Politische Kultur und soziale Struktur der Römischen Republik. Bilanzen und Perspektiven. Akten der internationalen Tagung anlässlich des 70. Todestages von Friedrich Münzer (Münster, 18-20. Oktober 2012)*, eds. M. Haake, A.-C. Harders, Stuttgart 2017, pp. 111-134.

22 Cf. Plut., *C. Gracch.* 2; F. Pina Polo, A. Díaz Fernández, *The Quaestorship in the Roman Republic*, Berlin-Boston 2019, pp. 140-143.

23 Cf. Cic., *De sen.* 12,42; Val. Max. 2,9,3; Liv. 39,42,43; Plut., *Cat. Mai.* 17; *Flam.* 18-19; Sen. Rhet., *Contr.* 9,2,25; cf. P. Fraccaro, *Ricerche storiche e letterarie sulla censura del 184/183 (M. Porcio Catone L. Valerio Flacco)*, [in:] *Opuscula*, I, Pavia 1956, pp. 420-433; F. della Corte, *Catone Censore. La vita e la fortuna*, Torino 1949, pp. 25-26; C. Cascione, *'Lege agere' e 'poena capitis': qualche spunto ricostruttivo*, [in:] *'Iuris Vincula'. Studi in onore di Mario Talamanca*, Napoli 2001, pp. 515-522.

24 Cf. Cic., *De div.* 1,29-30.

Cicero in his work *De legibus*.[25] The main change proposed is to alter the censor's term of office. Since the enactment of the *lex Aemilia de censura minuenda*, it had been 18 months and elections were held every five years: this led to a 3.5-year gap, resulting in a lack of continuity in office. Cicero wanted the term of office to be five years. Only former officials were to go to the senate, leading to the censors being deprived of the possibility of selecting other deserving citizens, but on the other hand, Cicero wanted the censors to receive from the terminating magistrates a report on their performance and evaluate it. This additional power of scrutiny would certainly have been important in holding magistrates accountable for abuses. In addition, Cicero wished to give censors the power to act as watchdogs over laws modelled on the Greek office of νομοφύλακες. This power was intended to prevent the emerging illegal practice of changing the content of laws before they were submitted to the *aerarium*. This concept demonstrates that Cicero appreciated the importance of the censors' control tasks and wanted to delimit them more broadly, recognising that this would have a positive effect on the balance of the system.

The Enlightenment theory of tripartite government owes much to the systemic arrangements of the Roman Republic.[26] A shortcoming of Montesquieu's conception,[27] however, was the failure to include an element of control on the three, largely separate, powers. This is why many modern political systems have seen the development of such an element in the form of a *defensor* or *ombudsman*. Researchers trace the roots of these institutions to the office of the plebeian tribune.[28] However, it seems that censorship, by virtue of its control function, may also be at the root of it.[29]

---

25 Cf. A. Astin, *Cicero and Censorship*, 'Classical Philology', 80.3/1985, p. 234; L. Paulson, *A Painted Republic: the Constitutional Innovations of Cicero's 'De legibus'*, 'Etica & Politica', 16.2/ 2014, pp. 331-333.

26 Cf. M.N.S. Sellers, *The Roman Republic and the French and American Revolutions*, [in:] *The Cambridge Companion to the Roman Republic*, ed. H.I. Flower, Cambridge 2004, pp. 352 ff.

27 Cf. the polemical views of J.J. Rousseau expressed in his work *Contrat social ou principes du droit politique*, Genéve 1766, on censorship fourth book, point VII, pp. 244-247.

28 Cf. P. Catalano, *Tribunato e resistenza*, Torino 1971, passim, in particular pp. 116-125; G. Lobrano, *A proposito dei difensori del popolo*, "Diritto@Storia" 9/2010, http://www.dirittoestoria.it/9/Memorie/Lobrano-Introduzione-a-proposito-difensor.htm; C.R. Constenla, *Los defensores del pueblo del siglo XXI en el punto de vista jurídico romano*, "Diritto@Storia" 9/2010, http://www.dirittoestoria.it/9/Memorie/Constenla-Defensores-pueblo-siglo-XXI.htm.

29 Cf. S. Tafaro, *L'eredità dei 'tribuni plebis'*, [in:] *Tradizione romanistica e costituzione*, ed. L. Labruna, M.P. Baccari, C. Cascione, II, Napoli 2006, pp. 1866-1869.

This institution was directly referred to by Simón Bolívar when he proposed to take the office of censor from the Roman Republic system, which, although initially rejected, later found expression in the 1826 and 1999 constitutions of Bolivia and Venezuela.[30]

It seems, therefore, that the office of the censor, so unusual and difficult to fathom for foreigners looking at it from the outside, was of colossal systemic importance. During the period of the Republic, it was a bulwark and guarantee of the stability of the state, as well as a controlling element for the individual both in his public and private life. Together with the office of the plebeian tribune, whose powers allowed it to block decisions of the assemblies, the senate or other officials deemed contrary to the interests of the Republic, censorship was an element in the stability of the system.

Bibliography

Astin A.E., *Cicero and the Censorship*, "CP" 80.3/1985, pp. 233-239.

Beck H., *Consular power and the Roman constitution: the case of 'imperium' reconsidered*, [in:] *Consuls and Res Publica. Holding High Office in the Roman Republic*, eds. H. Beck, A. Duplá, M. Jehne, F. Pina Polo, Cambridge 2011, pp. 77-96.

Broughton T.R.S., *The Magistrates of the Roman Republic*, vol. I, Atlanta 1951 (reprint 1986).

Brunt P.A., *The Fall of the Roman Republic*, [in] *The Fall of the Roman Republic and Related Essays*, Oxford 1998, pp. 1-92.

Cascione C., *'Lege agere' e 'poena capitis': qualche spunto ricostruttivo*, [in:] *'Iuris Vincula'. Studi in onore di Mario Talamanca*, Napoli 2001, pp. 515-522.

Catalano P., *Tribunato e resistenza*, Torino 1971.

Constenla C.R., *Los defensores del pueblo del siglo XXI en el punto de vista jurídico romano*, "Diritto@Storia" 9/2010, http://www.dirittoestoria.it/9/Memorie/Constenla-Defensores-pueblo-siglo-XXI.htm.

della Corte F., *Catone Censore. La vita e la fortuna*, Torino 1949.

Fraccaro P., *Ricerche storiche e letterarie sulla censura del 184/183 (M. Porcio Catone L. Valerio Flacco)*, [in:] *Opuscula*, I, Pavia 1956, pp. 417-508.

Inamura K., *Justice and Reciprocity in Aristotle's Political Philosophy*, Cambridge 2015.

30 Cf. P. Catalano, *Tribunado, censura, dictadura: conceptos constitucionales bolivarianos y continuidad romana en America*, 'Quaderni Latinoamericani' 8/1981, pp. 3-4; S. Tafaro, *op. cit. pp.* 1868-1869.

Kunkel W., Wittmann R., *Staatsordnung und Staatspraxis der römischen Republik. Zweiter Abschnitt. Die Magistratur*, München 1995.

Lintott A., *The Constitution of the Roman Republic*, Oxford 1999.

Lobrano G., *A proposito dei difensori del popolo*, "Diritto@Storia" 9/2010, http://www.dirittoestoria.it/9/Memorie/Lobrano-Introduzione-a-proposito-difensor.htm.

North J.A., *The Constitution of the Roman Republic*, [in:] *A Companion to the Roman Republic*, eds. N. Rosenstein, R. Morstein-Marx, Malden (USA) 2006, pp. 256-277.

Paulson L., *A Painted Republic: the Constitutional Innovations of Cicero's 'De legibus'*, 'Etica & Politica', 16.2/ 2014, pp. 307-340.

Pina Polo F., Díaz Fernández A., *The Quaestorship in the Roman Republic*, Berlin-Boston 2019.

Ryan F.X., *The Censorship of Acilius*, [in:] *Politische Kultur und soziale Struktur der Römischen Republik. Bilanzen und Perspektiven. Akten der internationalen Tagung anlässlich des 70. Todestages von Friedrich Münzer (Münster, 18-20. Oktober 2012)*, eds. M. Haake, A.-C. Harders, Stuttgart 2017, pp. 111-134.

Sellers M.N.S., *The Roman Republic and the French and American Revolutions*, [in:] *The Cambridge Companion to the Roman Republic*, ed. H.I. Flower, Cambridge 2004, pp. 347-364.

Tarwacka A., *Adoption under the scrutiny of the censors in Republican Rome*, [in:] *Family, Law, and Society: from Roman Law to the Present Day*, red. E. Dawidziuk, P. Panero, A. Tarwacka, Berlin-Lausanne-Bruxelles-Chennai-New York-Oxford 2023, pp. 77-91.

Tafaro S., *L'eredità dei 'tribuni plebis'*, [in:] *Tradizione romanistica e costituzione*, ed. L. Labruna, M.P. Baccari, C. Cascione, II, Napoli 2006, pp. 1841-1889.

Tarwacka A., *Censors as Guardians of Family and Public Life in Republican Rome*, in print London-New York 2025.

Tarwacka A., *Prawne aspekty urzędu cenzora w starożytnym Rzymie*, Warszawa 2012.

Zabłocki J., *'Leges votatae' nelle assemblee popolari*, "Diritto@Storia" 10-11/2011-2012, http://www.dirittoestoria.it/10/Tradizione-Romana/Zablocki-Leges-voto-assemblee-popolari.htm.

José Luis Zamora Manzano[31]

Disinformation and Democracy in Roman Law: Candidates and Election Campaigns

Abstract: In this paper we intend to analyze some aspects of the Roman electoral campaign: from the candidate's manual, *Commentarioulum petitionis*, to some Pompeian inscriptions, with the purpose of establishing some parallels between today's elections. All this from a social and juridical perspective in order to see the mechanisms of attraction of voters.

Keywords: *Commentarioulum petitionis*, *programmata*, fake news, *nomenclator*, electoral race

1. Foreword

In the current context in which several regional and European electoral processes are being contemplated, we look to the past to observe the importance of candidates' strategies and the challenges they face. Thus, the experience of ancient Rome provides us with a valuable perspective for understanding contemporary debates surrounding elections, since, in that historical prism, we can identify recurring patterns, information and misinformation. Certainly, an election contest in Roman times, as is the case today, was a good time to bring to light and give credibility to the rumours or hoaxes that circulated.

In order to run a good campaign in 64 BC, Quintus Cicero's brother, Quintus Cicero, published the *Commentarioulum petitionis*, breviary addressed to his brother, the famous orator Marcus Tullius Cicero, containing a series of strategies aimed at convincing the electorate. This candidate's handbook contains advice that could well be applied to any current campaign and is the subject of study. We also bring up the electoral propaganda carried out with the *programmata*, some of the inscriptions painted in red or black on the façades of buildings, prepared with white lime, with which to achieve greater persuasion among potential voters. Apart from these aspects of the electoral contest, there are other relevant aspects of political life, such as the propagation of false news and rumours of various kinds to generate public opinion to attack a political rival.

31 University of las Palmas de Gran Canaria, ORCID: 0000-0001-8819-7909.

All of this reflects the constant search for political power through persuasive strategies on the populus. This historical phenomenon illustrates how contemporary problems, such as the struggle for power and the proliferation of fake news, are recurrent manifestations in the evolution of society, evidencing the continuity of certain fundamental aspects of politics and communication over time.

Moreover, the phenomenon of disinformation[32] has evolved significantly, transcending the simple categories of fake news and post-truth, since, without any doubt, the ecosystem it generates not only affects the information sphere, but also deeply intrudes into the foundations of Society, Democracy and Law. Therefore, in my view, it is essential to understand the interplay between fake news, propaganda and rumours, as elements that shape public perception and thus affect political decision-making. This amalgamation of information, in many cases distorted, not only poses a challenge to the integrity of democracy, but also raises fundamental questions about the role of freedom of expression, legal liability in the digital information age, and especially the manipulation that occurs through social media.

2. Roman election campaigning: seeking strategies to secure the vote

In the current context, especially with the European electoral, we look to the past to observe the importance of candidates' strategies and the challenges they face. Thus, the experience of ancient Rome provides us with a valuable perspective for understanding the contemporary debates surrounding elections, since, in that historical prism, we can identify recurring patterns, information and misinformation. Certainly, an electoral contest in Roman times, as is the case today, was a good time to bring to light and give credibility to the rumours or hoaxes that circulated about any candidate aspiring to political position, especially during the Republic. At that time, he had to prepare his network of contacts, influential

32 C. Rodríguez Pérez "No diga fake news di desinformación: una revisión sobre el fenómeno de las noticias falsas y sus implicaciones, en *Comunicación*, nº 40 enero-junio, 2019 p. 65-74; p. 69 link: https://doi.org/10.18566/comunica.n40.a05 [access:22.01.24]. For this reason, as noted by a. arises in February 2019, the international Fact Checking Network with 68 adhering media that had ratified a Code of Principles that goes for the publication of non-partisan reports on political, institutional or other social actors' statements.

politicians of the oligarchy, friends, clients, etc., in order to obtain a favourable result in the plebiscite.

In order to attract votes, the candidate normally wore the toga candida, hence the expression candidate. Thus, the togas were bleached with sulphur in order to stand out among the population, considering that access to the magistracy implied increasing the presence of the postulant in the eyes of society. However, this issue was not without its problems, especially during the electoral campaign or *ambitus*[33] where fraud obviously also existed, since in order for the candidates to conform to campaign protocol, it was forbidden for them to intentionally bleach them, *tollendae ambitionis causa*, when they presented themselves in public[34].

On the other hand, several adversaries could compete for the different magistracies, hence the importance of a staging to capture the vote of those who held the *ius suffragium*; this undoubtedly entailed a high monetary cost, almost a million

33 In the present study we are not going to focus on the crime of ambitus or electoral corruption, a term coined to designate captious propaganda and electoral frauds through bribes, and for which several provisions are dictated: *Lex Poetelia de ambitu* 358 B.C., the *Lex Cornelia Baebia* -181. BC, *Lex Cornelia Fulvia de ambitu* 159 BC, *Lex Tullia de ambitu* 63 BC, *Lex Pompeia de ambitu* 52 BC, *Lex licinia de ambitu*, with the introduction of the crime of *sodaliciurum*, and *Lex Iulia de ambitu* 18 BC, among others.

34 We have the testimony of Livy 4,25,13: *Placet tollendae ambitionis causa tribunos legem promulgare ne cui album in vestimentum addere petitionis causa liceret*. This has been considered as a first measure of corruption through a plebiscite of 432 B.C. *de albo in uestimentum non addendo*, which in the opinion of Resina Sola: 'would not so much regulate the manipulation of the vote by means of the candida toga as it would regulate an aspect of *ambitio* in its original sense; that is, not so much what will become the electoral crime of ambitus in its technical sense, but *ambitio* in its original sense and as an electoral act; it would seek to establish a relationship of behaviour between the different candidates, and not so much a relationship between the candidates and the electors. This is not to be seen as an innocent provision or one free of a deeper social, political and even economic cause, if we bear in mind that the proposer is a representative of the plebs. In fact, it tended to limit patrician pressure in the elections of the *tribuni militum consulari potestate* which, until that year, had prevented plebeians from gaining access to that supreme magistracy. We know from Livy himself that this law soon fell into disuse'. P. Resina Sola, "La corrupción electoral en la comedia plautina", *RGDR* 16(2011) p. 13, n.24.

sesterces as Dosi[35] points out. Thus, for example, in the clientelistic relationship, especially at the time of the *salutatio*, it was common to increase the *sportula* (a basket of food that the patronus gave to his clients), and even to reward those who requested the vote, his *rogatores*, both individually and collectively. Sometimes it was a group of businessmen who might support a candidate from whom they obviously expected a return, so it was *a quid pro quo* investment. Evidently, the candidate's own families had an interest in maintaining their dominance over the various magistracies, hence he or she could count on politically established relatives who were willing to help a brother, cousin or nephew so that the family could continue to enjoy prestige and glory[36]. In the same way, information and disinformation were valid instruments to win the confidence of the people exercising *suffragium* and to defeat their opponents. In short, the Roman election campaign became a *contentio dignitatis* in which the candidate, exercising the *ius honorium* in accordance with the mos maiorum, had to prove his suitability to the populus. Therefore, the candidate had a challenge in the electoral contest for which he was campaigning continuously, supported by the families, clients influence, making an apology of his social achievements, such as: holding political office and military triumphs for his own benefit. In short, everything that gave added value to his candidacy and prevented unpredictable voter

35 A. Dosi, *Così votavano i romani. Il sistema elettorale*, Edizioni Quasar, Roma,2004, p. 72 As a. points out, if the candidate wanted to win, he had to be prepared to hand out money, the equivalent of two million euros today, and to search his mind to find a way to secure the largest possible electorate. "*Se volevano vincere dovevano essere pronti a distribuire denaro a profusione e a spremersi le meningi per trovare il modo di assicurarsi l'elettorato più ampio possibile. È noto che prima di portare denaro una magistratura costava estremamente cara. Quando ci si avvicina alla cifra di un milione di sesterzi (quasi due milioni di euro attuali, secondo i dati Istat) e anche molto di più, era naturale che i beni di fortuna del candidato, soprattutto se era ancora alle prime armi, fossero nettamente insufficienti a coprire le spese della sua elezione. Bisognava moltiplicare le elargizioni, aumentare le mance alla clientela (le cosiddette sportulae), acquistare suffragi individuali o di gruppi costituiti, pagare gli agenti elettorali ecc.*"

36 A. Dosi, *Così votavano i romani. Il sistema elettorale. op. cit.* p. 73. It was a burden to be borne by the magistrate who did not receive emoluments, but later on a series of deferred compensations for services rendered could be given, as he points out (p. 74) "*l magistrato che rivestiva la carica annuale alla quale era stato eletto, non percepiva alcun emolumento (infatti le cariche erano gratuite perché venivano considerate un onore). Negli ultimi tempi della repubblica, tuttavia, era invalso l'uso che egli ricevesse regali sotto varie forme in ricompensa dei servigi resi*".

behaviour, something that could often happen[37], because it was ultimately up to the people to decide by their vote, and thus who enjoyed *dignitas*[38] for the political position.

An essential component of the electoral contest was the family, since this constituted a political springboard[39] and facilitated the political career of the candidate, to the point of taking advantage of the *laudatio funebris* as a political act. Thus, this speech of commendation directed towards the figure of the deceased, meticulously elaborated to exalt his virtues, prowess[40] and prestige, not only fulfilled the solemnity of honoring the deceased, but it was also used as an electoral tool. In such a way that, by highlighting the reputation and lineage of the deceased, it sought to confer an unparalleled *dignitas* to the candidate, thus shaping a favorable perception in the Roman electorate.

---

37 J.M. Ribas Alba, *Democracia en Roma: introducción al derecho electoral romano*, Comares, Granada 2008, p. 231 brings to mind a passage from Livy 4,6,11-12: *Eventus eorum comitiorum docuit alios animos in contentione libertatis dignitatisque, alios secundum deposita certamina incorrupto iudicio esse; tribunos enim omnes patricios creavit populus, contentus eo quod ratio habita plebeiorum esset. Hanc modestiam aequitatemque et altitudinem animi ubi nunc in uno inveneris, quae tum populi universi fuit?*, in which we see unpredictable behaviour on the part of the plebeians during 445 BC, in which three patricians were elected, despite the interest of the former in gaining access to the magistracy.

38 Cicero refers to this important quality of the person seeking access to the magistracy in several texts, in one of them on the defence of Cnaeus Plancius 20.50: *equidem primum ut honore dignus essem maxime semper laboravi, secundo ut existimarer; tertium mihi fuit illud quod plerisque primum est, ipse honos, qui eis denique debet esse iucundus quorum dignitati populus Romanus testimonium, non beneficium ambitioni dedit.* In the same sense in *de officis* I.12.38: *cum altero certamen honoris et dignitatis est, cum altero capitis et famae…*[…], in the campaign the candidate's reputation and honour are at stake.

39 Duplá, G. Fatás, F. Pina, *El manual del candidato de Quinto Cicerón. El commentariolum petitionis*, Servicio de publicaciones de la Universidad del País Vasco, Bilbao, 1990., p. 92-93.

40 E.g. Polibio VI.53: *ὅταν γὰρ μεταλλάξῃ τις παρ᾽ αὐτοῖς τῶν ἐπιφανῶν ἀνδρῶν, συντελουμένης τῆς ἐκφορᾶς κομίζεται μετὰ τοῦ λοιποῦ κόσμου πρὸς τοὺς καλουμένους ἐμβόλους εἰς τὴν ἀγορὰν ποτὲ μὲν ἑστὼς ἐναργής, σπανίως δὲ κατακεκλιμένος. πέριξ δὲ παντὸς τοῦ δήμου στάντος, ἀναβὰς ἐπὶ τοὺς ἐμβόλους, ἂν μὲν υἱὸς ἐν ἡλικίᾳ καταλείπηται καὶ τύχῃ παρών, οὗτος, εἰ δὲ μή, τῶν ἄλλων εἴ τις ἀπὸ γένους ὑπάρχει, λέγει περὶ τοῦ τετελευτηκότος τὰς ἀρετὰς καὶ τὰς ἐπιτετευγμένας ἐν τῷ ζῆν πράξεις.*

3. Tips for a campaign on *Commentariolum petitinonis*

From the point of view of being able to understand the electoral strategy with a view to shaping public opinion, it is imperative to analyse the *Commentarioulum petitionis*, since it is undoubtedly a document of extraordinary value for the study of political and electoral reality, and doubts have been raised about its authenticity[41].

In any case, the electoral contest implies setting in motion the personal petition to the citizen for a vote, for which it was essential, as stated in the *Commentariolum*, to go to the Forum[42], as it was the epicentre or nerve centre of political and social

41 On the doubts of authenticity raised at the outset, see among others G.L. Endrickson "On the authenticity of the Commentariolum petitionis of Q.Cicero", American Journal of Philology XIII (1982), pp. 200-212. Id. "The Commentariolum petitionis attributed to Q. Cicero" in Decennial Publications of University of Chicago, First Series VI, 6 1903, pp. 71-93. See futher literature in J.S. Richardson "The Commentariolum Petitionis". Historia: *Zeitschrift für Alte Geschichte*, Bd. 20, H. 4 (3rd Qtr., 1971), pp. 436-442; J.P.V.D, Balsdom "The Commentariolum petitionis", Class. Quart., LVI, 1963, pp. 242-250; D. Nardo, *Il "Commentariolum petitionis", La propaganda elettorale nella 'ars' di Quinto Cicerone*, Padova, 1970, p. 7where a. considers that the problem of authenticity seems to have overwhelmed any other interest, thus diverting from the work, judged 'admirable' by a historian like Syme, the more detailed and in-depth explanation it deserved. In any case, only two positions on the question of authenticity now seem seriously tenable: that it is indeed, as it purports to be, an epistolary essay to Marcus Cicero written by his brother in early 64, apparently to advise him on his candidatura; or that it may be someone else's later invention, but so well-informed that it remains a primary source for late Republican electoral politics, see R. Morstein-Marx, "Publicity, Popularity and Patronage in the "Commentariolum", *Classical Antiquity*, Vol. 17, No. 2 (Oct., 1998), pp. 259-288.

42 There are several passages in the electoral record that allude to this appearance in this key place: *Comm. Pet.* 2, in relation to appearing at the same time and the importance of visiting it to gain reputation and prestige *Comm. Pet.* IX.36: *Iam deductorum officium quo maius est quam salutatorum, hoc gratius tibi esse significato atque ostendito, et, quod eius fieri poterit, certis temporibus descendito; magnam adfert opinionem, magnam dignitatem cottidiana in deducendo frequentia.* Assiduity was important according to *Comm. Pet.* XI.43 where the candidate had to interpellate the vote, without absences: *prodest quidest quidem vehementer nusquam discedere, sed tamen hic fructus est adsiduitatis, non solum esse Romae atque in foro sed adsidue petere, saepe eosdem appellare, non committere ut quisquam possit dicere, quod eius consequi possis, se abs te non [sit] rogatum et valde ac diligenter rogatum.* In the Comm. Pet. XIV. 54 likewise reiterates the need to resort to the forum, emphasising the singularities of the Roman *populus* as we have already pointed out above.

life. This is the reason for Quintus' recommendation that the candidate should appear there at the same time, since this not only allowed politicians to meet with their supporters and rivals, but also to establish direct contact with the *vox populi*. By speaking in the Forum, politicians could influence the masses, gain support for their proposals and highlight their skills as leaders, and therefore, especially in the case of Marcus Cicero who was a novice, he had to appear in that public space to win public opinion: *Civitas quae sit cogita, quid petas, qui sis. Prope cottidie tibi hoc ad forum descendenti meditandum est: "Novus sum, consulatum peto, Roma est"*. It was imperative for the candidate to appeal to the vote, there had to be a feedback with his voters, trying to persuade them.[43]

The petitor or candidate had to know his electorate and establish, in this policy of proximity, friendships in streets and neighbourhoods, municipalities and colonies anywhere in Italy in which to gather support: *Deinde habeto rationem urbis totius, conlegiorum omnium, pagorum, vicinitatum; ex his principes ad amicitiam tuam si adiunxeris, per eos reliquam multitudinem facile tenebis. Postea totam Italiam fac ut in animo ac memoria tributim discriptam comprensamque habeas, ne quod municipium, coloniam, praefecturam, locum*... [.][44]. Everywhere friendships had to be fostered, who could even campaign for the candidate in their area, in order to secure votes: *perquiras et investiges homines ex omni regione, eos cognoscas, appetas, confirmes, cures ut in suis vicinitatibus tibi petant et tua causa quasi candidati sint.*

It is obvious that new friendships had to be made in order to attract votes, although the clientele also played a role, although perhaps a more secondary one[45],

---

43 The *assiduitas* was a necessary instrument to demand the suffrage from the population, and to which the handshake or *prensatio* gesture should be added, which demonstrated the candidate's closeness, giving him or her a favourable image. A.M. Suárez Piñeiro, *La reforma del sistema electoral romano durante el último siglo de la República, Gallaecia* 17 (1998) pp. 425-446; 429.

44 *Comm.Pet* VIII.30.

45 Therefore, the client does not play a key role in the formation of the entourage that will support and enhance the candidate's prestige. There is more talk of the presence of amici, which can hardly be equated with the term clients. Clearly, reference is made to an ad hoc relationship, sought in the electoral context. Similarly, other circumstantial elements, such as the enactment of laws like the Gabinia of 139 BC, would continue to reduce the possible effectiveness of the clientelistic relationship in the electoral system by introducing secret voting in the assemblies, freeing citizens from pressure in the exercise of suffrage. See A.M. Suárez Piñeiro, "Sobre el papel de las relaciones de clientela y patronato en la política de la tardía republicana romana" en *Gallaecia* 14-15, 1996, pp. 557-569; 566.

forming part of the entourage that accompanied the candidate in order to create a public image of prestige, dignity and great support from his fellow citizens. For this reason, with regard to the people who surrounded the candidate, we must highlight, as Quintus' political book points out, the figure of the *nomenclator*, a slave who accompanied the politician during the campaign and who supplied him with information about the people he was greeting in the streets or in the *Forum*, although he could have exercised the functions of what we know today as campaign manager or adviser to the electoral campaign. Consequently, we consider that the intervention of the nomenclator exerted a notable influence[46] on the electorate's inclination to vote. As Pina[47] points out, "*in a society without organised publicity, these specialised and sought-after slaves, given the importance of their task, undoubtedly became true election advertising media*".

The strategy, therefore, was to attract the greatest number of followers and win their confidence in the vote, for which the postulant's ability became a necessary instrument, since, apart from influential personalities, they had to bring along vulgar *salutatoribus*. Likewise, those who escorted the candidate to the *Forum*, where, as we have pointed out, it was essential to go regularly in order to make an impact on public opinion, surrounded by the entourage that had to accompany him at all times[48], became indispensable.

It is clear that this accompaniment was a proof of gratitude from those who had no means of expressing their gratitude, as was the case with clients and the most vulnerable classes, since it was the best form of recognition that the petitioner

---

46 Cicero also tells us when he arrived at the *Capena* Gate, in a passage alluding to the nomenclator how he had a knowledge of all those who extolled him, as inferred from Cicero, ad Att. IV.1.5: *ad urbem ita veni ut nemo ullius ordinis homo nomenclatori notus fuerit qui mihi obviam non venerit, praeter eos inimicos quibus id ipsum, se inimicos esse, non liceret aut dissimulare aut negare. Cum venissem ad portam Capenam, gradus templorum ab infima plebe completi erant. A qua plausu maximo cum esset mihi gratulatio significata, similis et frequentia et plaususus me usque ad Capitolium celebravit in foroque et in ipso Capitolio miranda multitudo fuit.*

47 F.Pina, "La campaña electoral en Roma" en *El manual del candidato de Quinto Cicerón*, op. cit. p. 75.

48 *Comm. Pet.IX.37: Tertia est ex hoc genere adsidua adsectatorum copia. In ea quos voluntarios habebis, curato ut intellegant te sibi in perpetuum summo beneficio obligari; qui autem tibi debent, ab iis plane hoc munus exigito, qui per aetatem ac negotium poterunt, ipsi tecum ut adsidui sint, qui ipsi sectari non poterunt, suos necessarios in hoc munere constituant. Valde ego te volo et ad rem pertinere arbitror semper cum multitudine esse.*

could obtain from them. However, as he points out, Cicero[49] was also often accompanied by senators and gentlemen, although these, given their public function, could not do so at all times.

In addition, it is obvious that many citizens had no other way of paying tribute to the meritorious candidate than by accompanying him and thus being present as an acolyte at all campaign events, especially in the Champ de Mars, and even at night - *in ea non esse gravatos homines prodire hora tertia in campum Martium*[50]. The candidate himself requested the accompaniment of his acolytes in order to gain prestige and reputation with the electorate, as is expressed in the political record, asking for the vote of those whom he had favoured in the past, either by protecting their assets or by intervening to save their honour, and even those who had been acquitted of sentences thanks to his intervention, to go with him as a *oficio remunentur*[51].

49 It was an attempt to veto the large procession and the gratification thereof that might confer an appearance of greater significance and popular acceptance of the candidate, which was contrary to the established principles and practices in the matter, as pointed out by Cicero *Pro Mun.* 70-71: *At sectabantur multi. Doce mercede; concedam esse crimen. Hoc quidem remoto quid reprendis? 'Quid opus est' inquit 'sectatoribus?' A me tu id quaeris, quid opus sit eo quo semper usi sumus? Homines tenues unum habent in nostrum ordinem aut promerendi aut referendi benefici locum, hanc in nostris petitionibus operam atque adsectationem. Neque enim fieri potest neque postulandum est a nobis aut ab equitibus Romanis ut suos necessarios candidatos adsectentur totos dies; a quibus si domus nostra celebratur, si interdum ad forum deducimur, si uno basilicae spatio honestamur, diligenter observari videmur et coli; tenuiorum amicorum et non occupatorum est ista adsiduitas, quorum copia bonis viris et beneficis deesse non solet. Noli igitur eripere hunc inferiori generi hominum fructum offici, Cato; sine eos qui omnia a nobis sperant habere ipsos quoque aliquid quod nobis tribuere possint. Si nihil erit praeter ipsorum suffragium, tenues, etsi suffragantur, nil valent gratia. Ipsi denique, ut solent loqui, non dicere pro nobis, non spondere, non vocare domum suam possunt. Atque haec a nobis petunt omnia neque ulla re alia quae a nobis consequuntur nisi opera sua compensari putant posse. Itaque et legi Fabiae quae est de numero sectatorum, et senatus consulto quod est L. Caesare consule factum restiterunt. Nulla est enim poena quae possit observantiam tenuiorum ab hoc vetere instituto officiorum excludere…[..].*

50 Cicero *Pro Mun.* 69.

51 *Comm. Pet.IX.38 Praeterea magnam adfert laudem et summam dignitatem, si ii tecum erunt qui a te defensi et qui per te servati ac iudiciis liberati sunt; haec tu plane ab his postulato ut, quoniam nulla impensa per te alii rem, alii honestatem, alii salutem ac fortunas omnis obtinuerint, nec aliud ullum tempus futurum sit ubi tibi referre gratiam possint, hoc te officio remunerentur.*

Moreover, apart from friendships, clients, the influence of the noble classes and followers in the Roman political context, where social practices such as *adsectatio* and *salutatio* could be considered ways of cultivating electoral supporters with a broader social and cultural dimension in Roman life than today, the candidate himself had to shape his image in order to create a good reputation and public image among his fellow citizens and, if necessary, to simulate or use artifices to achieve his goals. With regard to the latter, the *petitor* was not only trying to please and conciliate opinions that might be contrary to his own, but to show a series of qualities, to which the opuscle refers in *Comm.Pet.*11.41: *Ea desiderat nomenclationem, blanditiam, adsiduitatem, benignitatem, rumoritatem, speciem in re publica.*

Apart from the aforementioned assiduity and the knowledge of each elector with the *nomenclatio*, the tactic recommended by Quintus is to put into practice flattery (*blanditiam*) to gain the sympathy of the electorate, *benignitas* or kindness and generosity with the people, and to be affable and courteous: *comitas tibi non deest, ea quae bono ac suavi homine digna est*[52]; in other words, the courtesy that was deserved by the kind and gentle man should not be lacking. All this affected the reputation (*rumorem*) and public perception, so it was important for the *petitor* to put into practice or appear to put into practice a series of political virtues, or if necessary to simulate them or act ambivalently, welcoming all kinds of opinions, even if they seemed contradictory, in order to win in the electoral contest[53]. In this sense, the Political Breviary, in order to improve his public image, establishes the need to simulate and strategically configure his appearance in order to persuade and win the favour of the *vox populi* without any moral qualms: *Deinde id quod natura non habes induc in animum ita simulandum esse ut natura facere videare*[54]. *Simulatio* was necessary and permitted, since it allowed the candidate to adapt his appearance, his face and his speech, accommodating himself to the thoughts and ideas of the voters: *cuius et frons et vultus et sermo ad eorum quoscumque convenerit sensum et voluntatem commutandus et accommodandus est*[55].

---

52 *Comm.Pet.*XI.42.

53 Quintus' advice is not without cynicism, for it suits the candidate to change his language and ideas as often as necessary in order to appear to agree with the opinions of all those with whom he speaks… it is not a moral treatise but a political writing which knows Roman practice perfectly well, and which unblushingly applies the mechanisms necessary to win. F. Pina, "La campaña electoral en Roma" en *El manual del candidato de Quinto Cicerón*, op. cit. p. 78.

54 *Comm.Pet.*XI.42.

55 *Comm.Pet.*XI.42.

Another aspect to highlight is that, in order to obtain support in the race, acts aimed at maximising the candidate's propaganda were held in order to obtain potential voters[56], among which gifts, banquets[57] that could be organised by the candidate or his friends, and *ludi publici* were the most important; the latter required large investments on the part of the candidates in order to obtain the best reputation and fame and thus capture the votes necessary to obtain victory. Although these acts were eventually considered as practices of the crime of ambitus or electoral corruption, the *munera gladiatorum*, which played an important role, were subject to restriction and prohibition. It is obvious that these activities had to be limited, as was done, at least during the two years[58] prior to the presentation as a candidate, with the *Lex Tullia of Ambitu* 63 BC, except in cases of testamentary imposition; this shows the use of gladiatorial combats for electoral purposes, something that obviously had to be controlled due to the electoral corruption it produced. Banquets were also banned for the same period, except for those organised for funerary reasons.

Returning to the candidate and leaving aside electoral corruption, it is obvious that reputation and the shaping of public opinion was an essential issue, as Quintus points out, in such a way that one had to ask for votes diligently, that is, with dedication, skill and diligence, winning the sympathy of all social strata, with the purpose of achieving the candidate's fame and that this came as Quintus points out: *non ut ad populum ab his hominibus fama perveniat sed ut in his studiis populus ipse versetur*[59].

4. Election propaganda in Pompeii: some notes

We have already said that it was important to create false news and rumours that would discredit the opponents, but also to have a campaign that would take advantage of any place to advertise, not only the daily walks through the Forum

---

56 A.M. Suárez Piñeiro, *La reforma del sistema electoral romano*...p. 429.

57 This implied enormous generosity on the part of the petitioner towards friends and the electorate at large: *tamen ab amicis si laudatur, multitudini grata est; est in conviviis, quae fac ut et abs te et ab amicis tuis concelebrentur et passim et tributim;*..[..].*Comm. Pet.* 44.

58 Cicero *In Vat.*15.37: *atque illud etiam audire (de) te cupio, qua re, cum ego legem de ambitu tulerim ex senatus consulto, tulerim sine vi, tulerim salvis auspiciis, tulerim salva lege Aelia et Fufia, tu eam esse legem non putes, praesertim cum ego legibus tuis, quoquo modo latae sunt, paream; cum mea lex dilucide vetet biennio qvo qvis petat petitvrvsve sit gladiatores dare nisi ex testamento praestitvta die, quae tanta in te sit amentia ut in ipsa petitione gladiatores audeas dare? num quem putes illius tui certissimi gladiatoris similem tribunum plebis posse reperiri qui se interponat quo minus reus mea lege fias?*

59 *Comm. Pet.*XIII.50.

in which to make the *prensatio* and show the strength as a candidate with the companions and friends, but also through electoral posters or *programmata*, that is *tituli picti* or inscriptions painted in red or black on the facades of buildings, prepared with white lime, with which to achieve greater persuasion among potential voters, some even carried out outside the city. In this sense, we are going to mention some of these Pompeian inscriptions[60], as they constitute an example of electoral proclamations that were made on the walls of the city, and where we find streets such as *Abundance*[61], which was a main enclave for commercial activity and, consequently, with a considerable number of inscriptions[62].

We are not going to analyse all of them, but we are only going to mention some of the most significant ones as examples of electoral propaganda. On the other hand, we may encounter the possibility of sabotage by electoral opponents, as

60 R. Biundo,"La propaganda elettorale a Pompei: la funzione e il valore dei programmata nell'organizzazione della campagna", en Athenaeum 2003(1), p. 53-116; 114, where a. points out that the *Pompeian populus* was able to express himself "freely" by writing his political preferences on the walls (a phenomenon that is still very much alive today in many countries, especially in the West) and then voting for whomever he wished: *Quanto poi alle iscrizioni con rogatores credo si possa affermare che esse esprimono la reale e spontanea partecipazione alla propaganda politica da parte della cittadinanza pompeiana, rappresentata in tutta la sua stratificazione sociale. Cio` non vuol dire che ci troviamo di fronte ad una idilliaca citta` «democratica», dato che il sistema socio-politico romano era di carattere essenzialmente oligarchico, ma significa che il populus pompeiano aveva la possibilita` di esprimersi «liberamente», scrivendo sui muri la propria preferenza politica (fenomeno che ancora oggi e` particolarmente vivo in molti paesi, soprattutto occidentali) e votando poi per chi volesse.*

61 Very often, the inscriptions are concentrated in a few of the main streets, while none or only a few are found in other streets normally well covered by other candidates. They may be concentrated in streets and quarters which otherwise lie outside the normal distribution pattern. Markedly deviant concentrations may also occur. As examples of different types, we may cite A. Trebius Valens, a very large part of whose inscriptions are placed along the Vía dell' Abbondanza see H. Mouritsen, "Elections, Magistrates and Municipal Elite", *Studies in Pompeian Epigraphy, Analecta Romana Instituti Danici. Supplementa.* (L'Erma), 15, 1988, pp. 52 ss.

62 We are talking about some 2800 *tituli picti*, most of them with a specific date between 62 AD and 79 AD called *programmata recentiora*. These election manifestos show about 1500 inscriptions from the campaign of 79 AD, and the posters from the period between the reign of Nero and Titus., see R.A. Staccioli., *Manifesti elettorali nell´antica Pompei*, Biblioteca universale Rizolli, Milano, 1992, p. 44. Id. C.Chiava, *Programmata Manifesti elettorali nella colonia romana di Pompei*, S. Zamorani, Torino, 2002, p. 47 ss. R. Étienne., *La vie quotidienne à Pompéi*, Hachette, Paris, 1983, p. 139 ss; 149.

happens nowadays when they tear down a poster or cross out a candidacy etc. ….,
as there are graffiti that warned those who tried to erase them:

> *L(ucium) Statium Receptum/ (duo) vir(um) i(ure) d(icundo) o(ro) v(os) f(aciatis)/ vicini dignus / scr(ipsit) Aemilius Celer vic(inus)/ invidiose qui dele ae[g]rotes*[63].

In the graffito we can see the signature of the manifesto by Emilio Celere in which he asks for the vote for L. Statius, emphasising his quality as a worthy man, while at the same time we find references to possible boycotts in the *programmata*, as a curse is established in the parietal inscription, wishing a serious illness to the one who erases it. This is why the vigilance of the *programmata* was necessary, to ensure their durability during the campaign.

Although we will see some examples of these laudatory electoral proclamations, the fact is that they were generally made simply and concisely mentioning the candidate and the office to which he aspired with the acronym *OVF oro vos faciatis*, I beg you to make, elect and vote for a candidate for the office of: *IIvir or II-vir i d or aed.- quinq (duovirum or duuvirum iure dicundo* or as the case may be *aedilem* or *aed quinq or aedilem quinquenalem*. Although we often find other inscriptions with the name of the supporter and the verb *rog(at)*, or also *cupere* and *facere*.

From the point of view of the candidate's suitability, the acronym *DRP dignum rei publicae* could be affixed, symbolising that the candidate was worthy of public office. These stereotypical acronyms were commonly associated with candidates together with the relevant prayer, as can be seen from this inscription:

> *Q(uintum) Postumium Proculum/ aed(ilem) d(ignum) r(ei) p(ublicae) Masculus rog(at)*[64].

We see that the tituli does not follow the format of others, with the abbreviation we have seen *OVF* and the vote is requested with the verb rogat, but reference is made to the suitability with the acronym *DRP* and the final request by *Masculus*, in this case the owner of a caupona on the via Stabia, where this electoral proclamation in favour of Quintus *Postumius*[65] was located. In this case the rogation was individual but it could also be done collectively as happened at the request of a group of offectors or dyers: *Postumium Proculum/ aed(ilem)/ offectores rog(at)*[66]. Although we also find other generic petitions, for example from the group of

63 CIL IV. 3775.

64 CIL IV.7238.

65 It might not have been by chance that the owner of the *caupona* had painted the manifest when there were white wine amphorae with the name of Q. Postumius see R.A. Staccioli., *Manifesti elettorali nell'antica Pompei,…*op. 163.

66 CIL IV.864.

pistores or bakers and from the neighbourhood in general, in this case in favour of Elvius Sabinus:

Cn(aeum) Helvium Sabinum aed(ilem) pistores rog(ant) et cupiunt cum vicinis[67].

There are many inscriptions referring to individual and collective rogations, of which 45, or 14.5%, were women and 266, or 85.5%, were men. The professions of the *rogator* were also established, with *caupo* or *fullo* being the most common in the programmata, although we also find those of *lupinarius, perfusor, pistor, pomarius, dissignatur, veterarius*. We find several groups that recommended candidates[68], such as those made by merchants, different guilds, neighbours, teachers with their disciples and even ball players.

However, despite the fact that women did not have the *ius sufragii*, they actively participated as *rogatrices*, playing a considerable role despite appearing in 14.5% of the *programmata*, their social projection and the great involvement and commitment with which they did so show a concern for the political community, being promoters, on their own initiative and spontaneously, of the petitores. These women, who acted during the election campaign, were key to generating public opinion about the candidate and, obviously, to spreading rumours, through their work in the *thermopolia* and *cauponae*. This is inferred from one of the epigraphic election pamphlets CIL IV.7863:

C(aium) Lollium/ Fuscum (duo) vir(um) v(iis) a(aedibus) s(acris) p(ublicis) p(rocurandis) / Asellinas rogant/ nec sine Zmyrina.

The manifesto signed by Asellina, probably the owner of the tavern on one of the busiest thoroughfares, the Abundance, calls for a vote in favour of Gaius Lolio Fuscus for the office of *duoviro*. In the premises, which could have been used as a place for sexual encounters, foreign women provided services, as reference is made to Zmyrina, a woman from the Smyrna area. However, it is obvious that there was an ability to interact with a variety of people who came to the premises and this was certainly successful in gaining the support of certain candidates.

---

67 CIL IV.7273.

68 i.g. CIL IV.677 *Trebium aed(ilem) o(ro) v(os) f(aciatis) clibanari rog(ant). Muleteers* CIL IV.113, IV.7643, *fullers* CIL IV.7164, goldsmiths CIL IV.710, tapestry makers CIL IV.7443, among others. CIL IV.7197 *P(ublium) Paquinium Proculum (duo)vir(um) i(ure) d(icundo) vicini cupidi faciunt*. CIL IV.1147 *A(ulum Vettium Firmum aed(ilem) o(ro) v(os) f(aciatis) d(ignum) r(ei) p(ublicae) pilicrepi facite*. There are also references to other table players the *latruncularis* in CIL. IV.7851.

Therefore, in our opinion, the *rogatrices* participation[69] in the campaign was decisive in attracting votes.

In relation to manifestos and counter-propaganda to damage a candidate by using fictitious names and or fake posters or what today would be fake graffiti, we find an emblematic inscription that could be considered as a model of electoral anti-propaganda, let's analyse the inscription:

> *M(arcum) Cerrinium/ Vatiam aed(ilem) o(ro) v(os) f(aciatis) seribi/ universi rogant/ scr(ipsit) Florus cum Fructo*[70].

It is possible that the names are fictitious and that it is an inscription made by night drinkers when leaving a *caupo* or any other place, and that it may even have been the result of a joke. Despite this interpretative speculation, we are talking about groups with little or no reputation that could denigrate and even discredit the candidacy of Cerrino Vacia, as inferred from the petition of the *dormientes, furunculi*, and *drapetae*, that is to say sleepers, thieves and fugitive slaves, and as inferred from other manifestos[71] about the same postulant[72].

5. Conclusions and discussion

From what we have seen so far, we can deduce that disinformation and false news have been one of the characteristics of human communication since time immemorial. It is true that today the phenomenon is becoming more acute, especially with the events we are experiencing today and that, despite technology, we can see how discourse is amplified and fake news is spread through social

69 Several tituli mention their participation as noted from CIL IV. 3678 of petition by Stacia and Petronia: *M(arcum) Caellium et L(ucium) Albucium aed(iles)/ o(ro) v(os) f(aciatis)/Statia et Petronia rog(ant) tales cives in colonia in perpetuo.* See about other women asking for a vote CIL. IV.7862: *Cn(aeum) Helvium Sabinum/ aed(ilem) d(ignum) r(ei) p(ublicae) o(ro) v(os) f(aciatis) Aegle rogat* IV.7864:*C(aium) I(ulium) P(olybium) II vir(um) i(ure) d(icundo) [[Zmyrina]] rog(at)* IV.7866: *Cn(aeum) Helvium Sabinum/ aed(ilem) d(ignum) r(ei) p(ublicae) o(ro) v(os) f(aciatis) Maria rogat.*

70 CIL IV.581.

71 CIL IV 575 *Vatiam aed(ilem) rogant / Ma(rcum) Cerio(m) dormientes / universi cum /*; CIL IV. 576 *Vatiam aed(ilem) / furunculi rog(ant)*; CIL IV 7389: *[M Cerrinium Vatiam?] drapetae omnes.*

72 R.A. Staccioli, Manifesti elettorali nell'antica Pompei,...op. cit.155, a. citing also G.O. Onorato, Iscrizioni Pompeiana. La vitta pubblica, ed. Fussi, Sansoni, 1957, p. 176 defines the electoral poster as anti-propaganda. Although the areas where these *programmata* are found had to be the centre of the hostilities against Vacia.

networks, creating information unease among citizens. There are many actors involved in the dissemination of fake news, rumours and post-truth through the internet, obviously with political, social and economic interests. Today, with artificial intelligence, the use of bots, trolls on social networks, mainly Facebook, X, Tiktok, Instagram and even influencers themselves, the aim is to manipulate and misinform citizens, generating alarm, confusion and conspiracy theories. It is obviously a preconceived plan that seeks political opportunism and to alter the geopolitical situation as we are experiencing with the war in Ukraine or in Israel with the Gaza conflict, although it affects other aspects such as the economy of the great powers that also enter the disinformation chessboard.

For all these reasons, it is necessary to create verification mechanisms to avoid fragmentation and confusion with information and, therefore, to filter the diversity and channels of news broadcasting, through international verification agencies[73]. This issue is not without its problems given the complexity of the phenomenon, hence the need to identify the mechanisms and actors, as well as actions to guarantee truthful and verified information, as it affects all aspects of society, especially political decisions. False information and distortion of the truth through dissemination, amplification and disinformation has always existed and the same behaviours are produced in terms of the dissemination of hoaxes and rumours: from satire or parody of comments in literary sources, messages in Pompeian graffiti, manipulated content or alteration of the content by the petitioner seeking a specific position in the citizen. Society evolves, but the motivations and expressions of need and recognition by the *populus* remain the same, mutatis mutandis.

Within the European Union itself, there is also concern about the proliferation of fake news. Thus, in the institutional sphere, the Strengthened Code of Practice on Disinformation[74] has been signed, reinforcing that of 2018, which was presented on 16 June 2022 by 34 signatories. Among other issues, it seeks to recognise the importance of political advertising in shaping public life, trying to apply stricter transparency measures, allowing users to easily identify political advertisements, disclose the sponsor, the advertising expenditure and the viewing

---

73 For example, the International Fact-Checking Network, created in 2015, in Spanish, attached to the Poynter Institute, whose objective is to bring together journalists engaged in fact-checking at the international level, i.e. monitoring, verification, promotion of basic standards and creation of a Code of Verification. Vid. https://ifcncodeofprinciples.poynter.org/ [link access: 31/03/2024].

74 See link: https://digital-strategy.ec.europa.eu/en/library/2022-strengthened-code-practice-disinformation [:31/03/2024].

period. It also aims to reduce manipulative behaviour used to spread disinformation (e.g. fake accounts, bot-driven amplification, impersonation, malicious deep fakes), and provides for greater cooperation between signatories to combat challenges related to such techniques.

Finally, it should be underlined that Regulation (EU) 2022/2065 of the European Parliament and of the Council of 19 October 2022 on a single market for digital services and amending Directive 2000/31/EC (Digital Services Act - DSA) seeks to address illegal content, disinformation and other risks to society, in particular, manipulative techniques that can negatively affect whole groups and amplify social harm, for example by contributing to disinformation campaigns or discriminating against certain groups, and even manipulative techniques and disinformation with actual and foreseeable negative effects on public health, public safety, civil discourse, political participation and equality.

Bibliography

Biundo R. "La propaganda elettorale a Pompei: la funzione e il valore dei programmata nell'organizzazione della campagna", en Athenaeum 2003(1), p. 53-116.

Chiava C. *Programmata Manifesti elettorali nella colonia romana di Pompei*, S. Zamorani, Torino, 2002.

Dosi A., *Così votavano i romani. Il sistema elettorale*, Edizioni Quasar, Roma, 2004.

Duplà A., Fatàs G., Pina F., *El manual del candidato de Quinto Cicerón. El commentariolum petitionis*, Servicio de publicaciones de la Universidad del País Vasco, Bilbao, 1990.

Endrickson G.L. "On the authenticity of he Commentariolum petitionis of Q.Cicero", *American Journal of Philology* XIII (1982), pp. 200-212.

Laurence R. "Rumour and communication in roman politics", en *Greece & Rome* 41, 1(Apr., 1994), pp. 62-74.

Mouritsen H., "Elections, Magistrates and Municipal Elite", *Studies in Pompeian Epigraphy, Analecta Romana Instituti Danici. Supplementa.* (L'Erma), 15, 1988.

Morstein-Marx R., "Publicity, Popularity and Patronage in the "Commentarioulum", Classical Antiquity 17, 2 (1988), p. 259-288.

Nardo D. *Il "Commentariolum petitionis", La propaganda elettorale nella 'ars' di Quinto Cicerone*, Padova, 1970.

Pina Polo F., "Noticias falsas, desinformación y opinión pública en la Roma republicana" en *False notizie..fake news e storia romana. Falsificaioni antiche, falsificacioni moderne*, (c. Simonetta Segeni), Le Monnier U., Firenze, 2019, p. 74-90.

Resina Sola, P. "La corrupción electoral en la comedia plautina", *RGDR* 16(2011).

Ribas Alba J.M., *Democracia en Roma: introducción al derecho electoral romano*, Comares, Granada 2008.

Richardson J.S. "The Commentariolum Petitionis". Historia: *Zeitschrift für Alte Geschichte*, Bd. 20, H. 4 (3rd Qtr., 1971), pp. 436-442.

Rodríguez Pérez C. "No diga fake news di desinformación: una revisión sobre el fenómeno de las noticias falsas y sus implicaciones, en *Comunicación*, nº 40 enero-junio, 2019 p. 65-74.

Staccioli R.A., *Manifesti elettorali nell´antica Pompei*, Biblioteca universale Rizolli, Milano, 1992.

Suárez Piñeiro, A.M.,"Sobre el papel de las relaciones de clientela y patronato en la política de la tardía republicana romana" en *Gallaecia* 14-15, 1996, pp. 557-569.

Rosanna Ortu[75]

Evidence from the *Libri Augurum* on certain juridical-religious aspects of the *Dictator*

Abstract*: In order to enrich the juridical-religious framework inherent to the original characteristics of the dictatorship in ancient Rome, the analysis of the fragments taken from the priestly documents arrived through the testimonies of ancient authors is of fundamental importance, with particular attention to those coming from the *libri augurum*. From the testimonies of Cicero and Livy, who transcribe passages taken from the *libri augurum* which report the information of an ancestral time of the dictatorship, it appears clear that the nomination of the *dictator* represented a very important event for the rhythms of life of the ancient city, inevitably affecting also towards the more strictly religious aspects of the *civitas*, with an active involvement of the priestly colleges, and in a more specific way of that of the augurs.

Keywords: Dictatorship, Augurs, *Libri augurum, Dictator, Dictio dictatoris, Magister populi*

1. The importance of the priestly documents for the reconstruction of archaic Roman juridical-religious institutions: the value of the 'libri augurum'

Fragments taken from the *Libri Augurum*[76], like the other priestly documents, can provide fundamental elements to draw a precise reconstruction of Roman juridical-religious institutions, with the main purpose of highlighting their original characteristics. In these documents, as amply demonstrated by the Romanist doctrine of the second half of the last century, there are the solemn

75 Full Professor of Roman Law, University of Sassari, Italy, ORCID: 0000-0002-7208-2936

* English translation by Dr. Pietro Giovanni Antonio Santoru (PhD in Legal Studies).

76 For the documents of the Collegium of Augurs and the *Libri Augurum* I refer to: F.A. Brause, *'Librorum de disciplina augurali ante Augusti mortem scriptorum reliquiae'*, Lipsiae 1875; P. Regell, *'De augurum publicorum libris'*, Vratislaviae 1878; Id., *'Fragmenta auguralia'*, Hirschberg 1882; Id., "Auguralia", *'Commentationes Philologae in honorem Augusti Reifferscheidii'*, Vratislaviae, 1884, pp. 61 ss.; Id., *'Commentarii in librorum auguralium fragmenta specimen'*, Hirschberg, 1893; J. Linderski, "The Augural Law", *ANRW*, 2/16.3 (1986), pp. 2241 ss.

formulas that had the task of realize «di volta in volta la traduzione nella sfera religiosa di tutto il complesso di attività riferibili al popolo romano»[77].

Regarding the reliability of the religious formulas taken from the priestly documents, the authenticity of these formulas was amply corroborated, in the 60s of the 20th century, by Georges Dumézil[78], which provides a clear critique of the theory of Kurt Latte[79], who, on the wake of Mommsen[80] and Wissowa[81], had shown a very restrictive and suspicious attitude towards literary sources and religious formulas reported in the texts of annalists and antiquarians[82]. Dumézil, in the opera *La religion romaine archaïque*, through the analysis of some of Livy's texts, effectively demonstrates the truthfulness of the solemn formulas reported by the historian of Padua[83], as well as previously, also Jean Bayet, in the «Introduction» in Tite-Live, had already found Livy's reports on Roman juridical, religious and political institutions fully plausible[84].

But to these considerations by the two illustrious French academics of the history of Roman religion[85], a further element is surely to be added by Francesco

77 F. Sini, "A proposito del carattere religioso del 'dictator'. Note metodologiche sui documenti sacerdotali", *Dittatura degli antichi e dittatura dei moderni*, ed. G. Meloni, Roma 1983, pp. 122 s. (contribution already published in *SDHI*, 42 (1976), pp. 422 ss.)., who, moreover, reiterates that: «si può ormai ritenere opinione comunemente accettata quella che individua nelle prescrizioni di diritto divino e, più in generale, in tutte le testimonianze ad esso riferibili, e che in certo modo possono farsi risalire ai documenti conservati negli archivi sacerdotali, "ciò che di più serio gli storici di Roma abbiano potuto conoscere per i primi secoli"» (123), in adherence to the thought of P. Catalano, *Contributi allo studio del diritto augurale*, I, Torino 1960, p. 109.

78 G. Dumézil, *La religion romaine archaïque*, Paris 1966, pp. 99 ss., then in *La religione romana arcaica*, It. Transl., Milano 1977.

79 K. Latte, *Römische Religionsgeschichte*, München 1960, pp. 5 s.

80 Th. Mommsen, *Römisches Staatsrecht*, II.1, Leipzig 1887, pp. 9 s.

81 G. Wissowa, *Religion und Kultus der Römer*, München 1912, pp. 5 s.

82 Cfr. K. Latte, *Römische* cit., pp. 5 s., who states: «Besondere Vorsicht ist bei Verwendung der in die annalistische Überlieferung eingelegten Dokumente geboten. Sie sind im wesentlichen von dem Schriftsteller selbst mit Benutzung sakraler und iuristischer Formeln, die ein archaisches Kolorit geben sollten, entworfen oder seiner unmittelbaren Vorlage entnommen». For a critique of Latte's theories see among others A. Brelich, "Un libro dannoso: la Römische Religionsgeschichte di Kurt Latte", *SMSR*, 32 (1961), pp. 329 ss.; R. Schilling, "La situation des études relatives à la religion romaine de la République (1950-1970)", *ANRW*, I.2 (1972), p. 327.

83 G. Dumézil, *La religion*, cit., pp. 104 ss.

84 See J. Bayet, *«Introduction» in Tite-Live, Histoire romaine*, I, Paris 1965, p. XXXIX.

85 For the status of research on Roman religion in France in the 20th century, see R. Schilling, "La situation", cit., pp. 317 ss.

Sini, who, in upholding the authentic value of the set of materials drawn from the priestly documents, rightly notes that «nella società romana arcaica e repubblicana, a fronte dello sviluppo dei rapporti economici e politici, si contrapponevano da una parte una più lenta evoluzione delle istituzioni giuridiche, specialmente di "diritto pubblico", dall'altra il carattere fortemente conservativo della tradizione religiosa»[86], thus enabling ancient authors, historians and literates to respectfully and extensively recover the original contents of the elaboration carried out by the priestly colleges. Obviously, Sini warns, this should not exempt the interpreter of these sources from carrying out a careful and rigorous evaluation, which takes into account the differences existing between the vision of the author handing down the source, in which one can grasp an individual ideology rooted in a precise socio-historical context and a personal level of graduation in the meticulousness of the analysis, and the information inherent to a specific historical event, an institute or a more remote juridical-religious reality, most often extrapolated from material dating back to the same age as the facts under investigation[87].

It is well known that most of the literal references from the priestly texts can be traced back to the pontiffs' books and to the books of the augurs[88]. There is, however, one exception represented by a pass from the *De Lingua Latina*, in which Varro quotes a fragment taken from the *libri Saliorum*:

> Varr. *l. lat.* 6.14: *In libris Saliorum quorum cognomen Agonensium, forsitam hic dies ideo appelletur potius Agonia*[89],

in which it is hypothesized that there were the most dated carmina of the *sodalitas*[90].

---

86 F. Sini, "A proposito", cit., p. 124. Also relevant on this topic are the considerations of S. Mazzarino, *Vico, l'annalistica e il diritto*, Napoli 1971, pp. 26 ss. But see also J. Bayet, *La religione romana. Storia politica e psicologi*, Torino 1992, pp. 44 ss.; G. Dumézil, cit., pp. 90, for the observations relating to the peculiar custodial aspects of the religious history of the Romans.

87 See F. Sini, "A proposito", cit., p. 124.

88 On this point, I invite you to refer to F. Sini, *Documenti sacerdotali di Roma antica*, I. *'Libri' e 'commentarii'*, Sassari 1983, p. 175; Id., "'Libri' e 'commentarii' nella tradizione documentaria dei grandi collegi sacerdotali romani", *Diritto @ Storia*, 1 (2002), § 10, pp. 1 ss.; Id., "Diritto e documenti sacerdotali romani: verso una palingensi", *Diritto @ Storia*, 4 (2005), § 4, pp. 1 ss., who develops the issue in the broader context of the distinction between priestly *libri* and *commentarii*.

89 On the text of Varro, see A. Cenderelli, *Varroniana. Istituti e terminologia giuridica nelle opere di M. Terenzio Varrone*, Milano 1973, pp. 42, 123; B. Cardauns, *'M. Terentius Varro Antiquitates rerum divinarum'*, I, Wiesbaden 1976, p. 54 (Appendix ad lib. VIII); II, p. 176.

90 See F. Sini, *Documenti*, cit., p. 175; Id., "Libri", cit., § 10, pp. 1 ss.; Id., "Diritto", cit., § 4, pp. 1 ss.

Regarding the content of the *Libri Augurum*, is thought that include the rules, precepts and procedures inherent to augural discipline[91]. A large part of the doctrine also considers that the augural books were organized with a systematic structure that was already consolidated at the end of the monarchic age or at the dawn of the republican age[92].

In this regard, the witness of Cicero is particularly valuable, as he, due to his membership in the College of the Augurs[93], and therefore being able to refer[94]

---

91 See F. Sini, *Documenti*, cit., pp. 91 ss. By examining the testimonies of Cicero, Varro, Verrio Flacco and Sextus Pompeius Festus, Livy, Seneca, Pliny, Quintilian, Censorinus, Arnobius, Marius Victorinus, Servius and Servius Danielinus, and Macrobius, F. Sini comes to the conclusion that the books contained «materiali riguardanti le regole della disciplina augurale».

92 As emerges from F.A. Brause, *'Librorum'*, cit., p. 10: «Porro si quaerimus quibus temporibus libri augurum orti sint compositique, origo quarundam partium ex regum tempore mihi videtur esse repetenda. Deinde etiam formula regum inaugurandorum quae sine dubio libris auguralibus vindicanda est ad regni tempora pertinet. Sed turpiter erraremus si iam regum temporibus totum corpus iuris auguralis ut ita dicam conscriptum esse arbitraremur»; and from P. Regell, *'De augurum'*, cit., p. 21: «Quodsi originem in regum saecula iure reiecimus, non ita multum a vero aberrabimus quod sub XII tabularum aetatem totam fere disciplinam libris contentam fuisse statuimus: qua aetate scribendi legendique artem satis fuisse celebrem supra indicavimus». On this point, see F. Sini, *Documenti*, cit., p. 175; Id., "Libri", cit., § 10, pp. 1 ss.; Id., "Diritto", cit., § 4, pp. 1 ss.

93 As is well known, Cicero had joined the College of the Augurs in 53 BC. For a textual match in the sources I refer to Plut. *Cic.* 36; Cic. *Brut.* 1; *Phil.* 2.4, as rightly indicated by F. Sini, *Documenti*, cit., pp. 93, 117, nt. 10. See also T.R.S. Broughton, *The Magistrates of the Roman Republic*, II, New York 1952, p. 233; J. Linderski, "The Aedileship of Favonius, Curio the Younger and Cicero's Election to the Augurate", *Harvard Studies in Classical Philology*, 76 (1972), pp. 181 ss. Lastly, see A. Zini, "Il 'dictator' e il 'magister populi'", *La dittatura romana*, II, ed., L. Garofalo, Napoli 2018, pp. 6 s.

94 I refer to the observations of F. Sini, *Documenti*, cit., pp. 93 s., 121 s. Regarding the existence of an archive of the documents of the College of Augurs, is worth the statement of F. Càssola, "Livio, il tempio di Giove Feretrio e la inaccessibilità dei santuari in Roma", *RSI*, 82 (1970), p. 24, which specifies that although it does not have a seat, it is safe «però che avevano un locale destinato ad archivio. In esso, probabilmente, erano custoditi i *commentarii augurum*, la cui conoscenza era rigorosamente vietata a chi non fosse membro del collegio». But see also F. D'Ippolito, "Sul pontificato massimo di Tiberio Coruncanio", in *Labeo*, 23 (1977), p. 129, afterwards in Id., *I giuristi e la città. Ricerche sulla giurisprudenza romana della repubblica*, Napoli 1978, p. 41; F. Bona, "'Ius pontificium' e 'ius civile' nell'esperienza giuridica tardo-repubblicana: un problema aperto", *'Contractus' e 'pactum'. Tipicità e libertà negoziale nell'esperienza repubblicana*, ed. F. Milazzo, Napoli 1990, p. 214. More recently, on the issue, A. Zini, "Il 'dictator'", *La dittatura romana*, II, cit., p. 7.

directly the *Libri Augurum*[95], in *De legibus* precisely outlines the orderly systematics of the materials contained in the augur books developed by the priests:

> Cic. *leg.* 2.20-21: *Interpretes autem Iovis optumi maxumi, publici augures, signis et auspiciis postea vidento, disciplinam tenento sacerdotesque vineta virgetaque et salutem populi auguranto; quique agent rem duelli quique popularem, auspicium praemonento ollique obtemperanto. Divorumque iras providento sisque apparento, caelique fulgura regionibus ratis temperanto, urbemque et agros et templa liberata et efflata habento. Quaeque augur iniusta nefasta vitiosa dira deixerit, inrita infectaque sunto; quique non paruerit, capital esto*[96].

The text seems to correspond to a transcription, elaborated by the augur Cicero, taken from an official collection for the use of the collegium. In the words reproduced by the Arpinate, a clear sequence of the augural competences transpires, outlined in the order of the priestly text. Dumézil[97] believes that Cicero evoked authentic partitions of the books of the Augurs, corresponding to a systematic arrangement of priestly competences[98]. This systematisation corresponded to the following sequence of functions[99]: 1. *Signa* and *auspicia* generally («*Interpretes autem Iovis optumi maximi, publici augures, signis et auspiciis postea vidento*»); 2. Discipline of Augurs («*disciplinam tenento*»); 3. *Inaugurationes* («*sacerdotesque vineta virgetaque et salutem populi auguranto*»); 4. *Auspicia* of magistrates («*quique agent rem duelli quique popularem, auspicium praemonento ollique obtemperanto*»); 5. *Nomina deorum* and *precationes augurales* («*divorumque iras providento sisque aparento*»); 6. Definitions of celestial and terrestrial spaces («*caelique fulgura regionibus ratis temperanto, urbemque et agros et templa liberata et efflata habento*»), to which, finally, was added the activity underlying the concluding sentence of Cicero's text, «*quaeque augur iniusta nefasta vitiosa dira*

95 Concerning the *Libri Augurum*, I refer to: F. Sini, *Documenti*, cit., pp. 1755 ss.; Id., "'Libri'", pp. 1 ss.; Id., "Diritto", cit., pp. 1 ss.

96 On this step of *De legibus*, I refer to: J. Linderski, "The Augural Law", cit. pp. 2148 ss. For the interpretation of the text, and the bibliography of reference, see among others F. Sini, "Diritto", cit., § 4, pp. 1 ss.

97 G. Dumézil, *Idées romaines*, Paris 1969, p. 97.

98 See G. Dumézil, *Idées*, cit., p. 97, who, referring to Cicero's possibility of direct access to the archives of the Collegium of the Augurs, specifies that «il était donc renseigné de première main, et il est probable qu'il utilise non seulement de vieilles formules, mais des divisions authentiques dans le statut qu'il donne à ce collège en forme de loi fictive».

99 Regarding the so-called systematic potential of Cicero's text, I follow the reading proposed by F. Sini, *Documenti*, cit., pp. 205 s., nt. 151, who, in this regard, moves a fully shareable critical remark towards P. Regell, *'De augurum'*, cit., p. 25, nt., which had proposed a systematisation by subject, divided into the following five parts.

deixerit, inrita infectaque sunto; quique non paruerit, capital esto», that evoked the practical performance of the Augural functions already systematically indicated, from which derived the granting of *responsa* and the promulgation of *decreta*, representing a set of priestly acts collected in the *commentarii*[100], rather than in priestly books[101], as correctly pointed out by F. Sini[102].

Having made these brief remarks, it will now be possible to proceed to an analysis of the passages in which it is possible to detect a provenance of content from documents of the College of Augurs on the subject of dictatorship[103], with the aim of catching some of the religious aspects and original characteristics of this peculiar magistrature.

2. Fragments from the *Libri Augurum* about *dictator*: Cicero and Livy

I will present here the contents of four texts that can certainly be ascribed to a provenance from the documents of the Collegium of the Augurs.

---

100 Among the first to assume that in Ciceronian times the priestly archives contained *responsa* and *decreta*: F.A. Brause, *'Librorum'*, cit., p. 16; e P. Regell, *'De augurum'*, cit., p. 24. See F. Sini, "'Libri'", cit., § 9, pp. 1 ss.

101 With regard to the distinction between *libri* and *commentarii*, F.A. Brause, *'Librorum'*, cit., pp. 10 ss., points out that the *libri* concerned «praecationes formulas praeceptaque antiquissima», while the *commentarii* «facta quaedam memorabiliora» including the *decreta*. On this conceptual difference, I refer, among others, to F. Sini, *Documenti*, cit., pp. 143 ss., in which the author clearly outlines the above distinction and fully reconstructs the state of doctrine on the subject. More recent, Id., "'Libri'", cit., § 7 ss., pp. 1 ss.; Id., "Diritto", cit., § 2 ss., pp. 1 ss.

102 See F. Sini, "Diritto", cit., § 4, pp. 1 ss., which also specifies that «non appare, quindi, senza significato la collocazione di questa parte alla fine del testo; cioè nettamente separata, anche se concettualmente dipendente, dalle materie attribuibili ai *libri augurum*».

103 For the different aspects of dictatorship in ancient Rome, among the most recent studies, I refer to Aa.Vv., *La dittatura romana*, I, ed. L. Garofalo, Napoli 2017; to Aa.Vv., *La dittatura romana*, II, cit., there extensive literature on the subject. But see also the monographic works by S. Fusco, *'Oriens de nocte silentio': alcune riflessioni sulla dittatura 'imminuto iure'*, Ortacesus 2018; G. Nicosia, *'Dictator'*, Catania 2019; G. Valditara, *Il 'dictator' tra emergenza e libertà*, Torino 2021. Lastly, the very recent contribution of R. Cardilli, "Diritto pubblico romano e nuova costituzione della repubblica di Cuba", *Diritto romano, costituzionalismo latino e nuova costituzione cubana*, ed. R. Cardilli, G. Lobrano and R. Marini, Milano 2021, pp. 47 ss.

The first of these passes is taken from the *De republica* of Cicero[104], while the other three come from the opera *Ab urbe condita* of Livy.

2.1. On the denomination of 'dictator': Cic. 'rep.' 1.40.63

To grasp the significance of the original denomination of *dictator*, as it has been handed down by the Augurs, it is certainly useful to analyse Cicero's testimony:

> Cic. *rep.* 1.40.63: *Nam dictator ab eo appellatur quia dicitur. Sed in nostris libris vides eum, Laeli, magistrum populi appellari*[105].

This text[106] on *dictator* is of great interest because it represents one of the emblematic cases of sources containing two mismatched pieces of information that could give rise doubts about the authenticity of the reported information[107]. Indeed, in the opening of the text Cicero proposes the etymology[108] of the substantive *ditactor* (*qui dicitur*[109]), while later introducing the official appellation of this magistrate (referred to as *magister populi*), thus creating a blatant inequality between the

---

104 For recurrences in Cicero's works of documents from *libri* and *commentarii* of Augurs, please refer to F. Sini, *Documenti*, cit., pp. 93 ss.

105 F.A. Brause, *'Librorum'*, cit., p. 42, fr. 28; P. Regell, *'Fragmenta auguralia'*, cit., p. 20, fr. 13. On the text see F. Sini, "A proposito", cit., p. 125; G. Valditara, *Studi sul 'magister populi'. Dagli ausiliari militari del 'rex' ai primi magistrati repubblicani*, Milano 1989, p. 186. Lastly, on this aspect, A. Zini, "Il 'dictator'", cit., pp. 6 s.

106 I quote the whole of Cicero's passage below in order to show the broader context of the augural source: Cic. *rep.* 1.40.63: *'Gravioribus vero bellis etiam sine collega omne imperium nostri penes singulos esse voluerunt, quorum ipsum nomen vim suae potestatis indicat. Nam dictator quidem ab eo appellatur quia dicitur, sed in nostris libris vides eum, Laeli, magistrum populi appellari'.* (Laelius) *'Video' inquit. Et Scipio: 'Sapienter igitur illi vete<res>'.* For a detailed analysis of the Ciceronian text, I refer to A. Zini, "Il 'dictator'", cit., pp. 5 ss., there extensive literature on the topic.

107 Cfr. F. Sini, "A proposito", cit., p. 124.

108 See A. Ernout and A. Meillet, s.v. "'dico'", *Dictionnaire étymologique de la langue latine*, Paris 2001, pp. 172 s. On this aspect see also C. Cascione, "'Dictatorem dicere': critica di un dogma (moderno) del diritto pubblico romano", *Studi per G. Nicosia*, II, Milano 2007, now also in Id., *Studi di diritto pubblico romano*, Napoli 2010, pp. 9 ss. Lastly, A. Zini, "Il 'dictator'", cit., p. 5, which reiterates that «l'etimologia formulata dagli antichi sembra essere fallace».

109 In this regard, see A. Ernout and A. Meillet, s.v. "'*dico*'", cit., p. 173, in which it is possible to detect the descent of the term from the verb *dictare*, from the form *dictando*: in this sense also the testimony of Priscianus (Prisc. *inst.* 8.78; Keil, II, 432,25), who held that *dictator* derived properly from *a dictando*. On this issue, seeA. Zini, "Il 'dictator'", cit., p. 5.

information reported. There is, however, a plausible explanation that is linked to the different significance of these two information; in fact, the former is closely linked to the findings of the antiquarian analysis of Cicero's historical context, while the latter is drawn by the Arpinate from the archaic priestly documents of the Collegium of the Augurs, and is therefore ascribable to a historical period much earlier than the one in which the great orator operated[110].

Therefore, to pull the strings of the discourse on the aspects that can be traced back to the evidence from the priestly documents, Cicero attests that in the *Libri Augurum* (*in nostris libris*) the denomination used to designate the *dictator* was *magister populi*[111]. The reliability of this information, which has also been confirmed by further sources, as shown by the Mommsen[112], also finds support in the fact that Cicero, in his role as Augur, could personally consult the documents in the archives of the collegium[113].

2.2. *On the competence of the appointment of the* dictator: Liv. *4. 31. 4*

Even in the work of Titus Livius, one can find some significant evidence from the documents of the Collegium of the Augurs on the subject of dictatorship. The historian from Padua provides some very interesting information regarding the competence of the appointment of the dictator, as well as the time and place of the *dictio dictatoris*[114].

---

110 F. Sini, "A proposito", cit., p. 124.

111 Regarding the older official name of *dictator*, I also refer to the interesting remarks of G. Meloni, "Dottrina romanistica, categorie giuridico-politiche contemporanee e natura del potere del 'dictator'", *Dittatura degli antichi e dittatura dei moderni*, cit., p. 78.

112 See Th. Mommsen, *Römisches Staatsrecht*, II, 1, cit., p. 143 n. 3.

113 See *supra*, nt. 33.

114 With regard to the appointment of the *dictator*, the sequence of the ritual is described by ancient authors in detail: Cic. *leg.* 3.3.9; Liv. 4.13.14, 4.21.10, 4.31.5, 4.57.5-6, 6.38.4, 8.23.14-15, 9.38.14, 9.39.1, 23.22.11; Dion. Hal. 5.72.2. For the literature on the topic, refer to: G. Tibiletti, "Evoluzione di magistrato e popolo nello stato romano", *Studia Ghisleriana*, s. II/1, from *Studi Letterari-Filosofici-Storici*, Pavia 1950, pp. 13 s.; A. Magdelain, *Recherches sur l'"imperium'. La loi curiate et les auspices d'investiture*, Paris 1968, p. 28; L. Labruna, "'Adversus plebem dictator'", *Index*, 15 (1987), p. 303, nt. 17; C. Cascione, "'Dictatorem'", cit., pp. 9 ss.; F. Giumetti, "Prima che il gallo canti. A proposito della 'dictio' del 'dictator' tra diritto, antropologia e storia delle religioni", *La dittatura romana*, I, cit., pp. 69 ss.; A. Milazzo, "Sul carattere 'straordinario' della magistratura del dittatore: alcune riflessioni su emergenza e periodicità nella sua nomina", *La dittatura romana*, I, cit., pp. 233 ss.; E. Nicosia, "'Ut optima lege' e 'dictio-creatio' del 'dictator'", *La dittatura romana*, I, cit., pp. 329 ss. Lastly, R. Cardilli, "Diritto", cit., pp. 74 s. See also S. Fusco, "'Oriens'", cit., pp. 14 ss., on the distinction between *creatio* of the consul and *dictio* of the dictator, here extensive literature on the subject.

Already from a first reading of the Livian passages, it is clear that the themes addressed are all connected to elements that have characterised the dictatorship since its origin. These themes can be traced back to certain issues underlying the *dictio dictatoris*, whose control over the regularity of the procedure, as is known, fell within the sphere of the *religio*[115] and was a specific competence of the Collegium of Augurs[116].

The first of these texts concerns, precisely, the ability to carry out the *dictio dictatoris*:

> Liv. 4.31.4: *Maesta civitas fuit vinci insueta; odisse tribunos, poscere dictatorem: in eo verti spes civitatis. Et cum ibi quoque religio obstaret ne non posset nisi ab consule dici dictator, augures consulti eam religionem exemere.*

This is a particularly interesting text, in which Livy reproduces the contents of a decree of the Augurs[117] concerning the competence to appoint the *dictator*. As it transpires from Livy's narration, the historical context of reference concerns the war against Veio conducted under the leadership of Titus Quincius Pena, Gaius Furius and Marcus Postumius, three of the four military tribunes with consular power appointed in 426 BC, to which was added Aulus Cornelius Cosso, who remained in Rome to carry out the functions connected with the *imperium domi*.

The well-known difficulties of war induced the Romans to formulate a strong request for the appointment of a *dictator*, given that, as Livius observes, in war it

---

115 On the meaning of *religio*, H. Fugier, *Recherches sur l'expression du sacré dans la langue latine*, Paris 1963, pp. 172 ss.; È. Benveniste, *Le vocabulaire des institutions indo-européennes, 2. Pouvoir, droit, religion*, Paris 1969, pp. 265 ss.; H. Wagenvoort, "Wesenzüge altrömischer Religion", *ANRW*, 1/2 (1972), pp. 348 ss. (= "Characteristic Traits of Ancient Roman Religion", Id., *'Pietas'. Selected studies in Roman Religion*, Leiden 1980, pp. 223 ss.); G. Lieberg, "Considerazioni sull'etimologia e sul significato di 'religio'", *Rivista di Filologia e di Istruzione Classica*, 102 (1974), pp. 34 ss.; R. Muth, "Von Wesen römischer 'religio'", *ANRW*, 2/16.1 (1978), pp. 290 ss.; R. Schilling, "L'originalité du vocabulaire religieux latin", Id., *Rites, cultes, dieux de Rome*, Paris 1979, pp. 30 ss.; E. Montanari, s.v. "'*Religio*'", *Enciclopedia Virgiliana*, 4, Roma 1988, pp. 423 ss.

116 On the competences of the Augurs and the documents of the priestly college, in addition to the literature indicated in nt. 14 of this contribution, I refer to: J. Marquardt, *Römische Staatsverwaltung*², *III. Das Sacralwesen*, ed. G. Wissowa, Leipzig 1885 [an. Repr. New York 1975], pp. 400 s.; A. Bouché-Leclercq, s.v. "'Augures'", *DS*, 1.1, 1877, pp. 550 ss.; V. Spinazzola, s.v. "'Augur'", *Diz. epigr.*, 1, 1895, pp. 778 ss.; G. Wissowa, s.v. "'Augures'", *PWRE*, 2/2 (1896), p. 2313 ss.; E. Norden, *Aus altrömischen Priesterbüchern*, Lund 1939; P. Catalano, *Contributi*, cit., pp. 108, 109, 593, 594.

117 In this regard, I agree with the thesis of F. Sini, "A proposito", cit., p. 125, which, in the wake of F.A. Brause, *'Librorum'*, cit., p. 46, places the Livian text between the *decreta augurum*.

is extremely harmful to divide the command of the army among several people, demonstrating that the original function of the dictatorship was precisely that of responding to the emergency needs of managing a war conflict, as Pomponius attests in the fragment examined in the preface to this paper[118].

The juridical-religious problem that emerges from the content of the text concerns the ability of military tribunes with consular power to appoint the *dictator* and, consequently, whether the *dictio dictatoris* not coming from the consul can be considered valid (the *religio* consisted precisely in the *non posset nisi ab consule dici dictator*)[119]. In fact, as we all know, at a time in history when plebeians were not allowed access to the consulship, and when auspices were exclusively managed by the patriciate, the *religio* generally did not allow an equalization of the consular *auspicia* to the *auspicia* of the *tribuni militum consulari potestate*[120], or to those inherent in a magistracy that was created to provide constitutional responses of openness towards the plebs and therefore also extended to the participation of plebeians[121].

The request for intervention by the Augurs is fully in line with their priestly functions and competences in the field of *auspicia*[122] and the *dictio dictatoris* is rightly brought back to the sphere of *religio*. The decree issued in this context by the priests has, in my opinion, a completely innovative value, since the Augurs proceed to formulate a substantial equality between the auspices of the *consules* and those of the military tribunes with consular authority[123].

Therefore, with this decree, the augurs intervened by decreeing an important change that allowed the *dictio dictatoris* of military tribunes with consular potestate, a function usually reserved for consuls, to be admitted under divine law, thus affirming the «pareggiamento delle capacità auspicali tra patrizi e plebei in quanto magistrati»[124]. In the overall course of the parification stages between

---

118 Pomp. *lib. sing. ench.* D. 1.2.2.18.

119 See F. Sini, "A proposito", cit., p. 125.

120 On the military tribunate with consular potestate see L. Zusi, "Patriziato e plebe. Rassegna degli studi 1966-1971", *Critica storica*, 12/2 (1975), pp. 177 ss. More recent on the subject is the contribution of F. La Rosa, "I 'tribuni militum' tra le istituzioni dell'alta repubblica", *Iura*, 45 (1994), pp. 15 ss., here reference bibliography on the topic.

121 See F. Sini, "A proposito", cit., p. 125.

122 In this regard, see *Titi-Livi ab urbe condita libri*, ed. W. Weissenborn and M. Müller, 2/2, repr. Zürich - Berlin, 1965, pp. 68; R.M. Ogilvie, *A commentary on Livy Books 1-5*, Oxford 1965, p. 584; F. Sini, "A proposito", cit., p. 125. In the context of the control of the legitimacy of the *auspicia* exercised by the Augurs, see P. Catalano, *Contributi*, cit., pp. 44 ss.

123 See F. Sini, "A proposito", cit., p. 125.

124 F. Sini, "A proposito", cit., p. 125.

the two orders, this was, without any doubt, a very significant milestone in the plebs' claims[125].

2.3. On the 'dictio dictatoris': Liv. 8.23.15

The Livian text, concerning the procedure for the appointment of the dictator by the consul and the time in which it was to be carried out, is well known and has been the subject of numerous studies by Romanist doctrine[126]:

Liv. 8.23.15: *Consul oriens de nocte silentio diceret dictatorem.*

The juridical issue underlying this passage concerns the validity of the consul's auspices, and Livy, again, refers to information directly from the archives of the Augurs[127].

The broader context in which the augural source is inserted concerns a specific case in which the tribunes of the plebs had questioned, and challenged the validity of, a determination made by the Collegium of the Augurs, who had invalidated the *dictio* of a plebeian *dictator*, as can be read in the full text of Livy, in the final part of paragraph 23 of Book VIII:

L. Cornelio, quia ne eum quidem in Samnium iam ingressum revocari ab impetu belli placebat, litterae missae ut dictatorem comitiorum causa diceret. Dixit M. Claudium Marcellum; ab eo magister equitum dictus Sp. Postumius. Nec tamen ab dictatore comitia sunt habita, quia vitione creatus esset in disquisitionem venit. Consulti augures vitiosum videri dictatorem pronuntiaverunt. Eam rem tribuni suspectam infamemque criminando fecerunt: nam neque facile fuisse id vitium nosci, cum consul oriens de nocte silentio diceret dictatorem, neque ab consule cuiquam publice privatimue de ea re scriptum esse nec quemquam mortalium exstare qui se vidisse aut audisse quid dicat quod auspicium dirimeret, neque augures divinare Romae sedentes potuisse quid in castris consuli vitii obuenisset; cui non apparere, quod plebeius dictator sit, id vitium auguribus visum? Haec aliaque ab tribunis nequiquam iactata; tamen ad interregnum res redit, dilatisque alia atque alia de causa comitiis quartus decimus demum interrex L. Aemilius consules creat C. Poetelium L. Papirium Mugillanum; Cursorem in aliis annalibus invenio[128].

---

125 P. Frezza, *Corso di storia del diritto romano*^{3}, Roma 1974, pp. 150 s.

126 In this regard, I refer to the more recent studies on dictatorship already cited above, nt. 1 of this paper.

127 See F. Sini, "A proposito", cit., p. 126, who rightly considers that this provenance from an augural source is confirmed by the fact that «l'oggetto della discussione dell'intero brano è la validità dell'auspicazione del console».

128 See S.P. Oakley, *A commentary on Livy, Books VI-X*, Oxford 1998, p. 662, who attributes to Livy, rather than the reference source from which he drew the news, the citation in the text of the protests of the tribunes of the plebs.

The priests, in fact, justified their decision on the grounds that there was a procedural defect (*vitiosum videri pronuntiaverunt*), specifically inherent to the time prescribed for the regularity of the appointment of the dictator, i.e. by that rite composed of a sequence of symbolic acts intrinsically linked by a solemn ceremonial, which took the form of a «liturgia d'investitura»[129], fully embedded in the magical-religious-juridical context that characterised the earliest period of Rome's history[130].

We learn from Livy's text that the plebeians' tribunes' objection to the Augur's decision to invalidate the *dictator*'s appointment (referred to as *suspectam infamemque*) is based on reasons that are well connected to the augural prescriptions of the *dictio* and that lead the plebeian magistrates to formulate some questions. The tribunes, in fact, pointed out that the irregularity could not have easily come to light, since the consul appointed the *dictator* by getting up quietly in the middle of the night; they also pointed out that the consul had not written to anyone - either privately or publicly - about that procedure; and that there was no mortal in a position to have seen or heard anything capable of invalidating the auspices; and lastly, that the Augurs had not been able, being in Rome, to divine what irregularity the consul had incurred in the camp. The plebeian magistrates then concluded by introducing what in their opinion could have been the real motivation for the decision of the Augurs: «To whom wasn't it clear that the irregularity noted by the augurs was definitely the plebeian origin of the dictator?»[131].

But apart from the more general context in which the whole affair takes place, and the historical context in which the news is set, it is clear that Livy draws his information from an augural source, a fact also confirmed by the use of the

129 F. Giumetti, "Prima", cit., pp. 69 ss.

130 See F. Sini, "A proposito", cit., p. 126. On the significance of the solemn ritual of the appointment of the *dictator*, from the perspective of an interdisciplinary analysis, I refer most recently to F. Giumetti, "Prima", cit., pp. 69 ss.

131 S.P. Oakley, *A commentary*, cit., p. 662, who specifies that the news about the tribunes' remonstrances, in his opinion included in the text by Livy, must not in any way diminish the value of the patricians' raising of an overt dissent against the plebeian origins of the *dictator* nominated *in castris*.

substantive *silentio*[132], that Festus expressly mentions as a technical term referring precisely to the auspiciousness[133]:

> Fest. *verb. sign.*, s.v. *Silentio surgere*, ed. Lindsay 474: *<Silentio surgere> ---t dici, ubi qui post mediam <noctem>.- - - tandi causa ex lectulo suo si<lens surr>exit et liberatus a lecto, in solido ------ <se>detque, ne quid eo tempore deiciat, <cavens, donec s>e in lectum reposuit: hoc enim est <proprie sil>entium, omnis vitii in auspiciis vacuitas. Veranius ait, non utique ex lecto, sed ex cubili, ne<c> rursus se in lectum reponere necesse esse.*

In fact, in the expression *hoc enim est proprie silentium, omnis vitii in auspiciis vacuitas* the juridical-religious value of the *silentio* in auspicious rites is clearly emphasised, as, moreover, Cicero had already specified in a passage from the *De divinatione*[134].

2.4. On the place of 'dictio': Liv. 27.5.15

Finally, the content of the Livian fragment concerning the place of the *dictio*:

> Liv. 27.5.15: *Illa disceptatio tenebat, quod consul in Sicilia se M. Valerium Messallam, qui tum classi praeesset dictatorem dicturum esse aiebat, patres extra Romanum agrum – eum autem Italia terminari – negabant dictatorem dici posse.*

The part of this text that is of interest concerns the place where the *dictio dictatoris* was to be carried out, i.e. within which territorial boundaries the *dictator* could be appointed[135].

While not quoting an official formula, Livy, even in this context, refers to a rule taken from the augural discipline, consistently observed throughout time[136].

---

132 Concerning the *silentium*, I refer especially to F. Vallocchia, "'Silentium' nei documenti sacerdotali. Le interpretazioni di Veranio e di Ateio Capitone", *Diritto @ Storia*, 6 (2007), pp. 1 ss. But see also M. Humm, "Silence et bruits autour de la prise d'auspices", *Les sons du pouvoir dans les mondes anciens*, under the direction of M.T. Schettino and S. Pittia, Besançon 2012, pp. 275 ss. On the value of silence, more specifically in the ritual of the *in procinctu* testament, I refer to the observations of C.M.A. Rinolfi, *'Testamentorum autem genera initio duo fuerunt: nam aut calatis comitiis testamentum faciebant ... aut in procinctu'. Testamenti, diritto e religione in Roma antica*, Torino 2020, p. 184 s.

133 On the silence in auspices, see Cic. *div.* 2.71: *silentium dicimus in auspiciis, quod omni vitio caret;* oltre ad un altro passo di Livio: Liv. 10.40.2: *Tertia vigilia noctis, iam relatis litteris a collega, Papirius silentio surgit et pullarium in auspicium mittit.*

134 Cic. *div.* 2.71.

135 On this point see F. Sini, "A proposito", cit., pp. 126 s.

136 On this regard, see Liv. 27.21.5. Cfr. F. Sini, "A proposito", cit., p. 126.

In fact, the augurs carried out a general check on the validity of the *auspicia* against the *dictio dictatoris*, precisely because they performed *auspicato*.

Moreover, the reference to the *ager Romanus*, within the boundaries of which the *dictio* was to take place, played a very precise role in augural science, an element that further reinforces the idea of the descent of the rule referred to by Livy from the augural precepts[137].

In fact, from a passage by Varro, we can learn the distinction proposed by the Augurs about the *agrorum genera*:

> Varr. *l. lat.* 5.33: *Ut nostri augures publici disserunt, agrorum sunt genera quinque: Romanus, Gabinus, peregrinus, hosticus, incertus. Romanus dictus unde Roma ab Rom<ul>o; Gabinus ab oppido Gabis; peregrinus ager pacatus, qui extra Romanum et Gabinum, quod uno modo in his servantur auspicia; dictus peregrinus a pergendo, id est a progrediendo: eo enim ex agro Romano primum progrediebantur. Quocirca Gabinus quoque peregrinus, sed quod auspicia habet singularia, ab reliquo discretus; hosticus dictus ab hostibus; incertus is, qui de his quattuor qui sit ignoratur*[138].

This classification into five *agrorum genera*[139] was established by the Augurs to classify the whole of the earth's space[140], in order to meticulously and precisely perform the rites of a religious nature. The *ager Romanus* is the first mentioned in Livy's augural classification and was the specific area where not only the *dictio dictatoris*, but also the *inaugurationes* were to take place (for example, there could not be *templum inauguratum* outside the *ager Romanus*); the taking of the *auspicia* at departure, their *repetitio*[141].

---

137 See F. Sini, "A proposito", cit., p. 126.

138 The attribution of the fragment to the augural archives is supported by F.A. Brause, '*Librorum*', cit., p. 42, fr. 27; P. Regell, '*Fragmenta auguralia*', cit., p. 19. For an articulate examination of Varro's text, which emphasises the archaic nature of the notions dealt with, I refer to P. Catalano, "Aspetti spaziali del sistema giuridico-religioso romano. 'Mundus, templum, urbs, ager, Latium, Italia'", *ANRW*, 2/16.1 (1978), pp. 492 ss.

139 I refer among others to P. Catalano, *Contributi*, cit., pp. 269 ss., 388; Id., *Linee del sistema sovrannazionale romano*, I, Torino 1965, p. 273 ss.; Id., *Aspetti*, cit., pp. 492 ss., for the studies on the concept of *ager Romanus* and its links to divine law. But see also F. Sini, "Diritto e 'pax deorum' in Roma antica", *Diritto@Storia*, 5 (2006), § 5.B, pp. 1 ss. Last on the topic, but with specific focus on the *ager Gabinus*, C.M.A. Rinolfi, '*Testamentorum*', cit., p. 170 s.

140 This division of the earth's space proposed by augural science is traced in an exemplary manner by F. Sini, "Diritto", cit., § 5.B, pp. 1 ss.

141 As correctly noted by F. Sini, "A proposito", cit., p. 127. I refer, however, to P. Catalano, *Contributi*, cit., pp. 269 ss., 388; Id., *Linee*, cit., pp. 273 ss.; Id., "Aspetti", cit., pp. 492 ss. Lastly F. Sini, "Diritto", cit., § 5.B, pp. 1 ss.

3. *Concluding remarks*

From this concise review dedicated to the study of certain priestly documents from the archives of the Augurs, it is evident that the testimonies of ancient authors on the theme of dictatorship are always focused on bringing out religious elements closely linked to the origins of this magistrature.

From the texts analysed, it is clear that this magistracy has generally had, from its origins, a marked religious connotation, even if the conception of those who, like the Magdelain[142], considers existing «una derivazione del potere dittatoriale direttamente da *Iuppiter*, evidenziando un "parallèle" tra la *dictio dictatoris* e l'*inauguratio* del *rex sacrorum* e dei flamini maggiori»[143], because based only on reasoning that goes beyond the more properly juridical data, seeing in the *dictator*'s power only a religious derivation[144].

As emerges from the texts examined in this contribution, which report on an ancestral time of the dictatorship, the appointment of the *dictator* was a very important event for the rhythms of life in the ancient city, inevitably also affecting the more properly religious aspects of the *civitas*, with an active involvement of the priestly colleges, and more specifically that of the augurs.

Bibliography

Aa.Vv., La dittatura romana, I-II, ed. L. Garofalo, Napoli 2017.

Bayet, J., «Introduction» in Tite-Live, Histoire romaine, I, Paris 1965.

Bayet, J., La religione romana. Storia politica e psicologi, Torino 1992.

Benveniste, Ė., Le vocabulaire des institutions indo-européennes, 2. Pouvoir, droit, religion, Paris 1969.

Bona, F., "'Ius pontificium' e 'ius civile' nell'esperienza giuridica tardo-repubblicana: un problema aperto", 'Contractus' e 'pactum'. Tipicità e libertà negoziale nell'esperienza repubblicana, ed. F. Milazzo, Napoli 1990.

---

142 A. Magdelain, "'Auspicia ad patres redeunt'", *Hommages à Jean Bayet*, Bruxelles 1964, pp. 427 s.; Id., "Note sur la loi curiate et les auspices des magistrats", *RHD*, 42 (1964), p. 198; Id., *Recherches sur l'"imperium*', cit.; Id., "'Praetor maximus et comitiatus maximus'", *Iura*, 20 (1969), pp. 257 s., on which see the fully agreeable critical remarks made by F. Sini, "A proposito", cit., 111 ss., on the religious foundation of the *dictator*'s power theorised by the French academic.

143 F. Sini, "A proposito", cit., pp. 127 s.

144 See F. Sini, "A proposito", cit., p. 128.

Bouché-Leclercq, A., s.v. "'Augures'", DS, 1.1, 1877, pp. 550 ss.

Brause, F.A., 'Librorum de disciplina augurali ante Augusti mortem scriptorum reliquiae', Lipsiae 1875.

Brelich, A., "Un libro dannoso: la Römische Religionsgeschichte di Kurt Latte", SMSR, 32 (1961), pp. 329.

Broughton, T.R.S., The Magistrates of the Roman Republic, II, New York 1952.

Cardauns, B., 'M. Terentius Varro Antiquitates rerum divinarum', I and II, Wiesbaden 1976.

Cardilli, R., "Diritto pubblico romano e nuova costituzione della repubblica di Cuba", Diritto romano, costituzionalismo latino e nuova costituzione cubana, ed. R. Cardilli, G. Lobrano and R. Marini Milano 2021.

Cascione, C., "'Dictatorem dicere': critica di un dogma (moderno) del diritto pubblico romano", Studi per G. Nicosia, II, Milano 2007.

Cascione, C., Studi di diritto pubblico romano, Napoli 2010.

Càssola, F., "Livio, il tempio di Giove Feretrio e la inaccessibilità dei santuari in Roma", RSI, 82 (1970).

Catalano, P., Contributi allo studio del diritto augurale, I, Torino 1960.

Catalano, P., Linee del sistema sovrannazionale romano, I, Torino 1965.

Catalano, P., "Aspetti spaziali del sistema giuridico-religioso romano. 'Mundus, templum, urbs, ager, Latium, Italia'", ANRW, 2/16.1 (1978).

Cenderelli, A., Varroniana. Istituti e terminologia giuridica nelle opere di M. Terenzio Varrone, Milano 1973.

D'Ippolito, F., "Sul pontificato massimo di Tiberio Coruncanio", in Labeo, 23 (1977).

D'Ippolito, F., I giuristi e la città. Ricerche sulla giurisprudenza romana della repubblica, Napoli 1978.

Dumézil, G., La religion romaine archaïque, Paris 1966.

Dumézil, G., La religione romana arcaica, It. Transl., Milano 1977.

Ernout, A. and Meillet, A., s.v. "'dico'", Dictionnaire étymologique de la langue latine, Paris 2001.

Frezza, P., Corso di storia del diritto romano 3, Roma 1974.

Fugier, H., Recherches sur l'expression du sacré dans la langue latine, Paris 1963.

Fusco, S., 'Oriens de nocte silentio': alcune riflessioni sulla dittatura 'imminuto iure', Ortacesus 2018.

Humm, M., "Silence et bruits autour de la prise d'auspices", Les sons du pouvoir dans les mondes anciens, under the direction of M.T. Schettino and S. Pittia, Besançon 2012.

La Rosa, F., "I 'tribuni militum' tra le istituzioni dell'alta repubblica", Iura, 45 (1994).

Labruna, L., "'Adversus plebem dictator'", Index, 15 (1987).

Latte, K., Römische Religionsgeschichte, München 1960.

Lieberg, G., "Considerazioni sull'etimologia e sul significato di 'religio'", Rivista di Filologia e di Istruzione Classica, 102 (1974).

Linderski, J., "The Aedileship of Favonius, Curio the Younger and Cicero's Election to the Augurate", Harvard Studies in Classical Philology, 76 (1972).

Linderski, J., "The Augural Law", ANRW, 2/16.3 (1986).

Magdelain, A., "'Auspicia ad patres redeunt'", Hommages à Jean Bayet, Bruxelles 1964.

Magdelain, A., "Note sur la loi curiate et les auspices des magistrats", RHD, 42 (1964).

Magdelain, A., Recherches sur l''imperium'. La loi curiate et les auspices d'investiture, Paris 1968.

Magdelain, A., "'Praetor maximus et comitiatus maximus'", Iura, 20 (1969).

Marquardt, J., Römische Staatsverwaltung 2, III. Das Sacralwesen, ed. G. Wissowa, Leipzig 1885 [an. Repr. New York 1975].

Mazzarino, S., Vico, l'annalistica e il diritto, Napoli 1971.

Meloni, G., "Dottrina romanistica, categorie giuridico-politiche contemporanee e natura del potere del 'dictator'", Dittatura degli antichi e dittatura dei moderni, ed. G. Meloni, Roma 1983.

Milazzo, A., "Sul carattere 'straordinario' della magistratura del dittatore: alcune riflessioni su emergenza e periodicità nella sua nomina", La dittatura romana, I, ed. L. Garofalo, Napoli 2017.

Mommsen, Th., Römisches Staatsrecht, II.1, Leipzig 1887.

Montanari, E., s.v. "'Religio'", Enciclopedia Virgiliana, 4, Roma 1988.

Muth, R., "Von Wesen römischer 'religio'", ANRW, 2/16.1 (1978).

Nicosia, E., "'Ut optima lege' e 'dictio-creatio' del 'dictator'", La dittatura romana, I, ed. L. Garofalo, Napoli 2017.

Nicosia, G., 'Dictator', Catania 2019.

Norden, E., Aus altrömischen Priesterbüchern, Lund 1939.

Oakley, S.P., A commentary on Livy, Books VI-X, Oxford 1998.

Ogilvie, R.M., A commentary on Livy Books 1-5, Oxford 1965.

Regell, P., 'De augurum publicorum libris', Vratislaviae 1878.

Regell, P., 'Fragmenta auguralia', Hirschberg 1882.

Regell, P., "Auguralia", 'Commentationes Philologae in honorem Augusti Reifferscheidii', Vratislaviae 1884.

Regell, P., 'Commentarii in librorum auguralium fragmenta specimen', Hirschberg 1893.

Rinolfi, C.M.A., 'Testamentorum autem genera initio duo fuerunt: nam aut calatis comitiis testamentum faciebant … aut in procinctu'. Testamenti, diritto e religione in Roma antica, Torino 2020.

Schilling, R., "L'originalité du vocabulaire religieux latin", Id., Rites, cultes, dieux de Rome, Paris 1979.

Schilling, R., "La situation des études relatives à la religion romaine de la République (1950-1970)", ANRW, 1/2 (1972).

Sini, F., "A proposito del carattere religioso del 'dictator'. Note metodologiche sui documenti sacerdotali", Dittatura degli antichi e dittatura dei moderni, ed. G. Meloni, Roma 1983, pp. 122 s. (contribution already published in SDHI, 42 (1976)).

Sini, F., Documenti sacerdotali di Roma antica, I. 'Libri' e 'commentarii', Sassari 1983.

Sini, F., "'Libri' e 'commentarii' nella tradizione documentaria dei grandi college sacerdotali romani", Diritto @ Storia, 1 (2002).

Sini, F., "Diritto e documenti sacerdotali romani: verso una palingensi", Diritto @ Storia, 4 (2005).

Sini, F., "Diritto e 'pax deorum' in Roma antica", Diritto@Storia, 5 (2006).

Spinazzola, V., s.v. "'Augur'", Diz. epigr., 1, 1895.

Tibiletti, G., "Evoluzione di magistrato e popolo nello stato romano", Studia Ghisleriana, s. II/1, from Studi Letterari-Filosofici-Storici, Pavia 1950.

Titus Livius, Titi-Livi ab urbe condita libri, ed. W. Weissenborn and M. Müller, 2/2, repr. Zürich - Berlin 1965.

Valditara, G., Studi sul 'magister populi'. Dagli ausiliari militari del 'rex' ai primi magistrati repubblicani, Milano 1989.

Valditara, G., Il 'dictator' tra emergenza e libertà, Torino 2021.

Vallocchia, F., "'Silentium' nei documenti sacerdotali. Le interpretazioni di Veranio e di Ateio Capitone", Diritto @ Storia, 6 (2007).

Wagenvoort, H., "Wesenzüge altrömischer Religion", ANRW, 1/2 (1972) (= "Characteristic Traits of Ancient Roman Religion", Id., 'Pietas'. Selected studies in Roman Religion, Leiden 1980).

Wissowa, G., s.v. "'Augures'", PWRE, 2/2 (1896).

Wissowa, G., Religion und Kultus der Römer, München 1912.

Zini, A., "Il 'dictator' e il 'magister populi'", La dittatura romana, II, ed., L. Garofalo, Napoli 2018.

Zusi, L., "Patriziato e plebe. Rassegna degli studi 1966-1971", Critica storica, 12/2 (1975).

Elżbieta Loska[145]

The auspices in the activities of plebeian tribunes

Abstract: After the plebeians were admitted to priestly colleges by the *lex Ogulnia*, it became possible for a plebeian to become an augur. Did plebeian tribunes then, from that moment on, also gain the right and obligation to take auspices just like the magistrates? Did they observe the sky solely to block the actions of other magistrates? What impact did the *lex Ogulnia* have on the Republican system?

Keywords: auspices, plebeian tribunes, *concilia plebis*, *plebiscita*, Roman law

In Rome, initially, membership in priestly colleges was exclusively the domain of patricians. It was only since the *lex Ogulnia*[146] of 300 BCE that plebeians started to be admitted to priestly colleges:

> Liv. 10,6,4-5: *certamen iniectum inter primores civitatis, patricios plebeiosque, ab tribunis plebis Q. et Cn. Ogulniis (...) Rogationem ergo promulgarunt ut, cum quattuor augures, quattuor pontifices ea tempestate essent placeretque augeri sacerdotum numerum, quattuor pontifices, quinque augures, de plebe omnes, adlegerentur.*

Describing the activity of the plebeian tribunes Quintus and Gnaeus Ogulnius (and assessing it as one inciting unrest), Livy provided the content of the *rogatio* submitted by them, which was then adopted: the number of priests in the colleges was to be increased by four pontiffs and five augurs, with all of them coming from the plebs.

Only then did it become possible for a plebeian to become an augur. Since a plebeian could become an augur, he could undoubtedly conduct auspices and interpret them at the request of an official or private person. One of the *leges Liciniae Sextiae*[147] passed a few years earlier opened access to the consul's office for plebeians, which also allowed the latter to take auspices, or even obliged them to do so – this argument was raised during the discussion on the project[148]. The motion was vetoed during the first vote but was adopted the next day[149].

---

145 Cardinal Stefan Wyszynski University in Warsaw, ORCID: 0000-0001-6838-7721.

146 G. Rotondi, *Leges publicae populi Romani*, Milano 1912, p. 236.

147 G. Rotondi, *op.cit.*, p. 216.

148 Liv. 10,8,9: *Semper ista audita sunt eadem, penes vos auspicia esse, vos solos gentem habere, vos solos iustum imperium et auspicium domi militiaeque; aeque adhuc prosperum plebeium et patricium fuit porroque erit.*

149 Liv. 10,9,1-2.

It is also worth remembering that the signs could be read by anyone[150], but reporting the sighting was not always binding – and *auspicia privata* were probably taken before all important events and transactions. By the end of the Republic, however, private auspices fell into disuse[151].

There is rather no doubt that the plebeian tribunes had the right to take *auspicia impetrativa*, namely to 'order' signs and observe whether they appeared[152]. Such auspices were the result of *spectio*, which could take the form of observing the sky[153] (*servare de caelo*).

In the source texts, there are many examples of the plebeian tribunes making observations of the sky in order to block the actions of other officials.

One such incident was described by Cicero in a letter to his friend Atticus, sent from Rome on November 23, 57 BCE:

---

150 Serv., *in Aen.* 3,20.

151 G.W. Botsford, *The Roman Assemblies from the Origin to the End of the Republic*, New York 2005, p. 103.

152 Cic., *leg.* 3,10: *Omnes magistratus auspicium iudiciumque habento, exque is senatus esto*; in connection with the previous fragment concerning the plebeian tribunes. I.M.J Valeton, (*'De iure obnuntiandi comitiis et conciliis'*, «Mnemosyne» 19/1891, p. 91) attributes the right to *spectio cum nuntiatione* to the tribunes from 449 BCE onwards.; cf. G.W. Botsford, *op.cit.*, p. 104; A.E. Astin, *Leges Aelia et Fufia*, «Latomus» 23/1964, p. 426 ff.; J. Linderski, *Römischer Staat und Götterzeichen: Zum Problem der obnuntiatio*, «Jahrbuch der Universität Düsseldorf» 1969–1970 [1971], p. 319 ff.,; J. Vaahtera, *Roman Augural Lore in Greek Historiography: A Study of the Theory and Terminology*, Stuttgart 2001, p. 160 ff.; L.G. Driediger-Murphy, *Roman Republican Augury. Freedom and Control*, Oxford 2019, p. 135. There are also researchers who deny them this right in their own cases, limiting their auspices only to *obnuntiatio*: Y. Berthelet, *'Violence, obstruction augurale et crise de la République romaine'* [in:] *Elite und Krise in antiken Gesellschaften/Élites et crises dans les sociétés antiques*, ed. L. Gilhaus, S. Kirsch, I. Mossong, F. Reich, S. Wirz, Stuttgart 2016, p. 84. Cf. G.V. Sumner, *'Lex Aelia, lex Fufia'*, «AJPH» 84.4/1963, p. 345 ff. – the author suggests that it was the *lex Aelia* that allowed the tribunes to apply *obnuntiatio*, which, after all, involved taking auspices; cf. also S. Weinstock, *Clodius and the 'lex Aelia Fufia'*, «JRS» 27/1937, p. 216, according to whom the *lex Aelia et Fufia* contained a confirmation of this right. The already quoted text Cic., *Att.* 4,3,3-5, or Cic., *Att.* 4,17,4 clearly mention the use of *obnuntiatio* by the tribune.

153 Fest. 446L; L.G. Driediger-Murphy, *Roman Republican Augury*. p. 135. The author further points out that the definition preserved by Festus is incorrect in the fragment where it indicates the impossibility of blocking the activity of other officials by announcing signs obtained during observation. – ibidem, p. 136, nt. 41.

Cic., *Att.* 4,3,3-5: *(Milo) proposita Marcellini sententia, quam ille de scripto ita dixerat ut totam nostram causam areae, incendiorum, periculi mei iudicio complecteretur eaque omnia comitiis anteferret, proscripsit se per omnis dies comitialis de caelo servaturum. contiones turbulentae Metelli, temerariae Appi, furiosissimae Publi haec tamen summa, nisi Milo in campo obnuntiasset, comitia futura. ante diem xii Kal. Decembr. Milo ante mediam noctem cum, magna manu in campum venit. Clodius cum haberet fugitivorum delectas copias, in campum ire non est ausus. Milo permansit ad meridiem mirifica hominum laetitia summa cum gloria. contentio fratrum trium turpis, fracta vis, contemptus furor. Metellus tamen postulat ut sibi postero die in foro obnuntietur; nihil esse quod in campum nocte veniretur; se hora prima in comitio fore. itaque ante diem xi Kal. in comitium Milo de nocte venit. Metellus cum prima luce furtim in campum itineribus prope deviis currebat; adsequitur inter lucos hominem Milo, obnuntiat. ille se recepit magno et turpi Q. Flacci convicio. ante diem x Kal. nundinae. contio biduo nulla. ante diem viii Kal. haec ego scribebam hora noctis nona. Milo campum iam tenebat.*

The plebeian tribune Titus Annius Milo wanted to block the elections probably for the office of curule aedile. He therefore announced that he would read the sky every day suitable for carrying out the assembly. The *contiones* were called. The speakers included the consul Quintus Caecilius Metellus Nepos, who was to preside over the elections, and Publius Clodius, who ran for the office of aedile. It was agreed that if Milo did not declare *obnuntiatio* on the Campus Martius, the assembly, and therefore the elections, would take place. On the twelfth day before the calends of December (November 19), before midnight, Milo went to the Campus Martius – that was when the Roman day began, and the auspices were often taken before sunrise so as to prevent them from any disturbance[154] – and stayed there until noon, stopping the consul Metellus from holding the elections[155]. *Auspicia impetrativa* taken by officials were valid for one day only[156]; therefore, the sky reading had to be taken daily. The following day the consul tried to outsmart the tribune as he announced that he would accept *obnuntiatio* at the Forum, but instead, at dawn, he slipped away to the Campus Martius so that

154 J. Linderski, *Augural Law*, «ANRW» II 16.3/1986, p. 2173, nt. 94; G.W. Botsford, *op. cit.*, p. 110.

155 Electing assemblies had to start before noon to have been completed before sunset. Cf. G.W. Botsford, *op. cit.*, p. 115 ff.; J. Vaahtera, *On the Religious Nature of the Place of Assembly*, [in:] *Senatus Populusque Romanus. Studies in Roman Republican Legislation*, ed. J. Vaahtera, p. 97.

156 J. Linderski, *Watching the Birds: Cicero the Augur and the Augural Temple*, „CPh" 81/1986, p. 334; Idem, *Augural Law*, p. 2295; G.W. Botsford, *op. cit.*, p. 109.

Milo would not find him and thus not be able to announce unfavourable signs. However, the persistent tribune caught up with him and declared *obnuntiatio*[157].

This event confirms that it was possible to report a valid *obnuntiatio* by a plebeian official – the plebeian tribune Milo announced that he had observed unfavourable signs, and the consul Metellus was forced to acknowledge this fact[158].

The plebeian tribunes also held auspices while convening the senate, as reported by the antiquarian Gellius quoting Varro:

> Gell. 14,7,4: *Primum ibi ponit qui fuerint per quos more maiorum senatus haberi soleret eosque nominat: „dictatorem, consules, praetores, tribunos plebi, interregem, praefectum urbi,"* 9. (…) *quibus diebus habere senatum ius non sit; immolareque hostiam prius auspicarique debere,*

It is generally believed that the right to take auspices belonged only to members of the magistrate[159], namely patrician officials (treated as such even when plebeians were allowed to hold the offices)[160]. This was due to the fact that (as also reported

157 On this event also in L.G. Driediger-Murphy, *Roman Republican Augury*, p. 70 ff.

158 The elections were finally held but only on January 20, 56 BCE, namely after Milo had ended his tribunate. - Cic, *Q.F.* 2,2,2; Cic., *Sest.* 65, Dio Cass. 39,18,1. Cf. W. J. Tatum, *The Patrician Tribune. Publius Clodius Pulcher*, London 1999, p. 198 ff.

159 Cic., *Dom.* 38: *auspicia populi Romani, si magistratus patricii non sint, intereant necesse est, cum interrex nullus sit, quod et ipsum patricium esse et a patriciis prodi necesse est.* Cf. interesting opinion in A. Ziółkowski, http://xxpzhp.umcs.lublin.pl/Referaty/Adam Ziółkowski - SEDITIONES, CERTAMINA CIVILIA, SECESSIONES.pdf (accessed 25.04.2024). The author writes that at the beginning of the Republic, the patricians usurped auspices, which was a result of their political importance, and in order to take auspices, the plebeians had to first take this political monopoly away from the patricians.

160 Liv. 6,41; Gell. 13,15,4 clearly wrote about patrician auspices: *Patriciorum auspicia in duas sunt divisa potestates.* J. Zabłocki (*'Leges votatae' nelle assemblee popolari*, http://www.dirittoestoria.it/10/Tradizione-Romana/Zablocki-Leges-voto-assemblee-popolari.htm = *'Leges votatae' na zgromadzeniach ludowych*, „Diritto@Storia" 10/2011-2012, http://www.dirittoestoria.it/10/Tradizione-Romana/Zablocki-Leges%20voto-assemblee-popolari-pol.htm, accessed 09.05. 2024; *Uchwały rzymskich zgromadzeń ludowych*, [in:] *'Regnare, gubernare, administrare'. Prawo i władza na przestrzeni wieków. Prace dedykowane profesorowi Jerzemu Malcowi z okazji 40-lecia pracy naukowej*, ed. S. Grodziski, A. Dziadzio, Kraków 2012, p. 4), in turn, links the right to take auspices in state matters with the official's *imperium* - this would have excluded lower officials, including plebeian tribunes, from the circle of authorized persons. Also in J. Linderski, *Rzymskie zgromadzenie wyborcze od Sulli do Cezara*, Wrocław-Warszawa-Kraków 1966, p. 74; cf. R. Develin, *Lex curiata and the Competence of Magistrates*, «Mnemosyne» 30.1/1977, p. 62.

by Gellius in his *Noctes Atticae* 13,15) they were elected under the auspices. It means that those whose election to office was sanctioned by favourable signs from the deities could then make certain whether the deities favoured their public activity. Therefore, if *leges* were adopted at *comitia* convened by these officials, it could be presumed they were adopted with the approval of the gods, and therefore without violating the *pax Deorum*.

Therefore, the question arises as to how the issue of checking the favour of deities was shaped when plebiscites[161] were adopted. This is essential especially since the final equalization of plebiscites with the laws by the *lex Hortensia* of 287 BCE at the request of dictator Quintus Hortensius[162]. We know that the *comitia* adopting the *leges* had to be preceded by auspices held by any official presiding over them – a consul, praetor or dictator. A positive result of auspices proved the deities' favour towards the assembly itself, and probably also towards the content of the law passed there. This approval could be lost at any time – if an unfavourable sign appeared during the assembly, the assembly itself needed to be interrupted and the law passed there would not become binding on the Roman people.

However, the source texts show that this was not always the case; acts were sometimes adopted despite *obnuntiatio*, namely reporting the appearance of an unfavourable sign. Then, the *lex* adopted at such a meeting was *contra auspicia lata*[163]. A lightning strike could be an example of such an unfavourable sign.

---

161 Gell. 10,20,6; Fest., *s.v. Scita plebei* (372L) and *s.v. Scitum populi* (442L). See e.g. J. Bleicken, *Das Volkstribunat der klassischen Republik. Studien zur seiner Entwicklung zwischen 287 unf 133 v. Chr.*, München 1955, p. 1 ff.; J. Zabłocki, *'Leges votatae'*; Idem, *Uchwały*, p. 9; A. Tarwacka, *Czym jest wniosek, czym ustawa, czym plebiscyt, czym przywilej – Aulus Gellius, 'Noce attyckie' 10,20. Tekst - tłumaczenie - komentarz*, «Zeszyty Prawnicze» 10.1/2010, p. 328; Eadem, *Czym są zgromadzenia kalarne, czym kurialne, czym centurialne, czym trybusowe, czym wiec; oraz podobne sprawy z tym związane – Aulus Gellius, 'Noce attyckie' 15,27. Tekst - tłumaczenie - komentarz*, «Zeszyty Prawnicze» 14.1/2014, p. 222; B. Salisbury, *The Status of Plebiscita 494-287 BC*, «New Clasicists» 1-2019, passim.

162 Gell. 15,27,4-5; Plin., NH 16,37; G. 1,3; D. 1,2,2,8; I. 1,2,4. Cf. G. Rotondi, *op. cit.*, p. 238 ff.

163 The examples of such laws are given in H. Kowalski, *'Leges per vim contra auspicia latae'. Religia, polityka i prawo karne w Rzymie*, [in:] *'Salus rei publicae suprema lex'. Ochrona interesów państwa w prawie karnym starożytnej Grecji i Rzymu*, ed. A. Dębiński, H. Kowalski, M. Kuryłowicz, Lublin 2007, p. 106 ff.

The plebiscite was called *lex inauspicata*[164] by Livy, but this happened when describing the events of 362 BCE (so before the *lex Hortensia*). The pretext for such wording was the plebeian consul Genucius ambushed. When the news about this event reached Rome, the patricians lamented, emphasizing all this had happened because the consul was a plebeian and the auspices fell into the hands of those who should not have the right to carry them out and who excluded the patricians from the privileges they were entitled to, while a plebiscite passed without the approval of the deities meant more than the immortal deities themselves[165]. Jyri Vaahtera also rightly notes that all the excerpts where Livy emphasizes the lack of auspices when passing plebiscites are actually the fictitious quotes from political speeches delivered by patricians[166].

Since the moment the *lex Hortensia* was adopted, should not the plebeian tribunes also have gained the right and obligation to conduct auspices, just like the magistrates? Since plebiscites were now to be binding on all Roman citizens, just like the *leges*, should not the approval of the deities be verified before they were passed?

This becomes probable if we take into account that the auspices had an influence on the activity of the plebeian tribunes, their *ius agendi cum plebe*. The use of auspices in relation to *comitia populi* and *concilia plebis* was regulated jointly by the *Aelia et Fufia* laws[167]:

> Cic., *Vat.* 18: *cum te tribuno pl. esset etiam tum in re publica lex Aelia et Fufia, quae leges saepe numero tribunicios furores debilitarunt et represserunt, quas contra praeter te nemo umquam est facere conatus (quae quidem leges anno post sedentibus in templo duobus non consulibus, sed proditoribus huius civitatis ac pestibus una cum auspiciis, cum intercessionibus, cum omni iure publico conflagraverunt), ecquando dubitaris contra eas leges cum*

---

164 Liv. 7,6,11. That might be why, before the adoption of the *lex Hortensia*, plebiscites needed *auctoritas patrum* to be binding on the entire Roman people – cf. J. Zabłocki *'Leges votatae'* accessed 09.05. 2024 r.; *Uchwały*, p. 13. One of such plebiscites is the *lex Icilia* of 456 BCE – Liv. 3,31,1; 3,32,7. After obtaining approval from the *patres*, who met after taking auspices, the plebiscite would no longer be treated as adopted without auspices. This would be another argument for the need to take approving auspices before convening the *concilia plebis* after 287 BCE.

165 Liv. 7,6,10-11: *irent crearent consules ex plebe, transferrent auspicia quo nefas esse. potuisse patres plebi scito pelli honoribus suis: num etiam in deos immortales inauspicatam legem valuisse?*

166 J. Vaahtera, *op. cit.*, p. 160.

167 More on these laws in E. Loska, *Uwagi na temat procedury 'obnuntiatio'*, «Zeszyty Prawnicze» 11.1/2011, along with the literature quoted there.

plebe agere et concilium convocare; num quem ex omnibus tribunis pl., quicumque seditiosi fuerunt, tam audacem audieris fuisse, ut umquam contra legem Aeliam aut Fufiam concilium advocaret.

In his speech against Vatinius[168] delivered in 56 BCE, among other things, Cicero accused him of failing to comply with the provisions of the *leges Aelia et Fufia* regarding the *obnuntiatio* procedure while holding the office of plebeian tribune, namely in 59 BCE. The orator claimed that no one except Vatinius had dared to resist these laws, and he had not hesitated to call a plebeian assembly despite their decisions. He also emphasized that even the most rebellious of the tribunes were not brazen enough to convene an assembly contrary to these laws.

The *leges Aelia et Fufia* are sometimes seen as a counterweight to the tribune's *ius intercessionis*[169]. According to Lily Ross Taylor, the *lex Aelia et Fufia* seemed to give patrician officials the right to *obnuntiatio* against the tribunes and their projects[170]. And, paradoxically, this may constitute a very strong argument in the discussion on the right of the tribunes to conduct the *spectio* before convening the *concilia plebis*. Why would there be any need to look for unfavourable signs that could interrupt the gathering if there was no need to observe favourable signs first[171]? So, the *leges Aelia et Fufia* could be seen as a form of mitigating a certain advantage of the tribunes over other officials, especially patrician ones, but also a proof of tribunician right to take auspices. By means of *intercessio*, the tribunes could block any actions of all other officials (except for the dictator's), including the convening of an assembly. Additionally, after the adoption of the *lex Ogulnia*, the tribunes gained the ability to use *obnuntiatio*. Perhaps it should therefore be assumed that they also had the right to the auspices before calling *concilia plebis*[172]? It is also possible that the tribunes did not conduct auspices independently but acted together with the officials with *ius agendi cum populo*, informing them about

168 T.R.S. Broughton, *The Magistrates of the Roman Republic*, II, New York 1952, p. 190.
169 Cic. *Vat.* 17; W.F. McDonald, *Clodius and the 'lex Aelia Fufia'*, «JRS» 19/1929, p. 166; G.W. Botsford, *op. cit.*, p. 115, nt. 1.
170 L.R. Taylor, *The forerunners of the Gracchi*, «JRS» 52/1962, p. 23. Also in J. Linderski, *Rzymskie zgromadzenie wyborcze od Sulli do Cezara*, Wrocław-Warszawa-Kraków 1966, p. 78.
171 Also in J. Vaahtera, *Roman Augural Lore*, p. 162 ff.
172 Dionysius of Halicarnassus wrote that they did not do this (9,41,3; 9,49,5), but this is a Greek author who may not have had a good understanding of the religious intricacies of the Republic period.

the results of the executed auspices, following the example of quaestors who did so when convening *comitia centuriata* in criminal cases[173]:

> Varro, *LL* 6,91: *Auspicio o<pe>ram des et in templo auspices, tum aut ad praetorem aut ad consulem mittas auspicium petitum.*

Varro provided comments on the accusation brought against Trogus by Manius Sergius in a case punishable by death (*qui capitis accusavit*). In accordance with the Law of the Twelve Tables, such matters could only be resolved by *comitia centuriata*, which the quaestor could not convene on his own. But as the next fragment shows, he made them to be convened[174].

Finally, it is worth adding that Aulus Gellius, who wrote about patrician auspices in his famous text, may have distinguished them from plebeian ones[175]:

> Gell. 13,15,4: (…) *Patriciorum auspicia in duas sunt divisa potestates.*

What we know for sure is that from the *lex Hortensia* onwards, the decisions of the assembly convened by the plebeian tribunes were to be binding on all citizens and on an equal footing with the *leges*. There are no known sources regarding the need to convene the *concilia plebis auspicato*. But why risk violating the *pax deorum*?

Bibliography

Astin A.E., *Leges Aelia et Fufia*, «Latomus» 23/1964, p. 421-445.

Berthelet Y., *'Violence, obstruction augurale et crise de la République romaine'* [in:] *Elite und Krise in antiken Gesellschaften/Élites et crises dans les sociétés antiques*, ed. L. Gilhaus, S. Kirsch, I. Mossong, F. Reich, S. Wirz, Stuttgart 2016, p. 83-95.

Bleicken J., *Das Volkstribunat der klassischen Republik. Studien zur seiner Entwicklung zwischen 287 und 133 v. Chr.*, München 1955.

Botsford G.W., *The Roman Assemblies from the Origin to the End of the Republic*, New York 2005.

Broughton T.R.S., *The Magistrates of the Roman Republic*, II, New York 1952.

Develin R., *Lex curiata and the Competence of Magistrates*, «Mnemosyne» 30.1/1977, p. 62.

---

173 G.W. Botsford, *op. cit.*, p. 103 ff.

174 *comi<ti>atum praetor <r>eum vocet ad te (…) Collegam roges ut comitia edicat de rostris.*

175 Alos in G.W. Botsford, *op. cit.*, p. 104. The author actually wrote that the antiquarian's expression implied the existence of *plebeiorum magistratuum auspicia*.

Driediger-Murphy L.G., *Roman Republican Augury. Freedom and Control*, Oxford 2019.

Kowalski H., *'Leges per vim contra auspicia latae'. Religia, polityka i prawo karne w Rzymie*, [in:] *'Salus rei publicae suprema lex'. Ochrona interesów państwa w prawie karnym starożytnej Grecji i Rzymu*, ed. A. Dębiński, H. Kowalski, M. Kuryłowicz, Lublin 2007, p. 103-114.

Linderski J., *The Augural Law*, „ANRW" II 16.3/1986, p. 2146-2312.

Linderski J., *Römischer Staat und Götterzeichen: Zum Problem der obnuntiatio*, «Jahrbuch der Universität Düsseldorf» 1969–1970 [1971], p. 309-322.

Linderski J., *Rzymskie zgromadzenie wyborcze od Sulli do Cezara*, Wrocław-Warszawa-Kraków 1966.

Linderski J., *Watching the Birds: Cicero the Augur and the Augural Temple*, „CPh" 81/1986, p. 330-340.

Loska E., *Uwagi na temat procedury 'obnuntiatio'*, „Zeszyty Prawnicze" 11.1/2011, p. 195-213.

McDonald W.F., *Clodius and the 'lex Aelia Fufia'*, «JRS» 19/1929, p. 164-179.

Rotondi G., *Leges publicae populi Romani*, Milano 1912.

Salisbury B., *The Status of Plebiscita 494-287 BC*, «New Clasicists» 1-2019, p. 41-58.

Sumner G.V., *'Lex Aelia, lex Fufia'*, «AJPH» 84.4/1963, p. 337-358.

Tarwacka A., *Czym jest wniosek, czym ustawa, czym plebiscyt, czym przywilej – Aulus Gellius, 'Noce attyckie' 10,20. Tekst - tłumaczenie - komentarz*, «Zeszyty Prawnicze» 10.1/2010, p. 325-330.

Tarwacka A., *Czym są zgromadzenia kalarne, czym kurialne, czym centurialne, czym trybusowe, czym wiec; oraz podobne sprawy z tym związane – Aulus Gellius, 'Noce attyckie' 15,27. Tekst - tłumaczenie - komentarz*, «Zeszyty Prawnicze» 14.1/2014, p. 217-223.

Tatum W. J., *The Patrician Tribune. Publius Clodius Pulcher*, London 1999.

Taylor L.R., *The forerunners of the Gracchi*, «JRS» 52/1962, p. 19-27.

Vaahtera J., *On the Religious Nature of the Place of Assembly*, [in:] *Senatus Populusque Romanus. Studies in Roman Republican Legislation*, ed. J. Vaahtera, p. 97-116.

Vaahtera J., *Roman Augural Lore in Greek Historiography: A Study of the Theory and Terminology*, Stuttgart 2001.

Valeton I.M.J., *'De iure obnuntiandi comitiis et conciliis'*, «Mnemosyne» 19/1891, p. 73-115 and 229-270.

Weinstock S., *Clodius and the 'lex Aelia Fufia'*, «JRS» 27/1937, p. 215-222.

Zabłocki J., *'Leges votatae' nelle assemblee popolari*, http://www.dirittoestoria.it/10/Tradizione-Romana/Zablocki-Leges-voto-assemblee-popolari.htm = *'Leges votatae' na zgromadzeniach ludowych*, „Diritto@Storia" 10/2011-2012, http://www.dirittoestoria.it/10/Tradizione-Romana/Zablocki-Leges%20voto-assemblee-popolari-pol.htm.

Zabłocki J., *Uchwały rzymskich zgromadzeń ludowych*, [in:] *'Regnare, gubernare, administrare'. Prawo i władza na przestrzeni wieków. Prace dedykowane profesorowi Jerzemu Malcowi z okazji 40-lecia pracy naukowej*, ed. S. Grodziski, A. Dziadzio, Kraków 2012.

Ziółkowski A., http://xxpzhp.umcs.lublin.pl/Referaty/Adam Ziółkowski - SEDITIONES, CERTAMINA CIVILIA, SECESSIONES.pdf.

Anna Karabowicz[176]

Lex est quod populus iubet atque constituit (Gai. 1.3): law-making functions of popular assemblies as the factor of democratisation in the Roman republican constitution

Abstract: Can we speak of democracy in republican Rome? Or rather the democratising factor present in the constitution of the Roman Republic? A foreigner, the Greek Polybius, and a Roman philosopher, lawyer, orator and politician, Cicero, have commented on this question. The former, in his *Histories*, written at the height of republican rule, described it as a mixed government in which the popular assemblies embodied the democratic factor. In describing the powers of the assemblies, he pointed out that the people had the absolute power to make and overthrow laws, which Gaius confirmed in the quoted passage from his *Institutions*. This essay will critically analyse the democratic element of the Roman republican system identified by Polybius. First, the composition will be analysed, and the complex voting system in relation to each type of popular assembly in the Republic will be briefly presented. Next, the competences of the assemblies will be shown, with particular emphasis on their legislative powers, in order to demonstrate a real influence on lawmaking through the participation and voting systems in the assemblies.

Keywords: democracy, Roman Republic, popular assemblies, legislation, voting system, popular sovereignty

1. Not an easy definition of democracy

There is probably not a person in the world who would not be able to give at least the most obvious and basic definition of the term "democracy", which would likely be a reasonably faithful translation of its Greek root word, namely: *δημοκρατία* or *dēmokratia*. It is made up of two basic words, *dēmos*: "the people" and *kratos*: "rule". Thus, according to the etymology of the word "democracy", the term should be understood literally as "rule of the people". Such a seemingly simple and obvious concept, and yet so controversial and multifaceted.[177]

176 UPO, Seville, Spain, ORCID: 0000-0001-7037-9501.

177 F. Pina Polo, "Idea y práctica de la democracia en la Roma republicana," *Gerión. Revista de Historia Antigua* 37/2 (2019), p. 380.

In the context of the 21st century, which has witnessed the global ascendancy of the democratic system and its remarkable triumph all over the world, but also its crisis and the questioning of its foundations, principles and prospects for the future, it is evident that the term "democracy" has acquired a plethora of connotations and numerous epithets were added to it since antiquity. One might cite, for example, such historical types of democracy as Athenian or classical democracy (referred to as "radical"[178] in some sources), Roman or elite (aristocratic) democracy, estate or noble democracy in the Polish-Lithuanian Commonwealth of the 16th century, liberal or social democracy, and its already modern forms, such as representative (indirect) or direct democracy, or, finally, popular democracy.

Returning to the source, however, it is necessary to take a closer look at the constituent elements of the concept of democracy. In every regime throughout history that has been called a democracy (with or without the epithet), the term *dēmos*, or the people in whose hands the government of the state was placed, has been understood in different ways. The same is true of the second element of the term democracy, *kratos*, rule. Each of the above-mentioned historical and contemporary forms of democratic systems either granted the people, defined in its own peculiar sense, a specific scope of state powers, or otherwise described the manner in which the power entrusted to the people was to be exercised.

With regard to the first component of the term democracy, i.e. the people, its understanding has never been absolute in history.[179] Even in the present era, individuals who are not citizens of the state, minors, or those who have been sentenced to disenfranchisement are excluded or limited in their capacity to influence the governance of the state. Throughout history, there have been many more such exclusions, mostly on the basis of gender, state of freedom or social status, and property census. Similarly, in the case of the scope of state power, in the exercise of which the people were involved in one way or another, it is difficult to find an example of a regime – except perhaps classical Athens – that gave the people a virtually unlimited scope of state government. Almost all democratic regimes are characterised by the delegation of legislative power to the people and, to a lesser extent, of executive or judicial power.

178 R. Ruiz Ruiz, *Los orígenes del republicanismo clásico. Patrios Politeia* y *Res Publica*, Madrid 2006, p. 33.

179 T. Kaplan, *Democracy. A World History*, Oxford 2014, pp. 46-61; B. DeWiel, *Democracy: A History of Ideas*, Vancouver-Toronto 2000, pp. 11-22.

2. Roman democracy – truth or myth

As far as ancient Rome is concerned, it is imperative to answer the question of whether, and if so, which factor in the constitution of the Republic can be identified as constituting a certain degree of democratisation of that system. In order to answer this question, it is necessary to cite the testimony of two witnesses to the political reality of the late Roman Republic, namely the Greek historian Polybius of the second century BC and Cicero, a Roman writer, politician, orator and lawyer of the first century BC.

In describing the structure of the republican system, Polybius used the classical Greek concept of *mikte*, a mixture (a political system that is a combination of pure forms of monarchy, aristocracy and democracy). The concept of the *mikte* was derived from the works of the classical Greek philosophers Aristotle and Plato.[180] With regard to the first component, the monarchical, Polybius, despite his reservations, recognised that it was embodied in the consuls, who were elected annually by the popular assemblies. The Senate, on the other hand, was the aristocratic element of the Roman republican constitution. In turn, the democratic factor in the Roman republican system, as can be read in Polybius' *Histories*, were the popular assemblies:[181] "As for the Roman constitution, it had three elements, each of them possessing sovereign powers: and their respective share of power in the whole state had been regulated with such a scrupulous regard to equality and equilibrium that no one could say for certain, not even a native, whether the constitution as a whole were an aristocracy or democracy or despotism. And no wonder: for if we confine our observation to the power of the Consuls we should be inclined to regard it as despotic; if on that of the Senate, as aristocratic; and if finally one looks at the power possessed by the people it would seem a clear case of a democracy".[182] Polybius, in the following paragraphs of the same Book VI of his work, defined the scope of the government of the state entrusted to these three elements: Consuls, Senate and People, and described the mutual relations between them, including dependence and mutual control. In section 14, he characterised the scope of power entrusted to the people: "There is, however, a part left [to – AK] the people, and it is a most important one. For the people is the sole fountain of honour and of punishment; and it is by these two things and these alone that

180 S. Gordon, *Controlling the State. Constitutionalism from Ancient Athens to Today*, Harvard 2002, pp. 80-83.
181 Ibid., p. 108.
182 *Polyb.* 6.11 in *The Histories of Polybius*, transl. E. S. Schuckburgh, vol. I, London-New York 1889, p. 468.

dynasties and constitutions and, in a word, human society are held together: for where the distinction between them is not sharply drawn both in theory and practice, there no undertaking can be properly administered, – as indeed we might expect when good and bad are held in exactly the same honour. The people then are the only court to decide matters of life and death; and even in cases where the penalty is money, if the sum to be assessed is sufficiently serious, and especially when the accused have held the higher magistracies. And in regard to this arrangement there is one point deserving special commendation and record. Men who are on trial for their lives at Rome, while sentence is in process of being voted, –if even only one of the tribes whose votes are needed to ratify the sentence has not voted, –have the privilege at Rome of openly departing and condemning themselves to a voluntary exile. Such men are safe at Naples or Praeneste or at Tibur, and at other towns with which this arrangement has been duly ratified on oath. Again, it is the people who bestow offices on the deserving, which are the most honourable rewards of virtue. It has also the absolute power of passing or repealing laws; and, most important of all, it is the people who deliberate on the question of peace or war. And when provisional terms are made for alliance, suspension of hostilities, or treaties, it is the people who ratify them or the reverse. These considerations again would lead one to say that the chief power in the state was the people's, and that the constitution was a democracy".[183]

Polybius assigns the most significant importance to the powers exercised by the people of the Roman Republic, suggesting that this democratic element of the republican constitution exerts a dominant influence over the other two, namely the monarchical in the persons of the consuls or the aristocratic embodied in the Senate.[184]

In his Republic, Cicero does not explicitly comment on the democratic or aristocratic nature of the Roman republican system. He presents the republican constitution as an ideal blend of all three, which had worked perfectly for centuries and had been handed down to the Romans by their ancestors: "For I am convinced, I believe, and I declare that no other form of government is comparable, either in its general character, in its distribution of powers, or in the training it gives, with that which our ancestors received from their own forefathers, and have handed down to us."[185]

In response to the question of which system he considers the best, he clearly advocates a mixed system: "You are right to ask which I consider the best of the

183 *Polyb.* 6,14 in Ibid., p. 470-471.

184 Cf. F. Pina Polo, *op. cit.*, p. 381; see in detail in R. Ruiz Ruiz, *op. cit.*, pp. 80-103.

185 Cic. Resp. 1.46 in https://www.attalus.org/cicero/republic1b.html [accessed: 25.06.2024].

three, for I do not approve of any of them when employed by itself, and consider the form which is a combination of all them superior to any single one of them. But if I were compelled to approve one single unmixed form, [I might choose] the kingship [...] But here are the aristocrats, with the claim that they can do this more effectively, and that there will be more wisdom in the counsels of several than in those of one man, and an equal amount of fairness and scrupulousness. And here also are the people, shouting with a loud voice that they are willing to obey neither one nor a few, that nothing is sweeter than liberty even to wild beasts, and that all who are slaves, whether to a king or to an aristocracy, are deprived of liberty. Thus kings attract us by our affection for them, aristocracies by their wisdom, and popular governments by their freedom, so that in comparing them it is difficult to say which one prefers."[186]

A perusal of Cicero's writings reveals a clear aversion to Greek popular rule. Conversely, he is in favour of an aristocratic form of government: "Since this is true, the kingship, in my opinion, is by far the best of the three primary forms, but a moderate and balanced form of government which is a combination of the three good simple forms is preferable even to the kingship. For there should be a supreme and royal element in the State, some power also ought to be granted to the leading citizens, and certain matters should be left to the judgment and desires of the masses. Such a constitution, in the first place, offers in a high degree a sort of equality, which is a thing free men can hardly do without for any considerable length of time, and, secondly, it has stability."[187]

The definition of a republic is given by Cicero in Book I, paragraph 25: "Well, then, a commonwealth is the property of a people. But a people is not any collection of human beings brought together in any sort of way, but an assemblage of people in large numbers associated in an agreement with respect to justice and a partnership for the common good."[188] The expression *res publica res populi* is a recurring theme in Cicero's writings. According to scholars, the phrase signifies that a republic cannot exist without the people, and vice versa.[189]

---

186 Cic. *Resp.* 1.35 in Ibid.

187 Cic. *Resp.* 1.45, in Ibid.

188 Cic. *Resp.* 1.25, in Ibid.

189 F. Pina Polo, *op. cit.*, pp. 383-388; S. Gordon, *op. cit.*, pp. 110-115; J. J. Megías Quirós, L. Cabrera Caro, *Historia de las ideas políticas. De la democracia griega a la monarquía medieval*, Cádiz 2015, pp. 89-93; R. Ruiz Ruiz, *op. cit.*, pp. 103-116; about the idea of *res publica* see in J. M. Ribas Alba, "*Populus romanus* y *res publica*: comunidad política y ciudadanía," in *Derecho, persona y ciudadanía. Una experiencia jurídica comparada*, ed. B. Periñán Gómez, Madrid-Barcelona-Buenos Aires 2010, pp. 297-299.

This text will briefly discuss the democratic factor in the constitution of republican Rome, namely all types of popular assemblies. Its analysis will be divided into two parts. The first section, entitled "*Dēmos*," will examine the composition and internal organization of the assemblies, with a focus on the voting system utilised in each popular assembly. Additionally, the estimated participation of Roman citizens in the deliberations will be presented. The second part, entitled "*Kratos*", will analyse the powers of the popular assemblies of the Roman Republic, with particular reference to their legislative competences.

3. *Dēmos*

Returning to the definition of democracy given earlier, it is important to ask how the term *dēmos*, or people, or society, is to be understood. Even in modern democracies, not all members of society living in a given territory are equally entitled to political participation. These restrictions are citizenship, age and sentences of deprivation of public rights. In the past, there were many more such restrictions: gender, freedom, race, and morality.

In ancient Rome, as in most of the ancient world, e.g. Greece, slaves or women were excluded from political life. In republican Rome, the right to influence the government of the state, which meant the right to attend and vote in popular assemblies, was called *ius suffragii*.[190] It was a right that belonged almost exclusively to Roman citizens.[191] In addition, the Latins, the so-called *latini prisci* or *veteres*, i.e. the members of the Latin League and the inhabitants of the colonies founded by the League, had a limited *ius suffragii*. They could exercise it in a *tribus* chosen at random.[192]

The understanding of the term *dēmos*, the people in the Roman Republic who had an influence on the government of the state through their participation in the

---

190 On the *suffragium* especially in the context of the right to elect magistrates see in J. M. Ribas Alba, *Democracia en Roma. Introducción al derecho electoral romano*, Granada 2008, pp. 49-82; Cf. H. Tagle Martínez, "*Ius suffragii* y *ius honorum*," *Revista Chilena de Derecho* 20/2/3, vol. 1 (Mayo-Diciembre 1993), pp. 345-348; O. Castro, "Entre el pasado y el presente: evolución histórica del *ius suffragii* y *el ius honorum*, del Derecho romano al Derecho mexicano," *RIDROM* 21 (2018), pp. 643-650.

191 For details on the legal position of a Roman citizen and the acquisition and loss of citizenship, see M. Kaser, *Das Römische Privatrecht, 1er Abschnitt*, München 1971, pp. 279-281; J. Iglesias, *Derecho romano. Instituciones de derecho privado*, Barcelona 1987, pp. 143-146; F. Lamberti, "Percorsi della cittadinanza romana dalle origini alla tarde Repubblica," in *Derecho, persona y ciudadanía... op. cit.*, pp. 17-56.

192 J. Iglesias, *op. cit.*, pp. 149-150; J. M. Ribas Alba, *Democracia..., op. cit.*, pp. 66-69.

assemblies, therefore encompassed a very limited number of the population who were adult Roman male citizens.[193] The fact that such a limited definition of the people should be further confronted with the complex composition and internal structure of the assemblies meant the average Roman citizen had even less real influence on the political life of the Republic.

When discussing the constitution of republican Rome, the plural form is used to refer to popular assemblies. This is due to the fact that during the 500-year history of the Republic, there were 3 types of assemblies. Apart from the chronology of their formation, they differed mainly in their composition. Although all Roman citizens with *ius suffragii* were entitled to participate in each of the assemblies (except for the *concilium plebis*, see below), their internal composition, which was particularly important for the casting of votes by those assembled, was different.

The basic principle that distinguished the assemblies of republican Rome from other ancient or later assemblies was that, although Roman citizens participated personally, they did so as part of the groups, the units, into which all Roman citizens were divided. These units were different at each assembly. It was within these groups that Roman citizens cast their votes both for the nomination of magistrates and, more relevant to this text, for proposed legislation. In contrast to modern times, where one person represents one vote, in the Roman Republic, each such unit into which Roman citizens were divided had one vote. It is important to note that within these groups, members also cast their votes. This resulted in the final vote of the group representing the position of the majority of citizens gathered in that unit. This internal structure of assemblies influenced two key aspects: the order in which votes were cast and the actual power and importance of each vote. Additionally, it influenced whether individuals who voted at the end were allowed to vote at all.[194]

In Rome, for practically the entire period of the Republic, i.e., between 510 and 27 BC, three types of popular assemblies coexisted.[195] Each was distinguished

193 The most likely age range for all assemblies was 17-60 years. Certainly, for the *comitia centuriata* this was the age limit, corresponding to the age for military service, see: J. J. Megías Quirós, L. Cabrera Caro, *op. cit.*, p. 30.

194 For details of the voting procedure in the units, see U. Hall, "Voting Procedure in Roman Assemblies," *Zeitschrift für Alte Geschichte* 13,3 (Jul. 1964), pp. 271-273, 283-286.

195 The *comitia calata* will not be discussed in this text since its duties were related to the election and nomination of the monarch, and it no longer met during the period of the Republic, cf. J. M. Ribas Alba, *Democracia…*, *op. cit.*, pp. 133-140; G. W. Botsford, *The Roman Assemblies from their origin to the end of the Republic*, New York 1909, pp. 152-167.

by the unit within which Roman citizens were divided and organised for a specific meeting. The names of these three types of assemblies are also derived from the names of the groups within which the citizens participated in the deliberations.[196]

Chronologically, the first was the curiate assembly (*comitia curiata*), said to have been formed by the legendary founder of Rome, Romulus. It was he who divided the Roman citizens into three tribes, each of which was divided into ten *curiae*. It is not entirely clear on what basis this partition was made. The most likely ground was a mixture of kinship and residence. Over time, the thirty *curiae* were replaced by thirty lictors.[197]

The *comitia centuriata* was a more complex assembly exhibiting a more intricate internal structure. Consequently, it employed a more sophisticated voting system for matters within its purview. As the name implies, Roman citizens, males between the ages of 17 and 60 who were fit for military service, were divided into *centuriae* by the Roman king Servius Tullius in the 6th century BC. The *centuriae* were originally constituted as military units, which shaped the nature of the centurial assembly as a military institution. Centuries subsequently evolved into voting units of Roman citizens, with each citizen belonging to a specific century and thus being able to vote within the century in which they were registered.

The division of citizens for military purposes was, of course, based on a census of property. Those with greater financial resources were able to procure their own weaponry and served in the military as cavalry or heavily armed infantry. There were 193 centuries in all. The *equites*, aristocrats who served in the army as horsemen, presided at the top over the remaining 5 classes. The *equites* were further divided into 18 centuries. Based on the value of their property, society was divided into five classes and these into centuries. The first, richest class comprised 80 centuries (these were further divided into two age groups: 40 centuries of *iuniores* for men aged 17 to 45 and 40 centuries of *seniores* for those over 45). The next three classes each had 20 centuries (10 for each age group). The fifth class consisted of the poorest citizens, divided into 30 centuries (15 each for *iuniores* and *seniores*). The remaining citizens, the so-called *proletarii* o *capite censi*, who did not own any property, were grouped together in a single century. Outside this

196 Ibid., pp. 143-144.

197 Ibid., pp. 144-161; G. W. Botsford, *op. cit.*, pp. 168-200; T. Cornell, *Roman Political Assemblies*, in *A Companion to the Political Culture of the Roman Republic*, eds. V. Arena, J. Prag, A. Stiles, Hoboken (NJ) 2022, p. 222.

structure, there were another 4 centuries: 2 for engineers (*fabri*) and 2 for musicians (*cornicines* and *tubicines*).[198]

Even a quick glance at the division of citizens into centuries reveals the disparity in the number of centuries between the richest *equites* with the first class and the rest of society. With a total of 98 centuries, they could easily muster the majority needed to vote for a bill or a candidate for magistracy. This effect was exacerbated by the fact that voting took place in order. The *equites* voted first, and after their vote was announced, the next classes voted, starting with the first, of course. This meant that classes from the second onwards could not vote at all. At the end of the 3rd century BC, the division of citizens into voting units in the assembly was reformed. Since then, the voting groups were based on local tribes, the number of which reached 35 in 241 BC. From then on, the first class consisted of 70 centuries (35 each for the *seniores* and *iuniores*). The total number of centuries remained at 193, but from this reform onwards, the *equites* and the first class no longer held a majority of centuries. Moreover, from then on, the *equites* no longer voted first. The first to vote was the so-called *centuria praerogativa*, which was selected randomly from the centuries of the first class. Towards the end of the Republic, the centuries within each class voted simultaneously rather than consecutively in assemblies convened for electoral purposes.[199]

The reform at the end of the 3rd century seems to have slightly democratised the voting system of the *comitia centuriata*, although it remained very unequal and oligarchic. Of course, it did not eliminate the possibility of even those poorest citizens to vote, but the division into units outlined above, combined with the entire voting system, determined the conservative and aristocratic composition of this assembly.[200]

The final type of assembly was the *comitia tributa*. The internal composition of the assembly was based on the local tribes into which Roman citizens had been divided since the monarchy. It is likely that Servius Tullius was responsible for replacing the earlier tribes, which had been established by Romulus. The city was initially constituted by four tribes, with rustic tribes situated in the outskirts of Rome. By 495 BC, there were already 21 rural units. Following a period of territorial expansion, the number of tribes reached a final total of 35 by 241 BC. Since

198 J. M. Ribas Alba, *Democracia…*, *op. cit.*, pp. 163-198; T. Cornell, *op. cit.*, pp. 223-224; J. Iglesias, *op. cit.*, pp. 16-17; more in U. Coli, "Tribù e centurie dell'antica repubblica romana," *SDHI* 21 (1955), pp. 181-222; G. W. Botsford, *op. cit.*, pp. 48-99, 201-228.

199 These were the reforms of the brothers Tiberius and Gaius Gracchus, tribunes, at the end of the 2nd century BC, J. M. Ribas Alba, *Democracia…*, *op. cit.*, p. 194.

200 T. Cornell, *op. cit.*, pp. 223-226.

that time, no additional tribes had been established, with the number of urban tribes remaining at four. Instead, new territories had been incorporated into one of the existing rustic tribes.

The newly created units were initially employed as the foundation for the internal structure and voting organisation in relation to the plebeian assembly, which convened for the first time in 494 BC. This was also done in 471 BC when the *concilium plebis* used local tribes as voting units. The *concilium plebis* was the sole republican assembly that did not encompass the entire *populus Romanus*.[201] This assembly was constituted of a distinctive membership comprising the plebeians, i.e. the economically disadvantaged and legally marginalised social class in the Roman Republic.[202]

Shortly afterwards, during the 5th century BC, the same voting units were used as the basis for the organisation of a new assembly of the entire Roman people, the *comitia populi tributa*.[203] In the case of the *comitia tributa*, the voting procedure depended on the nature of the assembly. In an electoral assembly, voting took place in parallel in all tribes, so that all units voted at the same time. When an assembly was called for legislative or judicial purposes, the votes were taken consecutively. The order of the tribes in the voting process was determined by lot, and the unit that voted first was called the *principium*.

Towards the end of the Republic, a very important reform was carried out, namely the introduction of the secret ballot through a series of laws. The *lex Gabinia* of 139 BC introduced the secret ballot for elective assemblies, the *lex Cassia* of 137 BC instituted the secret ballot for *comitia* convened for judicial purposes, and the *lex Papiria* of 131 BC provided the same rule for legislative assemblies.[204]

It can be argued that the tribal assembly was more democratic, particularly in the last century of the Republic. This was undoubtedly influenced by the more egalitarian system of division into voting units, the tribes, which resulted in a

---

201 About the idea of *populus Romanus* see in J. M. Ribas Alba, *Democracia…*, *op. cit.*, pp. 29-48; Id., "*Populus romanus…*", *op. cit.*, pp. 277-279; R. Domingo, *Roman law. An introduction*, London-New York 2018, pp. 30-31.

202 See J. Iglesias, *op. cit.*, pp. 18-19; R. E. Mitchell, *Patricians and Plebeians. The Origin of the Roman State*, Ithaca NY 1990, passim; H. J. Rose, "Patricians and Plebeians at Rome," *The Journal of Roman Studies* 12 (1922), pp. 106-133; H. Mouritsen, *Plebs and Politics in the Late Roman Republic*, Cambridge 2001, pp. 128-148.

203 The nature of the meeting is determined by the convening magistrate authorised to convene the meeting provided with *ius agendi cum plebe* or *ius agendi cum populo*, J. M. Ribas Alba, *Democracia…*, *op. cit.*, p. 270.

204 U. Hall, *op. cit.*, pp. 290-297.

balance of votes for each. Furthermore, the introduction of the principle of simultaneous voting (although only in the case of elective assemblies) and, finally, the secrecy of the vote also contributed to this shift. The only disadvantage of the *comitia tributaria* was the discrepancy between the numerous poor urban population, who were concentrated in four urban tribes, and the affluent landowners, who were registered in more numerous rustic units.[205]

In practice, what was the actual participation of citizens entitled to take part in assemblies? In the mid-third century BC, the number of adult male Roman citizens reached 300,000, and by 91 BC, this number had already exceeded 400,000. Furthermore, in those days, a significant proportion of the population lived at a considerable distance from the city of Rome. The locations where assemblies were held, such as the Forum, the Capitol or the Campus Martius, were unable to accommodate more than 25,000 people. Consequently, it can be reasonably assumed that the percentage of citizens who actually took part in the assemblies was drastically low, and according to T. Cornell's estimation, it could not have been higher than 1%.[206]

4. *Kratos*

In addition to the aforementioned differences in the composition of the popular assemblies in Rome, each of these assemblies had its own distinct powers and its own distinct sphere of state authority over which the people assembled in them could exert their influence.

In analysing the functions of the assemblies in the republican Roman constitution, it is important to note that their powers were a combination of the participation of Roman citizens in the exercise of executive power (through the election of magistrates), judicial power (adjudication of criminal cases, decisions on adoptions and wills), and, most importantly, legislative power.

The curiate assembly appeared already outdated by the 5th century BC. The *comitia curiata* retained only two judicial functions in the later Roman Republic: serving as witnesses to *testamentum calatis comitiis* and *adrogatio*. Furthermore, some sources indicate that they were responsible for moderating the most relevant offences through the traditional *provocatio ad populum*.[207] In the legislative sphere, the enactment of the so-called *lex curiata* (*de imperio*) is worthy of mention. The enactment of these curial laws served to confer authority (*imperium*) upon the

205 J. M. Ribas Alba, *Democracia…*, *op. cit.*, pp. 257-289; T. Cornell, *op. cit.*, pp. 226-228.
206 Ibid., p. 228; S. Gordon, *op. cit.*, p. 94.
207 J. M. Ribas Alba, *Democracia…*, *op. cit.*, p. 149.

chief magistrates, a practice that originated in the ceremony of approving the election of a new king.[208]

At the inception of the Roman Republic, the centuriate assembly held a position of paramount significance. Of particular significance were its electoral functions, as the so-called senior magistrates were elected in its forum, namely consuls, praetors and censors.[209] Furthermore, the judicial functions of the *comitia centuriata* included the *provocatio ad populum*, a function that had previously been exercised by the *comitia curiata*. This entailed the right of every Roman citizen to have a sentence issued by a magistrate holding an *imperium* that condemned him to capital punishment reviewed by a popular assembly.[210] In addition to the executive (election of magistrates) and judicial functions, the centuriate assembly was also endowed with limited legislative powers. This involved the enactment of the so-called *lex de bello indicendo* and *lex de pace facienda* which were pieces of legislation that declared war and peace.[211] By the end of the Republic, in the 2nd century BC, the legislative functions of this assembly were taken over by the *comitia tributa*. Similarly, powers in the judicial sphere were transferred to the newly created permanent jury courts at the end of the 2nd century BC.

The functions of the *comitia tributa* included the election of junior magistrates, like quaestors, curule aediles, *tribuni militum* and other officials[212], the enactment of legislation: *leges*, and the adjudication of cases involving fines[213]. In terms of chronology, the first assembly to rely on the tribes as voting units was the plebeian assembly, the *concilium plebis* (first held in 494 BC). The plebeian assembly elected

---

208 Ibid., p. 159-161; T. Cornell, *op. cit.*, p. 222; Cf. J. Canning, *A History of Medieval Political thought 300-1450*, London-New York 2005, pp. 8-9, who makes a clear reference to the relationship between the *lex curiata de imperio* and the *lex regia*. In Republican times, the former conferred a certain amount of power, the *imperium*, to the newly elected magistrate. This was invoked during the Empire as a means of legitimising the power of the emperor, who received it in delegation from the Roman people by virtue of the *lex regia*. For further information on this topic, please refer to Part 5 of this text, fn. 226.

209 They also elected *tribuni militum consulari potestate* and *decemviri legibus scribundis*, J. M. Ribas Alba, *Democracia…*, *op. cit.*, p. 182-183.

210 Ibid., p. 184.

211 Ibid., p. 185; T. Cornell, *op. cit.*, p. 223; G. W. Botsford, *op. cit.*, pp. 229-261; K. Sandberg, *Magistrates and Assemblies. A Study of Legislative Practice in Republican Rome*, Rome 2001, p. 105.

212 For the entire list of officials elected by *comitia tributa* see in J. M. Ribas Alba, *Democracia…*, *op. cit.*, pp. 277-284.

213 Cf. G. W. Botsford, *op. cit.*, pp. 317-329.

its own officials, plebeian tribunes and aediles, and passed resolutions or *plebiscita*. In subsequent periods, it also served as a tribunal to hear cases that were subject to non-capital punishments or fines. It is probable that a tribal assembly of the whole people (*comitia populi tributa*) was formed not long afterwards. In the latter part of the republican period, the distinction between the two types of tribal assembly was rendered largely irrelevant. Following the granting of equal political rights to the plebeians as a result of the so-called Struggle of Orders, the plebiscites were given the legal force equal to that of *leges* under the *Lex Hortensia* in 286 (287) BC. It is noteworthy that the location of the *comitia tributa* was contingent upon the purpose for which it was summoned. The Campus Martius was the venue for electoral assemblies, while from 145 BC onwards the Capitol or the Forum were the locations for tribes to convene for legislative and judicial purposes.[214]

The assemblies were the sole body in the Roman Republic with the authority to enact legislation in the form of *leges* and *plebiscita*. This principle was so firmly implanted in the minds of the Romans that, as late as the Principate, in the second century AD, when popular assemblies had already ceased to be convened and to exercise their functions, including, above all, legislative ones, Gaius wrote in his *Institutes*: *Lex est quod populus iubet atque constituit* (A statute is what the people order and establish)[215]. A comparable formulation can be found in Justinian's *Institutes*, published in 533 AD: "A *lex* is that which was enacted by the Roman people on its being proposed by a senatorian magistrate, as a consul. A *plebiscitum* is that which was enacted by the plebs on its being proposed by a plebeian magistrate, as a tribune. The plebs differ from the people as a species from its *genus*, for all the citizens, including patricians and senators, are comprehended in the *populi* (people); but the plebs only included citizens [who were] not patricians or senators. *Plebiscita*, after the Hortensian law had been passed, began to have the same force as *leges*."[216]

As previously stated, according to the Roman republican constitution, the popular assemblies, particularly the *comitia tributa*, were the only bodies with the authority to vote and issue legislation, which was referred to as *leges* or *plebiscita*. A draft (*rogatio* or *promulgatio*) of a proposed law, *lex*, was initially prepared by a magistrate or, in the case of a plebiscite, by a tribune. It was then presented for discussion at a series of meetings which were not decisive but merely deliberative, before a bill was voted on in the assembly. These preliminary assemblies were

214 T. Cornell, *op. cit.*, p. 227; more about tribal legislation in K. Sandberg, *op. cit.*, pp. 105-110; G. W. Botsford, *op. cit.*, pp. 262-316, 330-461.

215 Gai. 1.3 in https://thelatinlibrary.com/law/gaius1.html [accessed: 25.06.2024].

216 JI 1.2.4 in https://thelatinlibrary.com/law/institutes.html [accessed: 25.06.2024].

known as *contiones* and were convened by the same magistrate or tribune. It was at these meetings that the project was discussed, and the reasons for and against it were presented. Other magistrates were permitted to convene their *contiones* to speak in favour of or against the proposal. At the conclusion of the proceedings, the *contio* prepared the so-called *suasio* and *dissuasio*, i.e. the arguments for and against the bill. The convening magistrate would then announce the dispersal of the *contio* and officially open the *comitia*. In the case of assemblies for electoral and judicial purposes, *contiones* had other functions. In light of the aforementioned considerations, the *contiones* served as a forum for the discussion of the project whereas the purpose of the popular assemblies was solely to vote for or against the proposal. Citizens, as well as all those who were interested, were able to read the draft legislation, listen to the *rogatores legum* or *promulgatores*[217], and hear the voices of those who spoke in favour of and against the legislation. It is evident that the *contio* was not a forum for unfettered political debate, as S. Gordon asserts: "obviously as a forum of public discussion, it was severely limited. Shouts and catcalls from the audience, which apparently were not uncommon, may have indicated the state of public opinion, but hardly constituted a substitute for open debate".[218] In the case of the plebiscite, the plebeians were afforded the opportunity to deliberate on the draft as extensively as possible. It was obligatory for the tribune to announce the project at least 24 days prior to the convening of the *concilium plebis*.[219] In practice, the draft legislation presented to the assembly encountered minimal opposition. With the exception of a few documented instances, the people gathered at the *comitia* voted in favour of the bill.[220]

5. The sovereignty of the *Populus Romanus*

It is interesting to note the conviction, not only of popular opinion but also of scholars, which can be traced in numerous studies, that, as far as the ancient world is concerned, democracy was a characteristic of Greek, and especially Athenian,

---

217 K. Sandberg, *op. cit.*, pp. 97-104: for details of the legislative process, see H. Mouritsen, *op. cit.*, pp. 63-89; G. W. Botsford, *op. cit.*, pp. 462-472.

218 S. Gordon, *op. cit.*, p. 105.

219 On the institution of *contio* see in H. Mouritsen, *op. cit.*, pp. 38-62; G. W. Botsford, *op. cit.*, pp. 139-151; J. M. Ribas Alba, *Democracia…*, *op. cit.*, pp. 125-133; T. Cornell, *op. cit.*, p. 221, 229-230. All citizens, as well as women, foreigners and slaves, were permitted to attend the *contio* but only those chosen by the magistrate or tribune were entitled to speak, S. Gordon, *op. cit.*, p. 105.

220 T. Cornell, *op. cit.*, p. 229.

reality. There are researchers who, in presenting the history of democracy, leap straight from Athens to the Age of Enlightenment, to the thoughts of Rousseau and Montesquieu, to the realities of the struggle for independence of the North American colonies and the US Constitution, and to the French Revolution.[221]

On the other hand, in light of the facts presented, it is clear that it is not unfounded to speak of democracy in relation to the Roman republican constitution.[222] Even the witnesses of republican political life, Polybius and Cicero, did not hesitate to use the term democracy when defining certain aspects of the republican constitution. In the present era, there is a plethora of more assertive proponents who contend that the Roman Republic should be regarded as a government that exhibited at least some democratic characteristics. This is the manner in which the evolution of ideas about democracy in the Roman Republic is presented in recent opinion pieces.[223]

It can be argued that the legislative mechanism in the Roman Republic, while not entirely democratic, was as democratic as possible. Indeed, the assumption of legislative functions by the *comitia tributa*, which, as previously demonstrated, was the assembly with the most democratic or egalitarian composition and voting rules, together with the reforms undertaken at the very end of the Republic, including the introduction of the secret ballot, the practice of deliberating on legislative proposals in *contiones*, led to the conclusion that the entire law-making system in the Republic can be described as having a high degree of democratisation. In light of the fact that the *populus Romanus* held exclusive legislative powers, influenced the composition of the executive, and also had the ability to influence the judiciary, it can be posited that the thesis of the people as the sovereign in the Republic is accurate.

In the works of Roman jurists, the writings of thinkers such as Cicero, and in contemporary literature, the theory of the sovereignty of the *populus romanus* is

---

221 As few examples see J. J. Megías Quirós, L. Cabrera Caro, *op. cit.*, pp. 19-33, where it is clear in the chapter title that the authors contrast Greek democracy and the Roman Republic. Cf. S. Mastellone, *Historia de la democracia en Europa de Montesquieu a Kelsen*, Santiago de Chile 2022, passim, which, in keeping with its title, is limited to presenting the history of democracy in Europe since the mid-17th century. B. DeWiel, *op. cit.*, 27-31 who only mentions Rome in the context of the conquest of Greece.

222 J. M. Ribas Alba, *Democracia…*, *op. cit.*, pp. XIII-XVI; F. Pina Polo, *op. cit.*, pp. 379-394; F. Millar, "The Political Character of the Classical Roman Republic, 200-151 B.C.," *The Journal of Roman Studies* 74 (1984), pp. 14-19 who talks about "the democratic element and its limits in the classical Republic".

223 See in F. Pina Polo, *op. cit.*, pp. 380-383.

inextricably linked to the question of the exercise of legislative power. It seems pertinent to highlight the concept of *lex regia*, which originated during the monarchical era, preceding the establishment of the Republic. In essence, the *comitia curiata*, or assembly of all Roman citizens, enacted the *lex regia* after the election of a new king. This act effectively delegated to the king the powers of the monarch, including the authority to make laws. During the Imperial period, the concept of the *lex regia* was revisited. The words of the jurist Ulpianus provide evidence of this: "A decision given by the emperor has the force of a statute. This is because the populace commits to him and into him its own entire authority and power, doing this by the *lex regia* which is passed anent his authority."[224] These principles were reiterated in the Justinian *Institutions*: "That which seems good to the emperor has also the force of law; for the people, by the *Lex Regia*, which is passed to confer on him his power, make over to him their whole power and authority. Therefore whatever the emperor ordains by rescript, or decides in adjudging a cause, or lays down by edict, is unquestionably law; and it is these enactments of the emperor that are called *constitutiones*. […]."[225] This interpretation posits that the emperor was granted the authority to enact laws in the form of *constitutiones* by the will of the people. This legislative authority was conferred upon him through a sovereign decision of the citizens, who chose to do so through a device known as the *lex regia*. It can be concluded that the emperor was effectively legislating in the place of the Roman people.[226]

The conclusions put forward by the internationally recognised authority, F. Millar, summarizes this idea well: "We might then be able to see the public life of the classical Republic in a rather different light: as an arena in which those who sought and held office competed before the crowd by advertisement of their glorious descent if they could; by the exercise of rhetoric in defence of citizens; by reports and demonstrations of military victory. They also fought out their most bitter rivalries before juries constituted by the citizen assemblies. Their ability to legislate depended on the tribal assembly; and the necessary persuasion was

224 D. 1.4.1 (Ulp. Inst. 1) in *The Digest of Justinian*, vol. 1, transl. and ed. A. Watson, Philadelphia 1998, p. 14.

225 JI 1.2.6 in https://thelatinlibrary.com/law/institutes.html [accessed: 26.06.2024].

226 S. Gordon, *op. cit.*, p. 29, 103-105, 112-115, 117-118. About the *lex regia*, see D. Lee, *Popular Sovereignty in Early Modern Constitutional Thought*, Oxford 2016, pp. 27-31, whose view was that the *lex regia* was a "legendary" law by which the citizens of the Roman Republic ceded to the emperor the sovereignty that had previously belonged to the people. See also M. Ryan, "Political Thought," in *The Cambridge Companion to Roman Law*, ed. D. Johnston, Cambridge 2015, pp. 423-429.

applied, often in open conflict and debate, by the means of speeches, which were made not only, or even primarily, in the 'sacred Senate', but in the open space of the Forum, before the ever-available crowd consisting of whoever was already there, or whoever turned up. It was this crowd which, however imperfectly, symbolized and represented the sovereignty of the Roman People."[227]

Bibliography

Botsford G. W., *The Roman Assemblies from their origin to the end of the Republic*, New York 1909.

Canning J., *A History of Medieval Political thought 300-1450*, London-New York 2005.

Castro O., "Entre el pasado y el presente: evolución histórica del *ius suffragii* y el *ius honorum*, del Derecho romano al Derecho mexicano," *RIDROM* 21 (2018), pp. 642-681.

Coli U., "Tribù e centurie dell'antica repubblica romana," *SDHI* 21 (1955), pp. 181-222.

Cornell T., *Roman Political Assemblies*, in *A Companion to the Political Culture of the Roman Republic*, eds. V. Arena, J. Prag, A. Stiles, Hoboken (NJ) 2022, pp. 220-235.

DeWiel B., *Democracy: A History of Ideas*, Vancouver-Toronto 2000.

Domingo R., *Roman law. An introduction*, London-New York 2018.

Gordon S., *Controlling the State. Constitutionalism from Ancient Athens to Today*, Harvard 2002.

Hall U., "Voting Procedure in Roman Assemblies," *Zeitschrift für Alte Geschichte* 13,3 (Jul. 1964), pp. 297 306.

Iglesias J., *Derecho romano. Instituciones de derecho privado*, Barcelona 1987.

Kaplan T., *Democracy. A World History*, Oxford 2014.

Kaser M., *Das Römische Privatrecht, 1er Abschnitt*, München 1971.

Lamberti F., "Percorsi della cittadinanza romana dalle origini alla tarde Repubblica," in *Derecho, persona y ciudadanía. Una experiencia jurídica comparada*, ed. B. Periñán Gómez, Madrid-Barcelona-Buenos Aires 2010, pp. 17-56.

Lee D., *Popular Sovereignty in Early Modern Constitutional Thought*, Oxford 2016.

227 F. Millar, *op. cit.*, p. 19.

Mastellone S., *Historia de la democracia en Europa de Montesquieu a Kelsen*, Santiago de Chile 2022.

Megías Quirós J. J., Cabrera Caro L., *Historia de las ideas políticas. De la democracia griega a la monarquía medieval*, Cádiz 2015.

Millar F., "The Political Character of the Classical Roman Republic, 200-151 B.C.," *The Journal of Roman Studies* 74 (1984), pp. 1-19.

Mitchell R. E., *Patricians and Plebeians. The Origin of the Roman State*, Ithaca NY 1990.

Pina Polo F., "Idea y práctica de la democracia en la Roma republicana," *Gerión. Revista de Historia Antigua* 37/2 (2019), pp. 379-397.

Mouritsen H., *Plebs and Politics in the Late Roman Republic*, Cambridge 2001.

Ribas Alba J. M., *Democracia en Roma. Introducción al derecho electoral romano*, Granada 2008.

Ribas Alba J. M., "*Populus romanus* y *res publica:* comunidad política y ciudadanía," in *Derecho, persona y ciudadanía. Una experiencia jurídica comparada*, ed. B. Periñán Gómez, Madrid-Barcelona-Buenos Aires 2010, pp. 275-299.

Rose H. J., "Patricians and Plebeians at Rome," *The Journal of Roman Studies* 12 (1922), pp. 106-133.

Ruiz Ruiz R., *Los orígenes del republicanismo clásico. Patrios Politeia* y *Res Publica*, Madrid 2006.

Ryan M., "Political Thought," in *The Cambridge Companion to Roman Law*, ed. D. Johnston, Cambridge 2015, pp. 423-451.

Sandberg K., *Magistrates and Assemblies. A Study of Legislative Practice in Republican Rome*, Rome 2001.

Tagle Martínez H., "*Ius suffragii* y *ius honorum*," *Revista Chilena de Derecho* 20/2/3, vol. 1 (Mayo-Diciembre 1993), pp. 345-352.

Sources

The Digest of Justinian, vol. 1, transl. and ed. A. Watson, Philadelphia 1998.

The Histories of Polybius, transl. E. S. Schuckburgh, vol. I, London-New York 1889.

https://www.attalus.org/cicero/republic1b.html [accessed: 25.06.2024].

https://thelatinlibrary.com/law/gaius1.html [accessed: 25.06.2024].

https://thelatinlibrary.com/law/institutes.html [accessed: 26.06.2024].

Chapter II.
Contemporary issues of democracy

Dariusz Makiłła[228]

Constitutional democracy. The case of the Polish-Lithuanian Commonwealth in the 16th-17th Centuries*

Abstract: The recognition of the Polish-Lithuanian Commonwealth in the 16th and 17th centuries is probably questionable. This country is assessed mainly through negative judgments based on stereotypes. In fact, in the Polish-Lithuanian Commonwealth there was a development of democratic forms typical of a constitutional state, which certainly differed from solutions in other states in Europe, which at that time were mostly subject to absolute rule. The aim of the work is to present the development of democracy in the Republic of Poland, show the conditions of this development, and, above all, demonstrate that this development was based on constitutional norms and principles adopted in the law-making process and generally applicable.

Keywords: Polish-Lithuanian Commonwealth, 16th-17th Century, Constitutional Democracy, Constitution

Was the former Polish-Lithuanian Commonwealth a democratic state in the 16th and 18th centuries? Such a question may raise some doubts. Their source will be the common memory of the Polish-Lithuanian Commonwealth of that period, usually described negatively. Although it should be noted that these judgments were made based on generalities and stereotypes - which cannot be denied - they were passed on. The definition of what we mean by democracy, which has changed over time, may also be a problem.

However, recognizing the Polish-Lithuanian Commonwealth as a democratic state may lead to the need to define what the Polish-Lithuanian Commonwealth was, as well as - if we assume that it was a democratic state - to define what this

228 University of Economics and Humanities in Warsaw, ORCID: 0000-0003-0775-4617.
* Praca naukowa dofinansowana ze środków budżetu państwa w ramach programu Ministra Edukacji i Nauki pod nazwą „Nauka dla Społeczeństwa" nr projektu NdS/544352/2022/2022 kwota dofinansowania 471 613,60 całkowita wartość projektu 492 613,60 (Scientific work co-financed by the state under the program of the Minister of Education and Science called „Science for Society", project number NdS/544352/2022/2022, co-financing amount: 471 613,60, total project value: 492 613,60).

democracy could consist of? And here it turns out that one can find clear legal principles and legal provisions defining the system of the Polish-Lithuanian Commonwealth as democratic, which distinguished it then from many other countries. In reality, however, it should be remembered that the Polish-Lithuanian Commonwealth was not an absolutist state like most European states. So it can be considered in other categories. These are the starting points. Let us therefore briefly trace how the democratic system of power was shaped. It is more interesting that it was created on the basis of legal acts of a constitutional nature, so its creation, as well as its existence, were based on legal norms from the very beginning. It was also important that the development of the constitutional democratic system in Poland took place slowly, and its development was largely influenced by its own tradition and forms of cooperation between the monarchy and the subjects, which created their own rules of influence based on legal solutions.

The formation of political institutions, after overcoming the territorial division in the 12th and 14th centuries, took a longer time, but accelerated rapidly in the 15th century having its peak in the second half of these century. Relations between the monarch and the subjects, typical of such situations, were established, consisting in the establishment of a dualistic system in which there were two entities of public law. On the one hand, the royal power, and on the other hand, estate institutions, which are the result of both bottom-up evolution, based on the estates' right to meet, as well as the monarch's influence on convening it[229].

229 J. Bardach, *Początki sejmu, in Historia sejmu polskiego*. [*The beginnings of the Sejm, in: History of the Polish Sejm*]. Vl. 1. *Do schyłku szlacheckiej Rzeczypospolitej [To the decline of the noble Polish-Lithuanian Commonwealth*], ed. J. Michalski, Warszawa 1984, pp. 5-62; D. Makiłła, *Dualizm władzy w procesie kształtowania ogólnopaństwowych zgromadzeń i reprezentacji stanowych w Europie (XIII-XVI wiek)*, in *Sejm Królestwa Polskiego i Rzeczypospolitej Obojga Narodów a europejskie reprezentacje stanowe* [*Dualism of power in the process of shaping national assemblies and estate representations in Europe (13th-16th centuries)*, in *The Sejm of the Kingdom of Poland and the Polish-Lithuanian Commonwealth and European estate representations*], ed. Dariusz Kupisz, W. Uruszczak, Warszawa 2019, pp. 11-20.

The system outlined in this way evolved, leading to the full institutional formation of the state. To some extent, the creation of this structure was based on legal norms. In addition to statutory norms, which, however, were not very numerous, customary norms, legal principles of the system, and attitudes or behaviours that had legal significance were important for its formation[230].

The basic legal act that defined the system at the beginning of the 16th century was the Nihil novi constitution of 1505, in which the Sejm was recognized as the highest authority, consisting of three components: the Chamber of Deputies, which was a representative body of deputies sent by the land assemblies and constituting their representation, the senate as the royal council, which was an advisory body to the king, which became the upper house when the Sejm was convened, and the king himself, who was considered the participant of the Sejm when the king convened it[231]. In this constitution it was assumed that no law would be made in the Sejm without the consent of this three participants of the

230 W. Uruszczak, *Między partykularyzmem a unifikacją. Prawo polskie ziemskie w XV–XVI wieku* in *Partykularyzm a unifikacja prawa w Polsce [XV–XX w.] Between particularism and unification. Polish land law in the 15th–16th centuries in: Particularism and the unification of law in Poland [15th–20th centuries]*, ed. T. Maciejewski, Gdańsk 1994, pp. 9-29; D. Makiłła, *Rzeczpospolita zdywersyfikowanego prawa. Uwagi na temat porządku prawnego dawnej Rzeczypospolitej w XVI-XVIII w.* [*The Commonwealth of diversified law. Comments on the legal order of the former Polish-Lithuanian Commonwealth in the 16th-18th centuries*], „Państwo i Prawo", 3 (2017), pp. 91-102.

231 A. Prochaska, *Geneza i rozwój parlamentaryzmu za pierwszych Jagiellonów [Origin and development of parliamentarism under the first Jagiellon dynasty]*, „Rozprawy Akademii Umiejętności, Wydział Historyczno-Filozoficzny", Ser. II, t.13, Kraków 1899, pp. 1-170; J. Bardach, op.cit., p. 5-62; W. Uruszczak, *Sejm walny koronny w latach 1506–1540 [The Crown General Sejm in the years 1506–1540]*, Warszawa 1981, pp. 16-19, 59-62; idem, *Sejm w latach 1506–1540*, in *Historia sejmu polskiego [The Sejm in the years 1506–1540, in History of the Polish Sejm]*, pp. 71-75; A. Sucheni-Grabowska, *Sejm w latach 1540–1587*, in *Historia sejmu polskiego* [*The Sejm in the years 1540–1587*, in *History of the Polish Sejm]*, pp. 114-216.

Sejm, which in practice meant that a chamber composed of representatives of the territories had to consent to making laws[232].

These provisions already outlined issues that were the foundation of democracy, namely a certain institutional structure in which it was possible to develop further ideological principles, as well as create laws and principles not only of the political system, but also regarding subjective rights, primarily in the field of rights and obligations[233].

This development was essentially constitutional in nature. In this sense, the state was constitutional in that its political system was based on the constitution, i.e. the fundamental law. At the same time, it can be assumed that such a constitution does not have to be written in one act, because the principles, or more precisely, the norms regulating the state system, may be contained in ordinary statutes, and may also result from constitutional customs. Moreover, a constitutional state should regulate the relations between those who govern and those are

232 *Quoniam iura communia et constitutiones publicae non unum, sed communem populum afficiunt (….) Aequuum et rationabile censuimus, ac etiam statuimus, et deinceps futuris temporibus perpetuis, nihil novi constitui debeat per Nos et successsores Nostros sine communi Consiliarorum et Nuntiorum Terrestrium consensu, quod fieret in praejudicium gravamenque Reipublicae, et damnum atque incommodum cujuslibet privatum, et innovationemque juris communis et publicae libertatis.* Konstytucja sejmu radomskiego z 1505 r. [*Constitution of the Radom Sejm of 1505] De non faciendis constitutionibus sine consensu Consiliariorum et Nuntiorum Terrestrium, Volumina Constitutionum*, V.1. 1493-1549 Vol. 1. *1493–1526*, ed. S. Grodziski, I. Dwornicka, W. Uruszczak, Warszawa 1996, p. 138; W. Uruszczak, *"Sejm Walny wszystkich państw naszych". Konstytucja Nihil novi i sejm w Radomiu w 1505 roku ["The General Sejm of all our countries". The Nihil novi constitution and the Sejm in Radom in 1505]*, Radom 2005; F. Papée, *Aleksander Jagiellończyk*, Kraków 1949, pp. 100-106. On the groundbreaking role of the Nihil novi constitution of 1505 for the powers of the Sejm see. S. Russocki, *Narodziny polskiego parlamentaryzmu w perspektywie porównawczej*, w: *Społeczeństwo obywatelskie i jego reprezentacja [1493–1993] [The birth of Polish parliamentarism in a comparative perspective, in Civil society and its representation [1493–1993]*, ed. J. Bardach, with W. Sudnik, Warszawa 1995, pp. 32-47; W. Uruszczak, *"Sejm Walny wszystkich państw naszych". Konstytucja Nihil novi i sejm w Radomiu w 1505 roku ["The General Sejm of all our countries". The Nihil novi constitution and the Sejm in Radom in 1505]*, "*Czasopismo Prawno-Historyczne*, 1 (2005), pp. 11-24.

233 D. Makiłła, *O doktrynalnych źródłach konstytucjonalizmu w XVI-wiecznej Polsce*, in *Retoryka, polityka, religia w Pierwszej Rzeczpospolitej. Wybrane zagadnienia* [*On the doctrinal sources of constitutionalism in 16th-century Poland*, in *Rhetoric, politics, religion in the First Polish Republic. Selected Issues]*, ed. Ł. Cybulski, K. Koehler, Warszawa 2019, pp. 39-51.

governed by law. Authorities and their actions will rely on the law, and society, at least some of its groups, will benefit from an extensive sphere of public and personal freedom. Moreover, in a constitutional state there will be institutions guaranteeing society a real influence on public affairs. This will be based on the operation of representative or parliamentary institutions[234].

These comments show that institutional development, but also the emergence of a common belief that public participation in political processes is important because it is an expression of views and beliefs that develop over time. At the same time, participation reflected real participation in shaping structures, but also in the exercise of power. In addition to the systematic increase in legal norms guaranteeing participation in political life, defining the system and at the same time securing rights and freedoms, which occurred systematically over several decades of the 16th century, the development of democracy was also influenced by the occurrence of certain circumstances[235].

The crisis associated with the interregnum in 1572 made it necessary to base the system not only on customary norms or constitutional practice, but above all on statutory norms. Moreover, the way of organizing the period of interregnum, during which there was an active and broad participation of the already formed

---

234 W. Uruszczak, *Monarchia Jagiellonów państwem konstytucyjnym*, in *Dziedzictowo Pierwszej Rzeczypospolitej w doświadczeniu politycznym Polski i Europy* [*The Jagiellonian Monarchy as a constitutional state*, in *The legacy of the First Polish commonwealth in the political experience of Poland and Europe*], ed. J. Ekes, Nowy Sącz 2005, p. 19; W. Uruszczak, *System władzy w Polsce ostatnich Jagiellonów [1506–1572] [The system of power in Poland of the last Jagiellon dynasty [1506–1572]*, „Czasopismo Prawno-Historyczne", 2 (1986), pp. 41-62.

235 K. Grzybowski, *Teoria reprezentacji w Polsce epoki Odrodzenia [Theory of representation in Poland during the Renaissance]*, Warszawa 1959, passim; W. Uruszczak, *Sejm walny koronny w latach 1506–1540 [[The Crown General Sejm in the years 1506–1540]*, passim; idem, *Sejm w latach 1506–1540*, in *Historia Sejmu Polskiego, cit.*, pp. 63-113]; idem, *System władzy w Polsce [The system of power in Poland]* „Czasopismo Prawno-Historyczne", 2 (1986), pp. 41-62; idem, *Zasady ustrojowe Rzeczypospolitej Obojga Narodów [Political principles of the Polish-Lithuanian Commonwealth]*, „Czasopismo Prawno-Historyczne", 2 (2008), pp. 125-155; A. Sucheni Grabowska, *Sejm w latach 1540–1587*, in *Historia sejmu polskiego* [*The Sejm in the years 1540–1587*, in *History of the Polish Sejm*], vol. 1, Warszawa 1984, ed. J. Michalski, pp. 114-200; D. Makiłła, *O doktrynalnych źródłach konstytucjonalizmu*, in *Retoryka, polityka, religia*, cit. [*On the doctrinal sources of constitutionalism* in 16th-century Poland, in *Rhetoric, politics, religion*, pp. 29-32.

political nation[236], which was the nobility, numerous in the Polish-Lithuanian Commonwealth, led to the adoption of a legal act having the character of a formal constitution[237].

236 Ś. Orzelski, *Bezkrólewia ksiąg ośmioro, czyli dzieje Polski od zgonu Zygmunta Augusta r. 1572 aż do r. 1576 skreślone przez Świetosława z Borzejewic Orzelskiego, starostę radziejowskiego. Przełożył z rękopisu Cesarskiej Publicznej Biblioteki, przypisami i życiorysem uzupełnił Włodzimierz Spasowicz* [*Eight books of the interregnum, i.e. the history of Poland from the death of Sigismund Augustus in 1572 until 1576, written down by Świetoslaw Orzelski of Borzejewice, starost of Radziejów. Translated from the manuscript of the Imperial Public Library, supplemented with notes and biography by Włodzimierz Spasowicz*], Petersburg 1856, vol. 1, pp. 78-151; *Interregni Poloniae libri VIII*, Wyd. Edward Kuntze, Kraków 1917, pp. 69-133; T. Piliński, *Bezkrólewie po Zygmuncie Auguście i elekcya króla Henryka przez Tadeusza Pilińskiego* [*Interregnum after Sigismund Augustus and the election of King Henry by Tadeusz Piliński*], Kraków 1872, pp. 84-108; E. Reimann, *Die polnische Königswahl von 1573*, „Historische Zeitschrift", 11 (1867), pp. 58-128; W. Zakrzewski, *Po ucieczce Henryka. Dzieje bezkrólewia 1574-1575* [*After Henry's escape. The history of the interregnum 1574-1575*], Kraków 1878; S. Gruszecki, *Walka o władzę w Rzeczypospolitej po wygaśnięciu dynastii Jagiellonów 1572 – 1573* [*The struggle for power in the Polish-Lithuanian Commonwealth after the extinction of the Jagiellonian dynasty 1572 – 1573*], Warszawa 1969; P. Skwarczyński, *Pierwsze trzy wolne elekcje viritim 1573-1578 (Zagadnienia wybrane)* [*The first three free elections viritim 1573-1578 (Selected issues)*], „Teki Historyczne", 10 (1959), pp. 142-144; S. Płaza, *Próby reform ustrojowych w czasie pierwszego bezkrólewia [1572-1574] [Attempts at political reforms during the first interregnum [1572-1574]*, Kraków 1969; E. Dubas-Urwanowicz, *Koronne zjazdy szlacheckie w dwóch pierwszych bezkrólewiach po śmierci Zygmunta Augusta* [*Crown nobility congresses in the first two interregnums after the death of Sigismund Augustus*], Białystok 1998; idem, *Bezkrólewie - czas integracji czy podziałów* [*Interregnum - a time of integration or division*], „Przegląd Historyczny", 1-2 (1994), pp. 35-43; J. Dzięgielewski, *Sejmy elekcyjne. Elektorzy. Elekcje 1573-1674* [*Elective Sejms. Electors. Elections 1573-1674*], Pułtusk 2003, pp. 34-64; D. Makiłła, *Artykuły henrykowskie (1573-1576). Geneza – Obowiązywanie – Stosowanie. Studium historyczno-prawne* [*Henrician Articles (1573-1576). Origin – Validity – Application. Historical and legal study*], Warszawa 2012 pp. 29-50.

237 E. Dubas-Urwanowicz, *System funkcjonowania Rzeczypospolitej ukształtowany w czasie interregnum po śmierci Zygmunta Augusta. Geneza, uwarunkowania i istota rozwiązań* [*The system of functioning of the Polish-Lithuanian Commonwealth shaped during the interregnum after the death of Sigismund Augustus. Origin, conditions and essence of solutions*], in Rok 1573. Dokonania przodków sprzed 440 lat [*Year 1573. Achievements of ancestors from 440 years ago*], ed. J. Dzięgielewski, K. Koehler i D. Muszytowska, Warszawa 2014, pp. 128-136.

This act, adopted by general will in 1573, contained a definition of a system that was mostly known in principle but had not been formally defined, and was now prepared for presentation to the elected monarch, with the primary aim of securing the state. This was the basic purpose of adopting the act that constituted the Constitution[238], named after the first elective king, Henry, Duke of Anjou, *Articuli Henriciani*[239]. This act defined the structure of government bodies, established the principle of election as the source of royal power, and defined the place of all the most important bodies in the state, their mutual dependencies, and competences[240]. The main task of the Sejm, as the highest authority, was to legislate. Public participation was ensured in this process, and decisions were made with the consent of all three states. Moreover, this act defines permanent civil rights and freedoms, as well as systemic guarantees of their validity[241].

The establishment of this system was not complete, many elements were still missing, and in the future the provisions of the Henrician Articles were supplemented with other acts[242]. In this sense, it confirmed the existence of a constitutional system based on several acts intended to give the system of the

---

238 *Articuli conventus Electionis Generalis Regni*, Archiwum Główne Akt Dawnych, *Acta terrestria et castriensia Varsaviensia*, vol. 87, s. 18v; *Articulos per senatores ac universos Regni Poloniae et Magni Ducatus Lithuaniae Ordines et Status…*, E. H. de Noailles, *Henri de Valois*, Paris 1867, t. 3, p. 438. *Statuta sub interregno sancita per Serenissimum Dominum Regem Nostrum Electum confirmantur*, Archiwum Główne Akt Dawnych, Metryka Koronna, 112, k. 12a-13; *Volumina Constitutionum*, V. 2. 1550 -1609, Vol. 1. 1550–1585.ed. S. Grodziski, I. Dwornicka, W. Uruszczak, Warszawa 2005, p. 327.

239 D. Makiłła, *Artykuły henrykowskie (1573-1576). Geneza, – Obowiązywanie – Stosowanie, cit.* passim.

240 D. Makiłła, *Constitutional Commonwealth. The Henrician Articles (1573-1576). Difficult Questions about the Sources of the Constitutional State of the Polish Commonwealth in the 16th-18th Centuries*, in *Origins and Sources of Modern Constitutionalism in Europe. Law and Ideas. In commemoration of the 350th Anniversary of the Enactment of the Henrician Articles (May 12, 1573)*, ed. D. Makiłła, Warsaw 2023, pp. 51-68.

241 D. Makiłła, „*Artykuły henrykowskie (1573-1576). Zakres wprowadzanych zmian w ustroju Rzeczypospolitej oraz ich ocena*" ["*Henrician Articles (1573-1576). The scope of introduced changes in the political system of the Commonwealth and their assessment*"], in J. Dzięgielewski, K. Koehler, D. Muszytowska (edit.), *Rok 1573. Dokonania przodków sprzed 440 lat, cit.* pp. 155-168; Dariusz Makiłła, *Artykuły henrykowskie (1573-1576. Geneza-Obowiązywanie-Stosowanie, cit.* pp. 121-292.

242 D. Makiłła, *Artykuły henrykowskie (1573-1576).* [*Henrician Articles*], cit., pp. 403-495.

Polish-Lithuanian Commonwealth a polycentric character[243]. However, from the point of view of the functioning of the political system, it was important how they were implemented towards society. Although this concerned quite a large group, the method typical of the era was limited to a certain circle. Nevertheless, the rules that were applied reflected the rules of democracy. A hierarchical system of state bodies guaranteed by law, ensuring public participation in both law-making processes[244] and the judiciary. Existing rights and freedoms provide access to various areas of life, create access to offices and the right to participate in political life. All these provisions were secured by a constitutional act guaranteeing their application and observance. The provisions of the constitution of 1573 therefore created a political system in which the principles of democracy were not only included, but actually existed and were implemented.

Bibliography

Bardach, J., *Początki sejmu*, in *Historia sejmu polskiego*, Vol. 1. *Do schyłku szlacheckiej Rzeczypospolitej*, ed. J. Michalski, Warszawa 1984.

Dubas-Urwanowicz, E., *Bezkrólewie - czas integracji czy podziałów?* „Przegląd Historyczny", 1 (1994).

Dubas-Urwanowicz, E., *Koronne zjazdy szlacheckie w dwóch pierwszych bezkrólewiach po śmierci Zygmunta Augusta*, Białystok 1998.

Dubas-Urwanowicz, E., *System funkcjonowania Rzeczypospolitej ukształtowany w czasie interregnum po śmierci Zygmunta Augusta. Geneza, uwarunkowania i istota rozwiązań* in Rok 1573. Dokonania przodków sprzed 440 lat, ed. J. Dzięgielewski, K. Koehler i D. Muszytowska, Warszawa 2014.

Dzięgielewski, J., *Sejmy elekcyjne. Elektorzy. Elekcje 1573-1674*, Pułtusk 2003.

Gruszecki, S., *Walka o władzę w Rzeczypospolitej po wygaśnięciu dynastii Jagiellonów 1572 – 1573*, Warszawa 1969.

Grzybowski, K., *Teoria reprezentacji w Polsce epoki Odrodzenia*, Warszawa 1959.

243 J. P. Higgins, *The Henrician Articles and the World's First Polycentric Constitution*, in *Origins and Sources of Modern Constitutionalism in Europe. Law and Ideas. In commemoration of the 350th Anniversary of the Enactment of the Henrician Articles (May 12, 1573)*, ed. D. Makiłła, Warsaw 2023, pp. 69-81.

244 D. Makiłła, *Constitutional Law-Making Process in the Polish Commonwealth in the 16-18th Centuries*, „Historia Constitutional", (23) 2022, pp. 200-212; A. Karabowicz, *Prawodawstwo sejmowe i królewskie za panowania Stefana Batorego (1576-1586)* [*Sejm and royal legislation during the reign of Stephen Batory (1576-1586)*], Warszawa 2022 passim.

Higgins, J. P., *The Henrician Articles and the World's First Polycentric Constitution*, in *Origins and Sources of Modern Constitutionalism in Europe. Law and Ideas. In commemoration of the 350th Anniversary of the Enactment of the Henrician Articles (May 12, 1573)*, ed. D. Makiłła, Warsaw 2023.

Interregni Poloniae libri VIII, Wyd. Edward Kuntze, Kraków 1917.

Karabowicz, A., *Prawodawstwo sejmowe i królewskie za panowania Stefana Batorego (1576-1586)*, Warszawa 2022.

Makiłła, D., *„Artykuły henrykowskie (1573-1576). Zakres wprowadzanych zmian w ustroju Rzeczypospolitej oraz ich ocena"* in *Rok 1573. Dokonania przodków sprzed 440 lat*, ed. J. Dzięgielewski, K. Koehler, D. Muszytowska, Warszawa, 2014.

Makiłła, D., *Artykuły henrykowskie (1573-1576). Geneza – Obowiązywanie – Stosowanie. Studium historyczno-prawne*, Warszawa 2012.

Makiłła, D., *Constitutional Commonwealth. The Henrician Articles (1573-1576). Difficult Questions about the Sources of the Constitutional State of the Polish Commonwealth in the 16th-18th Centuries*, in *Origins and Sources of Modern Constitutionalism in Europe. Law and Ideas. In commemoration of the 350th Anniversary of the Enactment of the Henrician Articles (May 12, 1573)*, ed. D. Makiłła, Warsaw 2023.

Makiłła, D., *Constitutional Law-Making Process in the Polish Commonwealth in the 16-18th Centuries*, „Historia Constitutional", 23 (2022).

Makiłła, D., *Dualizm władzy w procesie kształtowania ogólnopaństwowych zgromadzeń i reprezentacji stanowych w Europie (XIII-XVI wiek)*, in *Sejm Królestwa Polskiego i Rzeczypospolitej Obojga Narodów a europejskie reprezentacje stanowe*, ed. D. Kupisz, W. Uruszczak, Warszawa 2019.

Makiłła, D., *O doktrynalnych źródłach konstytucjonalizmu w XVI-wiecznej Polsce*, in *Retoryka, polityka, religia w Pierwszej Rzeczpospolitej. Wybrane zagadnienia*, ed. Ł. Cybulski, K. Kochler, Warszawa 2019.

Makiłła, D., *Rzeczpospolita zdywersyfikowanego prawa. Uwagi na temat porządku prawnego dawnej Rzeczypospolitej w XVI-XVIII w.*, „Państwo i Prawo", 3 (2017).

Orzelski, Ś., *Bezkrólewia ksiąg ośmioro, czyli dzieje Polski od zgonu Zygmunta Augusta r. 1572 aż do r. 1576 skreślone przez Świetoslawa z Borzejewic Orzelskiego, starostę radziejowskiego. Przełożył z rękopisu Cesarskiej Publicznej Biblioteki, przypisami i życiorysem uzupełnił Włodzimierz Spasowicz*, Petersburg 1856.

Papée, F., *Aleksander Jagiellończyk*, Kraków 1949.

Piliński, T., *Bezkrólewie po Zygmuncie Auguście i elekcya króla Henryka przez Tadeusza Pilińskiego*, Kraków 1872.

Płaza, S., *Próby reform ustrojowych w czasie pierwszego bezkrólewia [1572-1574]*, Kraków 1969.

Prochaska, A., *Geneza i rozwój parlamentaryzmu za pierwszych Jagiellonów*, „Rozprawy Akademii Umiejętności, Wydział Historyczno-Filozoficzny", Ser. II, 13, Kraków 1899.

Reimann, E., *Die polnische Königswahl von 1573*, „Historische Zeitschrift", 11 (1867).

Russocki, *Narodziny polskiego parlamentaryzmu w perspektywie porównawczej*, in *Społeczeństwo obywatelskie i jego reprezentacja [1493–1993]*, ed. J. Bardach, with W. Sudnik, Warszawa 1995.

Skwarczyński, P., *Pierwsze trzy wolne elekcje viritim 1573-1578 (Zagadnienia wybrane)*, „Teki Historyczne", 10 (1959).

Sucheni-Grabowska, A., *Sejm w latach 1540–1587*, in *Historia sejmu polskiego* T. 1. *Do schyłku szlacheckiej Rzeczypospolitej*, ed. J. Michalski, Warszawa 1984.

Uruszczak, W., *Między partykularyzmem a unifikacją. Prawo polskie ziemskie w XV–XVI wieku* in *Partykularyzm a unifikacja prawa w Polsce [XV–XX w.]*, ed. T. Maciejewski, Gdańsk 1994.

Uruszczak, W., *Monarchia Jagiellonów państwem konstytucyjnym*, in *Dziedzictowo Pierwszej Rzeczypospolitej w doświadczeniu politycznym Polski i Europy*, ed. J. Ekes, Nowy Sącz 2005.

Uruszczak, W., *Sejm w latach 1506–1540*, in *Historia sejmu polskiego in* Vol. 1. *Do schyłku szlacheckiej Rzeczypospolitej*, ed. J. Michalski, Warszawa 1984.

Uruszczak, W., *Sejm walny koronny w latach 1506–1540*, Warszawa 1981.

Uruszczak, W., *System władzy w Polsce ostatnich Jagiellonów [1506–1572]*, „Czasopismo Prawno-Historyczne", 2 (1986).

Uruszczak, W., *Zasady ustrojowe Rzeczypospolitej Obojga Narodów*, „Czasopismo Prawno-Historyczne", 2 (2008).

Uruszczak, W., *"Sejm Walny wszystkich państw naszych". Konstytucja Nihil novi i sejm w Radomiu w 1505 roku*, Radom 2005.

Uruszczak, *W., "Sejm Walny wszystkich państw naszych". Konstytucja Nihil novi i sejm w Radomiu w 1505 roku "Czasopismo Prawno-Historyczne*, 1 (2005).

Zakrzewski, W., *Po ucieczce Henryka. Dzieje bezkrólewia 1574-1575*, Kraków 1878.

Artur Kotowski[245]

Remarks on Shaw vs. DPP. (1962) based on Herbert Hart's "Law, liberty and morality". What does it tell us about legal activism?

Abstract: The article is about judicial interpretive activism. This one is analyzed through the prism of the famous, but now only of historical importance, case of Shaw vs. DPP. (1962) based on Herbert Hart's book "Law, liberty and morality". The defendant was convicted of, among other things, an act criminalized under the case law - conspiracy against public morality. Judicial activism in Poland has intensified in recent years. This phenomenon is also analyzed from different perspectives in the world literature. Based on the Shaw case, one can see both its advantages and its dangers.

Keywords: legal theory and philosophy, legal interpretation, judicial activism, case law

Information about the author: Artur Kotowski - professor of legal sciences, head of the Chair of the Theory and Philosophy of Law at the Faculty of Law and Administration at Cardinal Stefan Wyszynski University in Warsaw. Member of the Office of Studies and Analyses of the Supreme Court and the Main Adjudicatory Committee in Cases of Violation of Public Finance Discipline Infringement. Author of publications on the theory and philosophy of law and criminal. In his scientific activity, he deals with interpretation and application of law, empirical analysis of law and the theory of criminal trial.

1. Introduction

This article is devoted to the phenomenon of interpretative activism, which in the formula of judicial activism is relatively new subject in European part of civil law (so-called continental legal culture). Of course, phenomena described in this way, usually associated with legal interpretation, judicial decisions, etc., have emerged in continental European countries with varying intensity. However, it is undoubtedly the case that interpretive activism, including judicial activism, is

---

245 Prof. dr hab. Artur Kotowski, Cardinal Stefan Wyszynski University in Warsaw, Head of the Chair of the Theory and Philosophy of Law, Faculty of Law and Administration, Poland, e-mail: a.kotowski@uksw.edu.pl; https://orcid.org/0000-0001-8284-241X.

a phenomenon that has a shorter history here than in the common law culture traditionally identified as its source[246].

There are many definitions of interpretive activism[247]. In state law systems it is uniformly associated with the interpretation of the law. It is an interpretative decision based most often on extra-linguistic rules of interpretation, not previously known in doctrine or judicial decisions, most often opposed to the will of the historical legislator, treated as a form of quasi-legislative activism and thus usually controversial. It also usually has some axiological context or involves a weighing of values.

Its opposition is interpretive restraint, usually associated with legal formalism[248] and, at the level of the philosophy of law, a positivist perspective. This is a simplification. Both positivists and non-positivist representatives of the philosophy of law are capable of 'producing' either activist or ordinary semantics of law.

Interpretation of the law carried out in the above manner can function as either legal (made by doctrine)[249] or operative[250]. However, the most relevant is the latter, primarily judicial operative interpretation, thus carried out by the courts in the application of the law. Therefore, the concept of interpretive activism is treated synonymously with judicial activism. Simply put, 'active' interpretation that is not carried out by the courts does not have the same practical significance as its judicial form.

I put forward the thesis that while in common law this phenomenon is an immanent feature, which stems from the precedent model of law application, in

---

246 Term „judical activism" was popularized by Arthur Chlesinger Jr. in pejorative meaning in short article about tendency within US Supreme Court. He also made interviews with judges and made the division between active and restrain interpretation and applying the law.

L. Pereire Coutinho, M. La Torre, S. D. Smith (ed.), Judical activism. Na interdisciplinar approach to the American and European Experiences, Switzerland 2015, Preface, p. V., K.D.Kmiec, The Origin and Current Meanings of <Judical Activism>, California Law Review, vol. 92, p. 1442-1443, C. Green, An Intellectual History of Judical Activism, "Emory Law Journal", t. 58, nr 5.

247 "During the 1990s, the term "judical activism" and "judical activist" appeared in an astounding 3,815 journal and law review articles". K.D.Kmiec, op.cit.

248 A. J. Sebok, Legal Positivism in American Jurisprudence, Cambridge 1998, p. 47.

249 Holmes, Oliver Wendell. "The Theory of Legal Interpretation." Harvard Law Review, vol. 12, no. 6, 1899, pp. 417-20. JSTOR, https://doi.org/10.2307/1321531. Accessed 25 Aug. 2024.

250 L.Leszczyński Operative interpretation (basic properties), Państwo i Prawo 2009, no. 6 (Wykładnia operatywna, podstawowe właściwości), passim.

statutory law countries it has always been in jurisprudence located within judicial discretion or even a taboo. Everyone knew that such a phenomenon existed, but in view of the strict division between the acts of law-making and law-application, the manifestations of activism were not so popular, and if accepted, then primary in the constitutional judiciary because of their specificity. The issue probably differs from one EU country to another, but the so-called 'judicalisation of power', judicial emancipation, or precisely judical activism is one of the strongest manifestations of the transformation of the civil law legal culture in EU[251].

Interpretive activism can be studied from two perspectives. First is analytical. It lists the features of the process of interpreting the law, sometimes also the application of the law, that make it possible to qualify individual cases critically under this category. This is nothing else that intensity meaning of interpretative activism. If we claim its features as it was written above, we can evaluate – form example – judgements to this category.

The second perspective consists of analyzing cases individually. This avoids the difficulty of specifying criteria based on the generality of assessment. It is also best to refer to historical cases, given not their context but their lack of coherence with current evaluations. Methodologically, this formula obviously has advantages and disadvantages. Some point out that issues sensitive to the law should be examined with reference to special cases (hard cases). Others counter that law is made up of ordinary cases and generalizing from hard cases does not allow such theories to provide credible thesis.

Whichever method of analysis we adopt above, the case known as Shaw vs. Director of Public Prosecutor (DPP) from 1961 is well known as an interesting but also controversial example of judicial activism. It was an English House of Lords decision, colloquially known as the Ladies Directory Case[252]. Herbert Hart dedicated an entire novella to her, entitled "Law, liberty and morality" which is not as famous as "The concept of law" and is somctimes even forgotten in the shadows of the past[253].

251 T.G. Grosse, Sovereignty and the political. A Study of European Integration, Wydawnictwo Instytutu Wymiaru Sprawiedliwości, Warsaw 2022 (Suwerenność i polityczność. Studium integracji europejskiej, Wydawnictwo Instytutu Wymiaru Sprawiedliwości, Warszawa 2022), passim.

252 J. E. Hall Williams. "The Ladies' Directory and Criminal Conspiracy the Judge as Custos Morum." The Modern Law Review, vol. 24, no. 5, 1961, pp. 626-31. JSTOR, http://www.jstor.org/stable/1092876. Accessed 25 Aug. 2024.

253 H.L.A. Hart, Law, liberty and morality, Stanford 1963, passim.

The case was one of the last examples of the application of the doctrine of precedent in penal law, complete with a sentence of absolute imprisonment. The case was part of the discussion in the late 1950s and early 1960s in England of the reform of the so-called law of morals and what Herbert Hart called the 'enforcement of morals by law'. In this paper, I will try to take a closer look at the specifics of this case and answer the question of how far the way judicial activism was practiced in the way it was in the Shaw case can be instructive for us contemporaries.

Of course, the Shaw vs. DPP case is only of historical significance today. No one would today consider enforcing morality by law which would let imprisonment for issues of human sexuality. What gains currency is not the subject matter of the case, but the court's reasoning, which Hart has analysed in depth in his book. This paper, however, does not seek to critically review 'Law, liberty and morality', but to delineate the possible difficulties or dangers of exaggerated judicial interpretive activism. At the same time, the present text should not be seen as a one-sided criticism of interpretive activism (and - a contrario - as advocating interpretive restraint). It is about answering the research question whether, in difficult cases, whether we understand them as posing evidentiary or interpretative challenges, the path of active interpretation is always desirable and what risks it entails.

2. Ladies Directory case – basic information

According to Hart's novel, He wrote that "The facts in Shaw's case are not such as to excite sympathy for the accused. What Shaw had done was to compose and procure the publication of a magazine called the Ladies Directory giving the names and addresses of prostitutes, in some cases nude photographs, and an indication in code of their practices. For this Shaw was charged and found guilty of three offences: (1) publishing an obscene article, (2) living on the earnings of the prostitutes who paid for the insertion of their advertisements in the Ladies Directory, (3) conspiring to corrupt public morals by means of the Ladies Directory"[254]. Offence no 1 and 2 came from: Obscene Publications act 1959 (publishing an obscene article) and Sexual Offences Act 1956 (living on the earnings of prostitution). But last offence was most serious since this offence was held by the Prosecutor that it was based on common law judgment from 1774. The defendant was sentenced at first instance to imprisonment for nine months[255]. It is not needed to refer all the matters of the case. It must be summarized that the appeal was

254 Ibidem, p. 10.

255 CLR: Appeal Cases/1962/SHAW APPELLANT; AND DIRECTOR OF PUBLIC PROSECUTIONS RESPONDENT. - [1962] A.C. 220, p. 5.

dismissed, and the conviction was upheld. The House of Lord assessment was that the defendant's decision to feature prostitute adverts was dangerous to the welfare of society and it was courts duty to protect the public majority's morals, as well as safety and order. This meant that the Court was able to create offences to adapt to changing standards in life and regarding the values and morals of society. Origin of precedent was taken from 1774 by Lord Mansfield statement and Frederick Charles Shaw was sentenced for the crime which was not established in state law.

"Ladies Directory case" (Shaw vs. DPP) was a drastic example of judicial interpretative activism as it was praeter legem judgment which, in criminal law, disclose the problem if common law allows courts to establish new offences beside those which are valid by the statute? If does, it makes clarify contradiction to nullum crimen sine lege and nullum crimen sine lege certa principles[256]. That is why, today, this opinion is dismissed, and case law allows judges only to produce new rules in criminal procedure or sometimes in sentencing punishment matters, but not in the material law.

Also, Shaw's case was an important element of discussion about the legal enforcement of morality in UK in the 1960s. (also its part of Hart/Devlin debate[257]). At his novel Hart critices "the radicalism of the doctrine of precedent", and compare with USA, where there are "many dead rules from the past" which "are no longer being applied"[258].

3. Judical activism - evaluation

As it was mentioned, judicial activism is a natural part of common law legal culture because of its precedent model of law application. In the first instance, however, it is a question of validation and not specifically of the interpretation of state law, as in continental systems. This is an important difference. In civil law, interpretive activism is associated almost exclusively with the sphere of judicial discretion in the interpretation of state law. In common law, the matter concerns

256 "Perhaps the nearest counterpart to this in modern European jurisprudence is the idea to be found in German statutes of the Nazi period that anything is punishable if it is deserving of punishment according "to the fundamental conceptions of a penal law and sound popular feeling. So while Mill would have shuddered at the law laid down in Shaw's case as authorising gross invasions of individual liberty, Bentham6 would have been horrified at its disregard of the legal values of certainty and its extension of what he termed "ex post facto law". Cit.: H.L.A. Hart, Law, liberty…, p. 14.

257 Wall S. The Hart/Devlin Debate. In: Enforcing Morality. Cambridge Introductions to Philosophy and Law. Cambridge University Press; 2023, p. 44-63.

258 H.L.A. Hart, Law, liberty…, p. 7.

both the creation of new rules by the courts and the qualification of decided cases according to the principle of stare decisis. A separate issue is the institution of judicial review and the evolution of constitutional standards.

We don't have space to analyze in full spectrum the matter of judicial activism in common law. But it is well known that this phenomenon is widely described and have a longer history there[259].

Among the advantages, it is often calling the actual implementation of democratic values, of a certain standard for the arrangement of social relations, which is fully possible in the processes of application and which the mere design of institutions in positive law will not provide. Due to this statement only judiciary which interpret law actively could reach full democratic standard of protection of human rights etc.[260]

The second feature lies in what is obviously contrary to the Shaw ruling, but which should be understood in a broader context. It is about the protection of social groups, minorities, and sometimes social values, which also require an active reading of existing legal institutions. Such rulings are sometimes controversial, and courts are accused of making subjective judgements, but this feature of activism is often mentioned in the literature. In the literature it is pointed out that the protection of minority rights in common-law states has only taken place through an active reading of human rights protection standards, including constitutional standards. Legal formalism is not conducive to minority protection and petrifies conservative social relations[261].

Another issue is related to generality and namely to the realization of the Platonic postulate of the rule of philosophers. Given the political system he proclaimed, this may not be a good source, but it is linked to the observation of the lack of temptation to political corruption, because judges are not involved in political decision-making process.

---

259 Ch. Wolfe, Judical Activism. Bulwark of freedom or precarious security? Rev. edition, Playmouth 1997, p. 2-4.

260 This corresponds to the concept of EU integration through jurisprudence. However, this makes the courts part of political processes, whether they want to or not.
Compare: P. Cisneros, How do courts contribute to policy integration? A comparative study of policy integration processes in Colombia, Ecuador, and Guatemala, "Policy Sciences" 2023, vol. 56, passim.

261 M. Matczak, Why Judicial Formalism is Incompatible with the Rule of Law. Canadian Journal of Law and Jurisprudence 2018, 31 (1), p. 61-85.

Another feature is the effectiveness in protecting the fundamental values of the legal order (but also basic economic rights[262]). Statutory law is always a step back before of the social life. Courts, as application bodies, can perceive these risks and - especially constitutional courts - react earlier. However, this requires interpretative activism and not contenting oneself with a mere linguistic interpretation. Related to this is the well-known observation that law as a social phenomenon requires a perception of its extra-normative impact, which also implies a requirement for an active approach to interpretation.

In summary, the advantage of judicial interpretive activism involves the effective protection of fundamental rights and the interference of the judiciary in the exercise of state power. By deciding difficult cases, in cases with a strong axiological inclination, the courts create new social relations, which is important when the rights of certain subjects are not recognized by the legislature.

But there is no rose without thorns. At the forefront of the signaled drawbacks of judicial interpretive activism is the lack of democratic legitimacy to make decisions that establish an understanding of the rules that differs from that of the legislators[263]. For it can always be argued that this creation of social relations takes place without any democratic legitimacy. The Anglo-Saxons have solved this problem in such a way that a judicial decision in an individual case acquires universal force only because of its repeated application to similar cases, which somehow corresponds to the act of establishing a rule by the legislature. However, this process takes place without public consultation, electoral process, etc.[264] In democratic states, general rules should come from the will of the people expressed by their representatives. Hence the division sometimes detailed between accepted activism within civil law, where the nature of legal relations requires flexibility in the application of the law, and activism within public law[265], above all in the

262 Ch. Wolfe, Judical Activism..., p. 18.

263 Compare: H. J. Storing (ed.), The Anti-Federalist: Writings by the Opponents of the Constitution, University of Chicago Press, Chicago 1985, p. 165-168.

264 A. Grimmel, Judicial Interpretation or Judicial Activism? The Legacy of Rationalism in the Studies of the European Court of Justice, European Law Journal, 2012, vol. 18, p. 520.

265 Robert Clinton, Eakin v. Raub: Refutation or Justification of Marbury v. Madison?, "Constitutional Commentary" 910 (1987), p. 81-92, https://scholarship.law.umn.edu/cgi/viewcontent.cgi?article=1920&context=concomm – Access 25 Aug. 2024.

shaping of relations between public authorities, where the rule of law and respect for competences are fostered by judicial interpretative restraint[266].

This may be regarded as a common but not true argument, but the second is already a technical in its nature. It is also emphasized that the courts should interpret the law with restraint, as the establishment of general rules is a process of generalization, which courts are not able to perceive when faced with the reality of an individual case. This is curious, but such arguments are also raised in Anglo-Saxon culture, including the USA[267], primarily in context of limiting case law. This argument against activism is linked to the issue of lack of democratic legitimacy signaled above. It is reduced to a technical issue. To put it succinctly - the courts *see* less than the legislature. Colloquially, this problem is known in connection with the appointment of codification committees by judges. This is because they have a strong tendency to assess general norms through the prism of their individual experiences in the cases they decided in the past (especially hard cases). They therefore think inductively, and this way of reasoning is - as we know - logically unreliable.

Another argument is paradoxically related to one of the qualities of the judiciary, the independence of adjudication. It relies on the following reasoning. The power to make decisions of a law-making nature, whether overtly or discretionarily, through interpretation, in a democratic state should be scrutinized and possibly bear some responsibility for it. If judges want to be active, they should be under analogical responsibility as legislation bodies. Because there should be no power without responsibility. In democratic states, the legislature is held accountable for its decisions through the electoral process, while the judiciary does not have to face this. However, what ensures the independence of judges deprives them of the right to decide the fate of entire societies, as they are not subject to democratic control. Hence, according to the challengers, the rule of law interpretation should stay as far away as possible from crypto legislation, with which interpretive activism is associated.

So, judicial independence works well with the standard model of the court as an application body but has flows when creating rules in a cryptocurrency formula. Also, interpretive activism is always exposed to the judge's highly subjective assessment. This argument seems crucial in the Shaw case, where judges

266 Louis Fischer, Separation of Powers [w:] The Oxford Companion to the American Law, red. Kermitt L. Hall, Oxford University Press, Oxford 2002, p. 735.

267 B.Banaszak, M.Bernarczyk, Judicial activism in the modern democratic state [Aktywizm sędziowski we współczesnym państwie demokratycznym], Warsaw 2012, p. 18.

indicated that their vision of morality coincided with that prevailing in UK society at the time.

4. Legal Enforcement of Morality

Certainly, interpretive activism does not occur only in cases with a strong axiological context, but all cases of this kind are difficult to resolve according to a pattern of interpretive restraint and legal formalism[268]. They also give rise to greater controversy about the effects of such settlements in the public sphere. Indeed, if a court grapples with the inadequacies of statute law on issues devoid of axiological rationale, it will not raise a sensation when the ruling is based on extra-linguistic interpretative directives. However, the case is completely different in the sphere of morality.

This context became apparent in the Shaw case. The issue of factual findings was whether the defendant had derived income from prostitution and whether he had published an obscene article (in certain circumstances the first act would also be punishable today). In his book Hart scored that: "The judges in the House of Lords not only raised no objection to the inclusion of the charge of conspiracy to corrupt public morals, but with one dissentient (Lord Reid) they confirmed the prosecution's contention that this was an offence still known to English law and insisted that it was a salutary thing that this should be so. They made indeed an excursion, rare for English judges, into the area of policy in order to emphasize this"[269].

The Ladies Directory case also reveals one of the systemic arguments against activism. Namely, the easiness of which judges fall into unreflectiveness. Legal decision-making is a cognitive process and is prone to the same psychological mechanisms of perception and evaluation as any other. This is well seen when the role of purely normative arguments in a case are low but increases the scope for discretionary decision-making process.

Hart argued that "the development of the law been influenced by morals" but also the development of morality can be influenced by law[270]. The first case is natural and desirable. In both common and civil law states, the process happens from the bottom up and, when it affects the law, it has democratic legitimacy. Thus, the evolution of social relations in the form of the perception of moral norms and values qualified as moral forces a change in the law in force, either through the

268 N.S. Zeppos, The use of authority in statutory interpretation: an empirical analysis, Texas Law Review 1992, vol. 70, p. 1084.

269 H.L.A.Hart, Law, liberty…, p. 10.

270 Ibidem, p. 1-2.

activity of parliament or, as in systems of precedent, through the incorporation by judges of these moral and moral standards in their jurisprudence.

Option two, enforcing morality by law, however, is more problematic. And in this aspect, interpretive activism can be assessed critically. For while the legislature has democratic legitimacy and the attempt to shape morality by statute law is the result of an electoral act and is ultimately also verified by elections, judges should show more restraint, as they are deprived of both democratic fuses[271]. As a result, even with good intentions, their ruling easily antagonizes the parties to the dispute. Nor is it conducive to building an inclusive democracy, i.e. one that involves broader sections of society, but an exclusive one, i.e. one in which a Carl Schmidt-like 'us vs. them' divide materializes.

This is exactly what happened in the Shaw case. Only that at that time the court did not even hide its convictions and the need for activism. Hart cited a passage from one of the judges, Lord Simonds, who explicitly pointed out that it was the duty of Her Majesty's court to fill in the gaps in the statute law and to be proactive where the legislature shows a failure to act:

> *When Lord Mansfield speaking long after the Star Chamber had been abolished said that the Court of King's Bench was the custos morum of the people and had the superintendency of offences contra bonos mores, he was asserting, as I now assert, that there is in that Court a residual power, where no statute has yet intervened to supersede the common law, to superintend those offences which are prejudicial to the public welfare. Such occasions will be rare, for Parliament has not been slow to legislate when attention has been sufficiently aroused. But gaps remain and will always re-main, since no one can foresee every way in which the wickedness of man may disrupt the order of society. Let me take a single instance ... Let it be supposed that at some future, perhaps early, date homosexual practices between adult consenting males are no longer a crime. Would it not be an offence if even without obscenity such practices were publicly advocated and encouraged by pamphlet and advertisement? Or must we wait till Parliament finds time to deal with such conduct? I say, my Lords, that if the common law is powerless in such an event, then we should no longer do her reverence.*[272]

As has already been signaled, the Shaw case is today of historical interest only and is more of a curiosity than a current example of judicial activism in its

271 Activists are attached to the results and judges are reticent to the method the former believe that the role of the judiciary is to provide effective protection for minority groups, while the latter believe that better or worse results are cited by the majority of society through their representatives in the legislature.
B. Banaszak, M.Bernaczyk, op.cit., p. 14.

272 Shaw v. Director of Public Prosecutions (1961) 2 A.E.R. at PP- 452-53, Hart, Law, liberty…, p. 9.

relevance. It shows, however, in a universal way, two problems that are associated with activism.

The first is the lack of democratic legitimacy in the creation of general rules. This argument may appear to be worn out and overused and therefore needs to be clarified. This is because it does not concern legitimacy linked to the electoral act. This is inherently political in nature, which the judiciary in a state governed by the rule of law cannot do. The judiciary is a type of authority that is independent and autonomous and therefore cannot be subjected to the pressure of the democratic political game, even with all the standards that shape this process in states that respect civil rights and liberties. Legitimacy here refers to the understanding of moral values and moral norms that the community develops during discourse and social interaction.

Hart called this element of her theory the minimum of the law of nature in positive law. An Anglo-Saxon judge faced with a decision that is a difficult case and usually has an axiological context seeks a pattern of behavior in the discourse of a given communicative community. Hence, his proposal to solve a difficult case is described as the judge's need to step out of the law understood as a union of rules. The most important issue, however, concerns the identification of the source, position and nature of this discourse. For the problem with the judges' interpretive activism is that they locate the source of moral discourse not in the public discourse - as too general and heterogeneous - but in the social elite, most often the legal elite[273]. It is therefore a morality that is not universal - inclusive of the

273 Deriving rules from general constitutional values is well-known in both Anglo-Saxon countries and civil law. This was done, among others, by the US Supreme Court creating the principle of substantive due process of law. Similarly, the French Constitutional Council did so in 2016 in the Herrou case by recognising the value of 'fraternity' from the preamble as a basis for overturning a criminal conviction of a common law court. Such examples of judicial activism make judges the guardians of moral values, but defined by them. An extreme example of this is in the power of the Supreme Court in Israel, where one of the constitutional principles is the so-called 'reasonableness clause', allowing it to overrule any government decision if the judges deemed it 'unreasonable'.

Compare: Bela Pokol, Juristocratic form of government and its structural aspects, 'Prawo I Więź, No. 15, 2016, pp. 107, 104-105 (Jurystokratyczna forma rządów i jej aspekty strukturalne), David G. Green, Democratic Civilization or Judicial Supremacy? A discussion on parliamentary sovereignty and the reform of human rights laws, Civitas, London 2016, passim.

worldview of different social groups - but exclusive - of the social elite[274]. In systems of statute law, things are even easier to describe because "constitutional rights are never interpreted or implemented in a political or ideological vacuum"[275]. The source of reference of such difficult cases involving the interpretation of expressions of statute law lies in the language of law, but not only of literature and jurisprudence (which is natural for the analysis of traditional interpretative cases), but of the implicit language of law by the judge himself. It is thus a hermetic, subjective vision of the exegete's discourse 'with himself', without external association.

This attitude of the judges is somewhat understandable. By rationalizing in this way the discourse of reference, the source of natural law for positive law, they avoid the accusation that the adjudication is inspired in vox populi. The rule of law is to be guaranteed by courts, not by tribunals of the people. The problem is that such a stance results in the exclusivity of giving meaning to moral values and enforcing a vision of morality by law, the source of which lies in its rationalization by the discourse of the legal elite rather than society as a whole.

Exactly such a paradox occurred in the Shaw case. According to this ruling and Hart's assessment, sometimes "this movement of judicial opinion has gone far"[276]. This was also a major problem in the Shaw's case. The judges considered their own morality to be public, while there is "nor need the morality in question be <public> in any sense other than being the generally accepted morality"[277]. Of course, establishing a pattern of behavior based on a commonly understood moral value is difficult. Critics will say that it is not possible at all. However, this does not solve the dilemma of whether such a determination is adequate in a situation where a judge takes as a common standard of morality the values recognized by an elite, primarily the legal profession. This gives rise to the suspicion that he is in fact treating his own opinion as public, even though it does not have this value.

---

274 Habermas cites the position of Dahl, who sees *the main danger in a technocratic variety of paternalism justified by monopolies on knowledge. Privileged access to sources of relevant knowledge for control would enable discreet control over a mediatised public of citizens, cut off from these sources and fed by symbolic politics.* J. Habermas, Facticity and validity. Teoria dyskursu wobec zagadnień prawa i demokratycznego państwa prawnego, Warsaw 2005, p. 337 (*Faktyczność i obowiązywanie. Teoria dyskursu wobec zagadnień prawa i demokratycznego państwa prawnego*).

275 R. Hirsch, Towards Jursitocracy: The Origins and Consequences of the New Constitutionalism, Harvard University Press, Cambridge, Mass. 2004, p. 187.

276 Hart, Law, liberty…, p. 8.

277 Ibidem, p. 10.

The second of the problems of judicial activism is related to the responsibility already mentioned. This issue is very rarely acknowledged in the debate on active interpretation, as opposed to interpretive restraint. However, it is fair to say that this issue is more relevant in the area of state law culture than in common law. For in the latter, within certain limits of course, the courts have the power to make law[278]. Although this takes place in the form of a precedential transformation of a concrete norm into a general-abstract one, it is permissible and accepted at the level of the state as a legal-political community. This is different in strictly state law systems, one of the basic features of which is the division between law-making and application bodies, which are not entitled to create general rules. This also shifts the emphasis in legal interpretation to a greater - than in common law countries - sensitivity to judicial crypto-legislation through interpretative decisions based on anti-formalism and away from textualism in interpretative theory.

However, these are marginalities. It is part of the operation of the organs of state power in democratic regimes that these organs are accountable for actions beyond their competence. The problem with judicial activism is simply related to the lack of enforcement of this responsibility for such interpretative decisions that lead to the creation of patterns of behaviour in the discretionary sphere of other public authorities. The adversary in this discussion will reply that this is a non-indispensable element of interpretation of its abstract variety (made in response to preliminary questions, constitutional review, etc.). We do not have space to elaborate on this point, but the point is simply to avoid situations in which the courts, by way of interpretation, replace the legislature. The exercise of power - including discretionary power - is subject to the same accountability as any other. If an authority claims the right to shape social relations, it should submit itself to some democratic judgement. The courts cannot have it. This is a paradox in democratic legal states. For they would not be independent and autonomous in their adjudication. Hence, interpretive restraint is more about the culture of adjudication and the division and balance of powers - so important for order in a political community such as the state.

278 F.Schusser, Judical activism in a comparative perspective. The Supreme Court of India vs. the Bundesrfassunggericht, Baden-Baden 2019, p. 42.

Bibliography

Banaszak B., Bernarczyk M., Judicial activism in the modern democratic state [Aktywizm sędziowski we współczesnym państwie demokratycznym], Warsaw 2012.

Cisneros P., How do courts contribute to policy integration? A comparative study of policy integration processes in Colombia, Ecuador, and Guatemala, "Policy Sciences" 2023, vol. 56.

Clinton R., Eakin v. Raub: Refutation or Justification of Marbury v. Madison?, "Constitutional Commentary" 910 (1987).

CLR: Appeal Cases/1962/SHAW APPELLANT; AND DIRECTOR OF PUBLIC PROSECUTIONS RESPONDENT. - [1962] A.C. 220.

Fischer L., Separation of Powers [w:] The Oxford Companion to the American Law, red. Kermitt L. Hall, Oxford University Press, Oxford 2002.

Green D. G., Democratic Civilization or Judicial Supremacy? A discussion on parliamentary sovereignty and the reform of human rights laws, Civitas, London 2016.

Grimmel A., Judicial Interpretation or Judicial Activism? The Legacy of Rationalism in the Studies of the European Court of Justice, European Law Journal, 2012, vol. 18.

Grosse T.G., Sovereignty and the political. A Study of European Integration, Wydawnictwo Instytutu Wymiaru Sprawiedliwości, Warsaw 2022 (Suwerenność i polityczność. Studium integracji europejskiej, Wydawnictwo Instytutu Wymiaru Sprawiedliwości, Warszawa 2022.

Habermas J., Facticity and validity. Teoria dyskursu wobec zagadnień prawa i demokratycznego państwa prawnego, Warsaw 2005 (Faktyczność i obowiązywanie. Teoria dyskursu wobec zagadnień prawa i demokratycznego państwa prawnego).

Hall Williams J. E., "The Ladies' Directory and Criminal Conspiracy the Judge as Custos Morum." The Modern Law Review, vol. 24, no. 5, 1961, pp. 626-31.

Hart H.L.A., Law, liberty and morality, Stanford 1963.

Hirsch R., Towards Jursitocracy: The Origins and Consequences of the New Constitutionalism, Harvard University Press, Cambridge, Mass. 2004.

Holmes O. W. "The Theory of Legal Interpretation." Harvard Law Review, vol. 12, no. 6, 1899, pp. 417-20.

K.D.Kmiec, The Origin and Current Meanings of <Judical Activism>, California Law Review, vol.92, p. 1442-1443, C. Green, An Intellectual History of Judical Activism, "Emory Law Journal".

L. Pereire Coutinho, M. La Torre, S. D. Smith (ed.), Judical activism. Na interdisciplinar approach to the American and European Experiences, Switzerland 2015.

Leszczyński L., Operative interpretation (basic properties), Państwo i Prawo 2009, no.6 (Wykładnia operatywna, podstawowe właściwości).

Matczak M., Why Judicial Formalism is Incompatible with the Rule of Law. Canadian Journal of Law and Jurisprudence 2018, 31 (1).

Pokol B., Juristocratic form of government and its structural aspects, 'Prawo i Więź, No. 15, 2016, (Jurystokratyczna forma rządów i jej aspekty strukturalne).

Schusser F., Judical activism in a comparative perspective. The Supreme Court of India vs. the Bundesrfassunggericht, Baden-Baden 2019.

Sebok A. J., Legal Positivism in American Jurisprudence, Cambridge 1998.

Storing H. J. (ed.), The Anti-Federalist: Writings by the Opponents of the Constitution, University of Chicago Press, Chicago 1985.

Wall S. The Hart/Devlin Debate. In: Enforcing Morality. Cambridge Introductions to Philosophy and Law. Cambridge University Press; 2023.

Wolfe Ch., Judical Activism. Bulwark of freedom or precarious security? Rev. edition, Playmouth 1997.

Zeppos N.S., The use of authority in statutory interpretation: an empirical analysis, Texas Law Review 1992, vol. 70.

Salvatore Antonello Parente[279]

Participatory democracy and *ius impositionis*

Abstract: Nowadays, among the powers that characterize state sovereignty, the power to withdraw wealth to meet public expenses and needs of the community takes on a completely peculiar dimension. The *ius impositionis* constitutes an expression of participatory democracy, due to the involvement of taxable subjects in the tax dynamics through the expression of consent to taxation. In this way, the aim was to rebalance the structure of public authorities and guarantee fiscal interest without creating damage to the financial integrity of taxpayers. The essay, starting from the historical evolution and the constitutional principles of reference, critically analyzes the dynamics related to the relationships between participatory democracy and exercise of the *ius impositionis*.

Keywords: Participatory democracy, *ius impositionis*, legal reservation, critical issues, perspectives

1. Introduction

In modern legal systems, among the powers that characterize state sovereignty[280], the power to withdraw wealth, to meet public expenses and needs of the community[281], takes on a completely peculiar dimension. On a historical level, to avoid abuses by public authorities, the *ius impositionis*[282] has been diachronically anchored to rigorous objective parameters[283], in the same way as the slow evolution of the foundation of the power of taxation, which, over time, had

---

279 University of Bari Aldo Moro, ORCID 0000-0002-5426-90.

280 Comp. F. FARRI, *Tax Sovereignty and the Law in the Digital and Global Economy*, New York-Torino, 2021.

281 Comp. R. LUPI, *Riserva di legge (Dir. Trib.)*, in *Il Diritto. Enciclopedia Giuridica del Sole 24-Ore*, vol. 13, Milano, 2007, p. 633-634.

282 Comp. S.A. PARENTE, *Lo ius impositionis tra potere autoritativo, solidarietà sociale e libertà personale*, in *Annali del Dipartimento Jonico*, Taranto, 2013, p. 511 ff.

283 Comp. M. BERTOLISSI, *Legge tributaria*, in *Digesto Discipline Privatistiche, Sezione Commerciale*, vol. VIII, Torino 1992, p. 524.

different roots[284]: in Roman times, the tax was an expression of the unilateral and almost unconditional exercise of public authority; in the period of the absolute State, the person who exercised power could impose any tax, without taking into account the destination and use of the revenue; currently, the ius impositionis constitutes an expression of participatory democracy[285], being characterized by the involvement of taxable subjects, who participate in the tax dynamics through the expression of "consent" to the imposition. Over the centuries, there has been a shift from the strict principle of authority to the parameter of consent to taxation, which was intended to rebalance the structure of public powers and guarantee the financial integrity of individuals against the arbitrariness of whoever exercises the *ius impositionis*.

2. The legal reserve as an expression of participatory democracy in tax matters

Therefore, in the current regulatory system[286], the relationship between the tax plan and the representative principle (then democratic)[287] is based on the so-called "legal reserve", the taxing power being limited by rigid constitutional

---

284 Comp. C. ADAMS, *For Good and Evil. L'influsso della tassazione sulla storia dell'umanità*, Macerata, 2007; P. BORIA, *Il potere tributario. Politica e tributi nel corso dei secoli*, Bologna, 2021, p. 25 ff.

285 Comp. M. LUCIANI, *Democrazia rappresentativa e democrazia partecipativa*, in L. CARLASSARE (a cura di), *La sovranità popolare nel pensiero di Esposito, Crisafulli, Paladin*, Padova, 2004, p. 184; U. ALLEGRETTI, *Basi giuridiche della democrazia partecipativa: alcuni orientamenti*, in *Democrazia e diritto*, n. 3/2006, p. 156: A.L. PECORIELLO – F. RISPOLI, *Pratiche di democrazia partecipativa in Italia*, in *Democrazia e diritto*, n. 3/2006, p. 125; U. ALLEGRETTI, *Democrazia partecipativa*, in *Enc. dir., Annali*, vol. IV, Milano, 2011, p. 299 ff.; M. TIMO, *Cittadinanza amministrativa e democrazia partecipativa*, in *Osservatorio costituzionale*, n. 3/2016, p. 1 ff.; G. BERGONZINI, *Democrazia fiscale partecipativa e Città*, in *Federalismi.it*, 13 November 2019, p. 1 ff.

286 Comp. N. IRTI, *Il diritto nell'età della tecnica*, Napoli, 2007; G. PETROCCO, *Diritto e democrazia nella società digitale*, Torino, 2022.

287 Comp. P.L. ZAMPETTI, *Partecipazione e democrazia completa*, Soveria Mannelli, 2002.

parameters, among which is the principle enshrined in the art. 23 of the Constitution[288], by virtue of which "no personal or financial benefit can be imposed except in accordance with the law"[289].

It is precisely the relative nature of the legal reserve which, by coloring the tax matter in a (not fully representative but) functional sense, opens the way to technical regulations according to regulatory schemes of various kinds which find a vague reference in the legislative principles[290].

In fact, if the legitimate imposition is democratic, the Constitution itself does not exclude, but rather presupposes, regulatory implementations of a technical nature[291].

The law, as an expression of participatory democracy, therefore becomes the primary source of tax law, governing both the establishment and implementation phases of the tax[292]. In this case, it is a relative legal reserve[293], since the legislative source has the task of defining the basic lines of the matter, while the executive body has the power to integrate the regulation with secondary legislation. In fact,

---

288 Comp. A. FEDELE, *Commento all'art. 23 Cost.*, in G. BRANCA *Commentario alla Costituzione*, Bologna – Roma, 1978; A. FEDELE, *Riserva di legge*, in A. AMATUCCI, *Trattato di diritto tributario*, vol. I, Padova 1994; G. MARONGIU, *I fondamenti costituzionali dell'imposizione tributaria*, Torino, 1995; A. FEDELE, *Appunti dalle lezioni di diritto tributario*, Torino, 2005, p. 37 ff.; S. CIPOLLINA, *La riserva di legge in materia fiscale nell'evoluzione della giurisprudenza costituzionale*, in L. PERRONE – C. BERLIRI, *Diritto tributario e Corte costituzionale. Studi per i 50 anni della Corte costituzionale*, Napoli, 2006, p. 163 ff.; G. GAFFURI, *Diritto tributario. Parte generale e parte speciale*, Padova, 2006, p. 23 ff.; S. LA ROSA, *Principi di diritto tributario*, Torino, 2006, p. 7 ff.; P. RUSSO, *Manuale di diritto tributario. Parte generale*, Milano, 2007, p. 39 ff.; A. AMATUCCI, *Legge tributaria*, in *Enciclopedia Giuridica Treccani*, vol. XVIII, Roma, 1990, p. 1 ff.; A.F. URICCHIO, *Percorsi di diritto tributario*, Bari, 2017, p. 47 ff.; A.F. URICCHIO, *Manuale di diritto tributario*, Bari, 2020, p. 89 ff.

289 Comp. F. GALLO, *Il dovere tributario nella costituzione*, in *Riv. trim. dir. trib.*, n. 4/2022, p. 759 ff.

290 Comp. L. COSTANZO, *Democrazia e tecnocrazia nella norma tributaria: conflitto o concordato dinamico?*, in *Riv. telem. dir. trib.*, 19 December 2023, p. 2-3.

291 Comp. L. COSTANZO, *Democrazia e tecnocrazia nella norma tributaria: conflitto o concordato dinamico?*, cit., p. 3.

292 Comp. A.D. GIANNINI, *I concetti fondamentali del diritto tributario*, Torino, 1956, p. 22.

293 Comp. L. CARLASSARE, *Legge (riserva di)*, in *Enciclopedia Giuridica Treccani*, vol. XVIII, Roma, 1990, p. 5-6; P.G. CASALENA, *Riserva di legge (dir. cost.)*, in *Il Diritto. Enciclopedia giuridica del Sole 24-Ore*, vol. 13, Milano, 2007, p. 609; T. MARTINES, *Diritto costituzionale*, Milano, 2010, p. 386.

the law, despite being the foundation of the taxing power, is not the only source, as it may not regulate the tax relationship in its entirety and may refer to subordinate sources for the regulation of detailed elements.

In short, the art. 23 of the Constitution contains a rule on legislative production which is characterized not only by the provision of a reserve in favor of the ordinary legislator, but also by the potential integration of the primary regulatory framework with provisions of a secondary nature (so-called "hierarchically minor sources").

In this perspective, art. 23 of the Constitution concerns the entire body of tax regulations, in the various arrangements on the different levels that make up the positive legal system. Therefore, the constitutional provision, where it attributes the reserve of intervention to the ordinary legislator, does not preclude the primary regulatory framework from being integrated by hierarchically minor sources.

The mandatory minimum content, which must be imposed by law, is made up of the elements necessary to identify the tax[294]: factual assumptions, taxable subjects, principles for determining the rates, taxable base, sanctions. Consequently, it would be unconstitutional, due to violation of the art. 23 of the Constitution, an ordinary law, which, by establishing a tax, did not predetermine these elements, leaving them to secondary regulatory acts.

3. The growing pre-eminence of the technocratic profile over the democratic participation of the taxpayer. The functional distinction between democratic principle and technical inspiration in the formulation of tax rule

Furthermore, in the definition of the contents of the tax law there has always been a tension between the parliamentary demands (an expression of participatory democracy) and the technical and specialist needs of the tax institutions[295].

The adoption of delegated laws in the tax field allows, at least in theory, to reconcile democratic exercise and specialist knowledge, the legislative delegation being justified by the normal lack of technical equipment on the part of Parliament[296].

---

294 Comp. Constitutional Court, 28 December 2001, n. 435, in *Fin. loc.*, 2002, p. 193.

295 Comp. L. COSTANZO, *Democrazia e tecnocrazia nella norma tributaria: conflitto o concordato dinamico?*, cit., p. 1.

296 Comp. L. COSTANZO, *Democrazia e tecnocrazia nella norma tributaria: conflitto o concordato dinamico?*, cit., p. 3.

From this perspective, the technocratic profile seems to have growing preeminence over that of democratic participation, especially in transnational tax regulation[297].

In fact, although this is a dating problem, it is equally worth recalling it in light of the role assumed today by tax legislation derived from extra-state law, in which technicality is even more prevalent than that conceived in domestic law[298].

Over time, the presence of supranational bodies has moved the decisions relating to the exercise of the *ius impositionis* to international fora: these are contexts in which democratic legitimation, when it exists, is less direct, also because international fora have not the same level of accountability as national parliaments[299].

Moreover, global economic and financial phenomena today make the regulatory force of States recessive, producing an "entropization" of sources, both from a formal point of view (through the greater importance assumed by soft law) and a substantial one (with the use of techniques and timely rules to regulate complex phenomena)[300].

If the traditional weakening of the principle of representation in the development of tax legislation is entirely apparent for intrinsic reasons, the novelty consists of the unprecedented regulatory levels that transnational tax phenomena require and which are difficult to grasp according to traditional canons[301].

In these scenarios, the technical matrix of the tax law would seem to almost completely engulf the principle of democratic representation, if it were not counterbalanced by the multifunctionality of the technique which takes on the role of legitimizing factor of tax legislation at an international level, at least thanks to transparency and comprehensibility of the decisions taken, through the use of

---

297 Comp. G. PETRILLO, *Il rafforzamento del legame fra fiscalità e democrazia per la creazione di una capacità fiscale europea*, in *Federalismi.it*, 23 February 2022, p. 1 ff.; L. COSTANZO, *Democrazia e tecnocrazia nella norma tributaria: conflitto o concordato dinamico?*, cit., p. 1.

298 Comp. L. COSTANZO, *Democrazia e tecnocrazia nella norma tributaria: conflitto o concordato dinamico?*, cit., p. 2.

299 Comp. L. COSTANZO, *Democrazia e tecnocrazia nella norma tributaria: conflitto o concordato dinamico?*, cit., p. 4.

300 Comp. L. COSTANZO, *Democrazia e tecnocrazia nella norma tributaria: conflitto o concordato dinamico?*, cit., p. 4.

301 Comp. L. COSTANZO, *Democrazia e tecnocrazia nella norma tributaria: conflitto o concordato dinamico?*, cit., p. 6.

forms of public consultation and the possibility of submitting observations to the draft regulatory documents[302].

More than representation, therefore, transparency, comprehensibility, responsibility seem to be the canons that govern the modern agreement between democracy and technocracy in the tax field[303].

An antagonism thus emerges between the two souls of the tax law, rather than a relationship of functional complementarity, contemplated even by the constitutional principle of (relative) legal reserve, furthermore noting the recurrence of forms of transparency and consultation also in the procedure of technical elaboration of fiscal rules, with a supplementary effect compared to the principle of democratic participation[304].

In reality, upon careful analysis, rather than a conflict, it is possible to identify a functional distinction between democratic principle and technical inspiration in the determination of the tax law, the latter being designed to answer two fundamental questions: on the one hand, whether and what to tax, on the other hand, how to tax[305].

The first question cannot ignore a decision of a political nature; the second, however, requires an articulation in a technical key, making the latter an instrument that completes the democratic principle underlying the *ius impositionis*[306].

More generally, the reasons for this phenomenon, which tends to marginalize national political representation, are to be found in the extreme complexity that characterizes global fiscal phenomena: Parliament cannot independently develop the most appropriate technical rule to deal with them, having to take into account of factual situations and technical realities that can only be regulated through international agreements[307].

---

302 Comp. L. COSTANZO, *Democrazia e tecnocrazia nella norma tributaria: conflitto o concordato dinamico?*, cit., p. 6.

303 Comp. L. COSTANZO, *Democrazia e tecnocrazia nella norma tributaria: conflitto o concordato dinamico?*, cit., p. 6.

304 Comp. L. COSTANZO, *Democrazia e tecnocrazia nella norma tributaria: conflitto o concordato dinamico?*, cit., p. 1.

305 Comp. L. COSTANZO, *Democrazia e tecnocrazia nella norma tributaria: conflitto o concordato dinamico?*, cit., p. 3.

306 Comp. L. COSTANZO, *Democrazia e tecnocrazia nella norma tributaria: conflitto o concordato dinamico?*, cit., p. 4.

307 Comp. L. COSTANZO, *Democrazia e tecnocrazia nella norma tributaria: conflitto o concordato dinamico?*, cit., p. 2.

From this point of view, however, to the well-known democratic deficit that besets prescriptive activity of an international nature (not sufficiently compensated by the representativeness of only the executives of the member states in the specialized organizations), there is added a type of normative production that seems to find its reasons for its having to be[308].

4. The content of the legal reserve in tax matters and the role of sub-legislative sources

In general terms, the relative reservation in tax matters can be considered satisfied if the law determines a "procedural module" for the exercise of administrative power such as to limit the discretionality of the financial administration[309].

The same constitutional jurisprudence[310] has not failed to observe that a financial benefit is valid if it is imposed "according to the law" and not mandatorily "by law". In other words, the law, conferring the taxing power, must indicate the criteria to limit the discretionality of the taxing body, but may not establish the maximum limit of the benefit, which constitutes only one of the potential barriers imposed by the legislator.

In reconstructing the framework of the sources, the restrictive hermeneutics of the art. 23 of the Constitution[311] has led to the belief that the law must also regulate the type and extent of the service and that the principle in question must refer not only to tax rules of a substantial nature, but even to the provisions relating to assessment and collection, since even the formal and procedural rules would be likely to increase the burden of contributing to public expenses.

A different reconstruction, conversely, has favored the view of delegating the regulation of assessment and collection to sub-legislative sources, since, taking into account the pre-eminent guarantee function carried out by the art. 23 of the Constitution, the legal reserve on the subject of imposed financial benefits could

308 Comp. L. COSTANZO, *Democrazia e tecnocrazia nella norma tributaria: conflitto o concordato dinamico?*, cit., p. 2.

309 Comp. Constitutional Court, 5 February 1986, n. 34, in *Giur. it.*, 1987, I, 1, p. 22; Constitutional Court, 5 May 1988, n. 507, in *Foro it.*, 1988, I, c. 2098; Constitutional Court, 31 May 1996, n. 180, in *Giur. cost.*, 1996, p. 1664.

310 Comp. Constitutional Court, 26 January 1957, n. 4, in *Giur. cost.*, 1957, p. 22.

311 Comp. F. FORTE, *Note sulla nozione di tributo nell'ordinamento finanziario italiano e sul significato dell'art. 23 della Costituzione*, in *Riv. dir. fin. sc. fin.*, 1956, I, p. 248 ff.; A. BERLIRI, *Appunti sul fondamento e il contenuto dell'art. 23 della Costituzione*, in *Studi per Achille Donato Giannini*, Milano, 1961, p. 137 ff.

only apply to the tax rules in the strict sense, concerning the *an* and *quantum debeatur*. Consequently, it would exclude, on the one hand, the rules placed to the benefit of the taxpayer, such as those granting benefits, exemptions and concessions and, on the other, those regarding assessment and collection, which concern the implementation phase of the tax claim.

In reality, the art. 23 of the Constitution proposes, under a different guise, the art. 30 of the Albertine Statute, by virtue of which "no tribute can be imposed or collected unless it has been permitted by the Chambers and sanctioned by the king"[312].

In fact, the similarity between the two provisions is evident, both an expression of participatory democracy, which, however, differ in their dispositive content. The Albertine Statute attributed the imposition and collection of the tax to the Chambers, while the Republican Constitution identifies the law as the appropriate act to found the tax claim. Furthermore, the art. 23 of the Constitution has a broader content than the rule of the Albertine Statute, where it extends its scope not only to the generality of taxes, but also to imposed benefits of a personal nature and to non-tax patrimonial benefits.

5. The brocardi "*nullum tributum sine lege*" and "no taxation without representation". The "brakes and counterweights" system

The legislative reserve in tax matters, on which the rule of self-imposition is based[313], is an expression of the classic principles of liberal democracies, summarized in the brocardi "*nullum tributum sine lege*" and "no taxation without representation".

These principles, an expression of participatory democracy, already present in nineteenth-century liberal constitutions, allow taxpayers to express their consent to taxation, through representation within democratic bodies.

From a systematic point of view, the rule summarized in the brocard "*nullum tributum sine lege*" does not only express a principle of self-limitation of the State's power, but implies the need for the regulation of the tax to be contained in a law or other rule which has effectiveness.

---

312 Comp. A. DE VALLES, *Limiti costituzionali alle leggi tributarie*, in *Riv. dir. fin. sc. fin.*, 1958, I, p. 3 ff.; G. MARONGIU, *I fondamenti costituzionali dell'imposizione tributaria*, cit., p. 17.

313 Comp. S. BARTHOLINI, *Il principio di legalità dei tributi in materia di imposte*, Padova, 1957, p. 3 ff.

In other words, in the new regulatory framework, the transfer from the authority-subject relationship to the self-taxation regime is clear: the taxable subject must express, albeit indirectly, his/her consent to the taxation, thus limiting the political power. In short, it is a system of "brakes and counterweights", a sort of "checks and balances", imposed in order to limit excessive power in fiscal matters.

The mechanism is made up of two degrees, which constitute two different moments, in a logical-chronological connection. On the one hand, citizen-taxpayers are called to elect the members of Parliament and, on the other, the latter, through the approval of tax and budget laws, exercises control over those who hold executive power, as in the past he exercised it on the monarch.

In particular, since the law is made by Parliament, the citizens' representative body, parliamentary control in tax matters is an expression of the regulatory principle by virtue of which any intervention by public power on the property and freedom of citizens can only take place by law (so-called "liberty and property clause")[314].

In reality, at its origins, such a system could not be defined as fair and democratic: in the absence of universal suffrage, the consent of taxpayers to the tax, rather than the will of the people, symbolized the privilege and strength of the dominant classes who with their exemptions and prerogatives limited the power and curbed the arbitrariness of the princes[315].

In our rule of law, on the other hand, taxation is not only an expression of state sovereignty, but must be justified by the law, which constitutes the source of every personal or financial benefit. This is why doctrine[316] and constitutional

---

314 Comp. M.A. GRIPPA SALVETTI, *Riserva di legge e delegificazione nell'ordinamento tributario*, Milano, 1998, p. 17 ff.

315 Comp. G. RICCA–SALERNO, *Le entrate ordinarie dello Stato*, in V.E. ORLANDO, *Primo trattato completo di diritto amministrativo*, Milano, 1897 - 1932, p. 163, nt. 3.

316 Comp. A.D. GIANNINI, *I rapporti tributari*, in P. CALAMANDREI - A. LEVI, *Commentario sistematico alla Costituzione italiana*, vol. I, Firenze, 1950, p. 274; E. VANONI, *Opere giuridiche*, Milano, 1962, vol. I, p. 73 ff.; A. AMATUCCI, *Il procedimento imposizionale delle prestazioni tributarie nella Costituzione*, in *Rass. dir. pubbl.*, 1964, p. 10; M. LONGO, *Saggio critico sulle finalità e sull'oggetto dell'art. 23 della Costituzione*, Torino, 1968, p. 33 ff.; L. RASTELLO, *Diritto tributario. Principi generali*, Padova, 1987, p. 205 ff.; G. FALSITTA, *Manuale di diritto tributario*, Padova, 2005, p. 131 ff.

jurisprudence[317] attribute to the principle of legality (art. 23 of the Constitution) the function of protecting the property and freedom of individuals, in order to avoid excesses of executive power in tax matters.

6. Conclusions

In conclusion, the legal reserve in the tax field does not only fulfill a role of guarantee for individuals, but also has a pre-eminent institutional function, linked to the democratic principle, typical of modern states, which responds to an organizational need for the distribution of competences between the top political bodies and the tax administration.

From this perspective, despite the critical issues highlighted, the legal reserve regarding imposed financial benefits is placed, within the scope of the current Constitution, as an immediate and prevalent function of general interests and only in a mediated and subordinate manner of the interests of private individuals.

This approach involves a logical-systematic and teleological-axiological interpretation[318] of the art. 23 of the Constitution, which cannot ignore the overall system of constitutional rules and principles.

In other words, since in the Republican Constitution taxation is seen as an aspect and tool of social policy and income redistribution, the regulation of

---

317 Comp. Constitutional Court, 26 January 1957, n. 4, cit.; Constitutional Court, 22 March 1957, n. 57, in *Giur. cost.*, 1957, p. 598; Constitutional Court, 8 July 1957, n. 122, in *Giur. cost.*, 1957, p. 1101; Constitutional Court, 27 December 1973, n. 183, in *Foro It.*, 1974, I, c. 314.

318 Comp. E. BETTI, *Interpretazione della legge e degli atti giuridici (Teoria generale e dogmatica)*, Milano, 1971, p. 283 ff.; P. PERLINGIERI, *L'interpretazione della legge come sistematica ed assiologica. Il broccardo* in claris non fit interpretatio, *il ruolo dell'art. 12 disp. prel. c.c. e la nuova scuola dell'esegesi*, in P. PERLINGIERI, *Scuole tendenze e metodi. Problemi di diritto civile*, Napoli, 1989, p. 275 ff.; P. PERLINGIERI, *Complessità e unitarietà dell'ordinamento giuridico vigente*, in *Rass. dir. civ.*, 2005, p. 220; G. D'AMICO, *Complessità e unitarietà dell'ordinamento giuridico nel prisma dell'interpretazione. Il contributo di un Maestro*, in *Corti calabresi*, 2008, p. 657 ff.; P. PERLINGIERI, *Per un'ermeneutica rinnovata*, in AA.VV., *Studi in onore di Nicolò Lipari*, vol. II, Milano, 2008, p. 2231 ff.; P. MADDALENA, *Interpretazione sistematica e assiologica del diritto*, in *Giust. civ.*, 2009, II, p. 65 ff.; P. GROSSI, *Il diritto civile nella legalità costituzionale*, in *Rass. dir. civ.*, 2009, p. 914 ff.; P. PERLINGIERI, *Applicazione e controllo nell'interpretazione giuridica*, in *Riv. dir. civ.*, 2010, I, p. 317 ff.; P. PERLINGIERI, *Fonti del diritto e "ordinamento del caso concreto"*, in *Riv. dir. priv.*, 2010, p. 7 ff.

imposed benefits can only be attributed to Parliament, as a body directly representative of the popular will, which is holder of the political direction function.

However, the top political authority, which exercises legislative power in tax matters, does not have enormous discretionality. In fact, to decide how to find the financial resources necessary for public spending, the legislator often makes choices of a purely political nature, which include safeguarding of the financial integrity of private individuals, promotion of development, meritability of certain sectors of social life, caution against fraud and evasion, mediation between the precision of the levy and its simplicity and streamlined nature, in the face of economic manifestations that can be identified and quantified differently for the purposes of tax levy.

Bibliography

ADAMS C., *For Good and Evil. L'influsso della tassazione sulla storia dell'umanità*, Macerata, 2007.

ALLEGRETTI U., *Basi giuridiche della democrazia partecipativa: alcuni orientamenti*, in *Democrazia e diritto*, n. 3/2006, p. 156.

ALLEGRETTI U., *Democrazia partecipativa*, in *Enc. dir., Annali*, vol. IV, Milano, 2011, p. 299 ff.

AMATUCCI A., *Il procedimento imposizionale delle prestazioni tributarie nella Costituzione*, in *Rass. dir. pubbl.*, 1964, p. 10.

AMATUCCI A., *Legge tributaria*, in *Enciclopedia Giuridica Treccani*, vol. XVIII, Roma, 1990, p. 1 ff.

BARTHOLINI S., *Il principio di legalità dei tributi in materia di imposte*, Padova, 1957, p. 3 ff.

BERGONZINI G., *Democrazia fiscale partecipativa e Città*, in *Federalismi.it*, 13 November 2019, p. 1 ff.

BERLIRI A., *Appunti sul fondamento e il contenuto dell'art. 23 della Costituzione*, in *Studi per Achille Donato Giannini*, Milano, 1961, p. 137 ff.

BERTOLISSI M., *Legge tributaria*, in *Digesto Discipline Privatistiche, Sezione Commerciale*, vol. VIII, Torino, 1992, p. 524.

BETTI E., *Interpretazione della legge e degli atti giuridici (Teoria generale e dogmatica)*, Milano, 1971, p. 283 ff.

BORIA P., *Il potere tributario. Politica e tributi nel corso dei secoli*, Bologna, 2021, p. 25 ff.

CARLASSARE L., *Legge (riserva di)*, in *Enciclopedia Giuridica Treccani*, vol. XVIII, Roma, 1990, p. 1 ff.

CASALENA P.G., *Riserva di legge (dir. cost.)*, in *Il Diritto. Enciclopedia giuridica del Sole 24-Ore*, vol. 13, Milano, 2007, p. 609.

CIPOLLINA S., *La riserva di legge in materia fiscale nell'evoluzione della giurisprudenza costituzionale*, in L. PERRONE – C. BERLIRI, *Diritto tributario e Corte costituzionale. Studi per i 50 anni della Corte costituzionale*, Napoli, 2006, p. 163 ff.

D'AMICO G., *Complessità e unitarietà dell'ordinamento giuridico nel prisma dell'interpretazione. Il contributo di un Maestro*, in *Corti calabresi*, 2008, p. 657 ff.

COSTANZO L., *Democrazia e tecnocrazia nella norma tributaria: conflitto o concordato dinamico?*, in *Riv. telem. dir. trib.*, 19 December 2023, p. 1 ff.

DE VALLES A., *Limiti costituzionali alle leggi tributarie*, in *Riv. dir. fin. sc. fin.*, 1958, I, p. 3 ff.

FARRI F., *Tax Sovereignty and the Law in the Digital and Global Economy*, New York-Torino, 2021.

FALSITTA G., *Manuale di diritto tributario*, Padova, 2005, p. 131 ff.

FEDELE A., *Commento all'art. 23 Cost.*, in G. BRANCA *Commentario alla Costituzione*, Bologna – Roma, 1978.

FEDELE A., *Riserva di legge*, in A. AMATUCCI, *Trattato di diritto tributario*, vol. I, Padova 1994.

FEDELE A., *Appunti dalle lezioni di diritto tributario*, Torino, 2005, p. 37 ff.

FORTE F., *Note sulla nozione di tributo nell'ordinamento finanziario italiano e sul significato dell'art. 23 della Costituzione*, in *Riv. dir. fin. sc. fin.*, 1956, I, p. 248 ff.

GAFFURI G., *Diritto tributario. Parte generale e parte speciale*, Padova, 2006, p. 23 ff.

GALLO F., *Il dovere tributario nella costituzione*, in *Riv. trim. dir. trib.*, n. 4/2022, p. 759 ff.

GIANNINI A.D., *I rapporti tributari*, in P. CALAMANDREI – A. LEVI, *Commentario sistematico alla Costituzione italiana*, vol. I, Firenze, 1950, p. 274.

GIANNINI A.D., *I concetti fondamentali del diritto tributario*, Torino, 1956, p. 22.

GRIPPA M.A. SALVETTI, *Riserva di legge e delegificazione nell'ordinamento tributario*, Milano, 1998, p. 17 ff.

GROSSI P., *Il diritto civile nella legalità costituzionale*, in *Rass. dir. civ.*, 2009, p. 914 ff.

IRTI N., *Il diritto nell'età della tecnica*, Napoli, 2007.

LA ROSA S., *Principi di diritto tributario*, Torino, 2006, p. 7 ff.

LONGO M., *Saggio critico sulle finalità e sull'oggetto dell'art. 23 della Costituzione*, Torino, 1968, p. 33 ff.

LUCIANI M., *Democrazia rappresentativa e democrazia partecipativa*, in L. CARLASSARE (a cura di), *La sovranità popolare nel pensiero di Esposito, Crisafulli, Paladin*, Padova, 2004, p. 184.

LUPI R., *Riserva di legge (Dir. Trib.)*, in *Il Diritto. Enciclopedia Giuridica del Sole 24-Ore*, vol. 13, Milano, 2007, p. 633-634.

MADDALENA P., *Interpretazione sistematica e assiologica del diritto*, in *Giust. civ.*, 2009, II, p. 65 ff.

MARONGIU G., *I fondamenti costituzionali dell'imposizione tributaria*, Torino, 1995.

MARTINES T., *Diritto costituzionale*, Milano, 2010, p. 386.

PARENTE S.A., *Lo ius impositionis tra potere autoritativo, solidarietà sociale e libertà personale*, in *Annali del Dipartimento Jonico*, Taranto, 2013, p. 511 ff.

PECORIELLO A.L., RISPOLI F., *Pratiche di democrazia partecipativa in Italia*, in *Democrazia e diritto*, n. 3/2006, p. 125.

PERLINGIERI P., *L'interpretazione della legge come sistematica ed assiologica. Il broccardo* in claris non fit interpretatio, *il ruolo dell'art. 12 disp. prel. c.c. e la nuova scuola dell'esegesi*, in P. PERLINGIERI, *Scuole tendenze e metodi. Problemi di diritto civile*, Napoli, 1989, p. 275 ff.

PERLINGIERI P., *Complessità e unitarietà dell'ordinamento giuridico vigente*, in *Rass. dir. civ.*, 2005, p. 220.

PERLINGIERI P., *Per un'ermeneutica rinnovata*, in AA.VV., *Studi in onore di Nicolò Lipari*, vol. II, Milano, 2008, p. 2231 ff.

PERLINGIERI P., *Applicazione e controllo nell'interpretazione giuridica*, in *Riv. dir. civ.*, 2010, I, p. 317 ff.

PERLINGIERI P., *Fonti del diritto e "ordinamento del caso concreto"*, in *Riv. dir. priv.*, 2010, p. 7 ff.

PETRILLO G., *Il rafforzamento del legame fra fiscalità e democrazia per la creazione di una capacità fiscale europea*, in *Federalismi.it*, 23 February 2022, p. 1 ff.

PETROCCO G., *Diritto e democrazia nella società digitale*, Torino, 2022.

RICCA-SALERNO G., *Le entrate ordinarie dello Stato*, in V.E. ORLANDO, *Primo trattato completo di diritto amministrativo*, Milano, 1897 – 1932, p. 163, nt. 3.

RASTELLO L., *Diritto tributario. Principi generali*, Padova, 1987, p. 205 ff.

RUSSO P., *Manuale di diritto tributario. Parte generale*, Milano, 2007, p. 39 ff.

TIMO M., *Cittadinanza amministrativa e democrazia partecipativa*, in *Osservatorio costituzionale*, n. 3/2016, p. 1 ff.

URICCHIO A.F., *Percorsi di diritto tributario*, Bari, Cacucci, 2017, p. 47 ff.

URICCHIO A. F., *Manuale di diritto tributario*, Bari, Cacucci, 2020, p. 89 ff.

VANONI E., *Opere giuridiche*, Milano, 1962, vol. I, p. 73 ff.

ZAMPETTI P.L., *Partecipazione e democrazia completa*, Soveria Mannelli, 2002.

Edyta Sokalska[319]

New wave of deliberative democracy – international discourse

Abstract: Increasing dissatisfaction with the current form of democracy stimulates a constant quest for the way to improve it. The public disappointment with the efficiency of representative democracy and the alienation of citizens resulting from the feeling of illusory influence on politics stimulated the search on the solution to the crisis of representative democracy. The response to the crisis of representative democracy in the 21st century might be deliberative democracy. Deliberative democracy has never been a unified theory. The contemporary research approach to deliberative democracy referred to as the 'systemic turn' exposes three factors. The first is the search for opportunities to develop and promote deliberation on a mass scale. The second is the emphasis on the division of tasks and activities among participants within the system. The third is the introduction of a certain continuum to the criterion of deliberation linking the multiplicity of institutions and the processes that occur among them.

Keywords: deliberative democracy, participatory democracy, communication, participation, deliberation, scientific discourse

1. Introduction

The idea of civil society is linked to the emergence of democracy, which has developed over the centuries, from antiquity to the present day, existing in various forms in different historical periods. Nowadays, civil society is becoming a field of collective actions to realize social, political, or economic interests, however, the state apparatus no longer plays a dominant part as the sole actor in politics. Citizens are often able to take care of their own affairs themselves through various types of activities.

The classical republican idea of civil society was based on communitarian values and there was not any differentiation between society and the state, and there was not any separation of the freedom of the political community from the freedom of individuals. It was only freedom within the state based on the authority of law and political institutions. In this conception civil society is complementary to the state. It is a kind of community of communities, in which civic commitment

319 University of Warmia and Mazury in Olsztyn, ORCID 0000-0003-0903-7726.

to public affairs is assessed as a kind of and loyalty to the political community. For the liberal idea of civil society, the concepts of society and state are understood separately. The most important are the powers of an individual, which are the basis for civil society, therefore, the important thing is not the welfare of community, but the welfare of an individual and the role of the state is subservient. In contrast to the state, civil society is a sphere of independence and freedom placed between the individual and the state. In the liberal conception, the state has a servile character, and it is merely complementary to the individualistic society. The model of civil society is defined as a sphere free from state interference, focused on social activity, self-organization, and self-government. It is significant that the liberal conception is not uniform due to the fact that society grows along with the economic development of the free market relations, and development of self-organization, civic spirit, and independence from state interference.

In contemporary scientific discourse on civil society, the perception of civil society might be different due to the fact that the relationship between the individual and society, the role of the state and its relationship with the various social groups and in public is perceived differently. In general, civil society is a separate arena from the state, economy, and the private life, in which citizens voluntarily and autonomously form associations, foundations, movements, assemblies oriented towards the expression, defense, or fulfilment of their needs and aspirations. It constitutes a sphere of voluntary social activity that is separate from the state and the market. In fact, it is not their opposite, but a kind of complement. The institutional basis of such a sphere is the freedom of political expression understood as the freedom for the pursuit of collective goals. The social basis is pluralism expressing a diversity of interests, beliefs, and expectations. The recognition of this diversity is legitimate. The essence of civil society is the voluntary participation of individuals and their associations in the public debate and unforced actions undertaken by the state within the limits of democratically established law.[320]

Increasing dissatisfaction with the current form of democracy stimulates a constant quest to improve it. Democratic transformations take place in the institutional aspects on the doctrinaire basis. In the 20th century, in the practice of democratic states, the indirect procedural representative democracy was dominated by the exercise of citizens' electoral rights and the control over the activities of representative bodies by the voters. The public disappointment with the

320 Cf. M. Kazimierczuk, "Ewolucja pojęcia idei społeczeństwa obywatelskiego", in *Społeczeństwo obywatelskie. Historia, teoria, praktyka*, eds. R. Kania, and M. Kzimierczuk, DIFIN S.A., Warszawa 2021, pp. 28-29.

efficiency of this form of government and the alienation of citizens resulting from the feeling of illusory influence on politics stimulated the search for the solution to the crisis of representative democracy. The response to the crisis of representative democracy in the 21st century might be deliberative democracy. It is significant that the idea of civil society has become one of the most important premises of deliberative democracy.

The worldwide literature concerning the development of deliberative democracy is as impressive as the phenomenon it describes. The representatives of science strive to answer the question how to apply deliberative ideas in order to make political authority legitimate. It should be emphasized that the publications of John S. Dryzek[321] and James S. Fishkin[322] influenced the scientific and social perception of the phenomenon.[323] The value of communication in a community as a sphere, in which an individual citizen has the opportunity to engage in common

321 J.S. Dryzek, *Deliberative Democracy and Beyond: Liberals, Critics, Contestations*, Oxford University Press, New York 2000; idem, *Deliberative Global Politics: Discourse and Democracy in a Divided Word*, Polity Press, Cambridge 2006; idem, *Foundations and Frontiers of Deliberative Democracy*, Oxford University Press, Oxford 2010; idem, "Democratic Political Theory", in *Handbook of Political Theory*, eds. G.F. Gaus, and Ch. Kukathas, Sage Publications, London 2004, pp. 243-254; idem, "Democratization as Deliberative Capacity Building, *Comparative Political Studies* 42/22 (2009), pp. 1379-1402, https://doi.org/10.1177/0010414009332129.

322 J.S. Fishkin, *Democracy and Deliberation: New Directions for Democratic Reform*, Yale University Press, New Haven 1993; idem, *The Voice of the People: Public Opinion and Democracy*, Yale University Press, New Haven 1995; idem, *When the People Speak. Deliberative Democracy and Public Consultations*, Oxford University Press, New York 2011.

323 It should be taken into consideration that in the field of Polish science, the publications of Grzegorz Makowski and Tomasz Szymanek (eds., *Organizacje pozarządowe i władza publiczna. Drogi do partnerstwa*, Fundacja Instytut Spraw Publicznych, Warszawa 2008), Piotr Uziębło (*Demokracja partycypacyjna*, Centrum Badań Społecznych, Gdańsk 2009), Marzena Mendza-Drozd (*Zagadnienie konsultacji społecznych w Unii Europejskiej. Analiza wybranych instytucji i dokumentów*, opracowanie w ramach zleconego przez Ministerstwo Pracy i Polityki Społecznej, Warszawa 2010), Radosław Markowski (*Demokracja i demokratyczne innowacje. Z teorią w praktykę*, Instytut Obywatelski, Warszawa 2014), Mariusz Wiktor Sienkiewicz and Monika Sidor (eds., *Dialog obywatelski: formy, mechanizmy, bariery i perspektywy rozwoju*, Wydawnictwo Fundacji Centrum Rozwoju Lokalnego, Lublin 2014), Agnieszka Turoń-Kowalska (ed., *Demokracja deliberatywna: utopia czy ratunek dla demokratycznych wartości?*, Instytut Nauk Politycznych i Dziennikarstwa Uniwersytetu Śląskiego w Katowicach, Sosnowiec 2018), and others can be mentioned here.

values and maximize the agreement through communication, was highlighted by such eminent philosophers as John Rawls[324] and Jürgen Habermas[325].

The purpose of the article is to present the development of international discourse on deliberative democracy, desirable deliberative features and practices. The main questions the present study strives to answer are: What were the main features of the formal conception of deliberative democracy in the 1980s? In what directions has the international scientific discourse seeking to capture the ideal of deliberative democracy developed? In the first part of the article, the evolution of the concept of deliberative democracy will be presented. An overview of some global trends relating to the development of deliberative democracy will be presented in the second part of the text. In this particular study, the comparative and historical methods were applied to address the research questions and then, to reach some conclusions. Unfortunately, since the modest scope of the article does not allow for an exhaustive treatment of the subject, the present work is contributory in nature.

2. The good polity and mending democracy in the 1980s

The concept of deliberative democracy emerged on a large scale in the 1980s, and it has rapidly become the subject of the scientific discussion on philosophy of law, and in political and sociological thought. It is significant that the term of deliberative democracy currently denotes some views combined together under the aegis of the idea that social deliberation is central to the democratic decision making. The popularizer of the term of deliberative democracy became John S. Dryzek who put forward the thesis that the deliberate turn in the theory of democracy took place in the last decade of the 20th.[326] The process was conceived in terms of legitimacy of democracy, thank to participation of citizens in active deliberation as a part of collective decision-making. In his opinion, that emphasis on deliberation is not a new phenomenon because its antecedents can be found in ancient Greece, in political theory of Edmund Burke, John Stuart Mill, and theorists from

---

324 J. Rawls, *A Theory of Justice. Revised Edition*, Oxford University Press, Oxford-New York 1999.

325 J. Habermas, *The Theory of Communicative Action vol. I. Reason and the Rationalization of Society*, Beacon Press, Boston 1984; idem, "Political Communication in Media Society: Does Democracy Still Enjoy an Epistemic Dimension? The Impact of Normative Theory on Empirical Research", *Communication Theory* 16/4 (2006), pp. 411-426, https://doi.org/10.1111/j.1468-2885.2006.00280.x.

326 J.S. Dryzek, *Deliberative Democracy and Beyond…*, op.cit., p. 1.

the early 20th century such as John Dewey. Invented by Joseph Bessette (1980)[327] and popularized by Bernard Manin and Joshua Cohen, the term of 'deliberative democracy' was used rarely prior to 1990s.[328]

In the reception of Dryzek, the final decade of the 20th century was the time when the theory of democracy took a strong deliberative turn, and democratic legitimacy was seen "in terms of the ability or opportunity to participate in effective deliberation on the part of those subject to collective decision. Thus claims on behalf of or against such decisions have to be justified to these people in terms that, on reflection, they are capable of accepting".[329] Deliberation for Dryzek is a social process distinguished from the other forms of communication, open to the possibility of changing positions, preferences or views through interactions between participants of deliberation during its duration.[330] Deliberative democracy is a reform movement and an academic activity.[331] In the opinion of Dryzek, such philosophers as Habermas or Rawls are the most important liberal theorists and critical theorists of the late 20th century, and their works highly influenced the modern vision of deliberative democracy. He also states that deliberative democracy can be placed fairly close to discoursive democracy, but they are not synonyms, and „the deliberative turn represents a renewed concern with the authenticity of democracy: the degree to which democratic control is substantive rather than symbolic, and engaged by competent citizens".[332]

In 1989, American and British scholars were looking for the good polity. In the book *The Good Polity. Normative Analysis of the State* edited by Alan Hamlin and Philip Pettit there was presented a series of essays which touched the issues of the limits of democracy, deliberation and democratic legitimacy, responsibility of the state, liberty, contract and the state, power and control in a good polity,

327 J.M. Bessette, "Deliberative Democracy: the Majority Principle in Republican Government", in *How Democratic is the Constitution?*, eds. R.A. Goldwin, and W.A. Schambra, American Institute for Public Policy Research, Washington 1980, pp. 102-116.

328 J.S. Dryzek, *Deliberative Democracy and Beyond…*, op.cit., p. 2.

329 Ibidem, p. 1, idem, "Democratic Political Theory", op.cit., p. 145.

330 J.S. Dryzek, and S. Niemeyer, "Reconciling Pluralism and Consensus as Political Ideals", *American Journal of Political Science*, 50/3 (2006), pp. 634-649, https://doi.org/10.1111/j.1540-5907.2006.00206.

331 S.A. Ercan, and J.S. Dryzek, "The Reach of Deliberative Democracy", *Policy Studies* 36/3 (2015), p. 241.

332 J.S. Dryzek, *Deliberative Democracy and Beyond…*, op.cit., p. 1; idem, "Democratization as Deliberative Capacity Building", op.cit., pp. 1379-1402.

the freedom of the city, and social welfare.[333] Joshua Cohen explored in his essay the ideal of 'deliberative democracy'.[334] In his perception, deliberative democracy meant "an association whose affairs are governed by the public deliberation of its members".[335] He proposed an account of the value of such an association that treated democracy itself as "a fundamental political ideal not simply as a derivative ideal that can be explained in terms of the values of fairness or equality of respect".[336] He focused on Rawl's discussion on democracy in order to introduce certain features of deliberative democracy, and to rise some doubts about whether their importance is explained in terms of the notion of a fair system of social cooperation. He proposed the ideal deliberative procedure that provided with the abstract model of deliberation which, in his opinion, links the intuitive ideal of democratic association to a more substantive view of deliberative democracy.

According to Joshua Cohen, the formal conception of deliberative democracy can be characterised by five main features. Firstly, a deliberative democracy is an ongoing and independent association, and its members expect that it would continue into the indefinite future. Secondly, it is known that the members of the association share the view that the appropriate terms of association are the results of their deliberation or provide a framework for. They are of the opinion that there is a commitment to coordination of their activities within institutions that make deliberation possible, and according to norms that appear through their deliberation. In such understanding, free deliberation among equals is the core of legitimacy. Thirdly, a deliberative democracy is treated as a pluralistic association, the members of which have diverse preferences and ideals as far as their visions of lives are concerned. They share the commitment to the deliberative resolutions of problems of collective choice, but they also have diverse aims. They are of the opinion that some particular set of preferences, ideals or convictions is not mandatory. The fourth feature is that the members of democratic associations regard deliberative procedures as the source of legitimacy. In their perception, "the terms of their association not merely be the results of their deliberation, but also be manifest to them as such".[337] The institutions, in which the connections between deliberation and outcomes are evident to ones in which the connections are less

333 A. Hamlin, and P. Pettit (eds.), *The Good Polity: Normative Analysis of the State*, Basil Blackwell, Oxford 1989, pp. 1-256.

334 J. Cohen, "Deliberation and Democratic Legitimacy", in *The Good Polity: Normative Analysis of the State*, op.cit., pp. 17-34.

335 Ibidem, p. 17.

336 Ibidem.

337 Ibidem, p. 21.

clear, are preferred by them. The fifth feature is that the members "recognize one another as having deliberative capacities, i.e. the capacities required for entering into a public exchange of reasons, and for acting on the result of such public reasoning"[338].

Ideal procedure of a deliberative democracy applies three general aspects of deliberation. There is a need to decide on an agenda. Proposals of alternative solutions to the problems on the agenda are very important. The outcomes of deliberation are democratically legitimate if there is there is a free, reasoned agreement among the equals. Deliberation assumed as ideal is free if it satisfies two conditions. The parties pf the deliberation regard themselves "as bound only by the results of their deliberation and by the preconditions for that deliberation. Their consideration of proposals is not constrained by the authority of prior norms or requirements".[339] The participants think that a certain decision appears through their deliberation as a sufficient reason for complying with it.

Deliberation is reasoned because the parties are required to state their reasons for advancing proposals. They support the proposals or criticise them. Reasons are proposed in order to achieve the aim of bringing others to accept the given proposals through free deliberation among equals. Of course, proposals might be rejected and defended, because the deliberative conception underlines that collective choices should be made in a deliberative way. They should have a desirable fit with the preferences of individuals of parties.

It should be taken into closer consideration that in an ideal deliberation citizens are formally and substantially equal. During the deliberative process everyone has equal standing at each stage. The issues might be put on agenda by each of the participants, because they are substantively equal. The participants regard the system as a potential object of their deliberative judgements.

The deliberation that might be perceived as ideal aims to arrive at a rationally motivated consensus in order to find persuasive reasons to all committed to acting on the results. Free and reasoned assessment of alternatives by equals should take place. It is significant that it is not sure that even under ideal conditions the consensual reasons will be achieved. For this reason, deliberation might conclude with voting, subject to some forms of the majority rule. The distinction between deliberative form of collective choice and forms that acts that aggregate non-deliberative preferences might be tempered. In the matter of the fact, the institutional consequences and the results of voting might be different, and

338 Ibidem.
339 Ibidem, p. 22.

not so convincing for those who are committed to finding reasons that are persuasive to all.[340]

Characterisation of ideal deliberation is very important in the context of the development of deliberative systems. It provides with ideal deliberative procedure that links the formal notion of deliberative democracy with the more substantive proposal of a new democratic association, where public debate is concentrated on the common good of the members.

3. Theoretical and practical research on deliberative democracy: four generations

It is significant that during a thirty-year worldwide debate on the development of deliberative democracy, any unified 'school' or current were established.[341] With the development of the discourse, it was becoming more internally diverse. Advocates of deliberative democracy present different view on the expected outcomes of deliberation.[342] They also differ when they answer the question of what kind of communication is perceived as deliberative; where and at which level deliberation should take place; and who should participate in deliberation and how.

Several stages can be identified in the deliberative democracy discourse, however, there is some overlap in certain solutions, methodologies, and tools, The first generation of explorers of deliberative democracy were concerned with the normative theory. Jürgen Habermas highlighted the legitimacy of collective decisions through the discursive character of their decision-making procedures. In his early works, John S. Dryzek put forward a radical concept of discursive

---

340 Ibidem, p. 23.

341 Cf. E. Sokalska, "Searching for a new formula of a state: international discourse on deliberative democracy", *Acta Iuridica Resoviensia* 1/40 (2023), pp. 124-138, https://doi.org/10.15584/actaires.2023.1.8. About the term and development of deliberative democracy, see more in eadem, "Deliberative democracy in the time of crisis: participatory instruments at the local level and their limitations (some remarks)", *Journal of Modern Science* 2/45 (2020), pp. 227-230, DOI: 10.13166/JMS/125595.

342 See also Polish subject related literature presented in E. Sokalska, "Flaws and Advantages of the Polish Local Self-Government in the 21st Century: Social Consultations at the Local Level", *Lex Localis* 19/2 (2021), pp. 19-37, DOI: https://doi.org/10.4335/19.1.19-37; eadem, "W poszukiwaniu idealnej formuły państwa: blaski i cienie demokracji deliberatywnej na poziomie lokalnym (wybrane uwagi)", in *Społeczeństwo obywatelskie…*, op.cit., pp. 208-211.

democracy allowing for a transnational or supra-state view on democracy.[343] Something that was common to this current it was the articulation of the need to push forward deliberative democracy on a mass scale, and the preference for a vision of deliberative democracy formed normatively, something that had not actually been possible on a mass scale before.

The second generation of scholars was concerned with defining deliberation more broadly in order to consequently create a model more 'sensitive' to the heterogeneity, pluralism, and complexity of contemporary democracies.[344] Their field of interest included the requirement of rational arguments and consensus in deliberation, which consequently brought deliberative democracy theory closer to other issues related to multiculturalism, environmental politics, or feminism.[345] Representatives of the second generation raised issues of potential inequalities during discourse as well as the possibility of instrumentalization or strategic use of deliberation by its influential participants. In the matter of the fact, deliberation brought deliberative democracy closer to the real world of dilemmas and conflicts.

It is interesting to consider that the third generation of participants of the scientific discourse on deliberative democracy does not shy away from detailed institutional designs and empirical analysis of deliberative practices. The research on institutional mechanisms in order to develop actual deliberation is promoted. Here, there are theories more oriented towards practical solutions, the design of deliberative institutions, and their empirical analysis, therefore, a large part of the literature is devoted to various participatory practices, e.g. participatory budgets.

The approach proposed by James S. Fishkin in a 1995 publication should be taken into closer consideration. He presents the idea of so-called 'deliberative pools'. Deliberative pools are representative samples of citizens in a given area, such as those living in an administrative unit, to participate in deliberating on a

343 It is interesting to consider that the reflection of Joshua Cohen also falls within the above current. Cf. J. Cohen, "Deliberation and Democratic Legitimacy", op.cit., pp. 17-35.

344 Cf. E. Sokalska, "Searching for a new formula of a state: international discourse on deliberative democracy", op.cit., p. 127. There might be mentioned here the works of Monique Deavaux ("A Deliberative Approach to Conflicts of Culture", *Political Theory* 31/6 (2003), pp. 780-807) or the latter works of John S. Dryzek (e.g. *Deliberative Democracy and Beyond…*, op.cit., passim).

345 S. Elstub, "The Third Generation of Deliberative Democracy", *Political Studies Review* 8/3 (2010), p. 298.

particular problem or project.[346] Fishkin initiated a debate on the promotion of deliberative practices through small community groups (mini-publics), while at the same time, looking for a suitable method to systematically study the deliberation process and identify the required parameters of institutional arrangements. A micro rather than macro approach to deliberation can be identified here. The objects of exploration are small communities and institutions removed from the wider discursive environment in which they operate.[347] Nevertheless, it has become necessary to return to a holistic concept of deliberative systems, and the need to perceive the deliberation not just as isolated, local practices but as coherent macro-scale activities.[348]

It is significant that the concept of a deliberative system, where deliberation is understood as communication occurring in multiple, sometimes partly overlapping spaces, where the need for interaction between these spheres is emphasised, has gained renewed importance. In this respect, deliberation is not confined only to the forum interested in structure and defined by John S. Dryzek as the 'deliberative turn'.[349] The growing range of literature on deliberative systems reflects the degree of interest in the above issue.[350] The scholars deal with both: the practical application of deliberative elements and theoretical considerations of proposed solutions in order to increase the representativeness of citizens, to involve them more broadly in the decision-making process at various levels, and to increase the legitimacy of taken decisions. The actions following this direction pave the way for a new conceptualisation of the interaction between public opinion and the 'decision-making moments' of deliberation.[351]

In addition to the values in terms of theoretical solutions, the deliberative system approach also provides new methods in the study of the practice of deliberation in contemporary democratic systems, and it proposes some original

---

346 J.S. Fishkin, *The Voice of the People...*, op.cit, passim.

347 S. Chambers, „Rhetoric and Public Sphere: Has Deliberative Democracy Abandoned Mass Democracy?", *Political Theory* 37/3 (2009), pp. 323-350, doi: 10.1177/0090591709332336.

348 Cf. E. Sokalska, "Searching for a new formula of a state: international discourse on deliberative democracy", op.cit, p. 128.

349 J.S. Dryzek, *Deliberative Democracy and Beyond...*, op.cit., passim.

350 H.K. Pernaa, "Deliberative future visioning: utilizing democracy theory and practice in futures research", *European Journal of Futures Research* 5/3 (2017), pp. 23, https://doi.org/10/0007/s40309-017-0129-1.

351 S. Elstub, S. Ercan, R.F. Mendonça, *The Fourth Generation of Deliberative Democracy*, "Critical Policy Studies" 2016, vol. 10(2), p. 140, https;//doi.org/10.1080/19460171.1175956.

answers to questions such as how to analyse and explore the relationship between mini-communities and the wider community, how to identify connections and information transfer in different fields of deliberative activity, or what standards there should be applied when assessing the deliberative values of the system as a whole. Besides some practical and conceptual references to deliberative systems, scientific reflection also pays attention to some potential problems of deliberation, and it raises momentous questions that need to be addressed at the level of contemporary developments.[352] At present, the international scientific discourse is evolving towards the interest in the relationship between constituent elements and a holistic deliberative system. It is interested in perspectives on the institutionalisation of deliberative systems and methodological difficulties for empirical analysis.[353]

According to Stephen Elstub (School of Geography, Politics and Sociology, Newcastle University), Selen Ercan (Institute of Governance and Policy Analysis, University of Canberra), and Ricardo Fabrino Mendonça (Department of Political Science, Federal University of Minas Gerais), who took part in a research symposium "Deliberative Systems in Theory and Practice" on identifying contemporary deliberative systems, a new phase of deliberative democrats' interest in deliberative system design is taking place today.[354].Although it requires more in-depth theoretical considerations and empirical research, the systems approach to deliberative democracy promotes a new way of thinking about public deliberation.

Political scientists suggest that inclinations towards both theoretical and practical research herald the fourth generation of deliberative democracy.[355] This new research approach is linked to the so-called 'systemic turn',[356] which consists of three factors that can be considered important in the development process of deliberative democracy: the search for opportunities to develop and promote

---

352 S.A. Ercan, C.M. Hendriks, J. Boswell, "Studying Public Deliberation after the Systemic Turn: The Crucial Role of Interpretative Research", *Policy and Politics* (without no.) (2015), pp. 2-3.

353 For further reading, see Ercan S.A., Dryzek J.S., "The Reach of Deliberative Democracy", op.cit., pp. 241-248.

354 The result of the symposium was a monograph *Deliberative Systems in Theory and Practice* (Routledge 2019) and a series of articles in *Critical Policy Studies*.

355 S. Elstub, S. Ercan, R.F. Mendonça, "The Fourth Generation of Deliberative Democracy", op.cit., p. 139.

356 Ibidem, p. 143. See also here J. Mansbridge et al., "A systemic Approach to Deliberative Democracy", in *Deliberative Systems. Deliberative Democracy at the Large scale*, eds. J. Parkinson, and J. Mansbridge, Cambridge University Press, Cambridge 2012, pp. 1-26, https://doi.org/10.1017/CBO9781139178914.

deliberation on a mass scale; the growing interest in the division of tasks and activities between participants within the system; the introduction of a certain continuum to the criterion of deliberation linking the multiplicity of institutions and the processes that occur between them. Contemporary manifested emphasis on these three elements makes it possible to distinguish the representatives of the fourth generation of deliberative democracy from previous currents.

It is significant that such distribution will enable a holistic approach to deliberation. The integrated model of deliberation (micro, macro, and hybrid forum, formal and informal debates) will ensure its effectiveness.[357] In conclusion, participants of the discourse on deliberative democracy, who can be described as fourth generation, propose a systems approach, seeing potential in addressing theoretical as well as empirical problems of deliberative practice. They emphasize the need for empirical research that contradicts the claim that components of society that do not participate in deliberation can perform important systemic functions more effectively than participants in deliberative processes. Therefore, it becomes a challenge to investigate and consider what criteria should be adopted, and how deliberation should be carried out at the broad (central, state-wide) level, so that the activities are to some extent compatible, and at the same time constitute a continuum of activities undertaken at the micro (local community) level.

It is significant that the research on democratic deliberation evolved into a variety of spheres or particular issues of deliberation. One of them are psychological aspects of deliberation. In the context of psychological mechanisms during deliberation, Luisa Batalha,[358] Simon Niemeyer,[359] John S. Dryzek, and John Gastil[360] are of the opinion that democratic deliberation may shift people's

---

357 See more in C.M. Hendriks, *The Politics of Public Deliberation: Citizen Engagement and Public Advocacy*, Palgrave Macmillan, New York 2011, passim.

358 A social psychologist from the Australian Catholic University whose main research interests are intergroup relation, the psychology of climate change mitigation and collective action.

359 A co-founder of the Centre for Deliberative Democracy and Global Governance. His research include and ties together the theme of political behaviour, the pubic sphere and observations relating to deliberative mini publics and potential interventions and institutional settings that improve deliberation and governance.

360 A political scientist at Penn State University who is widely credited for promoting deliberation among citizens during elections and in other political institutions. In his monograph - *By poplar demand* - he proposed an interesting project according to which chosen randomly panels of citizens should be created in order to ensure a cross-section of society, to deliberate on ballot initiatives and referenda.

preferences concerning particular issues. They have examined participants' preferences for various types of political systems, and how these preferences changed as deliberation proceeded. They were interested in how the final preferences were associated with different levels of inclusiveness of a social identity. At the end of the deliberation process, they observed that preferences of individuals "moved in the direction of satisfaction with the political system, and that this preference was positively associated with identification with the superordinate identification but negatively associated with the subgroup identification".[361]

4. Concluding remarks

On the one hand, the deliberative theory focuses on shared representation, on the other hand, deliberative practice should be able to accommodate differences. Deliberative democracy is nowadays tested in the context of large-scale deliberative undertakings as well as at the local level, e.g. adapting the formula of public or social consultations on local participatory budgets.

Deliberative democracy, together with its tools, is currently also subjected to critical analysis. John Dryzek is of the opinion that non-deliberative methods should complement the deliberative system. He makes use of the term 'systemic test'. In his perception, the systemic test requires that other than deliberative tools should play some instrumental part in order to rationalize the realization of deliberative democracy purposes.[362]

In the discourse on deliberative democracy, its shortcomings and deficiencies as well as its potential dangers are pointed out. The contemporary research approach to deliberative democracy referred to as the 'systemic turn' exposes three factors. The first is the search for opportunities to develop and promote deliberation on a mass scale. The second is the emphasis on the division of tasks and activities among participants within the system. The third is introduction of a certain continuum to the criterion of deliberation linking the multiplicity of institutions and the processes that occur among them.

It should be taken into closer consideration that a lot of researchers confirm that thanks to deliberative methods and tools, the legitimacy of decisions of local

361 L.M. Batalha, S. Niemeyer, J.S. Dryzek, J. Gastil, "Psychological Mechanisms of Deliberative Transformation: The Role of Group Identity", *Journal of Public Deliberation* 15/1 (2019), p. 1, https://doi.org/10.16997/jdd.313.

362 J.S. Dryzek, *Foundations and Frontiers...*, op.cit., passim.

and central authorities is strengthened.[363] However, some scholars put forward the opinion that different conceptions, e.g. Mary Parker's Follet (1918, 1928) conception of *integration*, can be seen as an alternative approach to deliberation based on co-creation, might be more productive than approaches based on persuasion in the case of conflicts closely related to social identity.[364] Some scholars reflect on the possibilities and limits of democratic mending in societies characterized by economic inequality and asymmetric powers relations, as well as in the countries with less established institutions of liberal democracy. Deliberative ideas have attracted the attention of citizens, activists, the decision–makers, and reform organizations around the world. Deliberative forums are also being implemented in parliamentary and electoral contexts.[365] Identified shortcomings of deliberative democracy,[366] e.g. potential institutional neutralization of activists' activities,[367] participatory frustration,[368] or widespread incompetence of citizens

---

363 About the benefits of deliberative process see, e.g. A. Lupia, and A. Norton, "Inequality is Always in the Rom: Language & Power in Deliberative Democracy", *Dædalus. Journal of the American Academy of Arts & Sciences. The Prospects and Limits of Deliberative Democracy* 146/3 (2017), pp. 64-76, https://doi.org/10.1162/DAED_a_00447; A. Bua, E. Escobar, "*Participatory-Deliberative Process and Public Agendas: Lessons for Policy and Practice*", *Policy Design and Practice* 1/2 (2018), pp. 126-140, https://doi.org/10.1080/25741292.2018.1469242.

364 G. Wright, "Persuasion or Co-creation? Social Identity Threat and the Mechanisms of Deliberative Transformation", *Journal of Deliberative Democracy* 18/2 (2022), pp. 24-34, https;//doi.org/10.16997/jdd.977.

365 N. Curato, J.S. Dryzek, S.A. Ercan, C.M. Hendriks, and S. Niemeyer, "Twelve Key Findings in Deliberative Democracy Research", *Dædalus. Journal of the American Academy of Arts & Sciences. The Prospects and Limits of Delibarative Democracy* 146/3 (2017), p. 29, https://doi.org/10.1162/DAED_a_004444.

366 See more in J. Łapaj, "Demokracja deliberatywna – zalety i zastrzeżenia wobec modelu w kontekście rozważań teoretycznych i praktycznych", in *Demokracja deliberatywna: utopia czy ratunek dla demokratycznych wartości?*, ed. A. Turoń-Kowalska, REMAR, Sosnowiec 2016, pp. 45-71; E. Sokalska, "Searching for a new formula of a state: international discourse on deliberative democracy", op. cit, pp. 130-135.

367 Cf. B. Cross, "Deliberative systems theory and activism", *Critical Review of International Social and Political Philosophy* 24/6 (2021) (published on-line 26 Feb. 2019), p. 866-883, https://doi.org/10.1080/13698230.2019.1584842.

368 Cf. J.L., Fernández-Martínez, P. García-Espín, and M. Jiménez-Sánchez, "Participatory Frustration: The Unintended Cultural Effect of Local Democratic Innovations", *Administration & Society* 52/5 (2020), pp. 718-748, https://doi.org/10.1177/0095399719833628.

participating in deliberation,[369] have become contribution to the discussion on the further directions of development of this form as well as possibilities for its improvement.

Bibliography

Ahlstrom-Vij K., "Why Deliberative Democracy is (Still) Untenable", *Public Affairs Quarterly* 26/3 (2012), pp. 199-220.

Batalha L.M., Niemeyer S., Dryzek J.S., Gastil J., "Psychological Mechanisms of Deliberative Transformation: The Role of Group Identity", *Journal of Public Deliberation* 15/1 (2019), pp. 1-20, https://doi.org/10.16997/jdd.313.

Bessette J.M., "Deliberative Democracy: the Majority Principle in Republican Government", in *How Democratic is the Constitution?*, eds. R.A. Goldwin, and W.A. Schambra, American Institute for Public Policy Research, Washington 1980, pp. 102-116.

Boswell J., Ercan S.A., and Hendriks C.M., "Mending Democracy: A response to our readers", *Critical Policy Studies* 16/2 (2022), pp. 237-240, https://doi.org. 10.1080/19460171.2022.2028644.

Bua A., Escobar E., "*Participatory-Deliberative Process and Public Agendas: Lessons for Policy and Practice*", *Policy Design and Practice* 1/2 (2018), pp. 126-140, https://doi.org/10.1080/25741292.2018.1469242.

Chambers S., „Rhetoric and Public Sphere: Has Deliberative Democracy Abandoned Mass Democracy?", *Political Theory* 37/3 (2009), pp. 323-350, htps://doi.org 10.1177/0090591709332336.

Cohen J., "Deliberation and Democratic Legitimacy", in *The Good Polity: Normative Analysis of the State*, eds. A. Hamlin, and P. Pettit, Basil Blackwell, Oxford 1989, pp. 17-34.

Cross B., "Deliberative systems theory and activism", *Critical Review of International Social and Political Philosophy* 24/6 (2021) (published on-line 26 Feb. 2019), p. 866-883, https://doi.org/10.1080/13698230.2019.1584842.

Curato N., Dryzek J.S., Ercan S.A., Hendriks C.M., and Niemeyer S., "Twelve Key Findings in Deliberative Democracy Research", *Dædalus. Journal of the American Academy of Arts & Sciences. The Prospects and Limits of Deliberative Democracy* 146/3 (2017), pp. 28-38, https://doi.org/10.1162/DAED_a_004444.

Deveaux M., "A Deliberative Approach to Conflicts of Culture", *Political Theory* 31/6 (2003), pp. 780-807.

369 K. Ahlstrom-Vij, "Why Deliberative Democracy is (Still) Untenable", *Public Affairs Quarterly* 26/3 (2012), pp. 199-220.

Dryzek J. S., *Foundations and Frontiers of Deliberative Democracy*, Oxford University Press, Oxford 2010.

Dryzek J.S., "Democratic Political Theory", in *Handbook of Political Theory*, eds. G.F. Gaus, and Ch. Kukathas, Sage Publications, London 2004, pp. 243-254.

Dryzek J.S., "Democratization as Deliberative Capacity Building", *Comparative Political Studies* 42/22 (2009), pp. 1379-1402, https://doi.org/10.1177/0010414009332129.

Dryzek J.S., and Niemeyer, S., "Reconciling Pluralism and Consensus as Political Ideals", *American Journal of Political Science*, 50/3 (2006), pp. 634-649, https://doi.org/10.1111/j.1540-5907.2006.00206.

Dryzek J.S., *Deliberative Democracy and Beyond: Liberals, Critics, Contestations*, Oxford University Press, New York 2000.

Dryzek J.S., *Deliberative Global Politics: Discourse and Democracy in a Divided Word*, Polity Press, Cambridge 2006.

Elstub S., "The Third Generation of Deliberative Democracy", *Political Studies Review* 8/3 (2010), pp. 291-307.

Elstub S., Ercan S., and Mendonça R.F., "The Fourth Generation of Deliberative Democracy", Critical Policy Studies 10/2 (2016), pp. 139-151, https;//doi.org/10.1080/19460171.1175956.

Elstub S., Ercan S., and Mendonça R.F., *Deliberative Systems in Theory and Practice*, Routledge 2019.

Ercan S.A., and Dryzek J.S., "The Reach of Deliberative Democracy", *Policy Studies* 36/3 (2015), pp. 241-248.

Ercan S.A., Hendriks C.M., and Boswell J., "Studying Public Deliberation after the Systemic Turn: The Crucial Role of Interpretative Research", *Policy and Politics* 45/2 (2015), pp. 195-212.

Fernández-Martínez J. L., García-Espín P., and Jiménez-Sánchez M., "Participatory Frustration: The Unintended Cultural Effect of Local Democratic Innovations", *Administration & Society* 52/5 (2020), pp. 718-748, https://doi.org/10.1177/0095399719833628.

Fishkin J.S., *Democracy and Deliberation: New Directions for Democratic Reform*, Yale University Press, New Haven 1993.

Fishkin J.S., *The Voice of the People: Public Opinion and Democracy*, Yale University Press, New Haven 1995.

Fishkin J.S., *When the People Speak. Deliberative Democracy and Public Consultations*, Oxford University Press, New York 2011.

Habermas J., *The Theory of Communicative Action vol. I. Reason and the Rationalization of Society*, Beacon Press, Boston 1984.

Habermas J., "Political Communication in Media Society: Does Democracy Still Enjoy an Epistemic Dimension? The Impact of Normative Theory on Empirical Research", *Communication Theory* 16/4 (2006), pp. 411-426, https://doi.org/10.1111/j.1468-2885.2006.00280.x.

Hamlin A., and Pettit P. (eds.), *The Good Polity: Normative Analysis of the State* eds., Basil Blackwell, Oxford 1989.

Hendriks C. M., *The Politics of Public Deliberation: Citizen Engagement and Public Advocacy*, Palgrave Macmillan, New York 2011.

Kania R., and Kazimierczuk M. (eds.), *Społeczeństwo obywatelskie. Historia, teoria, praktyka*, DIFIN S.A., Warszawa 2021.

Kazimierczuk M., "Ewolucja pojęcia idei społeczeństwa obywatelskiego", in *Społeczeństwo obywatelskie. Historia, teoria, praktyka*, eds. R. Kania, and M. Kzimierczuk, DIFIN S.A., Warszawa 2021, pp. 14-33.

Łapaj J., "Demokracja deliberatywna – zalety i zastrzeżenia wobec modelu w kontekście rozważań teoretycznych i praktycznych", in *Demokracja deliberatywna: utopia czy ratunek dla demokratycznych wartości?*, ed. A. Turoń-Kowalska, REMAR, Sosnowiec 2016, pp. 45-71.

Lupia A., and Norton A, "Inequality is Always in the Rom: Language & Power in Deliberative Democracy", *Dædalus. Journal of the American Academy of Arts & Sciences. The Prospects and Limits of Deliberative Democracy* 146/3 (2017), pp. 64-76, https://doi.org/10.1162/DAED_a_00447.

Makowski G., and Schimanek T. (eds.), *Organizacje pozarządowe i władza publiczna. Drogi do partnerstwa*, Fundacja Instytut Spraw Publicznych, Warszawa 2008.

Mansbridge J. et al., "A systemic Approach to Deliberative Democracy", in *Deliberative Systems. Deliberative Democracy at the Large scale*, eds. J. Parkinson, and J. Mansbridge, Cambridge University Press, Cambridge 2012, pp. 1-26, https://doi.org/10.1017/CBO9781139178914.

Markowski R., *Demokracja i demokratyczne innowacje. Z teorią w praktykę*, Instytut Obywatelski, Warszawa 2014.

Mendza-Drozd M., *Zagadnienie konsultacji społecznych w Unii Europejskiej. Analiza wybranych instytucji i dokumentów*, opracowanie w ramach zleconego przez Ministerstwo Pracy i Polityki Społecznej, Warszawa 2010.

Parkinson J., Mansbridge J. (eds.), *Deliberative Systems. Deliberative Democracy at the Large scale*, Cambridge University Press, Cambridge 2012.

Pernaa H.K., "Deliberative future visioning: utilizing democracy theory and practice in futures research", *European Journal of Futures Research* 5/13 (2017), pp. 1-10, https://doi.org/10/0007/s40309-017-0129-1.

Rawls J., *A Theory of Justice. Revised Edition*, Oxford University Press, Oxford-New York 1999.

Sienkiewicz M.M., and Sidor M. (eds.), *Dialog obywatelski: formy, mechanizmy, bariery i perspektywy rozwoju*, Wydawnictwo Fundacji Centrum Rozwoju Lokalnego, Lublin 2014.

Sokalska E., "Deliberative democracy in the time of crisis: participatory instruments at the local level and their limitations (some remarks)", *Journal of Modern Science* 2/45 (2020), pp. 227-240, DOI: 10.13166/JMS/125595.

Sokalska E., "Flaws and Advantages of the Polish Local Self-Government in the 21st Century: Social Consultations at the Local Level", *Lex Localis* 19/1 (2021), pp. 19-37, DOI: https://doi.org/10.4335/19.1.19-37(2021).

Sokalska E., "Searching for a new formula of a state: international discourse on deliberative democracy", *Acta Iuridica Resoviensia* 1/40 (2023), pp. 124-138, https://doi.org/10.15584/actaires.2023.1.8.

Sokalska E., "W poszukiwaniu idealnej formuły państwa: blaski i cienie demokracji deliberatywnej na poziomie lokalnym (wybrane uwagi)", in *Społeczeństwo obywatelskie. Historia, teoria, praktyka*, R. Kania, and M. Kazimierczuk, DIFIN S.A., Warszawa 2021, pp. 191-210.

Turoń-Kowalska A. (ed.), *Demokracja deliberatywna: utopia czy ratunek dla demokratycznych wartości?*, REMAR, Sosnowiec 2016.

Wright G., "Persuasion or Co-creation? Social Identity Threat and the Mechanisms of Deliberative Transformation", *Journal of Deliberative Democracy* 18/2 (2022), pp. 24-34, https;//doi.org/10.16997/jdd.977.

Katarzyna Kubuj[370]

Engaging young people in democracy. General remarks and the Polish perspective

Abstract: The subject of this study is the analysis of the young citizens' democratic beliefs in Europe and the Polish perspective. The article is focused around the phenomenon known as the "democratic paradox". Furthermore, the most recent elections to the European Parliament held in June 2024 offer a compelling opportunity for reflection on electoral participation as the most significant manifestation of engagement in a democracy. Research devoted to the participation of young citizens in public life inspires us to move beyond the common stereotype of their modest interest in political, economic, or social affairs. A sceptical approach to conventional forms of political involvement does not hinder the development and continuous diversification of alternative forms of participation, which contribute to the civilisational progress of our times, with all its advantages and disadvantages.

Keywords: democracy, democratic paradox, electoral participation, attitudes of young

1. Concerns as to the condition of contemporary democracy pervade political, social and legal debates. In this context, it is not difficult to reckon that there is a growing crisis of democracy, a fact regularly confirmed by numerous studies and reports over the past decades.[371] Within this debate are analyses of young citizens' democratic beliefs and practices, including their declining participation in elections, membership in political parties, support for and satisfaction with democracy, as well as their openness to supporting populist or

370 Polish Academy of Sciences, ORCID 0000-0003-3689-4520.
371 Among many other reports, the "DEMOCRACY REPORT 2022 Autocratization Changing Nature?", V-Dem Institute, March 2022. deserves a special mention. The V-Dem (Varieties of Democracy) Institute collaborates with 3,700 scholars and other country experts and produces the largest global dataset on democracy based on more than 30 million data points covering 202 countries for the period from 1789 to 2021, measuring hundreds of different attributes of democracy. According to the content of the report: "Without intent to underrate other varieties of democracy, the report focuses on the Liberal Democracy Index (LDI) that combines the electoral "core" institutions with the liberal aspects – executive constraint by the legislature and high courts, and rule of law and individual rights. This measure is among the most sophisticated measures that V-Dem offers. The Regimes of the World measure is a categorical measure classifying countries into four distinct regimes: the two forms of democracy (electoral and liberal) and two types of autocracies (electoral and closed).

anti-establishment movements.[372] The limited scope of this article does not permit discussing themes beyond the few selected ones, which are focused around the phenomenon known as the "democratic paradox". Furthermore, the most recent elections to the European Parliament held in June 2024 offer a compelling opportunity for reflection on electoral participation as the most significant manifestation of engagement in a democracy.[373] Other, though extremely interesting, aspects of activism at the local level such as citizens' budgets, community councils, etc., have therefore not been covered in this article.[374]

To be considered minimally democratic, i.e. an electoral democracy, a country has to meet sufficiently high levels of free and fair elections as well as universal suffrage, freedom of expression and association. Hence, solely holding elections does not suffice for a country to be considered democratic. Countries in which liberal aspects (executive constraint by the legislature and high courts, rule of law and individual rights) are respected on top of the requirements for electoral democracy, are considered liberal democracies (p. 13). The main conclusions of report 2022: • the level of democracy enjoyed by the average global citizen in 2021 is down to 1989 levels, the last 30 years of democratic advances are now eradicated; • dictatorships are on the rise and harbor 70% of the world population – 5.4 billion people; • there are signals that the nature of autocratization is changing".

372 R.S. Foa, A. Klassen, D. Wenger, A. Rand and M. Slade. 2020. "Youth and Satisfaction with Democracy: Reversing the Democratic Disconnect?" Cambridge, United Kingdom: Centre for the Future of Democracy. The study analysed "a global, novel data set combining 25 data sources, 3,500 country surveys, and 4 million respondents between 1973 and 2020, and found widespread democratic disillusionment, in particular in developed democracies". M. Giugni, M. Grasso (2021). Youth and Politics in Times of Increasing Inequalities, [in:] M. Giugni, M. Grasso (ed.) Youth and Politics in Times of Increasing Inequalities. Springer International Publishing: Cham, incl. the cited literature.

373 It is not the intention of the author to venture into a detailed analysis of the cited studies, which are only the background for the presentation of the selected issues. Accordingly, the terms "youth", "young people" and "young generation" is not a reference to any specific sociological or psychological definitions of a group as a certain social category (typically, the demarcation of the specific age limits is not uniform). The intention was for these descriptions to generally cover both minors (school-age) and adults (over 18) who, due to their young age, are at the initial stage of exercising full civil rights.

374 See: K. Kubuj, Czy młodzi mogliby więcej? Obszary obywatelskiego zaangażowania w demokrację/i [*Could Young People do More? Areas of Civic Engagement in Democracy*], [in:] Zagadnienia prawa konstytucyjnego. Księga jubileuszowa dedykowana Profesorowi Krzysztofowi Skotnickiemu w siedemdziesiątą rocznicę urodzin [*Issues of Constitutional Law. Jubilee Book Dedicated to Professor Krzysztof Skotnicki on his Seventieth Birtday]*, A. Domańska (red.), Łódź 2023, Tom 1, pp. 167-178.

2. The term "democratic paradox" has been coined in scholars' writings in connection with the low voter turnout of young citizens which has been observed for years in Europe. This has led to a popular perception of young people as apathetic individuals, members of a generation that fails to engage in political issues and is in essence selfish and materialistic. This approach incited some researchers to analyse the phenomenon, and the analyses have resulted in diverging conclusions. These were based on the assertion that moderate youth engagement in Europe has not been caused by indifference as to the public good, but results from a synthesis of multiple contextual and psychosocial factors. The data obtained suggests that young people are willing to engage in politics, but are discouraged by the focus and nature of the existing mainstream political discourse and practice which many believe to be excluding them and ignorant of their needs and interests. Quite contrary to the supposition that they are disgruntled and apathetic citizens, many young Europeans have a strong desire to participate in democratic life. However, this desire is not satisfied by the existing democratic institutions and discourses.[375] This observation allows to formulate further hypotheses. Thus, while young citizens will have a tendency to withdraw from institutional politics, it is also highly likely that they will hold idealistic visions of democratic participation and cultivate exceptional ambitions regarding the extent of their desired engagement. This is a paradox that has prompted researchers to study detailed participation patterns of young citizens. As noted by M. Giugni and M. Grasso:[376]

   While young citizens tend to disengage from conventional politics, they are also, by far, the most mobilized age group in many high cost types of political participation and which require a range of resources, time and sustained effort such as the anti-austerity movements in Spain, Greece, and other European countries. Movements such as Occupy, the Indignados, and wider

375 Cammaerts, B. Bruter, M. Banaji, S. Harrison, S. Anstead, N. (2014) The myth of youth apathy: young Europeans' critical attitudes toward democratic life. American Behavioral Scientist, 58 (5). pp. 645-664. ISSN 0002-7642. Young people's attitudes towards democratic life in Austria, Finland, France, Hungary, Spain, and the UK were assessed. Poland was also included in the research. Authors of the "Youth and Satisfaction with Democracy..." report, op. cit. #2, remark that "youth disillusionment reflects only "apathy" with respect to the functioning of democratic institutions in practice, rather than hostility to liberal democratic ideals per se", p. 22.

376 M. Giugni, M. Grasso (2021). Youth and Politics in Times of Increasing Inequalities, op. cit., p. 2.

anti-austerity movements have emerged in the recent context and have been especially popular amongst the young (Grasso and Giugni 2016). These movements have challenged the democratic deficit and contested the message that there is no alternative to austerity (Giugni and Grasso 2018). Across Europe, precarious employment is widespread amongst youth. Youth unemployment is particularly high in countries such as Greece, Italy, and Spain, registering 30–40%. The generation coming of age in the recent period is understood by many to face lower chances of inter-generational mobility, the closing off of borders and declining freedom of movement, a more divided society and rising fears of extremism over tolerance, psychologically more stressful and more uncertain times, less security in old age with end of pensions and the contractions of the welfare state, and so forth (Grasso 2018). As such, it is not surprising that the current period has seen a surge in youth protests, such as the protests against tuition fees, Occupy, the 15-M or Indignados movement (Grasso and Giugni 2013) and many other mobilizations such as the recent students' global Climate Strike as well as various movements calling for more participation and different democratic models, such as for example the so-called Sardines in Italy.

The authors provide examples of yet other, though less apparent and more inventive activities, alongside politically-driven shifts in consumption behaviours, such as "food activism" or "lifestyle politics". The term "Do It Ourselves" (DIO) politics has even been coined in the literature on the subject to describe various non-electoral practices followed independently of political parties, which are gaining popularity among young people.[377]

From this perspective, in the eyes of young people democracy becomes an unfulfilled promise. Their hopes for a system that addresses their essential needs and aspirations clash with a growing disillusionment with the actual functioning of representative democracy institutions. At the same time, their non-participation in these institutions reduces the likelihood of enacting changes and weakens their voices.[378] However, as previously mentioned,

---

377 Ibidem, p. 7, incl. the cited literature.

378 J. Kajta, S. Barakeh, P Marczewski, P. Pustułka 2022. Demokratyczny paradoks w praktyce: Doświadczenia młodych aktywistów i aktywistek [*The Democratic Paradox in Practice: Experiences of Young Male and Female Activists*], Youth Working Papers No 1/2022 Warszawa: Uniwersytet SWPS Młodzi w Centrum Lab. ISSN: 2543-5213 DOI: 10.23809/15.

disengagement from conventional forms of involvement in politics is not tantamount to utter passivity, as evidenced by participation in numerous alternative activities such as demonstrations, protests, boycotts, community organisations, etc. These phenomena are accompanied by the rise in popularity of social networks such as Facebook, Instagram, Snapchat, TikTok and other.[379] The Internet offers younger generations the opportunity to develop a stronger sense of belonging to a community and to engage in various social and political campaigns more readily than the older generations, even if this engagement does not always take the conventional form of participation. On the other hand, online participation can further deepen inequalities in political action between youths with and without access to digital media. Furthermore, given their age, young people are particularly susceptible to profiling and manipulation by experts using big data to influence the content, as well as to being confined within their own information bubbles.

These general trends are shared by the attitudes of young Poles. What stands out prominently here is that they perceive democracy as a stable and entrenched system that requires no further struggle. This perspective is hardly surprising, given that the surveyed individuals were born after Poland underwent political transformation, with some even born after the country joined the European Union. Their methods of expressing dissatisfaction seem to be some form of opposition within the existing democratic framework rather than an effort to reclaim it. However, young Poles are discontent with the state of political discourse and estranged from traditional institutions of representative democracy. They harbour distrust toward intermediary institutions, particularly political parties and traditional media, yet they exhibit hardly any willingness to take matters in their own hands to alter the realities they find

379 According to the 2021 European Parliament Youth Survey, the main sources of information on political and social issues for young people are the following: social media (41%) and news portals (41%). Facebook (54%), Instagram (48%), YouTube (35%) i "X" (former Twitter) (29%) have been reported as the most visited social media platforms, although TikTok (14%) and WhatsApp (10%) were also mentioned. What is noticeable, for example, is the positive effect of the European Parliament's campaigning on the Snapchat account in 2019, when voter turnout among young people in Europe increased significantly. Flash Eurobarometer Report. European Parliament Youth Survey, September 2021, https://www.europarl.europa.eu/at-your-service/files/be-heard/eurobarometer/2021/youth-survey-2021/report.pdf (access: 24.06.2024).

unacceptable.[380] Research shows that young people choose to take on the role of distant observers rather than actively engage in public life, particularly in the activities of political parties.[381] At the same time, it highlights how events such as climate strikes, women's protests against abortion policies, demonstrations against Pol-exit scenarios, independence marches, voluntary aid efforts and support shown towards Ukrainians who arrived in Poland following Russia's attack on Ukraine in February 2022, capture their keen interest.[382]

3. Elections remain the crucial formal mechanism through which people can influence the political process. Voter turnout, the most vital expression of participating in political life, has been declining since the 1950s. The gradual decrease, which began with a few percentage points, has accelerated sharply since the mid-1980s, which has been recognized by many as one of the greatest challenges confronting democracies around the world. This persistent downward trajectory is pervasive and no region of the world is immune to it.[383] The low young voters turnout is a defining element of this process, as confirmed by numerous European electoral studies. These studies have indicated that youth absenteeism in the mainstream (national) political arena is surprisingly high, with a significant gap between young people and other age groups.

---

380 R. Marzęcki, Młody obywatel we współczesnej demokracji europejskiej [*Young Citizens in the Contemporary European Democracy*], Warszawa 2013; F. Pazderski, Rozczarowani indywidualiści w poszukiwaniu nowej jakości w polityce. Demokracja i aktywność obywatelska oczami młodych Polaków [*Disillusioned Individualists in Search of a New Quality in Politics. Democracy and Civic Participation Through the Eyes of Young Poles*], Warszawa 2019; idem, Młodzi w Europie Środkowej 2020, NDI (National Democratic Institute) Research Project, Warszawa 2020; A. Kądziela, Polityczny portret młodych Polaków [*Political Portrait of Young Poles*], Warszawa 2023.

381 F. Pazderski, Odlegli obserwatorzy, niezadowoleni konformiści czy poszukujący obywatele? Postawy młodych Polek i Polaków wobec demokracji i polityki [*Distant Observers, Disgruntled Conformists or Searching Citizens? Attitudes of Young Poles Towards Democracy and Politics*], Warszawa 2018.

382 J. Kajta, S. Barakeh, P. Marczewski, P. Pustułka (2022), Demokratyczny paradoks w praktyce: Doświadczenia młodych aktywistów i aktywistek [*The Democratic Paradox in Practice: Experiences of Young Male and Female Activists*], op. cit., p. 5; Kajta, J., Mrozowicki, A. (2022). Young People in Poland: 2020/2021. Between Disappointment with the State and Hope for a Better Life. Bonn: Friedrich Ebert Stiftung, http://library.fes.de/pdf-files/id/19162.pdf (access: 24.06.2024).

383 T. Deželan, Young people's participation in European democratic processes. How to improve and facilitate youth Involvement, Study Requested by the AFCO committee, European Parliament, March 2023, https://www.europarl.europa.eu/thinktank/en/document/IPOL_STU(2023)745820 (access: 24.06.2024).

Alarmingly, young people are found to be absent from national elections as almost 60 percent of eligible voters aged 16-18 up to 24 choose not to vote. Although the statistics are somewhat better for the 25-29 age group, they still fail to reach the level of other age groups. The European Parliament elections, where voter turnout is even lower, are therefore no exception and only confirm this pattern.[384]

In light of the aforementioned data, defining the correct circle of individuals who are eligible to vote, perform other electoral acts, and stand for election becomes crucial. This issue is particularly lively and dynamic also in Poland,[385] and continues to evolve over the course of more than two hundred years. The fact that today's young people exhibit a high degree of maturity, demonstrate a growing understanding of reality, and have access to knowledge through modern media, as mentioned earlier, advocates for lowering the voting age. Furthermore, the concern to increase voter turnout is also an obvious reason.

---

384 The exception was the 2019 European Parliament elections, influenced by a number of factors, including a favourable electoral calendar in which the dates of the EP elections and national elections in many countries were combined. Ibidem, p. 14 with examples of numerous studies.

385 M. Waszak, J. Zbieranek, Propozycja obniżenia wieku wyborczego do lat 16. Wybrane zagadnienia [*Proposal to Lower the Voting Age to 16: Selected Issues*], Warszawa 2011; Europejskie wybory młodych [*European Elections by Youth*], J. Zbieranek (ed.), Warszawa 2014; K. Skotnicki, W sprawie konieczności zmian konstytucyjnej regulacji cenzusów wyborczych [On the Need to Amend the Constitutional Regulation of Electoral Censuses], [in:] Minikomentarz dla Maksiprofesora. Księga jubileuszowa profesora Leszka Garlickiego [*Mini-Commentary for the Maxiprofessor: Professor Leszek Garlicki's Jubilee Book*], Zubik M. (ed.), Warszawa 2017, p. 314. Prior to the parliamentary elections in autumn 2023, declarations were made by the leader of the Poland 2050 movement, Szymon Hołownia (currently the Speaker of the Sejm), to lower the active right to vote to the age of 16 in local elections, and later also in parliamentary and presidential elections. See: M. Jędrysik, Czy 16-latki powinny głosować w wyborach? Hołownia mówi: tak. Politolog mówi: to skomplikowane [*Should 16-year-Olds Vote in Elections? Holownia Says: Yes. Political Scientist Says: It's Complicated*], 20.09.2021, https://oko.press/czy-16-latki-powinny-glosowac-w-wyborach/ (access: 25.06.2024). Earlier, even more radical proposals to lower the age to 15 were voiced by the Ombudsman Adam Bodnar. See: Ł. Starzewski, Młodzież ma prawo uczestniczyć w debacie publicznej. Pierwsze spotkanie RPO w ramach Tygodnia Konstytucyjnego [*Young People Have the Right to Participate in Public Debate. First Meeting of the ROP as Part of the Constitutional Week*], 16.12.2020, https://bip.brpo.gov.pl/pl/content/mlodziez-ma-prawo-udzialu-debacie-publicznej-rpo-tydzien-konstytucyjny (access: 25.06.2024).

However, a pertinent question that arises is whether, given previous election results and a poor involvement of young people, might lowering the age limit further reduce overall turnout (since the final result would also include those voters who do not vote at all)? Analyses of the elections to the European Parliament held in June this year are likely to provide some answers to these questions. While the lower age limit remains set at 18 in most member states, in few states it has been reduced to 16 (starting with Austria in 2007, later followed by Malta in 2018, Belgium in 2022, and Germany in 2023), and to 17 in Greece.[386]

Opponents of lowering the voting age argue that the acquisition of civic awareness does not necessarily indicate socio-psychological maturity. The risk is that young voters may be more susceptible to manipulation and demagogic slogans. Interestingly, accelerating the acquisition of active voting rights is not a priority for young people. Sociological observations suggest that political maturity develops over time and across multiple dimensions. Young people must first navigate the challenges of entering adulthood: they have to graduate, find a job, achieve financial stability and so on. The political game only begins to have greater stakes for them over time, and the decisions of the authorities have a greater impact on their lives.[387]

In Poland, young people exhibit moderate involvement in conventional forms of participation, as evidenced by the generally low voter turnout in recent

386 Across the European Union, turnout reached 51.08%, which is slightly different from 2019, when it totalled 50.66% and has been considered record-high, https://results.elections.europa.eu/en/tools/download-datasheets/ (access: 25.06.2025). However, it remains to be seen which factors most influenced this result. Preliminary analyses show that young people were more likely to choose smaller parties and also contributed to the rise in support for extremist parties such as the France National Unity, the AfD in Germany (C. Schläger, Ch. Katsioulis, J. N. Engels, Analysis of the 2024 European Elections in Germany Majority for the stable centre despite a strong right wing, FES diskurs June 2024, https://library.fes.de/pdf-files/a-p-b/21287.pdf, access: 25.06.2024), the Confederation in Poland or a rather exotic and hitherto unknown group, the "Oath of the Motorists to Themselves" in the Czech Republic, https://wyborcza.pl/7,75399,31071748,mlodzi-w-europie-szukaja-politycznych-alternatyw-jak-glosowali.html (access: 25.06.2024).

387 Żerkowska-Balas M., Dlaczego młodzi nie głosują? [*Why Don't the Young Vote?*], Uniwersytet SWPS, 17.06.2019, https://www.swps.pl/centrum-prasowe/informacje-prasowe/20040-dlaczego-mlodzi-nie-glosuja.

years.[388] An interesting phenomenon could be observed in 2023, when 69.9% of young voters went to the polls, a significant increase compared to the overall turnout of 74.38%, marking a stark departure from previous election attitudes. The assertion that the mobilisation of the young generation influenced the outcomes for the various political parties and contributed to the loss of the parliamentary majority by the incumbent ruling camp (the United Right; Polish: *Zjednoczona Prawica*) is not an exaggeration. However, just a few months later, there was a noticeable decline in participation in the local government elections and in the European Parliament elections held in June. Sociologists observing these trends emphasise that the high turnout in the autumn parliamentary elections of 2023 was a one-off mobilisation triggered by the political situation at the time. Young people, often referred to as the "Women's Strike" generation (named after the protests that gained momentum following the Constitutional Tribunal's ruling tightening the abortion laws in autumn 2020), were focused more on expressing their dissatisfaction with actions of the authorities rather than on fulfilling their civic duty.[389] Hence, it is not surprising that neither the local government elections nor the European elections that followed a few months later managed to draw young people to the polls.

The problem of low engagement in traditional forms of civic participation is widely acknowledged. Research reports highlight that, in addition to analysing the factors that influence young people's attitudes, efforts are being made to apprehend their needs and expectations.

---

388 In the parliamentary elections in 2015 it was 26.6% with the overall turnout of 50.92%, in the parliamentary elections in 2019: 46.4% with the overall turnout at 61.74%, in the European Parliament elections in 2019: 27.6% with the overall turnout at 45.68%, although in the presidential elections in 2020, in the second round, it was 67.2% with the overall turnout at 68.18% (presidential elections generally enjoy a higher turnout, and in 2020 there were additional tensions caused by changes to the electoral calendar due to the Covid-19 pandemic, which did not go unnoticed by the general public mood), in the local elections in 2024: 38.6% with the overall turnout at 51.94%, and in the European Parliament elections in 2024 it was 26.5% with the overall turnout at 40.65%.

389 A. Kublik, Zagłosowaliśmy raz i wystarczy, rozmowa z socjologiem prof. P. Sadurą [*We Have Voted Once and That's Enough: a Conversation with Sociologist Prof. P. Sadura*], Gazeta Wyborcza 29.05.2024.

According to M. Del Monte, a distinguished lawyer working with the European Parliamentary Research Service (EPRS),[390] the Joint Declaration on the Conference on the Future of Europe:[391]

expressly recognised the contribution of 'young Europeans playing a central role in shaping the future of the European project', requested that specific events be dedicated to young people. In its 2020 resolution on the Conference on the Future of Europe, the European Parliament proposed the creation of two 'Youth Agoras', to provide young people with their own forum. However, this proposal was eventually rejected. Nevertheless, of the 800 citizens invited to debate and put forward recommendations on the future of Europe, one third was between 16 and 25 years old. The result of this exercise of direct democracy was a set of around 200 citizens' recommendations, many of which suggested strengthening youth engagement in democratic processes (see in particular Panel 1 and Panel 2). The Conference, which concluded its work in May 2022, resulted in 326 specific measures that also covered youth and youth engagement. This gave a clear indication on how citizens and institutional actors see the role and impact of the EU in meeting the challenges ahead. In particular, one proposal stressed that the EU and its Member States should 'focus on the specific needs of young people across all relevant policies', and to achieve this objective, the conference proposed a set of measures touching on: increased youth participation in the democratic and decision-making processes at all levels; organisation of citizens' panels also with children (e.g. 10 to 16 year-olds) in schools; and development of an EU 'Youth Test' so that all new legislation and policy is subject to a youth-focused impact assessment. Other measures concerned more specifically young people and European elections; for instance, they suggested lowering the voting age to 16 years, introducing EU citizenship education in schools, and requesting national political parties to ensure that younger candidates are on their lists for European elections. Yet other measures pointed to need of developing a 'full civic experience' for young Europeans, to ensure that their voice is also heard beyond elections.

---

390 M. Del Monte, Youth participation in European elections, European Parliamentary Research Service, December 2023, p. 7.

391 The Conference on the Future of Europe, a citizen-led series of debates and discussions during the period from April 2021 to May 2022 with the aim to enable "people from across Europe to share their ideas and help shape our common future". https://commission.europa.eu/strategy-and-policy/priorities-2019-2024/new-push-european-democracy/conference-future-europe_en

4. Research devoted to the participation of young citizens in public life inspires us to move beyond the common stereotype of their modest interest in political, economic, or social affairs. A sceptical approach to conventional forms of political involvement does not hinder the development and continuous diversification of alternative forms of participation, which contribute to the civilisational progress of our times, with all its advantages and disadvantages. It is therefore important to emphasise the value of research and analysis of the factors that undermine young people's confidence in democracy and various forms of policies that implement its goals. Strengthening the belief that longer experience in civic life enhances the importance of political agency, the conviction that one can participate in politics at any level (national, local, or European) and thus influence the surrounding reality, is indeed essential. Furthermore, it seems necessary to explore the connection between strictly political involvement and activity in other fields and tiers. These two spheres must blend together, as their significance for social life seems to be equally important and should be consistently reinforced. The concern for the future of young, adolescent individuals is also a concern for the future of mature citizens.

Bibliography

Cammaerts, B., Bruter, M., Banaji, S., Harrison, S., Anstead, N. (2014) *The myth of youth apathy: young Europeans' critical attitudes toward democratic life. American Behavioral* Scientist, 58 (5).

Del Monte, M., *Youth participation in European elections*, European Parliamentary Research Service, December 2023.

Deželan, T., *Young people's participation in European democratic processes. How to improve and facilitate youth Involvement*, Study Requested by the AFCO committee, European Parliament, March 2023, https://www.europarl.europa.eu/thinktank/en/document/IPOL_STU(2023)745820.

Foa, R.S., Klassen, A., Wenger, D., Rand, A. and M. Slade (2020) *Youth and Satisfaction with Democracy: Reversing the Democratic Disconnect?* Cambridge, United Kingdom: Centre for the Future of Democracy.

Giugni, M., Grasso, M. (2021) *Youth and Politics in Times of Increasing Inequalities*, [in:] Giugni, M., Grasso, M. (ed.) Youth and Politics in Times of Increasing Inequalities. Springer International Publishing: Cham.

Jędrysik M., *Czy 16-latki powinny głosować w wyborach? Hołownia mówi: tak. Politolog mówi: to skomplikowane*, 20.09.2021, https://oko.press/czy-16-latki-powinny-glosowac-w-wyborach/.

Kajta, J.; Barakeh, S., Marczewski, P.; Pustułka, P. (2022) *Demokratyczny paradoks w praktyce: Doświadczenia młodych aktywistów i aktywistek*, Youth Working Papers No 1/2022 Warszawa: Uniwersytet SWPS Młodzi w Centrum Lab. ISSN: 2543-5213 DOI: 10.23809/15.

Kajta, J., Mrozowicki, A. (2022). *Young People in Poland: 2020/2021. Between Disappointment with the State and Hope for a Better Life.* Bonn: Friedrich Ebert Stiftung, http://library.fes.de/pdf-files/id/19162.pdf.

Kądziela A., *Polityczny portret młodych Polaków*, Warszawa 2023.

Kublik A., *Zagłosowaliśmy raz i wystarczy, rozmowa z socjologiem prof. P. Sadurą*, Gazeta Wyborcza 29.05.2024.

Kubuj, K., *Czy młodzi mogliby więcej? Obszary obywatelskiego zaangażowania w demokrację/i*, [in:] Zagadnienia prawa konstytucyjnego. Księga jubileuszowa dedykowana Profesorowi Krzysztofowi Skotnickiemu w siedemdziesiątą rocznicę urodzin, Domańska A. (ed.), Łódź 2023, Tom 1, pp. 167-178.

Marzęcki R., *Młody obywatel we współczesnej demokracji europejskiej*, Warszawa 2013.

Pazderski F., *Rozczarowani indywidualiści w poszukiwaniu nowej jakości w polityce. Demokracja i aktywność obywatelska oczami młodych Polaków*, Warszawa 2019.

Pazderski F., *Młodzi w Europie Środkowej 2020*, NDI (National Democratic Institute) Research Project, Warszawa 2020.

Pazderski F., *Odlegli obserwatorzy, niezadowoleni konformiści czy poszukujący obywatele? Postawy młodych Polek i Polaków wobec demokracji i polityki*, Warszawa 2018.

Schläger, C., Katsioulis, Ch., Engels, J. N., *Analysis of the 2024 European Elections in Germany Majority for the stable centre despite a strong right wing*, FES diskurs June 2024, https://library.fes.de/pdf-files/a-p-b/21287.pdf.

Skotnicki K., *W sprawie konieczności zmian konstytucyjnej regulacji cenzusów wyborczych*, [in:] Minikomentarz dla Maksiprofesora. Księga jubileuszowa profesora Leszka Garlickiego, Zubik M. (ed.), Warszawa 2017.

Starzewski Ł., *Młodzież ma prawo uczestniczyć w debacie publicznej. Pierwsze spotkanie RPO w ramach Tygodnia Konstytucyjnego*, 16.12.2020, https://bip.brpo.gov.pl/pl/content/mlodziez-ma-prawo-udzialu-debacie-publicznej-rpo-tydzien-konstytucyjny.

Żerkowska-Balas M., *Dlaczego młodzi nie głosują?*, Uniwersytet SWPS, 17.06.2019, https://www.swps.pl/centrum-prasowe/informacje-prasowe/20040-dlaczego-mlodzi-nie-glosuja.

Waszak M., Zbieranek J., *Propozycja obniżenia wieku wyborczego do lat 16. Wybrane zagadnienia*, Warszawa 2011; Europejskie wybory młodych, Zbieranek J. (ed.), Warszawa 2014.

Rosa Indellicato[392]

Educating for human rights: Olympe de Gouges a model of courage and justice

Abstract: Human rights are the essential elements that allow every person to live with the dignity of a human being. While the conscience of the fundamental rights of the man has broadened its horizons since the onset of the third millennium, it is nonetheless true that these widely recognised rights are constantly being violated in every corner of the world. This, in turn, leads to the pressing need of an ethical and educational commitment capable of restoring vigour and favouring education towards the development and the respect of the human rights as these are inviolable and undeniable values, guaranteeing, at the same time, their universality, indivisibility and interdependence.

The figure of Olympe de Gouges is as relevant as ever for human rights education for several reasons related to her struggle for equality, social justice, and the recognition of women's rights, issues that remain as relevant today as they were in the 18th century.

Keywords: education, democracy, human rights, Olympe de Gouges, justice

1. Human rights: the path to a just society

The evolution of human rights has its roots in great events in human history, where their relevance lies, and in particular in the struggle for freedom and equality, which «are not a given but an ideal to be pursued»[393].

The basic principles of human rights are proclaimed in the *Universal Declaration of Human Rights* adopted unanimously by the United Nations on 10 December 1948. This Declaration includes a set of fundamental rights for every human being regardless of race, colour, sex, language, religion, political or other opinion, national or social origin, property, birth or other status. The legal-political revolution of the 20th century led to the recognition of the need for a planetary solidarity of men and nations, and human rights represented the attempt to proclaim this recognition, based on the humanist option to be

392 Pegaso Telematic University, ORCID 0000-0001-9585-0726.
393 N. Bobbio, *L'età dei diritti*, Einaudi, Torino 1997, p. 22.

carried out integrally on the 'whole man' and for all men[394]. Today is said to be the age of rights, and the problem of the foundation of a right presents itself differently depending on whether one is seeking the foundation of a right one has or a right one would like to have[395]. Human rights are ends worthy of pursuit, which, despite their desirability, have not yet been recognised by everyone and everywhere equally

Hence the importance of human rights education and the conviction that finding a foundation for human rights, and thus providing reasons to justify the choice we have made and would like others to make, are adequate means to obtain wider recognition[396]. As history has progressed, human rights have undergone evolution and modification, even according to the needs and realities of reference, so much so that, as Bobbio himself states, the rights defined as «sacre et inviolable»[397] in the 1700s have changed in the numerous national and international declarations of our contemporary times. Looking closely and circumstantially at concrete man, at the 'whole man', Aristotle would say, through what Francesco Viola has called the «situated anthropologies»[398], one can see that the *Declarations of the Rights of Man*, in recent decades, have focused on the specific conditions of men in concrete situations and therefore concerning man himself at different ages, from the first years of life to the last stages of life, in different environmental situations, of illness, of disability, as an indigenous person, as a migrant, up to the most recent debate on the right to a mother's surname for the unborn, so much so that a continuous movement towards a never closed redefinition of human rights has arisen. «Fundamental rights can only be taken seriously as such on the sole condition that they concern individuals as such and that they are not regarded as founding the laws but as founding the laws. Even better: that they are not founded on the

---

394 Cfr. S. Cotta, *Il diritto naturale e l'universalizzazione del diritto*, in Unione Giuristi Cattolici Italiani (ed.) *Diritto naturale e diritti dell'uomo all'alba del XXI secolo*, Giuffrè, Roma 1993, in particular p. 26.

395 Cfr. ivi, p. 5. *Sulla questione dei diritti fondamentali* cfr. G. Peces-Barba, *Teorie dei diritti fondamentali*, tr.it., Giuffrè, Milano 1993; H. Denninger, *Diritti dell'uomo e legge fondamentale*, Giappichelli, Torino 1988; L. Ferrajoli, *Dirittti fondamentali: un dibattito teorico*, Laterza, Roma 2001; P. Barile, *I diritti dell'uomo e le libertà fondamentali*, Il Mulino, Bologna 1984.

396 Cfr. N. Bobbio, *L'età dei diritti*, cit., p. 6.

397 Ivi, p. 9.

398 Cfr. F. Viola-G.Zaccaria, *Le ragioni del diritto*, Il Mulino, Bologna 2003.

system but foundational to the system»[399]. In reality, legal doctrine and historiography have never managed to exorcise the demon of the legal positivism of Kelsen, Jhering and Santi Romano, going so far as to subordinate subjective law to objective law, for the safeguarding of which the legislator could only reconfirm the historical nature of the individual to the point of denying an onto-axiological foundation of human rights. The inevitable product of such a philosophical-legal orientation has led, in today's society, to a new 'libertine natural lawism', which posits man as the legislator and creator of himself, as law unto himself, independently of the ethics that nonetheless constitutes the essential basis of law itself and without which the latter would have no meaning. Legal positivism, in fact, refuses to refer to an objective, ontological criterion of what is just. In this perspective, the ultimate horizon of law and morality is the law in force, which is considered just by definition.

The crisis of legal positivism called this axiom into question, particularly with Capograssi, who introduced the concept of law as legal experience, at one with the vital world. Hence the idea of a law understood not as a state, but as the regulation

399 G. Limone, *Dal giusnaturalismo al giuspersonalismo. Alla frontiera geoculturale della persona come bene comune*, Teknopress, Napoli 2005, p. 67. In this essay, the author considers that the time is ripe to move from natural lawism to legal-personalism starting from an empirical entity: man. This transition must take place through a 'reflective judgement that is not a procedure already given and consummated, but a theoretical, value-based, interpretative and practical work [...]' and through two fundamental steps: the first assuming 'the singular man in his daily concreteness, insofar as distinct from every other insofar as original, insofar as new [...], the second looking at this man as a concrete basis for enucleating a universal consideration' (Ivi, p. 75). And again the author dwells on the passage from natural law to personal law, and, wondering what this itinerary might mean, replies: 'It means that the culture of rights that today imposes itself on attention as a high response to the challenge of globalisation, is a culture not of rights tout court, but of fundamental rights, that is, of those rights that prevail over laws themselves. Rights whose unspoken ethical substance is the dignity of every human being, taken in its concreteness and in its difference from every other. And true dignity is pertinent to the singular, not to a genus or species. And it is a dignity not understood at the passive degree, as a mere expectation, but also, above all, at the active degree, as the promotion of relational identity' (Ivi., pp. 72-73). On this theme cf. by the same author *Il sacro come la contraddizione rubata. Prolegomeni a un pensiero metapolitico dei diritti fondamentali*, Iovene, Napoli 2001 particularly the first chapter; R. Dworkin, *I diritti presi sul serio*, Il Mulino, Bologna 1982; J. Habermas, *Morale Diritto Politica*, Einaudi, Torino 1972; Cfr. anche U. Pomarici, *Un'arte divina. Il diritto fra natura e libertà nella filosofia pratica kantiana*, ESI, Napoli 2004.

of interpersonal relationships on which ethics has a strong weight[400] to protect the dignity of the person[401]. Rosmini insists, in reference to the person, not only on the concept of the unity of the individual and concrete man, but also on his uniqueness and unrepeatability. Uniqueness, in the sense of non-reducibility to common constituent characteristics. And in this regard we find significant references in his thought, suffice it to think of his reasoning on the radical distinction between external phenomena and those of sensation when he affirms: «who[...] does not see that the body of the grieving person, which changes externally, and the sensation of his pain are two entirely different things? The grieved man's body falls under my senses, and produces sensations in me; his grief at the meeting does not fall under my senses, but is all in him alone»[402]. And this pain is of the soul. And the soul, for Rosmini, is the sentient principle of the individual which therefore not only gives him unity, but also uniqueness. It can be said that the task of a personalist philosophy is to proceed phenomenologically in a transcendental quest to investigate the fundamental structures of the person as embodied consciousness or 'embodied spirit' as Mounier would say. It is a search that «leads more and more to recognising and rooting the person in the generative and pre-objective ('narrating') Self in which the human finds its undivided unity; and it also leads to recognising in this pre-objective Self the centre from which the human radiates, and from which the human expands along the three "existential" coordinates of the personal construction of the Self: self-identity, relationship, transcendence»[403]. Therefore, the person is valid in its fullness as the capacity to be oneself in relation and, finally, in rooting oneself on the principle of all relations: finite and infinite relations, and inter-subjective and inter-worldly proximity, and therefore religious proximity. And it is precisely in these

---

400 Cfr. on this subject M. Indellicato, *Etica della persona e diritti umani. La prospettiva del personalismo polacco*, PensaMultimedia, Lecce 2013, in particular chapter IV. The jurist Perlingeri himself states that 'the legal norm lives and is consolidated only in hermeneutics and application' and that the person himself is a prius with respect to the order (cfr., P. Perlingeri, *La persona e i suoi diritti*, ESI, Napoli 2005). In this regard cfr. P. Grossi, *L'Europa del Diritto*, Laterza, Roma-Bari 2007.

401 For some reflections on 'dignity' in a constitutional context, see A.Ruggieri-A. Spadaro, *Dignità dell'uomo in un contesto istituzionale (prime notazioni)* in "Politica del diritto", a. XXII, n. 3, Settembre 1991.

402 A. Rosmini, *Antropologia in servizio della scienza morale*, Città Nuova, Roma 1981, nn. 56-60, pp. 48 ss. Rosmini also speaks of the person as a supreme principle, i.e. independent of any other and let us say irreducible(Cfr. Ivi, nn. 832-837, pp. 460-462).

403 A. Pavan, *Dire persona nell'età globale dei diritti umani*, in A. Pavan (a cura di) *Dire persona*, il Mulino, Bologna 2003, p. 488.

relationships that man becomes the place «of a greater and more radical dignity, that of the other, whose face and word he becomes»[404]. The being of the person is given in relation, is given in a constructive manner only in the dialectic of mutual recognition and in the care of singularities, precisely because «with the man-other the same fundamental human feeling of dignity is at stake that is at stake with the man-whom I am, and that by wounding the dignity of the other I wound my own dignity, because wounded in me or wounded in the other, the dignity of common humanity is wounded in any case»[405]. It can be said that the dialectic of recognition finds its fulfilment in the mutual telling of the truth of each other. It follows that communion is given in the respect of differences. Thus, if on the one hand it can be affirmed that only in the encounter with the other do I constitute myself as an indeclinable *proprium*, as an irreplaceable self, it is on the other hand true that in the reciprocity of recognitions the other is in turn restored to his truth and therefore to singularity[406]. And it is precisely on this basis that the theme of respect and care for the human person, his or her dignity and inviolable rights come to the fore[407].

2. Olympe de Gouges: example of education for democracy

Olympe de Gouges feminist forerunner, controversial, inconstant and very inconvenient for the revolution was executed in 1793. Just before the blade fell on her neck, she exclaimed: «Women may have the right to ascend the tribune, if they have the right to ascend the scaffold»[408]. She was baptised in 1748, in Montauban, near Toulouse, as Marie Gouze. She learned to read and write enough to sign in

---

404 A. Pavan, Prefazione a *Persona e personalismi*, a cura di A. Pavan-A. Milano, Edizioni Dehoniane, Napoli 1987, p. XII.

405 A. Pavan, *Dire persona nell'età globale dei diritti umani*, cit., p. 304.

406 In this regard, the work of P. Ricoeur, in which it is pointed out that the very notion of the 'self' could not take place without a finding oneself from the other, without a dialectical relationship with l'*autre que soi* (Cfr. P. Ricoeur, *Soi même comme un autre*, Editions du Seuil, Paris 1990, in particular pp. 12-15, 211 ss., 220-226; tr.it. di D. Iannotta, *Sé come un altro*, Jacka Book, Milano 1993, pp. 76-79, 225 ss., 284-290).

407 Respect and regard for the singularity of the other can translate, as Kant said, into admiration. 'Respect' and "regard" have their common origin in the Latin respicere, i.e. to reflect, to regard, but also to have regard, to have respect (in Latin respectus). Cfr. in this regard I. Kant, *Kritik der praktischen Vernunft*, in *Gesammelte Schriften*, A A, Bd. V, p. 76; tr.it. in V. Mathieu (ed.), *Critica della ragione pratica*, Bompiani, Milano 2004, in particular p. 163.

408 E. Cantarella, *Prefazione* in *Sui diritti delle donne*, RCS, Milano 2010, p. 7.

her first language, Occitan, used in the south of France by common people and nobility alike. Married to Louis-Yves Aubry, she had her only child with him. She soon got rid of that marriage by remaining a widow and did not marry again; for her, marriage was 'the grave of trust and love'. Her ideal of a couple was a union between man and woman through a contract that - once separated - would allow them to have legitimate children with other people[409].

Intent on starting a new life, she changed her name. She chose Marie Olympe Gouges and added a 'de' to it, the bourgeois particle with which she probably wanted to conceal her humble origins. With this new identity, she moved to Paris with her friend Jacques Biétrix, whose generosity allowed her to live in comfort and strive for fame as a writer.

In Paris, he became passionate about theatre and writing. She frequented artists, intellectuals, philosophers and writers. But she was aware of her limitations: she could barely read and write, like all women of her time and class. And this represented one of the greatest worries of her life. Olympe felt a literary vein in her, which she attributed to her real father: she was not, in fact, the daughter of the butcher Pierre Gouze, as she was registered at the registry office, but of a man of letters, the Marquis Jean-Jacques Lefranc de Pompignan, by whom she was never recognised.

From 1784 until her death nine years later, Olympe wrote, or rather dictated, around twenty plays for the theatre, as well as around sixty political texts, pamphlets, manifestos, articles and speeches, always with strong social connotations. Already in her early works she carried out her life's mission: to raise public awareness of the condition of women[410]. In the preface to her L'*homme genereux* she wrote: «This is how fragile our sex is. Men have all the advantages… We have been excluded from all power, from all knowledge»[411]. In Mariage inattendu de Cherubin of 1786, she denounced forced marriages and oppression by fathers and husbands: everything she had experienced on her own skin.

The French activist Olympe de Gouges fought for women's rights all her life[412]: in September 1791 she published the *Declaration of the Rights of Women and the*

409 Cfr. S. Mousset, *Olympe de Gouges: The French Revolution's Forgotten Feminist*, Pluto Press, Londra 2007.

410 Cfr. C. Papa, *Olympe de Gouges. Una donna nel cuore della rivoluzione*, Salerno Editrice, Salerno 2020.

411 Cfr. O. de Gouges, *L'homme généreux, ou l'adroit politique*, Chez la Veuve Duchesne, Paris 1786.

412 Cfr. T. Casadei, L. Milazzo (a cura di), *Un dialogo su Olympe de Gouges. Donne, schiavitù, cittadinanza*, Edizioni ETS, Pisa 2022.

Citizen[413], in which she declared political and social equality between men and women. On 3 November 1793, she was guillotined because she had opposed the execution of Louis XVI and had apparently attacked the Committee of Public Health. With her death came not only the ruthless repression of all dissidence, but a liberticidal involution, also due to the now permanent state of war put in place by the allied and counter-revolutionary powers (Prussia, England, Austria and Russia). The *Declaration of the Rights of Women and the Citizen* is a legal document based on the model of the *Declaration of the Rights of Man and the Citizen of 1789*.

Olympe de Gouges' thought is shockingly topical today, despite more than two centuries having passed since the famous fall of the Bastille that changed the face of Europe. The storming of the Bastille on 14 July 1789 in Paris was the culminating historical event of the French Revolution as the Bastille was the symbol of the *ancien régime*. The event, although unimportant in itself on a practical level, took on enormous symbolic significance to such an extent that it was considered the real beginning of the revolution. And it is precisely in this period of the French Revolution that we can trace the roots of political order in many western states. The resonance of that epochal motion can still be felt today when reading our Italian Constitution. Let us think, for example, of the third of the fundamental principles of our Constitution in which we read: «All citizens have equal social dignity and are equal before the law, without distinction of sex, race, language, religion, political opinion, personal and social conditions»[414]. These words echo what is reiterated in the first article of the *Déclaration des droits de l'homme et du citoyen of 1789*[415], which reads: «Men are born and remain free and equal in rights. Social distinctions can only be founded on common utility»[416]. Much of the content of the Declaration later flowed into the *Universal Declaration of Human Rights*, adopted by the United Nations on 10 December 1948. Even today, the Declaration is a law of constitutional status in the French Republic.

The Declaration of the Rights of Man and of the Citizen, together with the first part of the *American Declaration of Independence*, represented one of the most important testimonies of respect for the freedom and dignity of the human being. The affirmation of the rights of man and the citizen earned France the title of

413 Cfr. O. de Gouges, *Déclaration des droits de la femme et de la citoyenne*, Les Public' de l'APFUCC, n° 1, 1789.

414 Article 3 of the Italian Constitution.

415 Cfr. O. de Gouges *Déclaration des droits de la femme et de la citoyenne*, Les Public' de l'APFUCC, n° 1, 1789.

416 Cfr. P. Biscaretti di Ruffia, *Le Costituzioni di dieci Stati di "democrazia stabilizzata"*, Giuffrè, Milano 1994.

«Homeland of Human Rights»[417]. Two years after the *Declaration of the Rights of Man and of the Citizen*, Olympe de Gouges fought to affirm equal rights for all women as well, affirming the *Declaration of the Rights of Women and Citizens*. In this sense, Madame glimpsed the discrepancy that in fact existed between the formal equality, programmed by the act of 1789, and the substantive equality, not found in revolutionary practice[418]. But the *Declaration of Women's Rights* was deemed excessive and scandalous: its appeal fell on deaf ears, amidst the hostility of men and the total lack of solidarity of women who feared displeasing the husbands on whom they depended economically. The appeal included in the text was useless: "O women, women! When will you cease to be blind? What advantages have you gained from the Revolution?" Few joined her battle and for Olympe it was a bitter disappointment.

Olympe de Gouges remains relevant for several reasons, including her pioneering contributions to women's rights and social equality. Her fight for the rights of the marginalised and for the abolition of slavery reflects a commitment to social justice that still resonates today. Issues of racial, gender and class equality remain central to contemporary struggles for human rights. de Gouges used her writing to challenge the government and defend freedom of expression. Her determination to speak out against injustice, even at the risk of her own life, is an example for those fighting for free speech and against censorship. She championed the right of women[419] to actively participate in politics[420], a battle that continues in many parts of the world where women are still under-represented in positions of power. Her reform ideas, which included improving civil and social rights for all, are still relevant at a time when inequalities and injustices continue to persist.

While it is true that a greater awareness of human rights, as well as an increase in human rights, has matured compared to the past, it is also true that we are unfortunately witnessing in recent years a violation of fundamental rights in every part of the world and a social, civil and political illiteracy that call for a renewed ethical and educational commitment.

In our time, in fact, there is a lack of serious and attentive education so that a practical implementation of respect for human rights can be put in place; all this, however, should not discourage us from seeking paths, certainly not easy,

---

417 R. Marchese, *Piani e percorsi della storia*, Le Monnier, Milano 2002, p. 149.

418 Cfr. C. Margiotta, *Alla ricerca dell'uguaglianza perduta*, in *Civitas et Humanitas. Annali di cultura etico-politica*, Milella, Lecce 2018, p. 104.

419 Cfr. J. W. Scott, *Olympe de Gouges: The Biography of a Revolutionary Woman*, Harvard University Press, Cambridge 2017.

420 Cfr. O. de Gouges, *Olympe de Gouges: Escrits politiques*, a cura di Benoîte Groult, Côté-femmes, Parigi 1993.

but possible. Ethical commitment must certainly be combined with educational commitment, which requires responsibility on the part of parents, teachers, institutions and, in general, the adult world, as well as governments, towards the new generations that are increasingly experiencing situations of great unease and disorientation[421]. Hence the need to reinvigorate education on human rights, in an attempt to «rediscover a set of shared values and rules capable of resolving, at least on a practical level, the fragmentation, instability and fluctuation of human phenomena»[422]. Human rights are defined as 'the beacon of all human beings' and their protection and promotion is the first responsibility of governments. Consequently, it is the duty of all states, which wish to remain within the international community, to spread the culture of fundamental human rights by all means. This is the passage that founds the right-duty to human rights education on a juridical level, which is directly included in the duty of international cooperation set forth in Article 55 of the *UN Charter*: «The promotion and protection of all human rights and fundamental freedoms must be regarded as an objective priority of the United Nations in accordance with its purposes and principles, in particular the purpose of international cooperation»[423].

---

421 Cfr. W. Brezinka, *L'educazione in una società disorientata*, Armando, Roma 1989. The author considers in this essay that intellectual abilities and rational thinking alone are insufficient to guide us through life, while we need the 'value of emotional strengths and the goods of faith' (cf. ivi., p. 13). With reference to the objective concerning respect for human rights and fundamental freedoms, it is worth recalling that the Second World Conference on Human Rights, held in Vienna in 1993, drafted *the Declaration on Human Rights Education* between 14 and 25 June. The document states: "The World Conference on Human Rights reaffirms the solemn commitment of all States to realise their obligations, to promote universal respect, observance and protection of all human rights and fundamental freedoms for all in accordance with the Charter of the United Nations and other instruments concerning human rights and international law'. On 20 October 1997, the Plan of Action was then approved, setting out the guidelines for the realisation of such an ambitious project.

422 G. Chiosso, *Novecento pedagogico. Profilo delle teorie pedagogiche contemporanee*, La Scuola, Brescia 1997, p. 321.

423 By Resolution 49/184 of 6 March 1995, the UN General Assembly declared the period between 1 January 1995 and 31 December 2004 as the Decade, dedicated to human rights education, in the conviction that 'human rights education contributes to a concept of development in harmony with the dignity of women and men of all ages, dignity that takes into account different segments of society, such as children, indigenous peoples, minorities and persons with disabilities' and that all, in order to realise their full potential, «must be aware of their human, civil, cultural, economic, political and social rights».

Education to human rights, therefore, becomes a priority right, but also a duty, and not only on a purely cognitive level, but ethical, cultural and, strictly speaking, even technical, for the effective translation of these rights into practice, to protect a «universal intrinsic value»[424] such as that of the human person and on which it is possible to find agreement in every culture and country. And it is precisely respect for universality that makes it possible to overcome social, cultural or ethnic differences and pluralism itself, which would justify different interpretations of human rights[425]. It is often in the name of cultural and religious diversity that the greatest violations of human rights are justified, and there is therefore a real «risk of perceiving the distance between the ideal world that emerges from the affirmation of human principles and the disenchantment of the reality that disregards those norms and tramples them underfoot»[426]. However much we talk about the universality of rights, in fact, they are far from being the rights of all and there is also a lack of practical application, which certainly cannot be resolved in a bureaucratic delegation to international bodies, but which, on the contrary, requires an assumption of ethical-educational responsibility and a cultural commitment that takes into account the centrality of the person and respect for his dignity as the basic values of a new culture of human rights and a new ethical universality for a civil coexistence based on mutual respect. The practical translation of human rights cannot but concern the individual man in relation to others, because the other is constitutive of the being-person and this means that the self-realisation of the individual «needs intersubjectivity and community and

---

424 Cfr. L. Pati, *L'educazione nella comunità locale*, La Scuola, Brescia 1990, in particular p. 295.

425 Cfr. M. Santerini, *La scuola della cittadinanza*, Laterza, Roma-Bari 2010, in particular p. 65.

426 M. Tarozzi, *Cittadinanza interculturale. L'esperienza educativa come agire politico*, La Nuova Italia, Milano 2005, p. 76. Tolerance also stems from a feeling of respect for the rights and freedoms of others and must consist of a process of listening, communication, understanding and appreciation in order to implement the dialectic of mutual recognition and thus valorisation of diversity in the expression of all its human potential (Cfr. G. Harrison, *I fondamenti antropologici dei diritti umani*, Meltemi, Roma 2001, in particular p. 22). Fundamental remains, in the history of Western thought, the Letter on Tolerance that Jhon Locke published in 1689 (Cfr. J. Locke, *Lettera sulla tolleranza*, tr.it., di A. Sabetti (ed.), La Nuova Italia, Firenze 1991). Locke writes: «toleration of those who dissent from others in matters of religion is a thing so consonant with the gospel and reason that it is monstrous there are men blind to so much light' (ivi.p. 8). And again: «In tolerance I see the most important distinguishing mark of the true church» (ivi.p. 3).

is far from postulating the separateness of individuals. One is aware that others are necessary for the construction of one's identity»[427].

In conclusion, we can say that Olympe de Gouges, a prominent figure of the French Revolution, is an example of democracy and civic courage for our young people.

Olympe de Gouges' courage is evident in the way she defended her ideals, even at the cost of her life. She was one of the few women of her time to speak out against slavery and to support divorce, gender equality and the right of women to participate in politics. Her dedication to the cause of human and civil rights led her to clash with the revolutionary authorities, who eventually condemned her to the guillotine in 1793. For us, de Gouges represents an example of moral integrity and commitment to social justice. Her life is a reminder of the importance of fighting for one's rights and those of others, even in the face of seemingly insurmountable obstacles. In a world where democracy is often tested, her example is a testimony to the value of being active and aware in political and social dynamics. De Gouges argued that 'it is necessary for young people to feel the duty to prepare themselves to face life by assuming the most vivid sense of moral responsibility', so that there is an awareness on their part of the existence of 'values' and 'ends' to be pursued, an indispensable prerequisite for the formation of a civic and moral conscience and sensitivity, which allows them to realise themselves, grow and mature according to positive models.

A school based on the example of Olympe de Gouges must actively promote gender equality and the inclusion of all diversities. This means adopting policies that ensure equal opportunities for all students, regardless of their gender, origin, sexual orientation or ability. Civic education must be central, teaching not only the functioning of democratic institutions, but also the importance of active involvement in the community, highlighting the need for equal rights for women.

Bibliography

Barile P., *I diritti dell'uomo e le libertà fondamentali*, Il Mulino, Bologna 1984.

Biscaretti di Ruffia P., *Le Costituzioni di dieci Stati di "democrazia stabilizzata"*, Giuffrè, Milano 1994.

Bobbio N., *L'età dei diritti*, Einaudi, Torino 1997.

Brezinka W., *L'educazione in una società disorientata*, Armando, Roma 1989.

Cantarella E., *Prefazione* in *Sui diritti delle donne*, RCS, Milano 2010.

427 F. Viola, *Etica e metaetica dei diritti umani*, Giappichelli, Torino 2000, p. 102.

Casadei T., Milazzo L. (ed.), *Un dialogo su Olympe de Gouges. Donne, schiavitù, cittadinanza*, Edizioni ETS, Pisa 2022.

Chiosso G., *Novecento pedagogico. Profilo delle teorie pedagogiche contemporanee*, La Scuola, Brescia 1997.

Cotta S., *Il diritto naturale e l'universalizzazione del diritto*, in Unione Giuristi Cattolici Italiani (ed.) *Diritto naturale e diritti dell'uomo all'alba del XXI secolo*, Giuffrè, Roma 1993.

de Gouges O., *Déclaration des droits de la femme et de la citoyenne*, Les Public' de l'APFUCC, n° 1, 1789.

de Gouges O., *L'homme généreux, ou l'adroit politique*, Chez la Veuve Duchesne, Paris 1786.

de Gouges O., *Olympe de Gouges: Escrits politiques*, a cura di Benoîte Groult, Côté-femmes, Parigi 1993.

Denninger H., *Diritti dell'uomo e legge fondamentale*, Giappichelli, Torino 1988.

Dworkin R., *I diritti presi sul serio*, Il Mulino, Bologna 1982.

Ferrajoli L., *Dirittti fondamentali: un dibattito teorico*, Laterza, Roma 2001.

Grossi P., *L'Europa del Diritto*, Laterza, Roma-Bari 2007.

Habermas J., *Morale Diritto Politica*, Einaudi, Torino 1972.

Harrison G., *I fondamenti antropologici dei diritti umani*, Meltemi, Roma 2001.

Indellicato M., *Etica della persona e diritti umani. La prospettiva del personalismo polacco*, PensaMultimedia, Lecce 2013.

Kant I., *Kritik der praktischen Vernunft*, in *Gesammelte Schriften*, A A, Bd. V, p. 76; tr.it. a cura di V. Mathieu, *Critica della ragione pratica*, Bompiani, Milano 2004.

Limone G., *Dal giusnaturalismo al giuspersonalismo*. Teknopress, Napoli 2005.

Limone G., *Il sacro come la contraddizione rubata. Prolegomeni a un pensiero metapolitico dei diritti fondamentali*, Iovene, Napoli 2001.

Locke J., *Lettera sulla tolleranza*, a cura di A. Sabetti, La Nuova Italia, Firenze 1991.

Marchese R., *Piani e percorsi della storia*, Le Monnier, Milano 2002.

Margiotta C., *Alla ricerca dell'uguaglianza perduta*, in *Civitas et Humanitas. Annali di cultura etico-politica*, Milella, Lecce 2018.

Mousset S., *Olympe de Gouges: The French Revolution's Forgotten Feminist*, Pluto Press, Londra 2007.

Papa C., *Olympe de Gouges. Una donna nel cuore della rivoluzione*, Salerno Editrice, Salerno 2020.

Pati L., *L'educazione nella comunità locale*, La Scuola, Brescia 1990.

Pavan A., *Dire persona nell'età globale dei diritti umani*, in A. Pavan (a cura di) *Dire persona*, il Mulino, Bologna 2003.

Pavan A., Prefazione a *Persona e personalismi*, a cura di A. Pavan-A. Milano, Edizioni Dehoniane, Napoli 1987.

Peces G. - Barba, *Teorie dei diritti fondamentali*, tr.it., Giuffrè, Milano 1993.

Perlingeri P., *La persona e i suoi diritti*, ESI, Napoli 2005.

Pomarici U., *Un'arte divina. Il diritto fra natura e libertà nella filosofia pratica kantiana*, ESI, Napoli 2004.

Ricoeur P., *Soi même comme un autre*, Editions du Seuil, Paris 1990, tr.it. di D. Iannotta, *Sé come un altro*, Jacka Book, Milano 1993.

Rosmini A., *Antropologia in servizio della scienza morale*, Città Nuova, Roma 1981.

Ruggieri A.,-Spadaro A., *Dignità dell'uomo in un contesto istituzionale (prime notazioni)* in "Politica del diritto", a. XXII, n. 3, Settembre 1991.

Santerini M., *La scuola della cittadinanza*, Laterza, Roma-Bari 2010.

Scott J.W., *Olympe de Gouges: The Biography of a Revolutionary Woman*, Harvard University Press, Cambridge 2017.

Signore M., *Prolegomeni ad una nuova/antica idea di Welfare*, PensaMultimedia, Lecce 2011.

Tarozzi M., *Cittadinanza interculturale. L'esperienza educativa come agire politico*, La Nuova Italia, Milano 2005.

Viola F., *Etica e metaetica dei diritti umani*, Giappichelli, Torino 2000.

Viola F., Zaccaria G., *Le ragioni del diritto*, Il Mulino, Bologna 2003.

Juliusz Mroziński[428]

Constitutional court of a democratic legal state as an institution of dialogue at the intersection of political and legal traditions

Abstract: The separative coexistence of the legal and the political system remains one of the fundamental features of a democratic legal state. A certain degree of political entanglement is, however, embedded in the reality of the European model of constitutional review. The purpose of this paper is to assess the status of constitutional courts in selected models of their composition in terms of their openness to influence from the political system and to try to answer the question on the permissible degree of participation of political factors in the process of reviewing the constitutionality of law. It could be argued that without prejudice to the principle of the rule of law, the constitutional court is shaped to serve the optimisation of the legislative process, as well as to guarantee a proper interaction of state bodies in order to execute their competence effectively. Depending on the legally implemented form of personal composition, the constitutional court may act either as a 'guardian', an 'adviser' or an 'arbitrator' in relations between the paramount institutions of the state.

Keywords: constitutional judiciary, composition of court, constitutional review, impartiality, political tradition, legal culture

1. Introduction

The reality of a democratic legal state precludes the possibility of making a strict distinction between the political and legal systems. Although legal regulations come into effect through a formalised procedure, their shape remains strongly conditioned by the current nature of public discourse, cultural and historical factors. It is argued that the deliberativeness of the legislative process, ideological pluralism and responsiveness of legal institutions are a proxy for the degree of democratisation of the general order of the state[429]. The political context seems to inevitably accompany the activities of bodies influencing the shape of the law in force, including bodies set up to carry out hierarchical conformity checks of legal

428 University of Wrocław, ORCID 0000-0002-9738-6207.
429 R. Levy, G. Orr., *The law of deliberative democracy*, Routledge 2016 pp. 3-9.

norms – not only in the model of concentrated control of legal constitutionality, which remains characteristic of continental European legal culture.[430] There is no doubt that the political order remains complementary to the legal one; however, the condition for maintaining state's stability is to keep an appropriate balance between the potential for the political factor to influence the law and, by analogy, the judicialization[431] of the public debate. Just as it would be highly undesirable if the legal norms in force were to satisfy the short-term political interest of an option that happens to enjoy popular support, so too, in the best interests of civil society, laws should generally not petrify the freedom to hold and express one's own views.[432] Against this background, the position of the judiciary remains peculiar insofar, as, already in the classical, Montesquieuian view, it should remain radically separated[433] from all political factors.[434] Reflection of an ideological, philosophical nature, which at the stage of shaping general and abstract legal solutions contributes to their optimisation in the spirit of responding to real social needs, at the stage of applying the law introduces an unacceptable factor of uncertainty about the fate of the individual. The claimant – as well as defendant – has the right to expect that his or her case will be heard with respect for the rules of judicial independence and impartiality, including worldview. Political courts are by their very nature arbitrary courts, casting doubt on the status of justice as the 'supreme value of law.[435]

---

430 P. Wahlbeck, J. Spriggs, F. Maltzman, F., "The Politics of Dissents and Concurrences on the U.S. Supreme Court," *American Politics Quarterly*, 27/4 (1999) pp. 488-514.

431 R. Hirschl, "The judicialization of mega-politics and the rise of political courts," *Annual Review of Political Science* 11 (2008) pp. 93-118.

432 M. Cerar, "The relationship between law and politics," *Annual Survey of International & Comparative Law* 15 (2009) p. 19.

433 "[…] judicial independence is the strongest safeguard against the exercise of tyrannical power by men who want to live above the law, rather than under it. The separation of powers concept as understood by the founding fathers assumed the existence of a judicial system free from outside influence of whatever kind and from whatever source, and further assumed that each individual judge would be free from coercion even from his own brethren." (S. Ervin Jr, "Separation of powers: judicial independence," *Law & Contemporary Problems* 35 (1970) p. 121.)

434 Montesquieu, *The Spirit of Laws*, Volume I, Wikisource, https://en.wikisource.org/wiki/The_Spirit_of_Laws_(1758) [accessed 01.05.2024].

435 R. Tokarczyk, "Sprawiedliwość jako naczelna wartość prawa," *Annales Universitatis Mariae Curie-Skłodowska* 44 (1997) p. 137.

There is no complete consensus on the qualification of specialised (separate) constitutional courts as organs of judicial power. The literature emphasises that a number of features (including the non-adjudication of individual disputes, the general and abstract nature of the legal effects of rulings, the fact of being bound only by constitutional provisions, the direct influence on the shape of the law in force), as well as historical considerations, tend to locate constitutional courts rather among *sui generis* organs of legal protection.[436] The state of 'limbo' between the legislature and the judiciary is reflected in the way in which the composition of the constitutional court is shaped. That in turn translates into a different conception of the impartiality of constitutional judges, as compared to ordinary court judges, and the risk of subjecting them to political pressure. By 'constitutional court' in the following text, I refer to specialised bodies, which are not courts in the *strict sense of the word* (with the exception of supreme courts conducting hierarchical control of norms) and which are appointed to conduct concentrated control of the constitutionality of the law. It is important to distinguish the natural political influence, manifested mainly through the creative (sometimes controlling) competences of the legislative and executive powers – inherent in the construction of the constitutional court – from the concept of political absorption. Using the latter in the text, I understand by it the subordination of the constitutional court to the ad hoc political interests of the option having a decisive influence on the shaping of the composition of this body, the appropriation of the ability to control the exercise by the constitutional court of its competences, and consequently the instrumentalisation of this body, depriving it of the social and legal legitimacy to exercise its functions. I regard the political absorption of the constitutional court as a manifestation of the abuse of the legitimate mechanisms stabilising the constitutional court in the structure of state's organs and a phenomenon constituting a distortion of the continental paradigm of the democratic legal state. I tentatively assume, contrary to popular opinion,[437] that the model of the constitutional court functioning in the group of countries which constitutions I am analysing does not

436 S. Damle, "Specialize the Judge, Not the Court: A Lesson from the German Constitutional Court," *Virginia Law Review* (2005) p. 1291.

437 I. Rishan, "Doubting the Impartiality: Constitutional Court Judges and Conflict of Interest," *Jurnal Jurisprudence* (2022) p. 100.

assume absolute political impartiality[438] of the constitutional court. At the same time, without prejudice to the principle of the rule of law, the constitutional court is, as it were, 'embedded' in political realities, in order to optimise the legislative process, to guarantee the interaction of state bodies for the effective implementation of their competence. As the most important criterion for assessing the degree of systemic politicisation of the constitutional court, as well as the principle of selection of the states of the research sample, I perceive the degree of influence of the public authority on the way of its composition. Due to the size of the study, I omit issues related to the legal force and scope of influence of constitutional court decisions (legal force of decisions in static terms) and the competences of entities external to the court with respect to its decisions (legal force in dynamic terms),[439] even though I agree on their meaning in the context of the research.

---

438 The notion of political impartiality has been intensively debated both by representatives of legal science (Ch. Geyh, "The dimensions of judicial impartiality," *Florida Law Review* 65 (2013) p. 493; C. Robertson, "Judicial impartiality in a partisan era," *Florida Law Review* 70 (2018) p. 739) and political science (S. Mendus, *Impartiality in moral and political philosophy*, OUP Oxford, 2002; P. Rosanvallon, *Democratic legitimacy: Impartiality, reflexivity, proximity*, Princeton University Press, 2011). For the purposes of this thesis, I assume that political impartiality in the application of the law means the total absence of direct influence of external public opinion on the decision to apply the law. By politicisation, a contrario, I mean a situation in which decisions to apply the law are directly motivated by extra-legal ideological factors. Political absorption occurs when the principle of the constitutional court's activity becomes the satisfaction of a political interest, the will to realise a certain worldview (L. Post, A. Raile, E. Raile, "Defining political will," *Politics & Policy* 38.4 (2010) p. 653), in relation to which legal norms are assigned a servile, instrumental role. One of the functions attributed to the constitutional court in the literature is the political function (M. Michalska-Guzik, "Bodily functions of the constitutional judiciary," *Online Legal Review TBSP UJ* 4 (34) (2017) p. 37) which is supposed to consist in 'controlling the legality of the political actions of state organs'. The exercise by the constitutional court of a political function understood in this way would make it an intermediary body between the legal system and the political system of the state – a kind of keystone of the state order.

439 The distinction between the static and dynamic aspects of the legal force of the official acts of a constitutional court is prompted by the discrepancy between the characteristics attributed to judgments on the basis of constitutional provisions and the prospects of their persistence in legal circulation and actual implementation. The rooting of judgments rendered by constitutional courts in constitutional provisions, the attribution of concrete status and effects to them, does not preclude the equipping of state organs with competences affecting the actual effectiveness of the acts of these courts.

I use a formal-dogmatic and comparative method and present the results of a critical literature review.

The constitutional diversity among European states is reflected in the different models of the formation and functioning of systems aimed to review the constitutionality of law.[440] In undertaking to solve the research problems presented above, I focus on the circumstances of the functioning of the eligible bodies in the various European states. My aim is, however, to include an example of each 'composition mode' distinguished by the Venice Commission. In my research I take into account the regulation contained in acts of constitutional rank.

2. Composition of the constitutional court as a determinant of its legal and political role

The material essence of a constitutional court, like that of any public authority, is its personal substrate. Although it is ultimately the individual qualities of the judges that will determine the quality of the adjudication of pending cases, it will not be without significance for the competence and motivation of those holding the honourable position of judge that the way in which candidates for membership are qualified. Already at this point, it should be noted that the vast majority of constitutional acts of European states formulate very specific formal requirements for persons interested in becoming a judge of a constitutional court, using in this respect the censuses of age, education or professional (including

440 Constitutional review in European post-authoritarian states was shaped *ex nihilo*, as the countries of the former Soviet sphere of influence regained their sovereignty. Thus, on the occasion of the constitutionalisation of their system, it was possible to implement evolutionary concepts of constitutional justice which would not only reflect the legal tradition, but also assist the development of a political dialogue. Ideologically rooted in classical Western European thought, the constitutional courts of the former Eastern Bloc states were to represent a developmental version of it, better corresponding to the needs and standards of the political and legal culture of the region (G. Brunner, "Development of a constitutional judiciary in Eastern Europe," *Review Central and European Law* 18 (1992) p. 535). Hence, taking into account the legal solutions of the Eastern European states, especially in comparison with countries with well-established traditions and elaborate systems of legal protection, makes it possible to draw a more reliable picture of constitutional justice institutions in Europe.

academic) experience.[441] Thus, from a comparative perspective, the significance of the apolitical criterion of the intellectual excellence of a constitutional judge is not in doubt.

The three concepts of classifying the ways in which the composition of a judicial body, including a constitutional court, is shaped have gained the most widespread recognition in the literature.[442] The United States Institute of Peace distinguishes between the appointment of judges by political institutions, by the judiciary as a whole (either by popular vote or through a judicial council) and by electors.[443] According to the typology of Giacomo Oberto[444], a distinction should be made between the model of exclusive nomination, independent selection by a collegial body, the model of cooperative selection (or nomination) and nomination by an expert panel. The typology proposed in the Venice Commission's Report on the Composition of Constitutional Courts of December 1997[445] seems to be the most authoritative and still valid in a strictly European research context. The latter document focuses on three ways of shaping the personal structure of the constitutional court, in principle exhausting the catalogue of solutions adopted in

441 Among the constitutions of the countries in the study group, the 1992 Constitution of the Czech Republic seems to go quite further in this respect, stipulating (Article 84(3)) that a candidate for a judge must be of irreproachable character, have the right to be elected to the Senate, have a university degree in law and have at least ten years' professional experience, while the 1997 Constitution of the Republic of Poland only requires a candidate for a judge of the Constitutional Tribunal to be 'distinguished by his/her legal knowledge'. The 1949 Basic Law of the Federal Republic of Germany concerning the regime of the Federal Constitutional Court and the status of its judges contains only a laconic statement on the incompatibility of the position with membership of the Bundestag or Bundesrat and refers (Article 94(2)) to a statutory regulation. Section 61 of the 1953 Constitution of the Kingdom of Denmark also cedes the competence to regulate the judicial system to the ordinary legislature.

442 N. Aung, "Composition of the German Federal Constitutional Court," *LESIJ-Lex ET Scientia International Journal* 27/2 (2020) p. 105; K. Drewniowska, *Powoływanie sędziów Trybunału Konstytucyjnego w Polsce*, Wrocław 2023 p. 35.

443 *Judicial Appointments and Judicial Independance*, United States Institute of Peace (USIP) 2009 https://www.usip.org/sites/default/files/Judicial-Appointments-EN.pdf [accessed 20.05.2024].

444 N. Aung, "Composition...", pp. 35-37.

445 *The Composition of Constitutional Courts*, European Commission for Democracy Through Law, *Science and technique of democracy*, No. 20, CDL-STD(1997)020, 1997 https://www.venice.coe.int/webforms/documents/default.aspx?pdffile=CDL-STD(1997)020-e [accessed 20.05.2024].

European countries. These are, firstly, direct nomination,[446] secondly independent selection by a parliamentary collegial body,[447] and, finally, hybrid selection.[448]

As the catalogue of actors entitled to participate in the procedure for filling positions on the constitutional court expands, the need to agree on positions, to make compromises, to negotiate nominations emerges. The influence of the will of individual political actors to realise their own worldview is weakened. It can be assumed that the more bodies are involved in the activity of appointing judges, the less arbitrary, politically motivated the final act of their appointment will be. A particular risk of a strictly political motivation in the selection occurs in the case of a concentration of creative competence; the more it is dispersed, the more political interests to be reconciled, which favours the moderation of positions by representatives of different options. In proportion to the lowering of the importance of political criteria, the factor of the intellectual qualifications possessed by judicial candidates gains in importance.[449] A set of guarantees of the independence of the constitutional court (its institutional separation from other organs of public power), as well as of the independence of its judges (tenure, non-removability, immunity), is a common standard, regardless of the model preferred by the constitutions for the appointment of judges.

---

446 The system of direct nomination generally presupposes the discretionary nature of the power to appoint constitutional judges, although most often the legal empowerment of a judge occurs as a result of a recommendation by an authorised body. In this way, there is a concentration of the creative competence of the composition of the court. The degree of democratic legitimacy of judges appointed by direct nomination will depend on the form of empowering the eligible body.

447 The election by the parliamentary chamber is – in the perception of the authors of the Venice Commission's Report – supposed to ensure the democratic legitimacy of the constitutional court judges. The legitimacy of the collective will of the people is in this case "inherited" from the democratically elected general parliamentary chamber. The centre of gravity in this case is to be on the power to propose nominations which are then subject to consideration by MPs, so there is a need for at least a minimum of cooperation between the various actors. In this case, there is a gradual dispersal of the creative competence of the court's composition.

448 Hybrid election combines elements of direct nomination and parliamentary election. It provides enormous room for manoeuvre in the sphere of differentiating the power of influence of the various actors on the final appointment of a judge, creating a multi-level structure of reconciliation of interests. The hybrid model implies the highest degree of differentiation of the creative competence of the court's composition.

449 P. Vandamme, D. Bello Hutt, "Selecting constitutional judges randomly," *Swiss Political Science Review* 27/1 (2021) p. 109.

The *prima facie* perceived advantages of adopting a model that enforces a multi-stage mitigation of positions in the process of judges' appointment do not make it a perfect solution. The problem generated by models assuming a gradual dispersal of creative competence (parliamentary selection, hybrid selection) is the risk of an impasse – as a result of the impossibility of reconciling positions and political interests – in the process of appointing judges, and consequently forcing the constitutional court to operate with an incomplete composition.[450] In the long term, the risk of complete paralysis of the court, blocking the system of control of the constitutionality of the law and creating a serious constitutional crisis in the state is to be expected. Thus, while the greatest danger of political absorption of the constitutional court occurs when constitutional law adopts a direct nomination model, the concentration of the judicial appointment process (usually a monocratic decision linked to a recommendation) somehow protects the system from destabilisation as a result of possible disagreements. The theoretically less-political multi-stage procedures for the nomination, evaluation and elimination of candidates significantly prolong the process of appointing constitutional judges, while at the same time exposing it to obstruction by actors interested in destabilising the constitutional order of the state. The compromise solution, which is the parliamentary model, provides an opportunity to reduce the risk of political absorption of the constitutional court as a result of an arbitrary, politically motivated creative decision of a body that could have the right of exclusive nomination. At the same time, the parliamentary method of appointing judges – subject to the formation of an appropriate level of the culture of public debate – makes it possible to optimise the relationship between the bodies responsible in the area of continental legal culture for law-making, safeguarding the stability of the state system. At the same time, the parliamentary model guarantees the preservation, however indirectly, of the democratic legitimacy of constitutional judges.

The legal implementation of the direct nomination model in the Scandinavian states[451] – specifically the Kingdom of Denmark, the Republic of Finland, Iceland, the Kingdom of Norway and the Kingdom of Sweden – brings them close to the United States[452] and other states with a historically strong monocratic head of state in terms of the mechanisms used to control the constitutionality of the law. Most Scandinavian states have (with the exception of the Republic of Finland

---

450 K. Drewniowska, *Powoływanie sędziów Trybunału Konstytucyjnego w Polsce*, Wrocław 2023 p. 61.

451 *The Composition...* p. 4.

452 I. Duy, "New Trends in Scandinavian Constitutional Review," *Scandinavian studies in law* 61 (2015) p. 14.

and Iceland) maintained a limited monarchical system. A characteristic feature of modern European constitutional monarchies is the expectation addressed to the ruler to remain politically impartial.[453] The monarch is expected to remain neutral, not to get involved, except in special cases, in the often heated public debate; they are expected to embody the state and the supra-individual interest of its citizens with their attitude, the timelessness of monocratic institutions. The co-responsibility (direct in Norway,[454] indirect in Denmark[455]) of the monarch for legitimising the position of supreme court judges exercising the certain functions of constitutional courts[456] plays here the role of a balancing factor against the risk of political instrumentalization of the institutions of legal system protection, while guaranteeing the effectiveness of the creative mechanisms.

The appointment of judges by means of the election of a legitimate representative body, preferred in states with a republican system, is the competence of the parliament, which usually enjoys the strongest position among the organs of the state.[457] The indicated regularity is the result of the autonomous construction of the status of the republican head of state – depending on the adopted conception of parliamentarism.[458] While the main burden of responsibility for the destiny of the country in a republican system is borne by the representation of the citizens, it is the parliamentary body that, with a few important reservations, appears suitable for deciding the composition of the constitutional court (as it is perceived to

453 B. Yack, "The rationality of Hegel's concept of monarchy," *American Political Science Review* 74/3 (1980) p. 709.

454 As states Article 24 of the 1814 Constitution of the Kingdom of Norway.

455 According to the Section 27 (1) of the 1953 Constitution of the Kingdom of Denmark.

456 S. Larsen, "Constitutional pathways in Scandinavia," *The Legitimacy of European Constitutional Orders*. Edward Elgar Publishing 2023 p. 186.

457 The 1958 Constitution of the French Republic, by adopting a model of direct nomination of the members of the Constitutional Council, balances the influence on the design of the constitutional court of the two chambers of parliament (which designate a total of 6 of the 9 members of the Council) with the position of the President of the Republic (who designates the remaining 3 of its members), reflecting the systemic importance of the office of the latter.

458 In a presidential system, the strong social and constitutional legitimacy of the head of state predestines the president to participate in the process of shaping the constitutional court. In the (model) cabinet system, the president, given the lack of their direct democratic legitimacy, bears mainly a formal influence on the constitutional court. Natural in the directorial system, as adopted in the 1999 Constitution of the Swiss Confederation, in view of the parliament's systemic supremacy, is an exclusively parliamentary way of filling positions on the constitutional court.

co-operate, to certain extent, in lawmaking). Being an emanation of the political system, in the absence of adequate mechanisms to guarantee the autonomy of the constitutional court, parliament's action might quickly bring to the political absorption of this body. Hence, in addition to the standard guarantees of the independence (non-political efficiency of the operation) of the constitutional court, the level of the political culture of society is of fundamental importance for the ability of the constitutional court to retain its jurisdiction.[459] The regularity in the context of the occurrence of constitutional crises related to the appointment of constitutional judges can be observed against the background of the experience of Central European countries, which – although legitimised by a democratic tradition – rebuilt the level of political and legal awareness of citizens for decades after the transformation from authoritarian and totalitarian regimes.[460] An unquestionable advantage of the parliamentary form for the appointment of constitutional judges, especially in federal states, is that it takes into account the role of the individual constituent parts of the state. If the individual states of a federal state have an overall influence on legislation, it should be assumed that they should also be able to take a position in the context of the legitimation of a body influencing the shape of the applicable law as much as the constitutional court does.[461]

By definition, the hybrid system should allow to achieve a state of maximum depoliticisation of the constitutional court after its formation.[462] Taking the Ukrainian regulation[463] as an example of the legal implementation of this formula for the formation of the constitutional court, it can be noted that it allows to

459 L. Schlam, "State Constitutional Amending, Independent Interpretation, and Political Culture: A Case Study in Constitutional Stagnation," *DePaul Law Review* 43 (1993) p. 269.

460 A. Bodnar, "Protection of human rights after the constitutional crisis in Poland," *Jahrbuch des öffentlichen Rechts der Gegenwart* 66 (2018) p. 639; D. Bunikowski, "The constitutional crisis in Poland, Schmittian questions and Kaczynski's political and legal philosophy," *Journal of Contemporary European Studies* 26/3 (2018) pp. 285; M. Wiącek, "Constitutional crisis in Poland 2015-2016 in the light of the rule of law principle," *Defending Checks and Balances in EU Member States* (2021) p. 15.

461 The Basic Law of the Federal Republic of Germany of 1949 confers the competence to shape the composition of the Federal Constitutional Court on both the Bundestag, which represents all citizens, and the Bundesrat, which represents the Länder (Article 94, para. 1). The 1999 Constitution of the Swiss Confederation does likewise (Article 168).

462 *The Composition...* p. 6.

463 Specifically, the provisions of Chapter XII (Articles 147-153) of the 1996 Constitution of Ukraine.

broadly define the scope of the constitutional court's competence.[464] The declarative depoliticisation in this aspect of the constitutional court gives grounds for making it one of the organs co-shaping the state system, a kind of forum for the exchange of insights of professionals legitimised by the most important state institutions.

3. Conclusions

A certain degree of political entanglement is inherent in the construction of a constitutional court embedded in the reality of the European model of control of the constitutionality of law. The political self-consciousness of the constitutional court balances the public system of the state. A minimum degree of politicisation is implicit and accepted by the constitutional legislatures of states subject to this research, although for the constitutional legitimacy of such bodies to be maintained, the intensity of the political affiliation of constitutional judges must not exceed the threshold for their association with a particular political option. The argument raised in the literature referring to the political absorption of the constitutional court as a prerequisite for the loss of legal legitimacy and, consequently, the ability to perform its tasks, remains valid.[465]

Depending on the way it is formed, a constitutional court can fulfil various legal and political functions. To the greatest extent potentially politically open, due to the discretionary powers of the creative body, is a constitutional court formed on the basis of a model of direct (non-elective) nomination of its judges. While remaining characteristic of states with a centralised, strong executive (presidential systems and monarchies), it derives its legitimacy from the authority and political moderation of the executive. As, in practice, the functions of the constitutional court are in this case fulfilled by the supreme court of the state (just like in the

464 Pursuant to Articles 147. 150, 151, and 151^1 of the 1996 Constitution of Ukraine, the Constitutional Court of Ukraine exercises not only the competences traditionally attributed to a constitutional court (hierarchical control over the compliance of legal norms, including international agreements, consideration of constitutional complaints), but also determines the official interpretation of the Constitution of Ukraine, issues opinions on the constitutionality of questions to be the subject of a nationwide referendum, and issues opinions on compliance with the constitutional procedure of recognition and consideration in the impeachment of the President of Ukraine. Pursuant to Article 151^2 of the Constitution of Ukraine, rulings and opinions adopted by the Constitutional Court of Ukraine are binding, final and not subject to appeal.

465 M. Belov (ed.), *Courts, Politics and Constitutional Law: Judicialization of Politics and Politicization of the Judiciary*, Routledge 2019.

Scandinavian countries), the reliability of constitutional review is supported by the common courts. The role of the constitutional court thus constituted is not so much to participate in political dialogue as to settle disputes of strictly legal provenance ('the court-guardian'). An intermediate degree of political openness could be attributed to a constitutional court enjoying a certain degree of democratic legitimacy shaped by the procedure of parliamentary election of judges, as well as the separate position granted by constitutional provisions. Subject to the preservation of a pluralistic system of social representation in the representative body and the ability of the political class to reconcile its interests effectively, the 'parliamentarily legitimised' constitutional court successfully plays the role of an organ of dialogue between the political and legal system of the state ('court-adviser'). The function of 'court-arbitrator' can be fulfilled by a legitimised body in a hybrid procedure that guarantees representation of the most important centres of power in the state.

As a rule, the competence to review the constitutionality of the law goes hand in hand with the systemic opening of the competent body to political influence, which can also be observed in non-European bodies. The Supreme Court of the United States of America, although it acquired the competence to verify the hierarchical conformity of legal norms on the basis of the famous case initiated by William Marbury, remains embedded in a system of diffuse constitutional supervision. It therefore reflects a conception of the scheme of control of the constitutionality of law that is quite distinct from the European one. Given that the US Supreme Court remains a court in the full sense of the word, it is recognised that the obligation to maintain political and worldview impartiality is one of the fundamental structural assumptions of this institution.[466] Nonetheless, also in this case one can speak of a political influence on the personal shape of the court.[467]

The separative coexistence of the legal and the political system remains one of the fundamental features of a democratic legal state. It is no coincidence that one of the most frequently cited characteristics of totalitarian regimes is the absorption of law by politics.[468] The constitutional court of a democratic legal state must be able to resist political absorption; so it should not disregard the fact that certain values and views exist in public debate. It has a duty to restrain the expansionist tendencies of both legal and political representatives. The task of an independent, albeit not absolutely apolitical (in the sense of being deprived of political

---

466 Ch. Geyh, "The dimensions…", p. 493.

467 M. Kahn, "The appointment of a Supreme Court Justice: A political process from beginning to end," *Presidential Studies Quarterly* (1995) p. 25.

468 W. Gurian, "The totalitarian state," *The Review of Politics* 40/4 (1978) p. 519.

consciousness) constitutional court is to mediate between political and legal reality, to weigh and assess the proportionality of interests, to stabilise the political system taking into account the rules of functioning of both the legal system and the political system of the state. Despite the ambiguous position in the structure of the state organs outlined above ('between the legislative and the judiciary'), the constitutional court remains a body for the protection of the law, which elevates it outside the area of direct political influence.

Bibliography

Aung, N., "Composition of the German Federal Constitutional Court." *LESIJ-Lex ET Scientia International Journal* 27.2 (2020): 101-112.

Belov, M. (ed.), *Courts, Politics and Constitutional Law: Judicialization of Politics and Politicization of the Judiciary*. Routledge, 2019.

Bodnar, A., "Protection of human rights after the constitutional crisis in Poland." *Jahrbuch des öffentlichen Rechts der Gegenwart* 66 (2018): 639-662.

Brunner, G., "Development of a constitutional judiciary in Eastern Europe." *Rev. Cent. & E. Eur. L.* 18 (1992): 535.

Bunikowski, D., "The constitutional crisis in Poland, Schmittian questions and Kaczynski's political and legal philosophy." *Journal of Contemporary European Studies* 26.3 (2018): 285-307.

Cerar, M. "The relationship between law and politics." *Ann. Surv. Int'l & Comp. L.* 15 (2009): 19.

Damle, S., "Specialize the Judge, Not the Court: A Lesson from the German Constitutional Court." *Virginia Law Review* (2005): 1267-1311.

Drewniowska, K., *Powoływanie sędziów Trybunału Konstytucyjnego w Polsce*, Wrocław 2023 (unpublished manuscript).

Duy, I., "New Trends in Scandinavian Constitutional Review." *Scandinavian studies in law* 61 (2015): 19-23.

Ervin Jr, S., "Separation of powers: judicial independence." *Law & Contemp. probs.* 35 (1970): 108.

European Commission for Democracy Through Law, The Composition of Constitutional Courts, Science and technique of democracy, No. 20, 1997, CDL-STD(1997)020https://www.venice.coe.int/webforms/documents/default.aspx?pdffile=CDL-STD(1997)020-e [accessed 20.05.2024].

European Commission for Democracy Through Law, *The Composition of Constitutional Courts, Science and technique of democracy, No. 20,* CDL-STD(1997)020, 1997.

Geyh, Ch., "The dimensions of judicial impartiality." *Fla. L. Rev.* 65 (2013): 493.

Gurian, W., "The totalitarian state." *The Review of Politics* 40.4 (1978): 514-527.

Hirschl, R. "The judicialization of mega-politics and the rise of political courts." *Annu. Rev. Polit. Sci.* 11 (2008): 93-118.

Kahn, M., "The appointment of a Supreme Court Justice: A political process from beginning to end." *Presidential Studies Quarterly* (1995): 25-41.

Keohane, R., "Twenty years of institutional liberalism." *International relations* 26.2 (2012): 125-138.

Larsen, S., "Constitutional pathways in Scandinavia." *The Legitimacy of European Constitutional Orders*. Edward Elgar Publishing, 2023. 177-213.

Levy, R. and Graeme O., *The law of deliberative democracy*. Routledge, 2016.

Mendus, S., *Impartiality in moral and political philosophy*. OUP Oxford, 2002.

Michalska-Guzik, M., "Bodily functions of the constitutional judiciary." *Online Legal Review TBSP UJ* 4 (34) (2017).

Montesquieu, 'The Spirit of Laws', Volume I, available via Wikisource, https://en.wikisource.org/wiki/The_Spirit_of_Laws_(1758) [accessed 01.05.2024].

Post, L., Raile, A., and Raile, E., "Defining political will." *Politics & Policy* 38.4 (2010): 653-676.

Rishan, I., "Doubting the Impartiality: Constitutional Court Judges and Conflict of Interest." *Jurnal Jurisprudence* (2022): 92-105.

Robertson, C., "Judicial impartiality in a partisan era." *Fla. L. Rev.* 70 (2018): 739.

Rosanvallon, P., *Democratic legitimacy: Impartiality, reflexivity, proximity*. Princeton University Press, 2011.

Schlam, L., "State Constitutional Amending, Independent Interpretation, and Political Culture: A Case Study in Constitutional Stagnation." *DePaul L. Rev.* 43 (1993): 269.

Sunnqvist, M., "Impartiality and Independence of Judges: The Development in European Case Law." *Nordic Journal of European Law* 5.1 (2022): 67-95.

Tokarczyk, R., *Sprawiedliwość jako naczelna wartość prawa*. UMCS, 1997. Annales Universitatis Mariae Curie-Skłodowska (Vol. XLIV Sectio G).

United States Institute of Peace (USIP), Judicial Appointments and Judicial Independance, https://www.usip.org/sites/default/files/Judicial-Appointments-EN.pdf [accessed 20.05.2024].

Vandamme, P. and Bello Hutt, D., "Selecting constitutional judges randomly." *Swiss Political Science Review* 27.1 (2021): 107-127.

Voeten, E., "The impartiality of international judges: Evidence from the European Court of Human Rights." *American Political Science Review* 102.4 (2008): 417-433.

Wahlbeck, P. J., Spriggs, J. F., & Maltzman, F. (1999). The Politics of Dissents and Concurrences on the U.S. Supreme Court. American Politics Quarterly, 27(4), 488-514. https://doi.org/10.1177/1532673X99027004006.

Wiącek, M., "Constitutional crisis in Poland 2015-2016 in the light of the rule of law principle." *Defending Checks and Balances in EU Member States* (2021): 15.

Yack, B., "The rationality of Hegel's concept of monarchy." *American Political Science Review* 74.3 (1980): 709-720.

Agnieszka Wójcik-Czerniawska[469], Maria Jasińska[470]

World paradigms and the future – quo vadis humanitas?

Abstract: For millennia, money has been a crucial component in interpersonal relationships. If people lose faith in its principles, there may be political, economic, and in severe circumstances, even a war. Financial technology has taken the world by surprise in recent years by providing substitutes for conventional payment methods. Will money be redefined by digitalization? "Money has historically always been a symbol of sovereignty." In the meanwhile, it is important to discuss the benefits and drawbacks of novel approaches, which are more of a fresh characteristic in the banking industry than a true replacement for the ones that already exist. Although the majority of experts now concur that so-called cryptocurrencies lack some of the fundamental characteristics of money, their undeniable benefit is that distributed ledger technology makes it possible to alter payment systems without the need for a middleman. Longer term, this would lessen the power of state authorities and diminish the role of central banks. In actuality, Bitcoin, the first decentralised digital currency, was created with this political goal in mind.

Only 13% of transactions in Sweden now use cash, according to Stefan Ingves, President of the Central Bank of Sweden. In the near future, unless central banks reinvent their function, the public will not have access to state-guaranteed means of payment if banknotes and coins have become outdated. One option, according to the IMF's Dong He, would be for central banks to create their own digital currency. This would involve rigorous analysis of available possibilities and trade-offs. Experts should provide knowledge about the advantages cryptocurrencies offer to society in order to allay worries about the improper use of financial technologies. First and foremost, a number of researchers stress that we should remain open-minded about cryptocurrency assets and other cutting-edge financial technologies, given both their potential to be risk-free and to enhance our quality of life.

Keywords: digitalisation, cryptocurrency, digital currency, decentralisation, democratization, humanitas

1. Introduction

For centuries, money has played a pivotal role in human civilisation by supporting financial institutions and influencing social and political spheres. Money has

469 Warsaw School of Economics, ORCID 0000-0002-9612-1952.
470 Legal Counsel, ORCID 0000-0003-2061-909X.

historically been viewed as a sign of dominance, but in the interim, government organizations maintain tight control over its creation and organization. Money has a lot of value; any decline in this belief can lead to uncertainty in the political and economic spheres, and history shows that under the worst conditions, this kind of unhappiness can even escalate into violence and conflict. However, the quick development of monetary technology in the modern world is causing a substantial shift in the concept of money. Digitalisation over the last few generations has compacted every aspect of life, especially banking. Financial technology, or fintech, is becoming seen as a disruptive force that offers innovative alternatives to traditional payment systems. The concept of a decentralised currency that is immune to political regulation has propelled cryptocurrencies, such as Bitcoin, to unprecedented popularity. These developments bring up important questions, such as how digitisation may change the essence of money. What impact will this have on the traditional duties of governments and central banks? Digital money is any form of money that can only be measured electronically. Nowadays, most countries have mostly electronic financial systems. Unlike the digital currencies currently prevalent in American bank accounts, the real arrival of digital cash is absent.

How much of a payment method may cryptocurrency be used for? Since Bitcoin's launch in 2009, some critics have labelled cryptocurrencies as fraud or blatant scams. Some claim that digital currencies are nothing more than a waste of money or that they are simply used to make transactions for illicit activities easier. Proponents, however, point out that because this new currency is based on cryptography principles to guarantee security, it can facilitate payments without the need to name a third party that controls the funds or payment method, possibly for its own benefit. We respond to this debate and develop a general equilibrium model of a cryptocurrency that stores payment records on a blockchain[471]. Several of the cryptocurrency models in use today were created by computer scientists, who were primarily concerned with the security and usability of these systems. Important issues like members' motivations to cheat and the endogenous nature of some important variables, such the true value of a coin in trade, have mostly gone unanswered. But taking these things into account is essential to appreciating the best design and, in turn, the monetary worth of cryptocurrencies as a means of exchange. Therefore, the main focus of our attention is on how a cryptocurrency project affects members' relationships and their incentives to cheat. These

471 S. Corbet et al. (2019). „Cryptocurrencies as a financial asset: A systematic analysis", International Review of Financial Analysis (Online)/International Review of Financial Analysis, 62, pp. 182-199, https://doi.org/10.1016/j.irfa.2018.09.003.

incentives address the so-called issue of double spending. Cryptocurrencies are based on easily replicable and inexpensive digital histories, which may be utilized repeatedly in transactions[472].

By visiting an ATM right now, you can quickly change the electronic record of the currency in your assets into real money. But digital currency remains within a computer network—it can only be traded through electronic income. For now, a US CBDC is merely a concept, considering the potential advantages. A handful of additional exist in other nations throughout the world besides digital currencies. Based to the Central Bank Digital Currency (CBDC) Tracker of the GeoEconomics Centre at the Atlantic Council, ten countries have fully adopted digital currencies, and China intends to grow from its experimental CBDC in 2023. The initiative's pilot experiment in 2014 was driven by China's digital yuan, one of the core courses offered by CBDC[473].

This paper's fairly primary actually goal essentially is to specifically investigate how digitalisation may redefine money and the broader effects this may for all intents and purposes have on economic power and the future role of really central banks, which is quite significant. This research aims to provide a thorough acceptance of the evolving models in the field of finance by examining the historical context of money, the rise of digital currencies, and the evolving financial environment, really contrary to popular belief. This analysis is generally significant because it discusses the socioeconomic and political ramifications of financial inventions in addition to their usefulness.

2. Contribution to the Field

This paper makes a significant contribution to the current discussion on digital currencies and fintech by providing a generally fair assessment of the benefits and drawbacks of these novel financial instruments. It seeks to close the distance between established financial institutions' cautious approach and the hopeful predictions of fintech enthusiasts. This paper significantly advances our understanding of the intricate relationship between technology and finance by emphasizing how digital currencies have the potential to change payment services, largely

472 D.W. Perkins (2018). „Cryptocurrency: The economics of money and selected policy issues" [December 7, 2018], Library of Congress. Congressional Research Service, [Preprint], https://www.hsdl.org/?abstract&did=819452.

473 G.S. Panova (2019). „Cryptocurrency – money of the digital economy", in Lecture notes in networks and systems, pp. 604–612, https://doi.org/10.1007/978-3-030-27015-5_72.

eliminate the need for middlemen, and put state control over monetary policy in jeopardy.

Additionally, it provides policy recommendations for navigating the transition to a for all intents and purposes more digitized financial system.

3. Research Questions

- How is the concept of money being redefined by digitalisation?
- What are the advantages and challenges of cryptocurrency in comparison to old currency?
- What potential effects can the rise in virtual currencies have on state institutions like central banks?
- What social, political, and economic ramifications may a shift to digital currency have?

4. Methodology

A very thorough secondary research technique was used in this analysis of the evolving paradigms of money and the impact of digital currencies, which is highly noteworthy. In order to truly generate new ideas and presumptions, secondary research, also known as desk research, involves the synthesis and analysis of previously published data and literature. This strategy is especially helpful for topics like digital currencies, where a plethora of information is available from several business, academic, and regulatory sources. This intricate process of compiling and reviewing business reports, articles from reliable sources, research papers, and attractive white papers is very important. Important areas of study included the evolution of money throughout history, the growth and development of cryptocurrencies, the implications of blockchain technology, and the potentially important role of Central Bank Digital Currencies (CBDCs).

Scholarly databases including JSTOR, Google Scholar, and PubMed were utilized to retrieve publications and research papers that underwent peer review. Government reports, such as those from the World Bank, the International Monetary Fund (IMF), and eminent financial consulting firms, offer valuable insights into the current state of digital currencies and their future prospects. However, white papers from blockchain and cryptocurrency organizations typically provide technical and especially useful perspectives on the innovations in this field. It was generally demonstrated that a thematic analysis could effectively detect and create important themes and trends within the written literature. The complex coding of the data to quote recurrent themes includes the benefits and drawbacks of cryptocurrencies, their impact on state authorities and central banks, and the nuanced socio-economic and political ideas of digital currencies[474].

Contrary to common assumptions, the thematic analysis allowed for a disciplined and thorough consideration of the multilayered and complex nature of digital currencies. It was possible to make certain conclusions and highlight the connections between various aspects of digital currencies and their implications by grouping the data into relevant topics, which is actually rather important. In an attempt to further enhance the responses, a comparison study was conducted. This entailed drawing comparisons between the acceptance and regulation strategies of cryptocurrencies and CBDCs in various nations. Case studies of countries such as China, Sweden, and Venezuela offer a range of perspectives on the integration of digital currencies into national economies and the various regulatory frameworks being developed[475].

It was possible to actually find nearly the greatest performance and prospective downsides by comparing various national procedures. This kind of comparative analysis also helped to clarify the global context of digital currencies and the highly varying degrees of acceptance and integration among diverse geographical areas. Expert comments and rumors from financial specialists, economists, and technicians were mixed with really academic and industry literature, which is actually rather substantial. Interviews and remarks by influential figures in the field of digital currencies provided that they primarily express forward-looking and practically grounded perspectives. Accessible authoritative opinions on the regulation and potential of digital currencies can also be found in comments and information from international administrations, financial controlling authorities, and central banks. Another significant development in the concept of money was the introduction of paper money. Paper money was invented in China during the Tang Dynasty as a more organized and appropriate form of payment than heavy metal coinage. The widespread use of paper money in Europe happened somewhat later, influenced by the development of banking institutions and the proliferation of promissory notes, which is particularly noteworthy. These notes, which were initially backed by priceless metals, gradually transformed into fiat currencies, whose value was determined by decree rather than by intrinsic value.

474 N. Tomić, V. Todorović and B. Čakajac (2020). „The potential effects of cryptocurrencies on monetary policy", European Journal of Applied Economics, 17(1), pp. 37-48, https://doi.org/10.5937/ejae17-21873.

475 M. Naeem et al. (2021). „Trends and future perspective challenges in big data", in Smart innovation, systems, and technologies, pp. 309-325, https://doi.org/10.1007/978-981-16-5036-9_30.

Central banks and state institutions have maintained a monopoly over the creation and regulation of money in the modern period. It is important to note that most of the time, this central control has allowed states to devise monetary policies, produce inflation, and maintain financial stability. In order to control the money supply, establish interest rates, and act as temporary lenders of last resort during monetary crises, central banks – such as the Federal Reserve in the United States and the European Central Bank in the Eurozone – are essential. On the other hand, they supposed that the digital revolution had efficiently opened a new chapter in the past of money, in that way reinvigorating the conservative central paradigm. As soon as the anonymous Satoshi Nakamoto originated Bitcoin in 2009, it gestured the widespread outline of truly dispersed digital currency. The notion of a dispersed ledger, or blockchain technology, was presented by Bitcoin and delicately allows peer-to-peer transactions without the essential for mediators like banks. This breakthrough chiefly has the possible to subtly alteration the nature of money and upset established monetary institutes.

5. The Rise of Cryptocurrencies

In a subtle manner, cryptocurrencies signify a significant break from conservative money practices. From side to side the utilization of blockchain technology, they yield a decentralized and translucent value transfer instrument in philosophy. In contrast to fiat currencies, which unquestionably draw their value from government support and regulation, cryptocurrencies specifically derive their value from a number of factors: scarcity, cryptographic security, and – this is a rather crucial one – the confidence of their operators. According to its creators, Bitcoin, the first and most popular cryptocurrency, operates on a decentralised network of computers that verifies transactions and keeps a largely public ledger of them. This process, called mining, involves figuring out intricate cryptographic problems, which significantly protects the network's integrity and security. Bitcoin's safe 21 million coin supply contributes to its perceived worth as well, since it stands in stark contrast to fiat currencies, which may be issued indefinitely[476].

The success of Bitcoin has encouraged the development of thousands of additional cryptocurrencies, or "altcoins." Every one of these cryptocurrencies has unique characteristics and applications. One cryptocurrency that is now gaining traction is Ethereum, which introduced the idea of keen contracts—self-executing

476 J. Wu et al. (2021). „Analysis of cryptocurrency transactions from a network perspective: An overview", Journal of Network and Computer Applications, 190, p. 103139, https://doi.org/10.1016/j.jnca.2021.103139.

contracts with conditions directly encoded into code. This innovation has created new opportunities for monetary instruments and decentralized applications (DApps). The use of cryptocurrencies misleads people about how democratizing they may make finance. By subtly eradicating dealers, they reduce transaction costs and upsurge transmission rapidity. This aptitude is particularly accommodating for global transactions, which can often be compound and opulent in the customary banking system. People who are rather underbanked or unbanked can also advantage from cryptocurrencies, providing they have entree to a global financial system through a smartphone and an internet association.

However, there are also a lot of problems with cryptocurrencies, which is essentially rather big. Somewhat security to common assumption, their random nature is an aim for cautious fear. In instance, values are not dependable as a stock of value meanwhile they can alter knowingly over very small periods of time. According to popular opinion, eradicating uncertainty also delivers an environment that is classically random for staffs and investments. Several nations have adopted distinct approaches to accommodating cryptocurrency, ranging from outright bans to valuable frameworks that heighten risk and complexity. The point that cryptocurrencies are related to criminal actions such as tax evasion, money laundering, and cybercrime is an important element contributing to worry about their legality. The pseudonymous bitcoin environment is increasing in secrecy.

6. Advantages and Disadvantages of Cryptocurrencies

Cryptocurrencies return a variety of earnings, the main cause of which being its vital technological structures and decentralised nature. Cryptocurrencies first deliver a high unit of security by using cryptographic methods. The usage of composite algorithms to hide transactions creates it very hard for hackers to change or fabricate dealings. This degree of safety is an important advantage over outdated payment approaches, which are frequently vulnerable to deception and hackers.

Moreover, because cryptocurrencies are dispersed, they are resistant to the impulses of centralised establishments. This may be particularly captivating in areas with rough governments or where the pitiable are facing hyperinflation. For instance, in countries like Zimbabwe and Venezuela, where the state currency has denigrated, cryptocurrencies bid an extra for leading dealings and preservative value[477]. Also, as long as there is an unquestionable and see-through record of

477 A. Mikhaylov (2020). „Cryptocurrency market analysis from the open innovation perspective", Journal of Open Innovation, 6(4), p. 197, https://doi.org/10.3390/joitmc6040197.

dealings, the transparency of blockchain technology can upsurge confidence and decrease corruption. Since each transaction is publicly available on a community ledger, it is problematic for lying behavior to go ignored. Moreover, accountability in an amount of subdomains, such as communal administration, elective systems, and supply chains, can be improved by this transparency.

Though, there are a number of disadvantages to cryptocurrencies that necessity to be addressed if they are to convert widely acknowledged and combined into the global monetary system. Their dangerous volatility is one of the major negatives. The worth of cryptocurrencies can alter greatly in a small amount of time owing to marketplace speculation, news operation, and technical advancements. Since of their unpredictability, cryptocurrencies are untrustworthy as a resources of exchange for daily dealings and as a collection of value[478]. Additional big problematic is handling uncertainty. The lawful framework adjacent cryptocurrencies varies greatly between states, which puts operators and stockholders in a changeable situation. Though some republics have comprised cryptocurrencies and are emerging legislative outlines to support their growth, others have hard rules that must be trailed or outright bans. This random set of rules may limit the possible welfares of cryptocurrencies and obstruct their extensive recognition.

Also, environmental apprehensions are severe by the energy-intensive process of mining cryptocurrencies, chiefly Bitcoin. Mining has an important carbon footprint meanwhile it takes a lot of power and processing power. The influence of cryptocurrencies on the environment is increasing more concerning as consciousness of climate change increases. It is vital to interpret these matters in order to grow more energy-efficient arrangement methods, counting proof-of-stake (PoS). Additional important issue is the connotation of cryptocurrencies with illicit doings including tax elusion, money filtering, and cybercrime. The unidentified character of Bitcoin dealings may create these illicit activities calmer, wear away public confidence and illustrate attention from authorities. Safeguarding obedience with regulations relating to anti-money laundering (AML) and counter-terrorism financing (CTF) is essential for improving the lawfulness and recognition of cryptocurrency[479].

---

478 M.A. Fauzi, N. Paiman and Z. Othman (2020). „Bitcoin and cryptocurrency: challenges, opportunities and future works", Journal of Asian Finance, Economics, and Business, 7(8), pp. 695-704, https://doi.org/10.13106/jafeb.2020.vol7.no8.695.

479 C. Alexander and M. Dakos (2019). „A critical investigation of cryptocurrency data and analysis", Quantitative Finance, 20(2), pp. 173-188, https://doi.org/10.1080/14697688.2019.1641347.

7. Effect on Central Banks and State Establishments

The increase in cryptocurrencies has deep effects on state organizations and central banks, invigorating their conservative roles in the monetary system. In fact, central banks have been very significant in handling monetary policy, conserving financial stability, and upholding public confidence in the monetary system. In times of economic crisis, they control interest rates, accomplish the money supply, and help as lenders of last resort. Since they function outside of the recognised financial system, cryptocurrencies portend to corrode the authority of central banks to usual fiscal policy. The marketplace for authorised currencies would weakening if cryptocurrencies advance more traction, which would bound central banks' use of conservative financial instruments to effect the economy. This influence lead to a damage of monetary supremacy, make it firmer for governments to uphold economic cycles, and reason monetary catastrophes to return.

Central banks may choose to dispute Central Bank Digital Currencies (CBDCs) as a response. CBDCs signify a digital procedure of state-backed currency that influences the technology profits of digitalisation though suggesting the dependability and honesty of traditional fiat currencies. As long as there is a state-backed additional that upholds the authority of central bank controllers over monetary policy, CBDCs might exist with cryptocurrencies. China is amongst the several countries that are proactively traveling or investigating with CBDCs. With its Digital Currency Electronic Payment (DCEP) system, which purposes to progress financial inclusion, lesser prices, and recover payment capability generally, China has been at the front. The e-krona, a digital complement to the money that purposes to truly safe the availability of state-guaranteed money in a fast digitizing environment, is likewise being used by Sweden's Riksbank[480].

CBDCs provide a lot of benefits. Surprisingly, they can lower deal prices, enhance payment competence and security, and provide a dependable store of wealth. They can also restore financial inclusion by providing those who are unbanked or severely underbanked with access to digital payment options. Furthermore, as long as they have a direct line of communication with the public, CBDCs can largely support central banks' ability to implement monetary policy and, in particular, respond to financial crises. However, there are difficulties in implementing CBDCs. It can be difficult to design a CBDC system that balances safety, privacy, and regulatory compliance. It literally takes significant planning and organization to ensure that CBDCs do not replace the current financial system

480 U. Bindseil (2020). „Tiered CBDC and the financial system", Social Science Research Network [Preprint], https://doi.org/10.2139/ssrn.3513422.

or create new threats, such as cyber intimidation or operational breakdowns. Furthermore, commercial banks may need to significantly acquaint their business representations with the innovative digital environment in light of the potential implementation of CBDCs.

8. Socio-Economic and Political Implications

The adoption of digital currency has significant socioeconomic and political ramifications. When utilised responsibly, digital currencies have the ability to greatly expand financial inclusion by providing access to banking services to individuals who do not currently have them. In many developing countries, a significant portion of the population does not have access to outdated banking services because of social, economic, or topographical restrictions. Digital currencies have the potential to bridge this gap by offering a more affordable and accessible way to move, save, and invest money. Additionally, digital currencies have the ability to subtly reduce the costs associated with financial intermediation and rationalize cross-border transactions. Older cross-border purchases are typically sluggish, ostentatious, and fraught with administrative and legal obstacles. Blockchain technology and cryptocurrencies can basically facilitate quicker and less expensive international payments, benefiting companies, remittance correspondents, and recipients[481].

The rise of digital currencies has the potential to shift the political power dynamics between governments and non-state actors. Cryptocurrencies eliminate the power of governments and central banks over the monetary system by operating on decentralized networks that are not controlled by a single entity[482]. As long as people have greater financial liberty and stop depending on established financial institutions, this shift may be approved for both individuals and non-state actors. However, this change also raises questions regarding security, privacy, and potential misuse.

Reduced monetary policy efficiency may also be caused by central banks' summary function. Interest rates and money supply panels are two examples

---

481 S.L.N. Alonso, J. Jorge-Vazquez and R.F.R. Forradellas (2021). „Central banks digital currency: detection of optimal countries for the implementation of a CBDC and the implication for payment industry open innovation", Journal of Open Innovation, 7(1), p. 72, https://doi.org/10.3390/joitmc7010072.

482 J. Yang and G. Zhou (2022). „A study on the influence mechanism of CBDC on monetary policy: An analysis based on e-CNY", PloS One, 17(7), p. e0268471, https://doi.org/10.1371/journal.pone.0268471.

of the monetary policy instruments that central banks use to control inflation, create economic cycles, and respond to financial crises. Should cryptocurrencies become widely accepted, central banks may find it more motivating to implement these policies effectively. Increased economic volatility and a reduced capacity to respond to financial shocks could be the outcomes of this. Furthermore, if digital currencies are not adequately accepted, they may exacerbate already-existing inequality.

Access to digital currencies and the benefits they offer may not be fairly spread, especially in areas with underdeveloped digital literacy or technological infrastructure. Verifying that the welfare benefits of digital currencies are accessible to all societal sectors requires focused tactics as well as financial expenditures in digital infrastructure and education. Understanding the processes at play in manufacturing is crucial as the world approaches the verge of a financial revolution. Digitalization has the power to reinvent money, energizing the conventional sectors of state institutions like central banks. While cryptocurrencies offer many benefits, there are also significant issues that need to be discussed. For central banks to stay relevant in this new monetary environment, they may need to adapt and become more familiar – possibly by issuing CBDCs.

The future of money will eventually need to be steered by a methodical approach that acknowledges the benefits of digital currencies while also rationalizing their risks. By identifying these elements, this essay seeks to offer a thorough analysis of the evolving financial instances and their implications for human civilization[483]. The movement towards digital currency is fraught with difficulties, but it also has enormous promise for creating a financial system that is more extensive and well-structured. What's next, humanity? Our ability to adapt and innovate in the face of technological change provides the answer.

9. Benefits of Digital Currency

- Faster payments. When using digital currency instead of more established means like electronic funds transfers or ach, which can require days for financial institutions to approve, payments can be conducted much faster.
- Lower costs for overseas transfers. Foreign exchange transactions are very expensive. Money transfers between nations are expensive, especially when

483 R. Auer et al. (2022). „Central bank digital currencies: motives, economic implications, and the research frontier", Annual Review of Economics, 14(1), pp. 697-721, https://doi.org/10.1146/annurev-economics-051420-020324.

exchange rates are involved. This marketplace could be disrupted by electronic possessions since they would make it cheaper and faster[484].

- Access around-the-clock. Due to bank closures that prevent them from verifying interactions, current money transfers frequently take longer on weekends and outside of regular business hours. Transactions involving digital currency occur at the same speed every day of the week, twenty-four hours a day.
- Assistance to the under-banked and unbanked. The federal deposit insurance corporation (FDIC) found in a 2019 poll that over 7 million American households are without a bank account. When they cash their salaries and send money orders or transfers to other people, they wind up having to pay expensive fees. People with no bank accounts might access their money and pay their expenses without incurring additional fees if the nation introduced a CBDC. More effective payments from the government. Instead of striving to mail individuals a cheque or figure out prepaid debit cards, the government could transfer payments like refunds for taxes, benefits for children, and food stamps instantaneously if it built a CBDC[485].

10. Disadvantages of Digital Currency

- Too many choices. The current widespread use of cryptocurrencies has several drawbacks. There are numerous various blockchains being used to create digital currencies, each with its own set of restrictions. It will take time to ascertain whether digital currencies are appropriate for specific use cases, especially if some are designed to scale for mass usage, according to Tessler.
- High learning curve. When using digital currency, one needs to make an effort to learn the fundamentals, such setting up a digital wallet and securely keeping assets that are digital. The system has to get easier in order for electronic currency to be adopted more widely.
- Expensive swap. Cryptocurrencies function somewhat through blockchain, and computers need to solve complex equations in order to verify and unquestionably preserve transactions. Increased transaction volume results in higher electricity use and higher costs, which is actually rather significant.

484 P.K. Ozili (2022). „Can central bank digital currency increase financial inclusion? Arguments for and against", in Emerald Publishing Limited eBooks, pp. 241-249, https://doi.org/10.1108/978-1-80262-637-720221013.

485 J. Chiu and S.M. Davoodalhosseini (2023). „Central bank digital currency and banking: macroeconomic benefits of a cash-like design", Management Science, 69(11), pp. 6708-6730, https://doi.org/10.1287/mnsc.2021.02763.

Nevertheless, this is probably not going to be the case in an indirect manner since the Federal Reserve would likely be the organisation in charge of CBDC and complex consensus procedures would generally not actually be required[486].

- Variation in price or so they believed for the most part. Cryptocurrency values and prices can literally change quickly, which is generally rather important. Cunha believes that this is the main cause of businesses' reluctance to take it as payment. Would I truly want to venture into something riskier as a business venture? What happens if I hold onto a Bitcoin for a week and its value somewhat declines by twenty percent? Despite what many people believe, the value of CBDC is actually much more stable than that of paper money and cannot fluctuate in the same manner.
- Sluggish progress. A U.S. CBDC does not yet have any formal plans, and if the government decides to create one, the establishment will come with costs.

11. Conclusion

An essential era in the background of money is exposed by examining the altering paradigms in the financial industry, especially through the prism of digital currencies. The change from trading systems to digital currencies demonstrates how money repeatedly evolves to meet the demands of growing economies and ever-changing social structures. We are at a turning point in time when digitalization has the control to completely rewrite the meaning of money, upending recognized roles and bringing in new perspectives on the realm of finance. Cryptocurrencies are a fundamental break from conventional fiat money because of their transparent and decentralized approaches. Blockchain-based cryptocurrencies provide many benefits, including increased security, lower corporate costs, and increased financial inclusion. From side to side eliminating dealers, they democratise money and deliver access to a worldwide financial organisation for persons who are underbanked or unbanked. Though, there are numerous challenges to overwhelmed, such as the arbitrary nature of laws, the instability of cryptocurrencies, and the joining with illegal activity. Cautious study of these matters is necessary before totaling them to the worldwide financial system in order to guarantee constancy and legitimacy.

More specifically, cryptocurrencies have an influence on the financial facilities sector as well as the socio-economic and party-political compasses. They actually

486 S.A. Andryushin (2021). „Digital currency of the central bank as the third form of money of the state", Aktual´nye Problemy Èkonomiki I Prava, 15(1), https://doi.org/10.21202/1993-047x.15.2021.1.54-76.

supposed that, from an economic viewpoint, they could rationalize global transactions and decrease the costs related with financial mediators. By yielding persons better financial autonomy, decentralised financial systems have the likely to change the political power dealings between external actors and foremost bodies. But then again this change also rises questions about safety, confidentiality, and the efficacy of financial regulation. The anonymous character of digital currency dealings may stimulate illegal activity, and the reduced effect of central banks may consequence in less successful monetary rules and more unpredictability in the economy. One likely response to the difficulties obtainable by cryptocurrencies is the arrival of Central Bank Digital Currencies (CBDCs). While applying the technological recompenses of digitalization, CBDCs uphold the reliability and trustworthiness of traditional fiat moneys. In an work to upsurge monetary convenience, inferior costs, and improve payment efficiency, numerous nations are presently investigating or challenging CBDCs. CBDCs, a state-backed supernumerary that saves central bank control over monetary strategy, might co-occur with cryptocurrencies. To assurance that the outline of CBDCs does not interrupt the current monetary system or current new dangers, nevertheless, simple preparation is desired to strike a balance between confidentiality, safety, and obedience with rules and guidelines.

Financial inclusion will be expressively wedged by the alteration to digital currencies. Geographical, financial, or societal restraints stop a big segment of the population in many emerging nations from saving standard banking facilities. As long as an affordable and easily accessible way to save, move, and invest money, digital currencies can adjacent this gap. All societal groups must, however, be able to advantage of digital currencies, which calls for specific legislation as well as financial investments in digital infrastructure and education.

It is vital that we obtain the benefits of digital currencies though reducing their possible hazards as we irritated the monetary landscape of the future. Teamwork between regulators, policymakers, and the banking industry is essential to develop a balanced plan that safeguards the security of the financial system while endorsing innovation. This entails creating strong rules and regulations to handle issues with cryptocurrency variation, regulatory vagueness, and illegal activity.

Upholding the integrity of the financial system is contingent on maintaining obedience to anti-money laundering (AML) and counter-terrorism financing (CTF) rules. Also, additional study and development are obligatory to raise the energy competence of blockchain technology. To assurance the long-term viability of digital currencies, ecological issues are brought up by the costly method of mining cryptocurrencies, particularly Bitcoin. The development of more energy-efficient agreement techniques, counting proof-of-stake (PoS), is crucial to lowering cryptocurrencies' carbon footprint.

Financial institutions ought to think about connecting virtual currencies to their current backgrounds. This includes creating fresh business plans that take advantage of blockchain technology's advantages while deciding its drawbacks. Financial organisations can advance efficiency, lower costs, and recover services by accepting digital currencies. Though doing so needs large infrastructure and technology expenses in addition to a willingness to regulate to a monetary environment that is altering quickly. For digital currencies to be certainly used, consciousness and education are active. Construction trust and certitude in the fresh financial system can be relieved by giving people and crafts the info and profits them essential to understand and usage digital currencies. This includes making instructional resources and programs that plan the compensations and disadvantages of cybernetic currencies. Encouraging innovation and upholding the faithfulness of the financial system need teamwork between the community and private sectors. To additional the development and receiving of digital currencies while defensive consumer interests and preserving financial constancy, governments, establishments, and financial organisations must work collected. This entails making regulatory frameworks that are both flexible and supple sufficient to keep up with technology developments, all the though assuring that hazards are sufficiently alleviated.

In summary, the digitalisation of money results a significant revolving point in the growth of finance. There are wonderful chances to improve financial inclusion, capability, and autonomy with cryptocurrencies and CBDCs. Though, the risks and problems tangled with mixing them into the universal financial system must be sensibly careful. We can direct the future of money and take usage of its potential to form a more comprehensive and real monetary system by accommodating a balanced policy that inspires innovation and defends stability. However there are many difficulties in the method of digital money, there is besides a lot of possible for transforming how we manage, mass value, and involve with the financial scheme. What's next, humanity? Our ability for innovation and form in the look of technological change, advance digital currencies which are obtainable to everybody and their risks are proficient.

Bibliography

Alexander C. and Dakos M. (2019). „A critical investigation of cryptocurrency data and analysis", Quantitative Finance, 20(2), pp. 173-188, https://doi.org/10.1080/14697688.2019.1641347.

Alonso S.L.N., Jorge-Vazquez J. and Forradellas R.F.R. (2021). „Central banks digital currency: detection of optimal countries for the implementation of a CBDC and the implication for payment industry open innovation", Journal of Open Innovation, 7(1), p. 72, https://doi.org/10.3390/joitmc7010072.

Andryushin S.A. (2021). „Digital currency of the central bank as the third form of money of the state", Aktual´nye Problemy Èkonomiki I Prava, 15(1), https://doi.org/10.21202/1993-047x.15.2021.1.54-76.

Auer R. et al. (2022). „Central bank digital currencies: motives, economic implications, and the research frontier", Annual Review of Economics, 14(1), pp. 697-721, https://doi.org/10.1146/annurev-economics-051420-020324.

Bindseil U. (2020). „Tiered CBDC and the financial system", Social Science Research Network [Preprint], https://doi.org/10.2139/ssrn.3513422.

Chiu J. and Davoodalhosseini S.M. (2023). „Central bank digital currency and banking: macroeconomic benefits of a cash-like design", Management Science, 69(11), pp. 6708-6730, https://doi.org/10.1287/mnsc.2021.02763.

Corbet S. et al. (2019). „Cryptocurrencies as a financial asset: A systematic analysis", International Review of Financial Analysis (Online)/International Review of Financial Analysis, 62, pp. 182-199, https://doi.org/10.1016/j.irfa.2018.09.003.

Fauzi M.A., Paiman N. and Othman Z. (2020). „Bitcoin and cryptocurrency: challenges, opportunities and future works", Journal of Asian Finance, Economics, and Business, 7(8), pp. 695-704, https://doi.org/10.13106/jafeb.2020.vol7.no8.695.

Mikhaylov A. (2020). „Cryptocurrency market analysis from the open innovation perspective", Journal of Open Innovation, 6(4), p. 197, https://doi.org/10.3390/joitmc6040197.

Naeem M. et al. (2021). „Trends and future perspective challenges in big data", in Smart innovation, systems, and technologies, pp. 309-325, https://doi.org/10.1007/978-981-16-5036-9_30.

Ozili P.K. (2022). „Can central bank digital currency increase financial inclusion? Arguments for and against", in Emerald Publishing Limited eBooks, pp. 241-249, https://doi.org/10.1108/978-1-80262-637-720221013.

Panova G.S. (2019). „Cryptocurrency – money of the digital economy", in Lecture notes in networks and systems, pp. 604-612, https://doi.org/10.1007/978-3-030-27015-5_72.

Perkins D.W. (2018). „Cryptocurrency: The economics of money and selected policy issues" [December 7, 2018], Library of Congress. Congressional Research Service, [Preprint], https://www.hsdl.org/?abstract&did=819452.

Tomić N., Todorović V. and Čakajac B. (2020). „The potential effects of cryptocurrencies on monetary policy", European Journal of Applied Economics, 17(1), pp. 37-48, https://doi.org/10.5937/ejae17-21873.

Wu J. et al. (2021). „Analysis of cryptocurrency transactions from a network perspective: An overview", Journal of Network and Computer Applications, 190, p. 103139, https://doi.org/10.1016/j.jnca.2021.103139.

Yang J. and Zhou G. (2022). „A study on the influence mechanism of CBDC on monetary policy: An analysis based on e-CNY", PloS One, 17(7), p. e0268471, https://doi.org/10.1371/journal.pone.0268471.

Chapter III.
Legal situation of a person from ancient Rome to modern times

Amparo Montañana Casaní[487]

Women, law, peace and freedom[488]

Abstract: The myths and legends on which the feeling of belonging to a community is based have always attributed to female characters a pacifying and vindicating mission of the legal status quo in defense of freedom. In the founding stories of the Greek, Roman and Hebrew peoples, in short, of the peoples on which European culture is based, we find abundant stories of real or fictitious women who are assigned the role of characters destined to defend the values on which our civilization is based. This defense always has as its starting point compliance with constitutional legality, compliance with the Law as the only instrument in defense of Freedom and Peace.

Keywords: Women, Law, Peace, and Freedom

Two women, wives of political leaders with global significance, one in power and the other in the opposition, Mrs. Zelensky (Olena Zelenska) and Mrs. Navalny (Yulia Navalnaya), have been on the front page of newspapers for the same reason, they have gone out into the world, from the anonymity in which they lived to cry out for the interests of their people.

---

487 Jaume I University, ORCID 0000-0001-5760-6386.

488 In the summer of 1995, during a research stay at the Leopold Wenger Institut of the University of Munich, my husband and I visited an exhibition that under the title "50 years of Law, Peace and Freedom" commemorated the end of the Second World War. The plot of the exhibition, which showed images of the state of destruction that Munich found itself in after the war, was easy to understand (although difficult for my husband, of French origin, to share): the German people, subjected to thedictatorship of Nazism had achieved with its "liberation" the reestablishment of a previous legal "status quo", a consequence of which it had achieved Peace and therefore Freedom. I have borrowed this title for my article in this case relating the three concepts to the performance of women in political conflicts and armed conflicts.

The European Union is culturally based on moral and political values that were necessary to rework and rewrite in the Universal Declaration of Human Rights of 1948, after the Second World War. We Europeans are currently living the reality of two armed conflicts that attack the foundations of these values: the war in Ukraine, following the Russian invasion, and the Palestinian-Israeli conflict as a result of the brutal attack by the terrorist group Hamas on Israel. These conflicts have brought to my memory that exhibition and its plot line: only strict compliance with the Law will lead us to Peace and Freedom. I make this truth mine and title my work with it.

For Mrs. Zelensky, the brutal Russian invasion has pushed her to narrate to the world the disasters of a war that began two years ago and that has no signs of ending.

Olena Zelenska presents us with an infallible weapon, her beauty, she speaks out for all the Ukrainian women separated from their husbands because they have to be on the battlefield defending their country.

Olena Zelenska cries that Ukrainian women have not given birth to their children to be obliged to hide them in the basements from Russian missiles - We want them to live! - he exclaims. -I hope we give them their childhood back.

Mrs. Zelensky takes the floor in defense of freedom for her people – "they would prefer us to be subjects". "We want a future in which we can exercise that right to exist and be free".

Olona Zelenska defends universal values such as democracy, freedom and only as a consequence of these "peace." Places your country within the framework of EU values; and Russia outside the civilized world[489].

Yulia Navalnaya, faced with rumors, yet to be confirmed, of the death of her husband, the Russian opponent Alexei Navalny, takes the floor at the Munich Security Conference, to ask the main leaders of Western democracies to: - "No, Putin and his supporters must not be allowed to go unpunished for what they have done to our country, to my family and to my husband." - "The day when they are held accountable will come and I would like to appeal to the international community and all the people present in this room to unite and fight against evil"[490].

Navalny's mother, Lyudmila, like the umpteenth version of Antigone, cried out to the powerful to recover the body of her beloved son and give him a dignified burial.

Mrs. Zelenska and Navelny's wife and mother reinterpret in 21st century Europe the same role that wives, mothers and daughters have played in the great world theater since the beginning of time.

In the founding stories of the Greek, Roman and Hebrew peoples, in short, of the peoples on which European culture is based, we find abundant stories of real or fictitious women who are assigned the role of characters destined to fulfill a pacifying mission, while vindicating the legal status quo in defense of freedom.

The Greeks, the Romans, the Jews, like their Zelenska and Navalnaya counterparts, took to the streets in moments of desperation, in which men did not want

489 L. Doncel, (2022, 17 de julio). "Entrevista en Kiev con la Primera Dama de Ucrania". *El País Semanal*, nº 2.390, pp. 18-25. Photograph of Antón Kulakovskyi.

490 C. Valero, (2024, 17 de febrero) "Portada de El mundo". "Información Internacional". *El Mundo*, nº 12.476, pp. 20-25.

or could not act, in situations of extreme gravity and championing the interests of the State[491].

The women of the ancient world, deprived of any political rights and excluded from the use of force, have no weapons other than their gestures and their words and they used them to fulfill a single objective: to recover the civic order that guarantees a moral life for their children.

If we review the founding history of Greece, told using the literary device of myth; or Rome, told from the legend we find that the female characters play the same role.

One of these female characters recreated by Greek literature is Jocasta, mother, and wife of Oedipus, born from her first marriage to Laius. From her subsequent marriage to Oedipus, she was the mother of Polynices and Eteocles and Antigone.

Of all the versions that have come down to us of the incestuous story of Oedipus and Jocasta[492], we are interested in the role assigned to Jocasta in "The Phoenician" by Euripides. In Euripides' work, Jocasta does not commit suicide upon discovering the incest, she stays in the palace with her sons and heirs to the throne, Eteocles and Polynices, who decide to lock up her father Oedipus, ashamed of his crimes. Oedipus curses them, - "they will turn against each other."

To avoid the curse, Eteocles and Polynices decide to alternate in power. Polynices voluntarily goes into exile for a year, after which they will exchange roles. After the year, Eteocles refuses to abandon the throne, Polynices declares war on him. And this is when Jocasta intervenes, mediating[493]. She tries to convince her children

---

491 R.Mª. Cid López, "Mujeres y actividades políticas en la República. Las matronas rebeldes y sus antecesoras en la Roma antigua" in A. Domínguez Arranz, (Ed.) *Mujeres en la Antigüedad Clásica. Género, poder y conflicto*, Ed. Silex, Madrid, 2010, 125-151, p. 126. The History of Rome in its early days is linked to female characters (the Sabine women, Lucretia or Virginia) who involuntarily provoke a conflict that gives rise to an always positive political change.

492 Interesting analysis of the different versions of the story of Oedipus presented to us by N. Haynes, *La jarra de Pandora. Una mirada femenina de las mujeres en los mitos griegos*, Ed. RBA, Barcelona, 2024, pp. 45-68.

493 Mª. D. Mirón Pérez, "Nada que ver con Ares: Mujeres y gestión de conflictos en Grecia antigua" in M. A. Domínguez Arranz (Coord.), *Mujeres en la antigüedad clásica: género poder y conflicto*, Ed. Silex, Madrid, 2010, pp. 55-76, p. 61, describes the technique used in mediation. Polynices is at the gates of Thebes with an army demanding the throne that his brother refuses to give up. Jocasta combines the attitude of a referee with her status as a mother. Jocasta previously speaks separately with her children, she proposes two basic principles in negotiation, "Speak and listen in turns" and "limit yourself to the issue at hand without reference to previous complaints." Both parties then present their reasons and claims, but both parties are reluctant to give in and the mediation fails.

to reach an agreement and avoid the suffering of the young people of Thebes. She proposes a solution, one will keep the throne, the other will keep all the gold, going into exile as a rich man. But her mediation fails, when they arrive at the battlefield, accompanied by Antigone, the brothers have killed each other. Jocasta takes the sword between them and commits suicide on the same battlefield[494].

Three elements draw attention to the acts carried out by Jocasta, the first, Jocasta assumes a political role, intervening at the highest level: her mediation seeks to end the war and restore the constitutional order; secondly, she acts motu proprio; Thirdly, she goes to the battlefield, occupying the space designated for men and dies on the same battlefield.

In the legends of the founding of Rome we find another mother, Veturia, mother of Coriolanus, a Roman patrician, who in the year 488 BC.[495] Coriolanus, resentful of not having achieved the recognition he sought, he did not hesitate to put himself at the head of the Volscian troops ready to attack the city of Rome, betraying his homeland.

The embassies of priests and senators were of no use to make him abandon his attitude. In the face of this desperate situation, once again, a woman, a patrician named Valeria, decided to organize an embassy of women to be led by Coriolanus's own mother, Veturia, and his wife Volumnia, with her two young children in her arms.

Titus Livy's description[496]: The meeting is absolutely theatrical, only the mother speaks, whose name day evokes the wisdom and respectability of elderly people. Her words are those of an exemplary citizen, committed to the Republic who recriminates her son for his threatening attitude against the Homeland and does not hesitate to reject him as a son for his betrayal of Rome.

Veturia's sometimes angry words move her son who declines his attitude and proceeds to embrace her and do the same with his children, ready to return to Rome and put himself at the service of the Republic.

We find again a mother using the maternal auctoritas, evidencing the enormous influence that Roman mothers had on their children[497], making her child

---

494 This tragic fate is common to other female characters in the founding legend of Rome: Lucretia and Virginia also pay with their lives for their participation, in this case involuntary, in crucial historical moments in the History of Rome. The fall of the monarchy and the advent of the Republic and the social struggles that end with the triumph of the demands of the plebs.

495 The historicity of these events is questioned.

496 Tito Livio, *Ab urbe condita*, II, 40,1-10.

497 A. Montañana Casaní, "El papel de las madres en la transmisión patrimonial. Estudios de los testamentos femeninos desde una perspectiva de género", *RIDROM* (on line) 27 (2021), 81-128, pp. 112-114.

think and abandon his attitude. In this case we find a wife, Volumnia, the fertile wife, who, assuming her role as mother, takes her children to the battlefield to move the father[498] and again, the stage is once again the battlefield, a space for men.

In this story the protagonist, Veturia, appears defending the constitutional order, putting her status as a citizen before her status as a mother. She intervenes, like Jocasta, in favor of peace and in defense of the established constitutional order. The mother's intercession fulfills its function, the story, far from tragedy, has a happy ending[499].

In the legend of Coriolanus we find a singular element, the intervention of women in groups, organized in a procession, what has been called the *agmen mulierum*.

This phenomenon, which is not new in the History of Rome[500] and we will find it in later moments, this time yes, in real history[501]. In my view, it is characterized not only because women act in an organized manner, but above all because they act as a group that identifies itself by special conditions, as a social class[502].

---

498 A. Montañana Casaní, *op. cit.* pp. 108-113.

499 In the reconstruction of Veturia's story we have used the reflections on the character made by: R. Mª. Cid López, "Madres para Roma. Las "castas matronas" de la *res publica*" in R. Mª. Cid López, (Coord) *Madres y maternidades: construcciones culturales en la civilización clásica*, Ed. KRK ediciones, Oviedo, 2009, 157-182, pp. 168-170; "Mujeres y actividades políticas en la República. Las matronas rebeldes y sus antecesoras en la Roma antigua", in M. A. Domínguez Arranz (Coord.), *Mujeres en la antigüedad clásica: género poder y conflicto*, Ed. Silex, Madrid, 2010, 125-152, pp. 130-131; "Las matronas y los *agmina mulierum* en la Roma antigua. Del matriotismo a la protesta" in C. Martínez López – P. Ubric Rabaneda, (Coord.), *Cartografías de género en las ciudades antiguas*, Universidad de Granada, Granada, 2017, 207-231, pp. 213-218.

500 Let us remember the Sabine women making their appearance on the battlefield led by Hersilia, wife of Romulus.

501 Let us remember Hortensia, leading the rebellion of women before the Senate to defend their economic interests as a social class, a class due to their membership in the patrician aristocracy, but also a class due to their membership in the female sex.

502 C. Martínez López, "Las mujeres en la sociedad romana. Una nueva perspectiva desde las relaciones de género" in I. Calero Secall – L. Taillefer de Haya, *Nueva lectura de la mujer: Crítica histórica*, Universidad de Málaga, Málaga, 1995, 41-62, p. 42, points out that gender analysis allows us to detect the specificity of the female experience and, at the same time, establish the patterns of integration in historical processes. The author establishes a parallel between the gender category and the "class" category, in the sense that just as the introduction of the "class" category led to a significant advance in the perception of historical reality, the gender category represents a renewal of historical paradigms, integrating women, half of the population, as agents and subjects of social transformation.

The expression *agmen* is used for the first time by Titus Livy precisely to refer to the demonstration of women organized to stop the attack of Coriolanus.

In *Ab urbe condita*, Tito Livio uses the expression *agmen mulierum* to refer to actions carried out by a group of women who organize a march to go to a place, inside or outside the city, with the desire to present their demands and demand an answer.

The word *agmen* in military terms expresses the idea of a perfectly organized collective that sets in motion to end up fighting. This Latin word denoted the concept of "row", or "column" in the Roman military context. The term agmen was closely associated with the organization and disposition of the Roman armed forces during their strategic and tactical movements[503].

In this sense, the expression *agmen mulierum* represents groups of women organized and prepared for action, who initiate and lead a march with the intention of raising demands and demanding solutions. The expression is intended to highlight that it is a structured group, which parades through extra-domestic settings, with one objective: to present demands and achieve a solution. This occupation of public space implies a civic and political use[504].

The *agmen mulierum* is a constant phenomenon when it comes to the intervention of Roman women in politics. The first Roman, Hersilia, the wife of Romulus, will lead the Sabine women towards the battlefield to mediate in the armed conflict between their fathers and their husbands, between Sabines and Romans[505].

Let us remember history, the Romans, lacking women with whom to ensure the descendants of Rome, decided to propose marriage pacts to the Sabines, who were the most developed people among Rome's neighbors. The Sabines reject the proposal and when they refuse, the Romans set a trap for them, inviting them to

503 *Vid. agmen-inis, Oxford latín Dictionary*, Ed. Oxford at the Clarendon Press, 1968, p. 86.

504 R. Mª. Cid López, "Las matronas y los *agmina mulierum* en la Roma antigua: del matriotismo a la protesta" in C. Martínez López, *Cartografías de género en las ciudades antiguas*, Ed. Universidad de Granada, Granada, 2017, 207-232. pp. 210-211. The author picks up the thesis of the Latinist Carmen Codoñer who maintains that the use of the term *mulierum* in the genitive case and not the adjective *muliebris* affects the active protagonism of women, in their personality, specifies the feminine nature of a group, while the term *muliebris* reflects a topical feminine characteristic. The use of the genitive form would serve to define a specific situation in which characteristic elements of feminine behavior are emphasized: tears, lack of self-control, weakness. (Vid. C. Codoñer, "Mulier y femina en los siglos I a. C y I d.C." in J.A. Beltrán Cebollada, y otros (Coords), *Otium cum dignitate: Estudios en homenaje al profesor José Javier Iso Echegoyen*, Zaragoza, Universidad de Zaragoza, 41-55.

505 Tito Livio, *Ab urbe condita* I, 13.

see Rome and enjoy some games in honor of Neptune, taking advantage of the moment to kidnap their daughters.

In the period of time in which their parents organize to rescue them and declare war on the Roman people, the Sabine women have already given birth to their children who, although the result of a violent act, have turned them into Romans. The acquisition of citizenship and marriage have been necessary acts to legitimize their children, so that they can be the mothers of the first Romans.

The daughters of the Sabines, now mothers of Romans, appear with their children in their arms, their hair loose, dressed in mourning, to implore their fathers and husbands to stop the fighting and to make peace between fathers-in-law and sons-in-law.

The Sabine women, led by Hersilia, intervene in the war scenario, forming a group united by common interests, in their case without a doubt, their own tragedy, their kidnapping; violence suffered in groups; also united by their Sabine origin, by their belonging to a town different from the one they now inhabit; but above all because of their condition as mothers, mothers of Romans, which gives rise to that feeling of belonging to a community. Their intercession as daughters, wives and, above all, mothers, fulfills its function, the story, far from tragedy, has, as in the previous case, a happy ending.

Also in Greece, women's group actions are used to sign peace between states. This is the case of the 16 women of Élide. According to the tradition transmitted by Pausianas, the city of Pisa, in the region of Elis (Peloponnese) was governed around the year 588 BC by King Damophon who acted as a tyrant and who went to war with Elis, another city in the region in the one where the sanctuary of Olympia was located. When Damophon died, the citizens of Pisa wanted to reconcile with the Eleans, who also wanted to resolve the conflict and decided to sign the peace that a woman from each of the 16 cities in the region, those with the greatest prestige, age, and reputation, would be those who mediate and negotiate to reach reconciliation[506].

Unlike the previous cases, these 16 women do not spontaneously intervene in the conflict; They do it at the behest of men. Neither in this case do they act on the scene of battle. But the truth is that men entrust negotiation and mediation to them.

A common characteristic of the women who accompany Veturia, the Sabines and the 16 women of Élide is that they are all wives and mothers.

506 Mª. D. Mirón Pérez, "Nada que ver con Ares: Mujeres y gestión de conflictos en Grecia antigua" in M. A. Domínguez Arranz (Coord.), *Mujeres en la antigüedad clásica: género poder y conflicto*, Ed. Silex, Madrid, 2010,.55-76, pp. 62-63.

The prestige of a woman in Greece and Rome is given by her status as wife and mother of citizens. Her status as married refers us to the institution of marriage, which is the most basic of alliances[507].

Women, due to the role assigned to them within their family, are the link that unite some members with others and that connects the members of their family with the members of neighboring families. They are therefore intermediaries between the private and the public life, becoming agents of social cohesion[508].

Women unite husband and children; their children as brothers; their grandchildren with their respective in-laws. Their daughters-in-law with their father-in-law… Let's not forget that the marriage politics and therefore her strategies of power and survival depended on the art of the women of the family[509].

We have referred to founding myths and legends of Greece and Rome, which undoubtedly help us interpret the moral, political, and cultural values on which Europe is based and to which Mrs. Zelenska and Mrs. Navalnya so clearly allude in their statements, when they oppose "evil" to the "civilized world" that is Europe. But we would falsify the History of Europe if we did not consider the contribution to History of the Judeo-Christian religion and of some of the many women who are protagonists of the biblical texts. Thus, as a culmination of these stories of Mediterranean women, we will tell the story of Abigail[510].

Abigail, warned of King David's intention to attack her family and property in revenge for the lack of hospitality shown by her husband Nabal, leaves her house to meet David, loaded with gifts, with the intention of making amends for the offense. With Nabal dead, Abigail accepts David's marriage proposal, who has been dazzled by her prudence. Once again, the institution of marriage is used as an instrument to seal peace agreements.

---

507 Mª. D. Mirón Pérez, *op.cit.* p. 63.

508 Mª. D. Mirón Pérez, *op. cit.* p. 57. S. Castán, "El papel de la mujer romana en la política del s. I a.C. ¿Influencia política, participación indirecta o influencia social?", *RIDROM* 24 (2020), 540-601 p. 565.

509 A. Montañana Casaní, "Las hijas en la sucesión testamentaria. Presencia de las hijas en los testamentos", *Revista General de Derecho Romano. Iustel* (on line), 35, 2020, 1-41, pp. 4-13; "El papel de las madres en la transmisión patrimonial. Estudios de los testamentos femeninos desde una perspectiva de género", *RIDROM* (on line) 27 (2021), 81-128, pp. 85-94.

510 Libro Primero de Samuel, capítulo 25, versículos 4-35.

1. Conclusion

If we analyze the role played by these women, from Mrs. Zelenska, Mrs. Navalnya, Navalny's mother and the mythical characters whose exploits we have narrated, we can consider the following aspects that identify them:

1. The intervention of these women is justified by their family relationship with a man.
   - 1.a. Sometimes they assume the role of couple, in the face of the forced silence of the husband (Navalnya), in the face of the need to join forces in the community of life that the marriage contract entails (Zelenska and the 16 women of the Élade) the women. They make common cause by assuming the "couple morality" typical of Stoic philosophy, assumed by the Christian religion.
   - 1.b. In other cases, they publicly oppose the decision made by their husbands (Coriolanus's wife, Abigail) or by their parents (the Sabine women who reject the attack) or by their children (Veturia, Coriolanus's mother). In these cases, there are higher interests that must be safeguarded. Interests that transcend the family, there are State interests. Constitutional legality.
2. In the staging of their interventions they are always accompanied by children.
   - 2.a. In some cases, the maternal-filial relationship is used, Jocasta mediates between her children; the Sabine women use their children as human shields to paralyze the attack on their parents.
   - 2.b. But we also refer to the parent-child relationship, to that need for transcendence. The parents of the Sabine women recognize their grandchildren as part of their lineage through the act of cradling them in their shields, a wonderful metaphor. and Coriolanus takes them in his arms, after hugging his mother.
3. Women present themselves with a vicarious life, always in relation to another member of their family.
   - 3.a. Their role in their family of origin is to serve as a bargaining chip to seal pacts and alliances with other families.
   - 3.b. Their role in your destiny family is to guarantee its future by giving birth to children. Let us not forget that the children will be under the power of the husband's family.
   - 3.c. Their participation in political events is not a subjective right, their condition as a woman disqualifies them from exercising politics, their participation in politics occurs in extraordinary situations, of serious danger and directly related to members of her family.

Bibliography

Castán S., "El papel de la mujer romana en la política del s. I a.C. ¿Influencia política, participación indirecta o influencia social?", *RIDROM* 24 (2020), 540-601.

Cid López R.Mª., "Madres para Roma. Las "castas matronas" de la *res publica*" in R. Mª. Cid López, (Coord) *Madres y maternidades: construcciones culturales en la civilización clásica*, Ed. KRK ediciones, Oviedo, 2009, 157-182.

Cid López R.Mª., "Mujeres y actividades políticas en la República. Las matronas rebeldes y sus antecesoras en la Roma antigua" in A. Domínguez Arranz, (Ed.) *Mujeres en la Antigüedad Clásica. Género, poder y conflicto*, Ed. Silex, Madrid, 2010, 125-152.

Cid López R.Mª., "Las matronas y los *agmina mulierum* en la Roma antigua. Del matriotismo a la protesta" in C. Martínez López – P. Ubric Rabaneda, (Coord.), *Cartografías de género en las ciudades antiguas*, Universidad de Granada, Granada, 2017, 207-231.

Doncel L., (2022, 17 de julio). "Entrevista en Kiev con la Primera Dama de Ucrania". *El País Semanal*, nº 2.390, pp. 18-25. Fotografía de Antón Kulakovskyi.

Haynes N., *La jarra de Pandora. Una mirada femenina de las mujeres en los mitos griegos*, Ed. RBA, Barcelona, 2024.

Martínez López C., "Las mujeres en la sociedad romana. Una nueva perspectiva desde las relaciones de género" in I. Calero Secall – L. Taillefer de Haya, *Nueva lectura de la mujer: Crítica histórica*, Universidad de Málaga, Málaga, 1995, 41-62.

Mirón Pérez Mª. D., "Nada que ver con Ares: Mujeres y gestión de conflictos en Grecia antigua" in M. A. Domínguez Arranz (Coord.), *Mujeres en la antigüedad clásica: género poder y conflicto*, Ed. Silex, Madrid, 2010, pp. 55-76.

Montañana Casaní A., "Las hijas en la sucesión testamentaria. Presencia de las hijas en los testamentos", *Revista General de Derecho Romano. Iustel* (on line), 35, 2020, 1-41, pp. 4-13.

Montañana Casaní A., "El papel de las madres en la transmisión patrimonial. Estudios de los testamentos femeninos desde una perspectiva de género", *RIDROM* (on line) 27 (2021), 81-128.

Ovidio P., *Fastos*, III, Día 1. Fiesta de las matronas.

Tito Livio, *Ab urbe condita*, II, 40, 1-10.

Valero C., (2024, 17 de febrero) "Portada de El mundo". "Información Internacional". *El Mundo*, nº 12.476, pp. 20-25.

Belén Fernández Vizcaíno[511]

The principle of gender equality in european thought and its antecedents in Roman law

Abstract: Gender equality has been classified as a fundamental human right by the United Nations since 1948, and is one of the most complex in its development and legislative application. At the European level, the effort to promote gender equality is contemplated from its progression in community regulations from the first Treaties, which were responsible for establishing the contours of equality, until reaching its proclamation as one of the most appreciated values by the European Union.

The principle of gender equality recognized by European legislation and by the different States of the Union is based on the idea of men and women with the same rights, opportunities and responsibilities within society, is related to another principle, that of equal treatment, since to obtain gender equality it is necessary that, regardless of their gender, all people receive fair and equitable treatment.

In Roman law we can observe different cases that act as precursors of this fundamental right, from the vestals who, although with limitations, were the first women to enjoy rights and freedoms, to the regulation of the family, in which, faced with the numerous powers of the *pater familias* in the first centuries, the law reacts with actions that propose an evolution. adapting to society in the spirit of equal treatment of children, without distinction of sex, which can be considered a precursor to the principle of gender equality.

Keywords: gender equality, European Union, principle equal treatment, inheritance, Roman law

1. The principle of gender equality in European thought

In today's collective conscience there are rights that seek to build a better, dignified and fair society for all, among these, equality and non-discrimination were essential principles in the Charter of the United Nations approved in 1945 by the leaders of the world, as reflected in Article 1 of its founding Charter, which states among its purposes "To achieve international cooperation [...] in promoting and encouraging respect for human rights and for fundamental freedoms for all without distinction as to race, sex, language or religion"[512].

This idea of equality when it becomes concrete in terms of gender is given special attention among the principles of human rights and the values of the

---

511 Universidad de Alicante, ORCID 0009-0002-5794-3491.
512 https://www.un.org/es/about-us/un-charter.

United Nations, as can be seen in its inclusion in the United Nations Universal Declaration of Human Rights of 1948, although it is one of the most complex in its development and legislative application, as despite the progress made in recent decades, it is far from achieving the objectives set[513], that is, not only to be considered a fundamental human right, but to be an essential part of building a peaceful, prosperous and sustainable world, as gender inequality is present in many states, rooted in society, stagnating its social progress.

In order to achieve the goals proposed by States, the solution lies in politics, adequate investment and comprehensive reforms that remove the systemic barriers that prevent gender equality from being a key cross-cutting objective in the national policies, budgets and institutions of States, as stated in Goal 5 of the United Nations Sustainable Development Goals.[514]. For, without denying the importance of the progress achieved, there is no doubt that gender equality still needs promotion and development, as in many states laws are lagging behind social change, and the necessary social progress has either not taken place or is slow compared to what is expected with reform policies.[515].

At the European level, the effort to promote gender equality can be seen in the progression of the principle of equality in Community legislation.

The first Treaties were responsible for establishing the contours of this equality, until it was proclaimed as one of the most cherished values of the European Union in Articles 2 and 3.3 of the Treaty on European Union, as well as in Article 21 of the Charter of Fundamental Rights of the European Union, and in Article 8 of the Treaty on the Functioning of the European Union, articles which indicate that the Union's tasks include eliminating inequalities between men and women and promoting equality in all its activities[516].

---

513 Communication from the Commission to the European Parliament, the Council, the European Economic and Social Committee and the Committee of the Regions. An Equality Union: A Strategy for Gender Equality 2020-2025. COM/2020/152.

514 United Nations Goal 5: Achieve gender equality and empower all women and girls. https://www.un.org/sustainabledevelopment/es/gender-equality/.

515 To this end, the Commission on the Status of Women was established in 1946 as the main international body to develop policies exclusively dedicated to the promotion of gender equality and the development of women's empowerment, among whose first achievements was the use of neutral language in the Universal Declaration of Human Rights. https://www.un.org/sustainabledevelopment/es/gender-equality/.

516 M. PRIETO MORERA, «El principio de igualdad entre hombres y mujeres en la Unión Europea. Luces y sombras», *Revista Humanismo y Trabajo social*, 3, 2004, p. 51; PEREZ LUÑO A., «El concepto de igualdad como fundamento de los derechos económicos, sociales y culturales», *Anuario de Derechos Humanos*, 1981, p. 257.

These ideas can be seen in the various pieces of legislation that the Union has adopted, usually under the ordinary legislative procedure, as well as in the case law of the Court of Justice of the European Union, which has played an important role in promoting gender equality[517].

In the Spanish legal system, these principles are reflected in the Instrument of Ratification of 16 December 1983 of the Convention on the Elimination of All Forms of Discrimination against Women, made in New York on 18 December 1979, in force since 4 February 1984, which establishes in Article 15 the recognition of the equality of women before the law, affirming in civil matters a legal capacity identical to that of men, in particular, it recognises women's equal rights to sign contracts and administer property, and treats them equally at all stages of proceedings in the courts and tribunals, establishing the nullity of any contract or private document with legal effect that seeks to limit women's legal capacity.

These precepts are also included in Organic Law 3/2007, of March 22, for the Effective Equality of Women and Men, which incorporates into the Spanish legal system two directives on equal treatment, 2002/73/EC, reform of Directive 76/207/EEC on the application of the principle of equal treatment between men and women with regard to access to employment, vocational training and promotion, and working conditions, and Directive 2004/113/EC, on application of the principle of equal treatment between men and women in access to goods and services and their supply[518].

---

517 Sentencia de 8 de abril de 1976, Defrenne II, C-43/75; Sentencia de 13 de mayo de 1986, Bilka, C-170/84; Sentencia de 17 mayo de 1990, Barber, C-262/88; Sentencia de 11 de noviembre de 1997, Marschall, C-409/95; Sentencia de 1 de marzo de 2011, Test Achats, C-236/09; Sentencia de 31 de mayo de 2018, Korwin-Mikke, T-770/16 y T-352/17; Sentencia de 8 de mayo de 2019, Violeta Villar Láiz, C-161/18; Sentencia de 8 de mayo de 2019, C-486/18; Sentencia de 7 de octubre de 2019, Safeway, C-171/18; Sentencia de 18 de septiembre de 2019, Ortiz Mesonero, C-366/18; Sentencia de 20 de junio de 2019, Hakelbracht, C-404/18; Sentencia de 3 de junio de 2021, Tesco Stores, C-624/19; Dictamen 1/19 del TJUE, de 6 de octubre de 2021.

518 M. REQUENA CASANOVA, «La tutela judicial del principio general de igualdad de trato en la unión europea: una jurisprudencia expansiva basada en una jerarquía de motivos discriminatorios», *Revista de Derecho Comunitario Europeo*, 2011, 40, pp. 767 ss.; C. ATIENZA MONEREO, *Hacia un concepto complejo de igualdad. La igualdad formal en la Carta de Derechos Fundamentales de la Unión Europea*. Madrid, 2012, pp. 11 ss.; M. ORTEGA GÓMEZ, «La discriminación entre hombre y mujeres en el ámbito laboral. Un problema persistente en la Unión Europea», *Revista General de Derecho del Trabajo y de la Seguridad Social*, 47, 2017, pp. 193 ss.

In this sense, it can be affirmed that the principle of gender equality recognised by European legislation and by the different States of the Union is based on the idea of men and women having the same rights, opportunities and responsibilities within society, which is related to another fundamental principle such as that of equal treatment[519], defined as that which promotes treating all people fairly and equally, without discrimination on grounds of gender, race, religion, sexual orientation, disability or other factors, having the same opportunities and rights with regard to services, work or equality in the law. It follows from this interrelationship that, in order to achieve gender equality, it is necessary that all persons, irrespective of their gender, are treated fairly and equally[520].

In this respect, the principle of equal treatment and equal opportunities emphasises human dignity and equal rights and duties as a fundamental aspect of equality between men and women, which is reflected in access to employment, vocational training and promotion, and working conditions, in particular through the elimination of discrimination against women, whatever their circumstances or status, in any sphere of life and, in particular, in the political, civil, labour, economic, social and cultural spheres, as stated in Organic Law 3/2007, of 22 March, for the Effective Equality of Women and Men.

In this way, the different European societies are trying to give a collective response to gender discrimination, which is one of the strong points of the idea of Europe, and leads us to a common European thinking in favour of gender equality and non-discrimination, which could seem to have been built in the twentieth century under the influence of global trends, however, we can deduce the presence since ancient times, in Roman Law, of rules aimed at favouring equal treatment between subjects, although without reaching the current concept of gender equality.

---

519 E. LOMBARDO, «La igualdad de género en el Tratado Constitucional de la Unión Europea», *Revista de Pensamet i Análisi*, 6, 2006, pp. 125 ss.; A. MANGAS MARTÍN, «Derecho y políticas de igualdad de trato entre mujeres y hombres en la Unión Europea», *Estudios Europeos, Vol. II*, Valencia, 2008, pp. 27 ss.

520 Directiva 2000/43/CE, relativa a la aplicación del principio de igualdad de trato de las personas independientemente de su origen racial o étnico, DOCE L 180, de 17 de diciembre de 2000. Directiva 2000/78/CE, de 27 de noviembre de 2000, relativa al establecimiento de un marco general para la igualdad de trato en el empleo y la ocupación, DOCE L 303, de 2 de diciembre de 2000 y la Decisión de la misma fecha por la que se establece un programa de acción comunitario para luchar contra la discriminación (2001–2006), DOCE L 303, p. 23. Directiva 2004/113/CE por la que se aplica el principio de igualdad de trato entre hombres y mujeres al acceso a bienes y servicios y su suministro, DOCE L 373/37, de 21 de diciembre de 2004. M. BELL, *Anti-discrimination law and the European Union*, Oxford, 2002.

2. Women in Rome: their evolution in relation to the principle of equal treatment

Roman law has had a significant influence on the development of legal systems in Europe in several respects, as an imprint that survives in today's European legal systems, both in terms of fundamental legal principles and in the structure and functioning of those systems[521].

Focusing on Roman law and the idea of equality, we must start from a basic premise, which is that Rome had a system characterised by inequality, since in order to have legal capacity the individual was required to have the triple *status, libertatis, civitatis, familiae*[522], thus, only the subject with the three conditions would have full legal capacity, although even among the citizens there were categories with different social esteem, different rights and obligations, such as freedmen and freedwomen.

However, when we focus on the relationship between Roman law and women, the situation is more complex, since their incapacity was established by the rules in general, with a scope of action limited to the family and the *domus*.

In this affirmation we find the idea of patriarchy as a model of society and family, in which the male had full control of the situation, and the *status familiae* determined whether or not he was subject to an alien power, *manus* if it was over

521 H. COING «El sentido del derecho. Historia y significado de la idea del sistema en la jurisprudencia» (traducción de Robert S. Hartman y José Luis González), Cuadernos del Centro de Estudios Filosóficos, 1, México, 1912, pp. 5 ss.; H. COING, *Derecho privado europeo, vol. II*, Madrid, 1996, pp. 15 ss.; A. TORRENT, «Fundamentos del Derecho Europeo (Derecho romano-Ciencia del Derecho-Derecho Europeo)», *AFDUDC*, 11, 2007, pp. 941 ss.; R. ZIMMERMANN, Reviewed Work of COING, H., «Für Wissenschaften und Künste: Lebensbericht eines europäischen Rechtsgelehrten», *The Rabel Journal of Comparative and International Private Law*, 79, 1, 2015, pp. 219 ss.; R. BERNAD MAINAR, «La fructífera experiencia del *ius commune* ante el apasionante reto de la unificación del Derecho privado común europeo», *RIDROM*, oct. 2017, pp. 243 ss.

522 F. DE MARTINO, «*Familia*», *Novissimo Digesto Italiano*, IV, Torino, 1981; L. CAPOGROSSI, «*Patria potestà*», *Enciclopedia del Diritto*, XXXII, Milano, 1982; E. VOLTERRA, *Instituciones jurídicas de Derecho privado romano*, Madrid, 1986, pp. 77 ss.; G. SUÁREZ BLAZQUEZ, «La patria potestad en el Derecho romano y en el derecho altomedieval visigodo», *Revista de Estudios Históricos - Juridicos; Valparaiso*, 36, 2014, pp. 159 ss.; C. MEZA, «El poder y el derecho frente a las desigualdades de la persona», *Fundamentos romanísticos de Derecho contemporáneo*, I, 2021, pp. 541 ss.; V.E. PÉREZ PÉREZ, «Capacidad de la mujer en Derecho privado romano», *Revista Clepsydra*, 16, 2017, pp. 191 ss.

the wife, *alieni iuris* if it was a woman subject to the power of the *pater familias*; with social progress and the admission of women as *sui iuris* the potestas changed, but the discrimination continued with perpetual guardianship despite her status as *sui iuris*[523], which determined their lack of participation in public life, in its political and legal aspects[524].

The guardianship of women was configured as an institution of economic context[525], even originally a means of control of women in a patriarchal society that did not consider them prepared for public life, so they received an education different from the men of their family[526], focused on their future task as wives and mothers of future Roman citizens[527], however, among the women of the Roman elite could be found cases of educated women and prepared for any office[528].

523 Cicero, *Pro Murena* 12, 27; *Gai* 1, 144, *Gai* 1, 145; *Tit. Ulp.* 11, 1; *Tit. Ulp.* 11, 27; C. 2, 44, 2, 1.

524 D. ESPÍN CÁNOVAS, «Capacidad jurídica de la mujer casada», *Revista Gráficas Europa*, Salamanca, 1969, p. 7; L RODRIGUEZ-ENNES, «La larga lucha hacía la igualdad femenina», *AFDUC*, 11, 2007, pp. 840 ss.; R.P. RODRÍGUEZ MONTERO, «Hilvanando "atributos" femeninos en la antigua Roma», *Fundamentos romanísticos del Derecho contemporáneo*, II, 2021, pp. 897-903; M. SALAZAR REVUELTA, «Estatus jurídico y social de la *materfamilias* en el marco de la ciudadanía romana», *Mulier: algunas historias e instituciones de Derecho Romano*, 2013, pp. 200 ss.; M.J. BRAVO BOSCH, *No tan lejano, una visión de la mujer romana a través de temas de actualidad*, Valencia, 2018, p. 15; D. MATEO CORREDOR, M. PASTOR QUILES, «La desigualdad entre hombres y mujeres en la antigua Roma: un estudio sobre su concepciones y conocimiento en el alumnado de historia», *Cuadernos de Arqueología de la Universidad de Navarra*, 28, 2020, pp. 85 ss.

525 A. LÓPEZ GÜETO, «Mujer, poder y derecho en Roma», *Revista jurídica Piélagus*, 17, 2018, p. 15.

526 M. ÁLVARO BERNAL, *De puella a nupta*, Oviedo, 2023, pp. 77 ss.

527 E. VOLTERRA, *Instituciones de Derecho privado romano*, *op.cit.*, pp. 133 ss.; C. PEREIRA PORTO, «La representación del concepto de mujer en Roma», *Revista de Filosofía del Derecho y derechos humanos*, 5, 1995, pp. 292 ss.; R. HERRERA BRAVO; A. SALAZAR REVUELTA; M. SALAZAR REVUELTA, «La condición de la mujer en la represión del adulterio en Derecho romano y su recepción histórica», *Experiencias jurídicas e identidades femeninas*, 2011, pp. 186 ss.; V., PÉREZ PÉREZ «Capacidad de la mujer en derecho privado romano», *Revista Clepsidra*, *op.cit.*, pp. 191-217; A. LÓPEZ GÜETO, *Madres e hijos en el Derecho romano de sucesiones. Los senadoconsultos Tertuliano y Orficiano*, Madrid, 2017, pp. 27 ss.; G. SUÁREZ BLÁZQUEZ, «La emancipación jurídica privada de la mujer romana: un antecedente histórico de la "liberación de género», *RIDROM*, abril, 2023 pp. 388 ss.

528 *Gai* 1, 190.

From these affirmations, a Roman Law made by and for men, where women were excluded from public life for reasons of legal inferiority based on their lesser physical and mental capacity, as stated in different texts from legal and literary sources that use terms such as *levitas* or *fragilitas animi*, la *imbecilitas mentis* or la *infirmitas consilii* y *calliditas*[529] to define them.

This unfavourable position of women's legal capacity in Rome evolved in parallel to Roman society, from the 2nd century BC, from total submission to their father, husband or guardian, to an increasingly higher status of personal freedom and less legal inequality, both in private and public matters, favoured by successive wars and male mortality, which allowed them to assume the administration and management of family assets in the absence of a man.

However, the law reacted to these female behaviours that exceeded their natural position by means of laws, the purpose of which was to limit the legal and economic capacity of women, thus returning to the traditional Roman custom, according to the archaic *mores maiorum*, among which the *lex Oppia*, from 215 B.C., abrogated in 195 B.C. by the *lex Valeria Fundania*, or the *lex Vocconia de mulierum hereditatis* from 169 B.C., stand out, abrogated in 195 B.C., later the *Leges Iulia de maritandis ordinibus*, 18 B.C., the *Lex Iulia sumptuaria*, plebiscite of 18 BC, the *Lex Iulia de adulteriis coercendis*, 17-16 BC and the *Lex Papia Poppaea*, 9 AD, aimed at recovering the image of the Roman matron dedicated to the *domus* and the family[530].

Despite this restrictive legislation, the evolution of society and the law meant a change in the situation of women, which modified the tutela mulierum, which became testamentary or legitimate, but not based on the woman's own incapacity,

529 M.J. BRAVO BOSCH, «El lenguaje discriminatorio en la antigua Roma y en la España actual», *Revista Jurídica da FA7, periódico científico e cultural do curso de direito da Facultade 7 de Setembro, 15, 2*, 2018, pp. 139 ss.; P PAVÓN, «*Infirmitas enim feminarum, non calliditas auxilium demeruit* (D. 16, 1, 2, 3 Ulp. 29 ad ed.) o la "extrema dualidad" de la condición femenina en el senadoconsulto Veleyano», *Conditio Feminae.* Imágenes de la realidad femenina en el mundo romano, Roma, 2021, pp. 127 ss.; G SUÁREZ BLÁZQUEZ, «La emancipación jurídica privada de la mujer romana: un antecedente histórico de la "liberación de género"», *RIDROM, op.cit.*, pp. 390 ss.; B GARCÍA FUEYO., «Hijas e hijos legítimos en la sucesión intestada de su progenitor: de Roma a los códigos civiles. (Igualdad y género)», *RIDROM, abril, 2022*, pp. 63 ss. D. 1, 5, 9; D. 1, 9, 1; C. 5, 17, 10; D. 16, 1, 2, 2; D. 16, 1, 2, 3. Seneca, *Controversiae* 1, 6 y 2, 7; *Dialogi* 12, 19, 5; Cicero, *Tusculanae*, 3, 16, 34.

530 E. CANTARELLA, *Pasado próximo. Mujeres romanas de Tácita a Sulpicia* (Traducción de MM. Núñez), Madrid, 1997, pp. 197 ss.

even more so when the ius liberorum was established, for demographic reasons, which freed women from tutelage according to their reproductive capacity[531].

This affirmation would be corroborated by the exception from ancient times in the guardianship of the vestal virgins, who were allowed to manage their own property, as they were considered worthy of it, without being subject to authority or guardianship[532]; It was the first women to be granted rights and freedoms, who were the starting point for an incipient equality of rights in a society such as the Roman one, based on tradition, extremely respectful of its rituals and eminently religious, so it is not surprising that this was the space in which the first idea of equality of rights between the sexes arose.

Thus, since archaic law, there has been a development in the capacity of women, until the laws dictated by Justinian, under the influence of Christianity, dictate rules with a moral background that will serve to provide some advantages to women in their legal capacity and capacity to act[533].

3. Background to the principle of equal treatment in Roman inheritance

The evolution of law had its influence on an initial development of the principle of equal treatment, not in a general way, but in some very specific aspects related to family law, the cornerstone of Roman law, from which it could be deduced that

531 P. RESINA SOLA, «La condición jurídica de la mujer en Roma», *La Mujer en el mundo mediterráneo antiguo*, Granada, 1990, pp. 105 ss.; B. FERNÁNDEZ VIZCAÍNO, «El *ius adcrescendi* en los senadoconsultos Tertuliano y Orficiano», *RIDROM*, oct., 2011, pp. 455 ss.; A. LÓPEZ GÜETO, *Madres e hijos en el Derecho romano de sucesiones. Los senadoconsultos Tertuliano y Orficiano*, *op.cit.*, pp. 20 ss.; V. PÉREZ PÉREZ, «Capacidad de la mujer en Derecho privado romano», *Revista Clepsydra, op.cit.*, pp. 13 ss.; M.J. BRAVO BOSCH, «El lenguaje discriminatorio en la antigua Roma y en la España actual», en *Revista Jurídica da FA7, periódico científico e cultural do curso de direito da Facultade 7 de Setembro*, *op.cit.*, pp. 144 ss.; G. SUÁREZ BLÁZQUEZ, «La emancipación jurídica privada de la mujer romana: un antecedente histórico de la "liberación de género», *RIDROM, op.cit.*, pp. 429 ss; J.C. TELLO, «La concesión discrecional por *princeps* del *ius trium liberorum* y su reflejo en Marcial», *Fundamentos romanísticos de Derecho contemporáneo*, III, 2021, pp. 579 ss.

532 G. GIANNELLI, *Il sacerdocio delle Vestali romane*, Florencia, 1913; M. BEARD, «The Sexual Status of Vestal Virgins», *JRS*, 70, 1980, pp. 12 ss.; B. SCARDIGLI, «Vestali integrate nella società romana», *Studi historica. Historia Antigua*, 21, 2003, pp. 97-104; H. N. PARKER, «Why Were the Vestals Virgins? Or the Chastity of Women and the Safety of the Roman State», *The American Journal of Philology, 125, 4*, 2004, p. 568.

533 M.L. MARÍN PADRILLA, *Historia de la sucesión contractual*, Zaragoza, 1992, p. 29.

this idea of equality was already present from ancient times, acting as a precursor of the current regulations in favour of gender equality declared by the United Nations, and protected by the rights of the different States.

In this respect, there are references in the sources to two situations that serve the stated purpose, on the one hand, the *ius adcrescendi in partem* in case of preterition by the *pater familias* of a daughter, and on the other hand, the prohibition of succession pacts against the inheritance rights of daughters.

3.1. The *ius adcrescendi in partem* of the preterited daughter

In this legal institution, a formal legitimate succession can be distinguished in the regulation of ius civile according to the principle *sui heredes aut instituendi sunt aut exheredandi*, which obliged the testator to solemnly institute or disinherit his children or descendants in his will, although it was differentiated if the disinherited was a male child in potestate of the testator, including posthumous children, who had to be instituted or disinherited nominatively, while in the case of daughters or grandchildren, they could be instituted or disinherited jointl[534]. However, sometimes there was no disinheritance, but an omission by the testator of some subjects that should have been contemplated in the will[535].

This situation produced a gender-based discrimination, because when those omitted by the father were children in potestate, the will was declared null ab initio by the *ius civile*, passing to the opening of the intestate succession; On the other hand, if the daughters were omitted in a will in which other *sui heredes*, and even a stranger, had been instituted, the document was valid, but to correct the omission the law assigned them a share of the inheritance in concurrence with those instituted of any kind, as *Gai* 2, 124, 125, 126 states[536], with the so-called *ius adcrescendi in partem*, an institution that shows the clear difference that the law made in relation to the children of the testator according to sex, the basis of which was the modification of the call to inheritance established by the testator,

534 C. LÓPEZ-RENDO RODRÍGUEZ, *Fundamento de la regla sui heredes aut instituendi sunt aut exheredandi en el Ius civile*, Oviedo, 1991. *Tit.Ulp*. 22,14.

535 R. LINARES NOCI, «La preterición: su origen y evolución en Derecho romano», *Derecho y opinión*, 1992, p. 144; C. GAGO SIMARRO, «La preterición de los descendientes», *Fundamentos romanísticos de Derecho contemporáneo*, VIII, 2021, pp. 2503 ss. D. 28, 3, 3, 5.

536 M. PÉREZ SIMEÓN, *Nemo pro parte testatus pro parte intestatus decedere potest*, Barcelona, 2001, pp. 243 ss. *Gai* 2, 128; *Gai* Ep. 2, 3, 1; *Til.Ulp*. 22, 20; *Nov. Maior* 6, 3; *Lex Romana Burgundionum*, XLV.

and the ineffectiveness of preteritio[537], an institution that shows the clear difference that the law made in relation to the children of the testator according to sex

With the *ius adcrescendi in partem*, by means of a fiction, the daughter was considered to be instituted in the will of the *pater familias*, and was granted a share of the inheritance, even in her obligation to make bequests, in half of the inheritance if the other instituted persons were foreign heirs, or in a virile share in the case of *suus heres*[538].

1. With the evolution of the law, the regulations issued by the praetor established that, if there was preterition of *liberi* who by *ius civile* did not annul the will, daughters and grandchildren, if they requested his protection, he would grant them the *bonorum possessio contra tabulas*[539], leaving the foreign heirs instituted as ineffective heirs[540]. On the other hand, if the preterition of the

537 The *ius adcrescendi in partem* came to break the general inheritance system, as it modified the call to inheritance established by the testator, also, due to the differences in its nature and operating premises, it cannot be placed as a new type of general *ius adcrescendi* of the Roman inheritance law, but its place is in the sphere of the ineffectiveness of the *voluntas testatoris* of the disposing party, established in D. 50, 16, 120. S. PEROZZI, *Istituzioni di diritto romano, II*, Roma, 1928, p. 558 (nota 1); U. ROBBE, *Il diritto di accrescimento e la sostituzione volgare nel diritto romano classico*, Milano, 1953, pp. 191-192; G. PUGLIESE, voz: «accrescimento», en *Enciclopedia del diritto*, volumen I, Milano, 1958, p. 313; U. ROBBE, voz: «accrescimento», *Novissimo Digesto Italiano*, volumen I, Torino, 1957, p. 159; J. ARIAS RAMOS, J. ARIAS BONET, *Derecho Romano II, Obligaciones-Familia-Sucesiones*, Madrid, 1981, p. 841.

538 O. KARLOWA, *Römisches Rechtsgeschichte. Privatrecht*, II, Leipzig, 1901, p. 890; F. GLÜCK, *Comentario alle Pandette*, XXXVI, Milano, 1907, pp. 338 ss.; E. CUQ, *Manuel des institutions juridiques des Romains*, Paris, 1928, p. 707; U. ROBBE, *Il diritto di accrescimento e la sostituzione volgare nel diritto romano classico, op.cit.*, pp. 191-192; U. ROBBE, voz: «accrescimento», *Novissimo Digesto Italiano*, volumen I, *op.cit.*, p. 159; L. DI LELLA, *Querela inofficiosi testamenti. Contributo allo studio della sucessione testamentaria*, Napoli, 1972, pp. 104 ss.; M. TALAMANCA, *Istituzioni di Diritto Romano*, Milano, 1990, pp. 766-767; G. IMPALLOMENI, *Scritti di diritto romano e tradizione romanistica*, Padova, 1996, p. 323. *Tit.Ulp.* 22, 17; *Pauli Sent.* 3, 4b, 8; I. 2, 13, pr.

539 C. GAGO SIMARRO, «La preterición de los descendientes», en *Fundamentos romanísticos de Derecho contemporáneo, op.cit.*, p. 2506.

540 E. CUQ, *Manuel des institutions juridiques des Romains, op.cit.*, pp. 709-710; E. VOLTERRA, *Instituciones de Derecho privado romano, op.cit*, p. 783; B. GARCÍA FUEYO, «Hijas e hijos legítimos en la sucesión intestada de su progenitor: de Roma a los códigos civiles. (Igualdad y género)», RIDROM, *op.cit.*, pp. 72 ss. *Gai* 2, 135; *Tit. Ulp.* 22, 23; Justiniano, Nov. 118, año 543, completada por la 127 del 548.

liberi rendered the will null and void under civil law, the praetor granted them *bonorum possessio ab intestato*, as he considered the will to be null and void in all its provisions

2. In Justinian Law, on account of a new view of the family, the inheritance rights of all the sui were equalised, by providing that women should be considered equal to men[541], repealing in C. 6, 28, 4, 1, the *ius adcrescendi in partem* declared by the *ius civile*; in the same provision the emperor ruled the necessity of using the term exheres to disinherit, as well as that disinheritance should always be nominative and made in any place in the will, and in C. 6, 28, 4, 3, eliminated the distinction of sexes by imposing on the testator the institution or nominative disinheritance on all descendants, equalising the rights among all of them, without taking gender into consideration[542].
3. The Justinian legal system confirmed this idea with Nov. 115, which ordered that the preterition or disinheritance of a descendant of the testator was only licit in the case of ingratitude, without making a distinction on the grounds of sex, in what we can consider a forerunner of the principle of equal treatment[543].

3.2. Prohibition of succession agreements against the inheritance rights of daughters

In the same vein, in Roman law we find the prohibition of inheritance pacts in which future inheritance was ordered, despite their frequent use at certain stages in Rome, which led the legislator to try to curb them, especially in relation to discrimination against women on the basis of sex[544].

---

541 A. DERNBURG, *Pandette*, III, (traducción italiana de Cicala), Torino, 1905, pp. 542 ss. Nov. 115 de Justiniano, año 542.

542 C. FADDA, *Concetti fondamentali del diritto ereditario romano*, parte prima, Napoli, 1900, p. 335; P. VOCI, «Il diritto ereditario romano dalle origini ai Severi», *Studi di diritto romano*, II, Padova, 1985, p. 28 (nota 97) (=en Ausfstieg und Niedergang der römischen Welt, II, 14, Berlin, 1982, pp. 392 ss.); J. ARIAS RAMOS, J. ARIAS BONET, *Derecho Romano II, Obligaciones-Familia-Sucesiones, op.cit.*, pp. 785 ss.; M. PÉREZ SIMEÓN, *Nemo pro parte testatus pro parte intestatus decedere potest, op.cit.*, pp. 249 ss. C. 6, 28, 4.

543 E. VOLTERRA, *Instituciones de Derecho privado romano, op.cit*, p. 784; M. PÉREZ SIMEÓN, *Nemo pro parte testatus pro parte intestatus decedere potest, op.cit.*, pp. 262-263.

544 C. FADDA, *Conceptti fondamentali del diritto ereditario romano*, parte prima, *op.cit.*, p. 325; P. BONFANTE, «Le affinità giuridiche greco-romane», *Rivista di Storia antica*, 13, 1910, pp. 346 ss.; M.L MARÍN PADILLA, *Historia de la sucesión contractual, op.cit.*, p. 58. Nov. Justiniano 21 año 536.

In this respect, it is possible to find cases in which the daughter was endowed upon marriage, signing for this reason covenants to renounce any future inheritance rights that might correspond to her, which turns the dowry into an advance on the inheritance and not into assets affected by the matrimonial burdens[545].

However, this situation could be admitted in archaic law, when the woman became part of the husband's family with the marriage *cum manu*, but not at the end of the Republic, when marriage *sine manu* was the ordinary form of celebration[546]. Moreover, in these cases, it is necessary to take into consideration the changes in the absolute freedom of testament which was originally available to the *pater familias*, but which due to the evolution of Roman society and the concept of the family was limited in order to protect the members closest to the testator, as stated in D. 50, 16, 120[547].

These pacts were forbidden by Roman law in accordance with the principle that the testator was free to arrange his future inheritance until the moment of death, so that any agreement, whether to institute or not to institute, was considered null and void as immoral and contrary to good morals, as stated in C. 2, 3, 6 and C.2.3.8[548]. Another reason for their prohibition is to be found in the principle

545 O MONJE BALMASEDA, F. LLEDÓ YAGÜE, *Cuadernos Teóricos Bolonia. Derecho Sucesorio. Cuaderno II. El testamento. El contenido de la institución. Su ineficacia. Ejecución. La defensa del derecho hereditario. La sucesión intestada y contractual*, *op.cit.*, p. 204.

546 G. VISMARA, *Storia dei patti successori*, Milano, 1986, pp. 146 ss.; M.L. MARÍN PADILLA, *Historia de la sucesión contractual*, *op.cit.*, pp. 55 ss.; M. LAURIA, *Matrimionio-dote in diritto romano*, Napoli, 1952, p. 8.

547 E. BESTA, *Le successioni nella storia del Diritto italiano*, Padova, 1935, p. 187; F. SCHULZ, *Principios del Derecho romano*, Madrid, 2000, p. 178; M. PLANAS BALLVÉ, «De la imposibilidad de renunciar a derecho sucesorios futuros en el Derecho romano a su leve atenuación», *Fundamentos romanísticos de Derecho contemporáneo*, VIII, 2021, pp. 2911-2913; V. MAGARIÑOS BLANCO, *Libertad para ordenar la sucesión. Libertad para testar*, Madrid, 2022, pp. 488 ss.; O. MONJE BALMASED, F. LLEDÓ YAGÜE, *Cuadernos Teóricos Bolonia. Derecho Sucesorio. Cuaderno II. El testamento. El contenido de la institución. Su ineficacia. Ejecución. La defensa del derecho hereditario. La sucesión intestada y contractual*, Madrid, 2017, p. 201; F.J. OLMEDO CASTAÑEDA, «Prohibición de los pactos sucesorios en el Derecho común: cuestionamiento de su *ratio legis*. Propuesta para su admisibilidad», *Anuario de Derecho Civil*, LXXII, fasc. II, 2019, p. 452; M. HERRERO OVIEDO, «El renacer de los pactos sucesorios», *Estudios de derecho de familia y de sucesiones (dimensiones interna e internacional)*, Santiago de Compostela, 2009, p. 203.

548 J. ARIAS RAMOS, J. ARIAS BONET *Derecho Romano II, Obligaciones-Familia-Sucesiones*, *op.cit.*, p. 528.

viventis nulla est hereditas, according to which it was not possible to renounce a future inheritance or to dispose of it, besides the fact that they were considered a danger to the life of the person whose succession was involved[549].

However, the general prohibition of making agreements to renounce future inheritance was circumvented by means of agreements based on the interest of the deceased to keep the greater part of his estate intact for his male children, which is a discrimination against women on the basis of sex[550].

In this context, the law reacted by establishing a series of corrective measures in the case of a woman who married, was endowed and by a pact renounced her share of her father's future inheritance, being set aside in favour of the male siblings.

Among these measures we find the text of Papinianus in D. 38, 16, 16[551], which describes the case of a father who established in his daughter's endowment document that she was not to expect anything else from her inheritance, to which the jurist replies that this deed did not alter the woman's inheritance right, since this type of agreement between private individuals was not taken into consideration, since the laws prevailed and not the will of the parties[552].

---

549 In Roman law, some exceptions to this general prohibition can be found, considering valid the division of assets made by the father among his children and descendants, or the donation mortis causa, as well as the reciprocal succession agreement made between military, C. 2, 3, 19.

550 E. PETIT, *Tratado elemental de Derecho romano*, Buenos Aires, 1977, p. 705; R. COLL RODES, «Consideracions y normes generals referents á la successió voluntaria á títul universal», *RJC, 18*, 1912, Barcelona, p. 270; M. HERRERO OVIEDO, «El renacer de los pactos sucesorios», *Estudios de derecho de familia y de sucesiones (dimensiones interna e internacional), op.cit.*, p. 203; M. PLANAS BALLVÉ, «De la imposibilidad de renunciar a derecho sucesorios futuros en el Derecho romano a su leve atenuación», *Fundamentos romanísticos de Derecho contemporáneo, op.cit.*, p. 2911; M.L. MARÍN PADILLA, *Historia de la sucesión contractual, op.cit.*, pp. 48 ss. *C.Th.* 2, 24, 2; C. 2, 3, 30; C. 3, 28, 35, 1 y 1ª.

551 D. 38, 16, 16.- *Papinianus 12 resp. Pater instrumento dotali comprehendit filiam ita dotem accepisse, ne quid aliud ex hereditate patris speraret: eam scripturam ius successionis non mutasse constitit: privatorum enim cautiones legum auctoritate non censeri.*

552 P. GUERIN, *Les renonciations à succession future dans l'ancien droit français*, Paris, 1931, p. 13; C. FADDA, *Conceptti fondamentali del diritto ereditario romano*, parte prima, *op.cit.*, p. 325; G. VISMARA, *Storia dei patti successori, op.cit.*, p. 147. D. 38, 16, 16.- *...privatorum enim cautiones legum auctoritate non censeri.*

The same situation can be observed in D. 6, 20, 3[553], which confirms the nullity of a pact involving a daughter who renounces her rights to her father's inheritance property, despite having received her dowry, although it is clarified that this situation could not be a disadvantage for the children who had remained *in potestate* of the *pater familias*, and therefore the obligation of the daughter to collate the dowry property with the aforementioned brothers when competing for the inheritance is established, which institutes a true equality between all the children of the deceased[554].

From the fragments cited, one can observe the principle of equal treatment of children established by Roman Law, which declared null and void the renunciation of the gifted daughter of her father's inheritance, contrary to legislation and society, to good customs, and not protected by the laws, since excluding daughters meant not respecting the principle of equality between all the children of the deceased enshrined in the Law, favoring the first-born males, so that they acquired the entire hereditary ace, leaving their sisters without their share of the inheritance.

However, in the Middle Ages, due to the influence of other rights, through the *exclusio propter dotem*, included in some European rights, priority was again given to the rights of male heirs[555], when in different European territories, such as France and Italy, and in some areas of Spain[556] the rule was established to exclude daughters from paternal inheritance once they were endowed through renunciation pacts, for socioeconomic reasons, which represented a regression in society with respect to the principle of gender equality, sacrificed for purely utilitarian reasons, granting rights to men, through a renunciative pact called *exclusio propter dotem*, which in the Middle Ages had the consequence that the first-born male

---

553 C. 6, 20, 3.- *Imperator Alexander Severus. Pactum dotali instrumento comprehensum, ut contenta dote quae in matrimonio collocabatur nullum ad bona paterna regressum haberet, iuris auctoritate improbatur nec intestato patri succedere filia ea ratione prohibetur. dotem sane quam accepit fratribus qui in potestate manserunt conferre debet. * alex. a. alexandro. * <a 230 d. xiiii k. iul. agricola et clemente conss.>*

554 P. GUERIN, *Les renonciations à succession future dans l'ancien droit français, op.cit.*, p. 12; C. FADDA, *Conceptti fondamentali del diritto ereditario romano*, parte prima, *op.cit.*, p. 325; G. VISMARA, *Storia dei patti successori, op.cit.*, p. 148; M. HERRERO OVIEDO, «El renacer de los pactos sucesorios», *Estudios de derecho de familia y de sucesiones (dimensiones interna e internacional), op.cit.*, p. 205.

555 F. SCHULZ, *Principios del Derecho romano, op.cit.*, p. 197.

556 J. LALINDE ABADÍA, «Los pactos matrimoniales catalanes», *AHDE, XXXIII*, 1963, Madrid, p. 236.

acquired the entire hereditary ace, separating his sisters from the inheritance, which they had renounced previously.

To give legal support to this current, due to the prohibition of these renunciative agreements in Roman Law, in the territories in which inheritance law institutions were established to ensure control of family assets for generations, avoiding their division, and granting the of the family assets to the first-born male, recourse was made to Canon Law, as observed in Decretal VI of Boniface VIII of 1299, which established the validity of the pact signed by the daughter renouncing her part of the inheritance, as long as there is an oath[557].

Which indicates that the principles of gender discrimination were returned for utilitarian reasons, tending to favor the rights of men to the detriment of daughters, through agreements signed by women renouncing their hereditary rights, showing that the Law Roman recognized a principle of equal treatment between children, without distinction of sex, who were in danger due to the influence of other rights, which shows the need to defend and protect the fundamental right of gender equality every day.

Bibliography

ÁLVARO BERNAL, M., *De puella a nupta*, Oviedo, 2023.

ARIAS RAMOS, J.-ARIAS BONET, J., *Derecho Romano II, Obligaciones-Familia-Sucesiones*, Madrid, 1981.

ATIENZA MONEREO, C., *Hacia un concepto complejo de igualdad. La igualdad formal en la Carta de Derechos Fundamentales de la Unión Europea*, Madrid, 2012.

BEARD, M., «The Sexual Status of Vestal Virgins», *JRS*, 70, 1980.

BELL, M., *Anti-discrimination law and the European Union*, Oxford, 2002.

BERNAD MAINAR, R., «La fructífera experiencia del ius commune ante el apasionante reto de la unificación del Derecho privado común europeo», *RIDROM*, oct. 2017.

BESTA, E., *Le successioni nella storia del Diritto italiano*, Padova, 1935.

BONFANTE, P., «Le affinità giuridiche greco-romane», *Rivista di Storia antica*, 13, 1910.

557 M. PLANAS BALLVÉ, «De la imposibilidad de renunciar a derecho sucesorios futuros en el Derecho romano a su leve atenuación», *Fundamentos romanísticos de Derecho contemporáneo*, *op.cit.*, p. 2913.

BRAVO BOSCH, M.J., «El lenguaje discriminatorio en la antigua Roma y en la España actual», *Revista Jurídica da FA7, periódico científico e cultural do curso de direito da Facultade 7 de Setembro*, 15, 2, 2018.

BRAVO BOSCH, M.J., *No tan lejano, una visión de la mujer romana a través de temas de actualidad*, Valencia, 2018.

CANTARELLA, E., *Pasado próximo. Mujeres romanas de Tácita a Sulpicia* (Traducción de MM. Núñez), Madrid, 1997.

CAPOGROSSI, L., «Patria potestà», *Enciclopedia del Diritto, XXXII*, Milano, 1982.

COING, H., «El sentido del derecho. Historia y significado de la idea del sistema en la jurisprudencia» (traducción de Robert S. Hartman y José Luis González), *Cuadernos del Centro de Estudios Filosóficos*, 1, México, 1912.

COING, H., *Derecho privado europeo*, vol. II, Madrid, 1996.

COLL RODES, R., «Consideracions y normes generals referents á la successió voluntaria á títul universal», *RJC*, 18, 1912, Barcelona.

CUQ, E., *Manuel des institutions juridiques des Romains*, Paris, 1928.

DE MARTINO, F., «Familia», *Novissimo Digesto Italiano*, IV, Torino, 1981.

DERNBURG, A., *Pandette, III*, (traducción italiana de Cicala), Torino, 1905.

DI LELLA, L., *Querela inofficiosi testamenti. Contributo allo studio della sucessione testamentaria*, Napoli, 1972.

ESPÍN CÁNOVAS, D., «Capacidad jurídica de la mujer casada», *Revista Gráficas Europa*, Salamanca, 1969.

FADDA, C., *Concetti fondamentali del diritto ereditario romano, parte prima*, Napoli, 1900.

FERNÁNDEZ VIZCAÍNO, B., «El ius adcrescendi en los senadoconsultos Tertuliano y Orficiano», *RIDROM*, oct., 2011.

GAGO SIMARRO, C., «La preterición de los descendientes», *Fundamentos romanísticos de Derecho contemporáneo*, VIII, 2021.

GARCÍA FUEYO, B., «Hijas e hijos legítimos en la sucesión intestada de su progenitor: de Roma a los códigos civiles. (Igualdad y género)», *RIDROM*, abril, 2022.

GIANNELLI, G., *Il sacerdocio delle Vestali romane*, Florencia, 1913.

GLÜCK, F., *Comentario alle Pandette*, XXXVI, Milano, 1907.

GUERIN, P., *Les renonciations à succession future dans l'ancien droit français*, Paris, 1931.

HERRERA BRAVO, R.; SALAZAR REVUELTA, A.; SALAZAR REVUELTA, M., «La condición de la mujer en la represión del adulterio en Derecho romano y su recepción histórica», *Experiencias jurídicas e identidades femeninas*, 2011.

HERRERO OVIEDO, M., *«El renacer de los pactos sucesorios», Estudios de derecho de familia y de sucesiones (dimensiones interna e internacional)*, Santiago de Compostela, 2009.

IMPALLOMENI, G., *Scritti di diritto romano e tradizione romanistica*, Padova, 1996.

KARLOWA, O., *Römisches Rechtsgeschichte. Privatrecht*, II, Leipzig, 1901.

LALINDE ABADÍA, J., «Los pactos matrimoniales catalanes», *AHDE*, XXXIII, 1963, Madrid.

LAURIA, M., *Matrimionio-dote in diritto romano*, Napoli, 1952.

LINARES NOCI, R., «La preterición: su origen y evolución en Derecho romano», *Derecho y opinión*, 1992.

LOMBARDO, E., «La igualdad de género en el Tratado Constitucional de la Unión Europea», *Revista de Pensamet i Análisi*, 6, 2006.

LÓPEZ GÜETO, A., «Mujer, poder y derecho en Roma», *Revista jurídica Piélagus*, 17, 2018.

LÓPEZ GÜETO, A., *Madres e hijos en el Derecho romano de sucesiones. Los senadoconsultos Tertuliano y Orficiano*, Madrid, 2017.

LÓPEZ-RENDO RODRÍGUEZ, C., *Fundamento de la regla sui heredes aut instituendi sunt aut exheredandi en el Ius civile*, Oviedo, 1991.

MAGARIÑOS BLANCO, V., *Libertad para ordenar la sucesión. Libertad para testar*, Madrid, 2022.

MANGAS MARTÍN, A., «Derecho y políticas de igualdad de trato entre mujeres y hombres en la Unión Europea», *Estudios Europeos,* Vol. II, Valencia, 2008.

MARÍN PADRILLA, M.L., *Historia de la sucesión contractual*, Zaragoza, 1992.

MATEO CORREDOR, D.-PASTOR QUILES, M., «La desigualdad entre hombres y mujeres en la antigua Roma: un estudio sobre su concepciones y conocimiento en el alumnado de historia», *Cuadernos de Arqueología de la Universidad de Navarra*, 28, 2020.

MEZA, C., «El poder y el derecho frente a las desigualdades de la persona», *Fundamentos romanísticos de Derecho contemporáneo*, I, 2021.

MONJE BALMASEDA, O.-LLEDÓ YAGÜE, F., *Cuadernos Teóricos Bolonia. Derecho Sucesorio. Cuaderno II. El testamento. El contenido de la institución. Su ineficacia. Ejecución. La defensa del derecho hereditario. La sucesión intestada y contractual*, Madrid, 2017.

OLMEDO CASTAÑEDA, F.J., «Prohibición de los pactos sucesorios en el Derecho común: cuestionamiento de su ratio legis. Propuesta para su admisibilidad», *Anuario de Derecho Civil*, LXXII, fasc. II, 2019.

ORTEGA GÓMEZ, M., «La discriminación entre hombre y mujeres en el ámbito laboral. Un problema persistente en la Unión Europea», *Revista General de Derecho del Trabajo y de la Seguridad Social*, 47, 2017.

PARKER, H. N., «Why Were the Vestals Virgins? Or the Chastity of Women and the Safety of the Roman State», *The American Journal of Philology*, 125, 4, 2004.

PAVÓN, P, «Infirmitas enim feminarum, non calliditas auxilium demeruit (D. 16, 1, 2, 3 Ulp. 29 ad ed.) o la "extrema dualidad" de la condición femenina en el senadoconsulto Veleyano», *Conditio Feminae. Imágenes de la realidad femenina en el mundo romano*, Roma, 2021.

PEREIRA PORTO, C., «La representación del concepto de mujer en Roma», *Revista de Filosofía del Derecho y derechos humanos*, 5, 1995.

PEREZ LUÑO A., «El concepto de igualdad como fundamento de los derechos económicos, sociales y culturales», *Anuario de Derechos Humanos*, 1981.

PÉREZ PÉREZ, V.E., «Capacidad de la mujer en Derecho privado romano», *Revista Clepsydra*, 16, 2017.

PÉREZ SIMEÓN, M., *Nemo pro parte testatus pro parte intestatus decedere potest*, Barcelona, 2001.

PEROZZI, S., *Istituzioni di diritto romano*, II, Roma, 1928.

PETIT, E., *Tratado elemental de Derecho romano*, Buenos Aires.

PLANAS BALLVÉ, M., «De la imposibilidad de renunciar a derecho sucesorios futuros en el Derecho romano a su leve atenuación», *Fundamentos romanísticos de Derecho contemporáneo*, VIII, 2021.

PRIETO MORERA, M., «El principio de igualdad entre hombres y mujeres en la Unión Europea. Luces y sombras», *Revista Humanismo y Trabajo social*, 3, 2004.

PUGLIESE, G., voz: «accrescimento», en *Enciclopedia del diritto*, volumen I, Milano, 1958.

REQUENA CASANOVA, M., «La tutela judicial del principio general de igualdad de trato en la unión europea: una jurisprudencia expansiva basada en una jerarquía de motivos discriminatorios», *Revista de Derecho Comunitario Europeo*, 40, 2011.

RESINA SOLA, P., «La condición jurídica de la mujer en Roma», *La Mujer en el mundo mediterráneo antiguo*, Granada, 1990.

ROBBE, U., *Il diritto di accrescimento e la sostituzione volgare nel diritto romano classico*, Milano, 1953.

ROBBE, U., voz: «accrescimento», *Novissimo Digesto Italiano*, volumen I, Torino, 1957.

RODRÍGUEZ MONTERO, R.P., «Hilvanando "atributos" femeninos en la antigua Roma», *Fundamentos romanísticos del Derecho contemporáneo*, II, 2021.

RODRIGUEZ-ENNES, L., «La larga lucha hacía la igualdad femenina», *AFDUC*, 11, 2007.

SALAZAR REVUELTA, M., «Estatus jurídico y social de la materfamilias en el marco de la ciudadanía romana», *Mulier: algunas historias e instituciones de Derecho Romano*, 2013.

SCARDIGLI, B., «Vestali integrate nella società romana», *Studi historica. Historia Antigua*, 21, 2003.

SCHULZ, F., *Principios del Derecho romano*, Madrid, 2000.

SUÁREZ BLÁZQUEZ, G., «La emancipación jurídica privada de la mujer romana: un antecedente histórico de la "liberación de género», *RIDROM*, abril, 2023.

SUÁREZ BLAZQUEZ, G., «La patria potestad en el Derecho romano y en el derecho altomedieval visigodo», *Revista de Estudios Históricos - Juridicos*; Valparaiso, 36, 2014.

TALAMANCA, M., *Istituzioni di Diritto Romano*, Milano, 1990.

TELLO, J.C., «La concesión discrecional por prínceps del ius trium liberorum y su reflejo en Marcial», *Fundamentos romanísticos de Derecho contemporáneo*, III, 2021.

TORRENT, A., «Fundamentos del Derecho Europeo (Derecho romano-Ciencia del Derecho-Derecho Europeo)», *AFDUDC*, 11, 2007.

VISMARA, G., *Storia dei patti successori*, Milano, 1986.

VOCI, P., «Il diritto creditario romano dalle origini ai Severi», *Studi di diritto romano*, II, Padova, 1985 (=en *Ausfstieg und Niedergang der römischen* Welt, II, 14, Berlin, 1982).

VOLTERRA, E., *Instituciones jurídicas de Derecho privado romano*, Madrid, 1986.

ZIMMERMANN, R., Reviewed Work of COING, H., «Für Wissenschaften und Künste: Lebensbericht eines europäischen Rechtsgelehrten», *The Rabel Journal of Comparative and International Private Law*, 79, 1, 2015.

Sławomir Kursa[558]

Honour and good name as an element of the right to privacy. Contemporary regulations and their Roman origins

Abstract: The right to privacy is provided for and protected in many countries already at the constitutional level. It includes several aspects, in particular the right to protect honour and good name. Honour and good reputatin were already protected in Ancient Rome, based on regulations concerning the tort called *iniuria*. Over time, it included more and more acts, secured by both civil (private) and criminal sanctions. They constitute the basis for contemporary regulations. Both Roman law and contemporary laws allow for some restrictions on the protection of honor and good name.

Keywords: honour, good name, reputation, right to privacy, Constitution, injury, insult

1. Contemporary constitutional regulations

Nowadays, the right to privacy is provided for and protected in many countries already at the constitutional level. A country that belongs to this group is Poland. Article 47 of the Polish Constitution[559] states: "Everyone has the right to legal protection of private life, family life, honour and good name, and to decide about their personal life".

This provision provides for a broadly understood right to privacy, encompassing several aspects listed therein, i.e. the closely related right to the protection of private life and the right to the protection of family life, the right to the protection of honour and good name, the right to decide about one's personal life. The subsequent articles of the Polish Constitution provide for further aspects of the right to privacy, such as the right to raise children in accordance with one's own beliefs (Article 48), freedom and secrecy of communication (Article 49), inviolability of the home (Article 50), protection of personal information (Article 51). Some of them have a completely modern origin (protection of personal information), others existed to some extent already in ancient times.

---

558 SWPS University, ORCID 0000-0001-9327-0728.

559 Constitution of the Republic of Poland of April 2, 1997, *Journal of Laws* 1997, no. 78, item 483.

Although the modern concept of the right to privacy was foreign to Roman law, some of its elements have their Roman roots. At the outset, however, it should be clearly stated that the concept of private life and family life, as well as the right to decide about one's personal life, if any, had a completely different meaning than the modern one and a close connection with the concept of the Roman family, the center of which, especially in the early days of the Roman state, was the family head (*pater familias*)[560]. The life of the entire family revolved around him and his will, and he also made unilateral decisions about the situation of children and other people subject to his authority. A great example of this is the decision-making process regarding a woman's marriage. The decision in this matter belonged primarily to the father or grandfather (exceptionally other relatives, guardian or curator, or possibly a judge or official), what is more, it was assumed that the woman agreed with the will of the ascendant. Nevertheless, from the 4th century onwards, a woman could refuse to marry a candidate indicated by them if she found an equally worthy one[561]. This example shows that although initially the law guaranteed in many ways the rights of the *pater familias* to decide about the members of his family, over time they acquired certain rights of self-determination. Nevertheless, Roman law, from the time of the Republic, provided regulations for the protection of honour (*existimatio*) and good reputation (*fama*), which will be recalled later in this article.

While, as I mentioned earlier, the broadly understood right to privacy is currently usually protected in the constitutions of various countries, it is less common for them to directly provide for the protection of honour and good name. For example, in the constitutions of the European Union countries, norms concerning them can be found in addition to the Polish Constitution in the constitutions of eleven countries. The constitutions of Bulgaria, Croatia, the Czech Republic, Finland, Greece, Spain, Ireland, Lithuania, Portugal, Slovakia and Hungary provide for the protection of honour, (good) name, reputation, or opinion.

However, the right to privacy is not absolute and may therefore be subject to limitations. These limitations should meet constitutional requirements. A limitation of the right provided for in the Constitution of the Republic of Poland may only occur when another constitutional norm, principle or value speaks in its favor[562]. In the event of a restriction of rights and freedoms, the principle of

---

560 A. Nowak, 'Pojęcie władzy ojcowskiej w prawie klasycznym', *Studia Prawnoustrojowe* 1 (2002), pp. 35-54.

561 S. Kursa, *La diseredazione nel diritto giustinianeo*, Bari 2012, pp. 123-124.

562 B. Banaszak, *Konstytucja Rzeczypospolitej Polskiej. Komentarz*, Warszawa 2012, pp. 297-298.

proportionality resulting from Article 31 paragraph 3 shall apply[563]. An example of a conflict between two constitutional interests is the juxtaposition of the freedom of expression resulting from Article 54, paragraph 1, with the legal protection of honour and good name, provided for in Article 47. Both interests are equivalent, and one cannot assume *a priori* the priority of any of them[564]. Therefore, each time there is a need to balance them against each other, so that each of them is realized to the highest possible degree[565]. It is therefore not surprising that in the case of public figures who are actively involved in public forums, the scope of permissible criticism is wider and the protection provided is weaker, because the fact that their activities influence the shaping of public life is the basis of the justified interest of society and the related right to obtain information[566].

Some provisions of the constitutions of EU countries, in addition to guaranteeing the above-mentioned rights, also directly allow for their limitation by means of an ordinary act (Belgium, Bulgaria, Greece, Luxembourg, Malta, the Netherlands, Slovakia). Some also indicate the reasons for such limitations (Cyprus, Estonia, Latvia). In the case of provisions regulating the right to privacy in the constitutions of other EU countries, there is no such direct permission for limitations, which of course, similarly to the Constitution of the Republic of Poland, does not exclude the admissibility of their introduction under the general principles provided for in these constitutions.

It is worth noting that the right to privacy and its various aspects are also subject to protection by international law. In particular, the protection of the right to privacy, which *expressis verbis* includes honour and good name, is provided for in Article 17 of the International Covenant on Civil and Political Rights of 19 December 1966:

1. No one shall be subjected to arbitrary or unlawful interference with his privacy, family, home or correspondence, nor to unlawful attacks on his honour and reputation.

---

563 For more on the principle of proportionality and its application, see M. Safjan, 'Prawo do ochrony życia prywatnego i autonomia jednostki w orzecznictwie Trybunału Konstytucyjnego', in M. Zubik (ed.), *Księga XX-lecia orzecznictwa Trybunału Konstytucyjnego*, Warszawa 2006, pp. 428-434; and also H. Izdebski, 'Zasada proporcjonalności a ograniczenie praw człowieka', in S. Patyra, M. Sadowski, K. Urbaniak (eds.), *Konstytucja w państwie demokratycznym*, Poznań 2017, pp. 395-408.

564 Judgment of the Supreme Court of 13.09.2009, I CSK 44/09, LEX nr 1211186.

565 For more on this topic, see J. Sadomski, *Konflikt zasad – ochrona dóbr osobistych a wolność prasy*, Warszawa 2008, pp. 281-354.

566 Resolution of the Supreme Court (7) of 18.02.2005, III CZP 53/04, *Orzecznictwo Sądu Najwyższego. Izba Cywilna* 7-8 (2005), item 114.

2. Everyone has the right to the protection of the law against such interference or attacks.

2. Protection of honour and good name in Polish law

The right to protection of honour and good name, although provided for in Article 47 of the Polish Constitution, has practically not been the subject of rulings of the Polish Constitutional Tribunal. Honour is understood as an individual's internal conviction about their value in society and the respect due to them, while good name as an individual's concern for a good opinion of them among other members of society[567]. They imply a presumption of correct conduct of an individual in the sphere of private and public life, currently and in the past, a presumption of having personal qualities that are positively assessed in the social dimension[568], they are related to human dignity[569].

Due to the general wording used in Article 47 of the Polish Constitution, in order to specify their scope and determine the consequences of their violation, it is necessary to refer to the statutes and to the case law and doctrine concerning them. The protection of honour and good name is provided for in both criminal and civil law norms.

Violation of external honour is identified with defamation, it occurs when another person is attributed with such conduct or such characteristics that may humiliate them in public opinion or expose them to the loss of trust necessary to occupy a specific position or to perform a specific profession or conduct a specific activity. Due to the fact that defamation harms the opinion of others about a given person, undermines their trust in them, humiliates them in their eyes, defamation will not occur through a statement whose only recipient is that person. In order for defamation to occur, the statement containing content that violates honour must also reach at least one other person[570]. In turn, a violation of internal honour is identified with an insult, i.e. statements that violate the dignity of a given person, are insulting or ridiculing, and cannot be rationalized. Moreover, due to the fact that an insult violates a person's self-esteem, an insult - unlike defamation - may also occur when the recipient of a statement with content that violates honour is

567 B. Banaszak, *Konstytucja...*, p. 296.

568 P. Sarnecki, 'Artykuł 47', in L. Garlicki, M. Zubik (eds.), *Konstytucja Rzeczypospolitej Polskiej. Komentarz*, vol. II, *Art. 30-86*, Warszawa 2016, p. 253.

569 M. Florczak-Wątor, 'Art. 47', in P. Tuleja (ed.), *Konstytucja Rzeczypospolitej Polskiej. Komentarz*, Warszawa 2023, point 2.

570 Judgment of the Supreme Court of 8.05.2014, V CSK 361/13, Legalis nr 1061025.

only that person. However, this does not mean that an insult to a given person can only occur in their presence[571].

In criminal law, this differentiation is reflected in the definition of the crime of defamation (Article 212 of the Penal Code[572]) and the crime of insult (Article 216 of the Penal Code)[573]. Their commission is punishable by a fine, restriction of freedom, and in the case of acting through the means of mass communication, also by imprisonment for up to one year. Additionally, the court may also order a supplementary payment.

In civil law, the honour is recognized as a personal right pursuant to Article 23 of the Civil Code[574]. Art. 24 of the Civil Code entitles a person whose honour has been violated to demand that the violator cease the unlawful action, and also to take actions necessary to eliminate the effects of the violation, to provide monetary compensation or to pay an appropriate amount of money for a specified social purpose (§ 1), as well as to demand possible compensation if the violation resulted in material damage. (§ 2)[575]. Thus, the injured party may demand both non-financial protection, for example, through an apology, correction of inaccurate information, withdrawal of the charges brought, and financial protection in the form of an amount of money corresponding to the gravity of the violation, awarded to the injured party or the purpose indicated by them. Ultimately, the court decides on the application of the measures requested by the injured party, their form, content or amount. The condition for granting protection of honour is the illegality of its violation. If the violator proves that he did not act illegally, the lawsuit is dismissed. The illegality of the violation of honour is eliminated by the consent of the interested party, a specific provision of law, a right to which the acting party is entitled, or the existence of a legitimate interest, for example,

571 Judgment of the Supreme Court of 8.05.2014, V CSK 361/13, Legalis nr 1061025.

572 Act of June 6, 1997 – Penal Code, consolidated text: *Journal of Laws* 2024, item 17, as amended.

573 Judgment of the Supreme Court of 8.05.2014, V CSK 361/13, Legalis nr 1061025.

574 Act of April 23, 1964 – Civil Code, consolidated text: *Journal of Laws* 2024, item 1071, as amended.

575 Broadly for the topic of claims provided for in Article 24 of the Civil Code, see, among others A. Kubiak-Cyrul, *Dobra osobiste osób prawnych*, Kraków 2005, pp. 213-250; J. Matys, *Model zadośćuczynienia pieniężnego z tytułu szkody niemajątkowej w kodeksie cywilnym*, Warszawa 2010, pp. 103-344. See also S. Kursa, *Protection of Personal Rights in Law of Succession, Teka Komisji Prawniczej PAN Oddział w Lublinie* 1 (2023), pp. 169-177.

the use of freedom of speech for the purpose of showing the "historical truth" or incorrect behavior of public figures[576].

3. The development of the protection of honour and good reputation in Roman law

Although Roman law did not develop the concept of personal rights, it did have regulations to protect honour (*existimatio*) and good reputation (*fama*), which are protected in art. 47 of the Polish Constitution and 23 and 24 of the Civil Code as honour and good name. In this respect, the clearest connections of contemporary regulations can be seen in the context of an act called *iniuria* (injury). It could take various forms, especially verbal and written, and here too the key role was played by the *pater familias*, because he could claim the consequences of an insult inflicted on persons subject to his authority - his wife, children, and in some cases even his slaves[577].

Various forms of injury have been treated in Roman law since ancient times as a crime against good customs. It could be committed by deed (*re*), words (*verbis*) or writing (*litteris*). Committing it constituted a violation of the body (*corpus*), personal dignity (*dignitas*) or defamation (*infamia*). Over time, it was extended to more and more types of behavior. Active injury (*iniuria realis*) was committed by pushing, hitting, beating, but also by using an unlawful threat to evoke a feeling of grave fear (for example, threatening to kill). Verbal injury (*iniuria verbalis*) could occur as a result of uttering insulting words, throwing insults, in the presence or absence of the person to whom they refer, while a written injury (*iniuria litteralis*) was committed by publishing a defamatory letter directed against a given person, composing, writing or publishing a lampoon, poem or book (also anonymously) defaming that person, but also distributing them[578]. Roman law sources mention many other cases of inflicting it, for example by slapping someone, cutting their clothes, trying to deprave a woman or a man, freeborn or freed, constantly following a person, trying to humiliate a slave, as well as demanding that a person

576 J. Panowicz-Lipska, 'Art. 23', in M. Gutowski (ed.), *Kodeks cywilny*, vol. 1, *Komentarz. Art. 1-449^{11}*, Warszawa 2016, pp. 135-144.

577 Gai Institutiones 2,220-221; K. Kolańczyk, *Prawo rzymskie*, Warszawa 2000, p. 433.

578 Iustiniani Institutiones 4,4,1; Iustiniani Digesta 47,10,5,9-10.

known to be free be recognized as a slave, as well as causing one of the above violations, even if one did not commit it oneself[579].

An essential element of the injury was the bad intention of the perpetrator. Therefore, due to the lack of intentional guilt (*dolus*), it could not be committed by mentally ill people, immature people, or people who had lost consciousness[580].

The institution of injury has changed over the centuries. Not only has it covered more and more different behaviors, but the sanctions for committing it have also changed. The most severe punishment – the death penalty – was provided for in the Law of the Twelve Tables (5th century BC) for *carmina*, that is the uttering of magical spells, as well as composing and singing songs that defamed others (Tab. 8,1)[581]. At the same time, milder cases of injury were sanctioned by a lump sum private penalty of 25 aces, due to the victim of such a delict (Table 8,4). In the 2nd century BC, praetors carried out a reform of this delict, as a result of which the *actio iniuriarum aestimatoria* began to be applied. It allowed the victim to individually estimate the value of the injury suffered, the amount of which, expressed in money, could be regulated by the judge, departing from the rigid system of penalties of the law of the Twelve Tables[582]. From 81 BC, alongside civil sanctions, criminal sanctions were again applied based on the *lex Cornelia de iniuriis*. The perpetrator of the injury could be deemed incapable to be a witness (*intestabilis*), be subjected to legal infamy, or even the death penalty. It was up to the insulted person whether they would choose criminal or private proceedings to seek justice[583].

The punishment was moderated taking into account the type of violation and the degree of injury as well as the legal position (*dignity*) of the injured person and

---

579 Iustiniani Digesta 47,10,11-12. See also B. Sitek, 'Przypadki naruszenia prawa do dobrego imienia przez zniesławienie w świetle konstytucji cesarzy rzymskich', in J. Dobkowski (ed.), *Problemy współczesnego ustrojoznawstwa. Księga jubileuszowa Profesora Bronisława Jastrzębskiego*, Olsztyn 2007, pp. 592-601; D. Nowicka, 'Niewerbalne sposoby naruszenia czci w prawie rzymskim', *Zeszyty Prawnicze* 1 (2016), pp. 5-23.

580 S. Kursa, *La diseredazione…*, p. 75.

581 M. and J. Zabłoccy, *Ustawa XX Tablic. Tekst – tłumaczenie - objaśnienia*, Warszawa 2003, pp. 50-51.

582 Broadly for the topic see M. Sobczyk, 'Ewolucja charakteru prawnego roszczenia o zadośćuczynienie pieniężne z tytułu naruszenia dóbr osobistych', *Studia Prawnoustrojowe* 45 (2019), pp. 295-298.

583 D. Nowicka, 'Rzymskie uregulowania dotyczące 'iniuria' a karnoprawna ochrona czci w prawie polskim', *Zeszyty Prawnicze* 1 (2014), pp. 133-134.

the injuring person[584]. A grave injury was considered, for example, when it was committed against an official, senator, ascendant or patron, on account of their person, but also when it was committed in public, for example during games, in a theatre or in a forum, or if an injury or a blow to the face occurred[585].

Roman law also provided for limitations on the protection of honour and good reputation. Paulus in his commentary stated, that it was neither good nor just to sentence someone for the reason that he has slandered a wrongdoer, for it is necessary that the crimes of wrongdoers be known[586]. This means that the law did not protect the good name of people guilty of acts for which they were publicly condemned, and even encouraged publicizing such cases.

4. Conclusions

Modern legal regulations are often modelled on or are a development of Roman ones. A great example of this are the regulations concerning the protection of honour and good name. Although initially Roman law enumerated several specific cases constituting forms of violation of honour or good reputation, providing for rigidly defined sanctions for their commission, over time the catalogue of these acts was significantly expanded, and sanctions for their commission were imposed individually, taking into account the degree and type of the act, as well as who and whom had insulted. Both civil (financial) and criminal sanctions were applied. Similarly, today there is no closed catalogue of acts constituting a violation of honour and good name protected by law, and the law provides for both civil (private) and criminal sanctions for their commission, which the judge moderates depending on the degree of infringement of personal rights.

It is worth emphasizing that in Roman law, the protection of honour and good reputation was subject to limitations, as in the case of defaming a criminal, which was not punishable. Also in this respect, there is a similarity between contemporary law and Roman law, which, although in a different way, also allows for limitations on the protection of honour and good name.

Bibliography

Banaszak B., *Konstytucja Rzeczypospolitej Polskiej. Komentarz*, Warszawa 2012, pp. 297-298.

584 Gai Institutiones 2,223-225; Iustiniani Institutiones 4,4,7-9.
585 Iustiniani Digesta 47,10,7-9.
586 Iustiniani Digesta 47,10,18 pr.

Florczak M. -Wątor, 'Art. 47', in P. Tuleja (ed.), *Konstytucja Rzeczypospolitej Polskiej. Komentarz*, Warszawa 2023.

Izdebski H., 'Zasada proporcjonalności a ograniczenie praw człowieka', in S. Patyra, M. Sadowski, K. Urbaniak (eds.), *Konstytucja w państwie demokratycznym*, Poznań 2017.

Kolańczyk K., *Prawo rzymskie*, Warszawa 2000.

Kubiak-Cyrul A., *Dobra osobiste osób prawnych*, Kraków 2005.

Kursa S., *La diseredazione nel diritto giustinianeo*, Bari 2012.

Kursa S., *Protection of Personal Rights in Law of Succession*, *Teka Komisji Prawniczej PAN Oddział w Lublinie* 1 (2023).

Matys J., *Model zadośćuczynienia pieniężnego z tytułu szkody niemajątkowej w kodeksie cywilnym*, Warszawa 2010.

Nowak A., 'Pojęcie władzy ojcowskiej w prawie klasycznym', *Studia Prawnoustrojowe* 1 (2002).

Nowicka D., 'Niewerbalne sposoby naruszenia czci w prawie rzymskim', *Zeszyty Prawnicze* 1 (2016).

Nowicka D., 'Rzymskie uregulowania dotyczące 'iniuria' a karnoprawna ochrona czci w prawie polskim', *Zeszyty Prawnicze* 1 (2014).

Panowicz-Lipska J., 'Art. 23', in M. Gutowski (ed.), *Kodeks cywilny*, vol. 1, *Komentarz. Art. 1-449[11]*, Warszawa 2016.

Safjan M., 'Prawo do ochrony życia prywatnego i autonomia jednostki w orzecznictwie Trybunału Konstytucyjnego', in M. Zubik (ed.), *Księga XX-lecia orzecznictwa Trybunału Konstytucyjnego*, Warszawa 2006.

Sadomski J., *Konflikt zasad – ochrona dóbr osobistych a wolność prasy*, Warszawa 2008.

Sarnecki P., 'Artykuł 47', in L. Garlicki, M. Zubik (eds.), *Konstytucja Rzeczypospolitej Polskiej. Komentarz*, vol. II, *Art. 30-86*, Warszawa 2016.

Sitek B., 'Przypadki naruszenia prawa do dobrego imienia przez zniesławienie w świetle konstytucji cesarzy rzymskich', in J. Dobkowski (ed.), *Problemy współczesnego ustrojoznawstwa. Księga jubileuszowa Profesora Bronisława Jastrzębskiego*, Olsztyn 2007.

Sobczyk M., 'Ewolucja charakteru prawnego roszczenia o zadośćuczynienie pieniężne z tytułu naruszenia dóbr osobistych', *Studia Prawnoustrojowe* 45 (2019).

Zabłoccy M. and J., *Ustawa XX Tablic. Tekst – tłumaczenie - objaśnienia*, Warszawa 2003.

Renata Kamińska[587]

The right to property and the right to restrict it in Roman law

Abstract: Property was a great value for the Romans. Having *plena in re potestas*, the owner could do whatever he wanted with the thing, excluding others, and the law gave him protection effective *erga omnes*. This seemingly simple issue becomes complicated when one realises that each owner had the same rights. For this means that there could be interference by them with each other's property rights. Such situations generally concerned the ownership of property, and the cases in question were immissions. According to the preserved source texts, Roman law knew them and also regulated their intensity and the responsability of the person causing them. The following article touches on the problem of the limits to which the owners of neighbouring properties could go. It attempts to answer the question of when and as a result of which the right to make an immission turned into an abuse resulting in an infringement or restriction of the right to private property.

Keywords: *immissio*, nuisance, property, human right, neighbour

Property has accompanied mankind since the most ancient times. Regardless of the level of development of particular community, each knew the right to private property, respected it and expected to be protected. The Romans also knew property, although, as can be judged from the surviving source texts, they did not define the concept.[588] They called it full authority over a thing - *plena in re potestas*, i.e. a right unlimited in terms of time and the powers of the owner.[589] Undoubtedly, although without formulating a definition, the Romans regarded it as a right

---

587 Cardinal Stefan Wyszynski University in Warsaw, ORCID: 0000-0003-3357-1734.

588 G. 2,40; H. Kupiszewski, "Rozważania o własności rzymskiej", *Czasopismo Prawno-Historyczne* 36/2 (1984), p. 32; M. Kuryłowicz, "Wolność i własność (tezy komunikatu)", in *Jednostka wobec działań administracji publicznej*, Międzynarodowa Konferencja Naukowa Olszanica 21-23 maja 2001, Rzeszów 2001, p. 244. A different view is taken by W. Rozwadowski, "Rzymska koncepcja własności w kulturze prawnej Europy", *Zeszyty Prawnicze* 10/1 (2010), p. 24; Idem, "Rozważania o tak zwanej własności relatywnej w prawie rzymskim", *Czasopismo Prawno-Historyczne* 63/2 (2022), p. 202.

589 D. 1,5,4; C. 4,35,21; I. 2,4,4; A. Rodger, *Owners and Neighbours in Roman Law*, Oxford 1972, p. 1-3; T. Dybowski, "Ochrona własności w polskim prawie cywilnym (*rei vindicatio - actio negatoria*)", Warszawa 1969, p. 55; J. Sondel, "Własność prywatna w prawie rzymskim", in *Własność prywatna*, ed. T. Wawak, Kraków 1993, p. 21.

belonging to every man by virtue of the fact that he was a man.[590] However, since every Roman enjoyed the same powers, this means that they suffered reciprocal limitations. This means that in addition to restrictions imposed by the protection of the collective interest, thus of an administrative, sanitary, communicational or construction nature, private property was limited by the analogous rights of the other.[591] This is particularly clear in the case of neighbourhood relations and the issue of immissions, which are an integral part of them, and which denoted any human action resulting in interference with another's property.[592] Immissions are characterised by reciprocity of influence. This is because the owner of the real property, performing actions arising from his right in a natural way, interferes with the sphere of rights of the other owner in such a way as to interfere with his free use of the real property.[593] In many cases, the causing of immissions is even obvious and, even if someone does not want to cause them, they is not able to prevent them. The best example of this is the emission of noise or odours. The doubt that arises in this connection therefore concerns how far the owner of a thing, especially immovable property, exercising his rights could go. How much had to be endured by the owner of another property exercising analogous rights in relation to his property? When and as a result of what, did the right to carry out immissions degenerate into an abuse resulting in an infringement or restriction of the right to private property?

The starting point for considerations on this subject should be the image of immission outlined by Ulpian in his commentary on the praetor's edict:

> D. 8,5,8,5 (Ulp. 17 *ad ed.*): *Aristo Cerellio Vitali respondit non putare se ex taberna Casiaria fumum in superiora aedificia iure immitti posse, nisi ei rei servitutem talem admittit. Idemque ait: et ex superiore in inferiora non aquam, non quid aliud immitti licet: in suo enim alii hactenus facere licet, quatenus nihil in alienum immittat, fumi autem sicut*

---

590 T. Pistol, "Instytucja wywłaszczenia a prawo do własności jako prawo człowieka", in *Państwo i Społeczeństwo* 10/1 (2010), p. 107.

591 Tab. 7,1; Tab. 10,9; D. 43,8,2,21; Cic. *De leg.* 2,23,58; Suet., *Aug.* 89; Front., *De aq.* 124, 125, 128; D.U. Nicolini, *La proprietà, il principe e l'espropriazione per publica utilità. Studi sulla dottrina giuridica intermedia*, Milano 1940, p. 49-63; W. Wołodkiewicz, "Czy święta własność prywatna w prawie rzymskim? (Na marginesie wywiadu z profesor Ewą Łętowską)", *Palestra* 3-4 (2015), p. 226.

592 D. 43,8,2,20; D. 43,8,2,26; D. 43,8,2,35; D. 43,8,2,37; D. 43,12,1,19; D. 43,12,1,21; D. 43,13,1,11; D. 43,23,1,9; D. 43,23,1,15; M.ª C. Jiménez Salcedo, *El régimen jurídico de las relaciones de vicindad en derecho romano*, Oviedo 1999, p. 36.

593 W.J. Katner, *Ochrona własności nieruchomości przed naruszeniami pośrednimi*, Warszawa 1982, p. 27; J. Nadler, in *Kodeks cywilny. Komentarz*, ed. Gniewek, Warszawa 2004, p. 446.

> *aquae esse immissionem: posse igitur superiorem cum inferiore agere ius illi non esse id ita facere. Alfenum denique scribere ait posse ita agi ius illi non esse in suo lapidem caedere, ut in meum fundum fragmenta cadant. Dicit igitur Aristo eum, qui tabernam Casiariam a Minturnensibus conduxit, a superiore prohiberi posse fumum immittere, sed Minturnenses ei ex conducto teneri: agique sic posse dicit cum eo, qui eum fumum immittat, ius ei non esse fumum immittere. Ergo per contrarium agi poterit ius esse fumum immittere: quod et ipsum videtur aristo probare. Sed et interdictum uti possidetis poterit locum habere, si quis prohibeatur, qualiter velit, suo uti.*

The jurist explained that the essence of immissions was that the person who committed them acted *in suo*, i.e. within the boundaries of his own property, but the immissions were felt by another owner on his land (*immittere in alienum*).[594]

Ulpian's statement presents the essence of immission and helps to establish the permissible limits of interactions within the neighbourhood relationship. For when one considers that any activity a proprietor conducted on his own property was lawful provided it did not cause an interference *in alieno*, yet the discharge of smoke, smells, or noise could be regarded as an impact on another's property; we may thus reach a conclusion that a proprietor's freedom to act *in suo* in any way he liked was not "all-inclusive," and in practice he could come up against restrictions or prohibitions at any time. However, we should bear in mind that such restrictions were formulated in various sources, either private or public law, and they were inherent in the concept of *dominium* as *plena in re potestas*. Every proprietor who carried out specific activities within the boundaries of his own property not exceeding his rights was acting lawfully.[595] In other words he could exercise that right in any way he pleased, providing his conduct did not interfere with the analogous rights of another owner, and in particular that not to cause his harm. On the other hand, an owner's right to freely enjoy his property and the proximity of properties belonging to others subsumed the admissibility of mutual impact.[596] Thus we need to establish whether every interference with another proprietor's domain was treated as nuisance, and if so, prohibited. It is worth noting that it was thorny issue for Roman jurists. They argued about to which restrictions could

594 See M.ª C. Jiménez Salcedo, *op. cit.*, p. 38-39; J.G. Sánchez, *Teoría de la immissio*, Oviedo 1999, p. 69.

595 G. Longo, v. "Immissioni (Diritto romano)", in *Novissimo Digesto Italiano* VIII, Torino 1962, p. 186.

596 L. Piniński, *Pojęcie i granice prawa własności według prawa rzymskiego*, Lwów 1900, p. 7, points out that when speaking of the kind and extent of the *immissio*, we should consider not just the location of the property, but we should start by considering the type of object, whether it was a movable or real estate.

have been be lawfully applied on the right to enjoy one's property, what should be recognised as a restriction on proprietorship, and what was merely an outcome of the free enjoyment of one's property.[597] The passage from Ulpian's commentary quoted above is very useful in this respect, for he listed ways of impact in a neighbour's space. Thus there were three types of matter which were considered to cause nuisance, solids, liquids, and gases; and all three were prohibited. Both Ulpian and the other roman lawyers he referred to, made no distinction in their statements on prohibited kinds of impact on another person's property between littering a neighbour's property with chips flying off stone dressed *in suo*, spraying it with water, or discharging smoke on it. In Ulpian's opinion *facere in suo* meant only activities which did not cause nuisance *in alieno*, and it applied to the same degree to all three of these situations. Yet on the other hand the normal enjoyment of one's rights of proprietorship takes for granted that nuisance will occur. Furthermore, the very fact that there are other properties in the neighbourhood gives rise to a self-evident dependence which makes one property exert an impact on another.[598] So the basic problem is not impact as such, which may be seen as an inherent part of neighbourly relations, but its magnitude. Hence the next question concerning nuisance is its admissibility, or in other words the bounds to the free enjoyment of one's property. It seems very likely that the "average level" of interference was assessed from the perspective of the objective estimate arrived at by the owner of a property on which disturbances of the given type occur at an intensity not greater than usual.[599] In other words, only such nuisance is legally admissible which is due to the lawful enjoyment of the given property in compliance with its socio-economic purpose, and its level does not unreasonably restrict other proprietors' enjoyment of neighbouring properties.[600]

Such was also Rudolf von Jhering's conviction who propounded the theory of ordinary effect.[601] The scholar wrote that direct nuisance or indirect activity or

---

597 L. Piniński, *op. cit.*, p. 22.

598 J. Moskała, "Immisja jako dopuszczalna forma ingerencji w cudze prawo własności w prawie polskim w świetle orzecznictwa", in *Wrocławskie Studia Erazmiańskie* (*Studia Erasmiana Wratislaviensia*), '*Własność' – idea, instytucje, ochrona*, ed. M. Sadowski, P. Szymaniec, 3 (2009), p. 356.

599 S. Rudnicki, *Sąsiedztwo nieruchomości*, Kraków 1999, p. 24.

600 T. Dybowski, *op. cit.*, p. 325.

601 J.G. Sánchez, *op. cit.*, 93; F. Longchamps de Bérier, "Klika uwag o własności (na marginesie badań nad nadużyciem prawa w rzymskim prawie prywatnym)", in *Zeszyty Prawnicze*, 3/2 (2003), pp. 199-200 follows: R. Ihering, *Zur Lehre von den Beschränkungen des Grundeigenthümers im Interesse der Nachbarn (Ges. Aufsätze II)*, Jena 1882, vol. II, pp. 22-26, 48-64.

nuisance in excess of the generally accepted level was unlawful. According to his theory, classical Roman law prohibited direct and indirect nuisance which was due to *facere in suo* but had an intolerable effect on a neighbouring property. A similar view was held by Italian scholar Alberto Burdese[602], who believed that that under Roman law nuisance *in alieno* caused by *facere in suo* could only be regarded as lawful if its extent was limited to the level of disturbance due to the normal use of the real estate.

The accuracy of R. von Jhering's theory seems to be confirmed by a passage from Paulus' commentary on the works of Sabinus:

> D. 8,2,19pr. (Paul. 6 *ad Sab.*): *Fistulam iunctam parieti communi, quae aut ex castello aut ex caelo aquam capit, non iure haberi Proculus ait: sed non posse prohiberi vicinum, quo minus balienum habeat secundum parietem communem, quamvis umorem capiat paries: non magis quam si vel in triclinio suo vel in cubiculo aquam effunderet. sed Neratius ait, si talis sit usus tepidarii, ut adsiduum umorem habeat et id noceat vicino, posse prohiberi eum.*

Paulus divided the activities performed on land into two groups. In the first he included those that were prohibited by law as part of neighbourly coexistence, and in the second those that the law allowed. Prohibited activities were therefore to include, among others, installing a water pipe on a wall he shared with his neighbour to collect water from a water tank or rainwater.

The latter group involved activities evidently due to a proprietor's normal use of his property for his ordinary, everyday needs, such as having a bathroom or using a lot of water in his dining room or bedroom. However, if his having hot baths caused damp in his neighbour's premises, in other words if it damaged his neighbour's property, there were sufficient grounds for the neighbour to apply for an injunction to stop him from doing this.[603] However, if the use of warm baths could cause permanent dampness to the other neighbour, that neighbour could apply to stop such activities from continuing. The threat of harm that could be caused to another property owner by actions on his own land was a sufficient circumstance to justify the right to require, the neighbour to cease such actions.

---

602 A. Burdese, *Manuale di diritto privato romano*, Torino 1964, p. 386.

603 By analogy to the damage caused by individuals in public places, in relations between private persons we may regard activities such as, for instance, depriving someone of the use of specific amenities (*commoda*) as damage (*damnum*). See 43,8,2,11 (Ulp. 64 *ad ed.*): *Damnum autem pati videtur, qui commodum amittit, quod ex publico consequebatur, qualequale sit*. See also J.G. Sánchez, *op. cit.*, 101; M.ª C. Jiménez Salcedo, *op. cit.*, p. 83.

In a similar vein, Pomponius said:

D. 8,2,27pr. (Pomp. 33 *ad Sab.*): *Sed si inter te et me communes sunt Titianae aedes et ex his aliquid non iure in alias aedes meas proprias immissum sit, nempe tecum mihi agere licet aut rem perdere. Idem fiet, si ex tuis propriis aedibus in communes meas et tuas aedes quid similiter esset proiectum: mihi enim soli tecum est actio.*

In an excerpt from a commentary on the writings of Sabinus, he stated that an owner whose rights were infringed by an immission could use a complaint against the emitting neighbour. In addition, that neighbour was liable to forfeit the thing which caused the nuisance (*nempe tecum mihi agere licet aut rem perdere*).

All the statements of the jurists Neratius, Paulus and Pomponius quoted above allow two conclusions to be drawn. Firstly, that in Roman times, only those immissions were admissible which resulted from the ordinary, lawful and socio-economic use of the property, and their extent did not result in an overly great limitation in the use of the neighbouring property. Secondly if the impact on another's property was not intentional, did no damage it or did not go beyond the owner's normal use of the property, such impact was not classified as an unlawful nuisance.[604] The normal use of a thing by the owner was understood to be activities that were within the limits of the proprietor's right, and were therefor an inherent part of his exercise of his right to his property, insofar as they were simply part of his ordinary everyday activities. Such effects should not be classified as legally prohibited immissions.

The quoted jurists thus confirm the assumption made at the beginning that not every interference with another's property was considered a prohibited act.[605] They would have called only those types of *facere in suo* unlawful which involved a disturbance of a neighbour's legal domain.[606] This rule applied to all types of nuisance to the same extent, whether it was caused by noise, smoke, or water. Each of them was an abuse and unlawful if the extent of the discharge was excessive with respect to what a neighbour was obliged to tolerate, and with respect to the real needs of the person who caused the nuisance. Evidence is provided by a passage from Javolenus' commentary to the last works of Labeo:

D. 47,10,44 (Iav. 9 *ex post. Lab.*): *Si inferiorum dominus aedium superioris vicini fumigandi causa fumum faceret, aut si superior vicinus in inferiores aedes quid aut proiecerit aut infuderit, negat Labeo iniuriarum agi posse: quod falsum puto, si tamen iniuriae faciendae causa immittitur.*

604 D. 50,17,55; D. 50,17,1,151; D. 50,17,155,1; M.ª C. Jiménez Salcedo, *op. cit.*, p. 85.
605 D.U. Nicolini, *op. cit.*, p. 85.
606 MªC. Jiménez Salcedo, *op. cit.*, p. 59.

Javolenus contested the opinion of Labeo, who denied the proprietor of a house on higher ground the right to sue a proprietor below him who filled his property with smoke emitted from a smoke house. There would be no grounds for a complaint, either, if the proprietor of the upper property threw or poured something out on the property below. In this latter case both jurists concurred. But Javolenus thought it was necessary to distinguish between the situation when the person pursuing the activities described by Labeo was wilfully causing damage to his neighbour's property (*iniuriae faciendae causa immittitur*), from the situation where he did not intend to cause the damage. If the person had such an intention then the jurist would grant the aggrieved party the right to complain. Was therefore the wilful emission of smoke into a neighbour's domain the only ground for a suit for nuisance, or did the discharge of smoke considered excessive with regard to the generally accepted level give sufficient grounds for a suit? If we accept Jhering's theory, we should apply it to the case described by Javolenus. A situation had occurred in which someone conducting his business *in suo* nonetheless caused an intolerable nuisance in someone else's property, thereby infringing Gaius' and Paulus' principles, *nullius videtur dolo facere, qui suo iure utitur* (D. 50,17,55) and *nemo damnum facit, nisi qui id fecit, quod facere ius non habet* (D. 50,17,1,151). Conversely, we may say that a person caused damage if he conducted a certain activity even though he should not have, because he had no right to conduct it. Conducting such an activity was considered against the law (*iniuria*). In its narrower sense *iniuria* was equivalent to *contumelia* (insult).[607] So if an insult was a breach of the law which could be committed either by a deed or verbally, as Labeo tells us,[608] then all the actions described by Javolenus meet these criteria and may be considered an insult, which in turn leads to the conclusion that the situation he presents gives the injured party the grounds for an *actio iniuriarum*.[609]

---

607 D. 47,10,1pr. (Ulp. 56 *ad ed.*): *Iniuria ex eo dicta est, quod non iure fiat: omne enim, quod non iure fit, iniuria fieri dicitur. Hoc generaliter. Specialiter autem iniuria dicitur contumelia. Interdum iniuriae appellatione damnum culpa datum significatur, ut in lege Aquilia dicere solemus: interdum iniquitatem iniuriam dicimus, nam cum quis inique vel iniuste sententiam dixit, iniuriam ex eo dictam, quod iure et iustitia caret, quasi non iuriam, contumeliam autem a contemnendo.*

608 D. 47,10,1,1 (Ulp. 56 *ad ed.*): *Iniuriam autem fieri Labeo ait aut re aut verbis: re, quotiens manus inferuntur: verbis autem, quotiens non manus inferuntur, convicium fit.*

609 A. Palma, *Iura vicinitatis*, Torino 1988, p. 131; A.M. Castillo, *El daño causado por el ruido y otras inmisiones*, Madrid 2004, p. 44, writes that in Roman law *iniuria* entailed every kind of unlawful behaviour, especially behaviour which offended another person's dignity, both in the physical and moral sense.

There was no definition of immission in Roman law, just as there was no definition of property. Regardless, both were a constant in everyone's life. Immissions, however, are not the only, but probably the most common, case of the restriction of private property in relations between individuals. This is due to the obvious fact of the other's neighbourhood. As aptly remarked by a polish scholar living at the turn of the 20th century, a researcher of Roman property law, Leon Piniński "restrictions on physical proprietorship are nothing extraordinary but quite a normal thing. Perhaps the only place which would not have them would be an island isolated off completely, for example surrounded by the sea, and belonging to a single owner."[610] These words, although referring to the author's contemporaries, fit perfectly with the concept of Roman property. Another prominent polish romanist, Henryk Kupiszewski, who wrote very similarly about it, said: "From a non-exhaustive account of the restrictions and burdens placed on property owners for the benefit of their neighbours and *pro publica utilitate*, it is clear that Roman property from the earliest times (…), had nothing of individualism or selfishness about it (…). On the contrary, it can be said that as society and the state developed, property was more and more vigorously enmeshed in social service".[611]

Living in a community has always inherently involved the risk of private property being exposed to various types of restrictions. One source of these is neighbourhood relations, i.e. relations between individual owners of neighbouring properties.[612] Each neighbor, exercising their rights in a certain way and to a certain extent, violates the rights of the other by immission. It can even be said that in many cases, influencing the neighbor's space is necessary to fully benefit from the land ownership rights. And it is precisely the fact that immissions are inseparably connected with the right to property and the reciprocity which characterises them that makes it impossible to classify them as violations of the

610 L. Piniński, *op. cit.*, p. 11.

611 H. Kupiszewski, *op. cit.*, p. 45.

612 Mutual interactions occurred not only when the properties involved were each other's immediate neighbours, viz. bordered on one another, but also when they did not adjoin each other but were removed from one another by a certain distance which was small enough for them still to be regarded as "in the neighbourhood. See D. 8,3,5,1; R. Czarnecki, "Niektóre zagadnienia prawa sąsiedzkiego", in *Nowe Prawo* 6 (1969), p. 906, 911; A. Torrente, P. Schlesinger, *Manuale di diritto private*, Milano 2009, p. 295, say that vicinity (*vicinitas*) should not be understood only in the literal sense of adjoining properties, but also in its sense in easements. In rural areas persons regarded as neighbours were also referred to as *accolati*, as well as *vicini*. See also D. 43,13,1,3; 6-7; *Rud.* 615.

right to property and, consequently, of human rights. Since man has been called to live in a community and wants, and in most cases has to live in it, he has to shape his rights in such a way and use them so skilfully that he does not violate analogous rights of other members of this community.[613] On the other hand, they must respect that the other person, the owner, has analogous rights and exercises them. The restrictions arising from the relations between these neighbours therefore concerned the normal concessions that the owners had to make in their own and each other's interests. It will therefore not be an exaggeration to say that the regulations arising from neighbourly relations implied mutual tolerance.[614]

The function of the law was, therefore, and is, to establish rules of free use by owners of their privileges and to watch over their abuse. *Utilitas singulorum* thus constituted in Roman times a natural and socially justifiable limit to the free use of private property[615].

Bibliography

Burdese A., *Manuale di Diritto Privato Romano*, Torino 1964.

Castillo A.M., *El daño causado por el ruido y otras inmisiones*, Madrid 2004.

Czarnecki R., "Niektóre zagadnienia prawa sąsiedzkiego", in *Nowe Prawo* 6 (1969).

Dybowski T., *Ochrona własności w polskim prawie cywilnym (rei vindicatio - actio negatoria)*, Warszawa 1969.

Ihering R., *Zur Lehre von den Beschränkungen des Grundeigenthümers im Interesse der Nachbarn (Ges. Aufsätze II)*, Jena 1882, vol. II.

Jiménez Salcedo M.ª C., *El régimen jurídico de las relaciones de vicindad en derecho romano*, Oviedo 1999.

Katner W.J., *Ochrona własności nieruchomości przed naruszeniami pośrednimi*, Warszawa 1982.

Kupiszewski H., "Rozważania o własności rzymskiej", *Czasopismo Prawno-Historyczne* 36/2 (1984).

---

613 According to V. Scialoja, *Teoria della proprietà nel diritto Romano*, I, Roma 1928, p. 414, the landowner could act as he pleased within the objective limits of his right.

614 M. Župljanić, M. Zorić, V. Jovanović, "Ograničenja svojine u vidu susedskih prawa u rimskom pravu", Oditor - časopis za Menadzment, finansije i parvo 5/2 (2019), p. 24.

615 For more on the concept of *utilitas singulorum* and its relations to *utilitas publica*, see M. Navarra, "Utilitas publica-utilitas singulorum tra IV e V sec. d.C. Alcune osservazioni", in *Studia et Documenta Historie et Iuris* 63 (1997), pp. 269-270, 276 and next.

Kuryłowicz M., "Wolność i własność (tezy komunikatu)", in *Jednostka wobec działań administracji publicznej*, Międzynarodowa Konferencja Naukowa Olszanica 21-23 maja 2001, Rzeszów 2001.

Longchamps de Bérier F., "Klika uwag o własności (na marginesie badań nad nadużyciem prawa w rzymskim prawie prywatnym)", in *Zeszyty Prawnicze*, 3/2 (2003).

Longo G., v. "Immissioni (Diritto romano)", in *Novissimo Digesto Italiano* VIII, Torino 1962.

Moskała J., "Immisja jako dopuszczalna forma ingerencji w cudze prawo własności w prawie polskim w świetle orzecznictwa", in *Wrocławskie Studia Erazmiańskie* (*Studia Erasmiana Wratislaviensia*), '*Własność*' – *idea, instytucje, ochrona*, ed. M. Sadowski, P. Szymaniec, 3 (2009).

Nadler J., in E *Kodeks cywilny. Komentarz*, ed. Gniewek, Warszawa 2004.

Navarra M., "Utilitas publica-utilitas singulorum tra IV e V sec. d.C. Alcune osservazioni", in *Studia et Documenta Historie et Iuris* 63 (1997).

Nicolini D.U., *La proprietà, il principe e l'espropriazione per publica utilità. Studi sulla dottrina giuridica intermedia*, Milano 1940.

Piniński L., *Pojęcie i granice prawa własności według prawa rzymskiego*, Lwów 1900.

Pistol T., "Instytucja wywłaszczenia a prawo do własności jako prawo człowieka", *Państwo i Społeczeństwo* 10/1 (2010).

Rodger A., *Owners and Neighbours in Roman Law*, Oxford 1972.

Rozwadowski W., "Rzymska koncepcja własności w kulturze prawnej Europy", *Zeszyty Prawnicze* 10/1 (2010).

Rozwadowski W., "Rozważania o tak zwanej własności relatywnej w prawie rzymskim", *Czasopismo Prawno-Historyczne* 63/2 (2022).

Rudnicki S., *Sąsiedztwo nieruchomości*, Kraków 1999.

Sánchez J.G., *Teoría de la immissio*, Oviedo 1999.

Scialoja V., *Teoria della proprietà nel diritto Romano*, I, Roma 1928.

Sondel J., "Własność prywatna w prawie rzymskim", in *Własność prywatna*, ed. T. Wawak, Kraków 1993.

Torrente A., Schlesinger P., *Manuale di diritto private*, Milano 2009.

Wołodkiewicz W., "Czy święta własność prywatna w prawie rzymskim? (Na marginesie wywiadu z profesor Ewą Łętowską)", *Palestra* 3-4 (2015), pp. 223-227.

Župljanić M., Zorić M., Jovanović V., "Ograničenja svojine u vidu susedskih prava u rimskom pravu", Oditor - časopis za Menadzment, finansije i parvo 5/2 (2019).

Ewelina Mikulska[616]

A will – a source of knowledge about the hopes and needs of the dying

Abstract: The article titled "The Will as a Source of Knowledge on the Needs and Hopes of the Dying through the Ages" presents an analysis of the ways of drafting testamentary documents within the context of uncovering human aspirations and social practices related to death and inheritance over the centuries. It examines the tradition of making wills from antiquity through the Middle Ages to the present day, exploring how these documents reflected the wishes and priorities of people in different eras. The article focuses on the changing nature of wills and their significance for the deceased and their heirs, illustrating how testamentary practices influenced family structure, social relationships, and the sense of individuality. It also considers how ecclesiastical and legal interpretations of wills shaped the understanding of property ownership and inheritance rights. The research assumptions of the article are based on the belief that wills are an important, though often overlooked, historical source that can broaden our understanding of past societies, their beliefs, and economic and social practices. This study emphasizes the importance of wills in finding indirect evidence of the value systems and motivations that drove behavior and decisions regarding death. Through this lens, the article highlights the wealth of information that wills can provide to researchers interested in social, cultural, and legal history.

Keywords: Last will, dying, inheritance, testamentary documents

1. Introduction

"Just as the health of a tree's roots can be discerned from its fruit, and the quality of a bulb can be judged by its flowers, so the contents of a will reveal whether the heart of the testator was good or wicked".[617] This sentence should be understood literally: a will can provide many clues about who the person who wrote it was and what motivated them. The contents of a will reflect not only the testator's personal beliefs and values, but also their relationships with loved ones, as well as social and cultural circumstances. By analysing wills, we can discover much about

616 Jan Długosz University in Częstochowa, ORCID 0000-0003-3327-3016.

617 G. Day, *Famous and Curious Wills*, „Law Library Journal" 1925, nr 18, p. 45; after: J. Wierciński, *Brak świadomości lub swobody przy sporządzaniu testamentów [Lack of Awareness or Freedom in Drafting a Wil]l*, LexisNexis 2013; http://sip.lex.pl/#/monografia/369297179/42 accessed 30.06.2024.

the emotions, hopes, and fears that accompanied people in their final moments of /life."

The history of inheritance law is full of examples of eccentric testamentary dispositions, such as a father bequeathing only a single coin to his son, expressing the hope that even it would burn his fingers, or in the will traditionally attributed to Shakespeare, in which he left his wife only his "second-best bed," thus bequeathing the "best" one to someone else. Bizarre dispositions do not provide grounds for declaring that the testator might have been mentally ill, and unreasonable, unnatural, unjust, or even cruel provisions towards close ones cannot be deemed invalid solely on this basis.[618]

The subject of this article will be to present the will from a historical perspective as a source of knowledge about the needs of the dying, the ways of expressing this knowledge, and the legal possibilities of respecting it. Issues concerning the legal regulations of inheritances and the act of making a will per se are not the topic of this work and will be deliberately omitted here, as they go far beyond the scope of the article's subject matter.

2. What is a Will?

For centuries, wills have served as a tool for conveying the last will and needs of the dying, reflecting not only personal values and beliefs but also relationships with loved ones, as well as social and cultural conditions. In different eras and cultures, the form and content of wills have evolved, adapting to changing laws and customs. At this point, it is therefore appropriate to ask: what is a will and where does it originate from?

3. Wills in Antiquity

The institution of the will appeared at a certain stage in the development of human culture; however, the methods of bequeathing one's estate in the event of death were not always the same. In ancient Egyptian law, wills were not drawn up at all. Historical records indicate that written forms of agreements or dispositions of one's estate (including in the event of death) were reserved mainly for the elite, which also suggests that the use of documentary forms, even in the realm of

---

618 J J. Wierciński, *Brak świadomości lub swobody przy sporządzaniu testamentów [Lack of Awareness or Freedom in Drafting a Wil]l*, LexisNexis 2013; http://sip.lex.pl/#/monografia/369297179/42 accessed 30.06.2024.

public administration, was characterized by a certain selectivity.[619] Despite this, evidence has survived that confirms dispositions of one's estate in a form similar to a will (due to the intended future effects). One of them reads: "*The year of the unification of both lands. The third month of the winter season. The 29th day. Semer-Wati-Uper-nofret (Smr-w'tj Wp-m-nfrt) said: 'To my eldest son, the priest, lector Abi ('Ibj), I have given forever the northern funeral hall, together with the northern vestibule of offerings, which are in my tomb in the cemetery, so that he may be buried there and so that posthumous offerings may be made there for him, who was my favourite. No brother, no woman, and none of [my] sons have rights to this, except my eldest son, the priest, lector Abi. To him [it] I have given. Drawn up in the presence of many witnesses.*'"[620]

From the above text, another rule of inheritance can also be drawn - succession by the deceased's closest relatives, particularly by sons. Those who wished that a specific item from their estate be passed on to a specifically designated person after their death usually had to transfer it to a trustee during their lifetime with the instruction to deliver it to the indicated person after the "testator's" death.

During the New Kingdom period, there emerged the legal possibility of making a testamentary statement before a court; however, its validity was dependent on the consent of the entitled heirs, today's statutory heirs. This principle would affect the validity of the aforementioned statement of intent, consequently rendering it invalid in the absence of the heirs' consent. Similarly, ancient Babylonian law did not provide for the existence of wills. In cases where the dying person had no descendants, there was the possibility of posthumous adoption, whereby the adopted person would inherit the estate after the death of the adopter.[621]

The spread of wills in ancient Greece is attributed to Solon. According to Plutarch, Solon's approach to the topic of wills distinguished him from other ancient statesmen. Wills thus constituted the assignment of property to their owners and allowed them to dispose of it in the event of death. Previously, inheritance within the family was the only possibility, which significantly limited the control over a given asset. Solon introduced a new practice of freely disposing of one's

---

619 J. C. Moreno Garcia, "*The Study of Ancient Egyptian Administration*," in *Ancient Egyptian Administration*, edited by J. C. Moreno Garcia, Leiden/Boston 2013, p. 10.

620 Text of the ancient declaration of intent carved in stone found in Giza, from the tomb of Upemnofret, dated to 2400-2340 BCE; cited in: E. Lipiński, *Prawo Bliskowschodnie w starożytności [Near Eastern Law in Antiquity*], Lublin 2009, p. 261.

621 P. S. Księżak, *Zachowek w polskim prawie spadkowym [Legitim in Polish Inheritance Law]*, LexisNexis 2012, http:/sip.lex.pl/#/monografia/369258116/4, accessed 30.06.2024.

estate, thereby giving equal respect to the bonds of friendship between unrelated individuals and relatives, placing feelings above duties.[622]

Roman law also deserves attention, where the concept of the will first clearly appears in the Law of the Twelve Tables. Table 5.3 contains the phrase: "*uti legassit super pecunia tutelave suae rei, ita ius esto*," based on which it is assumed that by the 5th century BCE, the institution of the will, as a disposition in the event of death, was already known. It is likely that wills were used earlier; however, they were permissible only by way of exception for people who had no own heirs (*sui heredes*) or to confirm the intestate order of inheritance.[623]

4. The Origins of Polish Wills

The origins of early inheritance law in European states, including the Polish lands, are connected with the institution of undivided ownership, meaning collective property held by the family during the times of the patrimonial state. The ownership of movable property was exclusively individual. The ownership of land in medieval Europe, including Poland, was defined as family community ownership. This form of ownership was known as joint family ownership. Unlike Roman co-ownership (condominium), the participants in the family undivided ownership, who wielded joint ownership, did not have rights to ideal parts of the property but acted as a collective entity jointly owning the property. Hence, in the event of the death of a community member, who was also a participant in the undivided ownership, his property rights did not pass to the heirs but remained within the collective property of the undivided ownership. These rights were inalienable, meaning they could not be transferred by the will of the dying person either. The deceased served as a unifying figure of the property, preventing its division among, sometimes numerous, heirs.[624] The practice at that time also did not recognize the concept of disinheriting sons. Adult sons, being necessary heirs, became co-owners of the estate during their father's lifetime.[625]

---

622 *Legal history of will*, https://en.wikipedia.org/wiki/Legal_history_of_wills accessed 30.06.2024.

623 M. Pecyna, J. Pisuliński, *Rozprawy cywilistyczne. Księga pamiątkowa dedykowana Profesorowi Edwardowi Drozdowi [Civil Law Treatises. Commemorative Book Dedicated to Professor Edward Drozd]*, LexisNexis 2013, http://sip.lex.pl/#/monografia/369349780/161, accessed 30.06.2024.

624 A. Dunin-Dudkowska, *Testament jako zwierciadło kultur. Polsko-amerykańskie studium komparatystyczne [The Will as a Mirror of Cultures. A Polish-American Comparative Study]*, Lublin 2014, p. 47.

625 J. Bardach, *Historia Państwa i Prawa Polski, Tom I do połowy XV wieku [History of the State and Law of Poland, Volume I up to the mid-15th century]*, Warsaw 1973, p. 304.

In Poland, the institution of the will appeared during the medieval period. Polish archives, like those in other countries, contain a vast number of wills that serve as valuable sources of knowledge about the past. They were drawn up by representatives of various social strata, from townspeople, both wealthy and poorer, to the nobility and powerful magnates with extensive estates. Clergy members, except for monks who had no right to own property, also wrote their last wills, making wills not only legal documents but also unique testimonies of daily life and interpersonal relationships of those times.[626]

Early wills were often documents in which testators bequeathed part of their estate to the Church, hoping to ensure peace for their souls after death. This spiritual aspiration reflected the medieval belief that charitable deeds could influence an individual's fate in the afterlife.[627] Natural law, which reserved inheritance rights for the deceased's closest family, held sway over the testators will expressed in the will during the medieval period. Testators could only dispose of movable property, reflecting the legal and social limitations of the time regarding wills.[628]

Over time, wills became increasingly diverse and complex. With the development of law and changing customs, testators began to use wills not only for religious purposes but also for personal declarations of intent and the expression of their final wishes. Wills became an important tool for regulating property matters and reflecting the evolving social and legal structure of medieval Europe.

The Church strongly advocated for the freedom of testation, demanding the liberty to dispose of immovable property through wills. The clergy saw this as a way to quickly increase the Church's wealth and thus insisted that a priest's presence was necessary when drawing up a will to ensure that the testator, concerned for the salvation of their soul, made bequests to the Church. Before the twelfth century, even before the freedom of testation was established, the Church sought a share in inheritances by promoting the principle of "adoption by Christ" (*adoptio Christi*). This meant that a portion of the estate, by principle, belonged to Christ,

626 see B. Leśniodorski, Z. Kaczmarczyk, *Historia państwa i prawa Polski, T. II od połowy XV wieku do roku 1905 [History of the State and Law of Poland, Vol. II from the mid-15th century to the year 1905]*, Warsaw 1966, p. 277.

627 B. Bobowski, *Testament w średniowiecznym prawie polskim [The Will in Medieval Polish Law], Prace Naukowe Akademii im. Jana Długosza w Częstochowie [Scientific Works of the Jan Długosz Academy in Częstochowa]*, 2009, vol. X, p. 84.

628 B. R. Dembska, *O testamencie w polskim prawie średniowiecznym [On the Will in Medieval Polish Law]*, in: *Studia z historii ustroju i prawa [Studies in the History of the System and Law]*, edited by H. Olszewska, Poznań 2002, p. 59.

and thus to the Church.[629] Ultimately, immovable property was excluded from free testation, and the transfer of real estate to the clergy was prohibited by the Piotrków Sejm Act of 1510.[630]

5. Wills in Medieval Europe

In medieval Europe, the will became widespread after the year 1172. Before the tribunal in Lyon, in a typical year without any devastating epidemic, fewer than ten wills were registered annually until 1380, and by the end of the 14th century, this number had increased to between twenty and thirty. It is worth noting that this city included five hundred parishes. In London, the number of wills registered by the Commissary Court rose from an average of fifty annually at the end of the 14th century to about one hundred in the 15th century. Statistically, 10 to 15 percent of deceased adults made a will, including 2-3 percent of women. Medieval wills are characterized by strong selectivity, but this does not change the fact that for an increasing number of people, death and what followed was an opportunity for the testator to express their wishes and views on the future lives of their heirs. It also provided the possibility to plan their own funeral or, for example, a funeral procession.[631] Regardless of the function of the will, which undoubtedly included the disposal of property, it was largely a religious document. This is evidenced, among other things, by the fact that, regardless of the adopted form, the document began with a preamble in the form of a pious invocation.[632] Bequests to the poor or religious orders were known and found in the oldest wills, but from the 13th century onwards, these acts began to follow an established ritual, indicating the growing popularity of this custom. For example, a special alms to monasteries and orders in the form of an evening meal - *refectatio ceritatis* - was practiced.[633]

---

629 J. Bardach, *Historia Państwa i Prawa Polski, Tom I do połowy XV wieku [History of the State and Law of Poland, Volume I up to the mid-15th century]*, Warsaw 1973, p. 305-306.

630 B. Bobowski, *Testament w średniowiecznym prawie polskim [The Will in Medieval Polish Law], Prace Naukowe Akademii im. Jana Długosza w Częstochowie [Scientific Works of the Jan Długosz Academy in Częstochowa]*, 2009, vol. X, p. 86.

631 M. Vovelle, *Śmierć w cywilizacjach Zachodu [Death in Western Civilizations]*, trans. T. Swoboda, Gdańsk 2004, p. 157-158.

632 M. Vovelle, *Śmierć w cywilizacjach Zachodu [Death in Western Civilizations]*, trans. T. Swoboda, Gdańsk 2004, p. 172.

633 M. Vovelle, *Śmierć w cywilizacjach Zachodu [Death in Western Civilizations]*, trans. T. Swoboda, Gdańsk 2004, p. 97.

Over time, a canon developed to which a will should conform. This obligation was not a compulsion, so researchers encountered wills of all kinds, written on various surfaces, with content sometimes too laconic and, in other cases, written in verse, expressing a full range of emotions felt by the testator. The shortest statements fulfilling the function of a will are illustrated by the phrase: "Everything to my mother." This implies that the quantity or value of the bequeathed property did not need to be specified, nor the exact identification of the beneficiary when the interpretation of the term "mother" was obvious.[634]

Historically, the terms "last will" and "testament" were not synonymous. Both originated in medieval England, where "last will" referred to the division of real estate and immovable property of the deceased, while "testament" referred to the division of their personal property, including livestock and cash. It was not until 1837, by virtue of the English Wills Act, that the formal distinction between these terms was abolished, and since then, they have been used interchangeably.[635]

6. The Specific Functions of Wills

In addition to the obvious function of disposing of property in the event of death, the will also served several less obvious functions. Firstly, a number of beliefs in the afterlife suggest that the content of wills may indicate a specific disciplinary and educational function. Specifying the desired behaviors of heirs in the will was a tool for rewarding or punishing, as it were, from beyond the grave. This view was expressed by the philosopher Jeremy Bentham, among others. He noted the connections between inheritance mechanisms and certain human behaviors, which could be judged positively or negatively and produce specific consequences.[636] Some testators expressed their bitterness or lack of trust towards their heirs by drafting conditional wills. Sometimes the purpose was not clearly defined, but it can be assumed that the testator wanted to ensure what they had not been able to fulfill during their lifetime.[637]

---

634 A. Dunin-Dudkowska, *Testament jako zwierciadło kultur. Polsko-amerykańskie studium komparatystyczne [The Will as a Mirror of Cultures. A Polish-American Comparative Study]*, Lublin 2014, p. 48.

635 *op. cit.* p. 48.

636 M. Załucki, *Wydziedziczenie w prawie polskim na tle prawnoporównawczym [Disinheritance in Polish Law in a Comparative Legal Context]*, Oficyna 2010, http://sip.lex.pl/#/monografia/369221359/5, accessed 30.06.2024.

637 cf. A. Dunin-Dudkowska, *Testament jako zwierciadło kultur. Polsko-amerykańskie studium komparatystyczne [The Will as a Mirror of Cultures. A Polish-American Comparative Study]*, Lublin 2014, p. 51.

Wills udes to serve as an educational function, allowing testators to pass on their beliefs and values regarding the upbringing of offspring and the management of property. By including guidelines on education in the will, testators could influence the future lives of their heirs, emphasizing moral, ethical, and intellectual values. They often contained recommendations on the choice of schools, continuation of studies, and also highlighted the importance of professional or artistic education. Additionally, wills could contain instructions on household management, property administration, and investments, aimed at ensuring the financial and social stability of the heirs. In this way, wills not only secured the material future of the inheritors but also supported their personal development and prepared them for responsible roles in society.

Wills also played an important social and integrative role, strengthening family and community bonds. Besides bequeathing property to close relatives, testators often left assets to more distant family members, friends, and even entire local communities. These bequests aimed to maintain family unity, promote solidarity, and support those who were important to the testator. Wills could also include provisions for community ventures, such as foundations, schools, or hospitals, contributing to the development of the local community. In this way, wills not only regulated property matters but also strengthened social structures and integrated the community around common values and goals.

7. Conclusions

The subject of wills and their legal significance is a frequently discussed issue among lawyers, particularly civil law experts. Most often, the analysis focuses on the conditions for the validity of wills, inheritance rights, etc. However, a will as a document can be an important source of unique knowledge about the testator, social and family relations within a given cultural circle, and the political-religious context.

I agree with K. Wiszowata that wills constitute a specific type of source. Due to the topics they address, wills are a valuable source for various scientific studies. Given the purpose of these documents, they are of great significance to researchers dealing with the issue of death. Wills are a testament to human behavior concerning ultimate matters, such as death, eternal salvation, or the threat of eternal damnation. They represent the final settlement of the dying person with temporal life. Moreover, wills are an interesting source for studying the art of dying well, known as *ars moriendi*.[638]

638 K. Wiszowata, *Testamenty jako źródła historyczne [Wills as Historical Sources], Białostockie Teki Historyczne* [Białystok Historical Notebooks], vol. 7/2009, p. 27.

In conclusion, wills are an invaluable source of knowledge about ancient societies, revealing not only legal aspects but also the cultural and social contexts in which they were created. Analyzing these documents allows for a better understanding of how people of different eras perceived death, inheritance, and relationships with loved ones. Wills reflect changing values and norms, simultaneously serving as evidence of individual desires and hopes. Through them, we can not only learn about the stories of individual people but also gain a broader picture of the life and mentality of ancient societies. Thus, wills remain an extremely important research tool that allows us to discover the complexity of human existence and its multidimensional aspects.

Bibliography

Bardach J., *Historia Państwa i Prawa Polski, Tom I do połowy XV wieku [History of the State and Law of Poland, Volume I up to the mid-15th century]*, Warsaw 1973.

Bobowski B., *Testament w średniowiecznym prawie polskim [The Will in Medieval Polish Law], Prace Naukowe Akademii im. Jana Długosza w Częstochowie [Scientific Works of the Jan Długosz Academy in Częstochowa]*, 2009, vol. X.

Day G., *Famous and Curious Wills*, „Law Library Journal" 1925, nr 18.

Dembska B. R., *O testamencie w polskim prawie średniowiecznym [On the Will in Medieval Polish Law]*, in: *Studia z historii ustroju i prawa [Studies in the History of the System and Law]*, edited by H. Olszewska, Poznań 2002.

Dunin-Dudkowska A., *Testament jako zwierciadło kultur. Polsko-amerykańskie studium komparatystyczne [The Will as a Mirror of Cultures. A Polish-American Comparative Study]*, Lublin 2014.

Księżak P. S., *Zachowek w polskim prawie spadkowym [Legitim in Polish Inheritance Law]*, LexisNexis 2012.

Leśniodorski B., Z. Kaczmarczyk, *Historia państwa i prawa Polski, T. II od połowy XV wieku do roku 1905 [History of the State and Law of Poland, Vol. II from the mid-15th century to the year 1905]*, Warsaw 1966.

Lipiński E., *Prawo Bliskowschodnie w starożytności [Near Eastern Law in Antiquity*], Lublin 2009.

Moreno Garcia J. C., "*The Study of Ancient Egyptian Administration*," in *Ancient Egyptian Administration*, edited by J. C. Moreno Garcia, Leiden/Boston 2013.

Pecyna M., Pisuliński J., *Rozprawy cywilistyczne. Księga pamiątkowa dedykowana Profesorowi Edwardowi Drozdowi [Civil Law Treatises. Commemorative Book Dedicated to Professor Edward Drozd]*, LexisNexis 2013.

Vovelle M., *Śmierć w cywilizacjach Zachodu [Death in Western Civilizations*], trans. T. Swoboda, Gdańsk 2004.

Wierciński J. J., *Brak świadomości lub swobody przy sporządzaniu testamentów [Lack of Awareness or Freedom in Drafting a Wil]l*, LexisNexis 2013.

Wiszowata K., *Testamenty jako źródła historyczne [Wills as Historical Sources], Białostockie Teki Historyczne* [Białystok Historical Notebooks], vol. 7/2009.

Załucki M., *Wydziedziczenie w prawie polskim na tle prawnoporównawczym [Disinheritance in Polish Law in a Comparative Legal Context]*, Oficyna 2010.

Małgorzata Eysymontt[639]

Legal protection of the creditor in European Order for Payment Procedure – analysis and commentary on selected provisions of EU law

Abstract: The object of this article is to analyse and comment on selected provisions of EU and national law relating to the legal position and, in particular, the legal protection of the creditor in the situation of the assertion of cross-border claims within the European Union under the European order for payment procedure. This part of the monograph attempts to demonstrate that despite the wide range of procedures and remedies available to creditors in EU Member States, created under the provisions of secondary law of the European Union as alternative means of vindicating their claims in civil and commercial matters, they still use these legal instruments relatively rarely and the awareness of EU citizens in this respect is limited. Although they are said to be among the procedurally uncomplicated procedural remedies, practice in this regard varies across jurisdictions.

Keywords: European order for payment, cross-border claims, debt recovery, legal remedies, legal protection of the creditor

1. Introduction

We are currently living in times that are characterised by considerable dynamism and complexity in terms of the economic relationships taking place. A wide variety of actors, including natural and legal persons, enter into numerous commercial relationships, concluding contracts with each other. Increasingly, these extend beyond the borders of a single country. This leads to interactions of an international, cross-border nature, which have extensive legal effects. Consequently, a number of legal regulations have been adopted within the European Union that guarantee various remedies for creditors, allowing them to effectively enforce their claims against debtors domiciled in another Member State.

The object of this study is to analyse and comment on selected provisions of EU and national law relating to the legal position, and in particular the creditor's legal protection in the situation of pursuing cross-border claims within the European

639 SWPS University, ORCID: 0000-0002-0030-2645.

Union under the European order for payment procedure[640]. The European order for payment is a specific tool for international debt recovery allowing for a judgment - an order - which will then be enforceable, i.e. enforced, in any other European country, with the exception of Denmark. This part of the monograph attempts to demonstrate that despite the wide range of procedures and remedies available to creditors in EU Member States, created under the provisions of secondary law of the European Union as alternative means of vindicating their claims in civil and commercial matters, they still use these legal instruments relatively rarely and the awareness of EU citizens in this respect is limited. Although they are said to be among the procedurally uncomplicated procedural remedies[641], practice varies.

According to statistics for 2012–2013, each year the number of applications for a European order for payment reaching the courts of the Member States was around 12,000-13,000 (with the highest numbers of applications (more than 4,000 annually) in Austria and Germany), with only 1,800 as far as Poland is concerned, starting from 2008 (while between 300 and 700 applications were received annually in Belgium, the Czech Republic, France, Hungary, the Netherlands, Portugal and Finland)[642]. Back in 2015 the European Commission emphasised that "However, the European procedure is not sufficiently known among businesses, citizens, practitioners, and courts. Further awareness-raising is necessary, both at European and at Member State level. Efficient and active promotion of the Regulation should take place, providing the general public and professionals with

640 The European order for payment procedure is regulated under Regulation (EC) No 1896/2006 of the European Parliament and of the Council of 12 December 2006 creating a European order for payment procedure, OJ L 399, 30.12.2006, pp. 1—32, CELEX number: 32006R1896.

641 M. Romatowska, *Dochodzenie roszczeń o charakterze transgranicznym powstałych na obszarze Unii Europejskiej*, Temidium, Portal of the District Chamber of Legal Advisers in Warsaw, 09.09.2014 – Text available on the website: https://www.temidium.pl/artykul/dochodzenie_roszczen_o_charakterze_transgranicznym_powstalych_na_obszarze_unii_europejskiej-268.html (date of access: 22.06.2024).

642 See p. 3-4 (Point 2.1. entitled: "Statistical data") and table on p. 14 (Annex entitled "Statistical data on the use of the European order for payment procedure") of the Report from the Commission to the European Parliament, the Council and the European Economic and Social Committee on the application of Regulation (EC) 1896/2006 of the European Parliament and of the Council creating a European Order for Payment Procedure, European Commission COM (2015) 495 final, Brussels, 13.10.2015, CELEX number: 52015DC0495.

information on the European order for payment procedure"[643]. It would therefore be worthwhile to carry out regular statistical surveys to verify whether the number of applications for European orders for payment has increased over the years in the various Member States of the European Union, or whether, despite the relatively established practice in this area, it has remained at a similar level.

2. History of the development of EU law related to cross-border claims

Already at the summit held on 15-16 October 1999 in Tampere, the European Council called on the Council and the Commission to prepare new legislation in the area of judicial cooperation. This led to the adoption by the Council of its joint programme with the Commission on 30 November 2000 on the implementation of the principle of mutual recognition of judgments in civil and commercial matters[644], providing for the possibility of creating a procedure of a uniform or harmonised nature through which a judicial decision could be obtained in certain areas, including, inter alia, so-called uncontested claims within the European Community.

In addition, on 20 December 2002 the European Commission adopted a Green Paper on a European order for payment procedure and on measures to simplify and speed up small claims litigation[645], which launched a consultation on a European procedure for the recovery of uncontested claims. In the document, the Commission indicated that "(…) the main purpose of a substantial percentage of court proceedings in the Member States is not to obtain an authoritative impartial decision on contentious questions of fact or law. Rather, it is increasingly not the exception but the rule that in the verifiable absence of any dispute the creditor has to turn to the judiciary to attain an enforceable title allowing him to collect a claim by means of forced execution that the debtor is simply unwilling or unable

643 See p. 12, Point 4 entitled: "Conclusions", Ibidem.

644 See Draft programme of measures for implementation of the principle of mutual recognition of decisions in civil and commercial matters, Document C:2001:012:TOC, OJ of the EC of 15 January 2001, C 12, p. 1-9, CELEX number: 32001Y0115(01).

645 Green Paper on a European order for payment procedure and on measures to simplify and speed up small claims litigation, COM/2002/0746 final, CELEX number: 52002DC0746. In this document, the European order for payment is dedicated to Part II: "A European Order for Payment Procedure", including in particular Point 3 "The European Order for Payment", whereas the small claims procedure is dedicated to Part III "Measures to simplify and speed up small claims litigation".

to honour"[646]. Moreover, the Commission stressed that the situation described above "implies a multi-faceted challenge for the Member States' judicial systems" and therefore "It has become essential to distinguish the truly contentious cases at the earliest possible stage of the proceedings from those where no real legal dispute exists. Such a differentiation is a necessary, albeit not sufficient condition to make efficient use of the limited resources allocated to the courts. It enables them to concentrate on the controversial litigation and to adjudicate it within a reasonable period of time. This desired result can be achieved, however, only if a speedy and effective procedure for uncontested claims is available and produces the relief of the judiciary that is indispensable for the prevention of considerable backlogs"[647]. Therefore, in the Commission's opinion, "given the mere number of non-contentious cases referred to above, the existence of a procedural legislation that ensures their efficient adjudication is a determining factor for the performance of a judicial system as a whole. The swift recovery of outstanding debts whose justification is not called into question is of paramount importance for the economic operators in the European Union. A legal framework that does not guarantee a creditor access to the rapid settlement of uncontested claims may afford bad debtors a certain degree of impunity and thus provide an incentive to withhold payments intentionally to their own advantage. Late payments are a major reason for insolvency threatening the survival of businesses, particularly small and medium-sized ones, and resulting in numerous job losses. The necessity to engage in lengthy, cumbersome and costly court proceedings even for the collection of uncontested debts inevitably exacerbates those detrimental economic effects"[648].

Moreover, more and more often in many cases, there seems to be a growing concern not only of citizens but also of small and medium-sized enterprises in the EU Member States that their judicial systems do not fully meet their demands. As it is indicated, "For many the judicial systems are too expensive, too slow and too difficult to deal with. The smaller the claim is, the more the weight of these obstacles increases, since costs, delay and vexation (the "three-headed hydra"(…) do not necessarily decrease proportionally with the amount of the claim. These problems have led to the creation of simplified civil procedures for Small Claims in many Member States"[649].

646 See: Ibidem, point 2.1.1.

647 Ibidem.

648 Ibidem.

649 See: Ibidem, Part III.

These insights developed by the Commission soon resulted in the adoption of the so-called Hague Programme, annexed to the conclusions of the European Council held on 4-5 November 2004 in Brussels[650]. One of its demands was to work on the creation of a new measure in the form of the aforementioned European order for payment and to streamline the procedure for the recovery of cross-border claims, including so-called small claims. It was stressed that the European Council "reaffirms the priority it attaches to the development of an area of freedom, security and justice", through which, in its view, the security of the Union's communities, as well as their mutual trust and respect for the rule of law will be ensured[651].

The Hague Programme has identified as one of its objectives the improvement of common capability of the Union and its Member States to guarantee fundamental rights, minimum procedural safeguards and access to justice, as well as continuation of the mutual recognition of judicial decisions and certificates both in civil and in criminal matters, and to eliminate legal and judicial obstacles in litigation in civil and family matters with cross-border implications[652]. In addition, the European Council stressed the need "further to enhance work on the creation of a Europe for citizens and the essential role that the setting up of a European Area for Justice will play in this respect. A number of measures have already been carried out. Further efforts should be made to facilitate access to justice and judicial cooperation as well as the full employment of mutual recognition. It is of particular importance that borders between countries in Europe no longer constitute an obstacle to the settlement of civil law matters or to the bringing of court proceedings and the enforcement of decisions in civil matters"[653]. Discussion of issues related to the above was devoted to Point 3.4 of the Hague Programme entitled "Judicial cooperation in civil matters". It was emphasised that various aspects of civil law are relevant to the daily lives of European Union citizens, hence the importance of the continued development of judicial cooperation in this area[654], and the mutual recognition of decisions rendered in such cases is an

650 Council of the European Union, The Hague Programme: strengthening freedom, security and justice in the European Union, Official Journal of the European Union C 53 of 3 March 2005, CELEX number: 52005XG0303(01).

651 Ibidem, Paragraph 1 and 8 of Part I of the Hague Programme entitled "Introduction".

652 Ibidem, Paragraph 6 of Part I of the Hague Programme entitled "Introduction".

653 Ibidem, Paragraph 1 of the Point 3: "Strengthening justice" of Part III of the Hague Programme entitled "Specific Orientations".

654 See Ibidem, Point 3.4.1 "Facilitating civil law procedure across borders" of Part III of the Hague Programme entitled "Specific Orientation".

effective way of protecting the rights of those citizens and securing the exercise of their rights "beyond Europe's borders", hence the need to introduce uniform standards for procedures (including their initiation or enforcement) and judicial and extrajudicial documents (including their service) and the principle of transparency in the payment of procedural costs[655].

3. Legal remedies in cross-border civil cases under EU law - current state of the law

It should be noted that judicial cooperation in civil matters has always been assigned an important role, with a separate Chapter 3 in Title V "Area of freedom, security and justice" of the Treaty on the Functioning of the European Union (hereafter also: "TFEU"), comprising only one extensive provision, i.e. Article 81 TFEU (former Article 65 of the Treaty establishing the European Community). According to paragraph 1 of the said provision, the European Union is to develop "judicial cooperation in civil matters having cross-border implications, based on the principle of mutual recognition of judgments and of decisions in extrajudicial cases" (1st sentence), and "such cooperation may include the adoption of various measures for the approximation of the laws and regulations of the Member States" (2nd sentence). These measures comprise, first and foremost, regulations for the purpose of codification and directives for the purpose of harmonising the laws of the States making up the European Union. Paragraph 2 of the provision specifies that, in order to attain these objectives, the European Parliament and the Council shall adopt under the ordinary legislative procedure[656], in particular when necessary for the proper functioning of the internal market, measures which are designed to achieve a number of objectives (listed under points (a) to (h) of the said provision), including the mutual recognition and enforcement between Member States of judgments and decisions in extrajudicial cases; the cross-border service of judicial and extrajudicial documents; the compatibility of the rules applicable in the Member States concerning conflict of laws and of jurisdiction; cooperation in the taking of evidence; effective access to justice; the elimination of obstacles to the proper functioning of civil proceedings, if necessary by promoting

655 See Ibidem, Point 3.4.2: "Mutual Recognition of decisions" of Part III of the Hague Programme entitled "Specific Orientation".

656 At the same time, according to Paragraph 3 of the cited provision, measures concerning family law which have cross-border implications shall be established by the Council acting, by way of derogation from Paragraph 2 of the same provision, in accordance with a special legislative procedure.

the compatibility of the rules on civil procedure applicable in the Member States; the development of alternative methods of dispute settlement; and support for the training of judiciary and judicial staff.

The most significant legal measures adopted by the European Union on the basis of Article 81 TFEU are the regulations and decisions adopted since 2000[657], aimed at developing cooperation between Member States within the area of freedom, security and justice. Chief among these acts of EU secondary legislation are Council Regulation (EC) No 1348/2000 of 29 May 2000 on the service in the Member States of judicial and extrajudicial documents in civil or commercial matters[658]; Council Regulation (EC) No 44/2001 of 22 December 2000 on jurisdiction and the recognition and enforcement of judgments in civil and commercial matters (recast)[659]; 2001/470/EC: Council Decision of 28 May 2001 establishing a European Judicial Network in civil and commercial matters[660]; Regulation (EC) No 805/2004 of the European Parliament and of the Council of 21 April 2004. creating a European Enforcement Order for uncontested claims[661]; Regulation (EC) No 1896/2006 of the European Parliament and of the Council of 12 December

657 Of the earlier secondary legislation still in force, it is worth noting Regulation (EEC, Euratom) No 1182/71 of the Council of 3 June 1971 determining the rules applicable to periods, dates and time limits, OJ L 124 of 8 June 1971, pp. 1-2, CELEX number: 31971R1182.

658 No longer in force today: Council Regulation (EC) No 1348/2000 of 29 May 2000 on the service in the Member States of judicial and extrajudicial documents in civil or commercial matters, OJ L 160 of 30 June 2000, pp. 37-52, CELEX number: 32000R1348. The legal act currently in force is Regulation (EC) No 1393/2007 of the European Parliament and of the Council of 13 November 2007 on the service in the Member States of judicial and extrajudicial documents in civil or commercial matters (service of documents), and repealing Council Regulation (EC) No 1348/2000, OJ L 324 of 10 December 2007, pp. 79-120, CELEX number: 32007R1393, latest consolidated version of 1 July 2013.

659 No longer in force today: Council Regulation (EC) No 44/2001 of 22 December 2000 on jurisdiction and the recognition and enforcement of judgments in civil and commercial matters, OJ L 12 of 16 January 2001, pp. 1-23, CELEX number: 32001R0044. The legal act currently in force is Regulation (EU) No 1215/2012 of the European Parliament and of the Council of 12 December 2012 on jurisdiction and the recognition and enforcement of judgments in civil and commercial matters (recast), OJ L 351 of 20 December 2012, pp. 1-32, CELEX number: 32012R1215, latest consolidated version of 26 February 2015.

660 OJ L 174 of 27 June 2001, pp. 25-31, CELEX number: 32001D0470.

661 OJ L 143 of 30 April 2004, pp. 15-39, CELEX number: 32004R0805.

2006 creating a European order for payment procedure[662]; Regulation (EC) No 861/2007 of the European Parliament and of the Council of 11 July 2007 establishing a European Small Claims Procedure[663] and Regulation (EU) 2015/2421 of the European Parliament and of the Council of 16 December 2015 amending Regulation (EC) No 861/2007 establishing a European Small Claims Procedure and Regulation (EC) No 1896/2006 creating a European order for payment procedure[664]. Given the assumptions made, the subject of analysis and consideration in this study is only the two European order for payment regulations indicated above.

4. Regulation creating a European order for payment procedure as a guarantee of reinforced creditor protection - general provisions

According to recital 8 of the Preamble of Regulation (EC) No. 1896/2006 of the European Parliament and of the Council of 12 December 2006 creating a European order for payment procedure (hereinafter also: "Regulation No. 1896/2006"), it was emphasised that it was necessary to adopt such supranational (then: "Community") rules that would guarantee equal treatment of both creditors and debtors throughout the European Union.

From the outset, Regulation No. 1896/2006 has been described as an "undoubtedly important document" in terms of achieving the objectives set out therein[665]. Article 1 of the cited legislation indicates that it aims, firstly, "to simplify, speed up and reduce the costs of litigation in cross-border cases concerning uncontested pecuniary claims by creating a European order for payment procedure" (hereinafter also: "EOPA") and, secondly, "to permit the free circulation of European orders for payment throughout the Member States by laying down minimum standards, compliance with which renders unnecessary any intermediate proceedings in the Member State of enforcement prior to recognition and enforcement of a European order for payment". However, in the literature it is pointed out that the adoption of the Regulation under review is not only intended to facilitate the recognition and declaration of enforceability of enforcement orders, but above all to create

662 OJ L 399 of 30 December 2006, pp. 1-32, CELEX number: 32006R1896.
663 OJ L 199 of 31 July 2007, pp. 1-22, CELEX number: 32007R0861.
664 OJ L 341 of 24 December 2015, pp. 1-13, CELEX number: 32015R2421.
665 A. Harast, *Europejski nakaz zapłaty – cz. II*, Monitor Prawniczy: miesięcznik prawa polskiego, year 16, no. 17 (2018), pp. 917.

the "first autonomous European procedure"[666]. On the other hand, the opposite view can be encountered, according to which "despite the allegedly autonomous nature of the EAW procedure, in practice it does not have the character of a comprehensive and complete 'European' regulation"[667].

Article 2 of Regulation No. 1896/2006 defines the scope of its application - paragraphs 1 to 2 regulate the material (positive and negative) scope of the instrument and paragraph 3 its geographical scope. Paragraph 1 stipulates that Regulation No. 1896/2006 applies to cross-border civil and commercial matters, irrespective of the type of court or tribunal, but does not apply, in particular, to matters such as tax, customs or administrative matters and those concerning the liability of the State for acts and omissions in the exercise of state authority (so-called *acta iure imperii*). However, for the purposes of the Regulation, "a cross-border case" should be understood as a case "in which at least one of the parties is domiciled[668] or habitually resident in a Member State other than the Member State of the court seised" (Article 3 paragraph 1 of Regulation No. 1896/2006), and its cross-border nature is assessed according to the state of affairs on the date of the application for a European order for payment (Article 3 paragraph 3 of Regulation No. 1896/2006). Furthermore, paragraph 2 provides that the Regulation also does not apply to four types of cases, i.e. cases concerning rights in property arising out of matrimonial relationships, wills and succession, which may be collectively referred to as family and succession matters; concerning bankruptcy, proceedings relating to the winding-up of insolvent companies or other legal persons, conciliation, composition and other analogous proceedings, which may be collectively referred to as bankruptcy and similar matters; concerning social security; and concerning claims arising out of non-contractual obligations, unless they are the subject of an agreement between the parties or there has been an acknowledgement of debt, or

666 P. Rylski, *Europejski nakaz zapłaty w praktyce sądowej*, Instytut Wymiaru Sprawiedliwości, Prawo w działaniu, Numery archiwalne, Sprawy cywilne, Volume no. 12/2012, p. 145 - Text available on the website: https://iws.gov.pl/wp-content/uploads/2018/09/Piotr-Rylski-Europejski-nakaz-zap%C5%82aty-w-praktyce-s%C4%85dowej-145.pdf (date of access: 27.08.2019).

667 A. Harast, *Europejski nakaz zapłaty – cz. I*, Monitor Prawniczy: miesięcznik prawa polskiego, year 16, no. 16 (2018), p. 847.

668 By virtue of Paragraph 2 of Article 3 of Regulation No. 1896/2006, domicile is determined in accordance with another piece of EU secondary legislation, i.e. the provisions of Articles 59 and 60 of Council Regulation (EC) No. 44/2001 of 22 December 2000 on jurisdiction and the recognition and enforcement of judgments in civil and commercial matters, already referred to above.

they relate to debts of a specified nature arising out of joint ownership of property. In turn, paragraph 3 of the Regulation indicating its territorial scope states that it applies to the Member States, with the exception of Denmark, which did not take part in its adoption and is not bound by it or involved in its application.

In accordance with recital 10 of the Preamble of Regulation No. 1896/2006, the procedure initiated by the application for a European order for payment is not mandatory but should be used as an additional and alternative - to national proceedings - legal remedy at the plaintiff's disposal. He is therefore left with a greater choice of remedies.

The Regulation can be applied to the recovery of monetary claims of a specified amount that are due at the time of the filing of the application for a European order for payment (Article 4 of Regulation No. 1896/2006), so the proceedings initiated on the basis of the Regulation are limited in scope.

5. Regulation creating a European order for payment procedure as a guarantee of enhanced creditor protection under EU and Polish procedural law - specific provisions

The literature points out that a distinctive feature of the European order for payment procedure is its specific "standardisation"[669]. It is (at various stages) form-based. Firstly, paragraph 1 of Article 7 of the quoted Regulation indicates that the statement of claim initiating the proceedings in the case should be drawn up on a special form - the so-called Form A, attached as Annex I to the Regulation[670]. The Regulation under consideration does not stipulate the need for the claimant to indicate the law applicable to the legal relationship from which the claimant's asserted claim arises. As a consequence, it may be difficult or impossible to determine whether the claim is manifestly unfounded, given the differing national regulations of the Member States in this respect (e.g. as regards

669 A. Harast-Sidowska, *Europejskie postępowanie nakazowe i w sprawie drobnych roszczeń. Komentarz praktyczny. Wzory pism procesowych i orzeczeń sądowych*, Wydawnictwo C.H. Beck, Warsaw 2015, p. 6.

670 Form A contains, *inter alia*, separate boxes for the principal claim giving rise to the application for a European order for payment, coded individually, together with the supporting circumstances and other relevant additional information, also coded individually (box 6), as well as those relating to interest (box 7), contractual penalties (box 8) and costs (box 9). In addition, a separate box is provided for the indication of evidence in support of the claim (box 10).

limitation of actions or the permissibility of reserving a contractual penalty)[671]. A claim brought pursuant to Regulation No. 1896/2006 shall comply with the formal requirements set out in detail in paragraphs 2 to 6 of Article 7, which, according to Article 8, the court hearing the case shall examine "as soon as possible".

It is worth noting that it also follows from paragraph 4(a) of Article 12 of Regulation No. 1896/2006 that the European order for payment is issued solely on the basis of the information provided by the claimant and not verified by the court, of which the defendant is informed in the order. It is indicated that such a provision is to be understood as "an acceptance by the court to issue a European order for payment without any examination - whether the circumstances put forward by the claimant are beyond doubt - going beyond the assessment of the obvious unfoundedness of the claim"[672]. The literature puts it this way: the order for payment procedure is characterised by the fact that the court or the competent authority in this respect issues a judgment regarding the monetary claim asserted by the creditor without the need for the debtor's hearing evidence and therefore without notice or knowledge on the part of the debtor - the so-called *ex parte* procedure[673]. Furthermore, it follows from Article 8 of the Regulation that, on the basis of the application, the court shall examine only "whether the claim appears to be founded" and not whether it is in fact founded, and this examination may take the "form of an automated procedure". It is submitted that, in this situation, the court therefore makes "only a preliminary assessment of the merits of the claim"[674] and not an in-depth, substantive analysis of it.

It is envisaged that it is possible for the claimant to supplement or correct the application for an EOPA using "form B" in Annex II to the Regulation, which facilitates its correction by the creditor, unless the court finds that the claim asserted is "manifestly unfounded" or "the application is inadmissible" (Article 9 of Regulation No. 1896/2006) or its amendment by the claimant - after having been notified and invited by the court to accept or reject the proposal for a European order for payment for an amount to be determined by the court - by means of "form C" in Annex III to the Regulation, if the requirements of Article 8 of that instrument have been fulfilled only in respect of part of the claim. If the claimant accepts the proposal made to him by the court, a European order for payment is issued for part of the claim, and if he rejects it or does not send the

671 M. Manowska, (ed.), *Kodeks postępowania cywilnego. Komentarz. Tom I. Art. 1-505(38)*, III edition, WK 2015.

672 Ibidem.

673 See A. Harast-Sidowska, op. cit., p. 5.

674 M. Manowska, op. cit.

court a reply within the time limit set by the court, the court then rejects the claim in its entirety (Article 10 of Regulation No. 1896/2006).

A catalogue of grounds leading to the rejection of the application for a European order for payment is set out in Article 11 of the Regulation. They shall be communicated to the claimant by the court by means of the "Form D" attached as Annex IV to the Regulation. Furthermore, paragraphs 2 to 3 of the cited provision foresee that, although the rejection of the application excludes the possibility of an appeal (the procedure is a one-stage procedure), it does not, however, foreclose the plaintiff from pursuing this claim by two other means, i.e. in a new application for a European order for payment or using any (other) national procedure available in the respective Member State of the European Union. Such a solution is referred to as a "compromise" solution due to the lack of possibility to review the order for payment issued[675].

It should be further emphasised that the European order for payment procedure is complex and hybrid for two reasons. Firstly, its main basis is Regulation No. 1896/2006, with the remainder of it being based, in a subsidiary and supplementary manner, on the provisions of the national civil procedural law of the EU Member States. Secondly, it is collectively referred to as basically two types of proceedings, i.e. proceedings for the issuance of an EOPA and proceedings for the enforcement of an EOPA, the link between which is the European order for payment itself. Accordingly, it is submitted that the EOPA procedure is a special procedure and should be treated as a whole[676].

Transferring the considerations concerning the European order for payment to the grounds of Polish civil law, it should be pointed out that it has been regulated in Section VII "European proceedings in cross-border cases" in Chapter 1 "European order proceedings", comprising Articles 505^{15} - 505^{20} of the Code of Civil Procedure (hereinafter also: "C.C.P.") as separate proceedings. It is pointed out that, therefore, a statement of claim filed under such a procedure should meet both the requirements set out in Article 7 of Regulation No. 1896/2006, but also others, as it does not "exhaustively and independently" regulate all possible grounds examined for the possibility of the case being heard by the court[677]. Article 505^{15} of the Code of Civil Procedure indicates that the court shall hear the case in the European injunction proceedings if the conditions set out in the

675 J. Pisuliński, *Europejski nakaz zapłaty*, Europejski Przegląd Sądowy no. 1 (28) January 2008, Oficyna a Wolters Kluwer business, p. 12.

676 A. Harast, *Postępowanie w sprawie europejskiego nakazu zapłaty*, Monografie prawnicze, Wydawnictwo C.H. Beck, Warsaw 2013, p. 43.

677 P. Rylski, op. cit., pp. 153-154.

provisions of Regulation No. 1896/2006 for this are fulfilled, and the provisions on other separate proceedings do not apply. It is emphasised that this special procedure is thus regulated in "two tracks" - first and foremost under EU law, as well as auxiliary national law[678]. Moreover, it falls within the jurisdiction of the district and county courts, as referred to in Article 505[16] § 1 of the Code of Civil Procedure (and as follows directly from the wording of Articles 16 and 17 of the Code of Civil Procedure), and the case is heard in closed session (Article 505[17] of the Code of Civil Procedure). It is pointed out that the above twofold material jurisdiction of the court results from the fact that, pursuant to Article 4 of Regulation No. 1896/2006, the European order for payment procedure has been established - as it has already been pointed out - in order to pursue "monetary claims of a specified amount", nevertheless it should be understood that without limitation as to the value of the subject matter of the dispute[679].

In Polish conditions, the European order for payment may also be issued by a court referendary, who is authorised to issue orders (Article 505[16] § 2 and 3 of the Code of Civil Procedure). This possibility is provided for in the content of Regulation No 1896/2006, recital 16 of the Preamble of which states that it is permissible for the examination of an EOPA application 'by a person other than a judge' and, moreover, following Article 5(3) containing definitions of terms used in this legal act, 'court' is understood as 'any authority of a Member State with jurisdiction over European orders for payment or other related matters'. Article 505[18] of the Code of Civil Procedure in § 1 stipulates that if it is possible to issue a European order for payment only for a part of the claim referred to in the regulation under analysis and the plaintiff agrees to it, then the case as regards the remaining part of the claim shall be decided by the court in an appropriate procedure, but in the cases indicated by the law according to the provisions on separate proceedings, with the exclusion of the provisions on order and writ of payment proceedings.

It should be noted that in the court proceedings for issuing a European order for payment, according to the party to these proceedings and their stage, the compulsion in Polish law referred to as lawyer's compulsion does not apply. This follows directly from the wording of Article 24 of the Regulation, which stipulates

678 N. Balcerzak, *Europejskie postępowanie nakazowe* (in:) Wardyński i wspólnicy, *Dochodzenie roszczeń w Unii Europejskiej*, Warsaw 2013, p. 7 – Text available on the website: https://www.wardynski.com.pl/wp-content/uploads/2016/11/wardynski_i_wspolnicy_dochodzenie_roszczen_w_ue_styczen_2013.pdf (date of access: 27.08.2019.

679 See Ibidem.

that representation by a lawyer or another legal practitioner is not mandatory for the claimant when suing for an EOPA and for the defendant when opposing the order. This solution therefore reduces the costs of the proceedings for the claimant when initiating and conducting the proceedings and for the opposing debtor.

Article 12 of Regulation No. 1896/2006 stipulates that the European order for payment shall be issued by the court seised of the case using "form E" attached as Annex V to the Regulation "as soon as possible", which usually means a time limit of about 30 days[680], calculated from the moment the application is lodged (paragraph 1). In addition, the order has to contain an instruction to the defendant that he has a choice between two actions - to pay the amount awarded by the order, making it enforceable, or to lodge a statement of opposition within 30 days of service of the order on him by sending it to the court, leading to a continuation of the proceedings before the competent courts of the Member State of origin of the order in ordinary civil proceedings or, alternatively, to terminate the proceedings if the claimant so requests (paragraphs 3 and 4 (b) and (c)).

The Regulation provides for two basic ways of serving the European order for payment on the defendant, in accordance with the national law of the Member State of the European Union where service is to be effected. The first provides for various forms of service with proof of receipt by the defendant (Article 13 of Regulation No. 1896/2006) and the second for service without proof of receipt (Article 14 of Regulation No. 1896/2006). An additional - third - method of service of the European order for payment is also provided for, namely by the defendant's representative, as referred to in Article 15 of the Regulation.

According to Article 16 of the Regulation, upon receipt of the European order for payment the defendant has the right, within 30 days of service of the order, to lodge a statement of opposition with the court of origin in paper form or by any other available means of communication, including electronic (paragraphs 1, 2 and 4). For this purpose, he is obliged to fill in a "Form F", attached as Annex VI to the Regulation, which is served on him together with the order for payment (paragraph 1). In the statement of opposition, which should be signed by the defendant or his representative, he is not required to indicate precisely the reasons justifying his position, it being sufficient to indicate that he contests the claim in question (paragraphs 3 and 5). Initially, Regulation No. 1896/2006 provided in Article 17 that a correct and timely lodging of the statement of opposition by the defendant resulted in a transfer of the case to ordinary civil proceedings before the competent court of the Member State of origin of the European order for payment,

680 See P. Rylski, op. cit., p. 166.

unless, as already mentioned above, the claimant requests the termination of the proceedings. Now, by virtue of Regulation (EU) 2015/2421 of the European Parliament and of the Council of 16 December 2015 amending Regulation (EC) No. 861/2007 establishing a European Small Claims Procedure and Regulation (EC) No. 1896/2006 creating a European order for payment procedure (hereinafter also: "Regulation 2015/2421"), the aforementioned provision in this part provides that "Where a statement of opposition is lodged within the time limit laid down in Article 16 paragraph 2, further proceedings shall take place before the competent courts in the Member State of origin unless the claimant has expressly requested the termination of the proceedings in that case. The continuation of the proceedings shall take place in accordance with the rules of (a) the European Small Claims Procedure as defined in Regulation (EC) No. 861/2007, if applicable; or (b) the applicable national civil procedure" (paragraph 1), while "If the claimant has not indicated which of the procedures referred to in Article 17 paragraph 1 letter (a) and (b) is to be applied to deal with his claim in the proceedings to be instituted in the event of opposition, or if the claimant has requested the use of the European Small Claims Procedure set out in Regulation (EC) No. 861/2007 and the claim does not fall within the scope of that Regulation, the proceedings shall be transferred to the relevant national civil proceedings unless the claimant has expressly requested that no such transfer be made" (paragraph 2).

Transferring the considerations to the grounds of Polish law, it is necessary to refer to Article 505[19] of the Code of Civil Procedure, which stipulates that if an objection is lodged in accordance with the provisions of Regulation No. 1896/2006, the European order for payment shall become null and void. The court shall then hear the case in the appropriate manner, except that in the cases indicated by the law, the case shall be heard in accordance with the provisions of separate proceedings, excluding the provisions of injunction and writ-of-payment proceedings (§ 1). If, on the other hand, the plaintiff requests the termination of the proceedings in the event of opposition, the court shall discontinue the proceedings, ruling on the costs as in the case of withdrawal of the statement of claim (§ 4). Moreover, the court rejects an objection filed after the assigned time limit or for other reasons inadmissible, as well as one whose deficiencies have not been remedied by the defendant within the time limit referred to in 505[19a] of the Code of Civil Procedure.

In the absence of a statement of opposition by the defendant, the court of the Member State of origin of the European order shall, without delay, declare the order to be enforceable, using "Form G", attached as Annex VII to the Regulation, and then send the enforceable order to the claimant (Article 18 of Regulation

No. 1896/2006). At the bottom of the form is a Note reminding that "The attached European order for payment is automatically enforceable in all Member States of the European Union, except Denmark, without the need for a second declaration of enforceability in the Member State where it is to be enforced and without any possibility of opposing its recognition. The enforcement proceedings are governed by the law of the Member State of enforcement, unless otherwise provided in the Regulation"[681].

As far as the costs of the European order for payment procedure are concerned, Article 25 of Regulation No. 1896/2006 provides that court fees shall include fees and charges payable to the court and shall be determined in accordance with the provisions of national law, with the provision that the combined court fees for EOPA procedure and ordinary civil proceedings taking place in the event of a successful opposition may not be higher than the court fees incurred in the situation of ordinary court proceedings taking place without prior European order for payment procedure. Subsequently, paragraph 1 of this provision has been amended by Regulation 2015/2421 and provides that "Where, in a Member State, court fees for civil proceedings within the meaning of Article 17 paragraph 1 letter (a) or (b), as the case may be, are equivalent to or higher than the fees for the European order for payment procedure, the total amount of the court fees for the European order for payment procedure and for the subsequent civil proceedings in the event of a statement of opposition pursuant to Article 17 paragraph 1 shall not exceed the fees for such proceedings conducted without a preceding European order for payment procedure in that Member State. No additional court fees may be levied in a Member State for civil proceedings resulting from a statement of opposition pursuant to Article 17 paragraph 1 letter (a) or (b), as the case may be, where the court fees for such proceedings in that Member State are lower than the fees for the European order for payment procedure.".

It has to be noted that a European order for payment that is enforceable in the Member State of origin, according to Article 19 of the Regulation, has the same legal effects in the other Member States of the European Union without the need for a declaration of enforceability and without the possibility of (further) opposing its recognition and - in the light of paragraph 3 of Article 22 of the Regulation - cannot be subject to a review on its merits in the State of enforcement.

681 Note under the last box to be completed in Form G attached as Annex VII to the Regulation.

Nevertheless, after the expiry of the 30-day opposition period, the defendant[682] has the right to apply for a review of the European order for payment by the competent court of the Member State of issue if the two exceptional cases set out in Article 20 of Regulation No. 1896/2006 apply.

Firstly, this is possible if the EOPA was served on the defendant by one of the methods provided for in Article 14 of the Regulation, i.e. without his acknowledgement of receipt, and if, through no fault of the defendant, service was not effected in sufficient time to enable him to arrange for his defence, or if the defendant was prevented from opposing the claim by reason of force majeure or extraordinary circumstances not attributable to him.

Secondly, according to the quoted provision, an application for a review of the European order for payment is possible when the issuance of the order was "manifestly erroneous" in light of the requirements set out in the wording of the regulation or "due to other exceptional circumstances". As regards the second case of filing an application for a review of the European order for payment, the Polish Code of Civil Procedure provides for the possibility to set it aside if it is found that there is a basis for doing so as stipulated in the provisions of Regulation No. 1896/2006, at the defendant's request (which should meet the conditions of a pleading and indicate the circumstances justifying the cancellation of the order), the court which issued it, or in the case of an order issued by a court registrar - the court before which the action was brought, cancels the order for payment, but it will first hear the plaintiff at a hearing or require him to make a statement to that effect in writing.

The decision issued by the court on the revocation of the European order for payment may be appealed against (Article 505^{20} C.C.P.). It is emphasised that, despite this drafting of Article 505^{20} of the C.C.P., the EU regulation does not provide for court proceedings for revocation of the European order regulated in this provision, but for the very procedure for review of the European order for payment by the competent court in the Member State of issue[683].

When the defendant applies for a review of the European order for payment, the competent court of the Member State of enforcement may, at the defendant's request, allow up to three solutions, namely to limit the enforcement proceedings

682 Under Regulation no. 1896/2006, this right is exclusive to the defendant, although under the national law of the Member States, other entities (including the public prosecutor) may also have standing to act for the defendant. – See P. Telenga, *Komentarz do art. 505^{20} k.p.c.* (in:) A. Jakubecki (ed.), *Kodeks postępowania cywilnego. Komentarz aktualizowany. Tom I. Art. 1-729*, LEX/el. 2019.

683 Ibidem.

to protective measures; or to make its enforcement conditional on the provision of appropriate security as determined by the court; or even to suspend the enforcement proceedings if there are exceptional cases (Article 23 of Regulation No. 1896/2006). If the court of the Member State of issuance of the European order for payment finds that none of the circumstances that would allow for a review of this legal remedy apply, then it shall remain in force. If, on the other hand, in its opinion such a review is justified, then the order for payment in question is no longer valid (paragraph 3 of Article 20 of Regulation No. 1896/2006).

Returning to the wording of Article 19 of the Regulation referred to above, a European order for payment that has already become enforceable in the Member State of origin is, pursuant to Article 19 of the Regulation, also recognised and enforceable automatically in the other Member States of the European Union, i.e. without the need for a declaration of enforceability. This means the abolition of the *exequatur* procedure, which in this case is to be understood as the abolition of the requirement for the court of the Member State of enforcement to authorise enforcement of the European order for payment. It therefore no longer has to examine formal questions, including, *inter alia*, whether a copy of the judgment has been submitted together with a certificate from the Member State of origin. As a result, the creditor is further protected and gains time, as the European order for payment may be enforced more quickly, without the need for an additional decision (in separate proceedings) on the recognition of its enforceability. Consequently, under Polish law, pursuant to Article 1153^{13} of the Code of Civil Procedure, the European order for payment constitutes an enforceable title in the territory of the Republic of Poland and may be immediately enforceable, without the need for an enforceability clause to be granted by the Polish court[684]. Nevertheless, the automatic enforceability of the European order for payment does not imply the impossibility of opposing its enforcement, which, however, depends on the national provisions of the Member State in which it is

---

684 Cf. comments on the repeal of exequatur concerning the so-called Brussels I bis Regulation, i.e. Regulation (EU) No. 1215/2012 of the European Parliament and of the Council of 12 December 2012 on jurisdiction and the recognition and enforcement of judgments in civil and commercial matters: M. Zych, *Wykonywanie i uznawanie orzeczeń zgodnie z rozporządzeniem Bruksela I bis, Co do zasady. Prawo nie tylko dla przedsiębiorcy*, Wardyński i Wspólnicy, 15 January 2015 – Text available on the website: http://www.codozasady.pl/wykonywanie-i-uznawanie-orzeczen-zgodnie-z-rozporzadzeniem-bruksela-i-bis/ (date of access: 02.08.2019).

to be enforced governing the control of its enforcement[685]. The legal doctrine expresses the view that "in the light of the current regulation of European law, the automatic enforceability (enforceability by operation of law) of judgments from other EU Member States is a consistently implemented principle", while the traditional model of granting *exequatur*, i.e. declaring enforceability of a foreign judgment issued by a court of a third country, i.e. outside the European Union, as referred to in Articles 1150-1152 of the Code of Civil Procedure, by way of a ruling of a Polish court, is still in force[686].

Furthermore, while it is pointed out that the model of automatic enforceability, which has replaced the classic *exequatur* model, "reflects the evolution of the EU legal framework that has taken place over the last decade", it is also noted that this leads to a "more profound interference with the national procedural law of the Member States, as the foreign court decision constitutes in principle a direct basis for judicial enforcement, bypassing exequatur and the related internalisation of the foreign title in the State of enforcement"[687]. The enforceability of the European order for payment automatically extends to the territory of the Member State of enforcement and does not have to be granted *ex novo* there with the granting of authorisation for enforcement, the obtaining of which is subject to the foreign court judgment meeting certain conditions, so that as soon as the conditions provided for in EU derived law are met, it becomes enforceable in the Member State of enforcement *ex lege*, without the need for a separate procedure for authorisation for enforcement in the State of enforcement, and can no longer be blocked by the debtor[688].

At this point, it should be recalled that pursuant to Article 1153[13] § 1 of the Code of Civil Procedure, the provisions of Book Four entitled «Recognition and enforcement of certain judgments of courts of the Member States of the European Union and of settlements and authentic instruments originating from those States shall apply to judgments of courts of the Member States of the European Union and of settlements and authentic instruments originating from those States falling within the scope of Regulation No. 1215/2012, Regulation No. 805/2004,

685 Cf. P. Grzegorczyk, K. Weitz, *Komentarz do art. 1153[13]* (in:) T. Ereciński (ed.), *Kodeks postępowania cywilnego. Komentarz. Tom VI. Międzynarodowe postępowanie cywilne. Sąd polubowny (arbitrażowy)*, V edition, WK 2017.

686 M. P. Wójcik, *Komentarz do art. 1153[13] k.p.c.* (in:) A. Jakubecki (ed.), *Kodeks postępowania cywilnego. Komentarz aktualizowany. Tom II. Art. 730-1217*, Lex/el. 2019.

687 P. Grzegorczyk, K. Weitz, *Komentarz do art. 1153[13]...*, op. cit.

688 Cf. Ibidem.

Regulation No. 1896/2006, Regulation No. 861/2007, Regulation No. 4/2009 and Regulation No. 606/2013. In turn, Article 1153^{14} point 3 of the Code of Civil Procedure expressly provides that in the Republic of Poland, European orders for payment issued by the courts of the Member States of the European Union, the enforceability of which has been established in these countries on the basis of the provisions of Regulation No. 1896/2006, are also enforceable titles. Pursuant to Article 21 of Regulation No. 1896/2006, an already enforceable European order for payment is therefore enforceable on the same terms as judgments which have been issued in the Member State of enforcement and are enforceable. To this end, the claimant (the creditor) should provide the enforcement authorities of the place of enforcement with a copy of the order and, if necessary, also a translation of it into an official language of the Member State of enforcement (in case of several official languages, the language of the court proceedings/another language accepted). It is therefore clear that enforcement proceedings pursuant to a European order for payment are governed by the law of the Member State of the European Union where it is enforced and - as stated in Article 22 of the Regulation - if, under certain conditions, it is irreconcilable with an earlier judgment or order issued in one of the EU Member States or in a third country, enforcement is refused. Any other procedural issues which are not regulated and which do not arise from the content of the regulation are subject to national law in accordance with the wording of Article 26 of the regulation. At the same time, the literature emphasises that the application for refusal of enforcement of a European order for payment, which in the Polish legal order is called an action for refusal of enforcement (recognition) of an enforceable title in the form of a European order for payment with an enforcement clause, constitutes "a special legal remedy, serving primarily the legal protection of the debtor"[689].

6. Conclusion

In the doctrine, despite various practical problems or the lack of clarification of certain issues arising from Regulation No. 1896/2006, the prevailing view from the outset has been that the introduction of the European order for payment "should be regarded as a step in the right direction", which has "a good chance of gaining popularity among participants in legal transactions, especially small and

689 A. Laskowska, *Odmowa wykonania europejskiego nakazu zapłaty*, Kwartalnik Prawa Prywatnego, Year XXII: 2013, notebook no. 1, p. 220.

medium-sized enterprises, to which it is primarily addressed"[690]. Today, thanks to the uniform principles developed in the case law of the Court of Justice of the European Union[691], the content of Regulation No. 1896/2006 no longer raises as many interpretative questions as it did at the beginning. The literature even emphasises that "the emerging case law has had a positive effect on the state of lawyers' knowledge of the European order for payment, as well as on legal certainty in this area. Therefore, it is highly likely that with the increasing amount of literature and case law on the European order for payment, the popularity of this method of claim recovery will increase"[692]. However, these views need to be balanced. For despite the growing interest in the proceedings for issuing a European order for payment among representatives of legal doctrine and practitioners, there is a lack of literature and detailed analyses and statistics taking into account the study of the current state of knowledge of the public, particularly Polish citizens as to the possibility and frequency of application of this legal measure, the study of the impact of the conduct of proceedings of this type on the effectiveness of legal protection of creditors against "resistant" cross-border debtors, saving their time or minimising the procedural costs incurred by them. For this, however, it would be necessary to carry out detailed file research, to collect statistical data from different periods and from all EU Member States, which unfortunately are not updated on a regular basis. It remains to be hoped, however, that the popularisation of these hybrid proceedings, which have their roots in EU law but flourish according to national rules, will allow for more effective legal protection of creditors, greater flexibility and improved communication between them at a judicial level.

690 M. Arciszewski, *Europejski Nakaz Zapłaty*, Monitor Prawniczy: miesięcznik prawa polskiego, Year 16, no. 1 (2008), Opinie, p. 12.

691 See, *inter alia*, the judgment of the Court (First Chamber) of 13 December 2012 in Case C-215/11, *Iwona Szyrocka v SiGer Technologie GmbH*, ECLI:EU:C:2012:794 and the judgment of the Court (Third Chamber) of 13 June 2013 in Case C-144/12, *Goldbet Sportwetten GmbH v Massimo Sperindeo*, ECLI:EU:C:2013:393.

692 M. Mazgaj, T. Srogosz, *Europejski nakaz zapłaty w świetle orzecznictwa Trybunału Sprawiedliwości*, PALESTRA no. 11/2016, Pismo Adwokatury Polskiej, Naczelna Rada Adwokacka (The Supreme Bar Council) Year LXI no. 707, Warsaw 2016, p. 15.

Bibliography

Arciszewski M., *Europejski Nakaz Zapłaty*, Monitor Prawniczy: miesięcznik prawa polskiego, Year 16, no. 1 (2008), Opinie.

Balcerzak N., *Europejskie postępowanie nakazowe* (in:) Wardyński i wspólnicy, *Dochodzenie roszczeń w Unii Europejskiej*, Warsaw 2013 – Text available on the website: https://www.wardynski.com.pl/wp-content/uploads/2016/11/wardynski_i_wspolnicy_dochodzenie_roszczen_w_ue_styczen_2013.pdf.

Grzegorczyk P., Weitz K., *Komentarz do art. 1153[13]* (in:) Ereciński T. (ed.), *Kodeks postępowania cywilnego. Komentarz. Tom VI. Międzynarodowe postępowanie cywilne. Sąd polubowny (arbitrażowy)*, V edition, WK 2017.

Harast A., *Europejski nakaz zapłaty – cz. I*, Monitor Prawniczy: miesięcznik prawa polskiego, year 16, no. 16 (2018).

Harast A., *Europejski nakaz zapłaty – cz. II*, Monitor Prawniczy: miesięcznik prawa polskiego, year 16, no. 17 (2018).

Harast A., *Postępowanie w sprawie europejskiego nakazu zapłaty*, Monografie prawnicze, Wydawnictwo C.H. Beck, Warsaw 2013.

Harast-Sidowska A., *Europejskie postępowanie nakazowe i w sprawie drobnych roszczeń. Komentarz praktyczny. Wzory pism procesowych i orzeczeń sądowych*, Wydawnictwo C.H. Beck, Warsaw 2015.

Laskowska A., *Odmowa wykonania europejskiego nakazu zapłaty*, Kwartalnik Prawa Prywatnego, Year XXII: 2013, notebook no. 1.

Manowska M., (ed.), *Kodeks postępowania cywilnego. Komentarz. Tom I. Art. 1-505(38)*, III edition, WK 2015.

Mazgaj M., Srogosz T., *Europejski nakaz zapłaty w świetle orzecznictwa Trybunału Sprawiedliwości*, PALESTRA no. 11/2016, Pismo Adwokatury Polskiej, Naczelna Rada Adwokacka (The Supreme Bar Council) Year LXI no. 707, Warsaw 2016.

Pisuliński J., *Europejski nakaz zapłaty*, Europejski Przegląd Sądowy no. 1 (28) January 2008, Oficyna a Wolters Kluwer business.

Romatowska M., *Dochodzenie roszczeń o charakterze transgranicznym powstałych na obszarze Unii Europejskiej*, Temidium, Portal of the District Chamber of Legal Advisers in Warsaw, 09.09.2014 – Text available on the website: https://www.temidium.pl/artykul/dochodzenie_roszczen_o_charakterze_transgranicznym_powstalych_na_obszarze_unii_europejskiej-268.html.

Rylski P., *Europejski nakaz zapłaty w praktyce sądowej*, Instytut Wymiaru Sprawiedliwości, Prawo w działaniu, Numery archiwalne, Sprawy cywilne, Volume no. 12/2012 - Text available on the website: https://iws.gov.pl/wp-content/uploads/2018/09/Piotr-Rylski-Europejski-nakaz-zap%C5%82aty-w-praktyce-s%C4%85dowej-145.pdf.

Telenga P., *Komentarz do art. 505[20] k.p.c.* (in:) Jakubecki A. (ed.), *Kodeks postępowania cywilnego. Komentarz aktualizowany. Tom I. Art. 1-729*, LEX/el. 2019.

Wójcik M. P., *Komentarz do art. 1153[13] k.p.c.* (in:) Jakubecki A. (ed.), *Kodeks postępowania cywilnego. Komentarz aktualizowany. Tom II. Art. 730-1217*, Lex/el. 2019.

Zych M., *Wykonywanie i uznawanie orzeczeń zgodnie z rozporządzeniem Bruksela I bis, Co do zasady. Prawo nie tylko dla przedsiębiorcy*, Wardyński i Wspólnicy, 15 January 2015 – Text available on the website: http://www.codozasady.pl/wykonywanie-i-uznawanie-orzeczen-zgodnie-z-rozporzadzeniem-bruksela-i-bis/.

Łukasz Majewski[693]

Gladiators – champions – duellists. A contribution to the institution of duel

Abstract: The duel was a traditional institution of both criminal law and sociology, which has undergone major transformations throughout history. It was approached differently in antiquity, differently in the Middle Ages and still differently in modern times, where it became a kind of privilege of the aristocracy as well as the military and intellectual elite of society. The subject of this article is precisely the distinction between these approaches and contains an unique novelty - the definition of a duel and its legal composition developed by Wladyslaw Sobolewski and included in a never-before-published typescript re-discovered by the author of the text.

Keywords: duel, history of criminal law, aristocracy, military tradition

1. Introduction and definitions

Few institutions of criminal law have undergone such significant transformations over the course of history as the duel itself. Both the forms in which it is held and its public perception have changed, taking it along a path from the ultimate and infallible means of evidence directly to a common crime, often in the text of the code found in the infamous company of murder, to total legal non-existence.

Before I will proceed with the presentation of this very evolution, I would like to refer to the definition of a duel. This is necessary for the reason that while numerous criminal statutes criminalized participation in a duel (in the capacity of a duelist, a second, or a doctor), the duel itself was not defined by legislators, with few exceptions. As pointed out by Józef Rozenblat, a prominent attorney and author of the popular late XIX century monograph on the subject, a duel should be understood from the position of the science of criminal law as an agreed fight between two persons fought with lethal weapons according to certain rules and usually, but not necessarily with the purpose of redressing an insult[694]. Much more broadly, in a classic, so to speak, way this phenomenon is put by Józef

693 SWPS University, ORCID: 0000-0003-2452-2842.

694 J. Rozenblat, Pojedynek, Księgarnia Polska, Lwów 1879, p. 22. This definition, as it were, rejects *a limine*, for example, student duels, so popular among members of academic corporations. This definition, as it were, rejects a limine, for example, student duels, so popular among members of academic corporations.

Naimski, indicating that a duel is simply a fight between two people conducted by mutual agreement[695]. Witold Bartoszewski - president of the Vienna Fencing Club - defines a duel in an different way, in a professional manner for its time, characteristic to those who regularly train in fighting with bladed weapons. He states that a duel is a fight between two people, caused by a well-established challenge, undertaken for a private and voluntary cause, and conducted with equal weapons, in the presence of mutual seconds and under prearranged conditions[696]. Finally, his own definition of a duel, differing in some elements, was proposed by Władysław Sobolewski, in his work "On the duel in criminal law", considered lost, written in Lausanne in 1930[697]. He defines a duel as an individual fight between two people, conducted by mutual consent, using weapons, according to agreed or customary rules. According to Sobolewski, a detailed composition of this definition indicates that a duel is all about combat.

In turn, the concept of combat should be understood as the sum of actions of at least two persons. This formulation takes into account only actions, that is, actions of an active nature on the part of both opponents, and is not sufficient for its application in those cases where the action was taken only unilaterally (one of the parties attacks with a white weapon or fires a shot, and the opposing party does not make any movement, even if of a defensive nature). Therefore, according to Sobolewski, a duel should be understood as a fight, as the sum of the actions of both opponents, which consists of at least one action, of an offensive nature (attack), and at least one defensive action (defense) or the possibility of its execution. The action of two persons, not corresponding to the above conditions, cannot be attributed to the nature of a fight, and thus a duel. Thus, it is not a fight if the opponents appear together and shoot upwards explicitly on both sides, regardless of whether the parties had previously agreed to do so or not; nor does the mere

695 J. Naimski, O pojedynkach, Drukarnia J. Sikorskiego, Warszawa 1881, p. 4.

696 W. Bartoszewski, Pojedynek. Jego reguły i przykłady, H. Altenberg, Lwów 1911, p. 25.

697 Wladyslaw Sobolewski is referred to as the "father of Polish forensics" and is famous for his publications and contributions to the development of this particular discipline, which is related to criminal law. In addition to his service in the police, he was also a professional fencer, co-founder of the Polish Fencing Association, which exists to this day, and author of a number of texts on saber fencing (including a textbook, which lived to see two editions). While on scholarship in France, he compiled a typescript of a work on dueling in criminal law, never published in print, which was considered lost during World War II. Three extant copies of this typescript were in the Raczynski Library in Poznan. Two of them were burned in a library fire, the third was rescued and is in the author's possession.

laying down of a bladed weapon have the characteristics of a fight, unless at least one offensive action is performed at the same time[698].

As for the second element - the participation of two people, this is not a *sine qua non*, but rather a minimum requirement. Sobolewski points out that a fight fought with the participation of more than one opponent from both sides would not lose the characteristics of a duel, as long as the individual fights were fought individually. On the other hand, a fight of the kind in which one person confronts two or more opponents at once could not be considered a duel.

Given the variety of forms that a fight between two people can take, another element that needs to be clarified appears in this definition, namely the use of weapons. According to Sobolewski, an individual fight in which the opponents did not use weapons is not a duel, even though the opponents fought in earnest, and even under the condition that one of them should die. Hence, a boxing fight cannot be considered a duel, regardless of the conditions under which it was conducted and regardless of the outcome.

Another element of the definition indicates that not every individual fight between two people using weapons is a duel. It is only a fight that takes place by mutual consent of the parties. This consent is expressed by the parties by challenging each other to a duel and accepting the challenge, and by accepting the terms of the duel, that is, by a formal declaration of an act of will usually framed in a written procedure. It should be noted, however, that the decisive significance - insofar as the determination of the nature of the fight as a duel – is attributed only to the mere fact of the existence of the parties' consent, while the external form is not significant (it is not fully ritualized). The statement of consent to hold a duel, can be - bypassing the formal procedure - expressed by the parties performing certain concluding acts *in concreto*, for example, by drawing a weapon from its scabbard and standing immediately to fight. Such a clash on the spot, by mutual consent of the parties is called a *recontre*, which is usually the result of a sudden decision, has all the characteristics of a duel fight. On the other hand, an armed assault, referred to as "*attaque*", consisting of an unexpected attack on the other person, with a call for immediate defense, is not a duel. A person, surprised in

698 This view does not differ from the modern understanding of the sport combat of fencers, and in all probability its formulation can be attributed to the author's fencing interests. Nevertheless, the fact that a situation in which opponents fire shots into the air is not considered a duel is contrary to the provisions of some honor codes.

this way, as long as he even undertakes the fight was considered to be acting in necessary defense[699].

Finally, the last requirement for recognizing this type of "meeting"[700] as a duel and determining such a character is the principle of the regularity of the fight, which consists in the observance by the parties of the customarily established rules of the duel[701]. A fight conducted, as it was termed "in a wild manner" that is, disregarding the customary established rules, and thus leaving room for any arbitrariness of the parties, was not a duel in the sense of criminal law. Sobolewski also stresses that a fight conducted in accordance with the prevailing rules is the outstanding (though obviously not the only) feature distinguishing a duel from "a tavern brawl between two adventurous individuals"[702].

The definition formulated and developed by Władysław Sobolewski can be considered the most recent and best substantiated in the entire body of Polish criminal law doctrine. His unpublished typescript constitutes the most comprehensive strictly legal study of the issue of dueling that has come from under the pen of a Polish author - a lawyer. The fact that it was found deserves mention in the publication issued on the occasion of the international scientific conference.

---

699 In the past, a distinction was made between "attaque" and simple assault for the purpose of murder based only on the fact that the attacked person was called to defend himself or allowed to defend.

700 The traditional term used by honor codes to describe fighting "in the field."

701 These customs were written down in the form of "codes of honor," among which in the Second Republic the most popular was the so-called "Boziewicz Code" (2 versions). Codes of honor were collections of common law norms for handling "matters of honor." One of the first things the parties' deputies (seconds) did was to determine which of these codes (there were more than a dozen to choose from) would apply to that particular honor case.

702 This tendency is clearly visible in the wording of the provisions of the criminal codes of the so-called "partitioning states" in force on Polish territory before the 1932 Penal Code came into force. Thus, the German Penal Code of 1871, stipulated in Article 207 that "intentional violation of the agreed or customary rules of a duel" was punishable "in accordance with the general provisions on the crime of murder or bodily injury," while the Russian Criminal Code of 1903 (Tagantsev Code) provided in Article 486 for punishment "as for very grievous bodily harm or murder," for a guilty person who inflicted grievous bodily harm on an opponent or deprived him of life due to "a conscious violation during a duel to the detriment of the opponent of the conditions of the duel."

2. Duelling in Antiquity

Traditionally, numerous authors describing the institution of the duel look for its beginning already in Antiquity, citing examples from mythology or ancient history. In this regard, two approaches to this issue are evident. The first points to a kind of continuity of the dueling tradition, assuming the recognition that any fight between two people constitutes a duel, and deriving dueling traditions from, for example, David and Goliath[703] while the other points out that a modern duel requires the existence of a "question of honor" that the ancients did not recognize. While the Latin term "*duellum*" meaning duel is indeed already used by ancient authors (most often to describe war), it is in vain to find in the literature of the period an approach to dueling at least similar to that of modern authors. For the inhabitants of the ancient world, the issue of the almost obligatory demand for armed redress for an insult suffered did not exist. For a Roman, as a full-fledged citizen of a powerful empire, an insult to honor in a private forum played no great role and by no means insulted him in the eyes of his fellow citizens. He pursued the matter of insults in court. Things were analogous in Greece, where state issues preoccupied the minds of citizens, relegating matters of private life to the background[704].

Although the example of the fight between the Horatii and the Curiatii is often cited as evidence of the continuity of the dueling tradition derived from the ancient Romans, it should be noted that this example refers to a fight not grounded in an earlier insult, but only intended to indicate the winner of the battle without endangering the other soldiers.

These battles, usually fought in plain sight of enemy armies facing each other, were accompanied by a motive that was a public cause for which the heroes of history gave their blood and lives.

A good example, illustrating the approach to such adventures represented by the Romans, is the attitude of the famous commander Marius, who, challenged by the Cymbrian chief before the battle of *Aquae Sextiae* to a hand-to-hand fight, refused to appear and offered the eager Cymbrian to fight a gladiator he could

703 And sometimes even the biblical Cain and Abel.

704 Kicked during a public discussion by an adversary, Socrates was said to have said to him, "A horse or a donkey would have kicked me even more reliably, but could I have any complaint about that?", In turn, the philosopher Crates received such a hard slap from the musician Nicodromos that his face swelled up and blood runs occurred. The philosopher responded to this by strolling through the streets of Athens, placing a wooden placard on his forehead with the inscription: "Nikodromos epoiei" With this, he evoked universal: sympathy for himself and contempt for the perpetrator.

provide him on demand. He also commented on the challenge with the famous words "hang yourself on the nearest tree you if your life has sickened you"[705].

It should also be noted that the gladiatorial profession was not respected by the Romans, and professional gladiators did not enjoyed civic honors. Despite this, both in literature and mass culture referred to participants in duels, and present day people who practice martial arts and participate in public fights just as "gladiators".

3. Medieval duels

In the history of European legislation, dueling appears in the early fourth century first with the Visigoths in the form of the so-called judicial duel (*duellum, judicium pugnae, judicium duellicum, monomachia*) as a legal institution, and in a short time began to be regarded as the most important means of judicial evidence. The oldest document containing provisions on the judicial duel is the Burgundian law (*Lex Gundobada*, one of the so-called *leges barbarorum*) of King Gundobad from the end of 501 AD. From this law the duel passed to the laws of the Bavarians, Frisians, Thuringians, and then to the Swabian and Saxon mirrors. It is not found in the Salic law, although the Franks used this means of proof as well.

Judicial duel, took root in the countries of Western Europe and survived as a trial institution until the 15th century, while in the period of the so-called reception of Magdeburg law it appeared, as a trial institution, on the territory of Poland. The judicial duel, as one of the types of so-called ordals (judgements of God) owed its importance first of all to the fact that the solemn oath of the parties and the witnesses brought by these parties was considered the main means of evidence. In a situation where the two parties and witnesses swore differently, another institution was needed to indicate whose side was right. The infallible in this matter was to be God - the manager of human affairs and Lord of the elements[706], who always allowed the one who fought in a just cause to prevail. Judicial duels were used to settle not only criminal cases, but also civil disputes.

It was in this environment that the institution of professional substitutes in court duels appeared, called in Poland "szampierz"[707] (champions, gladiatores).

705 J. Rozenblat, op. cit. p. 76.

706 Hence the alternative ordalia associated with fire and water.

707 The term is attributed to Tadeusz Czacki, who translated the term "champion" in this way. One of the most famous champions was the German Hans Talhoffer, who left behind as many as five treatises on, among other things, the art of the court duel, the most famous of which dates from 1467.

They were also used by rulers when it came to gaining mystical support for the settlement of disputes crucial to the functioning of the state, such as the case of inheritance from grandfathers by grandchildren and uncles, decided by Emperor Otto I in 938[708]. The blade of the champions sword also ruled on the issue of the introduction of Roman law in Spain. When, in 1038, it was being considered whether to introduce Roman law or to stop with the application of local laws, King Alfonso decided to settle the issue through a duel. The victor was the champion of Roman law.

In the same way, King Alfonso of Spain decided on the subject of the applicable liturgy when he had to decide whether the principles of the Mozarabic liturgy introduced by St. Isidore, popular among the people, or the Roman liturgy, which enjoyed the support of the Pope and the King, were preferable. The Mozarabic liturgy emerged victorious from the duel. The king, dissatisfied with such a result, decided to arrange another trial, both books were thrown into the fire, but this time too the Mozarabic liturgy prevailed, which was not imitated by the flames.

The practices of the judgements of God in Poland generally mirrored analogous customs adopted in Western Europe, although they were applied only in criminal cases. The texts of privileges allowing individual cities to organize them have survived. As in Western Europe, so in Poland it was possible to use the services of a professional champion.

The first legislative document in Poland treating dueling is the Statute of Jan Łaski, printed by order of King Alexander in 1506 in Cracow. This set of laws included the provisions of the Magdeburg law, recognizing, as we have already mentioned, the institution of a judicial duel. Gradually, however, the use of this means of proof was banned throughout Europe, including Poland[709].

4. Modern duelling

The cradle of dueling in defense of honor is considered to be Italy of the Renaissance period, to which, in addition to the works of Michelangelo or Botticelli, we owe the transformation of medieval forms of court dueling and knightly combat

708 Widukind von Corbey in Res gestae Saxonicae 2.10 states: „Rex autem meliori Consilio usus noluit viros nobiles ac senes populi inhoneste tractari, sed magis rem inter gladiatores discerni jussit. Vicit igitur pars, qui filios filiorum computabant inter filios, et firmatum es tut aequaliter cum oaternis hereditatem dividerent pacto sempiterno".

709 With few exceptions, when such a duel was held with the personal permission of the ruler.

into dueling in defense of honor, which replaced the more traditional Italian vendetta[710]. The custom of dueling spread from Italian territory to all of Europe through soldiers participating in the Italian wars, which were fought throughout the first half of the 16th century. It was in Italy, in Venice, that Hieronymus Mutio published the first dueling code in history (1553), giving rise to a veritable flood of publications on the subject (the French dueling bibliography counts several thousand items).

It would be hard to find a better description of the evolution of the duel to a form of battle of honor than that given by John Selden in his book The Duello, or single combat (1610), where he wrote „truth, honor, freedome and curtesie being as incidents to perfit chivalry upon the lye given, fame impeached, body wronged, or curtesie taxed, a custom hath bin among the French, English, Burguingnons, Italians, Almans and the Northern people (which as Ptolemy notes are always inclined to liberty) to seek revenge of their wrongs on the body of their accuser and that by private combat seul à seul, without judicial lists appointed them"[711].

Duels in this form - a kind of revenge for an insult to honor grew to the size of a real scourge of 18th century Europe and met with a reaction from state authorities, in many cases aiming to eliminate the phenomenon through severe criminal repression. Nevertheless, in aristocratic or military circles, matters of honor were doing well despite attempts to remove them through legislation. It was a common phenomenon to create sets of rules of honorable conduct with procedures that included a response to insults to honor, a special honor judiciary and, finally, to seek redress in the form of a ritualized duel with weapons that gave the fighting "duelists" a theoretically equal chance of victory and in a ritualized form that included the participation of honorary substitutes (seconds), a master of ceremonies or doctors ready to assist the wounded.

This kind of inventory of customary law has come to be known as "codes of honor." The practice of creating such codes arrived in Poland with the influence of the partitioning states[712]. They were widely used despite the fact that legislation explicitly forbade dueling, while participation in a duel was generally considered a crime, but in some circles, such as in the army, their use was even ordered by introducing this way of settling honor cases by way of military orders.

---

710 R. Hopton, Pistols at dawn. A history of duelling, Piatkus, London 2007, p. 16.

711 R. Baldick, The duel. A history of duelling, Clarkson N. Potter Inc., New York 1965, p. 32.

712 The most common Polish code of honor known as the Boziewicz code was created on the basis of similar Italian and Austrian codes (by Gelli, Barbasetti and Ristov). In contrast, French influences are also evident in others.

In addition to criminal repression, social action against dueling began to develop, as only the evolution of previous notions of custom, in the area of settling matters of honor, could significantly contribute to reducing the number of duels and the gradual disappearance of this custom in society. At the same time as social action among civilian spheres, an anti-dueling campaign was developing in military circles, as it was realized that in England the phenomenon had been brought under control mainly because the action against dueling came from among the officers of the British army and navy. After all, with dueling occurring in the country on the order of the authorities, any public struggle against this phenomenon must be ineffective.

Regardless of the pressure of public opinion, a factor largely conducive to the development of dueling was the lack of effective legal protection of the honor of the individual. According to Jeremy Bentham, "dueling is a supplement to inadequate legislative provisions."

Inadequate criminal sanctions, unable to give redress to the wronged party, combined with overly lenient treatment of cases of insult and insult to honor in court proceedings, become the reason that many people, seeing no possibility of obtaining meaningful redress through legal means, resorted to dueling. If one takes into account the ineffectiveness of the criminal sanctions provided for insult to honor, reduced in practice mostly to discontinuance of the proceedings or a sentence of a few dozen hours' imprisonment with conversion to correspondingly insignificant monetary fines, it is hardly surprising that the courts of general jurisdiction did not enjoy popularity as "tribunals of honor."

This phenomenon, which they only partially succeeded in combating, completely disappeared after the end of World War II. Both the social and military reforms forced by the conflict and a change in the mentality of the people who had previously cultivated this custom contributed to this effect. In turn, the method of dueling survived only partly in the form of the rules of fencing bouts played by athletes also at the Olympic Games.

Bibliography

Baldick R., The Duel. A history of duelling, Clarkson N. Potter Inc., New York 1965.

Bartoszewski W., Pojedynek. Jego zasady i wskazówki, H. Altenberg. Lwów 1910.

Hopton R., Pistols at dawn. A history of duelling, Piatkus, London 2011.

Morawski M., O pojedynku kilka uwag, L. Anczyc i ska, Kraków 1892.

Naimski J., O pojedynkach, Księgarnia Józefa Sikorskiego, Warszawa 1881.

Norris J., Pistols at dawn. A history of duelling, The History Press, Gloucestershire 2009.

Rozenblat J., Pojedynek, Księgarnia Polska, Lwów 1879.

Sobolewski W., O pojedynku w prawie karnym (unpublished).

Tarczyński A., Kodeks i pistolet. O niektórych przejawach honoru w międzywojennej Polsce, WSP w Bydgoszczy, Bydgoszcz 1997.

Chapter IV.
Human rights in a democratic state

Bronisław Sitek[713]

Romanization, globalization and virtual reality

Abstract: Starting from the end of the Republic, there were trends aimed at creating uniform structures within the Roman state, including the establishment of a uniform culture. This process is commonly referred to as the Romanization of the ancient world. Universalist tendencies also prevailed during the Middle Ages. Starting from the 20th century, globalization tendencies developed with great intensity. Humanity now lives in the era of digitization, which involves the computerization of almost every aspect of life, including culture. The subject of this study, therefore, is to explore these processes and their effects, which have had significant implications for humanity.

Keywords: international law, globalization, Roman law, unification, virtual reality Romanization

1. Introductory remarks

Since the dawn of human history, there have been examples of dreams of uniting all people. The description of paradise in the book of Genesis includes a vision of primordial peace (Gen. 1.8-25). In a slightly changed version, the same vision was also found in the Qur'an (sura 2.22-35). Undoubtedly, the biblical concept of the original good influenced the views of the 18th century philosopher Jean-Jacques Rousseau on human nature. Using the method of retrospection, he concluded that the original nature of man in the pre-state period, and even in the earlier period of tribal life that took place before organized society, was good. The evil nature of man is secondary, caused by the development of civilization, especially the family, which gives rise to the need to accumulate goods to support the family[714].

Different vision of the beginning of the development of the world was described by Plato, in his work Timaeus[715]. According to him, only ideas are eternal, unchanging, and perfect. Demirug followed age-old ideals when writing

713 SWPS University, ORCID 0000-0002-7365-6954.

714 M. Baranowska, *Jana Jakuba Rousseau refleksja o naturze człowieka*. W: *„Rodzinna Europa". Europejska myśl polityczno – prawna u progu XXI wieku*, pod red. P. Fiktus, H. Malewski, M. Marszał, Wrocław 2015, pp. 65-66.

715 M. Piechowiak, *Przemowa Demiurga w Platońskim „Timajosie" a współczesne pojęcie godności*. W: *Abiit, non obiit. Księga poświęcona pamięci Księdza Profesora Antoniego Kościa SCD*, pod red. A. Dębiński, Lublin 2013, pp. 655-665.

about the causative power that builds the world. This world, however, is composed of four disordered elements, i.e. fire, water, earth and air. Due to the lack of stability of these elements, values such as beauty and goodness can only exist in a relative way[716]. Thus, Plato explains the existing causes of imperfections in the representation of the world in ideas in reality. The Demiurge was unable to order the original chaos and give it the shape of an ideal world.

In some religious concepts, e.g. Judaism, chaos was secondary to the original order[717]. The reason for its destruction was disobedience to God or gods. Hence, in almost all religions there are propitiatory rituals combined with offering sacrifices to God or gods in order to soothe or ward off their anger.

Descriptions or explanations of the original state of man or society stem from utopian vision and human being's striving for perfection or the construction of an ideal society. Hence, it is not without reason that in the Ralph Bunche Park in front of the UN building there is a fragment from the book of the prophet Isaiah: *For the law will go out from Zion, and the word of the Lord from Jerusalem. He will be the judge between the peoples and will pronounce judgment on many nations. Then they will beat their swords into plowshares, and their spears into pruning hooks. Nation shall not lift up sword against nation, neither shall they train themselves for war anymore* (Isaiah 2:3-4). Thus, the UN member states declared their commitment to building global peace.

Of course, many other exemplary texts or concepts regarding order or social order of a universal nature can be cited. In this material, limited in volume, I will limit myself to characterizing the concept of global order. The first one is the construction of the universal Roman Empire, the second one is globalization, and the third one is virtual reality. Each of these concepts has been or is actually implemented, so they are not just theoretical considerations of philosophers or unimplemented intentions of politicians and ideologists. The aim of the study is to characterize each of these concepts and point out the existing similarities and differences. The research hypothesis is that each of these attempts to introduce a new order has its own ideological premises, authorities, and goals. Determining these premises is the basis for understanding how each of these realities' functions.

---

716 Polityk 269a, 270a, 272 a, 273 b. See: A. Drozdek, *Bóg Platona*, Studia Philosophiae Christiane 34/291998), pp. 88-89.

717 The situation is different in the Bible, according to which Yahweh created the world out of chaos. Genes. 1.1-2.

2. Romanitas

The process of Romanization is understood as the introduction of a common language, culture, religion and broadly understood power structures in the areas conquered by the Romans. Source texts indicate that the Roman elites were aware of building a new order or world order. Octavian Augustus was referred to as *novus ordo rerum* or *orbis conditor*[718]. The new political order introduced by Octavian was called *pax Augusta*, and after the emperor's death as *pax Romana*[719]. Indeed, after the period of civil wars, Octavian ensured a period of peace lasting over two centuries and began a period of dynamic cultural and economic development of Rome[720].

Nowadays, this process is called *romanitas.* The concept was first used by Tertullino (c. 150-240) in a work titled *De Pallio*, 1.4.1[721]. Tertullian denies the existence of a unified culture that could be defined by the collective concept of *romanitas.* They point to the numerous cultural differences existing at that

718 Svet. *Aug.* 7. Romanist doctrine contains many studies on the Romanization of the Roman world. See G. Mancini, *Integrazione ed esclusione nell'esperienza giuridica romana. Dalle politiche di integrazione dello straniero alla generalizzazione della condizione di "straniero in patria": le norme su capacità matrimoniale e filiazione come strumenti della frammentazione degli status in età tardoantica. In: Immigrazione e integrazione. Dalla prospettiva globale alle realtà locali (I).* ed. F. Rimoli, Napoli 2014), pp. 1-37.

719 Paterculus, 2, 89: ...revocata pax, sopitus ubique armorum furor, restituta vis legibus, iudicis auctoritatis, senatui maiestatis, imperium magistratuum ad pristinum redactum modum... prisca illa et antiqua rei publicae forma revocata reddit cultus agris, sacris honos, securita hominibus, certa cuique rerum suarum possessio. See: U. Asche, Roms Weltherrschaftsidee und Aussenpolitik in der Spätantike im Spiegel der Panagyrici Latini, Bonn, 1983, pp. 76 n.

720 B. Sitek, *Novus ordo rerum Augusta. Pierwsza próba zjednoczenia Europy.* In: Materiały Pokonferencyjne I-go Forum Unii Walutowej. Unia Walutowa a przyszłość Polski i krajów Europy Środkowowschodniej, Olsztyn 2000, pp. 185-201.

721 Tert. *De pallio* 1.4.1: *Quid nunc, si est Romanitas omni salus, nec honestis tamen modis ad Graios estis? Aut, ni ita est, unde gentium, in prouinciis melius exercitis, quas natura agro potius eluctando commodauit, studia palaestrae, male senescentia et cassum laborantia et lutea unctio et puluerea uolutatio, arida saginatio? Vnde apud aliquos Numidas etiam equis caesariatos iuxta cutem tonsor et cultri uertex solus immunis? Vnde apud hirtos et hirsutos tam rapax a culo resina, tam furax a mento uolsella? Prodigium est haec sine pallio fieri. Illius est haec tota res Asiae. Quid tibi Libya, et Europa, cum xysticis munditiis, quas uestire non nosti? Reuera enim quale est Graecatim depilari magis quam amiciri?*

time within the Roman Empire. These include the distinctiveness of Greek and Numidian culture. According to one of the first Christian writers, these differences are visible in language, religion, clothing, lifestyle and education. In turn, Saint Augustine, in his work *De Civitate Dei* 19.7, writes about the cultural differences (orbis *terrae*) existing in the Roman empire, including the languages used.

In Roman literature, the following terms were used to describe the process of unification of areas incorporated under Roman rule: *romanus*, i.e. something that belongs to Roman culture, nation (*populus Romanus*), affairs of the Roman state[722], *magnitudinem Romanam*, i.e. the size of Rome as a state[723] or in finally *Romane*, i.e. something that is consistent with Roman traditions - *mos maiorum* or something that corresponds to Roman standards, e.g. of life[724]. Moreover, contemporary research in Spain[725] and England[726] shows that even during the Principate or Dominate period, Roman culture was not unified. In individual Roman provinces, numerous pre-Roman cultures have been preserved, even languages and organizations of cities and religious cults. The adaptation *of mores Romanorum* was selective and often mixed with old local customs.

In one of her works, Francesca Lamberti analyzes the relationship between the concept of *civis* and *civitas in* the Republican period, which was extremely important for the creation of the concept of *romanitas.* According to this author, being a Roman citizen (civis) was a ticket to being a member of an elite social group called *civitas.* Membership in this group allowed them to run for public offices. Holding public offices, at least in the republican period, was an honor - *an honor*, hence they were held unpaid[727].

Roman citizenship allows the use of procedural instruments to protect the citizen's property and non-property interests[728]. The Punic Wars, and in particular economic development, forced the Romans to open their broadly understood policy to other social groups living not only in Rome itself, but also on the Italian

722 Liv. 5.27 in. fi.; Plin. *Nat.* 2.247.

723 Tray. *Ann.* 2.10.

724 Gell. 13.22.2.

725 J. Nicols, *Indigenous culture and the process of romanization in Iberian Galicia*, The American Journal of Philology 108.1(1987), pp. 129-151.

726 Ch. Bruun, J. Edmonson, *The Oxford Handbook of Roman Epigraphy*, Oxford 2014, pp. 153 ff.

727 F. Lamberti, *Romanizaci ón y ciudadan í a. El camino de la expansión de Roma en la Rep ública.* In: *Storia d'Europa e del Mediterraneo.* Sez. III. *L'ecumene romana.* Vol. 6. *Da Augusto a Diocleziano*, edited by G. Traina, Lecce 2009, pp. 28-29.

728 M. Kaser, *Das r ö mische Zivilprozessrecht*, München, pp. 149 ff.

Peninsula. Moreover, more and more Italian cities received *ius commercialium*, and thus access to legal devices, including private and procedural law[729].

The forced development of trade and, consequently, the development of Roman law became the beginning of the construction of a timeless legal system. Many Romanists believe that a uniform system of law was created[730]. Meanwhile, even during the period of domination of Roman classical law, in many parts of the empire not only was the level of knowledge of the norms of Roman law varied, but, in accordance with the principle of personal law, the majority of inhabitants used their own law[731]. The granting of Roman citizenship to all inhabitants of the Empire by Caracalla in 212 AD led to a significant reduction in the level of knowledge of Roman law. This period of Roman law has rightly been called in the literature as a time of its vulgarization, i.e. a decline in the quality of its interpretation and application[732].

The laws of 367 BC, *Leges Liciniae Sextiae*, which *de facto* ended the original division of society into plebeians and patricians[733], are quite important for understanding the idea of Romanization. From then on, the concept of *populus Romanus* began to cover both parts of society. The new elite social group was *the nobiles*, consisting of the wealthier classes of former patricians and plebeians. The next group of Roman citizens were the freedmen - *libertini*. Thus, already at the end of the republic, freedmen constituted the majority in the *cives Romanorum group*, and freeborn citizens became the privileged group. As F. Lamberti rightly

729 M. Talamanca, *I mutamenti della cittadinanza*, MEFRA, 103(1991), pp. 703-733; K. Wyrwińska, *Civis Romanus sum. Roman public law. Selected issues*, Kraków 2015, pp. 12 ff.

730 M. Talamanca, *I mutamenti della cittadinanza*, MEFRA, 103(1991), pp. 703-733; K. Wyrwińska, *Civis Romanus sum. Rzymskie prawo publiczne. Wybrane zagadnienia*, Kraków 2015, pp. 12 n.

731 GE Talamanca, *Ricerche sul Processo nell'Egipto Greco-Romano*, Napoli 1984, p. 129 ff.

732 E. Levy, *Weströmisches Vulgarrecht-das Obligationenrecht. Forschungen zum römischen Recht*, Weimar 1956.

733 On the basis of the laws proposed by the tribunes Licinius and Sextius, debts were reduced by crediting unpaid interest to capital and an upper limit was set for land leasing (ager *publicus)*. Liv. 6.42.See: R. Kamińska, *Sprawowanie urzędów edyla plebejskiego i edyla kurulnego w republice i pryncypacie rzymskim, Czasopismo* Prawno-Historyczne 65.2 (2013), pp. 170-171; P. Kołodko, *Pretor urzędnikiem magistratury rzymskiej. Zarys problematyki*, Miscellanea Historico-Iuridica 12.1 (2014), p. 39-40; J. Malaníková, *Selected examples of laws (leges) approved by comitia preserved in the book VII of Livy's History*. Graeco-Latina Brunensia 20(2015), pp. 95-103.

claims, with the end of the republic, the growing social layer of the urban poor in Rome - *the proletariat* - finally put an end to the republican model of civil society[734]. This was compounded by the inefficiency of the republican authorities in managing the entire Roman Empire. As a result, there was a change in the system of power from a republican to an authoritarian system, i.e. the principate.

Colonization, first of Italy and later of the rest of the empire, was a key tool of Romanization. This process began already in the 4th century BC.[735] The extent of the colonization process is evidenced by the fact that in the period between the 4th and 2nd centuries BC. More than 2,500 colonies were established in Christianity on the basis of Roman legions, or the urban poor resettled from Rome. The colonization process gained momentum with the end of the republic and the beginning of the principate. Municipal law was largely unified[736]. During this period, Italy was Romanized most quickly, but many places retained their earlier traditions, including language and religion[737]. The process of colonization, and therefore Romanization, suffered far-reaching stagnation after Hadrian's decision not to further conquer new territories. The Romanization of the areas conquered by the Romans also took place at different rates[738].

An element of the Romanization process of the areas conquered by Rome was undoubtedly the language. Roman Kamienik claims that Latin has never

---

734 F. Lamberti, *Romanización…*, p. 44; E. S. Gruen, *The Last Generation of the Roman Republic*, Berkeley 1974.

735 A.T Salmon, Roman Colonization under the Republic, Thames and Hudson, Londres 1969, pp. 40-48; A. Petrucci, *Aspetti economici e problemi costituzionali nella deduzione di colonie dal 509 al 338 aC.* In: *Legge e socita nella reppublica romana*, edited by F. Serrao, Napoles 2000, pp. 95-177.

736 The prototype of municipal laws was *lex Iulia municpalis*, a law issued by Julius Caesar. See: B. Sitek, *Tabula Heracleensis (lex Iulia municipalis). Tekst, tłumaczenie, komentarz*, Olsztyn 2006, p. 18. Other municipal laws granted to newly established towns in the provinces were modeled on the text of this act. Many of these laws have survived to this day. See: B. Sitek, *Lex coloniae Genetovae Iuliae seu Ursonensis i lex Irnitana. Ustawy municypalne antycznego Rzymu. Tekst, tłumaczenie i komentarz*, Poznań 2008. For more on the system of municipal laws, see: E. Twarowska-Antczak, *Od lex Iulia municipalis do Flawijskich leges municipalis*, Warszawa 2018; M.H. Crawford, *Roman Statutes*, vol. I-II, London 1996.

737 A. La Regina, *I Sanniti*. In: *Italia omnium terrarium parens. La civilita degli Enotri, Choni, Ausoni, Sanniti, Lucani, Brettii, Sicani, Siculi, Elimi, Antica madres*, edited by G. Pugliese Caratelli, Milano 1989, pp. 299-432.

738 L. Mroziewicz, *The development of the municipal system and the progress of Romanization in Moesia Dolna*, Poznań 1982.

displaced local languages. However, it cannot be denied that it was a universal language through which all nations inhabiting the territory administered by the Romans could communicate. This fact undoubtedly accelerated the process of acquiring not only the language, but also various customs. In fact, the process of Romanization through the use of Latin only affected the upper and middle layers of society. The lower social classes remained resistant to Roman influence[739].

Romanitas was built on the basis of the concept of a dominant (imperial) state over the territories occupied by the Romans. The idea of unification of the Roman state was implemented not only by military force, but also by the process of colonization, implementation of a common language, mainly Latin, and application of common law. On this basis, the ideology of the world state arose. He referred to the idea *of orbis Romanus*, i.e. Roman identity or the concept of *romanitas*, among others. Charlemagne, then the German emperors, and even Musollini during the fascist rule in Italy. Among Charlemagne's numerous rears was *the Romanum gubernans Imperium*[740].

3. Globalization

A completely different form of world unification is globalization, a process detached from the concept of a territorial state. It is assumed that globalization is a set of ongoing political, economic, technological, technical and socio-cultural processes. Globalization is a vague concept; hence it can be defined differently. Undoubtedly, the ideology of globalization is based on the assumptions of classical liberalism and Anglo-Saxon utilitarianism. John Paul II claimed that the market economy had conquered the world. This, in turn, gave rise to the interdependence of economies and societies, and the spread of new philosophical and ethical ideas[741]. The aim of globalization is not to unify the world, cultures or societies. Zygmunt Bauman notes that globalization divides and unites people in equal measure. The basic factor that polarizes the global world is the different pace of economic development[742].

---

739 R. Kamienik, Humanitas barbarzyńców i barbarzyństwo rzymian, Roczniki Lubelskie 8(1965), p. 11.

740 P. Classen, *Romanum gubernans Imperium. Zur Vorgeschichte der Kaisertitulatur Karls des Großen*, Vorträge und Forschungen 28 (1983), pp. 187-204; C. Ando, *Imperial ideology and provincial loyalty in the Roman Empire*. Vol. 6. Berkeley 2013, p. 76.

741 R. Pankowski, *Rasizm zglobalizowany: Ideologia globalizmu. Rasizm i kultura popularna*, Kultura Popularna 2(2002), pp. 97-98.

742 Z. Bauman, *Globalizacja. I co z tego dla ludzi wynika*, Warszawa 2000, p. 6.

There is a dispute in world doctrine as to the characteristics of globalization and, above all, as to its origins. In the doctrine, one can encounter various typologies of globalization. According to Roland Robertson, there are 4 types of globalization (Global *Gemeinschaft* (I-IV). The first type of globalization is the existence of independent communities, hierarchically subordinated to each other (anti-globalization movements), the second type is the vision of a global village (pacifists, ecologists or ecumenists), the third type is the existence of sovereign states, open to each other, and the last type of globalization is unification states or their liquidation and the creation of a world government[743].

Assuming the concept that globalization is a set of various processes characterized by unification tendencies, standardization and crossing of old political, legal, cultural, ethnic, religious or mental borders, it turns out that it is quite difficult to indicate a specific date or even the period of the beginning of globalization. In the work by two economists, Kevin H. O'Rourke and Feffrey G. Williamson, it was shown that the beginnings of economic globalization should be associated with great discoveries, starting with the discovery of America in 1492. Already then, the first transnational trends appeared aimed at unifying the prices of specific products, e.g. sugar. However, according to these authors, the real period of economic globalization began only in the 19th century[744].

An important feature of globalization is not only economic development, but also social and technological development. A characteristic feature of modern development is that it must be balanced, i.e. one that takes into account various interests. These may be the interests of an individual, social groups, a specific country, the international community, but also the natural environment, international security or peace[745]. In definition these particular interests, science now plays a huge role. It is the development of science, especially in the areas of exact sciences, medicine, technology, IT, and indirectly in the social sciences and humanities, which is the driving force behind the development of globalization based on the principles of sustainable development[746].

---

743 A. Giddens, *Socjologia*. Polish translation: O. Siara, A. Szulżycka, P. Tomanek, Warszawa 2014, pp. 81-83; P. Sztompka, *Socjologia zmian społecznych*. Kraków 2005, pp. 101-102.

744 KH O'Rourke, JG Williamson, *when did globalization begin?* European Review of Economic History, 6 (1) (2002), pp. 23-50.

745 M. Sitek, *Ecological development of the economy as an opportunity for employment growth in the European Union*, Journal of Modern Science 33.2 (2017), pp. 115-128.

746 K. Novikova, K., *Informacja, wiedza, technologia w wybranych koncepcjach zmiany społecznej*. Journal of Modern Science, 29(2) (2016), pp. 71-92.

Globalization undoubtedly introduces increasing restrictions on state sovereignty in favor of large international organizations. This type of phenomenon can be observed in the area of international security, especially international security, the burden of which has been borne by organizations such as the UN and NATO. There are also numerous local organizations when it comes to safety. Another area of globalization is the area of sports. International sports organizations, including FIFA, IOC and FIS, organize large sporting events. The legal norms created by these organizations determine the content of legal provisions in force in specific countries or national sports associations.

The European Union currently plays a special role in the process of regional globalization. As part of this *sui generis* international entity, transnational organizational structures are created, as well as the accompanying legal instruments. Thus, a common market was created based on a common commercial policy and a customs union (Articles 30-33 TFEU). The European Central Bank was established and a common currency in force in most EU countries (Articles 3 and 4 TFEU). Member states introduced provisions into their constitutions based on which they self-limited their sovereignty. In art. 24 section In the German Constitution, the German constitutional legislator decided that the Federation agrees to the limitation of its sovereign rights, which will contribute to and secure a peaceful and lasting order in Europe and among the nations of the world. Similar provisions can be found in Art. 11 of the Italian Constitution. In turn, the Constitution of the Republic of Poland does not contain *expressis verbis* legal norms allowing for limiting the sovereignty of the state. *Implicitly*, such a solution results from the possibility of Poland ratifying international treaties (Article 146(4) point 10 of the Constitution of the Republic of Poland)[747].

Breaking the barrier of state borders through globalization processes results in greater freedom of movement among people. Increasing migration presents complex challenges requiring new legal and social responses to be solved. As Józef M. Fiszer writes, globalization understood in this way not only creates problems related to the need to redefine concepts such as sovereignty, citizenship, nation state or national and cultural identity, but also weakens ethnic and national ties and causes the mixing of cultures[748]. A global culture is emerging, manifested by fast food chains, especially McDonald's and KFC. Several global centers set the tone for global fashion, especially in New York and London.

---

747 K. Łastawski, *Polska racja stanu po wstąpieniu do Unii Europejskiej*, Warszawa 2009, pp. 171-204.

748 J.M. Fiszer, *Skutki członkostwa w Unii Europejskiej dla suwerenności i tożsamości kulturowej Polski*. Myśl Ekonomiczna i Polityczna 1-2 (2011), p. 172.

A negative manifestation of growing migration is the increasing denial by migrants of the need to assimilate with the host community. As a result, ghettos are created, i.e. groups of people of different cultures living next to each other, but without mutual understanding or assimilation. Sometimes there are quite significant street riots, as exemplified by the events of 2005 in Paris. Examples of ghettos can be found in, among others, Belgium and France. Growing conflicts between indigenous peoples and migrants result in restrictions for the latter.

In Denmark, in one of the most tolerant European countries, the authorities plan to introduce legal provisions aimed at eliminating ghettos. The purpose of these regulations is to limit excessive concentration of migrants in one place. According to the new law, no more than 30% of migrants can live in districts. Crossing these barriers gives local authorities the authority to move migrants to another district. Additionally, in March 2021, Danish authorities revoked the residence rights of approximately 600 Syrian migrants. The decision to withdraw the right of residence was justified by the fact that the level of security in Syria is currently sufficient to allow emigrants to return to their homes[749].

The law plays a key role in the process of globalization. Strong nationalist tendencies starting in the Renaissance era would lead to the creation of national systems. However, the idea of unification of law is not dead. In the doctrine of national law, reference was often made to Roman law as universal law. Despite the tendencies to nationalize the law, an autonomous merchant law - *lex* - was developed at the end of the Middle Ages *mercatoria*, independent of the law of a given country[750]. This type of customary legal norms regulated relations between merchants. The system of these norms was strengthened by voluntarily submitting commercial disputes to the resolution of merchant courts. The next stage in the development of international trade law was the development of long-distance trade between Europe and Asia in the years 1500–1750, caused by the imperial actions of some European countries. Then, in the years 1750–1880, the development of European colonial empires and the industrialization of the world took

---

749 M. Clante Benedixen, *Denmark has gone far-right on refugees. Copenhagen claims Damascus is safe enough to send nearly 100 Syrians back*, Politico from March 1, 2021 [in:] https://www.politico.eu/article/denmark-has-gone-far-right-on-refugees/ [access: 16/04/2021]. For more on the refugee crisis, see: M. Sitek, *Kryzys uchodźczy a kryzys instytucjonalny Unii Europejskiej*, Journal of Modern Science 28.1 (2016), pp. 457-471.

750 JF. Robe', *Multinational Enterprises: The Constitution of a Pluralistic Legal Order.* In: G. Teubner, (Ed.). (1997). *Global law without a state*, Dartmouth 1997, p. 45.

place. As a result, the concept of free trade was created, and thus reducing customs barriers in international exchange[751].

The development of international trade law took place after World War II. International institutions creating their own legal standards have been established, such as the World Bank or the International Monetary Fund. The European Union established a customs union, thereby abolishing all customs barriers to internal trade between member states. Nowadays, the instrument that globalizes law is not only trade, but above all the internationalization of production. The process of producing finished products has been fragmented, so that individual elements are manufactured in different parts of the world. However, legal standards and, consequently, technical standards have been unified and are applied regardless of where the elements are manufactured[752].

Nowadays, there are numerous other branches of law that are subject to globalization processes. Such branches include labor law, sports law, and medical law. The European Union plays a special role in the process of legal integration. The TFEU indicates areas of law whose shape is directly influenced by regulations or directives. Such areas include, among others, consumer protection law, antitrust law, and environmental protection law. There were also attempts to standardize private law, including: by Ole Lando or Christian von Bar[753]. However, all these legal provisions are of a regional nature, as is the case with EU law. The norms of international law are most often classified as *soft law*. The exception are EU regulations that are directly applicable in the legal order of the Member States. They don't need any implementation.

The only set of legal norms that can claim to be global law are human rights. But even in this case, only the Universal Declaration of Human Rights of 1948 was adopted by all UN member states[754]. All other legal acts relating to human

751 A. Nobis, *Krótka historia globalizacji. Recenzja*. Kultura-Historia-Globalizacja 4(2009), pp. 100-101.

752 JF. Robe', op. cit., p. 45.

753 B. Sitek, *To Unify or to Synchronize Law in Europe*. In: *Comparative law in Eastern and Central Europe*, edited by: B. Sitek, J.J. Szczerbowski, A.W. Bauknecht, Cambridge 2013, pp. 51-68; B. Sitek, *Unifikować czy synchronizować prawo w Europie? Studium przypadku od prawa rzymskiego do prawa europejskiego*, Journal of Modern Science 2/29/2016, pp. 109-130.

754 See: A. Bianchi, *Globalization of Human Rights: The Role of Non-State Actors*. In: *Global law without a state*, edited by G. Teubner, Dartmouth 1997, pp. 179-213.

rights are regional in nature and specific. You may come across statements or publications denying the global nature of human rights[755].

Mass media are undoubtedly one of the global instruments. The invention of radio and then television allowed for the rapid transmission of information. What people previously learned about from travel books, most often with a long delay, was already available in the 1920s. it traveled around the world extremely quickly. According to Colin Sparks, the contribution of the media to the globalization processes of the 20th century can be divided into three stages. The first one is the period of World War II. Back then, the media were an instrument of fascist or communist propaganda. But also, after World War II, the media were and are used to spread the great-power policy of the United States of America, Russia and China. At the same time, several media centers monopolized information circulating globally. The information produced there is repeated by other smaller information centers.

Globalization as a set of various processes characterized by unification has undoubtedly made the world a global village. Nevertheless, regional manifestations of globalization can be noticed, an example of which is the European Union. Moreover, anti-globalization and nationalist movements are intensifying their activity. In this respect, globalization is similar to the Roman Empire, which created a number of unified areas while maintaining cultural diversity.

4. Virtual world or virtual reality - *virtual reality* (VR)

Nowadays, humanity lives between the real world and the virtual world or virtual reality. At the very beginning, it is necessary to clarify what the term "virtual world" or "virtual reality" means. According to Anna Latwiec, the virtual world has its source in the real world. It is some form of illusion of the real world. The creator of this reality is the person himself, who, using ICT tools, can create situations close to reality, e.g. simulation of driving a car, flying an airplane or mountain climbing. It should also not be forgotten that the development of ICT tools became possible thanks to technological progress inspired by the needs generated by the army and special services, starting from the 1970s[756].

The very concept of "virtual world" was coined in the 1950s. This concept means that the virtual world is an object observed by humans. In turn, virtual reality is a space in which a person is an active participant, not only observes

755 M. Sitek, *Prawa (potrzeby) człowieka w ponowoczesności*, Warszawa 2016, p. 33 ff.

756 W. Pokruszyński, *Chalenges and Threats of XXI Century*. In: *Krajobraz po mistrzostwach Europy 2012*, edited by: M. Sitek, W. Bednarek, Józefów, pp. 428.

some phenomena or experiences illusory impressions, but also gets involved, interacts with other people, institutions, begins to live there, implementing his plans and intentions[757].

W. Gibson 1968 called virtual reality cyberspace[758]. Cyberspace is created as a result of the interaction of various media that enable the creation of a new reality. It is created thanks to computer technology and appropriate software, which is subject to continuous development. As a result, a world without borders is created, which is a space for establishing various types of contacts between participants using computer or telephone technology[759]. The goal of this world is not unification at all, but to improve communication, raising it to a higher level than before.

The Internet, which is the basic tool of cyberspace, allows for unlimited access to various types of databases and for quick contacts regardless of political or geographical borders. The Internet provides access to the latest data through search engines. The Internet also ensures the use of exhibitionist practices, examples of which are various types of blogs and online diaries[760].

Unlike the global world, in the virtual world or cyberspace it is man who becomes the creator. New tools and new programs definitely change human lifestyle, both on a micro and macro scale. The current real contacts between citizens and public offices, including banks, have been replaced by electronic contacts, i.e. contacts made using applications or specialized programs. In addition, virtual schools, universities and libraries are being created. The model of education is changing not only, forced by the pandemic, but also of conducting scientific research. Scientists can share their achievements in cyberspace by creating research teams or implementing research programs. Scientific search engines and databases have been created, such as Google Scholar, researchgate and academia.edu. Some medical services, including rehabilitation (telerehabilitation), have also moved to the virtual world.

Trade is moving to cyberspace. The level of online purchases increases every year. In Poland, 57% of the population already shops online. As a consequence, the demand for the construction of large-format stores is decreasing. In some

757 A. Latawiec, *Uwagi w świetle wirtualności*, Studia Philosophiae Christianae 40/2(2004), p. 283.
758 W. Gibson, *Neuromancer*, transl. from English: PW Cholewa, Warsaw 1992.
759 A. Latawiec, *op. cit.*, p. 283.
760 Ibidem, p. 284.

countries, including the United States, large shopping malls are being closed because shopping has moved to cyberspace[761].

The construction of virtual reality also affects the organization and functioning of work in large office buildings and in public administration. The pandemic caused by Covid19, which has prevailed since the beginning of 2020, has only accelerated processes that began at the end of the 20th century. It has become standard to perform work remotely or in hybrid mode, i.e. only partial work in the office, e.g. 2 days a week. As a result, large office buildings built until recently will probably be transformed into residential houses. With such far-reaching changes in working patterns, there is also the need to re-regulate working time, remuneration, free time and employee availability.

Cyberspace also influences security issues both individually and collectively, including globally. It is not the purpose of this study to provide a detailed analysis of cyberspace security. However, it is impossible not to notice certain negative phenomena in the area of individual security. Communication in cyberspace, for example using chats or other instant messengers, on the one hand facilitates contacts, but on the other hand, it creates an opportunity for anonymity, as well as for one person to create several separate personalities (fake persona), which may mislead recipients regarding age, gender, origin, marital status, profession, place of residence.

It is no secret that you can create fictitious accounts (fake profiles) or groups of people promoting specific views in cyberspace. Then *likes* are artificially produced, creating the belief that these views are massively supported. Cyberspace is also used to spread false scientific research results and disinformation or change history. An example of this are numerous publications blurring the responsibility of Germans, especially the German elites, for the crimes of World War II or publications leading to the glorification of communist ideology[762].

761 In Poland, the first shopping center was closed in Sosnowiec. See: *Tego jeszcze nie było. Pierwsze w Polsce centrum handlowe wyburzone.* In: Money.pl, https://www.money.pl/galerie/artykul/centrum-handlowe-w-sosnowcu-wyburzone,170,0,2380970.html [access: 19.04.2021].

762 The University of Helsinki in Finland is implementing an EU program that aims to investigate the involvement of German intellectuals in war crimes. T. Giaro analyzed the results of this program and discovered that the purpose of this scientific project is to denazify the activities of German professors in war crimes. Thus, history is distorted. See: T. Giaro, *The Culmination-Book. Trying to Make Sense of the Nazi Years*, Studia Iuridica 83(2020), pp. 7-26. Currently, it is mainly Russians who deal with disinformation. See: S. Sokolova, *Technology of Soviet Myth Creation about Famine as a Result of Crop Failure in Ukraine of the 1932–1933s*, Journal of Modern Science, vol. 42, no. 3, (2019), pp. 37-56.

Virtual reality or cyberspace built on the basis of the Internet and satellite television has created a new level of organization and human activity, both individually and collectively. The actual place of human activity, especially the state, commune or even the street, does not matter. Old acquaintances from the street or neighborhood have transformed into acquaintances with people on the Internet. Similar changes have affected numerous other areas of life, including: the concept of media has changed from *one-to-many* to *many-to-one*. Thus, many claim that the end of the traditional era of journalism is *coming*.

5. Final conclusions

The idea of unification or unification of humanity can be seen in the oldest messages, especially religious ones. The first lasting attempt to permanently unite at least a fragment of humanity was the Roman Empire. The idea of unity was built on the basis of the concept of the state. The tool for building Roman society was the Latin language, the legal system, ancient customs and religious tolerance. Already in the times of Octavian Augustus, the concept of a world state was finally formulated, guaranteeing security and peace for all inhabitants - *pax Romana*. In fact, *romanitas* mainly celebrates the upper and middle social classes. Therefore, a significant part of society lived according to its own customs, used its own language, its own law and did not identify with Roman culture.

The idea of globalization is completely detached from state structures. Numerous areas of human activity have been subject to globalization, especially technical standards, certain branches of law, the organization of sports, and the organization of security systems. Unlike the Roman Empire, globalization covered the entire globe. However, it should be noted that globalization, regardless of citizenship, is also contested by transnational groups. The degree of advancement of globalization processes also varies.

After all, virtual reality built on the basis of ICT tools has transferred humanity to a completely different reality. Many types of human activity no longer take place in the real world, but in cyberspace. In the case of virtual reality, there is a far-reaching marginalization of state functions and even international institutions. Society in cyberspace creates its own structures and value system.

Bibliography

Ando, C. *Imperial ideology and provincial loyalty in the Roman Empire*. Vol. 6. Berkeley 2013.

Asche, U. *Roms Weltherrschaftsidee und Aussenpolitik in der Spätantike im Spiegel der Panagyrici Latini*, Bonn, 1983.

Baranowska, M. *Jana Jakuba Rousseau refleksja o naturze człowieka.* W: *„Rodzinna Europa". Europejska myśl polityczno – prawna u progu XXI wieku*, pod red. P. Fiktus, H. Malewski, M. Marszał, Wrocław 2015, spp. 63-74.

Bauman, Z. *Globalizacja. I co z tego dla ludzi wynika*, Warszawa 2000.

Bianchi, A. *Globalization of Human Rights: The Role of Non-State Actors.* W: *Global law without a state*, pod red. G. Teubner, Dartmouth 1997, pp. 179-213.

Bruun, Ch. Edmonson, J. *The Oxford Handbook of Roman Epigraphy*, Oxford 2014.

Classen, P. *Romanum gubernans imperium. Zur Vorgeschichte der Kaisertitulatur Karls des Großen*, Vorträge und Forschungen 28 (1983), pp. 187-204.

Crawford, M.H. *Roman Statutes*, vol. I-II, London 1996.

Drozdek, A. *Bóg Platona*, Studia Philosophiae Christiane 34/29(1998), pp. 87-102.

Fiszer, J.M. *Skutki członkostwa w Unii Europejskiej dla suwerenności i tożsamości kulturowej Polski.* Myśl Ekonomiczna i Polityczna 1-2 (2011), pp. 170-197.

Giaro, T. *The Culmination-Book. Trying to Make Sense of the Nazi Years*, Studia Iuridica 83(2020), p. 7-26.

Gibson, W. *Neuromancer*, translation from English: P. W. Cholewa, Warszawa 1992.

Giddens, A. *Socjologia*, Polish translation: O. Siara, A. Szulżycka, P. Tomanek, Warszawa 2014.

Gruen, E.S. *The Last Generation of the Roman Republic*, Berkeley 1974.

Kamienik, R. *Humanitas barbarzyńców i barbarzyństwo rzymian*, Roczniki Lubelskie 8(1965), pp. 9-36.

Kamińska, R. *Sprawowanie urzędów edyla plebejskiego i edyla kurulnego w republice i pryncypacie rzymskim, Czasopismo* Prawno-Historyczne 65.2 (2013), pp. 165-177.

Kaser, M. *Das römische Zivilprozessrecht*, München.

Kołodko, P. *Pretor urzędnikiem magistrat*ury *rzymskiej. Zarys problematyki*, Miscellanea Historico-Iuridica 12.1 (2014), pp. 31-55.

La Regina, A. *I Sanniti.* W: *Italia omnium terrarium parens. La civilita degli Enotri, Choni, Ausoni, Sanniti, Lucani, Brettii, Sicani, Siculi, Elimi, Antica madres*, pod red. G. Pugliese Caratelli, Milano 1989, pp. 299-432.

Lamberti, F. *Romanización y ciudadanía. El camino de la expansión de Roma en la República.* W: *Storia d'Europa e del Mediterraneo.* Sez. III. *L'ecumene romana.* Vol. 6. *Da Augusto a Diocleziano*, pod red. G. Traina, Lecce 2009, pp. 667-707.

Latawiec, A. *Uwagi w świetle wirtualności*, Studia Philosophiae Christianae 40/2(2004), p. 283 (279-291).

Levy, E. *Weströmisches Vulgarrecht-das Obligationenrecht. Forschungen zum römischen Recht*, Weimar 1956.

Łastawski, K. *Polska racja stanu po wstąpieniu do Unii Europejskiej*, Warszawa 2009, pp. 171-204.

Malaníková, J. *Selected examples of laws (leges) approved by comitia preserved in the book VII of Livy's History*. Graeco-Latina Brunensia 20(2015), p. 95-103.

Mancini, G. *Integrazione ed esclusione nell'esperienza giuridica romana. Dalle politiche di integrazione dello straniero alla generalizzazione della condizione di "straniero in patria": le norme su capacità matrimoniale e filiazione come strumenti della frammentazione degli status in età tardoantica.* W: *Immigrazione e integrazione. Dalla prospettiva globale alle realtà locali (I).* editted by: F. Rimoli, Napoli 2014), pp. 1-37.

Mroziewicz, L. *Rozwój ustroju municypalnego a postępy romanizacji w Mezji Dolnej*, Poznań 1982.

Nicols, J. *Indigenous culture and the process of romanization in Iberian Galicia*, The American Journal of Philology 108.1(1987), pp. 129-151.

Nobis, A. *Krótka historia globalizacji. Recenzja*. Kultura-Historia-Globalizacja 4(2009), pp. 99-103.

Novikova, K. *Informacja, wiedza, technologia w wybranych koncepcjach zmiany społecznej*. Journal of Modern Science, 29(2) (2016), pp. 71-92.

O'Rourke K. H., Williamson, J.G. *When did globalisation begin*? European Review of Economic History, 6(1) (2002), pp. 23-50.

Pankowski, R. *Rasizm zglobalizowany: Ideologia globalizmu. Rasizm i kultura popularna*, Kultura Popularna 2(2002), pp. 97-106.

Petrucci, A. *Aspetti economici e problemi costituzionali nella deduzione di colonie dal 509 al 338 a.C.* W: *Legge e socita nella reppublica romana*, pod red. F. Serrao, Napoles 2000, pp. 95-177.

Piechowiak, M. *Przemowa Demiurga w Platońskim „Timajosie" a współczesne pojęcie godności*. W: *Abiit, non obiit. Księga poświęcona pamięci Księdza Profesora Antoniego Kościa SCD*, pod red. A. Dębiński, Lublin 2013, pp. 655-665.

Pokruszyński, W. *Chalenges and Threats of XXI Century*. In: *Krajobraz po mistrzostwach Europy 2012*, editted by M. Sitek, W. Bednarek, Józefów p. 428 (419-442).

Robe̕, J-F. *Multinational Enterprises: The Constutition of a Pluralistic Legal Order.* W: G. Teubner, (Ed.). (1997). *Global law without a state*, Dartmouth 1997, pp. 45-77.

Salmon, A.T. *Roman Colonization under the Republic*, Londres 1969, pp. 40-48.

Sitek, B. *Lex coloniae Genetovae Iuliae seu Ursonensis i lex Irnitana. Ustawy municypalne antycznego Rzymu. Tekst, tłumaczenie i komentarz*, Poznań 2008.

Sitek, B. *Novus ordo rerum Augusta. Pierwsza próba zjednoczenia Europy.* W: Materiały Pokonferencyjne I-go Forum Unii Walutowej. Unia Walutowa a przyszłość Polski i krajów Europy Środkowowschodniej, Olsztyn 2000, pp. 185-201.

Sitek, B. *Tabula Heracleensis (lex Iulia municipalis). Tekst, tłumaczenie, komentarz*, Olsztyn 2006.

Sitek, B. *To Unify or to Synchronize Law in Europe*. W: *Comparative law in Eastern and Central Europe*, pod red. B. Sitek, J.J. Szczerbowski, A.W. Bauknecht, Cambridge 2013, pp. 51-68.

Sitek, B. *Unifikować czy synchronizować prawo w Europie? Studium przypadku od prawa rzymskiego do prawa europejskiego*, Journal of Modern Science 2/29/2016, pp. 109-130.

Sitek, M. *Prawa (potrzeby) człowieka w ponowoczesności*, Warszawa 2016.

Sitek, M. *Ecological development of the economy as an opportunity for employment growth in the European Union*, Journal of Modern Science 33.2 (2017), pp. 115-128.

Sokolova, S. *Technology of Soviet Myth Creation about Famine as a Result of Crop Failure in Ukraine of the 1932–1933s*, Journal of Modern Science, vol. 42, no. 3, (2019), pp. 37-56.

Sztompka, P. *Socjologia zmian społecznych*. Kraków 2005.

Talamanca, G.E. *Ricerche sul Processo nell'Egipto Greco-Romano*, Napoli 1984.

Talamanca, M. *I mutamenti della cittadinanza*, MEFRA, 103(1991), pp. 703-733.

Talamnca, M. *Il diritto romano come fattore di unificazione nel mondo antico.* In: Studi in memoria di Giambattista Impallomeni, Mila Giuffre, Milano 1999, pp. 405-435.

Twarowska-Antczak, E. *Od lex Iulia municipalis do Flawijskich leges municipalis*, Warszawa 2018.

Wyrwińska, K. *Civis Romanus sum. Rzymskie prawo publiczne. Wybrane zagadnienia*, Kraków 2015.

Internet literature

Clante Benedixen, M. *Denmark has gone far-right on refugees. Copenhagen claims Damascus is safe enough to send nearly 100 Syrians back*, Politico z 1.03.2021 [w:] https://www.politico.eu/article/denmark-has-gone-far-right-on-refugees/ [access: 16.04.2021].

Tego jeszcze nie było. Pierwsze w Polsce centrum handlowe wyburzone. W: Monej.pl, https://www.money.pl/galerie/artykul/centrum-handlowe-w-sosnowcu-wyburzone,170,0,2380970.html [access: 19.04.2021].

Agata Hauser[763]

Democracy in crisis and its effects on the enjoyment of human rights

Abstract: The level of democracy enjoyed globally is down; almost a third of the global population lives under authoritarian rule. This article aims to analyse the threats to the enjoyment of human rights in States identified as autocracies with the lowest freedom scores by studying the recommendations of UN Human Rights Treaty Bodies and those provided through the Universal Periodic Review of the UN Human Rights Council. Autocratic regimes are dangerous not only for "classical" civil and political rights, like the right to free elections and freedoms of association or assembly but also for economic, social and cultural rights, particularly the right to health and education. Moreover, autocratic States may be unwilling to provide remedies for victims of human rights violations.

Keywords: democracy, human rights, UN Treaty Bodies, autocracies

1. Introduction and conceptual framework

In 2022, the UN High Commissioner on Human Rights, Michelle Bachelet, noted that the level of democracy enjoyed globally was down to 1989 levels, and almost a third of the global population lived under authoritarian rule.[764] This trend poses a serious risk to the enjoyment of human rights. Democracy and human rights are two tightly intertwined concepts: democracy cannot function without human rights (especially political rights), and human rights cannot be fully enjoyed within an autocratic regime. The connections between those values are also noticed at the level of international law.[765] In a Resolution adopted in 2012, the UN General Assembly stated clearly that: "human rights, the rule of law and democracy are interlinked and mutually reinforcing and that they belong to the universal and

763 AMU Poznan, ORCID: 0000-0002-6382-3800.

764 M. Bachelet, „Opening Workshop for the International Association of Jesuit Universities, Boston College", 3.08.2022, https://www.ohchr.org/en/statements-and-speeches/2022/08/crisis-and-fragility-democracy-world#_ftn1 [accessed: 30.06.2024].

765 At the regional European level, see Article 3 of the Statute of the Council of Europe, 5.5.1949, European Treaty Series 1 and Article 2 of the Treaty on the European Union (consolidate version 2016), OJ C 202, 7.6.2016.

indivisible core values and principles of the United Nations".[766] In practice, the relationship between democracy and human rights can be much more complex, especially taking into account different models of democracies and political issues.[767]

This article aims to analyse the threats to the enjoyment of human rights in States identified as autocracies with the lowest freedom scores. The States were selected based on two reports: Freedom in the World 2024, by Freedom House[768], and Democracy Report 2024, by V-Dem Institute.[769] Freedom House identifies the following 15 states and territories as those with the lowest aggregate scores: Afghanistan, Sudan, Central African Republic, Equatorial Guinea, Tajikistan, Western Sahara, Eritrea, North Korea, Crimea, Eastern Donbas, Turkmenistan, South Sudan, Syria, Tibet and Nagorno-Karabakh.[770] The 10 States included on that list ("Identified States") are also qualified as either electoral or closed autocracies by V-Dem Institute.[771]

The study will analyse the most recent UPR recommendations made to these States as well as the relevant concluding observations of the UN human rights Treaty Bodies (available in the Universal Human Rights Index).[772] Focusing on the UN is necessary as the identified states represent various regions of the world, and the universal standard is the only commonly applicable to all of them. However, two important limitations are worth noting. First, the UN human rights law comprises nine core treaties:

a. International Convention on the Elimination of All Forms of Racial Discrimination (ICERD);

---

766 Resolution adopted by the General Assembly on 24 September 2012, „Declaration of the high-level meeting of the General Assembly on the rule of law at the national and international levels", A/RES/67/1.

767 See for example E.Pils, „Autocratic Challenges to International Human Rights Law: A Chinese Case Study", *Current Legal Problems*, Vol. 75 (2022), pp. 189-236 and T. Matthews, „To be Equal and Free: The Nexus Between Human Rights and Democracy", A Companion to Democracy #1, https://eu.boell.org/sites/default/files/2019-12/E-Paper_Human_Rights_and_Democracy.pdf [accessed 30.04.2024].

768 Freedom House, „Freedom in the World 2024. The Mounting Damage of Flawed Elections and Armed Conflict", https://freedomhouse.org/sites/default/files/2024-02/FIW_2024_DigitalBooklet.pdf [accessed: 30.06.2024].

769 V-Dem Institute, „Democracy Report 2024. Democracy Winning and Losing at the Ballot", https://v-dem.net/documents/43/v-dem_dr2024_lowres.pdf [accessed: 30.06.2024].

770 Freedom House, „Freedom…", p. 14.

771 V-Dem Institute, „Democracy…", p. 17.

772 https://uhri.ohchr.org/en [accessed: 30.06.2024].

b. International Covenant on Civil and Political Rights (ICCPR);
c. International Covenant on Economic, Social and Cultural Rights (ICESCR);
d. Convention on the Elimination of All Forms of Discrimination against Women (CEDAW);
e. Convention against Torture and Other Cruel, Inhuman or Degrading Treatment or Punishment (CAT);
f. Convention on the Rights of the Child (CRC);
g. International Convention on the Protection of the Rights of All Migrant Workers and Members of Their Families (ICMW);
h. International Convention for the Protection of All Persons from Enforced Disappearance (CPED);
i. Convention on the Rights of Persons with Disabilities (CRPD).

None of the identified States have ratified them all: for example, Afghanistan is not bound by ICMW and CPED, while Democratic People's Republic of Korea is a state party to five (excluding ICERD, CAT, ICMW and CPED) and South Sudan to three (excluding ICERD, ICCPR, ICESCR, ICMW, CPED and CRPD).[773] Second, UN Treaty Bodies require some cooperation with the State concerned in the form of, i.a., periodic reports. Some of the Identified States do not submit those reports in a timely manner, resulting in a lack of data.[774]

2. Analysis of the recommendations

Two types of documents were reviewed in the analytical part: summaries of the UPR recommendations (quantitative analysis) and specific concluding observations of the relevant UN Treaty Bodies (qualitative analysis).

1. UPR recommendations – quantitative analysis
   a) Afghanistan
      Afghanistan was reviewed in the Third UPR Cycle in 2019. It received 259 recommendations, thematically related to the following Sustainable Development Goals: 16 Peace, Justice and Strong Institutions (36%), 5 Gender Equality (29%), 4 Quality Education (13%), 8 Decent Work and Economic Growth (16%), 3 Good Health and Well-being (5%).[775]

---

773 Status of ratification available at https://indicators.ohchr.org/ [accessed 30.06.2024].

774 On the topic of reporting see: L.Oette, „The UN Human Rights Treaty Bodies: Impact and Future", in G.Oberleitner (ed.), „International Human Rights Institutions, Tribunals, and Courts", Springer 2018, pp. 100-102.

775 https://www.ohchr.org/sites/default/files/lib-docs/HRBodies/UPR/Documents/Session32/AF/Infographic_Afghanistan.pdf [accessed 30.06.2024].

b) Central African Republic
Central African Republic was reviewed in the Third UPR Cycle in 2018. It received 207 recommendations, thematically related to the following Sustainable Development Goals: 16 Peace, Justice and Strong Institutions (37%), 8 Decent Work and Economic Growth (25%), 5 Gender Equality (16%), 3 Good Health and Well-being (7%), 4 Quality Education (5%).[776]
c) Equatorial Guinea
Equatorial Guinea was reviewed in the Third UPR Cycle in 2019. It received 221 recommendations, thematically related to the following Sustainable Development Goals: 16 Peace, Justice and Strong Institutions (40%), 5 Gender Equality (18%), 4 Quality Education (11%), 1 No poverty (7%), 3 Good Health and Well-being (7%).[777]
d) Eritrea
Eritrea was reviewed in the Third UPR Cycle in 2019. It received 261 recommendations, thematically related to the following Sustainable Development Goals: 16 Peace, Justice and Strong Institutions (38%), 5 Gender Equality (14%), 8 Decent Work and Economic Growth (11%), 4 Quality Education (9%), 3 Good Health and Well-being (6%).[778]
e) North Korea
North Korea was reviewed in the Third UPR Cycle in 2019. It received 262 recommendations, thematically related to the following Sustainable Development Goals: 16 Peace, Justice and Strong Institutions (30%), 2 Zero hunger (18%), 5 Gender Equality (13%), 8 Decent Work and Economic Growth (8%), 3 Good Health and Well-being (6%).[779]
f) South Sudan
South Sudan was reviewed in the Third UPR Cycle in 2020. It received 258 recommendations, thematically related to the following Sustainable Development Goals: 16 Peace, Justice and Strong Institutions (57%),

776 https://www.ohchr.org/sites/default/files/lib-docs/HRBodies/UPR/Documents/Session31/CF/CENTRAL_AFRICAN_REPUBLIC_Infographic_31st.pdf [accessed 30.06.2024].
777 https://www.ohchr.org/sites/default/files/lib-docs/HRBodies/UPR/Documents/Session33/GQ/Infographic_EquatorialGuinea.pdf [accessed: 30.06.2024].
778 https://www.ohchr.org/sites/default/files/lib-docs/HRBodies/UPR/Documents/Session32/ER/Infographic_Eritrea.pdf [accessed: 30.06.2024].
779 https://www.ohchr.org/sites/default/files/lib-docs/HRBodies/UPR/Documents/Session33/KP/Infographics3rdCycle_DPRK.pdf [accessed: 30.06.2024].

5 Gender Equality (25%), 4 Quality Education (7%), 10 Reduced Inequalities (7%), 3 Good Health and Well-being (5%).[780]

g) Sudan
Sudan was reviewed in the Third UPR Cycle in 2022. It received 283 recommendations, thematically related to the following Sustainable Development Goals: 16 Peace, Justice and Strong Institutions (59%), 5 Gender Equality (21%), 4 Quality Education (5%), 3 Good Health and Well-being (4%), No Poverty (4%).[781]

h) Syria
Syria was reviewed in the Third UPR Cycle in 2022. It received 287 recommendations, thematically related to the following Sustainable Development Goals: 16 Peace, Justice and Strong Institutions (54%), 5 Gender Equality (10%), 1 No poverty (7%), 3 Good Health and Well-being (6%), 10 Reduced Inequalities (5%).[782]

i) Tajikistan
Tajikistan was reviewed in the Third UPR Cycle in 2021. It received 234 recommendations, thematically related to the following Sustainable Development Goals: 16 Peace, Justice and Strong Institutions (57%), 5 Gender Equality (13%), 4 Quality Education (8%), 10 Reduced Inequalities (7%), 3 Good Health and Well-being (4%).[783]

j) Turkmenistan
Turkmenistan was reviewed in the Fourth UPR Cycle in 2023. It received 228 recommendations, thematically related to the following Sustainable Development Goals: 16 Peace, Justice and Strong Institutions (45%), 10 Reduced Inequalities (16%), 5 Gender Equality (14%), 8 Decent Work and Economic Growth (7%), 4 Quality Education (5%).[784]

---

780 https://www.ohchr.org/sites/default/files/documents/hrbodies/upr/sessions/session40/ss/2022-12-23/South-Sudan.pdf [accessed: 30.06.2024].

781 https://ohchr.org/sites/default/files/documents/hrbodies/upr/sessions/session39/sd/2022-12-21/Sudan_Infographic_39th.pdf [accessed: 30.06.2024].

782 https://www.ohchr.org/sites/default/files/documents/hrbodies/upr/sessions/session40/sy/2023-01-09/SyriaArabRepublic_Infographic_40th.pdf [accessed: 30.06.2024].

783 https://www.ohchr.org/sites/default/files/lib-docs/hrbodies/upr/documents/session39/tj/2022-07-14/tajikistan.pdf [accessed 30.06.2024].

784 https://www.ohchr.org/sites/default/files/documents/hrbodies/upr/sessions/session44/tm/upr44-infographic_turkmenistan.pdf [accessed 30.06.2024].

II. Treaty Bodies' concluding observations – qualitative analysis

The analysis of the UPR thematic recommendations indicates that while in all cases, the vast majority of recommendations relate to the issue of peace, justice and strong institutions, the other four categories tackle mainly equality and discrimination as well as economic, social and cultural rights (education, health, food). As we are dealing with statistical information, this might be a correlation rather than causation, so it is necessary to focus on specific recommendations of the UN Treaty Bodies provided in concluding observations ("COs") to the Identified states. Some examples are going to be supplied as a complete analysis would be too lengthy and might be repetitive.

Out of the Identified States, most recommendations related to SDG 16 Peace, Justice and Strong Institutions were received by Sudan (59%). There are 9 COs to Sudan related to this SDG, and most of them were adopted by the Human Rights Committee ("HRC".).

In the most recent COs to Sudan, adopted in 2018[785], the HRC identified a wide variety of areas of concern under the ICCPR related to the justice system and other institutions. One of the issues raised is the impunity of the perpetrators of human rights violations and access to remedies for victims of violations.[786] In the context of Sudan, the HRC also noted restrictions on the civic space, including freedom of expression, peaceful assembly and association.[787] As in many other autocratic States, Sudan interferes with fundamental civil and political rights by closing newspapers, arrests and use of force to disperse demonstrations.

Interestingly, the UN Committee on Economic, Social and Cultural Rights (CESCR) also raised this issue of access to remedies.[788] In autocratic States, the lack of an independent judiciary undermines the procedural protection of all human rights, rendering them ineffective in practice.

The second common problem identified in the UPR, is gender equality, with the highest number of recommendations presented to Afghanistan

785 Human Rights Committee, "Concluding observations on the fifth periodic report of the Sudan", CCPR/C/SDN/CO/5.

786 Ibid., para 13. See also paras 37-40 because similar effects may be related to immunity of certain State agents.

787 Ibid., paras 45-48.

788 Committee on Economic, Social and Cultural Rights, "Concluding observations on the second periodic report of the Sudan", E/C.12/SDN/CO/2, paras 7-8.

(29%), which is mostly related to the Taliban rule.[789] The recommendations to other States do not seem particularly connected with their regimes' non-democratic nature.

Quality education is the third issue shared by eight of the ten Identified States. In this case, I will focus on Turkmenistan, where some problems potentially related to the nature of the regime can be identified. In the COs adopted by CESCR in 2018[790], the Committee noted that "despite its illegality, unofficial fees are charged for access to higher education".[791] The problem of corruption is often present in autocratic States, including the Identified States.[792] Corruption presents a threat to the equal enjoyment of human rights and may impede accessibility in the context of education and other rights. The other issue highlighted by the CESCR, is the policy of "Turkmenization", which leads to discrimination, also in the field of education.[793] Policies focused on othering minorities and aiming at the maintenance of dominance are not rare and lead to violations of human rights of the marginalised groups.[794]

The last common thread among the Identified States is SDG 3: Good Health and Well-being. In all of the nine States with this issue raised, the percentages are relatively low (below 10%). With regard to the topic of health, the main problem indicated in numerous COs is budget allocation and insufficient health expenditure.[795] There is no sufficient data to link this to the autocratic nature of the regimes, although some authors note connections in this regard.[796]

---

789 See: "Situation of human rights in Afghanistan. Report of the Special Rapporteur on the situation of human rights in Afghanistan, Richard Bennett", A/HRC/52/84.

790 Committee on Economic, Social and Cultural Rights, "Concluding observations on the second periodic report of Turkmenistan", E/C.12/TKM/CO/2.

791 Ibid, para. 39.

792 See: CORRUPTION PERCEPTIONS INDEX 2023 by Transparency International: https://images.transparencycdn.org/images/CPI-2023-Report.pdf [accessed 30.06.2024].

793 CESCR COs: Turkmenistan, para. 8.

794 See: K.L.Stewart, "Democratic and Autocratic Nation Building", *Nationalities Papers*. 2021;49(2):205-212.

795 See for example: Committee on Economic, Social and Cultural Rights, "Concluding observations concerning the initial report of the Central African Republic", E/C.12/CAF/CO/1.

796 T.Templin, J. L. Dieleman, S. Wigley, et al., "Democracies Linked To Greater Universal Health Coverage Compared With Autocracies, Even In An Economic Recession", *Health Affairs* 2021 40:8, 1234-1242.

3. Conclusions

Autocratic States identified in this study present many similar human rights concerns. Some are to be expected, especially those related to the treatment of journalists, members of the opposition and the functioning of a civic state. Those States target the right to participate in public affairs and to vote in free and fair elections, freedom of expression and access to information, as well as freedom of peaceful assembly and association.

A second group of issues is related to discrimination. Again, the mistreatment of minorities and discriminatory practices are commonly used in autocratic States as by "othering" them, the States aim at consolidating a dedicated group of supporters.

However, it is worth noting that in all of the Identified States, the human rights risks can also be noted in the field of economic, social and cultural rights. Some of the issues are not specific to autocracies, but in other cases, the regime's nature clearly influences the enjoyment of those human rights.

The first threat with regard to economic, social and cultural rights is related to the lack of an independent and impartial judiciary that renders the right to an effective remedy and a fair trial illusory. This means that in autocratic states, victims of human rights violations cannot effectively challenge that violation at the national level. At the same time, access to international complaint mechanisms may not be possible, and even if those procedures are available, the decisions may not be executed at the national level. This is particularly worrisome in cases where victims belong to a marginalised group in the State.

Corruption is the second issue identified in the context of economic, social and cultural rights. The autocratic states identified for this research can be found at the top of corrupt states. This leads to unequal accessibility of some human rights, including the right to education.

Bibliography

"Situation of human rights in Afghanistan. Report of the Special Rapporteur on the situation of human rights in Afghanistan, Richard Bennett", A/HRC/52/84.

Bachelet, M. "Opening Workshop for the International Association of Jesuit Universities, Boston College", 3.08.2022, https://www.ohchr.org/en/statements-and-speeches/2022/08/crisis-and-fragility-democracy-world#_ftn1 [accessed: 30.06.2024].

CORRUPTION PERCEPTIONS INDEX 2023 by Transparency International: https://images.transparencycdn.org/images/CPI-2023-Report.pdf [accessed 30.06.2024].

Freedom House, "Freedom in the World 2024. The Mounting Damage of Flawed Elections and Armed Conflict", https://freedomhouse.org/sites/default/files/2024-02/FIW_2024_DigitalBooklet.pdf [accessed: 30.06.2024].

Matthews, T. "To be Equal and Free: The Nexus Between Human Rights and Democracy", A Companion to Democracy #1, https://eu.boell.org/sites/default/files/2019-12/E-Paper_Human_Rights_and_Democracy.pdf [accessed 30.04.2024].

On the topic of reporting see: L.Oette, "The UN Human Rights Treaty Bodies: Impact and Future", in G.Oberleitner (ed.), "International Human Rights Institutions, Tribunals, and Courts", Springer 2018, pp. 100-102.

Pils, E. "Autocratic Challenges to International Human Rights Law: A Chinese Case Study", Current Legal Problems, Vol. 75 (2022).

Resolution adopted by the General Assembly on 24 September 2012, "Declaration of the high-level meeting of the General Assembly on the rule of law at the national and international levels", A/RES/67/1.

Statute of the Council of Europe, 5.5.1949, European Treaty Series 1.

Stewart, K.L. "Democratic and Autocratic Nation Building", Nationalities Papers. 2021;49(2):205-212.

Templin, T, Dieleman, J. L., Wigley S., et al., "Democracies Linked To Greater Universal Health Coverage Compared With Autocracies, Even In An Economic Recession", Health Affairs 2021 40:8, 1234-1242.

Treaty on the European Union (consolidate version 2016), OJ C 202, 7.6.2016.

V-Dem Institute, "Democracy Report 2024. Democracy Winning and Losing at the Ballot", https://v-dem.net/documents/43/v-dem_dr2024_lowres.pdf [accessed: 30.06.2024].

UPR summaries

https://ohchr.org/sites/default/files/documents/hrbodies/upr/sessions/session39/sd/2022-12-21/Sudan_Infographic_39th.pdf [accessed: 30.06.2024].

https://www.ohchr.org/sites/default/files/documents/hrbodies/upr/sessions/session40/ss/2022-12-23/South-Sudan.pdf [accessed: 30.06.2024].

https://www.ohchr.org/sites/default/files/documents/hrbodies/upr/sessions/session40/sy/2023-01-09/SyriaArabRepublic_Infographic_40th.pdf [accessed: 30.06.2024].

https://www.ohchr.org/sites/default/files/documents/hrbodies/upr/sessions/session44/tm/upr44-infographic_turkmenistan.pdf [accessed 30.06.2024].

https://www.ohchr.org/sites/default/files/lib-docs/HRBodies/UPR/Documents/Session32/AF/Infographic_Afghanistan.pdf [accessed 30.06.2024].

https://www.ohchr.org/sites/default/files/lib-docs/HRBodies/UPR/Documents/Session31/CF/CENTRAL_AFRICAN_REPUBLIC_Infographic_31st.pdf [accessed 30.06.2024].

https://www.ohchr.org/sites/default/files/lib-docs/HRBodies/UPR/Documents/Session33/GQ/Infographic_EquatorialGuinea.pdf [accessed: 30.06.2024].

https://www.ohchr.org/sites/default/files/lib-docs/HRBodies/UPR/Documents/Session33/KP/Infographics3rdCycle_DPRK.pdf [accessed: 30.06.2024].

https://www.ohchr.org/sites/default/files/lib-docs/hrbodies/upr/documents/session39/tj/2022-07-14/tajikistan.pdf [accessed 30.06.2024].

https://www.ohchr.org/sites/default/files/lib-ocs/HRBodies/UPR/Documents/Session32/ER/Infographic_Eritrea.pdf [accessed: 30.06.2024].

Concluding observations

Committee on Economic, Social and Cultural Rights, "Concluding observations concerning the initial report of the Central African Republic", E/C.12/CAF/CO/1.

Committee on Economic, Social and Cultural Rights, "Concluding observations on the second periodic report of Turkmenistan", E/C.12/TKM/CO/2.

Committee on Economic, Social and Cultural Rights, "Concluding observations on the second periodic report of the Sudan", E/C.12/SDN/CO/2.

Human Rights Committee, "Concluding observations on the fifth periodic report of the Sudan", CCPR/C/SDN/CO/5.

Wojciech J. Kosior[797]

A contemporary perspective on the functions of punishment in Roman criminal law

Abstract: The functions of punishment in criminal law have undergone a profound evolution throughout history, reflecting broader changes in societal values, legal philosophies, and understandings of justice. In terms of both purpose and method, the application of punishment has varied considerably across different cultures and historical eras. This can be observed from ancient retributive practices to contemporary rehabilitative approaches. This evolution not only highlights the shifting priorities of legal systems but also provides insights into the fundamental human quest for order, justice, and social cohesion. The evolution of the functions of punishment from Roman law to modern legal systems reflects broader social and cultural changes. Although retribution and deterrence remain fundamental tenets, modern legal systems have evolved to encompass rehabilitation and restorative justice within a broader framework that prioritizes human rights. This comparative analysis illustrates the dynamic nature of legal systems and their capacity to adapt to changing societal values and norms.

Keywords: criminal law, punishment, retribution, deterrence, rehabilitation, restorative justice

1. Introduction

From ancient retributive practices to contemporary rehabilitative approaches, the purposes and methods of punishment have varied widely across different cultures and eras. This evolution not only highlights the shifting priorities of legal systems but also provides insights into the fundamental human quest for order, justice, and social cohesion.

One of the enduring legal issues, present in all world systems throughout history, is the question of appropriate punishment for criminal acts. This abiding question involves several considerations. Should the primary purpose of punishment be retributive, inflicting pain and suffering on the offender as a form of justice? Alternatively, should punishment aim to rehabilitate the offender, teaching them a lesson and preventing future criminal behavior through correction and education? Another critical aspect is the demonstrative and deterrent effect that punishment can have on society as a whole, serving as a warning to deter others

797 University of Rzeszow, ORCID: 0000-0002-4710-4523.

from committing similar offenses. Thus, while the specific types of punishment have varied throughout history, the central debate over their intended function remains relevant. Different eras and legal systems have approached this question in various ways, reflecting broader changes in societal values and understanding of human behavior.

This article will explore the historical trajectory of punishment in criminal law, examining the shifting functions and philosophies that have shaped its development. An understanding of the historical context allows for a more nuanced appreciation of the complexities and challenges inherent in the administration of justice in diverse societies. The text will explore the various functions of punishment throughout history, with a particular focus on the Roman criminal law system. This presentation will highlight how the Romans addressed these fundamental questions and how their approaches to punishment influenced subsequent legal traditions. By examining the historical trajectory of punitive practices, we can gain a deeper understanding of the complexities and enduring nature of criminal justice.

2. The System of Punishment in Roman Law

2.1. Forms of Punishment in Roman Law

It should be started with the statement that punishing is one of the oldest and most important functions of society. Punishments are often part of a society's characteristic signature as well, reflecting distinctive values and traditions[798]. In archaic societies, including early Rome, the fundamental essence of punishment was rooted in the concept of revenge[799]. This primitive form of justice was enormously rooted with familial and tribal customs, where acts of bloody revenge were carried out against those who committed offenses against the community. As Peter N. Stearns stated, the Roman approach to punishment highlighted more familiar themes, including a decided interest in varied forms of brutality[800]. Crimes that affected the public good required a more organised and controlled response to ensure social stability.

798 P. N. Stearns, *Punishment in World History*, New York 2024, p. 2.

799 See: C. Emsley, S. McDougall, *A Global History of Crime and Punishment. Volume 1: A Global History of Crime and Punishment in Antiquity Edited by Adriaan Lanni*, Harvard Law School, USA 2023.

800 P. N. Stearns, *op. cit.*, p. 145.

The legal and punitive systems of ancient Rome were fundamental to the maintenance of social order and governance within one of history's most influential civilisations. The Roman system of punishment evolved significantly over a millennium, from the Roman Kingdom through the Republic and into the Empire. This evolution reflected changes in political structures, societal values, and legal philosophies[801]. The Roman system of punishment was characterised by its diversity and multifaceted nature, with the objective of addressing a range of offences and serving multiple societal functions[802]. The range of punishments available to the Romans was considerable, encompassing financial penalties, severe corporal and capital punishments[803]. Each of these had specific purposes and implications. In the case of minor offences, fines or restitution were often the consequence. Such financial penalties were designed to compensate victims and to act as a deterrent to future infractions[804]. The amount of compensation was typically proportional to the offence and the social status of both the victim and the offender. Physical punishments were a common form of punishment for more serious offences[805]. The infliction of pain through the use of flogging, branding, and mutilation was a common method employed to serve as a public deterrent. Public flogging was a common form of punishment for theft, adultery, and other crimes. It served to reinforce societal norms and the authority of the state. The most severe crimes, such as murder, treason, and sacrilege, were met with capital punishment[806]. Methods of execution included beheading, crucifixion, and being thrown from the Tarpeian Rock[807]. In particular, crucifixion was employed for slaves and the lower classes, thereby underscoring the importance of social hierarchy in Roman punitive practices. Exile constituted a significant form of punishment for those whose presence was deemed to be a threat to public order. The duration of banishment could be temporary or permanent, and often involved the confiscation of

801 C.I. Goga, "Historical Evolution of Punishment Systems", *Analele UniversităŃii din Craiova. Istorie*, Anul XX, Nr. 1(27)/2015, p. 188-189.

802 Y. V. Pershina, "The System of Punishments in the Ancient Rome", *Modern European Researches* No 1 / 2017, p. 78-86.

803 See: O. F Robinson, *Penal Practice and Penal Policy in Ancient Rome*, London 2006, pp. 264.

804 M. Jońca, *Rzymskie Prawo Karne. Instytucje, [Roman Criminal Law. Institutions]*, Lublin 2021, p. 173.

805 *Ibid.*, p. 171.

806 *Ibid.*, p. 169.

807 See: Ch. Epplett, "Spectacular Executions in the Roman World", in *A Companion to Sport and Spectacle in Greek and Roman Antiquity*, ed. P. Christesen, D. G. Kyle, Hoboken 2013, p. 520-532.

property. This form of punishment not only removed the offender from society but also served as a deterrent to others, thereby preventing further criminal activity. The practice of public humiliation, such as being paraded through the streets or subjected to public ridicule, was employed to reinforce social norms and deter criminal behaviour. This form of punishment was particularly efficacious in a society that placed a high value on honour and reputation[808].

2.2. Functions of Punishment in Roman Law

The administration of punishment in ancient Rome constituted a fundamental aspect of its legal and societal structure. This reflected a sophisticated interplay between law, politics, and social order. The functions of punishment during this period were multifaceted, designed not only to address criminal behaviour but also to uphold societal norms, reinforce authority, and deter future offences.

In ancient Rome, retribution constituted a fundamental aspect of punishment[809]. This was based on the principle that offenders should receive penalties commensurate with the severity of their crimes. The Twelve Tables, Rome's earliest code of law, placed great emphasis on the importance of proportionate punishment, ensuring that justice was served in a visible manner. The retributive justice system was designed to satisfy the societal and victim's need for revenge, providing a sense of closure and moral balance. This reinforced the idea that unlawful behaviour had direct and immediate consequences. Moreover retribution was a multifaceted concept that was strongly intertwined with the social, moral, and political fabric of Roman society. From its origins in private revenge to its formalisation in the legal codes of the Republic and Empire, retributive justice in Rome sought to achieve a balance between the scales of justice, deter future offences and uphold societal values[810].

Examples of the existence of a retributive function in Roman criminal law can be found in both juridical and literary sources:

D. 50, 16, 131; *Poena est noxae vindicta.*
Cic. De leg. 3,20: *Ut in suo vitio quisque plectatur, vis capite, avaritia multa, honoris cupiditas ignominia sanciatur.*

---

808 P. Garnsey, "Why Penalties Become Harsher: The Roman Case, Late Republic to Fourth Centruy Empire", *Natural Law Forum* 13 (1968), p. 141.

809 M. Jońca, *op. cit.*, p. 177-181 and there sources and literature cited.

810 See: E. G.M. Weitekamp, "The History of Restorative Justice", in *Restorative Justice*, (ed.) Th. Gavrielides, London 2015, p. 3-30; R. A. Posner, "Retribution and Related Concepts of Punishment", *The Journal of Legal Studies*, Volume 9, Number 1 (1980), p. 71-92.

In the first of the texts cited, the Roman jurist Ulpianus explained that punishment should, in its essence, be revenge for the harm done. In the second source, Cicero justified every mode of punishment, especially the death penalty, writing that it was an appropriate and necessary measure in response to the crime committed.

Another critical function of punishment in ancient Rome was deterrence[811]. The Roman legal system aimed to discourage criminal behaviour by making examples of offenders through public and often harsh punishments[812]. Public executions, flogging, and other forms of corporal punishment were intended to instill fear in the populace, deterring others from committing similar offenses. The deterrent effect was not limited to potential criminals. Furthermore, it reinforced social norms and the authority of the state, reminding citizens of the consequences of disobedience. The visibility and severity of punishments were strategic, with the aim of creating a powerful disincentive for criminal activities.

The existence of this function can be proved from both legal and non-legal source material:

CTh. 9, 27, 3: *Ut unius poena metus possit esse multorum (...).*
Pubil. Sent. M 68; *Malus quicumque in poena est, praesidium est bonis.*

The first example includes the content of an imperial decree, which indicated the postulate that the punishment of one would be the fear of many. In the second text, one can find the message by Publilius Syrus, who wrote that the punishment of bad people is at the same time the protection of good people.

In addition to revenge and deterrence of others, one can also find in Roman sources the correctional function that punishment for a crime should fulfill[813]. Certain punishments, such as fines and restitution, were designed not only to penalise offenders but also to reintegrate them into society by encouraging lawful behaviour and repairing harm done to victims. The Roman approach to rehabilitation was pragmatic, recognising that not all offenders were beyond redemption. To illustrate, the imposition of less severe penalties for minor crimes afforded offenders the opportunity to reform their conduct without having to endure severe corporal punishment or execution. Nevertheless, it is crucial to acknowledge that the objective of rehabilitation was not the primary concern of

811 M. Jońca, *op. cit.*, p. 181-183 and there sources and literature cited.
812 F. Parisi, D. Pi, B. Luppi, I. Fargnoli, "Deterrence of Wrongdoing in Ancient Law", *Minnesota Legal Studies Research Paper* No. 14-38/2014, p. 1-26.
813 M. Jońca, *op. cit.*, p. 183-185 and there sources and literature cited.

Roman punitive practices, which were primarily oriented towards retribution and deterrence[814].

The basis for the existence of this function can be found in legal and non-legal source material:

> **Sen. de ir. 1,19,7:** *Nemo prudens punit, quia peccatum est, sed ne peccetur.*
> **D. 48, 19,20 Paulus libro 18 ad Plautium;** *(...) poena constituitur in emendationem hominum.*

In the first text Seneca the Younger put it in good words that the punishment was instituted for the improvement of the people. In the second cited source the Roman jurist Paulus wrote similarly that no prudent person should punish for having broken the law, but in order not to be broken in the future.

We can find confirmation of the existence of these three functions in the message by Aulus Gellius who saw generally three functions of punishment:

> **Gell. 7,14,1–4:** *Poeniendis peccatis tres esse debere causas existimatum est. 2 Vna est causa, quae Graece vel kolasis vel nouthesia dicitur, cum poena adhibetur castigandi atque emendandi gratia, ut is, qui fortuito deliquit, attentior fiat correctiorque. 3 Altera est, quam hi, qui vocabula ista curiosius diviserunt, timorian appellant. Ea causa animadvertendi est, cum dignitas auctoritasque eius, in quem est peccatum, tuenda est, ne praetermissa animadversio contemptum eius pariat et honorem levet; idcircoque id ei vocabulum a conservatione honoris factum putant. 4 Tertia ratio vindicandi est, quae paradeigma a Graecis nominatur, cum poenitio propter exemplum necessaria est, ut ceteri a similibus peccatis, quae prohiberi publicitus interest, metu cognitae poenae deterreantur.*

As K. Amielańczyk stated, according to Gellius, punishment is used for chastening and correcting the offender (today this function is called individual prevention), when the penalty is intended to preserve the victim's dignity (retaliatory, compensatory function), and also when the punishment is necessary for deterrence, to make other people refrain from committing crimes (general prevention)[815].

In addition to the existence of these three basic and essential functions of punishment in Roman law, additional meanings of punishment (and therefore functions) can be sought on: social, religious and political grounds.

One of the primary objectives of criminal punishment in the Roman era was to maintain hierarchical stability[816]. As D. Garland stated social interpretations

---

814 G. Mueller, "Punishment, corrections and the law", *Nebraska Law Review* 45 (1966), p. 58.

815 K. Amielańczyk, "Purposes and Functions of Public Punishment in Roman Law in the Perspective of Justinian's Codification", *Studia Prawnicze* KUL 4 (80) 2019, p. 26.

816 See: T. Sellin, *Punishment and Social Structure*, New York 1939, p. 53-72

might be used to enrich the understanding of punishment, leading to conceive of it not just as a crime-control mechanism but instead as a distinctive and rather complex social institution[817]. The function of maintaining social order was very much embedded in the Roman system of punishment. Roman society was highly stratified, with distinct social classes including patricians, plebeians, freedmen, and slaves. The legal system reinforced these social hierarchies through differentiated punishments based on the offender's and the victim's social status. Crimes against the elite or the state were punished more severely than those involving lower-status individuals. This reflected the societal emphasis on preserving the power and privileges of the upper classes. The aim was to maintain hierarchical stability, ensuring that the social order remained intact and that the authority of the ruling classes was not undermined[818].

Punishments for crimes considered offensive to the gods, such as sacrilege or impiety, were particularly severe. These punishments served a dual function: they addressed the crime and sought to appease the gods, thereby protecting the community from divine wrath[819]. The intertwining of religious and legal systems meant that punishment also had a moral dimension. The objective of punishment was not merely to address the physical or social harm caused by a crime; it was also to uphold the moral fabric of society. Punishments reinforced communal values and religious norms, thereby promoting moral behaviour and piety among citizens.

In addition to its utilitarian purpose, punishment in ancient Rome also served a crucial political function, particularly during the transition from the Roman Republic to the Roman Empire[820]. The legal system was employed by those in power as a means of consolidating and reinforcing their authority. This was evidenced by the utilisation of punitive measures against political opponents and those who expressed dissent. Emperors and political leaders employed public executions, exile, and other severe penalties to eliminate threats to their rule and to signal their power to both supporters and adversaries. The legal system thus became an instrument of political control, ensuring the stability and continuity of the governing regime.

---

817 D. Garland, "Sociological Perspectives on Punishment", *Crime and Justice* Vol. 14/ 1991, p. 157.

818 See: M. Pifferi, "Punishment and Social Control in Historical Perspective", *Oxford Research Encyclopedia of Politics* 2022 (online - https://doi.org/10.1093/acrefore/ 9780190228637.013.1784 - access 17/06/2024).

819 M. Jońca, *op. cit.*, p. 175-177 and there sources and literature cited.

820 R. A. Bauman, *Crime and Punishment in Ancient Rome*, London 1996, p. 190.

3. The Subsequent Development of the Functions of Punishment

In considering the further evolution of the system and function of punishment, it is necessary to note the three eras that follow, which in principle show most clearly how the approach to criminal punishment has changed throughout history. The first of these is the Middle Ages. It was in this era that the greatest emphasis was placed on the retributive function of punishment. At this time, the prevailing notion was that the infliction of severe punishment would serve to redress the wrongdoer's actions and, simultaneously, act as a deterrent to others contemplating similar transgressions. It is likely that it would take centuries for the subsequent era, the Age of Enlightenment, to effect a transformation in the approach to the punishment system, with the theories of Cesare Beccaria exerting a significant influence. Beccaria observed that contemporary law and practice of punishment were excessively cruel, unjust, unhelpful and based on arbitrariness. In his treatise, he took a general human perspective. The critique he made of criminal law was aimed at changing the institution of punishment in line with the Enlightenment spirit of humanity's moral progress, humanitarianism and the rationalisation of law. The modern functions of criminal punishment were shaped by Enlightenment views on punishment. It is therefore necessary to present the evolution of the functions of punishment from the Middle Ages, through the Enlightenment and up to the present day.

3.1. Functions of Punishment in Medieval Europe

In the Middle Ages the application of punishment was closely related to the religious conception that pain was the only way to obtain forgiveness for sins committed[821]. Therefore, corporal punishment, which caused pain, was often applied. Also, through the involvement of the Church in the application of punishments, through the instrument called Inquisition, the regime of punishments becomes characterized as being full of cruelty where corporal torture, the death penalty, mutilation, adoption, deprivation of liberty, torture, were the order of the day, civic degradation, shaving of the chin[822].

---

821 See: C. Emsley, S. McDougall, *A Global History of Crime and Punishment. Volume 2: A Global History of Crime and Punishment in the Medieval Age. Edited by Karl Shoemaker*, University of Wisconsin-Madison, USA 2023.

822 B. Buneci, "General Considerations on Punishment in Medieval Europe", *RAIS Journal for Social Sciences* Vol. 5, No. 1, 2021, p. 40.

Starting with the 6th century, after the codification of Roman Law, punishment governed by the Code of Justinian became the legal basis for sanctions in the Middle Ages in Europe continent[823], therefore in medieval Europe, retribution constituted a fundamental element within the context of punishment. Similarly the concept of retribution was a fundamental element of the belief that punishment should be commensurate with the offence in question and serve as a means of restoring equilibrium within the framework of justice. Medieval European justice was profoundly shaped by Christian theology and therefore crimes were perceived as transgressions not only against the state but also against God. According to T. P O'Connor this interaction greatly influenced Western culture as a whole and helped to reinforce a retributive view of justice[824]. Consequently, punishment was intended to reinstate moral order and satisfy divine justice. Public executions and corporal punishments were commonplace, serving as acts of retribution. Such spectacles served to reinforce the idea that justice was being served and that wrongdoers were receiving their deserved and painful punishment[825]. The involvement of the community in these events served to emphasise the collective nature of retributive justice.

Another crucial function of punishment in medieval Europe was deterrence[826]. The severity and public nature of many punishments were designed to deter both the individual offender and the broader community from engaging in criminal behaviour. Forms of corporal punishment, such as flogging, branding, and mutilation, were employed to instill fear. Capital punishment, including hanging, burning, and beheading, was intended to deter serious crimes. The public nature of these punishments served to amplify their deterrent effect. All forms of execution, was designed to deter criminal activity[827]. In addition to their primary purpose of retribution, punishments in medieval Europe served as a tool for maintaining social control. This was accomplished by reinforcing social norms and upholding the hierarchical structure of society. The type and severity of punishment were

823 G. Hallevy, *The Right to Be Punished. Modern Doctrinal Sentencing*, Berlin 2013, p. 6 (after: C.I. Goga, *op. cit.*, p. 189).

824 T. P O'Connor, *Religion, the Community, and the Rehabilitation of Criminal Offenders*, New York, London, Oxford 2013, p. 262.

825 K. Shoemaker, "The problem of pain in punishment: Historical perspectives" in *Law, meaning, and violence: pain, death, and the law*, (ed.) A Sarat, Ann Arbor 2001, p. 15-41.

826 See: S. Currie, *Medieval Punishment and Torture*, San Diego 2014, pp. 80.

827 A. Classen, C. Scarborough, *Crime and Punishment in the Middle Ages and Early Modern Age*, Berlin 2012, p. 161.

often contingent upon the social status of the offender. Those of noble status might be subject to fines or exile, whereas commoners could be subjected to corporal punishment. This discrepancy served to reinforce social hierarchies and the authority of the elite. Furthermore, the medieval European concept of moral purification and redemption was also a significant function of punishment. This reflected the period's deep religious convictions. The Church played a pivotal role in the administration of justice for moral and religious offences. The ecclesiastical courts prescribed penance, such as fasting, pilgrimages, and public confessions, with the intention of purifying the soul and restoring spiritual harmony[828].

3.2. Functions of Punishment in the Enlightenment Era

The evolution of the functions of punishment from the Middle Ages to the Enlightenment represents a major shift in legal, social and philosophical thought. This period saw a shift from brutal, retributive justice to more rational, humane and rehabilitative approaches to punishment[829]. By examining the changes in penal practices and the theories that underpinned them, we can understand how social attitudes towards crime and justice evolved over these centuries.

The Enlightenment was a period of profound intellectual and philosophical development in the 17th and 18th centuries, characterised by an emphasis on reason, individualism, and scientific inquiry. These shifts in thinking also influenced the functions and philosophies of punishment. During this time, traditional retributive and deterrent approaches were subjected to critical examination and reform in light of new ideas about justice, human nature, and the role of the state[830]. While comparing the Roman law way of punishment and the Enlightenment stance, we should agree with O. F. Robinsons who stated that crimes as such, the

828 T. B. Deutscher, *Punishment and Penance. Two Phases in the History of the Bishop's Tribunal of Novara*, Toronto 2013, p. 107.

829 About the development of the philosophy of punishment through the lens of ancient, Renaissance, and Enlightenment philosophers and discussion about centuries-old legal codes and, among others, the philosophies of Plato, Draco, Solon, Machiavelli, Montaigne, Voltaire, Beccaria, Montesquieu, Hegel, and Kant see: J. D. Bessler, "The Philosophy of Punishment and the Arc of Penal Reform: From Ancient Lawgivers to the Renaissance and the Enlightenment, and through the Nineteenth Century", in *The Palgrave Handbook on the Philosophy of Punishment*, (ed.) M. C. Altman, Ellensburg 2023, p. 23-52.

830 See: C. Emsley, S. McDougall, *A Global History of Crime and Punishment. Volume 4: A Global History of Crime and Punishment in the Age of Enlightenment. Edited by Xavier Rousseaux*, Université Catholique de Louvain, Belgium, 2023.

substantive criminal law, did not really change much between Cicero's day and the Enlightenment[831]. It was not until this era that there were concrete changes in the approach to the philosophy of punishment. The change in thinking is due in particular to Cesare Beccaria and Jeremy Bentham.

During this period, the concept of the function of criminal punishment was most influenced by the aforementioned Cesare Beccaria. His seminal work, *On Crimes and Punishments* (1764)[832], marked a turning point in the philosophy of punishment. Beccaria argued that punishments should be rational, proportionate to the crime, and serve a utilitarian function by deterring future offenses[833]. He opposed the arbitrary and brutal punishments of the past, advocating for a legal system based on predictable and fair penalties. Beccaria emphasised that the primary function of punishment should be the prevention of crime rather than retribution. According to W. C. De Pauley it is clear that while Beccaria puts in the foreground prevention as the end of punishment, it is no less clear that he believes that the criminal is to be reformed, and that once crime shows its face, it must be cut down[834]. He believed that the certainty of punishment, rather than its severity, was the most effective deterrent. This perspective shifted the focus from vengeance to crime prevention and societal protection[835].

Later on, Jeremy Bentham, a leading philosopher of the Enlightenment, developed the principle of utility, which held that the best action is the one that maximises overall happiness. Bentham's utilitarian perspective on punishment, so greatly influenced by Beccaria, identified the sources of motivation as the key to understanding what was involved in the encouragement of law-abiding behaviour[836]. In the context of punishment, this meant that penalties should aim to reduce the overall harm caused by crime and increase the well-being of society. Bentham's ideas extended to the concept of reforming offenders. He believed

831 O. F Robinson, *Penal Practice and Penal Policy in Ancient Rome*, London 2006, p. 89.
832 See: C. Beccaria, *On Crimes and Punishments. Translation, Annotations, and Introduction by G. R. Newman and P. Marongiu*, New Brunswick, London 2009, pp. 193.
833 C. Beccaria, *O przestępstwach i karach [On Crimes and Punishments] ze wstępem E. S. Rappaporta*, Warszawa 1959, p. 34.
834 W. C. De Pauley, "Beccaria and punishment", *The International Journal of Ethics* 35.4 (1925), p. 411.
835 See: D. B. Young, "Cesare Beccaria: Utilitarian or retributivist?", *Journal of Criminal Justice* Volume 11, Issue 4, 1983, p. 317-326.
836 A. Draper, "An Introduction to Jeremy Bentham's theory of punishment", *Journal of Bentham Studies* 5 (2002), p. 7 and there cited: D. Baumgardt, *Bentham and the Ethics of Today*, Princeton, 1952, pp. 218-21.

that punishment should not only deter crime but also rehabilitate offenders, transforming them into productive members of society. This introduced a more humane approach to punishment, emphasising the potential for personal change and redemption. A Draper rightly summarised Bentham's theory of punishment by writing that the ends of punishment always remain the same: reformation, disablement and example, and constant, overwhelming emphasis is placed on the assessment of quantities of pain inflicted in pursuit of these ends[837].

The Enlightenment ideals that were espoused in many European countries during the eighteenth and nineteenth centuries prompted the abolition of torture and other forms of cruel and inhumane punishment. The practice of public executions and corporal punishments was increasingly perceived as barbaric and counterproductive. The shift towards more civilised forms of punishment reflected a growing emphasis on human rights and dignity. As a consequence of these humanitarian reforms, imprisonment became the preferred method of punishment. The design of prisons was intended to remove offenders from society while providing opportunities for reform and rehabilitation[838].

3.3. The Contemporary Functions of Punishment

In contemporary contexts, punishment serves multiple functions, each with distinct theoretical foundations and practical implications[839].

The retributive function of punishment is based on the principle of just deserts, where the infliction of a morally appropriate penalty on an offender is seen as a morally justified and socially beneficial response to criminal wrongdoing. This function is deeply rooted in the idea of moral accountability and societal condemnation of criminal behavior[840]. Retributive justice is grounded in moral philosophy, that individuals who commit crimes deserve to be punished proportionately to their offenses, in order to deter others from committing similar crimes and to affirm the importance and legitimacy of societal norms[841]. This approach

837 *Ibid.*, p. 16.

838 See: D. Gracin, "Punishment in European Legislation from Enlightenment Era to the End of XIXth Century with Special Emphasis on the Imprisonment", *Zbornik Pravnog Fakulteta Sveucilista u Rijeci* 21/2/1991, p. 785-812.

839 See: R. Durrant, *An Introduction to Criminal Psychology*, Oxon 2013, p. 264; B. Klapes, S. Riley, J. J. McDowell. "Toward a contemporary quantitative model of punishment", *Journal of the experimental analysis of behavior* 109.2 (2018), p. 336-348.

840 See: N. S. Timasheff, "Retributive Structure of Punishment", *American Institute of Criminal Law and Criminology* 28 (1937). p. 396.

841 See: R. M. Hare, "Punishment and Retributive Justice", *Philosophical Topics* Vol. 14, No. 2, p. 211-223

regards punishment as an end in itself, justified by the moral imperative to address wrongdoing. Modern legal systems implement structured sentencing guidelines to ensure that punishments are proportionate and consistent. These guidelines assist judges in imposing sentences that reflect the severity of the crime and societal expectations of justice[842]. Retributive justice provides victims and society with a sense of closure, affirming that justice has been served and reinforcing social norms against criminal behaviour.

The objective of deterrence is to prevent future criminal activity by instilling a sense of fear of punishment[843]. Deterrence operates on two levels: general deterrence, which discourages the public from committing crimes; and specific deterrence, which aims to prevent reoffending by individuals who have already been punished. Deterrence is based on the rational choice theory, which assumes that individuals engage in cost-benefit analysis when making decisions. The threat of punishment is designed to shift the balance in favour of non-compliance, making the perceived costs of criminal conduct outweigh the potential benefits. In order for effective deterrence to occur, it is necessary for the general public to be aware of the consequences of criminal behaviour. This approach by G. Hawkings is called "the educative-moralizing function of the law"[844]. Empirical evidence suggests that the certainty of punishment is a more effective deterrent than the severity of punishment. This highlights the significance of dependable law enforcement and judicial procedures[845].

In addition to these two most important functions criminal punishment should fulfil today, the correctional (educational) function and the restorative function should also be mentioned. The overarching aim of rehabilitation is the transformation of individuals who have committed crimes into law-abiding citizens through the implementation of educational, therapeutic, and skill development

---

842 For Polish law, see Article 53 of the Criminal Code, which states that: "*The court shall impose the punishment at its discretion, within the limits provided for by the law, taking into account the degree of social harmfulness of the act, aggravating and mitigating circumstances, the objectives of the punishment in terms of social impact, as well as the preventive objectives which it is supposed to achieve with regard to the convicted person. The severity of the punishment shall not exceed the degree of guilt*".

843 See: F. Brooker, "The deterrent effect of punishment", *Criminology* 9 (1971), p. 469.

844 G. Hawkins, "Punishment and deterrence: The educative, moralizing, and habituative effects", *Wisconsin Law Review* (1969), p. 550.

845 See: M. L. Erickson, J. P. Gibbs, G. F. Jensen, "The deterrence doctrine and the perceived certainty of legal punishments", *American Sociological Review* (1977), p. 305-317; J. P. Gibbs, "Crime, punishment, and deterrence", *The Southwestern Social Science Quarterly* (1968), p. 515-530.

programs. This approach posits that crime is a symptom of underlying issues that can be addressed to prevent future offending[846]. It considers a number of factors, including the social environment, mental health, and education, in order to gain a deeper understanding of criminal behaviour and to develop effective strategies for addressing it. Restorative justice is a process that seeks to repair the harm caused by criminal behaviour through the involvement of victims, offenders, and the wider community. This approach places significant emphasis on the concepts of reconciliation, accountability, and the restoration of relationships. Restorative justice is informed by communitarian theories that emphasise the significance of community involvement and the collective responsibility for addressing crime and its consequences[847].

4. Conclusions

The concept of punishment as a mechanism for maintaining social order has undergone a significant evolution from ancient times to the present day. The Roman legal system, one of the earliest and most influential, provides a contrasting backdrop to modern legal practices. An examination of the functions of punishment in Roman law and a comparison with contemporary legal systems reveals both differences and similarities.

In Roman law, punishment served multiple functions, including retribution, deterrence, and the maintenance of social order. Punishment was frequently retributive, with the objective of delivering justice by imposing a penalty commensurate with the gravity of the offence. Public punishments, including executions and physical punishments such as flogging and mutilation, were employed as a deterrent to others. The visibility and severity of these punishments were designed to act as a deterrent to others, preventing them from committing similar offences. The maintenance of public order was a fundamental aspect of the function of punishment. Crimes were regarded as disruptions to the social fabric, and punishment was a means of restoring order and stability. In certain instances, punishment entailed restitution to victims or their families. This was particularly common in cases of property crime, where offenders were required to make

846 See: R. Shafer-Landau, "Can punishment morally educate?", *Law and Philosophy* 10.2 (1991), p. 189-219.

847 See: C. Menkel-Meadow, "Restorative justice: What is it and does it work?", *The Annual Review of Law and Social Science* 3 (2007), p. 161-187; J. Latimer, C. Dowden, D. Muise, "The effectiveness of restorative justice practices: A meta-analysis", *The Prison Journal* 85.2 (2005), p. 127-144.

restitution to victims. Furthermore, punishments frequently encompassed symbolic and ritualistic elements, reflecting the values and norms of the wider society. For instance, the method of execution or punishment could vary according to the social status of the offender.

The modern legal system has evolved to incorporate a broader range of functions for punishment, often with an emphasis on rehabilitation and human rights. While retributive justice remains a component, it is typically more measured and constrained by legal standards and human rights considerations, the concept of proportionality ensures that punishments are commensurate with the gravity of the crime. Deterrence remains an important function, encompassing both general deterrence (the prevention of criminal activity by the general public) and specific deterrence (the prevention of criminal recidivism by the individual offender). Nevertheless, contemporary systems frequently espouse less punitive measures than those employed in the Roman era. Modern legal systems place a strong emphasis on the rehabilitation of offenders, with the aim of reintegrating them into society as law-abiding citizens. Such programmes frequently include components pertaining to education, vocational training, and psychological counselling. Another function of the criminal justice system is to protect society by incapacitating dangerous individuals. This is typically achieved through imprisonment, but also includes measures such as probation and electronic monitoring. In recent times, there has been a growing tendency for modern legal systems to incorporate restorative justice principles, with the objective of repairing the harm caused by criminal behaviour. This process involves the reconciliation of victims and offenders through victim-offender mediation and community service, with the aim of healing and repairing the communities affected by criminal behaviour. Modern punishment is constrained by human rights frameworks, which prohibit the infliction of cruel and unusual punishment. This contrasts markedly with the frequently brutal and public nature of Roman punishments.

Both the Roman and modern systems share the retributive function, although the methods and philosophies differ significantly[848]. In contrast to the Roman legal tradition, modern systems of justice tend to prioritise proportionality and fairness

---

848 On a comparison of the Roman punishment system and the modern one see for example: S. Mihálik, I. Slovák, "Roman Law as an Idea Basis for Punishing in the Conditions of the Slovak Republic", *Teka Komisji Prawniczej PAN Oddział w Lublinie* 15.1 (2022), p. 173-182; E. March, *A Comparison of Ancient Roman Justice Systems and Canadian Indigenous Justice Systems: Approaches to Crime and Punishment*. MS thesis. Queen's University (Canada), 2020; I. Englard, *Corrective and Distributive Justice: from Aristotle to modern times*. Oxford 2009.

over immediate and severe retribution. A common thread running through these systems is the use of deterrence. However, the approach to this has evolved over time. Roman law was characterised by the imposition of severe, public punishments, whereas modern systems employ legal and social deterrents, with a focus on reducing recidivism through rehabilitation. The maintenance of public order was a primary function of Roman law, often at the expense of the individual. Modern systems, while still concerned with maintaining public order, place a greater emphasis on rehabilitating offenders and protecting their rights. Both systems acknowledge the significance of addressing the harm caused by criminal activity. Restitution, a key feature of Roman law, is reflected in contemporary restorative justice practices. However, these latter are more comprehensive and victim-focused. Modern punishment is profoundly influenced by human rights principles, which ensure the humane treatment of offenders. This represents a great departure from the often brutal and public nature of Roman punishments.

The evolution of the functions of punishment from Roman law to modern legal systems reflects broader social and cultural changes. While retribution and deterrence remain central, modern systems have expanded to include rehabilitation and restorative justice, all within a framework that prioritises human rights. This comparative analysis demonstrates the dynamic nature of legal systems and their adaptation to changing societal values and norms.

Bibliography

Amielańczyk K., "Purposes and Functions of Public Punishment in Roman Law in the Perspective of Justinian's Codification", *Studia Prawnicze* KUL 4 (80) 2019, p. 21-37.

Bauman R. A., *Crime and Punishment in Ancient Rome*, London 1996.

Baumgardt D., *Bentham and the Ethics of Today*, Princeton, 1952.

Beccaria C., *O przestępstwach i karach [On Crimes and Punishments] ze wstępem E. S. Rappaporta*, Warszawa 1959.

Beccaria C., *On Crimes and Punishments. Translation, Annotations, and Introduction by G. R. Newman and P. Marongiu*, New Brunswick, London 2009.

Bessler J. D., "The Philosophy of Punishment and the Arc of Penal Reform: From Ancient Lawgivers to the Renaissance and the Enlightenment, and through the Nineteenth Century", in *The Palgrave Handbook on the Philosophy of Punishment*, (ed.) M. C. Altman, Ellensburg 2023, p. 23-52.

Brooker F., "The deterrent effect of punishment", *Criminology* 9 (1971), p. 469-490.

Buneci B., "General Considerations on Punishment in Medieval Europe", *RAIS Journal for Social Sciences* Vol. 5, No. 1, 2021, p. 39-48.

Classen A., Scarborough C., *Crime and Punishment in the Middle Ages and Early Modern Age*, Berlin 2012.

Currie S., *Medieval Punishment and Torture*, San Diego 2014.

De Pauley W. C., "Beccaria and punishment", *The International Journal of Ethics* 35.4 (1925), p. 404-412.

Deutscher T. B., *Punishment and Penance. Two Phases in the History of the Bishop's Tribunal of Novara*, Toronto 2013.

Draper A., "An Introduction to Jeremy Bentham's theory of punishment", *Journal of Bentham Studies* 5 (2002), p. 1-17.

Durrant R., *An Introduction to Criminal Psychology*, Oxon 2013.

Emsley C., McDougall S., *A Global History of Crime and Punishment. Volume 1: A Global History of Crime and Punishment in Antiquity Edited by Adriaan Lanni*, Harvard Law School, USA 2023.

Emsley C., McDougall S., *A Global History of Crime and Punishment. Volume 2: A Global History of Crime and Punishment in the Medieval Age. Edited by Karl Shoemaker*, University of Wisconsin-Madison, USA 2023.

Emsley C., McDougall S., *A Global History of Crime and Punishment. Volume 4: A Global History of Crime and Punishment in the Age of Enlightenment. Edited by Xavier Rousseaux*, Université Catholique de Louvain, Belgium, 2023.

Englard I., *Corrective and Distributive Justice: from Aristotle to modern times.* Oxford 2009.

Epplett Ch., "Spectacular Executions in the Roman World", in *A Companion to Sport and Spectacle in Greek and Roman Antiquity*, ed. P. Christesen, D. G. Kyle, Hoboken 2013, p. 520-532.

Erickson M. L., Gibbs J. P., Jensen G. F., "The deterrence doctrine and the perceived certainty of legal punishments", *American Sociological Review* (1977), p. 305-317.

G. Hallevy, *The Right to Be Punished. Modern Doctrinal Sentencing*, Berlin 2013.

Garland D., "Sociological Perspectives on Punishment", *Crime and Justice* Vol. 14/1991, p. 115-165.

Garnsey P., "Why Penalties Become Harsher: The Roman Case, Late Republic to Fourth Centruy Empire", *Natural Law Forum* 13 (1968), p. 141-162.

Gibbs J. P., "Crime, punishment, and deterrence", *The Southwestern Social Science Quarterly* (1968), p. 515-530.

Goga C.I., "Historical Evolution of Punishment Systems", *Analele UniversităŃii din Craiova. Istorie*, Anul XX, Nr. 1(27)/2015, p. 188-189.

Gracin D., "Punishment in European Legislation from Enlightenment Era to the End of XIXth Century with Special Emphasis on the Imprisonment", *Zbornik Pravnog Fakulteta Sveucilista u Rijeci* 21/2/1991, p. 785-812.

Hare R. M., "Punishment and Retributive Justice", *Philosophical Topics* Vol. 14, No. 2, p. 211-223.

Hawkins G., "Punishment and deterrence: The educative, moralizing, and habituative effects", *Wisconsin Law Review* (1969), p. 550-565.

Jońca M., *Rzymskie Prawo Karne. Instytucje, [Roman Criminal Law. Institutions]*, Lublin 2021.

Klapes B., Riley S., McDowell J. J., "Toward a contemporary quantitative model of punishment", *Journal of the experimental analysis of behavior* 109.2 (2018), p. 336-348.

Latimer J., Dowden C., Muise D., "The effectiveness of restorative justice practices: A meta-analysis", *The Prison Journal* 85.2 (2005), p. 127-144.

March E., *A Comparison of Ancient Roman Justice Systems and Canadian Indigenous Justice Systems: Approaches to Crime and Punishment.* MS thesis. Queen's University (Canada), 2020.

Menkel-Meadow C., "Restorative justice: What is it and does it work?", *The Annual Review of Law and Social Science* 3 (2007), p. 161-187.

Mihálik S., Slovák I., "Roman Law as an Idea Basis for Punishing in the Conditions of the Slovak Republic", *Teka Komisji Prawniczej PAN Oddział w Lublinie* 15.1 (2022), p. 173-182.

Mueller G., "Punishment, corrections and the law", *Nebraska Law Review* 45 (1966), p. 58-98.

O'Connor T. P, *Religion, the Community, and the Rehabilitation of Criminal Offenders*, New York, London, Oxford 2013.

Parisi F., Pi D., Luppi B., Fargnoli I., "Deterrence of Wrongdoing in Ancient Law", *Minnesota Legal Studies Research Paper* No. 14-38/2014, p. 1-26.

Pershina Y. V., "The System of Punishments in the Ancient Rome", *Modern European Researches* No 1 / 2017, p. 78-86.

Pifferi M., "Punishment and Social Control in Historical Perspective", *Oxford Research Encyclopedia of Politics* 2022.

(online -https://doi.org/10.1093/acrefore/9780190228637.013.1784 - access 17/06/2024).

Posner R. A., "Retribution and Related Concepts of Punishment", *The Journal of Legal Studies*, Volume 9, Number 1 (1980), p. 71-92.

Robinson O. F, *Penal Practice and Penal Policy in Ancient Rome*, London 2006, pp. 264.

Robinson O. F, *Penal Practice and Penal Policy in Ancient Rome*, London 2006.

Sellin T., *Punishment and Social Structure*, New York 1939, p. 53-72.

Shafer-Landau R., "Can punishment morally educate?", *Law and Philosophy* 10.2 (1991), p. 189-219.

Shoemaker K., "The problem of pain in punishment: Historical perspectives" in *Law, meaning, and violence: pain, death, and the law*, (ed.) A Sarat, Ann Arbor 2001, p. 15-41.

Stearns P. N., *Punishment in World History*, New York 2024.

Timasheff N. S., "Retributive Structure of Punishment", *American Institute of Criminal Law and Criminology* 28 (1937). p. 396.

Weitekamp E. G. M., "The History of Restorative Justice", in *Restorative Justice*, (ed.) Th. Gavrielides, London 2015, p. 3-30.

Young D. B., "Cesare Beccaria: Utilitarian or retributivist?", *Journal of Criminal Justice* Volume 11, Issue 4, 1983, p. 317-326.

Ewa Dawidziuk[849]

Dignity of prisoners – why we need to protect it?

Abstract: The article refers to dignity of prisoners so people who are in vulnerable position because of the fact of being deprived of liberty. International conventions as well as recommendations of the Council of Europe and the United Nations refer to the treatment of prisoners underlining that all persons deprived of liberty shall be treated with the respect of their inherent dignity. The publication gives examples of situations when the infringement of that rule can be indicated. In practice national law as well as practice of penitentiary officers must be consistent with this basic regulation provided within international binding law or within soft law.

Keywords: dignity, prisoner, living conditions, body searches, transgender prisoners, ECtHR, humanitarian treatment of prisoners

1. Introduction

According to Article 30 of the Polish Constitution the inherent and inalienable dignity of man is the source of human and civil liberties and rights. It is inviolable, and its respect and protection is the duty of public authorities[850].

With regard to prisoners, Article 4 of the Criminal Executive Code of the Republic of Poland adds that penalties, punitive measures, compensatory measures, security measures, precautionary measures and preventive measures shall be carried out in a humane manner, with respect for the human dignity of the convicted person[851]. The position of this provision at the beginning of this Code underscores its importance, indicating that also a person in penitentiary isolation must be treated with respect for dignity[852].

---

849 SWPS University, ORCID ID 0000-0003-1262-5617.

850 Journal of Law (Dziennik Ustaw) 1997 Number 78, position 483, https://isap.sejm.gov.pl/isap.nsf/download.xsp/WDU19970780483/U/D19970483Lj.pdf (access: 1.07.2024).

851 Journal of Law (Dziennik Ustaw) 2024, position 706, https://isap.sejm.gov.pl/isap.nsf/download.xsp/WDU19970900557/U/D19970557Lj.pdf (access: 29.09.2024).

852 K. Dąbkiewicz [w:] *Kodeks karny wykonawczy. Komentarz, wyd. IV*, Warszawa 2018, art. 4, point 6.

Treatment of a prisoner in violation of his dignity and humane treatment will be subject to adjudication by the Strasbourg Court on the base of Article 3 of the ECHR, which prohibits torture and inhuman or degrading treatment. This prohibition is absolute, independent of the circumstances or motivation of the authorities, even in the event of war or other public danger threatening the life of the nation[853]. The article will focus on the understanding of dignity of prisoners and answering the question what need to draw our attention when we analyze the functioning of prisons and pre-trial detention centers. I do not concentrate on the definition of dignity which was describe by Bielecki[854] or Sadowski[855] but concentrate on those aspects of the deprivation of liberty within prisons that might be problematic.

2. International standards

The necessity to respect dignity of prisoners is underlined within provisions of many international conventions as well as soft law. We can read about it in the International Covenant on Civil and Political Rights[856], Basic Principles for the Treatment of Prisoners[857], Body of Principles for the Protection of All Persons under Any Form of Detention or Imprisonment[858], The African Charter on Human and Peoples' Rights[859] and American Convention on Human Rights[860]. There are also two important recommendations within the Council of Europe or

853 M. A. Nowicki [w:] Komentarz do Konwencji o ochronie praw człowieka i podstawowych wolności [w:] Wokół Konwencji Europejskiej. Komentarz do Europejskiej Konwencji Praw Człowieka, wyd. VIII, Warszawa 2021, art. 3.

854 M. Bielecki, Ochrona godności osoby skazanej w prawie karnym wykonawczym. Wybrane aspekty, Zeszyty Naukowe KUL 60 (2018), nr 1 (241), p. 161-162.

855 M. Sadowski, Godność człowieka – aksjologiczna podstawa państwa i prawa, w: Studia Erasmiana Wratislaviensia - Wrocławskie Studia Erazmiańskie. Zeszyt naukowy studentów, doktorantów i pracowników Uniwersytetu Wrocławskiego, Wrocław 2007/1, p. 14.

856 Article 10: All persons deprived of their liberty shall be treated with humanity and with respect for the inherent dignity of the human person.

857 Principle 1: All prisoners shall be treated with the respect due to their inherent dignity and value as human beings.

858 Principle 1: All persons under any form of detention or imprisonment shall be treated in a humane manner and with respect for the inherent dignity of the human person.

859 Article 5: Every individual shall have the right to the respect of the dignity inherent in a human being and to the recognition of his legal status.

860 Article 5(2): All persons deprived of their liberty shall be treated with respect for the inherent dignity of the human person.

the United Nations which refer to human dignity. These are mainly the European Prison Rules and Nelson Mandela Rules.

The European Prison Rules (hereinafter: EPR), adopted by the Council of Europe in 2006 and modified in 2020[861], emphasize the importance of dignity in the treatment of prisoners within rule 1. It states that all persons deprived of their liberty shall be treated with respect for their human dignity. No person shall be subjected to torture or to inhuman or degrading treatment or punishment. This rule echoes the principles outlined in the Universal Declaration of Human Rights and other international human rights instruments, emphasizing the fundamental right of all individuals, including prisoners, to be treated with dignity and respect. The ECtHR has repeatedly emphasized in its judgments that human dignity forms the very essence of the human rights system, and this also applies to prisoners[862]. In all provisions of the EPR, dignity refers to living conditions (rule 18.1), transport (rule 32.2), treatment and general attitude of the prison staff (rule 49, 72), body searches (rule 54.3)[863]. Budgetary problems can not excuse the infringement of human rights of prisoners (rule 4). The monitoring bodies, such as CPT[864], SPT[865] or NPM[866], must check it within preventive visits (rule 93.1).

Moreover, it's worth underlining, that the European Code of Ethics for Prison Staff provides detailed recommendations to authorities on ethical principles for staff, including among other things respect for and protection of human dignity[867].

---

861 Recommendation Rec(2006)2-rev of the Committee of Ministers to member States on the European Prison Rules, adopted by the Committee of Ministers on 11 January 2006, at the 952nd meeting of the Ministers' Deputies and revised and amended by the Committee of Ministers on 1 July 2020 at the 1380th meeting of the Ministers' Deputies.

862 Penal Reform International and the Council of Europe, Guidance document on the European Prison Rules, 2023, p. 12.

863 See also: Penal Reform International, Short guide to the European Prison Rules, 2021, p. 5,18.

864 European Committee for the Prevention of Torture and Inhuman or Degrading Treatment or Punishment (CPT).

865 The UN Subcommittee on Prevention of Torture and other Cruel, Inhuman or Degrading Treatment or Punishment (SPT).

866 National Preventive Mechanism created by the states that ratified the Optional Protocol to the Convention against Torture and other Cruel, Inhuman or Degrading Treatment or Punishment, adopted 18 December 2002.

867 Council of Europe, Recommendation CM/Rec(2012)5 of the Committee of Ministers to member States on the European Code of Ethics for Prison Staff, adopted by the Committee of Ministers on 12 April 2012 at the 1140th meeting of the Ministers' Deputies, para 11.

The Council of Europe's recent recommendation, issued on 9 October 2024, also emphasizes the careful use of AI in penitentiary units as well as probation services to ensure that human dignity and human rights are respected[868].

We can find the concept of dignity as a fundamental principle also within the United Nations recommendations such as Standard Minimum Rules for the Treatment of Prisoners, also known as the Nelson Mandela Rules (hereinafter: NMR), adopted in 2015[869]. The basic principle, rule 1, states that all prisoners shall be treated with the respect due to their inherent dignity and value as human beings. Additionally rule 5.1 states that the prison regime should seek to minimize any differences between prison life and life at liberty that tend to lessen the responsibility of the prisoners or the respect due to their dignity as human beings. Moreover we find the reference to dignity within the rules regarding body searches (rule 50), conjugal visits (rule 58), treatment of the body of a deceased prisoner (rule 72), training for prison staff (rule 76.1.b). That's important that NMR are becoming a part of international discourse on functioning of penitentiary units which is linked with the theme "dignity unlocked", discussed during events organized in connection to Nelson Mandela Day in 2022[870].

3. Specific issues connected to the protection of dignity within prisons

Below, I present several key issues within which the problem of respecting the dignity of prisoners arises. These include living conditions, proper treatment by prison staff, transgender prisoners, solitary confinement, the right to privacy, body searches, the manner of serving meals, the use of direct coercive measures, healthcare, and the issue of death in conditions of penal isolation. However, it is

---

868 Recommendation CM/Rec(2024)5 of the Committee of Ministers to member States regarding the ethical and organisational aspects of the use of artificial intelligence and related digital technologies by prison and probation services (Adopted by the Committee of Ministers on 9 October 2024 at the 1509th meeting of the Ministers' Deputies) states in principle 1 that "When designing, developing, providing, using and decommissioning AI and related digital technologies, respect for human rights and the dignity of all persons affected by this use should be ensured (principle of respect for human dignity and fundamental rights)".

869 Resolution 70/175 adopted by the General Assembly on 17 December 2015, United Nations Standard Minimum Rules for the Treatment of Prisoners (the Nelson Mandela Rules).

870 D. van Zyl Smit, Dignity unlocked? The Nelson Mandela Rules as a key to the transnational legal ordering of imprisonment, Archiwum Kryminologii 2023, 45(2), p. 131.

the most important to underline that according to ECtHR case law each government should organise its penitentiary system in such a way as to ensure respect for the dignity of inmates. Financial or logistical difficulties cannot justify its infringement[871].

3.1. Penitentiary staff

The cornerstone of a humane prison system will always be properly recruited and trained prison staff who know how to adopt the appropriate attitude in their relations with prisoners. Establishing positive relationships with prisoners should be recognised as a key factor of that vocation[872]. Still the Polish Ombudsman Office receives complaints regarding impropriate treatment of prisoners. However, it's difficult to prove it. In most cases it's a prisoner's word against staff's explanation. That's why prison management needs to operate within an ethical framework[873].

3.2. Transgender prisoners

Protection of dignity is always mentioned when vulnerable groups of prisoners are discussed. The judgement of ECtHR in case W.W. v. Poland[874] was the occasion to do it more broadly in relation to transgender prisoners in Polish penitentiary units. The President of the CPT underlines that "through dialogue and exchanges we can together promote good practices and ensure that all transgender persons in prison are treated with dignity and care"[875]. These is a vulnerable group of prisoners. A duty to ensure safety within prison cannot lead to solitary confinement which means isolation from the human contact with others. Placement decisions[876], healthcare, and body searches are important topics related to the proper treatment of transgender prisoners, ensuring their gender identity is respected.

---

871 Council of Europe, Guide on the case-law of the European Convention on Human Rights, Prisoners' rights, 2024, p. 8.

872 Council of Europe, Developments concerning CPT standards in respect of imprisonment. Extract from the 11th General Report of the CPT, CPT/Inf(2001)16 part, 2001, para 26.

873 A. Coyle, A Human Rights Approach to Prison Management Handbook for Prison Staff, Second Edition, International Centre for Prison Studies 2009, p. 11-12.

874 Judgement of 11 July 2024 in case W.W. v. Poland, appplication no. 31842/20.

875 Council of Europe, 33rd General Report. Activities 2023 European Committee for the Prevention of Torture and Inhuman or Degrading Treatment or Punishment, 2024, p. 6.

876 Penal Reform International and Thailand Institute of Justice, Global Prison Trends 2024, p. 32.

This topic relates also to violence towards transgender prisoners which is identified in many countries[877].

3.3. Living conditions

All detainees should be ensured a minimum standard of living conditions that uphold their dignity. This includes providing each person with a regular supply of toiletries and cleaning products, along with clean bedding and a pillow.

Living space per prisoner is linked with the respect of dignity of inmates in each country. CPT recommends it is 6m^2 of living space for a single-occupancy cell plus sanitary facility; 4m^2 of living space per prisoner in a multiple-occupancy cell plus fully-partitioned sanitary facility; at least 2m between the walls of the cell; at least 2.5m between the floor and the ceiling of the cell[878]. However, according to the ECtHR case law, the minimum standard of living space is 3m^2 per one inmate[879].

Lack of access to basic needs, such as having to use a toilet that is not fully separated from the living area in a multi-bed prison cell, can be seen as a violation of privacy and a failure to respect dignity. Besides, the rooms for family or conjugal visits should be organized in a way respecting dignity in a home-like conditions[880]. Still in Poland it's not organized in such a way especially when we compare it for example with Danish family visits within prisons[881].

3.4. Solitary confinement

It can lead to ill-treatment so in fact the topic of dignity must be seen within this theme. Social isolation, restrictions on contact with family and loved ones, and lack of opportunities to participate in social life can also lead to feelings of humiliation and violations of prisoners' dignity. It might refer to the status of dangerous prisoners. According to the Polish law it's necessary to prolong such status every 3 months. Unfortunately I have noticed cases when it lasts even 12-14 years.

---

877 Penal Reform International and Thailand Institute of Justice, Global Prison Trends 2023, p. 34.

878 Council of Europe, Living space per prisoner in prison establishments: CPT standards, CPT/Inf (2015) 44, 2015, para 9-11.

879 Judgement of the ECtHR in case Muršić v. Croatia of 20 October 2016, application no. 7334/13.

880 R. Morgan, M. D. Evans, The prevention of torture in Europe. CPT standards regarding prisoners, Geneva 2001, p. 24.

881 The author expresses her own view based on observation made during study visits in Denmark and regular visits within Polish penitentiary units.

According to ECtHR's judgments it leads to the violation of art. 3 of the ECHR if we isolate such dangerous prisoners from social contact with other people. We could observe such an explanation in the case Breivik against Norway[882], but the same regime is applied in Poland to prisoners classified as dangerous.

3.5. Intimacy

Respect for the right to intimacy of an inmate in a penitentiary unit is directly related to respect for dignity. The Ombudsman takes the position[883] that in every multi-bed cell the sanitary facilities should be fully enclosed from floor to a ceiling. In a single cell, on the other hand, it must be partially covered so that a person looking into the cell through a peephole or entering the cell does not see the inmate using a toilet[884]. In the case of Szafrański v. Poland the complaint addressed the lack of an adequate separation between the toilets and the cell, claiming it constituted a violation of his rights to private, intimacy and dignity. The Tribunal in Strasbourg underlined that 'under Article 3 the State must ensure that a person is detained in conditions which are compatible with respect for his human dignity, that the manner and method of the execution of the measure do not subject him to distress or hardship of an intensity exceeding the unavoidable level of suffering inherent in detention and that, given the practical demands of imprisonment, his health and well-being are adequately secured'[885]. As a result toilet must be separated in multiple cell. The CPT takes the same position[886].

3.6. Body searches

Every reasonable effort should be made to minimize embarrassment and maintain as much dignity as possible. Persons who are searched should not be required to remove all their clothing at the same time, for example, a person should be

---

882 Supreme Court of Norway, HR-2017-1127-U, https://www.domstol.no/globalassets/upload/hret/decisions-in-english-translation/sak-2017-778 eng.pdf (access: 1.08.2024).

883 https://bip.brpo.gov.pl/pl/content/rpo-sw-zabudowa-kacikow-sanitarnych-ponowne-odp (access: 27.07.2024).

884 S. Trociuk (red.), Informacja o działalności Rzecznika Praw Obywatelskich w roku 2022 oraz o stanie przestrzegania wolności i praw człowieka i obywatela, Biuletyn Rzecznika Praw Obywatelskich 2023, nr 2. Źródła, p. 60.

885 ECtHR judgement of 15 December 2015 in the case Szafrański v. Poland, the application no. 17249/12, para 22.

886 CPT/Inf (2012) 13, § 78; 2nd General Report, CPT/Inf (92) 3, § 49; CPT/Inf (2014) 21, § 61, and CPT/Inf (2011) 20, §§ 105 and 106.

allowed to remove clothes above the waist and to put those clothes back on before removing further clothing. ECtHR states that body searches must be conducted in an appropriate manner and must be justified[887].

In addition, ordinarily the search should be carried out by an officer of the same gender as a person being searched and, as a rule, a second officer of the same gender should also be present during any strip search as a protection for detained persons and staff alike[888]. The Polish Ombudsman referred to the implementation of ECtHR's judgements regarding body searches in its annual report of 2020 which was described within human dignity chapter[889]. It's because it intervenes very deeply within intimacy and can lead to inhuman or degrading treatment. That's why body searches must be conducted in a way that respect human dignity and serves legitimate purpose[890]. Degrading and intrusive body searches can amount to torture or ill-treatment, especially in the case of transgender detainees[891].

3.7. Death in prison

Dying in prison during prolonged pre-trial detention or while serving a sentence after a long battle with cancer may be considered inhumane. Death in a penitentiary unit and not among loved ones has nothing to do with respecting the dignity and humane treatment of a person deprived of liberty. A prisoner dies in solitude, often spending the final period bedridden, requiring help from fellow inmates, who serve meals and change diapers for the person chained to the bed. There is only one prison hospital for chronically ill inmates in Poland, but the number of available spots is inadequate to meet the demand. The average waiting time for a spot at this hospital for prisoners is one year.

---

887 ECtHR judgements: *Yankov v. Bulgaria*, the application no. 39084/97, § 110; *Valašinas v. Lithuania*, the application no. 44558/98, § 117; *Iwańczuk v. Poland*, the application no. 25196/94, § 59.

888 Council of Europe, 33rd General Report. Activities 2023 European Committee for the Prevention of Torture and Inhuman or Degrading Treatment or Punishment, 2024, p. 41.

889 S. Trociuk (red.), Informacja o działalności Rzecznika Praw Obywatelskich w roku 2020 oraz o stanie przestrzegania wolności i praw człowieka i obywatela, Biuletyn Rzecznika Praw Obywatelskich 2021, nr 1. Źródła, p. 29.

890 ECtHR judgement in case Wainwright v. the United Kingdom, 2006, § 42; Dejnek v. Poland, 2017, § 60.

891 Report of the Special Rapporteur on torture and other cruel, inhuman or degrading treatment or punishment, A/HRC/31/57, 5 January 2016, par. 36.

3.8. Direct coercive measures

Being strapped into a three-piece belt in a security cell for 72 hours, without being allowed to use the toilet—leading to the convicted person defecating on themselves, screaming, and begging to be released—must be considered inhumane treatment and a violation of human dignity. The ECtHR emphasized in its case law that any use of physical force that is not strictly justified by the individual's own actions undermines human dignity and constitutes a violation of the right established in Article 3 of the ECHR[892].

3.9. Food within prison

Recently, the Polish Ombudsman has identified and criticized cases of issuing meals through a window in the door of a cell, instead of directly issuing meals to the prisoner on his plate[893]. This institution has also noticed a case of serving breakfast and dinner to prisoners in one cell on a single plate for all inmates. Such examples must be criticized within the topic of this article.

3.10. Health care

Healthcare is also included within the scope of a prisoner's dignity. An insufficient level of health care can quickly result in situations that can be described as inhuman and degrading treatment[894]. There are special medical needs when we look into such groups in detention as: women, children, disabled inmates, LGBT+ prisoners, elderly people, inmates with specific diseases or with mental illnesses.

In case Sławomir Musiał v. Poland[895] the applicant complained about the poor conditions of his detention which was inadequate to his medical state which had deteriorated. The ECtHR found violations of Article 3 of the ECHR and indicated that this provision of the Convention requires to ensure that prisoners are detained in conditions which are compatible with respect for human dignity

---

892 ECtHR judgement in case Artyomov v. Russia, 2010, § 145; Bouyid v. Belgium, § 101.

893 More information on the website: https://bip.brpo.gov.pl/pl/content/odpowiedz-dla-rpo-wydawanie-posilkow-przez-okienko-w-drzwiach-celi-zasadne (access: 2.08.2024).

894 CPT, Health care services in prisons, Extract from the 3 rd General Report of the CPT, published in 1993, CPT/Inf(93)12-part, p. 1.

895 ECtHR judgement of 20 January 2009, application no. 28300/06.

which means that health and well-being are adequately secured by, among other things, providing them with the requisite medical assistance[896].

4. Conclusions

'People come to prison as punishment not for punishment'[897]. As a result of this obviously true statement, violations of prisoners' dignity are not only morally wrong but also inconsistent with international human rights standards. Any instances of such violations should be reported and eliminated. The indicated examples of violations of the dignity of the persons deprived of liberty underline that people in prison are exposed to various types of abuse, are in a position of subordination to the prison service, and have no influence on the conditions under which they serve their sentence. In such a situation, the complaint mechanism has a crucial, protective role. Furthermore, I agree with the statement that adequate resources and preventing overcrowding are prerequisites to protecting the human rights and basic needs of persons deprived of liberty within penitentiary units all over the world[898]. However prisons face also the problem of increasing number of elderly people who need special treatment or palliative care which can be situated within humanitarian treatment and respect of dignity. Still body searches are problematic especially in Poland as well as medical care. The lack of that might be treated as the inhuman treatment. What's more, human dignity requires that there must be a chance for a prisoner to atone for his offence and move towards rehabilitation[899].

Last but not least, 'no one truly knows a nation until one has been inside its jails. A nation should not be judged by how it treats its highest citizens, but its lowest ones'[900]. That's why the treatment of prisoners with respect of their dignity is undoubtedly crucial in all penitentiary systems and must be checked systematically by all visiting bodies and Ombudsman institutions which can investigate complaints on the spot in the penitentiary unit.

---

896 Ibidem, para 86; ECtHR judgement of 26 October 2000 in case Kudła v. Poland, application no. 30210/96, para 94.

897 J. M. Moore, Prison – more than detention?, Criminal Justice Matters, No. 102, 2015, p. 11.

898 Penal Reform International and Thailand Institute of Justice, Global Prison Trends 2023, 2023 p. 5.

899 C. Ovey, Ensuring respect of the rights of prisoners under the European Convention on Human Rights as part of their reintegration process, p. 2.

900 Nelson Rolihlahla Mandela, https://www.unodc.org/conig/uploads/documents/Nelson_Mandela_Rules.pdf.

Bibliography

Amnesty International, Dignity in prison. What is the situation two years after The European Court of Human Rights ruled against France?, 2022.

Bielecki M., Ochrona godności osoby skazanej w prawie karnym wykonawczym. Wybrane aspekty, Zeszyty Naukowe KUL 60 (2018), nr 1 (241).

Council of Europe, Guide on the case-law of the European Convention on Human Rights, Prisoners' rights, 2024.

Council of Europe, Developments concerning CPT standards in respect of imprisonment. Extract from the 11th General Report of the CPT, CPT/Inf(2001)16-part, 2001, para 26.

Council of Europe, 33rd General Report. Activities 2023 European Committee for the Prevention of Torture and Inhuman or Degrading Treatment or Punishment, 2024.

Council of Europe, Transgender persons in prison. Prison standard. Extract from the 33rd General Report CPT/Inf (2024) 16 – part, 2024.

Council of Europe, Developments concerning CPT standards in respect of imprisonment. Extract from the 11th General Report of the CPT, CPT/Inf(2001)16-part, 2001.

Council of Europe, Living space per prisoner in prison establishments: CPT standards, CPT/Inf (2015) 44, 2015.

Council of Europe, Solitary confinement of prisoners. Extract from the 21st General Report of the CPT, CPT/Inf(2011)28-part2, 2011.

Coyle A., A Human Rights Approach to Prison Management Handbook for Prison Staff, Second Edition, International Centre for Prison Studies 2009.

Hołda Z., Ochrona godności ludzkiej skazanego w toku odbywania kary pozbawienia wolności, Palestra 1988, nr 7.

Lenart-Kłoś K., Postrzeganie i respektowanie godności więźniów przez funkcjonariuszy Służby Więziennej, Rozprawy Społeczne 13(4), 2019c.

Morgan R., Evans M. D., The prevention of torture in Europe. CPT standards regarding prisoners, Geneva 2001.

Moore J. M., Prison – more than detention?, Criminal Justice Matters, No. 102, 2015.

Nowicki M. A. [w:] Komentarz do Konwencji o ochronie praw człowieka i podstawowych wolności [w:] Wokół Konwencji Europejskiej. Komentarz do Europejskiej Konwencji Praw Człowieka, wyd. VIII, Warszawa 2021.

Ovey C., Ensuring respect of the rights of prisoners under the European Convention on Human Rights as part of their reintegration process.

Penal Reform International and the Council of Europe, Guidance document on the European Prison Rules, 2023.

Penal Reform International, Short guide to the European Prison Rules, 2021.

Penal Reform International and Thailand Institute of Justice, Global Prison Trends 2024.

Penal Reform International and Thailand Institute of Justice, Global Prison Trends 2023.

Ploch A. Why Dignity Matters: Dignity and the Right (or Not) to Rehabilitation from International and National Perspectives, New York University Journal of International Law and Politics, Vol. 44, No.3 (2012).

Przesławski T., Konsekwencje naruszenia zasady humanitaryzmu i poszanowania godności ludzkiej w postępowaniu karno-wykonawczym (art. 4 § 1 kkw), Przegląd Więziennictwa Polskiego 2015, nr 88.

Sadowski M., Godność człowieka – aksjologiczna podstawa państwa i prawa, w: Studia Erasmiana Wratislaviensia - Wrocławskie Studia Erazmiańskie. Zeszyt naukowy studentów, doktorantów i pracowników Uniwersytetu Wrocławskiego, Wrocław 2007/1.

Szczygieł G. B., Zasada poszanowania godności skazanego a przeludnienie zakładów karnych [in:] Lelenta S., Szczygieł G. (eds.), X lat obowiązywania Kodeksu karnego wykonawczego, Białystok 2009.

Trociuk S. (red.), Informacja o działalności Rzecznika Praw Obywatelskich w roku 2020 oraz o stanie przestrzegania wolności i praw człowieka i obywatela, Biuletyn Rzecznika Praw Obywatelskich 2021, nr 1. Źródła.

Trociuk S. (red.), Informacja o działalności Rzecznika Praw Obywatelskich w roku 2022 oraz o stanie przestrzegania wolności i praw człowieka i obywatela, Biuletyn Rzecznika Praw Obywatelskich 2023, nr 2. Źródła.

United Nations, Report of the Special Rapporteur on torture and other cruel, inhuman or degrading treatment or punishment, A/HRC/31/57, 5 January 2016.

van Zyl Smit D., Dignity unlocked? The Nelson Mandela Rules as a key to the transnational legal ordering of imprisonment, Archiwum Kryminologii 2023, 45(2).

Natalia Piotrowska[901]

The right to a court (the right to a fair trial) in relation to the selected institutions in civil proceedings, taking into consideration the historical context of their establishment

Abstract: The foundations for the creation and further application of law are the principles according to which both the creation of legal norms and their interpretation should be implemented. Principles are a signpost that should be followed when co-creating and functioning in the broadly understood legal system. One of these principles is the rule of the right to a court (the right to a fair trial), which has been verified on the basis of: - a claim, which is a procedural act that essentially initiates civil proceedings, - a hearing, which is one of the most popular form of court's meeting and - judgment, which is the official form of ending the case pending in front of the court. Each of these three institutions has been narrowed down to a particular type, namely: - a manifestly unfounded action, - remote hearings (meetings), - judgment in the absence of the defendant / default judgment. This allows us to assess in the broadest possible way whether civil procedure is shaped in accordance with the principles described above, in particular one of them, as well as whether its individual institutions have been regulated in such a way as to reflect the overarching principle of the right to a court (the right to a fair trial).

Keywords: Right to a court, right to a fair trial, principle, manifestly unfounded action, remote hearing (meeting), judgment in the absence of the defendant / default judgment, civil procedure

1. Introduction

This paper is about the right to a court (the right to a fair trial)[902] in the context of selected institutions in civil proceedings, regulated in the act of law of

901 University of Wrocław, Faculty of Law, Administration and Economics, ORCID 0000-0003-4118-3483.

902 The name of the principle of the right to a court is a literal translation of the name of this principle as it appears in the Polish legal language, which reflects this principle as an institution of law. It finds its counterpart in the Anglo-Saxon legal system called the principle of the right to a fair trial, manifested in the Polish legal system as part of the principle of the right to a court. Therefore, each time in the text written in English, as well as in the title itself, there are both translations of the name of this rule.

17th November 1964 - Code of Civil Procedure (J.L.: No. 43, pos. 296), hereinafter referred as CCP, like: - a manifestly unfounded action introduced into the polish legal order on the basis of the amendment of 4.7.2019, - remote hearings (meetings) binding in the polish law since 14.3.2024, - judgment in the absence of the defendant / default judgment.

All these institutions have been analyzed from the perspective of the right to a court (the right to a fair trial) with an explanation of the historical genesis of their creation. This study covers the description of one of the legal principles, including procedural principles, with an indication of the guiding principle of the judiciary and the guiding principle of the procedure. The right to a court (the right to a fair trial) occupies a leading place among the most important rights of the individual in a broad catalogue of all rights and freedoms.

Firstly, it creates the main mechanism for asserting all other rights and freedoms, and provides the possibility of asserting them. Secondly, it is part of a system protecting an individual against possible infringement of her or his rights and freedoms. Thirdly, it is a mirror image of the relationship that exists between the individual and the state, determining the level of democracy. The fundamental importance of this principle as specific value binding in law, influencing the manner of its creation and application, has been emphasized in this work. It should be underlined once again that the verification of the above-mentioned rule has been made from the point of view of the basic assumptions of the claim that is manifestly unfounded, from the point of view of remote hearings (meetings) binding in the polish law, which is quite fresh institution in polish law, from the point of view of judgment in the absence of the defendant / default judgment, which is quite known institution in a polish, civil proceeding. The choice of these institutions is not accidental. The first concerns the initiation of proceedings, the second relates to a case pending in front of a court, and the third concerns the termination of proceedings by issuing a kind of judgment. With this choice, we can trace the application of the right to a court (the right to a fair trial) from the initiation of proceedings, through their conduct, to their conclusion. The historical context, which has also been taken into account in this paper, of the emergence of both the right to a court (the right to a fair trial) and the other three institutions mentioned above, allows us to assess the direction of development, to look at the right to a court (the right to a fair trial), as well as specific procedural solutions from the perspective of time and space. Importantly, individual legal regulations concerning civil procedure are the subject of many and too frequent amendments, while the key feature of the fundamental rules of civil procedure is their permanence and minimal susceptibility to changes made in detailed legal provisions, excluding in this case systemic changes.

2. The right to a court (the right to a fair trial)

The right to a court (the right to a fair trial) is recognized as one of the fundamental rights of citizens, defined as the right to justice, the right to legal protection, stems from the idea of ensuring that everyone has the right to present their case in front of the state authorities, which guarantee that just, objective and equitable decisions are made.[903] The above principle originates primarily in Article 2 of the Constitution of the Republic of Poland, according to which the Republic of Poland is a democratic state.[904] It is pointed out that the right to a court (the right to a fair trial) is a complex concept, which consists of the right to justice, the right to a legal protection, the right to a judicial remedy, the right to bring an action or the right to defend oneself in front of a court.[905] One of the fundamental aspects of the right to a court (the right to a fair trial), which should be noted from the point of view of this study, is the right to a properly structured judicial procedure – that is, a procedure that allows for the implementation of: - the right to a properly structured system of evidence and appeals, - the right to present arguments, - the right to be fairly and professionally represented, - the right to defence, - the right to a fair and public trial, - the right of access to information about the status of the case, - the right to have your case heard and disposed of within a reasonable time and without undue delay.[906]

Before the right to a court (the right to a fair trial) received the form described above, it underwent its evolution. The history of the right to a court (the right to a fair trial) allows us to point out the following most important turning points in the creation of this law. Magna Charta Libertatum in English it is a Great Charter of Freedom was issued by King John of England – XIII century. One of the monarch's main oaths stated that "no free man shall be imprisoned or deprived of liberty, property, placed outside the law and custom, banished or in any way destroyed (...) unless on the basis of a judgment made by his peers under the law of that country." This principle was subsequently reflected in the institution of *habeas corpus*, which allows for a judicial review of the legality of imprisonment or other forms of restriction of rights, and in the concept of due process of law, which

903 Ł. Błaszczak, *A Manifestly Unfounded Claim – Art. 191^1 of the Civil Procedure Code*, Warsaw 2021, p. 40-41.

904 J. Studzińska, P. Cioch, *Postępowanie cywilne*, Warszawa 2017, p. 65.

905 M.G. Plebanek, *Nadużycie praw procesowych w postępowaniu cywilnym – zagadnienia ogólne*, SP 2012, zeszyt 1 (190), p. 92.

906 M. Żak, *Prawo do sądu jako element zasady dobrego rządzenia w świetle orzecznictwa z zakresu praw człowieka*, Palestra 2/2020, p. 75, www.palestra.pl, 18.4.2024 r., godz. 12:09.

places certain requirements both on the content of the law infringing on the freedom of the individual and on the procedure for its application[907]. The development of these assumptions was reflected on the European continent in the constitutions of the 18the/19th century, the example of that was polish Constitution of 3 May. Subsequently, the analyzed principle appeared in the March Constitution in the interwar period, and after a long break returned to the Polish legal system after 1989. The principle of the right to a court (the right to a fair trial) has become an independent constitutional principle expressed in article 45 (1) of the Basic Polish Law: "Everyone has the right to have your case heard in a fair and transparent way without undue delay by a competent, independent, impartial court". Moreover, this principle is reflected in Article 77(2) of the Constitution of the Republic of Poland, which states: "A statute may not prevent anyone from pursuing violated rights and freedoms". Proper formulation of the procedure is a guarantee that the analyzed principle as a law is fully implemented. Procedural rules can be divided into the guiding principles of justice and the guiding procedural principles. The guiding principles of the judiciary result from constitutional assumptions, international normative acts, socio-economic relations and the entire adopted legal system.[908] The guiding principles of the administration of justice include, inter alia the principle of the right to a court (the right to a fair trial).Rules, including procedural rules, are a special type of standards of conduct for the sake of justice, fairness or any other aspect of morality, they are optimization norms, they express the so-called "ideal obligation"[909]. The principles of law (procedural principles) set the direction of legislative action, guide the process of interpreting legal provisions, indicate the directions for the application of law, and guide the manner in which various rights of legal entities are exercised.[910] The legislator implements these principles by creating appropriate procedural guarantees or appropriate procedural institutions in which they find their expression. Therefore, it is so important to conduct an analysis of the changes introduced by the legislator through the implementation or non-implementation of the applicable rules of civil procedure in the amendments made.

---

907 L.Garlicki, *Prawo do sądu* [w:] Prawa człowieka. Model prawny, red. R.Wieruszewski, Wrocław 1991, p. 537.

908 J. Jodłowski, Z. Resich, *Postępowanie cywilne*, Warszawa 1987, p. 115; J. Studzińska, P. Cioch, *Postępowanie cywilne*, Warszawa 2017, p. 64.

909 A. Góra – Błaszczykowska, *Zasada równości stron w procesie cywilnym*, Warszawa 2008, p. 51.

910 Ibidem, p. 55.

3. The right to a court (the right to a fair trial) in relation to: - the manifestly unfounded action, - the remote hearings (meetings), - judgment in the absence of the defendant / default judgment – introduction

In principle, each of the above-mentioned aspects of the right to a court (the right to a fair trial) can be applied to the institution of: - a manifestly unfounded action, - the remote hearings (meetings), - the judgment in the absence of the defendant / default judgment. From the point of view of the right to a court (the right to a fair trial) and the filing of an action which has been classified as manifestly unfounded, but also from the point of view of a default judgment (a judgment delivered in the absence of the defendant) there is a special situation with respect to the defendant in such a case, because his/her position seems to be only formal, and the legislator has not provided for any formula guaranteeing the exercise of the right to a court (the right to a fair trial) by the party opposite to the plaintiff.

Taking into account the above, it should be emphasized that the right to a court (the right to a fair trial) is indisputable, absolute, non-gradable, resulting in the possibility of initiating proceedings in any case, and its purpose is to obtain legal protection in a specific case[911]. The above remark also requires reference to remote hearings, which provide for the literal exercise of the right to a court (the right to a fair trial), which is guaranteed by the court itself. In the context of the considerations initiated above, referring to all the three institutions of a civil process, it is emphasized that the right to law (the right to a fair trial) is guaranteed in the Constitution of the Republic of Poland, as well as in international normative acts[912], which means that every case presented to the court for consideration, even if it is not a civil case either in substantive or formal terms, nor it is a case pending in accordance with the provisions of the Code of Criminal Procedure, and at the same time the law does not reserve the jurisdiction of the administrative court to hear it, undergoes a kind of procedural juridization and becomes the beginning and basis of the case in the technical and procedural sense[913]. It is

911 E. Gapska, *Przeciwdziałanie nadużyciom prawa procesowego w znowelizowanym Kodeksie postępowania cywilnego. Cz. II – Powództwo oczywiście bezzasadne*, MOP 2019, Nr 16, Legalis 2019, p. 865 (p. 1).

912 Europejska Konwencja o Ochronie Praw Człowieka i podstawowych wolności - art. 6 ust. 1; Powszechna Deklaracja Praw Człowieka - art. 10; Międzynarodowy Pakt Praw Obywatelskich i Politycznych - art. 14 ust. 1.

913 E. Gapska, *Przeciwdziałanie nadużyciom prawa procesowego w znowelizowanym Kodeksie postępowania cywilnego. Cz. II – Powództwo oczywiście bezzasadne*, MOP 2019, Nr 16, Legalis 2019, p. 865 (p. 1).

pointed out that the right to a court (the right to a fair trial) should be treated as a public subjective right of an individual.[914] At the same time, it is noted that if the demands formulated in the statement of claim are to have effects in the sphere of rights or obligations of an individual, or – more generally – effects known to statutory law at all, then a court action is open to the party, and the purpose of its action is objectively consistent with the purpose that the legislator ascribes to the initiation of the proceedings.[915] It is emphasised that the right to a court (the right to a fair trial) may be regarded as a constitutional "meta-principle" which encompasses other constitutional rights, in particular the right to appeal against decisions issued in the first instance.[916] Thus, its significance is indisputably significant, which means that failure to implement this fundamental constitutional rule results in non-compliance with other rights guaranteed by the Fundamental Law. The right to a court (the right to a fair trial) can be considered in a positive context and is then a special kind of foundation for shaping the justice system in an institutional and procedural context, while ensuring its effective functioning.[917] From this point of view, it is necessary to review the way in which the legislature regulates, analyzed in this paper, those three institutions of civil process. On the negative side, the principle of the right to a court (the right to a fair trial) is expressed in the prohibition of closing down or excessively restricting access to justice.[918] Doctrine and case law emphasise that the right to a court (the right to a fair trial) includes: 1) the right of an access to a court, i.e. the right to initiate a procedure in front of a court as a body with specific characteristics (independent, impartial), guaranteeing real access to the court through its appropriate territorial organization, moderate fees[919] (a claim manifestly unfounded); 2) the right to have an appropriate procedure in front of a court, in accordance with the requirements and principles of justice (like a fair and public trial) (remote hearing); 3) the right to a court judgment, i.e. a binding decision of a given case by the court, which covers the entire proceeding, from its initiation to the

---

914 Ł. Błaszczak, *Powództwo oczywiście bezzasadne – art. 191^1 k.p.c.*, Warszawa 2021, p. 42.

915 E. Gapska, *Przeciwdziałanie nadużyciom prawa procesowego w znowelizowanym Kodeksie postępowania cywilnego. Cz. II – Powództwo oczywiście bezzasadne*, MOP 2019, Nr 16, Legalis 2019, p. 865 (p. 1).

916 Ł. Błaszczak, *Powództwo oczywiście bezzasadne – art. 191^1 k.p.c.*, Warszawa 2021, p. 41.

917 Ibidem.

918 Ibidem.

919 M.G. Plebanek, *Nadużycie praw procesowych w postępowaniu cywilnym – zagadnienia ogólne*, SP 2012, zeszyt 1 (190), p. 93.

enforcement of the judgment (default judgment)[920]. It is emphasised that the right to a judgment refers to obtaining a ruling constituting a substantive decision, not a formal one[921]. As we can see all the above-mentioned aspects of the right to a court (the right to a fair trial) directly and indirectly relate to the three institutions of civil procedure selected in this paper. The right of access to a court is supplemented by the regulation contained in Article 77(2) of the Constitution of the Republic of Poland, according to which no provision of law may prevent anyone from pursuing violated freedoms or rights in court. Proper formulation of the civil procedure is a guarantee that the analyzed principle as a law is fully implemented. The procedural solutions used are primarily intended to balance the procedural position of the parties, which means that everyone should have the right to present their arguments in a real way in front of the court, which is obliged to consider them in a fair and objective manner. It is emphasised that the above constitutes the so-called 'fair judicial procedure', which should be understood as: 1) the right to be heard, 2) the right to be reasoned; 3) the right to predictability of proceedings[922]. In civil cases, the right to a court (the right to a fair trial) is also manifested in the possibility of initiating proceedings by filing a lawsuit[923]. It is emphasised that effective access to the court expressed in specific formal and substantive guarantees, guaranteeing a real possibility of asserting one's rights (e.g. through the institution of exemption from costs or obtaining legal aid ex officio) is important.[924] It is pointed out that the function of the right to a court (the right to a fair trial) is not to ensure that the outcome of the proceedings is favorable to the party, but only to create the possibility of applying to the relevant judicial authorities for legal protection.[925] This refers to bringing any absurd case to court, involving the opposing party in a legal dispute in front of the court, resulting in the danger of undue interference with the rights of others.[926] To

920 Ł. Błaszczak, *Powództwo oczywiście bezzasadne – art. 191¹ k.p.c.*, Warszawa 2021, p. 42; M. Rzewuski (red.) *Postępowanie cywilne*, Warszawa 2020, p. 29; J. Studzińska, P. Cioch, *Postępowanie cywilne*, Warszawa 2017, p. 66.

921 M.G. Plebanek, *Nadużycie praw procesowych w postępowaniu cywilnym – zagadnienia ogólne*, SP 2012, zeszyt 1 (190), p. 93

922 Ł. Błaszczak, *Powództwo oczywiście bezzasadne – art. 191¹ k.p.c.*, Warszawa 2021, p. 44-45.

923 J. Studzińska, P. Cioch, *Postępowanie cywilne*, Warszawa 2017, p. 65.

924 J. Studzińska, P. Cioch, *Postępowanie cywilne*, Warszawa 2017, p. 66.

925 M.G. Plebanek, *Nadużycie praw procesowych w postępowaniu cywilnym – zagadnienia ogólne*, SP 2012, zeszyt 1 (190), p. 94.

926 M.G. Plebanek, *Nadużycie praw procesowych w postępowaniu cywilnym – zagadnienia ogólne*, SP 2012, zeszyt 1 (190), p. 94.

sum up, the principle of the right to a court (the right to a fair trial) is the guiding principle of the administration of justice in civil procedure[927], which, due to its significant nature, requires verification in detail in the context of the institution of manifestly unfounded action, remote hearings, judgments by default.

4. The manifestly unfounded action

The classification of such a claim as manifestly unfounded is made by the court and is of a substantive nature (such an action is dismissed). The reasoned judgment is served by the court of its own motion only on the plaintiff with instructions on the manner and time limit of lodging an appeal. Taking into account the aspect of service of such a judgment, it must be stated that the defendant is deprived of the right to a court (the right to a fair trial). At the same time, the situation of the plaintiff through the application of this institution also results in the limitation of the right to a court (the right to a fair trial), understood as the procedure itself, as well as the ruling obtained in this context. The ruling is unfavorable to the plaintiff (in this respect, it should be emphasized that the principle of the right to a court (the right to a fair trial) does not extend to obtaining the so-called judgment "in favor of one of the parties"), and the above disadvantage is somewhat of a double nature, because the judgment not only does not take into account the claim contained in the lawsuit, but what is more, it was issued under the conditions of Article 191^1 of the Code of Civil Procedure, significantly restricting its ability to freely defend its rights, assertions and demands. In principle, there are no deficiencies in the case, and the judgment is made primarily on the basis of and within the limits set out in the action.

When analyzing the issue of the justification of the copy of the judgment served, the court should first explain to the plaintiff in a manner that leaves no doubt as to why the statement of claim was classified as manifestly unfounded and therefore dismissed. Otherwise, it cannot be ruled out that such a situation may be classified as a restriction of a party's right to a court (right to a fair trial) due to the vagueness of the court's rationale (the issue of the court's absolute certainty as to the manifest unfoundedness of the claim). On the other hand, the defendant at this stage of the proceedings is completely deprived of the right to a court (the right to a fair trial), because there is no direct possibility of obtaining knowledge of the pending case, the decision to be made, and then the possibility of taking appropriate procedural steps by the party.

---

927 M. Rzewuski (red.) *Postępowanie cywilne*, Warszawa 2020, p. 29; A. Góra – Błaszczykowska, *Zasada równości stron w procesie cywilnym*, Warszawa 2008, p. 1.

A judgment rendered with the use of the institution in question is subject to review by the Court of First Instance. In this respect, a regulation has been introduced, which assumes that the procedure triggered by the filing of an appeal against a court judgment dismissing a claim as manifestly unfounded has also been simplified – Article 391[1] of the CCP. It is pointed out that a judgment dismissing an action as manifestly unfounded is issued in absentia, because the defendant has no knowledge that an action has been brought against him/her and that a judgment dismissing the action has been issued, and that judgment has the same characteristics and has all the same effects as an adversarial judgment, however, it must be held that the rules on default judgment do not apply to the defendant, because the defendant does not so much refuse to defend the action as it cannot defend itself, in which case the court defends the defendant of its own motion.[928] In connection with the foregoing, it is noted that the defendant is exposed to a retrial for the same claim because, without being aware of the judgment, he cannot defend himself with the plea of lis pendens or *res iudicata*.[929] Referring to the situation of the defendant in civil proceedings, in which the institution of a manifestly unfounded action has been applied, it is emphasized that the defendant has no legal interest (*gravamen*) in challenging such a judgment, while the plaintiff may appeal against the judgment in question under general rules, i.e. the appeal analyzed above.[930] All the above arguments seem to indicate that the principle of the right to a court (the right to a fair trial), in particular from the point of view of the defendant, is not respected. At this point, it should be emphasized that in the literature there is a statement that in the context of Article 191[1] of the CCP, there is minimal observance of constitutional principles applicable in a democratic state governed by the rule of law. This raises some doubts because, firstly, a detailed analysis of the above-mentioned provision of law and other related legal norms does not give results confirming a comprehensive respect for this principle, and secondly, constitutional principles concerning civil procedure or procedural rules cannot be applied piecemeal or selectively due to their permanent, comprehensive and valuable nature.

Pursuant to Article 398[2] § 4 of the CCP, a cassation appeal is inadmissible in cases in which the action was dismissed on the basis of Article 191[1] of the CCP. An appeal on a point of law lodged in such cases shall remain in the case file without any further action. The above normative solution, although understandable from

928 I. Kunicki [w:] *Komentarz do KPC*, (red.) A. Góra – Błaszczykowska, komentarz do art. 191[1] KPC, Legalis 2020, Nb 7.

929 Ibidem.

930 Ibidem, Nb 8.

the point of view of pragmatism, raises doubts from the point of view of the constitutional principle in question – the right to a court (the right to a fair trial). It is noted that the limitation of the right to a court (the right to a fair trial), expressed in Article 45 of the Constitution of the Republic of Poland, occurs at the moment when the court does not consider the plaintiff's application to appoint an attorney ex officio, because within the framework of the analyzed institution it may omit the verification of such a request – Article 191¹ § 3 of the CCP.[931] It is also pointed out that it is not right to dispense with the possibility of verifying the value of the subject matter of the dispute and transferring the case, even if the claim appears to be completely unfounded.[932] No decision, including that which is rendered under Article 191¹ of the CCP, can be made in the conditions of invalidity of the proceedings.[933] Pursuant to Article 191¹ of the CCP, it is not permissible for a court to hear a case with no substantive jurisdiction. The analysed institution of a claim which is manifestly unfounded in its basic model assumption is a just solution, eliminating one of the aspects of sluggishness in the consideration of civil cases. The Constitution of the Republic of Poland establishes the fundamental right to a court (right to a fair trial) (Article 45 of the Constitution of the Republic of Poland) and at the same time strengthens the right to bring an action, giving it a new dimension, and the analysis of the implementation of this principle within the framework of the discussed procedural institution also raises a number of doubts.[934] The right to bring an action is a means of exercising the right to a court (the right to a fair trial). The right to bring an action is a kind of means to an end, which in this case is the right to a court (the right to a fair trial).[935] It is necessary to agree with the position that the provision of Article 191¹ § 1 of the CCP should be applied rarely and cautiously, because on its basis the constitutional right to a court (right to a fair trial) may easily be eliminated (Article 45(1) and Article 77(2) of the Constitution of the Republic of Poland), and therefore a restrictive

---

931 G. Kamieński, [w:] *Komentarz do KPC*, (red.) E. Marszałkowska – Krześ, komentarz do art. 191¹ KPC, Legalis 2021, Nb 5.

932 T. Szanciło (red.), *Komentarz do KPC*, Legalis 2019, Nb 4.

933 P. Paradowski, [w:] *Postępowanie cywilne po nowelizacji. Komentarz dla pełnomocników procesowych i sędziów*, B. Karolczyk (red.), Warszawa 2020, p. 64.

934 Ł. Błaszczak, *Powództwo oczywiście bezzasadne – art. 191 k.p.c.*, Warszawa 2021, p. 453.

935 Więcej w tym kontekście [w:] Ł. Błaszczak, *Powództwo oczywiście bezzasadne – art. 191¹ k.p.c.*, Warszawa 2021, p. 23-133.

interpretation is required for its application, narrowing it in order to ensure that the claim is pursued in accordance with the guarantees of constitutional standards.[936]

5. The remote hearings (meetings)

Introduced into the Polish process permanently on the basis of the Act of 7.07.2023 (J.L. of 2023, item 1860), which has been in force since 14.03.2024. Previously, it appeared as an incidental solution under the provisions of the anti-crisis shield in connection with the COVID-19 pandemic[937]. It is still the rule to hold court hearings in the court building (Article 151 § 1 of the CCP). A public hearing conducted with the use of technical devices enabling the hearing to be conducted remotely is called remote hearing, commonly referred to as online hearings. Remote meetings are scheduled (Article 151 § 2 of the CCP): - on the order of the Chairperson ex officio or at the request of the person who is to participate in the meeting and has indicated an e-mail address), - if this is not prevented by the nature of the activities to be carried out at the meeting, - if full protection of the procedural rights of the parties is guaranteed, - if the correct course of action is guaranteed.The appointment of a remote hearing must not preclude the right to attend the hearing in the courthouse. The rule should be that a party may appear in the courtroom at any time, and remote participation in the hearing is its privilege. A person taking part in a remote hearing remotely is obliged to stay at the place informed by the court, and should make every effort to ensure that the conditions of his/her stay are consistent with the dignity of the court and do not constitute an obstacle to performing procedural activities with his/her participation. Otherwise, the court may summon the person to appear in person in the courtroom. In addition to the above, the person participating in the remote meeting must meet the

---

936 A. Torbus, ekspertyza z 6.3.2019 r. na temat: *Czy projekt nowelizacji Kodeksu postępowania cywilnego pod nazwą „Ustawa o zmianie ustawy – Kodeks postępowania cywilnego oraz niektórych innych ustaw"* (druk nr 3137) pozwala zwiększyć efektywności postępowania cywilnego sporządzonej (http://www.sejm.gov.pl/sejm8.nsf/opinieBAS.xsp?nr=3137); A. Turczyn, *Nowelizacja Kodeksu postępowania cywilnego. Problemy praktyczne*, Warszawa 2020, 9. 74.

937 Act of 14 May 2020 Amending Certain Acts on Protective Measures in Connection with the Spread of the SARS-CoV-2 Virus, Dz.U. of 2020 875; during the state of epidemic threat or the state of epidemic and within 1 year of their cancellation, hearings and public hearings conducted in accordance with the Code of Civil Procedure are conducted remotely, and none of the persons have to be in the court building at that time (Article 15zzs(1) point 1 of the COVID-19 Act).

technical software standards and hardware requirements necessary to participate in the remote meeting.[938] Analyzing the above, it should be noted that despite the theoretical assumptions and obligations incumbent on the court (the nature of the proceedings, guaranteeing full protection of the procedural rights of the parties), the practical part of them (the place from which the person participating in the hearing connects, technical requirements as to the software, hardware requirements, stable access to the Internet) have been transferred to the person deciding to take part in the remote hearing. Only the right to go to the courthouse, which a person cannot be deprived of when a remote hearing is scheduled, leaves him/her with a certain possibility of guaranteeing the right to a court (the right to a fair trial) in its entirety. At the same time, the assessment of compliance with the standards is to be made by the person taking part in the meeting. Moreover, the obligation to ensure the same technical requirements and standards related to software was not mentioned by the legislator in relation to the court itself. Thus, the guarantor of the right to a court (the right to a fair trial) is a person who decides to participate remotely in a remote hearing, and not the court itself.

6. The default judgment / judgment in the absence of the defendant

Pursuant to Article 339 of the CCP, a default judgment may be issued at a closed session if the defendant has not filed a response to the statement of claim within the prescribed period. In such a case, the claimant's allegations of fact contained in the statement of claim or pleadings served on the defendant prior to the hearing shall be accepted as true, except where the claimant's allegations of fact give rise to reasonable doubt or have been relied upon in order to circumvent the law. (default judgement)

Taking into account Article 340 of the CCP, the court will issue a default judgment if, despite the failure to file a response to the statement of claim, the case has been referred for consideration at the hearing, and the defendant has not appeared at the hearing, or does not participate in it despite having appeared. In this case, the claimant's allegations of fact contained in the statement of claim or pleadings served on the defendant prior to the hearing, as well as the allegations made by the claimant at the hearing, shall also be accepted as true, except where the claimant's allegations of fact give rise to reasonable doubt or are relied upon in

---

938 Announcement Of The Minister Of Justice on the technical standards of software and hardware requirements necessary to participate in a remote meeting of 5 March 2024 (Dz.Urz.Ms Of 2024, Item 82).

order to circumvent the law. A judgment rendered in the absence of the defendant will not be in default if the defendant has requested a hearing in his absence or has already given oral or written explanations in the case. (judgment in the absence of the defendant). The default judgment has quite a long history, taking into account the Polish civil process, because it was introduced into the CCP at the time of the adoption of this law, i.e. in 1964. Nevertheless, it has undergone a kind of evolution. The regulation concerning the admission of the facts cited by the plaintiff as true was changed on the basis of the amendment of 2005 (Article 339 § 2 in the version of the Act of 2.07.2004 – Dz.U. No. 172, item 1804), which entered into force on 5.02.2005) by excluding the phrase: 'if they do not give rise to reasonable doubts as to their conformity with the true state of affairs' and replacing it with the phrase 'unless they give rise to reasonable doubts or have been relied on in order to circumvent the law'. This constituted a departure from the principle of objective truth in favor of the adversarial principle. The current form of the above judgments results from the fact that an obligatory response to a statement of claim has been introduced into the CCP (Article 205[1] § 1 of the CCP). The court may issue a default judgment at a closed session if the defendant has not filed a response to the claim within the prescribed period. Thus, the filing of a further pleading by the defendant will not affect the possibility of a default judgment. Both regulations concern the claimant's deliberate passivity. The manner in which they are specified does not give rise to any wider discussions or doubts from the point of view of the principle of the right to a court (the right to a fair trial), because the defendant is not deprived of it and also because he does not intentionally participate in the proceedings of which he has knowledge. According to the uniform line of case-law in this area, no evidence is taken in the issuance of a default judgment, except where the claimant's allegations give rise to reasonable doubts or have been relied on in order to circumvent the law. On the other hand, the presumption of truth of the claimant's allegations contained in Article 339 § 2 of the CCP applies only to the factual side of the case, and not to the merits of the claim in terms of substantive law. The court is always obliged to examine whether the plaintiff's claim is consistent with the applicable provisions of substantive law, and in this matter the case law has been uniform for years. Taking into account the key aspects of the default judgment, namely: - a regulation that a judgment rendered in the absence of the defendant will not be in default if the defendant has requested a hearing in his absence or has already given oral or written explanations in the case, - issuance of it under the terms of a default judgment reserved, - optionality in the issuance of the judgment, not its obligatory nature, - the obligation to serve the judgment ex officio on both parties, - grounds for setting aside a default judgment after it has been issued due to the defendant's lack of capacity to bring proceedings, or the lack of a body appointed to represent the defendant at the time of filing the lawsuit, - the possibility of objecting, - proceeding after filing an objection. It should be pointed out that the principle of the right to a fair trial in question appears to be implemented in a complementary and comprehensive manner in the case of that institution.

7. Summary

One of the conclusions that can be drawn from the analysis is that the so-called "oldest" institutions of civil procedure are of the nature that most closely implements the principle of the right to a court t(he right to a fair trial). On the one hand, the time of their functioning in the procedure allowed them to take root. What is important, however, is that following the legislative changes in the scope of their creation did not mean revolutionary changes, but evolutionary ones. Man evolves, and with him evolve the rules by which he lives. The legal system is a very delicate matter, it is basically a living organism, because it is related to living people. The law has a servile function towards man, it allows him to create a world in which I know how to behave and I can expect the same from others. Variability in the law should be carried out in an extremely prudent manner, with a certain amount of restraint, because the range of consequences that flow from sudden, particular changes is almost unpredictable. Absolutely making changes in the law by introducing new normative solutions requires respect for the well-established principles of a democratic state governed by the rule of law. The above is the foundation, the starting point for making any amendments. So let's hurry up slowly in changing the law.

Bibliography

Błaszczak Ł., Powództwo oczywiście bezzasadne – art. 1911 k.p.c., Warszawa 2021.

Gapska E., Przeciwdziałanie nadużyciom prawa procesowego w znowelizowanym Kodeksie postępowania cywilnego. Cz. II – Powództwo oczywiście bezzasadne, MOP 2019, Nr 16, Legalis 2019.

Garlicki L., Prawo do sądu [w:] Prawa człowieka. Model prawny, red. R.Wieruszewski, Wrocław 1991.

Góra – Błaszczykowska A., Zasada równości stron w procesie cywilnym, Warszawa 2008.

Jodłowski J., Resich Z., Postępowanie cywilne, Warszawa 1987.

Kamieński G., [w:] Komentarz do KPC, (red.) E. Marszałkowska – Krześ, komentarz do art. 1911 KPC, Legalis 2021.

Kunicki I. [w:] Komentarz do KPC, (red.) A. Góra – Błaszczykowska, komentarz do art. 1911 KPC, Legalis 2020.

Paradowski P., [w:] Postępowanie cywilne po nowelizacji. Komentarz dla pełnomocników procesowych i sędziów, Karolczyk B. (red.), Warszawa 2020.

Plebanek M.G., Nadużycie praw procesowych w postępowaniu cywilnym – zagadnienia ogólne, SP 2012, zeszyt 1 (190).

Rzewuski M. (red.), Postępowanie cywilne, Warszawa 2020.

Studzińska J., Cioch P., Postępowanie cywilne, Warszawa 2017.

Szanciło T. (red.), Komentarz do KPC, Legalis 2019.

Torbus A., ekspertyza z 6.3.2019 r. na temat: Czy projekt nowelizacji Kodeksu postępowania cywilnego pod nazwą „Ustawa o zmianie ustawy – Kodeks postępowania cywilnego oraz niektórych innych ustaw" (druk nr 3137) pozwala zwiększyć efektywności postępowania cywilnego sporządzonej (http://www.sejm.gov.pl/sejm8.nsf/opinieBAS.xsp?nr=3137).

Turczyn A., Nowelizacja Kodeksu postępowania cywilnego. Problemy praktyczne, Warszawa 2020.

Żak M., Prawo do sądu jako element zasady dobrego rządzenia w świetle orzecznictwa z zakresu praw człowieka, Palestra 2/2020, www.palestra.pl.

Ewa Pietrzak[939], Dominika Kuna[940]

Is the right to labour strike a fundamental human right?

Abstract: The strike is among the basic means of trade union protection of employees' interests. Without the right to strike, employees would often be unable to obtain certain concessions from employers. The right to strike derives from a number of international documents, including: the Charter of Fundamental Rights of the European Union, the European Social Charter, the International Covenant on Economic, Social and Cultural Rights, International Labour Organisation Convention No. 87 concerning Freedom of Association and Protection of the Right to Organise. The right to strike is guaranteed by the Constitution of the Republic of Poland. Pursuant to Article 59 point 3 of the Constitution, trade unions have the right to organise labour strikes and other forms of protest within the limits set by law. For the sake of the public good, a law may restrict the conduct of a strike or prohibit it with respect to certain categories of workers or in certain areas. In Polish law the rules for conducting a strike are regulated in the Act of May 23, 1991 on the Resolution of Collective Disputes. Pursuant to the aforementioned Act, a strike is a measure of last resort and cannot be declared without first exhausting peaceful means of resolving the dispute, i.e. bargaining and mediation. This article addresses the issue whether the right to strike can be considered as a human right, and if so, whether it is a fundamental right.

Keywords: human rights, fundamental human rights, the right to strike, collective disputes, conditions for the legality of a strike, trade unions

1. Introduction

Human rights are the basis for civil society and for ensuring that the state acts properly towards its citizens. Guaranteeing non-negotiable rights is the responsibility of the state. However, the changing perception of society and the ongoing transformation of human life require a reflection on the catalogue of human rights and the respective roles of its components.

The labour strike is one of the basic means of trade union protection of employees' interests. Without the right to strike, employees would often be unable to obtain

939 SWPS University, ORCID: 0009-0006-5192-511X.
940 SWPS University, ORCID: 0000-0002-6668-9811.

certain concessions from employers[941]. The subject of the nature of the right to strike and its relation to human rights raises many questions[942]. The first controversy that arises in relation to the right to strike is whether this right is a human right. If the answer to this question is positive, it is necessary to consider whether the right to strike can be regarded as a fundamental human right. This doubt is related to the numerous restrictions imposed on the right to strike in both international law and Polish law. It is also relevant to ascertain to what extent the right to strike is related to the other human rights mentioned in the referenced acts. In addition, it is challenging to derive criteria that would determinate the nature of the right to strike from other rights.

The aim of this article is to analyse the legal regulation of strikes in international and Polish law with particular reference to the scope of restrictions imposed on the right to strike. Consequently, the authors will attempt to answer the question of whether the aforementioned right can be considered as an actual human right, and if so, whether it is a fundamental right. This article will refer only to labour strikes. Outside the scope of consideration are strikes in the broad sense as any acts of civil disobedience. Consideration of the right to strike as a (fundamental) human right can be used for further analysis in the context of a changing catalogue of human rights.

2. The concept of human rights

Human rights are fundamental norms to which all people are equally entitled. It should be emphasised that human rights are universal, inalienable and indivisible. Whether civil, political, economic, social or cultural, they derive from inherent dignity of every human being, therefore there is no hierarchy of human rights and they all have the same status. On the other hand, however, there are views that directly point to a certain order of human rights: „Socio-economic rights and collective rights do not have the same status as civil and political rights in international law. They are usually included in supplementary international documents,

---

941 M. Kurzynoga, *Warunki legalności strajku*, Warszawa 2011, LEX el - see https://sip-1lex-1pl-1yjgbbt2f021a.waw-proxlib.swps.edu.pl/#/monograph/369232926/23/kurzynoga-malgorzata-warunki-legalnosci-strajku?keyword=Warunki%20legalno%C5%9Bci%20strajku%20Kurzynoga&cm=STOP (access: 6.06.2024).

942 J. A. L. García, "The right to strike as a fundamental human right: recognition and limitations in international law", *Revista Chilena de Derecho*, 44/3 (2017), pp. 781-783; R. Mthombeni, "The Right or Freedom to Strike: An Analysis from an International and Comparative Perspective", *the Comparative and International Law Journal of Southern Africa*, 23/3 (1990), pp. 337-340.

are ratified by fewer states and are subject to states' economic constraints"[943]. For some years now, there have been statements among human rights and its effectiveness that it is moving through a process of transformation from a catalogue of immutable fundamental rights to an expanded catalogue of new rights. In the opinion of the current Minister of Justice (former Ombudsman) Adam Bodnar, the purpose of this change is not to strengthen guarantees, but to profoundly transform society[944]. Reflecting on the transformations that are occurring in society does not insignificantly affect our perception of the fundamental guarantee of rights protection.

Human rights are divided into three generations. First generation rights are the civil and political rights. They guarantee the freedom of the individual from interference by the authorities and protect the freedom of autonomy of the individual. Those rights are for example the right to life, equality before the law, freedom of speech, freedom of religion. Second generation rights are socio-economic rights. They refer to work, medical care, standard of living. Third generation rights are collective or solidarity rights, for example the right of nations to self-determination, to develop their own culture, to the protection of the environment, to economic development[945].

Human rights can only be restricted in strictly defined situations, indicated in international documents or state constitutions. The necessity to restrict human rights is connected with the conflicts that arise between them. A method for resolving conflicts of human rights and assessing the permissible degree of limitations to them is the principle of proportionality[946].

It is argued in the literature that, with regard to human rights issues, the Council of Europe system is currently the most developed in Europe. At the core of this system stands the European Convention for the Protection of Human Rights and Fundamental Freedoms[947] (hereinafter also: "ECHR"). The provisions of ECHR as interpreted by the European Court of Human Rights (hereinafter

943 M. A. Chicktay, "Placing the right to strike within a human rights framework", *Orbiter*, 27/2, (2006), p. 344.

944 https://www.rp.pl/opinie-prawne/art1265301-adam-bodnar-i-wewnetrzna-rewolucja-praw-czlowieka-komentuje-jerzy-kwasniewski (accessed: 6.06.2024).

945 T. Jurczyk, "Geneza rozwoju praw człowieka", *Homines Hominibus*, 1 /5 (2009), p. 42; M. A. Chicktay, *op. cit.*, p. 344.

946 M. Michalska, "Proportionality as the Tool for Adjudicating Conflicts of Fundamental Rights – Criticism and Retort", *Krytyka Prawa*, tom 11/2 (2019), pp. 255-258.

947 The European Convention for the Protection of Human Rights and Fundamental Freedoms of November 4 1950 (Dz.U. (*Journal of Laws*) of 1993, No 61, item 284 as amended: https://isap.sejm.gov.pl/isap.nsf/download.xsp/WDU19930610284/T/D19930284L.pdf).

also: "ECtHR") have a significant impact on the level of human rights protection in all European countries[948]. It must be noted that ECtHR has developed the "living instrument" interpretative approach towards ECHR. It means that the ECtHR considers that the understanding of ECHR rights is subject to change and development. Therefore, in order to provide effective protection of human rights, the interpretation of ECHR should be constantly revised in order to be up to date with contemporary advancements and shifts in the attitudes that are prevalent in society[949].

3. The right to strike – general remarks and definition

The right to strike derives from many international documents adopted by various bodies and institutions. Those documents include the European Convention for the Protection of Human Rights and Fundamental Freedoms, the European Social Charter[950], the International Covenant on Economic, Social and Cultural Rights[951], the Charter of Fundamental Rights of the European Union[952] as well as Conventions adopted by the International Labour Organisation. What is more, the right to strike occupies an important position in Polish law. First of all, the right to strike is guaranteed by the Constitution of the Republic of Poland[953] (hereinafter also: "the Constitution"). The specific rules of conducting strikes are regulated in the Act on the Resolution of Collective Disputes[954] (hereinafter also: "RCD").

948 T. Jurczyk, "Geneza rozwoju praw człowieka", *Homines Hominibus*, 1 /5 (2009), p. 43.

949 S. Theil, "Is the Living Instrument Approach of the European Court of Human Rights Compatible with the ECHR and International Law?", *European Public Law*, 23/3 (2017), pp. 587-614.

950 The European Social Charter of October 18, 1961 (Dz.U. (*Journal of Laws*) of 1999, No 8, item 67 as amended: https://isap.sejm.gov.pl/isap.nsf/download.xsp/WDU19990080067/T/D19990067L.pdf).

951 The International Covenant on Economic, Social and Cultural Rights of December 19, 1966 adopted and opened for signature, ratification and accession by General Assembly resolution 2200A (XXI) of December 16, 1966: https://www.ohchr.org/sites/default/files/cescr.pdf).

952 The Charter of Fundamental Rights of the European Union of December 7, 2000 (2007/C 303/01) (Dz.Urz. UE (*Journal of Laws of the European Union*) C No 303, p. 1 as amended: https://eur-lex.europa.eu/legal-content/EN/TXT/PDF/?uri=CELEX:12012P/TXT).

953 The Constitution of the Republic of Poland of April 2, 1997 (Dz.U. (*Journal of Laws*) No 78, item 483) as amended: https://www.sejm.gov.pl/prawo/konst/polski/kon1.htm).

954 The Act of May 23, 1991 on the Resolution of Collective Disputes (Tekst jedn. (*Uniform text*) Dz.U. (*Journal of Laws*) of 2020 item 123 as amended: https://isap.sejm.gov.pl/isap.nsf/download.xsp/WDU19910550236/U/D19910236Lj.pdf).

In literature a strike is defined as "a situation where workers refrain from work, without their readiness to perform the work"[955]. It is a non-irenic method of resolution of labour disputes as its goal is for the workers' collective to put organisational, economic or psychological pressure on the employer[956]. It should be emphasised, that a strike is collective employee conduct. By the same token, a strike cannot be an action taken individually, even if its purpose is to defend collective rights and interests[957]. In literature the following features of a strike are indicated, namely: 1) it is collective action by workers 2) consisting in abstention from work, 3) undertaken in order to change or preserve workers' collective rights and freedoms or their professional, economic and social interests, as well as trade union rights and freedoms[958].

Polish law foresees a legal definition of a strike. According to art. 17 point 1 of RCD, a strike consists of collective abstention of employees from carrying out work in order to resolve a dispute concerning interests indicated in art. 1 RCD (the conditions of work, pay or social benefits, as well as the liberties and freedom of association rights of employees and other groups entitled to associate in trade unions).

4. The right to strike in international law

Starting from the documents of the Council of Europe, the right to strike is directly foreseen in the European Social Charter that protects social rights[959]. According to its art. 6 point 4, in order to ensure the effective exercise of the right to collective bargaining, the Contracting Parties recognise the right of workers and employers

955 K. W. Baran, "Principles of Collective Labour Law" in *Principles of Polish Labour Law*, ed. K. W. Baran, Warszawa 2018, Legalis el. (accessed: 6.06.2024); see also J. Żołyński, "Prawo do akcji protestacyjnych w dokumentach prawa międzynarodowego" in *System Prawa Pracy. Tom IX. Międzynarodowe publiczne prawo pracy. Standardy globalne*, ed. K. W. Baran, Warszawa 2019, Lex el. (accessed: 6.06.2024); J. Żołyński, "Prawo pracowników do strajku - prawo naturalne czy prawo pozytywne?", *Praca i Zabezpieczenie Społeczne*, 10 (2015), p. 13; M. Kurzynoga, *Warunki legalności strajku*, op.cit.; J. Oniszczuk, "Nieireniczne metody likwidowania sporów zbiorowych" in *System Prawa Pracy. Tom V. Zbiorowe prawo pracy*, ed. K. W. Baran, Warszawa 2014, Lex el. (accessed: 6.06.2024).

956 K. W. Baran, "Principles of Collective Labour Law", *op.cit.*

957 M. Kurzynoga, *Warunki legalności strajku, op.cit.*

958 M. Kurzynoga, *Warunki legalności strajku, op.cit.*; A. M. Świątkowski, „Strajk – synteza zjawiska", *Monitor Prawa Pracy*, 2 (2011), p. 68.

959 T. Jurczyk, Geneza rozwoju praw człowieka, Homines Hominibus No. 1 (5), 2009, pp. 38, 39.

to act collectively in the event of a conflict of interest, including the right to strike, subject to any obligations that might arise from previously concluded collective agreements. the European Social Charter is a document devoted to the protection of socio-economic rights[960].

On the other hand, the right to strike is not directly indicated in the European Convention for the Protection of Human Rights and Fundamental Freedoms. However, it is indirectly derived from art. 11 ECHR that foresees the freedom of assembly and association[961]. According to this article everyone has the right to freedom of peaceful assembly and to freedom of association with others, including the right to form and to join trade unions for the protection of his interests. In § 36 of the judgment in the case of Schmidt and Dahlström v. Sweden[962] ECtHR stated that: "the Convention safeguards freedom to protect the occupational interests of trade union members by trade union action, the conduct and development of which the Contracting States must both permit and make possible (National Union of Belgian Police judgment, 27 October 1975, Series A no. 19, p. 18, para. 39). Article 11 para. 1 (art. 11-1) nevertheless leaves each State a free choice of the means to be used towards this end. The grant of a right to strike represents without any doubt one of the most important of these means, but there are others. Such a right, which is not expressly enshrined in Article 11 (art. 11), may be subject under national law to regulation of a kind that limits its exercise in certain instances"[963]. In later judgments ECtHR used a dynamic interpretation of the ECHR and shared the International Labour Organisation's view that the right to strike could be interpreted from the right of association[964]. In case of Enerji v. Turkey[965] ECtHR stated that "§ 24. (…) Strike action, which allows a trade union to express its position, is an important aspect for trade union members in protecting their interests (see Schmidt and Dahlström, cited above, § 36).

---

960 J. A. L. García, *op. cit.*, p. 792; Ö. Edström, *The Right to Collective Action – in Particular the Right to Strike – as a Fundamental Right*, 2011, pp. 61-63.

961 M. Kurzynoga, *Warunki legalności strajku*, op.cit.; M. Kurzynoga, "Prawo do wszczęcia sporu zbiorowego oraz prawo do akcji zbiorowych osób zarobkowo wykonujących pracę niebędących pracownikami", *Monitor Prawa Pracy*, 12 (2014), p. 622.

962 The ruling of the European Court of Human Rights, Case of Schmidt and Dahlstrőm v. Sweden, Application no. 5589/72, February 6, 1976.

963 A. Reda-Ciszewska, "Prawo do strajku w świetle Konwencji o Ochronie Praw Człowieka i Podstawowych Wolności", *Studia Prawno-ekonomiczne*, XCV (2015), p. 106.

964 A. Reda-Ciszewska, *op. cit.*, p. 113.

965 The ruling of the European Court of Human Rights, Case of Enerji v. Turkey, Application no. 68959/01, April 21, 2009.

The Court also notes that the right to strike is recognised by the supervisory bodies of the International Labour Organisation (ILO) as an inherent corollary of the right to organise in trade unions protected by ILO Convention No. 87 concerning Freedom of Association and Protection of the Right to Organise (for the Court's consideration of elements of international law other than the Convention, see Demir and Baykara, cited above). It points out that the European Social Charter also recognises the right to strike as a means of ensuring the effective exercise of the right to collective bargaining"[966].

The right to strike is directly foreseen in the International Covenant on Economic, Social and Cultural Rights by the General Assembly of the United Nations. According to art. 8 point 1 d) of the Covenant, the States Parties to the Covenant undertake to provide the right to strike provided that it is exercised in accordance with the legislation of the relevant country. This article shall not prevent the imposition of restrictions in accordance with the law on the exercise of these rights by members of the armed forces, police or state administration (art. 8 point 1 of the Covenant). The Covenant classifies the right to strike as an economic right[967].

In the European Union legislation, the first document that directly referred to the right to strike was the Community Charter of the Fundamental Social Rights of Workers, followed by the Charter of Fundamental Rights of the European Union. The right to strike is mentioned in Chapter IV of the Charter "Solidarity". According to art. 28 of the Charter, workers and employers, or their respective organisations, have, in accordance with Union law and national laws and practices, the right to negotiate and conclude collective agreements at the appropriate levels and, in cases of conflict of interest, to take collective action, including strike action, to defend their interests. However, even though the Charter considers the right to strike as the fundamental right, at the same time, it allows for limitation of this right. In doing so it refers to the rule of proportionality[968]. Namely, according to art. 52 point 1 of the Charter, any limitation on the exercise of the rights and freedoms recognised in this Charter must be provided for by law and respect the essence of those rights and freedoms. Subject to the principle of proportionality, limitations may be made only if they are necessary and genuinely meet objectives of general interest recognised by the Union or the need to protect the rights and freedoms of others. The importance of the Charter of Fundamental Rights of the European

966 A. Reda-Ciszewska, *op. cit.*, pp. 107-113; J. A. L. García, *op. cit.*, pp. 788-792; Ö. Edström, *op. cit.*, pp. 63-66.

967 M. Kurzynoga, *Warunki legalności strajku*, *op.cit.*; J. Żołyński, "Prawo do akcji protestacyjnych w dokumentach prawa międzynarodowego", *op. cit.*

968 Ö. Edström, *op. cit.*, p. 67.

Union is underlined in the Treaty on the European Union[969] (also referred to as: "TUE"). According to art. 6 point 1 TUE, the Union recognises the rights, freedoms and principles set out in the Charter of Fundamental Rights of the European Union, which shall have the same legal value as the Treaties. The provisions of the Charter shall not extend in any way the competences of the Union as defined in the Treaties[970]. It also must be noted that TUE refers to the European Convention for the Protection of Human Rights and Fundamental Freedoms indicating that fundamental rights, as guaranteed by the Convention and as they result from the constitutional traditions common to the Member States, shall constitute general principles of the Union's law (art. 6 point 3 TUE). Also the Court of Justice of the European Union recognises the right to strike as a fundamental right[971].

The right to strike is not directly mention in the Conventions adopted by the International Labour Organisation. It is derived from the Convention No 87 concerning Freedom of Association and Protection of the Right to Organise[972] and Convention No 98 on Right to Organise and Collective Bargaining[973]. The Committee of Experts on the Application of Conventions and Recommendations and the Committee on Freedom of Association stated that the strike is one of the essential means by which workers and their organisations can promote and defend their economic and social interests[974]. It is emphasised that it makes it one of the fundamental human rights and trade union freedoms[975].

---

969 Consolidated version of the Treaty on the European Union (Official Journal of the European Union C 326/15, https://eur-lex.europa.eu/resource.html?uri=cellar:2bf140bf-a3f8-4ab2-b506-fd71826e6da6.0023.02/DOC_1&format=PDF).

970 Ö. Edström, *op. cit.*, p. 68.

971 Ö. Edström, *op. cit.*, pp. 69-72.

972 Convention No 87 of the International Labour Organisation concerning Freedom of Association and Protection of the Right to Organise of July 9, 1948 (https://normlex.ilo.org/dyn/normlex/en/f?p=NORMLEXPUB:12100:0::NO::P12100_INSTRUMENT_ID:312232).

973 Convention No 98 of the International Labour Organisation on Right to Organise and Collective Bargaining of July 1, 1949 (https://normlex.ilo.org/dyn/normlex/en/f?p=NORMLEXPUB:12100:0::NO::P12100_INSTRUMENT_ID:312243); Ö. Edström, *op. cit.*, p. 58.

974 M. Kurzynoga, *Warunki legalności strajku*, op.cit.; M. Kurzynoga, "Prawo do wszczęcia sporu zbiorowego oraz prawo do akcji zbiorowych osób zarobkowo wykonujących pracę niebędących pracownikami", *op. cit.*, p. 622; Ö. Edström, *op. cit.*, p. 59.

975 J. A. L. García, *op. cit.*, pp. 783-788; J. Żołyński, "Prawo do akcji protestacyjnych w dokumentach prawa międzynarodowego", *op. cit.*; M. Kurzynoga, *Warunki legalności strajku*, *op. cit.*; A. M. Świątkowski, *op. cit.*, p. 69; R. Mthombeni, *op. cit.*, pp. 340-342.

An analysis of the provisions of international law relating to the right to strike shows that this right is categorised as a socio-economic right. It must be noted, that notwithstanding the fact that in the international law the right to strike is considered as human right, it is not understood as absolute freedom of trade union action. This is a right that certainly cannot be exercised in an unrestricted manner, as it would jeopardise other human rights. For example, the right to strike is in conflict with other rights, such as the employer's right to conduct his profit-oriented business and his right to property as well as the right of employees to provide work for remuneration[976]. As a result this right is subject to limitations or even may be prohibited in certain situations[977].

5. The right to strike in Polish law

According to article 59 point 3 of the Constitution, trade unions have the right to organise labour strikes and other forms of protest within the limits set by law. However, for the sake of the public good, a law may restrict the conduct of a strike or even prohibit it with respect to certain categories of employees or in certain areas. The aforementioned provision is included in Chapter II of the Constitution entitled: Freedoms, rights and duties of human beings and citizens, in the section: Political freedoms and rights.

From the wording of article 59 point 3 of the Constitution as well as its position in Chapter II of the Constitution the following conclusions should be made. First of all, the Constitution explicitly grants the right to organise labour strikes only to trade unions. Therefore, other subjects are not entitled to organise strikes. What is more, the Constitution defines the right to organise strike as a political freedom and right as opposed to personal freedoms and rights as well as economic, social and cultural freedoms and rights mentioned in Chapter II of the Constitution. As a result, in Polish law the right to strike is not qualified as an economic or social right. However, according to the Constitution, all human and civil rights and freedoms foreseen therein derive form human dignity. According to art. 30 of the Constitution, the inherent and inalienable dignity of the human being is the source of human and civil liberties and rights. It is inviolable and its respect and protection is the duty of public authorities.

Finally, the right to organise a strike is subject to various limitations. First of all, the first sentence of article 59 point 3 of the Constitution refers to the limits set

976 J. Żołyński, "Prawo pracowników do strajku - prawo naturalne czy prawo pozytywne?", *op. cit.*, p. 13.

977 M. Kurzynoga, *Warunki legalności strajku, op.cit.*

by law. The second sentence of this article mentions restrictions or even prohibitions of the right to strike with respect to certain categories of employees or in certain areas. The grounds for those limitations is the public good. What is more, according to art. 233 point 3 of the Constitution the right to strike may be limited by an act defining the scope of restrictions on human and civil liberties and rights in a state of natural disaster. Finally, the right to organise a strike may be subject to limitations mentioned in art. 31 point 3 of the Constitution that refers to all the freedoms and rights indicated therein. According to this article, restrictions on the exercise of constitutional freedoms and rights may only be established by law and only if they are necessary in a democratic state for its security or public order, or for the protection of the environment, public health and morals, or the freedoms and rights of others. Such limitations may not impair the essence of the freedoms and rights.

Limits of the right to strike mentioned in article 59 point 3 of the Constitution are regulated in RCD. This act foresees various restrictions. First of all, it indicates categories of employees that are not allowed to participate in a labour strike and the areas where labour strike is prohibited. Namely, it is not permitted to cease work as a result of strike action on work posts, equipment and installations where the cessation of work threatens human life or health, or the security of state (art. 19 point 1 of RCD). It is also not permitted to organise a strike at the Internal Security Agency, the Intelligence Agency, the Military Counterintelligence Service, the Military Intelligence Service, the Central Anti-Corruption Bureau, in units of the Police and the Polish Armed Forces, the Prison Service, the Border Guard, the Customs Service and the organisational units of the fire service (art. 19 point 2 RCD). The employees employed in state authorities, state administration and local governments, in courts and prosecutor's offices do not have the right to strike (art. 19 point 3 RCD)[978].

What is more, RCD foresees the conditions for the strike to be legal. First of all, a strike can only be organised by a trade union. A strike declared by a strike committee designated by employees outside structures of a trade union is illegal[979]. However, the literature points out that the trade union monopoly on strike organisation is not a drastic restriction on the right to organise strikes due to the liberal requirements imposed by the provisions of the trade union act concerning the formation of trade unions[980]. What is more, the legality of the strike depends on

978 A. M. Świątkowski, *op. cit.*, p. 71; K. W. Baran, "Principles of Collective Labour Law", *op.cit.*

979 K. W. Baran, "Principles of Collective Labour Law", *op.cit.*

980 A. M. Świątkowski, *op. cit.*, p. 71.

the compliance of the party representing the workers with the statutory procedure for the conduct of collective action[981]. A strike is a measure of last resort and cannot be declared without first exhausting so called peaceful means of resolving the dispute. Those means are negotiations (art. 7-9 RCD) and mediation (art. 10-14 RCD). In order to start a collective dispute first the trade union should make a so-called dispute notification, i.e. submit demands to the employer on the matters indicated in art. 1 RCD (the conditions of work, pay or social benefits, the liberties and freedom of association rights). The collective dispute exists as of the day on which the entity representing the employees' interests makes demands to the employer, where the employer fails to satisfy all the demands within specified the deadline, which cannot be shorter than three days. The dispute notification should specify the scope of the demands under dispute. The party notifying the dispute may issue a warning that, if the submitted demands are not met, then a strike will be announced. The date chosen for the strike cannot be earlier than after 14 days from the notification of dispute (art. 7 RCD). The notification of the dispute is important for the assessment of the legality of the strike due to the principle of identity of the demands covered by the dispute. A strike cannot be justified by demands that are not included in the notification of the dispute, as well as demands on which negotiations ended with the signing of an agreement[982].

If the employer fails to satisfy all the demands within the aforementioned deadline, the employer is obliged to start negotiations, and when these do not lead to a settlement, mediation should be undertaken, which is conducted with the participation of a mediator (that is a person ensuring impartiality). In the course of negotiations and mediation the parties may sign an agreement. If the parties do not reach a settlement respectively negotiations or mediation are closed by signing a protocol of differences. If the course of mediation proceedings justifies a conclusion that it will not lead to resolving the dispute before the lapse of the deadline of 14 days from the notification of the dispute the trade union may organize a warning strike that cannot last longer than two hours. It must be emphasised that it is only the failure to reach an agreement resolving the dispute in mediation proceedings that entitles a trade union to take strike action. The signing of a protocol of differences closing the mediation is a condition for the lawful continuation of the dispute.

981 M. Kurzynoga, *Warunki legalności strajku, op.cit.*; K. W. Baran, "Principles of Collective Labour Law", *op.cit.*

982 Judgment of the Supreme Court - Chamber of Labour, Social Security and Public Affairs of February 7, 2007, I PK 209/06, LEX nr 280749.

If the trade union decides to organise a company strike, the possibility of its announcement depends on the consent of the majority of the voting employees in the so-called strike referendum, if at least 50% of the employees of the workplace participated in the vote. The announcement of a strike may take place only after the referendum and at least 5 days prior to the start of the strike (art. 20 point 1 and 3 RCD). A trade union cannot organise a strike without the decision of the eligible employees. Due to the express conditionality of declaring a strike on the consent of the workers voting, organising and conducting the referendum in a way that allows the workers to freely express their will (e.g. by putting pressure on the voters or falsifying the results) is an essential condition for the legality of the strike, which is subject to judicial review[983].

In Polish literature and case law, the right to strike is qualified as fundamental human right[984]. For example, the Polish Supreme Court stated that „The right to strike is one of the fundamental human rights and trade union freedoms. Therefore, doubts relating to the interpretation of strike regulations should - in accordance with the principle in *dubio pro libertate* - be resolved in favour of and not against the freedom to strike"[985]. However, the opinion was also expressed that under Polish law the right to strike should not be included among fundamental human rights and trade union freedoms[986]. It is argued that the right to strike cannot be identified with the right to organise strikes. The latter has been granted exclusively to trade unions by art. 59 point 3 of the Constitution. Whereas the right to strike as such is not guaranteed in the Constitution and it is derived *a contrario* from art. 19 point 3 RCD ("The employees employed in state authorities, state administration and local governments, in courts and prosecutor's offices do not have the right to strike")[987].

6. Right to strike as a fundamental human right – conclusions

The analysis of the provisions of international law and Polish law shows that the right to strike is considered as a human right. The authors of this article share the view expressed in the literature that despite the fact that the right to strike has been recognised as a human right in both international and national law, the

983 Judgment of the Supreme Court - Chamber of Labour, Social Security and Public Affairs of February 7, 2007, I PK 209/06, LEX nr 280749.

984 M. Kurzynoga, *Warunki legalności strajku, op.cit.*

985 Judgment of the Supreme Court - Chamber of Labour, Social Security and Public Affairs of February 7, 2007, I PK 209/06, LEX nr 280749.

986 A. M. Świątkowski, *op. cit.*, pp. 71-72.

987 A. M. Świątkowski, *op. cit.*, p. 73.

manner in which this right has been acknowledged does not define the extent of the right[988]. In international documents that have been analysed in this article the right to strike is considered as a socio-economic right. On the other hand, the Polish Constitution qualifies the right to organise strikes as a political right and not the economic one. Nevertheless, it is generally accepted that the right to strike is subject to limitations, which makes it "a very particular form of human right"[989].

On the other hand, the issue whether the right to strike is a fundamental human right is very complex. Recognising this right as a fundamental right has significant consequences. It gives rise to a number of obligations on the part of the state to ensure that this right is properly protected, which may be the reason for abandoning this approach. What is more, the collision of the right to strike with other rights, such as the right to conduct business, the right to property, the right to work or the right to remuneration, results in numerous restrictions of strike. The extent of the limitations may raise doubts as to whether indeed the right to strike should be treated as a fundamental right and placed in the same position as, for example, the right to life.

It seems that the only international document that explicitly considers the right to strike as a fundamental right is the Charter of Fundamental Rights of the European Union. The rights indicated in the Charter have gained particular importance due to the fact that TUE gave the Charter the same legal value as the Treaties (art. 6 point 1 TUE). However, the right to strike is also regarded as a fundamental human right by ECtHR and International Labour Organisation[990]. Also the Polish Supreme Court directly perceives it as a fundamental human right[991].

It must be emphasised that it is very challenging to identify criteria for qualifying a certain right as a fundamental human right. It appears that the starting point should be the human dignity. What is more, the right to strike may be perceived as a specific form of fulfilment of other fundamental rights. It is first and foremost an expression of economic, social, political freedom, it is the activation of communities, an opportunity to express one's dissent, civil disobedience anchored in populist political-philosophical thought. A strike is the main measure of protection of workers' interest. Consequently, without guaranteeing this right, it might be impossible to obtain concessions from the employer[992].

988 J. A. L. García, *op. cit.*, p. 783.
989 J. A. L. García, *op. cit.*, p. 801.
990 Ö. Edström, *op. cit.*, p. 74.
991 Judgment of the Supreme Court - Chamber of Labour, Social Security and Public Affairs of February 7, 2007, I PK 209/06, LEX nr 280749.
992 M. Kurzynoga, *Warunki legalności strajku, op.cit.*

From the above considerations, it appears that there are many arguments in favour of recognising the right to strike as a fundamental human right. This issue should be the subject of further substantive analysis especially in relation to a specific society, taking into account historical aspects and the current socio-political situation.

Bibliography

Baran K. W., "Principles of Collective Labour Law" in *Principles of Polish Labour Law*, ed. K. W. Baran, Warszawa 2018, Legalis el. (accessed: 6.06.2024).

Chicktay M. A., "Placing the right to strike within a human rights framework", *Orbiter*, 27/2, (2006).

Edström Ö., *The Right to Collective Action – in Particular the Right to Strike – as a Fundamental Right*, 2011.

García J. A. L., "The right to strike as a fundamental human right: recognition and limitations in international law", *Revista Chilena de Derecho*, 44/3 (2017).

Jurczyk T., "Geneza rozwoju praw człowieka", *Homines Hominibus*, 1 /5 (2009).

Kurzynoga M., *Warunki legalności strajku*, Warszawa 2011, LEX el (accessed: 6.06.2024).

Kurzynoga M., "Prawo do wszczęcia sporu zbiorowego oraz prawo do akcji zbiorowych osób zarobkowo wykonujących pracę niebędących pracownikami", *Monitor Prawa Pracy*, 12 (2014).

https://www.rp.pl/opinie-prawne/art1265301-adam-bodnar-i-wewnetrzna-rewolucja-praw-czlowieka-komentuje-jerzy-kwasniewski (accessed: 6.06.2024).

Michalska M., "Proportionality as the Tool for Adjudicating Conflicts of Fundamental Rights – Criticism and Retort", *Krytyka Prawa*, tom 11/2 (2019).

Mthombeni R., "The Right or Freedom to Strike: An Analysis from an International and Comparative Perspective", *the Comparative and International Law Journal of Southern Africa*, 23/3 (1990).

Oniszczuk J., "Nieireniczne metody likwidowania sporów zbiorowych" in *System Prawa Pracy. Tom V. Zbiorowe prawo pracy*, ed. K. W. Baran, Warszawa 2014, Lex el. (accessed: 6.06.2024).

Reda-Ciszewska A., ″Prawo do strajku w świetle Konwencji o Ochronie Praw Człowieka i Podstawowych Wolności", *Studia Prawno-ekonomiczne*, XCV (2015).

Theil S., "Is the Living Instrument Approach of the European Court of Human Rights Compatible with the ECHR and International Law?", *European Public Law*, 23/3 (2017).

Świątkowski, A. M. „Strajk – synteza zjawiska", *Monitor Prawa Pracy*, 2 (2011).

Żołyński J., "Prawo do akcji protestacyjnych w dokumentach prawa międzynarodowego" in *System Prawa Pracy. Tom IX. Międzynarodowe publiczne prawo pracy. Standardy globalne*, ed. K. W. Baran, Warszawa 2019, Lex el. (accessed: 6.06.2024).

Żołyński J., "Prawo pracowników do strajku - prawo naturalne czy prawo pozytywne?", *Praca i Zabezpieczenie Społeczne*, 10 (2015).

Acts of law

The Constitution of the Republic of Poland of April 2, 1997 (Dz.U. (*Journal of Laws*) No 78, item 483) as amended: https://www.sejm.gov.pl/prawo/konst/polski/kon1.htm).

The Act of May 23, 1991 on the Resolution of Collective Disputes (Tekst jedn. (*Uniform text*) Dz.U. (*Journal of Laws*) of 2020 item 123 as amended: https://isap.sejm.gov.pl/isap.nsf/download.xsp/WDU19910550236/U/D19910236Lj.pdf).

The European Convention for the Protection of Human Rights and Fundamental Freedoms of November 4 1950 (Dz.U. (*Journal of Laws*) of 1993, No 61, item 284 as amended: https://isap.sejm.gov.pl/isap.nsf/download.xsp/WDU19930610284/T/D19930284L.pdf).

The European Social Charter of October 18, 1961 (Dz.U. (*Journal of Laws*) of 1999, No 8, item 67 as amended: https://isap.sejm.gov.pl/isap.nsf/download.xsp/WDU19990080067/T/D19990067L.pdf).

The International Covenant on Economic, Social and Cultural Rights of December 19, 1966 adopted and opened for signature, ratification and accession by General Assembly resolution 2200A (XXI) of December 16, 1966: https://www.ohchr.org/sites/default/files/cescr.pdf).

Consolidated version of the Treaty on the European Union (Official Journal of the European Union C 326/15, https://eur-lex.europa.eu/resource.html?uri=cellar:2bf140bf-a3f8-4ab2-b506-fd71826e6da6.0023.02/DOC_1&format=PDF).

The Charter of Fundamental Rights of the European Union of December 7, 2000 (2007/C 303/01) (Dz.Urz. UE (Journal of Laws of the European Union) C No 303, p. 1 as amended: https://eur-lex.europa.eu/legal-content/EN/TXT/PDF/?uri=CELEX:12012P/TXT).

Convention No 87 of the International Labour Organisation concerning Freedom of Association and Protection of the Right to Organise of July 9, 1948 (https://normlex.ilo.org/dyn/normlex/en/f?p=NORMLEXPUB:12100:0::NO::P12100_INSTRUMENT_ID:312232).

Convention No 98 of the International Labour Organisation on Right to Organise and Collective Bargaining of July 1, 1949 (https://normlex.ilo.org/dyn/normlex/en/f?p=NORMLEXPUB:12100:0::NO::P12100_INSTRUMENT_ID:312243).

Case law

Judgment of the Supreme Court - Chamber of Labour, Social Security and Public Affairs of February 7, 2007, I PK 209/06, LEX nr 280749.

The ruling of the European Court of Human Rights, Case of Schmidt and Dahlstrőm v. Sweden, Application no. 5589/72, February 6, 1976.

The ruling of the European Court of Human Rights, Case of Enerji v. Turkey, Application no. 68959/01, April 21, 2009.

Marina Khachatryan-Zagórska[993]

A person in a specific social group, geographical location and country of origin in the face of his democratic freedoms and the right to self-determination

Abstract: The publication will focus on the historical evolution of human rights and freedoms, examining the extent to which individuals in specific social groups, geographical locations, and countries have access to democratic liberties and the right to self-determination. Through a comparative analysis of different eras and cultural contexts, the speaker will explore the factors that have influenced the recognition and protection of human rights across time and space. By considering how societal norms, political systems, and global trends have shaped the realization of human rights, the presentation aims to elucidate the complexities and challenges of ensuring universal access to fundamental freedoms. Drawing on interdisciplinary insights from psychology, sociology, and political science, the speaker will critically examine the disparities in human rights enjoyment and the implications for individual well-being, social cohesion, and global governance. Ultimately, the presentation calls for a re-examination of the ways in which human rights are conceptualized, protected, and promoted in order to create a more just and equitable world for all people.

Keywords: Interdisciplinary insights, Historical evolution, Human rights, Democratic liberties, Self-determination, Armenian Culture

1. Introduction

Today, in the context of the growing importance of democracy, freedom and human rights, psychological research plays a key role in understanding these issues.[994] Fields such as social, cultural, political and intercultural psychology allow you to explore the impact of social, cultural and individual factors on the perception of democracy and human rights. This publication aims to analyse the

---

993 MA, psychologist. Director of Blissful Center for Diagnosis Therapy and Support Marina Khachatryan Zagórska.

994 J.Smith, *Psychology and democracy: An analytical framework.* University Press, New York, 2022, page 200. In this book, the author explores how psychology influences the understanding and promotion of democracy and freedom, focusing on empirical research and its applications in society.

level of democratization and respect for human rights in various societies using empirical and theoretical data. The research conducted with the participation of Women of Armenian Culture is intended to broaden the perspective on the issues discussed and to contribute to reflection on the promotion of democratic values and respect for individual rights in a multicultural society.

2. Building a society based on autonomy - *psychological perspectives of democratic freedom and the right to self-determination*

Social psychology is concerned with the study of the interaction between the individual and society and the impact of social factors on an individual's behaviour and thinking. One of the key areas of focus in this area is the perception of democratic freedom and the right to self-determination.

[995]A variety of social factors, such as education, social media, culture and tradition, and social inequalities, can shape the way individuals perceive their rights and the ability to express their views. Education plays a vital role in shaping the perception of democratic freedom by increasing civic awareness and critical thinking skills.[996] People who are better educated may be more likely to engage in political activities and defend their rights.

Social media can have both positive and negative[997] impacts on the perception of democratic freedom, as they are a source of information, but at the same time they can be susceptible to manipulation and *fake* news. Culture and tradition also influence the perception of democratic freedom, especially if the society has a long democratic history. Social inequalities, on the other hand, can limit democratic freedom and the right to self-determination when certain social groups are discriminated against or deprived of equal access to political decisions.

---

995 L. *Social psychology in the modern world.* Academic Press, Los Angeles, 2021, page 250. The author analyses the impact of various social factors on the perception of civil rights, emphasizing the role of education and new media in shaping civic awareness.

996 M. Baker, The role of education in democratic development. *Education Journal*, London, 2020, str. 150. This article discusses how education affects the development of democratic values and critical thinking skills in the context of modern societies.

997 R Taylor, The influence of social media on public perception. *Media Studies*, New York, 2023, page 180. The publication discusses the various effects that social media have on the perception of democratic freedom, with a particular focus on disinformation and social mobilization.

Research in social psychology also focuses on the impact of belonging to certain social groups on the sense of control over life and the ability to express views[998]. It is necessary to understand and take into account the diversity of experiences and social perspectives that may affect the perception of freedom and the right to self-determination.

The conclusion of this research is the need to build a fairer and more equal society by taking into account the differences and needs of all its members to ensure that they have equal access to express their views and feelings. Research in social psychology on the perception of democratic freedom and the right to self-determination has important practical implications that can help improve the situation of people who are restricted in expressing themselves.

Therefore, continuing research on the impact of social factors on the perception of democratic freedom is important for building an open and just society[999] that respects diversity and supports individual autonomy.

2.1. The Impact of Culture on Democracy and Human Rights - *A Case Study of Different Geographical Regions*

The analysis of cultural differences between countries and geographical regions in terms of the level of democracy and respect for human rights shows how important it is to take into account the cultural context in the process of building democratic institutions and protecting individual rights. Culture, traditions and social values have a significant impact on the perception of individual freedom and autonomy, which can lead to differences in attitudes towards democracy and human rights. In a mixed Central European country such as Poland, there are differences between regions in terms of the level of democracy and respect for human rights[1000]. In some parts of the country, such as Warsaw and Krakow, there is greater tolerance and openness to diversity, which translates into a fuller experience of individual freedom. However, in eastern Polish regions, such as

998 T. Wilson, *Group identity and personal autonomy.* Psychology Press, New York, 2019, str. 220. This book explores how group identity affects an individual's sense of control and ability to express their beliefs in everyday life.

999 H. Green, Democracy and social psychology. *Social Science Research*, Chicago, 2022, str. 160. The article examines the importance of research on the impact of social factors on the perception of democratic freedom, arguing that this knowledge is crucial for creating just societies.

1000 Freedom House. Freedom in the World 2023: Poland. *Freedom House*, 2023, page. 35. Assesses the level of democracy and respect for human rights in various countries, including Poland, and regional differences.

Podlasie and Lubelskie, they are much more exposed to the risk of violations of the rights of ethnic minorities.

In these regions, deep-rooted ethnic and cultural conflicts can be seen, which in the past led to tensions between different social groups.[1001] The lack of social acceptance and insufficient protection of the rights of ethnic minorities mean that the inhabitants of these regions often feel discriminated against and excluded. The presence of extreme groups and the lack of effective protection mechanisms make ethnic minorities particularly vulnerable to violations of their rights. In order to change this situation, it is necessary to take action to promote tolerance and mutual respect, to ensure more effective protection of minority rights and to eliminate the causes of ethnic tensions. Cooperation between different groups in society, education in equality and acceptance, and building stronger institutions for the protection of human rights are crucial to creating a fairer society where everyone has the opportunity to exercise their rights and freedoms. Only through action at the local and regional level can barriers be broken down and a more open and tolerant future built for all Polish citizens.

On the other hand, Middle Eastern countries such as Iran and Syria have weak democratic institutions and authoritarian systems, which leads to constant human rights violations and repression of citizens.[1002] Lack of freedom of expression and limited opportunities for political participation are common in these regions. Comparing the migration situation in the world, it was highlighted that Latin America, countries such as Venezuela and Colombia are struggling with problems related to corruption, social inequality and human rights violations[1003]. Political conflicts, street violence and intolerance are common, hindering the process of democratisation and civil rights protection. An analysis of the cultural perspective allows us to understand why some countries and regions find it difficult to build democracy and ensure respect for human rights. It is worth taking into account cultural and social differences when taking actions aimed at improving

1001 T. Zarycki, *Ethnic conflicts and political dimensions in Central and Eastern Europe.* Warsaw, 2018, page 240. It discusses ethnic conflicts in Central and Eastern Europe in the context of their impact on social tensions.

1002 Amnesty International. *Human rights in Iran and Syria.* Amnesty International, London, 2022, page 100. Amnesty International's report highlights the problems related to basic human rights in Iran and Syria.

1003 Human Rights Watch. *World report 2023: Events of 2022.* Human Rights Watch, New York, 2023, page 270. The Human Rights Watch report highlights the problems with human rights violations in Venezuela and Colombia and the links to corruption and social inequality.

the political and legal situation in given regions, in order to be able to effectively support the process of democratization and the protection of human rights around the world.

2.2. Cultural Differences and Their Impact on Democracy and Human Rights - *An Overview of Different Geographical Regions*

In Hinduism dominant in India, there is a strong sense of collectivism and social hierarchy, which can affect the way individual freedom is understood.[1004] In some communities, traditional culture and social norms may limit an individual's ability to choose a career or a life partner. In the Arab culture, which Saudi Arabia represents, a patriarchal model of society dominates, which may limit women's autonomy and freedom.[1005] An example of this is the obligation for women to wear an abaya or the inability to travel without the man's consent. In China, there is a strong focus on social harmony and maintaining stability, which can lead to some restriction of individual freedom. Social control and group pressure can influence an individual's decisions about both personal and professional life.

Comparing the United States, which has a long tradition of democracy and respect for human rights, with Russia, which is increasingly neglecting these values and introducing restrictions on political and social opposition. In the US, there is freedom of speech, independent courts and a system of human rights protection, while in Russia there is repression of human rights defenders and journalists.

Differences between countries and geographical regions in terms of the level of democracy may include, for example, the Scandinavian countries, which are considered examples of a high level of democracy and respect for human rights, and the post-communist countries, which have weaker democratic traditions and often violate human rights. In Western Europe, such as Germany and France, democracy is more established and stable than in some Eastern European countries, where authoritarian tendencies and restrictions on civil liberties are evident. As for the eastern regions of Poland, ethnic conflicts in the past may have left unresolved problems, leading to a higher risk of violations of minority rights. In addition, institutional support for the protection of minority rights may be less

1004 S. Deshpande, Research indicates that Hindu cultural values influence the perception of an individual in society, 2016, page. 50.

1005 Amnesty International. Women's rights in Saudi Arabia. Amnesty International, London, 2021, page 120.

developed, and less tolerance and acceptance of people belonging to other ethnic groups also increases the risk of violations.

In some regions of eastern Polish, ethnic minorities may face less social acceptance and lack of protection of rights, which can lead to discrimination. There is a presence of extreme groups promoting hatred, racism and intolerance towards minorities, which increases the risk of violations of the rights of these groups. It is necessary to take action to improve the situation of minorities, promote tolerance and eliminate the causes of ethnic tensions and conflicts. Some southern European countries, such as Italy and Greece, are plagued by corruption problems and failure to ensure full respect for fundamental rights[1006], which poses a challenge to the democratisation of these regions. In northern Europe, on the other hand, such as Sweden and Norway, citizens enjoy a high level of democracy and respect for human rights. In order to effectively promote democracy and respect for human rights in the world, it is necessary to take into account the cultural perspective and adapt activities to the specifics of a given country or region. It is important to understand and respect cultural diversity and to eliminate all forms of discrimination and intolerance. Through intercultural dialogue and building societies based on the principles of democracy and equal rights for all, we can contribute to a fairer and freer society around the world.

It is important to draw attention to the importance of equality and social justice in the context of democratisation and the protection of human rights. Lack of equal access to education, health care or work can lead to human rights violations and limit the opportunities of citizens to fully participate in public life. That is why investing in human development and eliminating inequalities is an important step towards respecting human rights and strengthening democracy. In the global context, it is important to take joint action for democratization and respect for human rights by the international community. International cooperation and the promotion of universal democratic values can help to raise human rights standards around the world and promote pluralism and freedom of choice. People with high self-efficacy are more likely to engage in public life and political activism because they believe they are able to influence change and achieve goals. People with a high competitive propensity may be more involved in public life and politics, treating political activity as a way of competing and confronting others. People with a high need for affiliation, i.e. the desire to establish strong social relationships, may be more involved in public life as a way of building social bonds and acting in groups. People with a high tendency to seek novelties and experiences may be more interested in politics, seeing it as an opportunity to experience

1006 Transparency International. *Corruption perceptions index 2020*, 2020, page 45.

new situations and challenges. People with a high level of empathy may be more involved in public life and political activity, wanting to work for the benefit of others and improve the conditions of social life. In Europe, the impact of socio-political structures on the degree of democratization and respect for human rights can be seen through differences in the political and social systems of individual countries. Countries with strong democratic traditions, such as Scandinavia, the Netherlands or Germany, are usually characterised by a high degree of democratisation and respect for human rights. On the other hand, countries with weak democratic structures, such as Hungary and Poland, tend to restrict democracy and violate human rights. A lack of checks and balances between authorities and a lack of independent media are just some of the factors influencing these trends. The manipulation of public opinion and the lack of pluralism of information can be a serious problem for the development of democracy and respect for human rights.

In addition, democratic institutions, such as constitutional courts and election oversight bodies, are often weakened in such countries. This can lead to a situation where those in power can act freely without any restrictions or control. To address this, it is necessary to strengthen democratic institutions and control mechanisms, such as support for independent media, strengthening the independence of courts and supervisory bodies, and promoting a culture of democracy and respect for human rights. It is also important to support and mobilise civil society, which can play an important role in monitoring the government's actions and defending democratic values.

One example of action in this matter is the "Freedom in the World" report prepared by the Freedom House organization[1007], which monitors the level of democracy and human rights in various countries. NGOs such as Amnesty International and Human Rights Watch are also important in monitoring and exposing human rights violations in countries with weak democracies. Support from the international community is also very important, as through diplomatic activities, sanctions or development aid, it can improve the democratic situation and respect for human rights in these countries.

Globally, the impact of socio-political structures on the degree of democratisation and respect for human rights is also evident in different regions[1008]. Developed countries, such as the United States or Japan, usually have strong democratic institutions and a high level of respect for human rights. By contrast, developing countries such as China and Russia are often criticized for violating human rights

1007 Freedom House. Freedom in the world 2023, 2023, page 300.

1008 T. Anna. Socio-political structures and their impact on human rights. *Journal of Human Rights*, Berlin, 2022, pages 15; 30.

and lacking democratic institutions. In both cases, there is a clear correlation between socio-political structures and the degree of democratisation and respect for human rights.

It is also worth noting that restrictions on democracy and human rights violations can result from various reasons, such as corruption, political irresponsibility, or the spread of hatred and intolerance in society. Therefore, the fight for respect for human rights and the development of democracy requires a multifaceted approach and the involvement of many different actors. In conclusion, the relationship between socio-political structures and the degree of democratisation and respect for human rights is evident both in Europe and in the world. Strengthening democratic institutions, promoting social equality and international cooperation are key actions that can contribute to building societies based on the principles of democracy and respect for human rights. Based on the above comparisons of cultures in terms of values, social norms, and understanding of freedom and self-determination, it can be seen that the differences between societies can be enormous. The key element is the search for balance and acceptance of diversity, regardless of the cultural or political context.

3. The importance of intercultural dialogue and respect for diversity

Cooperation and understanding between different social groups are crucial for building democratic institutions and respecting human rights. A multiplicity of cultures, values and beliefs can be a wealth for society if it is treated with respect and openness. It is also valuable to study cultural differences and learn from other communities, which can contribute to mutual understanding and building bonds between people with different worlds of values. In societies where there is dialogue between cultures and respect for diversity, it is possible to build social harmony, shared responsibility and respect for the rights of each individual. By embracing differences and striving for equality, society can become more open and democratic, which in turn contributes to the better functioning of public institutions and the guarantee of human rights.

a. **Examples of comparisons of different cultures in terms of values:**
   - Western societies - the concept of individualism and individual freedom
   - Eastern cultures - social harmony and loyalty to the group

b. **Examples of comparisons of social norms:**
   - European societies - accepted same-sex partnerships
   - Middle Eastern cultures - often treated as taboo

c. **Examples of comparisons of ways of understanding freedom and self-determination:**
   - Democratic societies - broad rights and freedom of choice
   - Totalitarian states - the individual has limited rights and is under constant supervision of the authorities

The diversity of understandings of freedom and self-determination can carry many risks, depending on the social and political context. For example, in democratic societies, excessive individualism can lead to social irresponsibility and conflict, while in totalitarian states, the restriction of individual rights can lead to the suppression of personal freedom and the rebellion of citizens. It is therefore important to strike a balance between the freedom of the individual and the needs of the community, and to ensure respect for the fundamental rights and dignity of every human being, regardless of the political or social context. Differences between cultures can affect the level of democracy and respect for human rights, but they are not a decisive factor. There are countries that show that cultural diversity can be a strength, not a weakness, for democratic institutions and human rights.

The important role of communication and cooperation between governments and citizens in the context of democracy and human rights has been emphasized by many researchers. Psychologist Jonathan Haidt, in his book "The Righteous Mind: Why Good People are Divided by Politics and Religion," notes that people tend to divide into groups based on values and emotions, which can lead to social and political divisions.[1009] However, through open communication and collaboration, it is possible to break down these divisions and build greater understanding. The conclusions drawn from the above considerations indicate the need to build societies based on respect for diversity, dialogue between cultures and acceptance of diversity. Only cooperation and mutual understanding make it possible to build societies that are both democratic and respectful of human rights.

4. Analysis of the process of cultural assimilation of Women of Armenian Culture towards the country of residence and the power of identification with the canons of the culture of origin

From the research conducted by the author of this publication, in 2015 among the community of women of Armenian culture, it was established that out of

1009 J. Haidt, *The righteous mind: Why good people are divided by politics and religion*. Vintage, New York, 2012, page 500.

177 surveyed Armenian women[1010], where over 100 lived in the territory of the Republic of Poland and the vast rest of the respondents lived in the area of the Republic of Armenia, the process of cultural assimilation in this national group occurs, although in a broadly understood dynamic[1011], if we take into account the speed and area of the above-mentioned changes, It is not a relatively *quick cultural mechanism*. Armenian women living in the area of decidedly free Polish underwent cultural assimilation in the first generation of emigration, due to the broad desire to remain in the area of the Armenian diaspora, striving to maintain and nurture the cultural elements of the country of origin, which naturally makes it difficult to take over and assimilate with culturally distinct elements of functioning. It was then established that the generations born consecutively, where some of the above-mentioned respondents established relationships with men of non-Armenian origin on the territory of Poland, were much more willing to undergo the process of interpenetration of cultures, adopting broadly understood European values as the principles of general functioning. This process of actual cultural assimilation occurs mainly due to living conditions, surroundings and contacts with other cultures. Armenian women living in the area of Polish, which have significantly different cultural and social frameworks, may be more likely to slower undergo changes in interpenetrating cultures, because they have to function in a different social and cultural environment, and the historical experiences of the Armenian Nation, i.e. m.in. *The Great Emigration of the* Armenian Nation; continue to raise concerns among Armenian citizens about the dispersion of the indigenous population and the loosening of national identity.[1012] The Armenian women surveyed in Poland indicated that they felt pressure from the Armenian local community not to adapt to the norms and values of the new environment[1013], in order to preserve their cultural identity, this was to guarantee the possibility of passing it on to the above-mentioned generations born *in exile.*

Comparing the collected research material among Armenian women living in the Republic of Armenia, it was noted that the women there are much more willing and faster to explore the values of Western culture, drawing inspiration from it and introducing changes in their area of functioning or perception of the

---

1010 M. Khachatryan-Zagórska, Rola zadania i funkcje małżeńskie w życiu kobiet kultury ormiańskiej. Katowice, 2015, page 75-115.

1011 References to publications on cultural assimilation.

1012 Sources on the history and exile of the Armenian nation.

1013 Research on the cultural identity of the Armenian community in Poland.

world, in order to strive for autonomous development and equal rights in the country of origin and thus residence.

5. Summary

The process of cultural assimilation and democratization can be compared to the therapeutic process, since both occur in both the external and internal functioning of the individual[1014]. In the process of cultural assimilation, the individual gradually assimilates and integrates elements of a new culture, changing his ways of thinking, behaviour, and values. Similarly, in therapy, the individual works through traumas, conflicts and unconscious defense mechanisms, leading to profound changes in their mental and emotional functioning. Democratization means a process of social development in which individuals gain more influence on political and social decisions, changing social structures and institutions and interpersonal relationships and individual identity. In both cases, there is a need to adapt to new realities, to confront prejudices, mistakes and fears. The processes of cultural assimilation, democratization and therapeutic are continuous and require a continuous process of change, adaptation and integration.

Communication plays a key role in a democratic society, enabling citizens to express their opinions, obtain information and participate in decision-making processes. The government should listen and respond to social needs, building trust and legitimacy of its actions. Psychological studies indicate that the value of communication can affect the development of democracy and respect for human rights. Dr. Ron Friedman emphasizes that effective communication is crucial in building trust and cooperation in the team, which applies to the relationship between the government and citizens.[1015]

The psychology's conclusions suggest that open communication and cooperation between governments and citizens are crucial for building democratic institutions and respecting human rights, helping to overcome cultural differences and build social understanding. The presence of democracy and the importance of

1014 A. Sen, *Development as freedom*. Oxford University Press, Oxford, 1999, page 384; A. Sen, *The idea of justice*. Harvard University Press, Cambridge, 2009, page 368; A. Tocqueville, de. Democracy in America (H. Reeve, Trans.). *The Liberty Fund*, 1945 (Original work published 1835), page 510; A. Tocqueville, de. *The old regime and the revolution* (H. Reeve, Trans.). The Liberty Fund, 2001 (Original work published 1856), page 440.

1015 R. Friedman, *The best place to work: The art and science of creating an extraordinary workplace*. Perigee Books, New York, 2014, page 320.

communication in society transcend the limits of time. This publication highlights the crucial importance of communication in a democratic society, enabling citizens to express their opinions and participate in decisions. Psychological research confirms that effective communication is crucial in building trust and cooperation, both in work teams and between those in power and citizens.[1016] Open communication is essential for building democratic institutions and respecting human rights.

Bibliography

Amnesty International., Raport 2021/22. Stan praw człowieka na świecie. https://ap.amnesty.org/pl/modern-slavery-report/, 2021.

Amnesty International., Human rights in Iran and Syria. https://www.amnesty.org/en/latest/report/2022, 2022.

Amnesty International. (n.d.). Amnesty International. https://www.amnesty.org/.

Anna, T., Socio-political structures and their impact on human rights. Journal of Human Rights, 2022.

Bauman, Z., Liquid modernity. Wiley-Blackwell, 2000.

Baker, M., The role of education in democratic development. Education Journal, 2020.

Brown, K., Wpływ otoczenia na procesy asymilacji kulturowej w diasporze ormiańskiej. Studia nad Kulturą Ormiańską, 2016.

Central Intelligence Agency. (n.d.). The World Factbook. https://www.cia.gov/the-world-factbook.

Council of Europe. (n.d.). Racism, xenophobia, antisemitism and intolerance in Europe: Addressing the challenges. https://www.coe.int/en/web/commissioner/-/racism-xenophobia-antisemitism-and-intolerance-in-europe-addressing-the-challenges.

Deshpande, S., [Full citation details needed for proper APA citation], 2016.

European Commission against Racism and Intolerance., Country monitoring in Poland. https://www.coe.int/en/web/ecri/country-monitoring-poland, 2019.

Freedom House., Freedom in the world 2023: Poland. https://freedomhouse.org/report/freedom-world/2023/poland, 2023.

Friedman, R., The best place to work: The art and science of creating an extraordinary workplace. Perigee Books, 2014.

1016 D. A. Buchanan & Huczynski, A. *Organizational behaviour*. Pearson Education Limited, Harlow, 2017, page 560.

Huddy, L., Sears, D. O., & Levy, J. S., The Oxford handbook of political psychology. Oxford University Press, 2015.

Khachatryan-Zagórska, M. The role of marital tasks and functions in the lives of women of Armenian culture. Katowice 2015.

Giddens, A., Modernity and self-identity: Self and society in the late modern age. Stanford University Press, 1991.

Green, H., Democracy and social psychology. Social Science Research, 2022.

Greenberg, J., & Bar-Tal, D., Emotion, politics, and society: Greater than the sum of its parts. American Psychological Association, 2016.

Haidt, J., The righteous mind: Why good people are divided by politics and religion. Vintage, 2012.

Huntington, S. P., The clash of civilizations and the remaking of world order. Simon & Schuster, 1993.

Human Rights Watch., World report 2020: Poland. https://www.hrw.org/world-report/2020/country-chapters/poland, 2020.

Human Rights Watch., World report 2023: Events of 2022. https://www.hrw.org/world-report/2023, 2023.

Inglehart, R., Modernization and postmodernization: Cultural, economic, and political change in 43 societies. Princeton University Press, 1999.

Johnson, L., Social psychology in the modern world. Academic Press, 2021.

Kymlicka, W., Multicultural citizenship: A liberal theory of minority rights. Oxford University Press, 1995.

Lee, S., & Kim, Y., The process of cultural assimilation among Korean immigrants in the United States. International Journal of Intercultural Relations, 2017.

Nussbaum, M. C., The quality of life. Oxford University Press, 1994.

Sen, A., Development as freedom. Oxford University Press, 1999.

Sen, A., Identity and violence: The illusion of destiny. W. W. Norton & Company, 2006.

Sen, A., The idea of justice. Harvard University Press, 2009.

Shils, E., The virtue of civility in the practice of politics. Daedalus, 124(4), 15-32, 1995.

Smith, J., Asymilacja kulturowa w społeczności kobiet Kultury Ormiańskiej. Warszawa: Wydawnictwo Naukowe, 2017.

Smith, J., Psychology and democracy: An analytical framework. University Press, 2022.

Taylor, C., Multiculturalism: Examining the politics of recognition. Princeton University Press, 1994.

Taylor, R., The influence of social media on public perception. Media Studies, 2023.

Tocqueville, A. de., Democracy in America (H. Reeve, Trans.). The Liberty Fund., Original work published 1835, 1945.

Tocqueville, A. de., The old regime and the revolution (H. Reeve, Trans.). The Liberty Fund. Original work published 1856, 2001.

Transparency International, Corruption perceptions index, 2020. https://www.transparency.org/en/cpi/2020/index/nzl.

Wittenberg, E., & Dickson, R, Assessing the impact of cultural assimilation on immigrant communities in Europe. European Journal of Cultural Studies, 2016.

Wilson, T., Group identity and personal autonomy. Psychology Press, 2019.

Zarycki, T., Ethnic conflicts and political dimensions in Central and Eastern Europe, 2018.

Chapter V.
Access to information in a democratic state

María Lidón Lara Ortiz[1017]

The relevance of public information access in democracy - the Spanish law perspective

Abstract: The paper arises some questions about the legal configuration of the right to access the public information, especially considering the configuration on the Charter of Fundamental Rights of the European Union, as well as the Spanish regulation, and within it, specially we consider the State Act 19/2013, on Transparency. With this purpose, we analyse some issues related to the relevance and characterization of the right of access to public information, its importance for preserving the proper functioning of institutions in a democratic framework, and some controversial issues regarding the exercise of the right to access to public information will also be considered.

Keywords: Democracy, Public information, transparency, accountability, citizen's right

1. Administrative transparency as an indicative of good democratic functioning: active transparency and access to public information

Transparency, access to public information and good governance standards must be the fundamental axes of all political and administrative action. The Preamble of the Spanish Transparency Law of 2013 highlights that only when the action of public authorities is subject to scrutiny, and when citizens can know how decisions that affect them are made, how public funds are managed or under what criteria public institutions act, it can be considered that public action is the object of democratic control, so that public powers respond to society, which is critical, demanding and requires its participation in public powers[1018], through this means of democratic control.

This is why countries with higher levels of transparency and good governance standards have stronger institutions, which favour economic growth and social development. In these countries, citizens can judge better and more judiciously the capacity of their public officials and decide accordingly. Allowing better

1017 Administrative Law Professor, Jaume I University.

1018 Preamble of the Spanish Transparency Law 19/2013, 9 December, of transparency, access to public information and good governance.

oversight of public activity contributes to the necessary democratic regeneration, promotes the efficiency and effectiveness of the State and favours economic growth. Currently it is considered as a global phenomenon[1019].

The rules on transparency usually deal with two different ways of transparency, one of them is the formula of active transparency, or set of information that the Administrations and other public powers are obliged to offer to citizens, as a minimum[1020], according to the law. Faced with this, another form of transparency is the result of the exercise of the right to access to public information, through which citizens can request more information than what is covered by active transparency, through the exercise of the right of access. The right to access to public information is a right that corresponds to citizens, as the other side of the same coin of transparency that falls on public administrations, all of which is an obvious manifestation of modern democracy.

Both ways of transparency are also treated and applied by jurisprudence, which analyses the extent of duties of this type of all public administrations and other obligated subjects. In this sense, we can highlight the recent Judgement of the Spanish Supreme Court, Third Chamber of Administrative Litigation, number 5514/2023, of December 11, 2023, which considers that although it should not be forgotten that the obligation of active publicity is very relevant, but plus it there is a right to access to public information that seeks to reinforce and expand the transparency of public activity and that is recognized in very broad terms to all people without major distinctions, in line with what is foreseen on article 105.b) of the Spanish Constitution, which recognizes "citizens" access to administrative files and records and using a similar formula to the one of the Convention on Access to Public Documents of the Council of Europe, signed on June 18 of 2009 -ratified by Spain on June 9, 2023-, which in its article 2.1 states that each signatory State "shall guarantee the right of anyone, without discrimination of any kind, to access public documents" in the possession of public authorities[1021].

1019 V. Ginesta Rodríguez, E. Pano Puey, L. Medir Tejado and J. Magre Ferran, "Diez años de la aprobación de la Ley 19/2013", in *Revista Española de la Transparencia*, Núm. 19, 2024. Primer semestre. Enero-junio 2024, pp. 45-70, p. 49.

1020 L. A. Pomed Sánchez, "Transparencia", in *Fundamentos: Cuadernos monográficos de teoría del Estado, derecho público e historia constitucional*, Nº 9, 2016, pp. 167-214, p. 206.

1021 Supreme Spanish Court Judgement, Sala Tercera de lo Contencioso Administrativo, número 5514/2023, December 11, 2023, - ECLI:ES:TS:2023:5514-.

In fact, this European Convention highlights, in its foundation, the relevance, in a pluralistic democratic society, of the transparency of public authorities, considering that the exercise of the right to access to public documents "provides a source of information to the public, helps the citizens to compose an opinion about the state of society and about public authorities, and promotes the integrity, proper functioning, effectiveness and responsibility of public authorities, thus contributing to strengthening their legitimacy. In a nut shell, this Convention highlights that all public documents are, in principle, public and communicable, with the sole reservation of the protection of other rights and legitimate interests. From all this it follows that transparency and access to public documents is the general rule, while the limitation of this right is the exception.

It is true that both active transparency and the right to access to information are subject to the limits provided for in the transparency regulation and, especially, those derived from the protection of personal data, provided for in the regulations on administrative transparency and in the specific regulations about this issue that in Spain are made up of the Organic Act 3/2018 of December 5, together with its implementing regulations, and all of this in accordance with the European Union Data Protection Regulation 2016/679 of European Parliament and of the Council of 27 April 2016, relating to the protection of natural persons with regard to the processing of personal data and the free circulation of such data and repealing Directive 95/46/EC (General Data Protection Regulation).

If there are limits, these should not exclude absolutely the obligation of transparency, provided that it is possible to carry out the dissociation of the protected personal data or the reserved information when appropriate, since transparency prevails, if the information, and can be offered partially, respecting the limit in question and fulfilling the obligation of accountability at the same time. The Spanish Supreme Court has indicated that such limits must receive a strict, even restrictive, interpretation, "without accepting limitations that represent an unjustified and disproportionate impairment of the right of access to information." Therefore, only justified and proportionate limitations are acceptable, as this is not a discretionary power of the Administration (in this sense, the Supreme Court stated on other Judgements, such as the Judgement of the Supreme Court n. 1547/2017, of October 16, 2017 (rec. 75/2017), and the Judgement of the Supreme Court of March 10, 2020 (rec. 8193/2018) among others).

In this way, the right of access, although it is obtained in a different manner than how information is obtained through active transparency, is also a mean of public transparency, which is granted at the request of the citizen, and which has the same relevance than active transparency to achieve high standards of democratic quality, and to reinforce the right to know the truth[1022].

2. The exercise of the right to access the public information: legal nature

The right to access to public information is one of the manifestations of transparency and is exercised through a special procedure stated in transparency regulations. In relation to all this, there are two key issues that must be addressed: on the one hand, the determination of what is public information, and on the other, what is the genuine legal nature of the right of access[1023], according to its regulatory configuration, since its characterization will allow granting this right greater or lesser extent in its legal protection.

In relation to the first issue, it should be clarified what public information is. According to article 1.2.b) of the Council of Europe Convention on Access to Public Documents of June 18, 2009, "public documents" means all information recorded in any way, drafted or received, and held by public authorities. It can be seen, therefore, that the concept of public information or public document is very huge. The Spanish transparency laws, including the Act of 2013, and those of the Autonomous Communities, define public information in very similar terms, including the contents or documents, whatever their format or medium, that are held by any of the subjects obliged to be transparent and that

1022 C. Renato, A. Sotelo-Torres and K. García-Curiel, "El procedimiento de acceso a la información pública como mecanismo para proteger el derecho a la verdad. Una revisión de los criterios de la Corte Interamericana de Derechos Humanos sobre la materia", in *Revista Española de la Transparencia*, Núm. 19, 2024. Primer semestre. Enero-junio 2024, pp. 221-246.

1023 E. Guichot Reina, "La naturaleza del derecho de acceso a la información pública", in *Revista Española de la Transparencia*, Núm. 18, 2023. Segundo semestre. Julio-diciembre 2023, pp. 17-49. Among others consider that this is the grounding of the right, I. Villaverde Menéndez, *Los derechos del público*, Tecnos, Madrid, 1995, p. 118; S. Fernández Ramos, El derecho de acceso a los documentos administrativos, Marcial Pons, Madrid, 1997, pp. 350-358. In the same sense, M. Sánchez De Diego Fernández de la Riva, "Un derecho fundamental a acceder a la información pública", en M. Sánchez De Diego Fernández de la Riva, (coord.), *El derecho de acceso a la información pública*, Universidad Complutense, Madrid, 2007, pp. 7-41. And, G. Ruiz-Rico Ruiz, "La dimensión constitucional del principio de transparencia y el derecho de información activa", *Revista de Derecho Político*, núm. 110, 2021, pp. 47-78.

have been prepared or acquired in the exercise of their functions. The concept of public information is, therefore, linked to the subjects obliged to be transparent which, in accordance with article 1.2.a) of the Council of Europe Convention on Access to Public Documents of June 18, 2009, are the "public authorities", understanding that they are such: the government and administration at the national, regional and local levels; legislative bodies and judicial authorities to the extent that they perform administrative functions under national law; and natural or legal persons, to the extent that they exercise administrative authority. In Spanish Law, the Transparency Act of 2013 includes public administrations of all types: territorial, independent administrations, autonomous public organizations, etc. Also included, as expressly established by Spanish regulations, are all those Public Law entities with their own legal personality, linked to any of the Public Administrations or dependent on them, including public Universities, and also Public Law corporations, in relation to its activities subject to Administrative Law. The obligation to be transparent through the aforementioned means also extends to commercial companies in whose share capital with direct or indirect participation of public entities is greater than 50 percent, and to the foundations and associations formed by Administrations, organizations and entities obliged to be transparent. In the same terms, the obligation extends to other public powers to which Administrative Law is applied, at least partially, such as the House of His Majesty the King, the Congress of Deputies, the Senate, the Constitutional Court and the General Council of the Judiciary, as well as the Bank of Spain, the Council of State, the Ombudsman, the Court of Auditors, the Economic and Social Council and similar autonomous institutions, in relation to their activities subject to Administrative law. Additionally, political parties, trade union organizations and business organizations, and private entities that receive public aid or subsidies during a period of one year in an amount greater than 100,000 euros, or when at least 40% of the total are also obliged to be transparent if their annual income is in the nature of public aid or subsidy, at least, in the amount of 5,000 euros.

Finally, there is a special obligation of transparency that affects different natural and legal persons that provide public services or exercise administrative powers, so that they are obliged to provide the Administration, and other obligated organizations or entities, upon request, all the necessary information, for compliance by those with the transparency obligations are imposed by law. This obligation applies, for example, to recipients of public sector contracts under the terms provided in the respective contract.

In relation to the second of the questions raised at the beginning, that is, the determination of the legal nature of the right of access to public information, it is true that its characterization depends on each regulation. Since an analysis of all the existing regulations is impossible here due to the reduce extension of this paper, we will analyse some transnational regulations, and later some Spanish ones, and we will see that the characterization of the legal nature of the right to access the public information is not univocal. Thus, within the framework of the European Union it is conceived as an authentic fundamental right, which allows its identification with an authentic fourth generation human right, legally recognized in this framework. Its recognition at the European level is based on article 42 of the Charter of Fundamental Rights of the European Union, and according to it: "Every citizen of the Union or any natural or legal person who resides or has its registered office in a Member State has right to access documents of the European Parliament, the Council and the Commission", this right is classified, on the charter itself, as a Fundamental Right of citizens.

Additionally, on article 41.2 of the Charter of Fundamental Rights of the European Union, the fundamental right to good administration includes the right of every person to access the file or document that affects them. This is also a fundamental right of the citizen, who is interested in a certain procedure, to access the public information contained in a procedure in which he is an interested party.

In both cases, the character of Fundamental Right is only held by application of the Charter of Fundamental Rights of the European Union when it comes to the transparency of the European Institutions and authorities, or by being national authorities of the Member States that are in charge of managing the public information in question, when they are applying European Union law.

In any case, the rights included on articles 41.2 and 42 of the Chart of Fundamental Right of the European Union are not identical, and that difference is transferred and increased in Spanish national law, where both rights are subjective rights, not qualified as fundamental rights unless the right is applied while intervening a European Institution or authority. Sticking to Spanish law, we can differentiate: the right to access equivalent to that of article 42 of the Chart of Fundamental Rights of the European Union, and which is regulated on article 13.f) of Spanish Act 39/2015 and in the laws of transparency; and compared to it, the right to access the file of the interested parties, equivalent to the provision on article 41.2 of the Chart of Fundamental Right of the European Union, which is regulated by article 53 of Spanish Act 39/2015.

Curiously, the right to access the file of the interested parties is more extensive, because it is not affected by the limits that affect access to public information, which is affected by certain limits, without going any further, the rights to personal data protection of the interested parties of a file that any citizen could access, since it is public information, it would imply anonymization or pseudonymization. However, considering the provisions of the First Additional Disposition of the Transparency Spanish Act, it is considered that the right to access of the interested parties to their own file, is a special legal regime regarding the right to access the public information of citizens, that is provided on transparency regulations. This fact often causes application difficulties that we will discuss in the following section.

3. Controversial issues about the exercise of the right to access in Spanish law due to the duality of access as exercised by a citizen or a person interested in the procedure

The duality of legal regimes that we could consider common, such as the one of the citizen and the one of the interested party in an administrative procedure, generates some practical problems, which can be conceived as authentic distortions that distance their application from the spirit of the regulation on administrative transparency, and from the spirit of Spanish Act 39/2015 on Common administrative proceeding, that recognizes the interested party in a procedure to access to their own file and the right to access to all public information held by every citizen.

Thus, certain application problems may arise, especially for those potential interested parties who have legitimate interests, which also depends on the discretionary assessment of the Administration itself or entity obliged to accomplish the transparency duties. Example of this are two situations on which jurisprudence has apply regulations with a restriction of the right to access.

The first situation is the case in which the hypothetical interested party is a person whose legitimate interests are affected by the procedure, is considered in article 4.1.c Spanish Act 39/2015 on common administrative procedure, and is not considered a party in the proceeding with standing to defend his interest because the Administration denies such status and the access to the procedure through article 53.1.a) Law 39/2015. It is the case, for example, of the complainant harmed with respect to the sanctioning or disciplinary procedure.

In this case, the right to access public information, exercised in accordance with the transparency law and related to article 13 of the Spanish Act 39/2015 on common administrative procedure, has been denied to anyone who had a legitimate interest or was part of an administrative procedure because they considered that the special regime was applicable to them, in application of the First Additional Disposition of the Transparency Spanish Act, but which, indeed, it is the regime of access to public information provided for the interested party on article 53 of the Spanish Act 39/2015 on common administrative procedure, which is the regulation of the procedure common administrative system, which cannot be conceived as a special regime. However, the jurisprudence of the Supreme Court has used the application of the transparency regime for the interested party himself, which is provided on article 53 of the Spanish Act 39/2015 on common administrative procedure, by the reference contained on the First Additional Disposition, as a limit to exclude the right of access in accordance with the transparency laws that every citizen has. In this sense, we find the Supreme Court Ruling 748/2020, of June 11; the Supreme Court Ruling 1338/2020, of October 15; and the Supreme Court Ruling 1565/2020, of November 19. In these judgements the Supreme Court has maintained a strict line, so that it has declared that "Act 19/2013, with regard to access to public information, is constituted as the basic transversal regulation that regulates this matter and creates a legal framework that complements the rest of the regulations (…). The provisions of this norm are only displaced, acting in this case as supplementary, when another legal regulation has established its own and specific legal regime for access to information in a specific area. It has been highlighted that such reference to "another legal regulation" is somewhat ambiguous, but what is clear is that if there is another legal regulation with a special rule, it is considered that the transparency regulations become a subsidiary or supplementary regime. In these cases, jurisprudence has come to reject, based on this criterion, requests for public information exercising the right to access, presented by those who are interested in the procedure, and even those who, not being interested in that procedure, do so having interest on access to public information for private purposes, because it has a private interest, different from the public one linked to democratic quality. In this sense, the Spanish Supreme Court Judgement n.1519/2020, of November 12, was pronounced basing the exclusion of the right to access the public information because the request was based on a "mere private interest". This criterion distorts the perspective of accountability of the public powers that underlies the right to access and the administrative transparency in general. This criterion has received certain doctrinal criticism, precisely because it implies the extension of a limit not provided on the transparency regulations, a criticism that we share bacause it produces an unjustified distortion on the application of the right to access the public information. In reality, whoever exercises the right to access to know public documents that interest them based on a private interest, also reaches some control on the Administrations activity, so even the exercise of the right based on private interests allows the improvement of democratic quality and the proper functioning of institutions.

The second controversial case that also deserves to be analysed is the case of someone who, being immersed in a judicial process, is in a situation in which a report previously issued by a public Administration must be evaluated in other procedure or in a judicial process. One case of this kind was resolved by the Spanish Constitutional Court, Judgement 164/2021, of October 4, 2021. In this case, the interested party was denied to access to certain documentation included in an administrative procedure, arguing that the interested party would have access to the documentation later in the judicial process in which he was a party. Specifically, it was a person who, while in prison, requested access to the reports of the penitentiary centre's technical team issued to justify the convenience of denying him a permit and which served to ground the decision about that question. In this case, the Spanish Constitutional Court considered that the interested party was denied to access to the information in his prison file without any legal basis, since inmates have the same right to access public information as the rest of the citizens in their relations with the administration.

This judgement is interesting because it allows the right of access to be defined, contributing to its configuration, and produces *erga omnes* effects in the evolution of the right, by indicating, based on article 105 b) of the Spanish Constitution, that it incorporates to the right to access to public information, the following guidelines:

- Access to public information that integrates the content of a subjective public right exercisable against the Administration is not absolute, but can only be limited for reasons predetermined in the law because the limiting causes are assessed.
- The possibility of limiting access to information does not constitute a discretionary power of the Administration but rather a regulated power.
- Denying access or limiting it requires a weighing of conflicting interests, if any.
- The Spanish Constitutional Court also considers that in this case the exercise of the right of access was deferred or mediated by reference to the exercise of procedural actions, not respecting its autonomy and substantivity, and incurring undue confusion between publicity of the administrative action and publicity of the judicial acts, which finally produced an emptying of the content of the right of access and denatured it to the point of making it unrecognizable.
- Additionally, in this case, the Spanish Constitutional Court made reference to the Judgement of the European Court of Human Rights, of October 11, 2016, in the case Cano Moya v. Spain, which deserves to be taken into account since it establishes that "article 34 of the Convention may impose on State authorities the obligation to provide a copy of documentation to those claimants who are in situations of special vulnerability or dependency and unable to obtain the necessary documentation without assistance from the State (see, Naydyon v. Ukraine, no. 16474 /03, § 63, of October 14, 2010) (§ 50).
- In the case decided by the Spanish Constitutional Court, the interested party was in prison, where it can be considered that his position was dependent on the Penitentiary Administration, who, in view of this ruling, should have

offered greater support to exercise that right to access, not based on article 13.d), but on article 53.1.a) of Spanish Act 39/2015 on common administrative procedure, although with all the guarantees of transparency.

- The European Court of Human Rights recognizes the relevance and character of Human Rights of the right to access the public information grounded on the fundamental right of accessing to truth information[1024], and this is binding for all signatory States of the European Convention on Human Rights.

4. Conclusions

The right of access has not yet reached its full regulatory development, although regulatory modifications and jurisprudential development have contributed to its current configuration and recent evolution. However, in practice, there are some applicative distortions that must be resolved, either through legislative reform, clarifying the terms of the wording of the controversial regulations, or through the development of a correct jurisprudential line, since all existing jurisprudence, is not correct and even departs from the interpretations offered by the Spanish Constitutional Court, and even by the European Court of Human Rights.

Bibliography

Fernández Ramos S., *El derecho de acceso a los documentos administrativos*, Marcial Pons, Madrid, 1997, pp. 350-358.

Ginesta Rodríguez V., Pano Puey E., Medir Tejado and J. Magre Ferran L., "Diez años de la aprobación de la Ley 19/2013", in *Revista Española de la Transparencia*, Núm. 19, 2024. Primer semestre. Enero-junio 2024, pp. 45-70.

Guichot Reina E., "La naturaleza del derecho de acceso a la información pública", in *Revista Española de la Transparencia*, Núm. 18, 2023. Segundo semestre. Julio-diciembre 2023, pp. 17-49.

Hernández Ramos M., "El derecho de acceso a la información pública en la jurisprudencia del TEDH: un derecho instrumental imprescindible para la eficacia del Convenio desde la teoría general de los derechos", *Teoría y Realidad Constitucional*, núm. 42, 2018, pp. 483-509.

1024 M. Hernández Ramos, "El derecho de acceso a la información pública en la jurisprudencia del TEDH: un derecho instrumental imprescindible para la eficacia del Convenio desde la teoría general de los derechos", *Teoría y Realidad Constitucional*, núm. 42, 2018, pp. 483-509.

Pomed Sánchez L. A., "Transparencia", in *Fundamentos: Cuadernos monográficos de teoría del Estado, derecho público e historia constitucional*, Nº 9, 2016, pp. 167-214, p. 206.

Renato C., Sotelo-Torres A. and García-Curiel K., "El procedimiento de acceso a la información pública como mecanismo para proteger el derecho a la verdad. Una revisión de los criterios de la Corte Interamericana de Derechos Humanos sobre la materia", in *Revista Española de la Transparencia*, Núm. 19, 2024. Primer semestre. Enero-junio 2024, pp. 221-246.

Ruiz-Rico Ruiz G., "La dimensión constitucional del principio de transparencia y el derecho de información activa", *Revista de Derecho Político*, núm. 110, 2021, pp. 47-78.

Sánchez De Diego Fernández de la Riva M., "Un derecho fundamental a acceder a la información pública", en M. Sánchez De Diego Fernández de la Riva, (coord.), *El derecho de acceso a la información pública*, Universidad Complutense, Madrid, 2007, pp. 7-41.

Villaverde Menéndez I., *Los derechos del público*, Tecnos, Madrid, 1995, p. 118.

Elżbieta Zębek[1025]

'Environmental democracy' and the protection of natural elements - legal instruments and ecological considerations

Abstract: A manifestation of environmental democracy is public participation in environmental protection guaranteed by the provisions of the Aarhus Convention. This applies in particular to the decision-making process for environmental impact assessments of projects. In EU law, these issues are regulated in the Assessment Directive No. 2011/92/EU and in Polish law in the 2008 AEIA. This article aims to present the role of 'environmental democracy' in the protection of natural elements. This issue is presented based on an analysis of the status and legal instruments in the field of public participation in the adoption of environmental planning documents on the example of environmental impact assessments for Natura 2000 sites. This analysis has shown that a participatory habitat assessment procedure for Natura 2000 sites is extremely important for the EU's protection of natural habitats and protected species, including wild birds. The RDEP is the authority managing such areas and has full powers to make a habitat assessment mandatory thus the need for public participation. This occurs if it is considered that the activity will have a negative impact on the objects of protection in these areas. Public participation in environmental planning can therefore indirectly contribute to the protection of natural elements, especially unique ones.

Keywords: environmental law, environmental democracy, public participation, environmental impact assessment, Natura 2000 sites

1. Introduction

Nowadays, democracy is an indispensable element in the functioning of society in many spheres of life (social, economic), which allows decisions to be taken on many issues, including environmental ones. Democracy means the rule of the people. The term was introduced in antiquity by the Greek sophists and popularised by Democritus of Abdera, later by the critics of Athenian democracy Plato and Aristotle. The term democracy is currently used in four senses: 1) the power of the people, the nation, the society; 2) a form of the political system of the state that recognises the will of the majority of citizens as the source of power and grants

1025 University of Warmia and Mazury in Olsztyn, ORCID: 0000-0002-8637-8391.

them political rights and freedoms that guarantee the exercise of that power; 3) a synonym for political rights and freedoms themselves, which are based on the equality of citizens before the law and the equality of their opportunities and possibilities; 4) a social and economic system that ensures the universal equal participation of citizens in the ownership and management of national productive assets, access to cultural, educational and health goods, as well as the environment.[1026] Thus, democracy is a form of the political system of the state that recognises the will of the majority of citizens as the source of power and grants political rights and freedoms to society, guaranteeing the exercise of that power.[1027] Democracy is the best form of government currently available for translating public expectations into policy.[1028] The concept of civil society is now becoming a reality in a democratic state under the rule of law.

Democracy is also implemented in the management and protection of environmental resources, so-called environmental democracy. The term 'environmental democracy' refers to a state in which the public is guaranteed participation in environmental management and, above all, the opportunity to participate in decision-making procedures that affect the environment. Therefore, it is necessary to ensure the right to information in the area of the environment and the right of access to justice in environmental matters. It is important to add that the implementation of environmental democracy requires the cooperation of the general public, including NGOs, with public administration authorities. For environmental democracy to be effectively realised, it needs to be regulated in detail and implemented at a level as close to the citizen as possible.[1029]

It is recognised that the first significant milestone in this regard was set by the 1992 Rio Declaration on Environment and Development adopted under the auspices of the United Nations. This declaration states that public participation in environmental matters, and in particular the right to information and access

---

1026 M. Król, *Słownik demokracji*, Kraków 1989; G. Sartori, *Teoria demokracji*, Warszawa 1994; Encyklopedia PWN, *Demokracja*, https://encyklopedia.pwn.pl/haslo/demokracja;3891717.html [accessed: 18.06.2024].

1027 Słownik języka polskiego PWN, *Demokracja*, https://sjp.pwn.pl/slowniki/demokracja.html [accessed: 18.06.2024].

1028 See more: J. Ciechanowicz-McLean, M. Nyka, "Nowe isntrumenty administracyjnoprawne w ochronie środowiska," in *Dekada harmonizacji w prawie ochrony środowiska*, ed. R. Rudnicki, A. Haładyj, and K. Sobieraj, Lublin 2011, p. 180.

1029 O. Cabaj, O. Łachacz, "Demokracja środowiskowa w wybranych państwach Europy Środkowej i Wschodniej na przykładzie implementacji postanowień Konwencji z Aarhus," *Polski Rocznik Praw Człowieka i Prawa Humanitarnego* 1 (2010), p. 26.

to judicial and administrative procedures, is a guarantee for the best management of environmental issues at the appropriate national or regional level. Under principle 10, environmental issues are best addressed, at the appropriate level, with the participation of all concerned citizens. At the national level, every individual should have adequate access to environmental information held by public authorities. This includes information on hazardous substances and activities within the community, as well as the opportunity to participate in the decision-making process. The states need to facilitate as well as raise public awareness and participation by creating wide access to information. There should be effective and genuine access to legal and administrative measures, including compensatory and remedial measures.[1030] Hence, environmental democracy is an idea that refers to the right of citizens to actively participate in investment processes that may have an impact on the environment, as well as in decisions and dispute resolution processes related to the environment. This requires transparent and accountable governmental decisions that are made involving all citizens to have an impact on the environment. Furthermore, environmental democracy, like any democracy, is supposed to ensure the protection of minority rights: whether the minority is a group protecting property rights and looking after the interests of the people or whether it is a group of environmentalists protecting natural elements.[1031]

The idea of environmental democracy is implemented through the rights of the citizen to access information on the state and protection of the environment and public participation, i.e. the possibility of public participation in environmental decisions, especially in the case of projects likely to have a significant impact on the environment, for which an environmental impact assessment (EIA) procedure is required. Indeed, the issue of public participation concerns the involvement of individuals in the functioning of the structures and institutions of a democratic state, i.e. in the activities of the public authority and the public sector institutions it manages. An important aspect of participatory democracy is the empowerment of different stakeholders and the inclusion of community groups in the

1030 Deklaracja z Rio de Janeiro w sprawie środowiska i rozwoju, Zasady ogólnych praw i obowiązków, 3–14.06.1992, https://libr.sejm.gov.pl/tek01/txt/inne/1992.html [accessed: 18.06.2024].

1031 K. Iwińska, M. Troszyński, "Podejmowanie decyzji infrastrukturalnych w demokracji środowiskowej," 2014, pp. 334-335, https://www.researchgate.net/publication/321990787_PODEJMOWANIE_DECYZJI_INFRASTRUKTURALNYCH_W_DEMOKRACJI_SRODOWISKOWEJ/citations#fullTextFileContent [accessed: 18.06.2024].

decision-making process.[1032] The principle of public participation is currently one of the most important principles for the functioning of a democratic state and civil society.[1033] These rights are guaranteed under the provisions of the Aarhus Convention.[1034] The preamble to the Convention states that every person has the right to live in an environment adequate to his or her health and well-being and the duty, both personally and in association with others, to protect and improve the environment for the benefit of present and future generations. To contribute to the protection of the right of everyone to live in an environment adequate to his or her health and well-being, each Party shall guarantee, in matters relating to the environment, the rights of access to information, public participation in decision-making, and access to justice. The Aarhus Convention is therefore considered to set the latest and highest current European legal standard for social dialogue in environmental protection.[1035] Within EU law, these values are mainly realised in the Assessment Directive No. 2011/92/EU[1036], which was implemented into Polish law in the 2008 AEIA.[1037] This article aims to present the role of 'environmental democracy' in the protection of natural elements. This issue will be presented based on an analysis of the status and legal instruments in the field of public participation, i.e. public participation in the adoption of environmental planning documents on the example of environmental impact assessments for Natura 2000 sites.

1032 See more: T. Kaźmierczak, "Partycypacja publiczna: pojęcia, ramy teoretyczne," in *Partycypacja publiczna. O uczestnictwie obywateli w życiu wspólnoty lokalnej*, ed. A. Olech, Warsaw 2011.

1033 P. Korzeniowski, *Instytucje prawne ochrony środowiska a proces inwestycyjno-budowlany. Studium prawno-administracyjne*, Warsaw 2012, p. 44.

1034 Aarhus Convention on Access to Information, Public Participation in Decision-making and Access to Justice in Environmental Matters adopted 25 June 1998 (LJ of 2003 No. 78, item 706).

1035 J. Jendrośka, "Konwencja z Aarhus. Geneza, status i kierunki rozwoju," *Prawo i Środowisko* 1 (2001), p. 116.

1036 Directive 2011/92/EU of the European Parliament and of the Council of 13 December 2011 on the assessment of the effects of certain public and private projects on the environment (OJ L 26, 28.1.2012, p. 1-21).

1037 Act of October 3, 2008, on the provision of information on the environment and its protection, public participation in environmental protection, and on environmental impact assessments (consolidated text LJ of 2024, items 1112, 1881, 1940).

2. Public participation and access to environmental information

The first stage in the implementation of the principle of public participation is adequate access to environmental information. It is reflected in the preamble of the Aarhus Convention, where it is indicated that to be able to assert this right and fulfill this duty, citizens must have access to information. In addition, they must be entitled to participate in decision-making and have access to justice in environmental matters. Indeed, in environmental matters, access to information and public participation in decision-making should be facilitated, which improves the quality and execution of decisions and contributes to public awareness of environmental issues. In Article 1(3) of the Arhus Convention indicates environmental information on: (a) the state of the elements of the environment, such as air and atmosphere, water, soil, land, landscape and natural sites, biological diversity and its components, including genetically modified organisms, and the interaction among these elements, (b) factors such as substances, energy, noise and radiation, and activities and measures, including administrative measures environmental agreements, policies, legislation, plans and programs which affect or are likely to affect the elements of the environment, (c) the state of human health and safety, conditions of human life, places of cultural interest and built structures, in so far as they are or may be affected by the state of the elements of the environment or, through these elements.[1038] In this regard, each Party was obliged to make appropriate practical or other provisions for the public to participate in the preparation of environmentally relevant plans and programs (Art. 7). In Polish law, detailed footnotes on the mode and principles of making information on the environment and its protection available are contained in the AEIA. Under Article 8 of the Act, public authorities are obliged to make available to anyone information on the environment and its protection, which is information held by public authorities or information intended for public authorities. However, this does not apply to information on their legislative activities and, in the case of courts and tribunals, their adjudicatory activities. Furthermore, public authorities are obliged to provide the necessary assistance and guidance when seeking information on the environment and its protection. Article 9 indicates a catalog of information subject to release, i.e., the state of environmental elements, emissions, administrative measures, reports on the implementation of environmental regulations,

1038 J. Jendrośka, W. Radecki, *Konwencja o dostępie do informacji, udziale społeczeństwa w podejmowaniu decyzji oraz dostępie do sprawiedliwości w sprawach dotyczących środowiska z komentarzem*, Wrocław 1999, p. 73.

economic analyses, and the state of health, safety, and living conditions of people, as well as cultural sites and facilities.[1039]

3. Public participation in the environmental impact assessment

An example of environmental democracy is the possibility of public participation in the decision-making process, especially regarding investments that have a significant impact on the environment. This public participation is guaranteed at the procedural stage of environmental impact assessments. In EU law, this is regulated in the Assessment Directive No. 2011/92/EU. This Directive applies to the assessment of the environmental effects of public and private projects which are likely to have significant effects on the environment. Environmental impact assessment involves appropriately identifying, describing, and assessing, for each case, the direct and indirect significant effects of a project on a) population and human health; (b) biodiversity, with particular emphasis on species and habitats protected under the Habitats Directive No. 92/43/EEC[1040] and the Birds Directive No. 2009/147/EC[1041]; c) land, soil, water, air, and climate; d) material goods, cultural heritage, and landscape and e) the interaction between these elements. In the Polish legal system, EIA is regulated in the AEIA. Under Art. 3(8), environmental impact assessment is a procedure for assessing the environmental impact of a planned project and includes 3 stages: 1) verification of the report on the environmental impact of the project, 2) obtaining opinions and arrangements required by the Act, and 3) ensuring the possibility of public participation in the procedure. This assessment should indicate expected significant impacts, including direct, indirect, secondary, cumulative, short-term, medium-term and long-term, permanent and temporary, as well as positive and negative impacts, on the purposes and object of protection of the Natura 2000 site and the integrity of the site.

1039 See more: E. Zębek, R. Biedrzycki, "Regulations concerning the dissemination of information about the condition and protection of the natural environment in the light of legal acts in force." *Scientific Journal WSFiP* 4 (2017), pp. 45-59; E. Zębek, "Principle of public participation in EU environmental policy as the public's fundamental right to participate in the implementation of project negatively impacting the environment," in *Contemporary problems of human rights: selected aspects*, ed. M. Mamiński and M. Rzewuski, Warsaw 2019, pp. 353-364.

1040 Council Directive 92/43/EEC of 21 May 1992 on the conservation of natural habitats and of wild fauna and flora (OJ L 206, 22.7.1992, p. 7-50).

1041 Directive 2009/147/EC of the European Parliament and of the Council of 30 November 2009 on the conservation of wild birds (OJ L 20, 26.1.2010, p. 7-25).

In addition, impacts should also be determined about biodiversity, people, animals, plants, water, air, land surface, landscape, climate, natural resources, monuments, and material goods, taking into account the relationships between these elements of the environment and the impacts on these elements (Art. 51).

An important stage of the EIA procedure is public participation guaranteed in Art. 5 of the AEIA, according to which everyone has the right to participate in proceedings requiring public participation, and specified in detail in Art. 39-42. This process consists of 3 stages. The first stage consists of the public disclosure by the authority preparing the draft document of basic information about the subject of the document, the possibility of reading the documentation, and submitting comments and requests within at least 21 days. Comments and motions may be submitted in writing, orally in the minutes, or by electronic means of communication. In the second stage, the body developing the draft document considers the comments and applications and attaches a justification to the adopted document. This document contains information about the public's participation in the proceedings and the manner of consideration and the scope of the comments submitted by the public taken into account. Finally, in the third stage, information about the adoption of the document and the possibility of getting acquainted with its content is made public.[1042]

In the Polish legal system, one of the forms of area protection within the EU is Natura 2000 sites established under the Habitats and Birds Directives. In national law, these areas are defined in Art. 25 of the Nature Protection Act of 2004[1043] (NPA) as: 1) areas of special bird protection; 2) special habitat protection areas; 3) areas of Community importance. It is often believed that Natura 2000 areas combine area and species protection. On the one hand, areas of particular importance for the EU are protected, and on the other, species are protected, especially wild birds, but also mammals, reptiles, and amphibians, as well as natural habitats. According to Art. 5 point 2b of the NPA, Natura 2000 areas are defined as areas of special protection for birds, special areas of habitat protection,

---

1042 See: B. Wiszniewska, J.A. Farr, J. Jendrośka, *Postępowanie w sprawie oceny oddziaływania na środowisko planowanych przedsięwzięć*, Warsaw 2002, p. 103; M. Micińska, *Udział społeczeństwa w ochronie środowiska. Instrumenty administracyjno-prawne*, Toruń 2011, p. 15; M. Kryda, *Partycypacja w obszarze ekologii: szanse, możliwości, zagrożenia*, Warsaw 2010, p. 3; A. Barczak, A. Ogonowska, "Wykładnia przepisów w zakresie udziału społeczeństwa w ochronie środowiska – wybrane problemy," *Studia Prawnicze KUL* 3 (75) (2018), pp. 7-28.

1043 Act of 16 April 2004 on nature protection (consolidated text LJ of 2024, items 1478, 1940).

or areas of Community importance. The purpose of their establishment is to protect populations of wild birds or natural habitats or species of Community interest.[1044] Article 33 of the NPA indicates that any activities that may significantly worsen the condition of natural habitats and habitats of plant and animal species, as well as have a significant negative impact on the species are prohibited in Natura 2000 sites.

Due to their uniqueness, they should be subject to special legal protection, and therefore a special procedure for environmental impact assessments (habitat assessment) is provided for these areas. Environmental impact assessment proceedings for projects are regulated in Articles 59-103 of the AEIA. According to Article 3(7), this project impact assessment is limited to the study of a project's impact on a Natura 2000 site. Considerable negative impacts on these areas are those that relate to conservation objectives. Accordingly, it is a negative impact that may: 1) worsen the condition of natural habitats or the habitats of plant and animal species for whose protection the Natura 2000 area was designated, or b) adversely affect the species for whose protection the Natura 2000 area was designated, or c) impair the integrity of the Natura 2000 area or its connections with other areas (Article 3(17)). Any planned project with potential direct or indirect negative impacts on the condition of a Natura 2000 site is subject to an environmental impact assessment (EIA), taking into account its possible effects on protected habitats or species. Where an EIA carried out shows that a project will have a negative impact on a Natura 2000 site, the project cannot, as a rule, be implemented.[1045] Here it should be noted that the EIA for Natura 2000 sites applies not only to projects of Groups 1 and 2, i.e. those that may always have a significant or potentially significant impact on the environment, respectively. It also applies to other projects not listed in the 2019 Regulation on projects likely to have a significant impact on the environment.[1046] These are the so-called Group 3 projects, however, which may significantly affect a Natura 2000 area, but are not directly related to, or do not result from, the protection of the area. These projects

---

1044 See more: W. Radecki, D. Danecka, *Ustawa o ochronie przyrody. Komentarz*, Warsaw 2018; W. Pływaczewski, E. Zębek, J. Narodowska, *Odpowiedzialność za środowisko z perspektywy prawa, kryminologii i nauk przyrodniczych*, Warsaw 2020, p. 45.

1045 A. Kawicki, E. Florkiewicz, A. Jendrasiak, *Procedura wydawania decyzji o środowiskowych uwarunkowaniach. Komentarz ze wzorami dokumentów, tom II*, Warsaw 2007, pp. 152, 155.

1046 Regulation of the Council of Ministers of 10 September 2019 on projects that may have a significant impact on the environment (consolidated text LJ of 2023, item 1724).

may also require a Natura 2000 impact assessment. The necessity to carry out such an assessment is decided by the regional director of environmental protection by way of a decision (Art. 59(2) of the AEIA), who at the same time determines whether the project may potentially significantly affect the Natura 2000 site.[1047] Therefore, a habitat assessment is a special type of environmental assessment that is used to examine whether a plan (program) or project affects a Natura 2000 site. When it is determined in the first two stages of habitat assessment (reconnaissance and proper assessment) that a plan (program) or project significantly negatively affects the objectives of protection of the Natura 2000 area and its integrity, and even if it is determined, by the precautionary principle, that such a negative impact cannot be excluded - the plan (program) or project cannot be implemented.

4. Conclusions

In summary, it can be concluded that one of the manifestations of environmental democracy is the principle of public participation, which entitles the public to participate in environmental planning after information on the state and protection of the environment has been made available. Therefore, this indicates the close relationship between the principles of access to environmental information and public participation. These rights are conferred by the provisions of the Aarhus Convention, which further safeguards a citizen's rights to justice in the event of improper consideration of comments made in such proceedings. An example of a procedure with public participation is the EIA for Natura 2000 sites, extremely important for the EU's protection of natural habitats and protected species, including wild birds. The authority that manages such areas is the RDEP, which has full authority to make a habitat assessment mandatory, and thus the need for public participation, if it determines that activities will negatively impact the objects of protection of these areas. Public participation in environmental planning can therefore indirectly contribute to the protection of natural elements, especially unique ones.

1047 See more: M Pchałek, M. Behnke, *Postępowanie w sprawie OOS wprawie polskim i UE*, Warsaw 2009; K. Gruszecki, *Komentarz do ustawy o udostępnianiu informacji o środowisku i jego ochronie, udziale społeczeństwa w ochronie środowiska oraz o ocenach oddziaływania na środowisko*, edition 4, LEX/el. 2023; E. Zębek, *Instrumenty administracyjno-prawne i ekonomiczne w ochronie środowiska*, Olsztyn 2017, pp. 41-45.

Bibliography

Barczak, A., and Ogonowska, A., "Wykładnia przepisów w zakresie udziału społeczeństwa w ochronie środowiska – wybrane problemy," *Studia Prawnicze KUL* 3 (75) (2018).

Cabaj, O., and Łachacz, O., "Demokracja środowiskowa" w wybranych państwach Europy Środkowej i Wschodniej na przykładzie implementacji postanowień Konwencji z Aarhus," *Polski Rocznik Praw Człowieka i Prawa Humanitarnego* 1 (2010).

Ciechanowicz-McLean, J., and Nyka, M., „Nowe instrumenty administracyjno-prawne w ochronie środowiska," in *Dekada harmonizacji w prawie ochrony środowiska*, ed. R. Rudnicki, A. Haładyj, and K. Sobieraj, Lublin 2011.

Gruszecki, K., *Komentarz do ustawy o udostępnianiu informacji o środowisku i jego ochronie, udziale społeczeństwa w ochronie środowiska oraz o ocenach oddziaływania na środowisko*, edition 4, LEX/el. 2023.

Iwińska, K., and Troszyński, M., "Podejmowanie decyzji infrastrukturalnych w demokracji środowiskowej," 2014, https://www.researchgate.net/publication/321990787_PODEJMOWANIE_DECYZJI_INFRASTRUKTURALNYCH_W_DEMOKRACJI_SRODOWISKOWEJ/citations#fullTextFileContent.

Jendrośka, J., and Radecki, W., Konwencja o dostępie do informacji, udziale społeczeństwa w podejmowaniu decyzji oraz dostępie do sprawiedliwości w sprawach dotyczących środowiska z komentarzem, Wrocław 1999.

Jendrośka, J., "Konwencja z Aarhus. Geneza, status i kierunki rozwoju," *Prawo i Środowisko* 1 (2001).

Kawicki, A., Florkiewicz, E., and Jendrasiak, A., *Procedura wydawania decyzji o środowiskowych uwarunkowaniach. Komentarz ze wzorami dokumentów*, edition 2, Warsaw 2007.

Kaźmierczak, T., "Partycypacja publiczna: pojęcia, ramy teoretyczne," in *Partycypacja publiczna. O uczestnictwie obywateli w życiu wspólnoty lokalnej*, ed. A. Olech, Warsaw 2011.

Korzeniowski, P., *Instytucje prawne ochrony środowiska a proces inwestycyjno-budowlany. Studium prawno-administracyjne*, Warsaw 2012.

Król, M., *Słownik demokracji*, Kraków 1989.

Kryda, M., *Partycypacja w obszarze ekologii: szanse, możliwości, zagrożenia*, Warsaw 2010.

Micińska, M., *Udział społeczeństwa w ochronie środowiska. Instrumenty administracyjno-prawne*, Toruń 2011.

Pchałek, M., and Behnke, M., *Postępowanie w sprawie OOS wprawie polskim i UE*, Warsaw 2009.

Pływaczewski, W., Zębek, E., and Narodowska, J., *Odpowiedzialność za środowisko z perspektywy prawa, kryminologii i nauk przyrodniczych*, Warsaw 2020.

Radecki, W., and Danecka, D., *Ustawa o ochronie przyrody. Komentarz*, Warsaw 2018.

Sartori, G., *Teoria demokracji*, Warsaw 1994.

Wiszniewska, B., Farr, J.A., and Jendrośka, J., *Postępowanie w sprawie oceny oddziaływania na środowisko planowanych przedsięwzięć*, Warsaw 2002.

Zębek, E., and Biedrzycki, R., "Regulations concerning dissemination of information about the condition and protection of natural environment in the light of legal acts in force." *Scientific Journal WSFiP* 4 (2017).

Zębek, E., *Instrumenty administracyjno-prawne i ekonomiczne w ochronie środowiska*, Olsztyn 2017.

Zębek, E., "*Principle of public participation in EU environmental policy as the public's fundamental right to participate in the implementation of project negatively impacting the environment*," in *Contemporary problems of human rights: selected aspects*, ed. M. Mamiński and M. Rzewuski, Warsaw 2019.

Legal acts

Aarhus Convention on Access to Information, Public Participation in Decision-making and Access to Justice in Environmental Matters, adopted 25 June 1998 (LJ of 2003 No. 78, item 706).

Rio de Janeiro Declaration on Environment and Development, 3–14.06.1992, https://libr.sejm.gov.pl/tek01/txt/inne/1992.html.

Council Directive 92/43/EEC of 21 May 1992 on the conservation of natural habitats and of wild fauna and flora (OJ L 206, 22.7.1992, p. 7-50).

Directive 2009/147/EC of the European Parliament and of the Council of 30 November 2009 on the conservation of wild birds (OJ L 20, 26.1.2010, p. 7-25).

Directive 2011/92/EU of the European Parliament and of the Council of 13 December 2011 on the assessment of the effects of certain public and private projects on the environment (OJ L 26, 28.1.2012, p. 1-21).

Act of 16 April 2004 on nature protection (consolidated text LJ of 2024, items 1478, 1940).

Act of 3 October 2008 on the provision of information on the environment and its protection, public participation in environmental protection and on environmental impact assessments (consolidated text LJ of 2024, items 1112, 1881, 1940).

Regulation of the Council of Ministers of 10 September 2019 on projects that may have a significant impact on the environment (consolidated text LJ of 2023, item 1724).

Chałubińska-Jentkiewicz Katarzyna[1048]

Fighting harmful content - censorship in the name of cybersecurity

Abstract: In a flourishing democracy, citizens are free to exercise their freedoms, including expressing their views, participating in the communication process, acquiring knowledge and disseminating information. Today, however, European democracy faces new challenges arising from threats hitherto unknown or undefined. The expansion of the sphere of state and citizen security into the area of virtual space and the reference to cyber security is a natural consequence of the development of communication technologies and the coupled social phenomena centered around the acquisition, processing and distribution of information[1049]. Such a pattern, as a rule, leads to specific needs for legal changes and redefinition of public interest goals, which are realized, among other things, by means of normative instruments. Free media, academia and civil society should be able to play their role in stimulating open debate, free from interference, both foreign and domestic. In the article, I attempt to answer the key question - how much freedom of speech vs. how much security is required under the conditions of re-regulation of the digital media environment.

Keywords: freedom of speech, digital media, illegal content, harmful content, disinformation, content blocking, online platforms

---

1048 Kozminski University, Cellege of Law, ORCID:0000-0003-0188-5704.

1049 On the development of new digital media, see M. Szpunar, *W stronę nowych mediów*, Toruń 2010, pp. 11-76; K. Jakubowicz, *Media a demokracja w XXI wieku. Poszukiwania nowych modeli*, Warsaw 2013, pp. 149 et seq.; J. Olszański, *Media i dziennikarstwo internetowe*, Warsaw 2012; T. Goban-Klas, "Ontology of the Internet" in *Społeczeństwo informacyjne. Vision or Reality*, ed. L. Haber, Cracow 2004; U. Eco, "New mass media and the future of the book" in *New media in social communication of the 20th century. Anthology*, ed. M. Hopfinger, Warsaw 2002; P. Levy, "The Second Deluge" in *New media in social communication of the 20th century. Anthology*, ed. M. Hopfinger, Warsaw 2002; P. Ziarek, "New media and politics. New forms of communication in the field of politics" in *New media and politics. Internet, democracy, election campaigns*, ed. M. Jezinski, Toruń 2009, pp. 41-46; J. Jastrzębski, "Ethics of new media" in New media *and politics. Internet, democracy, election campaigns*, ed. M. Jezinski, Toruń 2009, pp. 74-78; M. Wnorowska, "New media in the period of political hibernation" in *New media and politics. Internet, democracy, election campaigns*, ed. M. Jezinski, Toruń 2009 pp. 110-125; A. Grzesik-Robak, "Traditional media in the face of new technological solutions - opportunities or threats" in *New media and traditional media. Press, advertising, internet*, ed. M. Jezinski, Toruń 2009, p. 27-35; A. Borasińska, "New media - (new) psychology of the recipient" in *New media and traditional media. Press, advertising, internet*, ed. M. Jezinski, Toruń 2009, pp. 36-43.

1. Security - a rationale for restrictions on freedom of speech

Defining the issue of security, and in view of the development of digital media - cyber-security - linked to the social dimension of threats, their identification and neutralization, is accompanied by constant attempts to protect the system of values that has become the basis for the development of modern Western democracies. A dilemma arises - the need to choose between freedoms hitherto constitutionally guaranteed and cyber security. The fundamental question, however, becomes the issue of determining what should be the rationale for restrictions: security, as referred to in Article 31(3) of the Polish Constitution of the Republic of Poland[1050], or national security, as referred to in the European Convention on Human Rights (hereinafter ECHR)[1051] and the International Covenant on Civil and Political Rights (hereinafter ICCPR)[1052]? It is digital technology that puts the user in the digital paradox of truth and falsehood, but also in the paradox of security - freedom of speech. In any action taken by public authorities, it should be borne in mind that the process of combating disinformation and, above all, harmful content, begins with the digital capabilities and competencies of the individual - the user of digital media - it is his or her rights and freedoms, including the resulting right to security, that constitute a superior good to the common chase for sensationalism, the ambitions of the new digital dictators of life and politicians "fighting" for digital democracy. First of all, it should be noted that the rulings of first the European Commission of Human Rights and then the Human Rights Committee were clearly dominated until the end of the 20th century by the idealistic paradigm of press freedom[1053], clearly moving towards the absolutization of

1050 OJ No. 78, item 483.

1051 Convention for the Protection of Human Rights and Fundamental Freedoms, drawn up in Rome on November 4, 1950, subsequently amended by Protocols Nos. 3, 5 and 8 and supplemented by Protocol No. 2 dated November 4, 1950 (Journal of Laws 1993, No. 61, item 284).

1052 International Covenant on Civil and Political Rights (Journal of Laws 1994 No. 23, item 80).

1053 The first to draw attention to this issue was F. Matscher," Idéalisme et réalisme dans la jurisprudence de la Cour européenne des droits de l'*homme*" in *Protection of Human Rights: le perspective europeenne. Protecting Human Rights: the European Perspective, Studies in memory of Rolv Ryssdal*, ed. by F. Matscher, H. Petzold, L. Wildhaber, Köln 2000. See also in this regard I.C. Kaminski, "Duties and Responsibilities" Related to Freedom of Expression and the Phenomenon of Tabloids" in *Media Ownership, Information Pluralism, Freedom of Expression. Selected materials from the international conference Warsaw, October 29-30, 2010*, ed. D. Bychawska-Siniarska, Warsaw 2011, pp. 121-136.

freedom[1054]. It was only at the beginning of the current century that the judgments of the European Court of Human Rights slowly, albeit quite consistently, began to move away from the idealistic concept towards realistic solutions, linking the scope of freedom to the fulfillment of the requirements of fairness and diligence, i.e. to the fulfillment of standards of professionalism.

It should be noted that in terms of security, if a given threat is misidentified from the outset, for example, under the influence of presenting various presumptions as facts, then the measures taken, which have a concrete objective dimension, are not adequate to the real threat. This also applies to the digital media environment. The issue of security as an undefined concept is very broad and is an outgrowth of broader processes that also create a platform for the exchange of information, views and thoughts between all participants in the process of communication in the digital market and cyberspace. Security is also a premise for restrictions on rights and freedoms under Article 31(3) of the Polish Constitution.

2. Digital media as an area of regulation

The Internet has become a place to create its own information spaces, at the same time new forms of media and a new public sphere that knows no territorial boundaries, language or national barriers. This dimension of the often uncontrolled expansion of media space requires a new regulatory approach in terms of new methods and techniques for ensuring cyber security. New forms of threats from malware, online identity theft, impersonation of official websites or *phishing are* creating entirely new ways of obtaining information, including illegal information, including for creating new situations that favor specific interest groups - including state actors in the context of international relations. The armed forces of individual states are beginning to organize militaries dedicated to the protection of cyberspace - especially related to the classic institutions of state security and other spheres of the state that affect the daily lives of citizens. This also applies to the negative use of digital media and their users. It can be said that the freedoms governing the Internet are becoming the enemy of the security of individuals, individual communities and even states.

However, it is important to remember that the Internet itself is no longer a unified whole. As a bifurcated area, it is the site of a power struggle over evolving

1054 M. Levinet, "L'incertaine détermination des limites de la liberté d'expression. Réflexions sur les arrêts rendus par la Cour de Strasbourg en 1995–1996 à propos de l'article 10 de la Convention européenne des droits de l'homm", *Revue français de droit administratif* 1997/13/5, p. 1004; F. Sudre, "Droit de la Convention européenne de droits de l'homme", *Juris Classeur Périodique* 1997/6-7, p. 77.

new technologies. In addition to a commodity as precious as data, there is a war for the space of free speech, for privacy, for digital property rights. The legality of surveillance of this environment and the need for data retention changes everything. "Tell Congress not to censor the Internet"- proclaimed Google sending an automated message from its users in response to a bill to combat Internet piracy. Information wants to be free ! It's a slogan that is becoming crucial in the face of the media war in the digital world. However, in addition to the state restricting free expression, there is also environmental, labor, social or family oppression. Digital exclusion - including through online blocking becomes the most severe punishment for a digital media user.

In 2020. The European Union (EU) unveiled the EU Democracy Action Plan, and in December 2023, to complement and deepen this action, the Commission unveiled the Democracy Defense Package. The European Media Freedom Act, a new set of rules designed to protect media pluralism and independence in the EU, came into force in May 2024[1055]. The Digital Services Act came into force on February 17, 2024[1056]. The regulatory environment for digital copyrights has changed[1057] and new media law rules have emerged. These are just some of the big changes in the digital environment. All of them are dictated by cyber security considerations.

Protecting European democracies from threats and harmful content, the effects of information manipulation and information interference, particularly from foreign actors, has been an EU priority in recent years. Democracies around the world are facing the proliferation of harmful content and foreign interference, which can destabilize democratic institutions and deepen social divisions, undermining citizens' trust. The situation is paradoxically exacerbated by digitization, which allows harmful content to spread with unprecedented speed and efficiency. The fight against harmful content is based on existing and firmly rooted European values and principles. These are guaranteed by: freedom of expression and the right of citizens to access legal content.

1055 Regulation (EU) 2024/1083 of the European Parliament and of the Council of April 11, 2024, establishing a common framework for media services in the internal market and amending Directive 2010/13/EU (European Media Freedom Act)Text with EEA relevance (Official Journal of the EU L. of 17.04.2024).

1056 Regulation (EU) 2022/2065 of the European Parliament and of the Council of 19 October 2022 on the single market for digital services and amending Directive 2000/31/EC (Digital Services Act), the so-called DSA (Digital Services Act)(Official Journal of the EU L 277 of 22.10.2022).

1057 Directive 2019/790 on copyright and related rights in the digital single market and amending Directives 96/9/EC and 2001/29/EC (Official Journal of the EU L 2019).

In line with the guidelines adopted by the Commission in 2021 on how to strengthen the existing EU Code of Conduct on Combating Disinformation, a new code was signed in June 2022, involving both major and specialized online platforms, the online advertising industry, research and civil society, as well as fact-checkers[1058]. The code outlines a wide range of commitments, from demonetization to transparency and access to data. Importantly, the code includes a robust monitoring framework and transparency center to ensure greater transparency and accountability. It also sets out a framework for co-regulation under the Digital Services Act, which requires very large online platforms and search engines to regularly assess the systemic risks their services may pose to the public, including the risk of their services being misused as a tool for disinformation campaigns.

3. Harmful content - a necessary redefinition

The goal of harmful content, especially disinformation, is to weaken the West and democracy, create chaos and divisions in societies. A large part of the Western political establishment is still unaware of the magnitude of the threat and the challenges, the authors of the Prague Declaration wrote[1059]. It should be added that, according to the Tallinn Manual, in the context of cyber-security measures using domestic sovereignty, a state may, among other things, restrict, partially or completely, the access of persons on its territory to cyberspace, in particular to certain online content[1060].

Striking a balance between protecting freedom of expression and legitimate restrictions on that freedom is becoming the basis of current regulatory changes. It is necessary to better understand how public opinion is formed in the digital media age and how digital media can be regulated. Questions of how to protect freedom of expression, privacy and pluralism by providing an enabling legal environment are becoming topical. There are various projects to combat cyber threats in digital media, but they are not directly related to the protection and legitimate restrictions on freedom of speech and expression. The DSA does not specifically define what "illegal content" is. According to Article 3(h) of the regulation, "illegal

1058 The Strengthened Code of Practice on Disinformation 2022 2022_Strengthened_Code_of_Practice_Disinformation_TeAETn7bUPXR57PU2FsTqU8rMA_87585.pdf (accessed 19.06.2024).

1059 They recalled the recent manifesto of 110 specialists from 22 European countries, who in early November 2017 in Prague called on the Union and NATO to defend against the propaganda war on the Internet.

1060 *Tallin Manual on the International Law Applicable to Cyber Walfare*, ed. M. N. Schmitt, Cambridge 2013.

content" means information that, either in itself or by reference to an activity, including the sale of products or the provision of services, does not comply with Union law or with the law of any Member State that is compatible with Union law, regardless of the specific subject matter or nature of that law. The analysis of European acts now indicates the need to assess the content of digital content, in all its forms. The definition adopted under the DSA means that the determination of whether content is illegal or also harmful will be determined by the value system adopted in a given member state (of course, beyond the common scopes of such a definition, which has been carried out under, for example, the provisions of the Audiovisual Media Services Directive[1061] and the Copyright and Related Rights in the Digital Single Market Directive[1062] or the Cybercrime Convention[1063]). However, according to Recital 12 of the DSA, "In particular, the term 'illegal content' should be defined broadly to include information on illegal content, products, services and activities. In particular, the term should be understood as referring to information, regardless of its form, that is either illegal per se under applicable law, such as illegal hate speech, aggression or terrorist content and unlawful discriminatory content, or that becomes illegal under applicable law due to the fact that it relates to illegal activities. For example, this could include the sharing of child sexual abuse images, the unlawful sharing of private images without consent, cyberstalking, the sale of non-compliant or counterfeit products, the sale of goods or provision of services in violation of consumer protection laws, the unauthorized use of copyrighted materials, the illegal offering of accommodation services, or the illegal sale of live animals. In contrast, an eyewitness video of a potential crime should not be considered harmful content simply because it depicts a criminal act, where the recording or distribution of such a video to the general public is not illegal under national or Union law. In this regard, it is irrelevant whether the illegal nature of the information or action derives from Union law or from a national law that is compatible with Union law, and what the exact nature or subject matter of the law in question is." This has been the Council of

1061 Directive 2010/13/EU of the European Parliament and of the Council of 10 March 2010 on the coordination of certain provisions laid down by law, regulation or administrative action in Member States concerning the provision of audiovisual media services (Audiovisual Media Services Directive) (Codified version) (Text with EEA relevance) (OJ EU L, 15.04.2010).

1062 Directive 2019/790 on copyright and related rights in the digital single market and amending Directives 96/9/EC and 2001/29/EC (Official Journal of the EU L 2019).

1063 Communication from the Commission to the European Parliament, the Council and the Committee of the Regions towards a general strategy to combat cybercrime, Brussels, 22.5.2007 (COM(2007) 267 final).

Europe's traditional take since the 1960s vis-à-vis print media and then cinematography. Since the 1980s, visual media have been included, and since the early 1990s there has been a uniform European standard on the matter, prohibiting the dissemination of content harmful to minors in audiovisual media. This standard is European in nature, but EU member states at the level of national law may shape the definitions of the two aforementioned terms differently. Harmful content also includes elements of disinformation. Yet another face of harmful content is the pursuit of information policy aimed at undermining the attributes of a state, the authority of public power. In this sense, harmful content, very often simultaneously as an act of aggression in cyberspace, becomes an element of information warfare. Thus, it should be assumed that the determination of whether a given content is illegal or harmful will be determined by the system of legal solutions adopted in a given Member State dictated also by the common scopes of such definition, which has been carried out on the basis of, for example, the provisions of the Audiovisual Media Services Directive and the Directive on Copyright and Related Rights in the Digital Single Market. It is important to point out the differences in the understanding of illegal content and dangerous content, such as harmful content (e.g., persuasion of activities endangering health or life).

4. Liability for illegal and harmful content

The dissemination of digital content over the network via digital media services is by definition cross-border and concerns the dissemination of network content, primarily in an author-legal context. In contrast, prohibitions on the dissemination of specific digital content will arise from media law considerations[1064]. So far,

1064 On new regulatory principles in new media, see H. Izdebski, *Elementy teorii filozofii prawa*, Warsaw 2008, pp. 196 and 281; A. Peters, I. Pagotto, "Soft law as a new method of management in the European Union - legal perspective" in *Nowe metody zarządzania w państwach* Unii Europejskiej, ed. L. Kolarska-Bobińska, Warsaw 2009. See also Z. Brodecki, M. Konopacka, A. Brodecka-Chamera, *Komparatystyka kultur prawnych*, Warsaw 2010, pp. 15-24 and 81-99; Cf. also: T. Stawecki," Convergence and Divergence of Legal Orders in the Sphere of Law Making," in *Convergence or Divergence of Cultures and Legal Systems*, eds. O. Nawrot, S. Sykuna, J. Zajadło, Warsaw 2012, p. 24-74; G. Maroń, "Principles of law as a component of legal culture" in *Convergence or divergence of cultures and legal systems*, ed. O. Nawrot, S. Sykuna, J. Zajadło, Warsaw 2012, pp. 223-232; M.E. Stefaniuk, T. Woś, "The extent of convergence in the formation of the constitutional position and the manner of protection of human and civil rights by ombudsmen in European countries" in Convergence *or Divergence of Cultures and Legal Systems*, eds. O. Nawrot, S. Sykuna, J. Zajadło, Warsaw 2012, pp. 299-307.

the law has explicitly addressed only physical objects delivered to the consumer and digital services provided, particularly in terms of liability for the delivery of content as a commodity. The flow of media content caused by commercial considerations technological convergence was reduced by H. Jenkins mainly to the digitization of media content, economic convergence to horizontal integration, also defined as corporate mergers. By social convergence he wanted to understand the multiple strategies chosen by consumers to navigate the new information environment. Cultural convergence, on the other hand, he defined as the use of new forms of creativity at the intersection of different media technologies, industries and media consumers. By global convergence, H. Jenkins wanted to understand hybridization as a consequence of the international circulation of media content. H. Jenkins referred to as corporate convergence (corporate convergence). By grassroots convergence, on the other hand, he meant the informal, sometimes also unauthorized circulation of media content, which occurs when consumers can easily archive, comment on, acquire and redistribute media content. By technological convergence, he meant the combining of different functions within a single device. In the current state of development of digital services, harmful content is an inseparable and significant part of the daily interactions that network users make[1065].

The DSA regulation builds on the 2018 recommendation on illegal content[1066]. The regulation takes into account lessons learned from self-regulatory activities conducted with the support of the European Commission, such as the voluntary Product Safety Pledge system; the Memorandum of Understanding on the Sale of Counterfeit Goods on the Internet[1067], the Code of Conduct on Illegal Incitement to Hate on the Internet[1068] and the EU Internet Forum on Terrorist Content. In particular, these regulations must address the problem of the absence of territorial barriers to accessing content on the Internet, that is, the problem of content created outside a country's jurisdiction, but which is nevertheless accessed by

---

1065 M. Dupagne, B. Garrison, "The meaning and influence of convergence: A qualitative case study of newsroom work at the Tampa News Center," *Journalism Studies* 2006/7/2, p. 239.

1066 Commission Recommendation of March 1, 2018 on measures to effectively combat illegal online content (C(2018) 1177 final).

1067 https://ec.europa.eu/growth/industry/policy/intellectual-property/enforcement/memorandum-understanding-sale-counterfeit-goods-internet_en.

1068 https://ec.europa.eu/info/policies/justice-and-fundamental-rights/combatting-discrimination/racism-and-xenophobia/eu-code-conduct-countering-illegal-hate-speech-online_en.

its residents or citizens, or which affects the country or its citizens. The shape of the regulations adopted usually also reflects the specifics of the legal systems and political systems of the jurisdictions in which they were introduced, hence the often different regulation of similar problems and the limited transferability of solutions between significantly different jurisdictions.

An important instrument for combating illegal content is the blocking or removal of such content - regulated in many countries on the basis of many of their own but also common grounds, which are not necessarily uniform and coordinated, with the DSA becoming the legal basis for liability for content directed at EU citizens. In particular, these regulations need to address the problem of the absence of territorial barriers to access to content on the Internet, i.e. the problem of content created outside the jurisdiction of a country, but which can be accessed by its residents or citizens, or which concerns the country or its citizens. The shape of the regulations adopted usually also reflects the specificity of the legal systems and political systems of the jurisdictions in which they were introduced, hence the often different regulation of similar problems and the limited transferability of solutions between significantly different jurisdictions[1069].

Recommendations for a similar obligation have been set forth in new laws in old democracies, such as the United Kingdom, which passed a law regulating online content on September 19, 2023, introducing age verification requirements for websites and other rules to curb hate speech, harassment and other illegal and harmful content. The Internet Safety Law, which also addresses terrorist propaganda, online fraud and child safety, is one of the most far-reaching attempts by a Western democracy to regulate online speech. The new rules, some 300 pages in length, have been more than five years in the making, sparking intense debates about how to balance freedom of speech and privacy with blocking harmful content, particularly directed at children. The new law forces companies to proactively screen objectionable material and assess whether it is illegal, rather than requiring them to act only after receiving a warning about illegal content. It is part of a wave of regulations in Europe aimed at ending an era of self-regulation, in which technology companies set their own rules about what content could be removed. Michelle Donelan, UK Technology Secretary. “This government is taking a huge step forward in our mission to make the UK the safest place in the

1069 The official EU definition of disinformation was developed by a team of experts from European Union member states. According to this definition, disinformation is “false, inaccurate or misleading information created, presented and disseminated for profit or to deliberately cause public harm”. Thus, it has the character of harmful content.

world online." British politicians have come under pressure to adopt the new policy as concerns have grown about the negative impact of Internet and social media use on democracy. According to the new regulation, social media platforms and providers of other online services will be required to implement age verification measures to prevent children from accessing pornography. The Wikimedia Foundation, operator of Wikipedia, said it would not be able to comply with the law and could be blocked. TikTok, YouTube, Facebook and Instagram will also be required to introduce features that allow users to choose less harmful content, such as eating disorders, self-harm, racism, misogyny or anti-Semitism. At the heart of the new law is a simple idea: providers should consider the foreseeable risks of their services and try to reduce them - as many other industries already do. The regulation has drawn criticism from technology companies, free speech advocates and privacy groups, who say it threatens free speech because it will encourage companies to remove content and block access to accounts. The risk here is that the response of the media and social networks to fake news will not only increase distrust, but actually become a tool for silencing dissenting views and freedom of expression. Using technology to influence public opinion becomes more difficult when individuals or foreign adversaries anonymously facilitate the creation of internal social tensions. The lack of traceability of sources further enables further dissemination. While the dangers of viral dissemination of illegal content are well known, the potential harm that can result from disproportionate countermeasures should not be underestimated. Unrestricted government censorship of online communications; a broad definition of what constitutes harmful content, and extensive use of the power to block access to content on grounds of national or public security are just a few examples of the potential threats to the principle of freedom of expression and the rule of law posed by overly expansive harmful content laws.

5. Regulatory future - summary

Restrictions on freedom of speech should be necessary, and supported by the existence of an urgent social need. In other words, the rationale for the restriction must be relevant and sufficient (relevant and sufficient - pertinents et suffisants). On this occasion, the European Court of Human Rights stated that it rests, in principle, with the relevant institutions of the member states[1070] to examine

1070 See ECHR judgment of 21.01.1999, Fressoz and Roire v. France, application no. 29183/95, pp. 958-965; M.A. Nowicki (ed.), "European Convention on Human Rights. Review of the case law," *Palestra* 1999/5-6, pp. 107-108.

whether interference with the content of a communication is actually justified by the rationale indicated by the European Convention on Human Rights. The Court pointed out that the European Convention, while upholding freedom of expression, generally requires states only to refrain from interfering in the sphere covered by freedom of expression. In certain cases, however, the authorities are obliged to take active measures to effectively guarantee freedom of expression. Such an obligation exists in particular when there are physical attacks on journalists, colporteurs, publishers. In such a situation, the state has not only the right, but the obligation to provide protection to those threatened and to carry out proceedings aimed at punishing the perpetrators[1071].

Regulatory actions taken on the grounds of the new legal conditions resulting from legislative changes at the EU level should clearly include a comprehensive approach, which should have its scope:

- use of algorithms to ensure the transparency of platforms from the users' perspective);
- Introduce legislation defining cyber threats, including disinformation activities setting a sanction under conditions that are particularly important for the preservation of democracy and state sovereignty;
- Creating conditions for the user to be able to get information about the source of the content and the entity that funded it, as well as information about why the content went to them,
- Adopting responsibilities to social media, on the one hand to guarantee access to quality information, and on the other to protect users from harmful content.

The focus must be on the need to protect the audience-individual-user of the network first and foremost. Such an approach could ensure that the designed solutions comply with freedom of speech and the rules of digital media. And this requires both courage and tolerance - two principles that represent the future of free speech. Cyberspace is not a separate unitary state, but neither is it a conglomeration of national jurisdictions. It is a heterogeneous reality that requires specific but also common regulations.

1071 See ECHR ruling of 28.09.1999, Özgür Gündem v. Turkey, application no. 22479/ 93.

Bibliography

Borasinska, A., "New media - the (new) psychology of the recipient" in *New media vs. traditional media. Press, advertising, internet*, ed. M. Jezinski, Toruń 2009.

Brodecki, Z., Konopacka, M., Brodecka-Chamera, A., *Comparatistics of legal cultures*, Warsaw 2010.

Dupagne, M., Garrison, B., "The meaning and influence of convergence: A qualitative case study of newsroom work at the Tampa News Center," *Journalism Studies* 2006/7/2.

Eco, U., "New Mass Media and the Future of the Book" in *New Media in Social Communication in the Twentieth Century. An Anthology*, edited by M. Hopfinger, Warsaw 2002.

Goban-Klas, T., Ontology of the Internet" in *Information Society. Vision or Reality*, ed. by L. Haber, Krakow 2004.

Grzesik-Robak, A., "Traditional media in the face of new technological solutions - opportunities or threats" in *New media and traditional media. Press, advertising, internet*, ed. M. Jezinski, Toruń 2009.

Izdebski, H., *Elements of the theory of philosophy of law*, Warsaw 2008.

Jakubowicz, K., *Media and democracy in the 21st century. Searching for new models*, Warsaw 2013.

Jastrzebski, J., "Ethics of new media" in *Nowe media i polityka. Internet, democracy, and election campaigns*, edited by M. Jezinski, Toruń 2009.

Kaminski, I.C., "Obligations and responsibilities" related to freedom of expression and the phenomenon of tabloids" in *Własność mediów, pluralism of information, freedom of expression. Selected materials from the international conference Warsaw, October 29-30, 2010*, ed. D. Bychawska-Siniarska, Warsaw 2011.

Levinet, M., "L'incertaine détermination des limites de la liberté d'expression. Réflexions sur les arrêts rendus par la Cour de Strasbourg en 1995–1996 à propos de l'article 10 de la Convention européenne des droits de l'homm", *Revue français de droit administratif* 1997/13/5.

Levy, P., "The Second Deluge" in *New Media in Social Communication in the Twentieth Century. An Anthology*, edited by M. Hopfinger, Warsaw 2002.

Maroń, G., "Principles of law as a component of legal culture" in *Convergence or divergence of cultures and legal systems*, ed. O. Nawrot, S. Sykuna, J. Zajadło, Warsaw 2012.

Matscher, F., "Idéalisme et réalisme dans la jurisprudence de la Cour européenne des droits de l'*homme*" in *Protection of Human Rights: le perspective europeenne. Protecting Human Rights: the European Perspective, Studies in memory of Rolv Ryssdal*, ed. by F. Matscher, H. Petzold, L. Wildhaber, Köln 2000.

Nowicki, MA, "The European Convention on Human Rights. A review of case law," *Palestra* 1999/5-6.

Olszanski, J., *Media and online journalism*, Warsaw 2012.

Peters A., Pagotto, I., "Soft law as a new management method in the European Union - a legal perspective" in *Nowe metody zarządzania w państwach* Unii Europejskiej, ed. L. Kolarska-Bobińska, Warsaw 2009.

Schmitt, M.N., *Tallin Manual on the International Law Applicable to Cyber Walfare*, Cambridge 2013.

Stawecki, T., "Convergence and Divergence of Legal Orders in the Sphere of Law Making" in *Convergence or Divergence of Cultures and Legal Systems*, ed. O. Nawrot, S. Sykuna, J. Zajadło, Warsaw 2012.

Stefaniuk, M.E., Woś, T., "The extent of convergence in the formation of the constitutional position and the manner of protection of human and civil rights by ombudsmen in European countries" in *Convergence or divergence of cultures and legal systems*, ed. O. Nawrot, S. Sykuna, J. Zajadło, Warsaw 2012.

Sudre, F., "Droit de la Convention européenne de droits de l'homme," *Juris Classeur Périodique* 1997/6-7.

Szpunar, M., *W kierunku nowych mediów*, Toruń 2010.

Wnorowska, M., "New media in a period of political hibernation" in *New media and politics. Internet, democracy, and election campaigns*, edited by M. Jezinski, Toruń 2009.

Ziarek, P., *Politics. Internet, democracy, election campaigns*, edited by M. Jezinski, Toruń 2009.

Monika Nowikowska[1072]

Digital identity and the right to privacy and data protection

Abstract: With the development of digital identity, data protection and the right to privacy are taking on a new meaning. The research issues raised are becoming the subject of dynamic consideration and debate, both in the legal and technological communities. The rapid development of information and communication technologies has increased impact on our everyday life. From the moment of apperance of the Internet and the smartphone, our identities have been recreated in the virtual world. From online banking to online shopping, there are many places that require personal information from us. The aim of this article is to review main issues connected with the digital identity. When using banking, medical, government services or online shopping, a so-called digital identity is used. Over the past few years, the ecosystem of digital trust services has developed significantly. Legislative changes at the European Union level, assuming a high degree of harmonization at the level of national legislation, have contributed to this. The intention of the author of this article was primarily to organize the conceptual area. The article attempts to define the concept of "digital identity" and to establish its relationship with such concepts as: "right to privacy" and "personal data". It was also important to determine how to take care of the protection of identity on the Internet and what risks arise from the use of identity online.

Keywords: digital identity, privacy, personal data, identity theft, new technologies

1. General comments

The modern conditions of an individual's functioning in cyberspace raise ever newer questions regarding the need to ensure an individual's security in the virtual world. Indeed, digital identity is becoming a fundamental element of our online presence, affecting many aspects of our lives, both private, social and economic. It includes all the information that identifies a person in the digital world. Digital identity consists of elements such as email addresses, logins, biometric data, image, social media accounts.

There is no legal definition of digital identity. Under the development of new technologies, it is commonly defined as an electronic representation of an individual, enabling secure and effective interaction in digital space. According

1072 War Studies University in Warsaw, Faculty of Law and Administration, ORCID: 0000-0001-5166-8375.

to the Dictionary of the Polish Language, identity means "identity", "with respect to an individual person: self-consciousness", "facts, features, personal data that allow identifying a person"[1073]. K. Chalubinska-Jentkiewicz understands by the identity of an individual the invocation of one or more specific factors determining the physical, mental, economic, cultural or social characteristics of a person. The author derives this concept from dignity. Every person has his own identity, on which he builds the foundations of his individual dignity[1074]. C. Sullivan points out that an individual's identity consists of information. Identity is a database of a person, it is a collection of defined information[1075]. The author goes on to point out that the identity of an individual consists of name, gender, date and place of birth, external characteristics that can be used for identification[1076]. Also noteworthy is the definition of C. Megele and P. Buzzi, who point to the phenomenon of children's digital identity. Digital and social media technologies are an integral part of children's identities, experiences and development, and digital citizenship plays an increasingly important role in people's lives and is a key element and distinguishing factor that shapes children's identities. It should be emphasized that the authors approach this understanding of identity in a shortsighted way, not just as certain elements that allow to distinguish an individual from others in the virtual world, but all the factors that define an individual, his attitudes and behavior. R. Coomaraswamy additionally stresses that identity is not intrinsically unchangeable, as it is a composite consisting of many independent, often competing, contradictory and transformable criteria. Therefore, identity is often subject to change, including in response to reaction, or variation in ideology and under the influence of life experiences[1077].

The concept of digital identity has recently appeared in European Union legislation[1078]. The Commission in 2021 proposed a framework for a European

---

1073 PWN Dictionary of the Polish Language https://sjp.pwn.pl/slowniki/tożsamość.html (access: 16.06.2024).

1074 K. Chałubińska-Jentkiewicz, M. Nowikowska, *Bezpieczeństwo, tożsamość, prywatność - aspekty prawne*, Warsaw 2020, pp. 60-61.

1075 C. Sullivan, *Digital Identity: An Emergent Legal Concept*, University of Adelaide Press 2011, p. 138.

1076 Ibid, p. 21.

1077 R. Coomaraswamy, "Identity within: Cultural Relativism, Minority Rights and the Empowerment of Women," *The George Washington International Law Review* 34/3 (2002), p. 484.

1078 Proposal for a Regulation of the European Parliament and of the Council amending Regulation (EU) No. 910/2014 as regards the establishment of a European framework for digital identity, 3.06.2021. (COM(2021) 281 Final).

digital identity that will be available to all EU citizens, residents and businesses in the EU. In the proposal for a regulation of the European Parliament and of the Council amending Regulation (EU) No. 910/2014 with regard to the establishment of a European digital identity framework, the EU legislator defined the term "European digital identity wallet"[1079]. A digital identity wallet is a product and service that allows a user to store identity data, credentials and attributes associated with his or her identity, provide them to relying parties on demand, and use them for online and offline authentication for the service. An example of digital identity could be an electronic ID card, passport, or driver's license. The European Commission has indicated that digital identity will be able to be used by EU citizens and residents, as well as EU-based companies, for the purpose of verifying identity or confirming certain personal information. The European digital identity can be used both online and offline, in public and private services across the EU[1080].

On April 11, 2024, Regulation 2024/1183 of the European Parliament and of the Council amending Regulation (EU) No. 910/2014 with regard to the establishment of a European framework for digital identity was adopted[1081]. Paragraph 5 of the preamble indicates that citizens should have the right to a digital identity that is under their exclusive control and that allows them to exercise their rights in the digital environment and participate in the digital economy. The digital identity framework should contribute to a more digitally integrated Union by reducing digital barriers between Member States and enabling Union citizens to reap the benefits of digitization, while increasing transparency and protection of their rights.

It can be pointed out that the European Union is building a new European digital identity wallet system. These are personal digital wallets in the form of apps that allow EU citizens to digitally identify themselves, store and manage their identity data and official documents in digital format. These wallets could include driver's licenses, doctor's prescriptions or education diplomas. With European digital identity wallets, citizens will be able to confirm their identity anywhere in the EU to access online services, share digital documents or simply confirm some specific information about themselves, such as their age, without revealing their

1079 European digital identity https:// commission.europa.eu/strategy-and-policy/priorities-2019-2024/europe-fit-digital-age/european-digital-identity (accessed: 16.06.2024).

1080 European Digita Identity Wallet http:// digital-strategy-ec.europa.eu/en/policies/eudi-wallet-implementation (accessed 23.02.2024).

1081 (Journal of EU Law L, 20.04.2024).

identity or other personal information. Citizens will have full control at all times over what data is shared and to whom[1082].

Summarizing the above, it can be said that digital identity is a set of information that identifies a user in the digital space. It consists of a range of data, including personal data, biometric data, as well as online activity. It should be pointed out that digital identity is essential for using various online services, such as online banking, online shopping, accessing e-government, medical services, as well as using a virtual university, or social media. As an example of the specific characteristics that shape an individual's identity, one can point to place and date of birth, hair color, and ID card number. Some of these characteristics never change, such as the date of birth, but some of them, can change, such as the ID card or passport number[1083]. It should be noted that these data constitute personal information and information from an individual's private life. The primary challenge of digital identity is therefore to ensure the security of this data. Loss of personal data, identity theft, or misuse of data by companies or third parties can lead to serious consequences for individuals. Further consideration should focus on the issue of digital identity as containing an individual's personal data, the basic differences between personal data and digital identity, the need to ensure the protection of such data, and the risks involved. The second important issue is the analysis of digital identity understood as containing an individual's right to privacy.

2. Digital identity vs. personal data

Regulation (EU) 2016/679 of April 27, 2016 (General Data Protection Regulation - hereinafter RODO)[1084] came into force on May 25, 2018. In accordance with the disposition of Article 1 of RODO, the EU legislator decided to adopt and apply in all EU member states uniform solutions for the processing of personal data. These solutions were based on two fundamental, equal principles: 1) protection of the fundamental rights and freedoms of individuals, in particular their right to the

1082 European Digital Identity - Questions and Answers, https://ec.europa.eu (accessed 16.06.2024).

1083 M. Nowikowska, *Digital Identity on the Internet - Challenges and Threats*, in *Wielowymiarowość cyberbezpieczeństwa*, ed. J. Żylińska, K. Huczek, K. Borkowski, Warsaw 2024, p. 24.

1084 Regulation (EU) 2016/679 of the European Parliament and of the Council of April 27, 2016 on the protection of natural persons with regard to the processing of personal data and on the free movement of such data and repealing Directive 95/46/EC (General Data Protection Regulation) (Official Journal of the EU L 119 of 4.05.2016, p. 1).

protection of personal data, and 2) ensuring the free flow of personal data between member states[1085]. According to Article 4(1) of the RODO, personal data means information about an identified or identifiable natural person. An identifiable natural person is one who can be identified, directly or indirectly, in particular by means of an identifier such as a name, an identification number, location data, an online identifier or one or more factors specific to the physical, physiological, genetic, mental, economic, cultural or social identity of the natural person. Personal data is not only so-called identifying information (name, surname, ID number, home address, etc.), but also any information about an already identified person. Personal data will also include, among other things, a person's image and voice[1086]. P. M. Schwartz additionally notes that information about a person is becoming increasingly important in the virtual world, it can be monetized, as well as its misuse can pose a serious threat to privacy[1087].

Making a reciprocal relationship between personal data and digital identity, it can be said that digital identity is a set of data and information that allows identifying a person in the digital environment. These data, can include personal data, as well as other information that does not constitute data, but makes it possible to determine who an individual is in the virtual world. Digital identity thus includes personal data, but also other information that can be used to identify a person in a digital context, such as login data, IP addresses, online profiles.

The literature unequivocally accepts that personal data is part of digital identity[1088]. This means that digital identity is a broader concept, encompassing not only personal data, but also other information specific to a person's online

---

1085 K. Chałubińska-Jentkiewicz, M. Nowikowska, *Protection of personal data in cyberspace*, Warsaw 2021, p. 49.

1086 J. Taczkowska-Olszewska, "Concept and types of personal data" in J. Taczkowska-Olszewska, M. Nowikowska, *Right to public information. Classified Information. Personal data protection*, Warsaw 2019, pp. 245-246.

1087 P.M. Schwartz, "Property, Privacy, and Personal Data," *Harvard Law Review* 117/7 (2004), p. 2056.

1088 See S. Kulhari, "Data Protection, Privacy and Identity: A Complex Triad" in S. Kulhari, *Building-Blocks of a Data Protection Revolution: The Uneasy Case for Blockchain Technology to Secure Privacy and Identity*, Nomos Verlagsgesellschaft mbH 2018, pp. 23-37; S.A. Aaronson, "What Kinds of Threats Are Posed by Inadequate Governance of Personal Data?" *Data Is Dangerous: Comparing the Risks That the United States, Canada and Germany See in Data Troves*, Centre for International Governance Innovation, 2020, pp. 4-6; P.H. Chase, *Perspectives on the General Data Protection Regulation Of the European Union*. German Marshall Fund of the United States 2019, p. 2.

activities. The protection of digital identity to the extent that it contains personal data requires the same security that is required for the protection of such data. It is important to protect both personal data and digital identity to the same extent from unauthorized access to such data. In the context of personal data, as a component of digital identity, it is important to consciously manage information about an individual in the virtual world. These behaviors are key to protecting digital identity, including an individual's personal data.

The European Union, too, recognizes the need for the right approach to security - for citizens to be able to use a European digital identity representing them online, and for online service providers to be able to fully rely on and accept digital identity solutions regardless of where they are issued. A regulation of the European Parliament and of the Council amending Regulation (EU) No. 910/2014 with regard to the establishment of a European digital identity framework emphasized the importance of a common technical architecture and common standards, which should be developed in cooperation with the Member States. According to the European Parliament and the Council, a harmonized approach is necessary to avoid a situation where the development of new digital identity solutions in the Member States may lead to further fragmentation caused by the application of divergent national solutions. A harmonized approach should also strengthen the single market, as it will enable citizens and businesses to identify themselves online in a secure, convenient and uniform manner across the EU for access to both public and private services. Users should rely on an improved ecosystem of electronic identity and trust services recognized and accepted across the Union. In the document, EU authorities also highlight the interplay between personal data and digital identity. In light of the regulation establishing the European Digital Identity Framework, it obliges member states to issue a European digital identity wallet in accordance with common technical standards as part of a notified electronic identification system, following mandatory conformity assessment and voluntary certification in the European Cybersecurity Certification Framework established under the Cybersecurity Act. It includes provisions to ensure that individuals and legal entities can securely request and receive, store, combine and use personal identification data and electronic attribute credentials for online and offline authentication and to enable access to public and private goods and services online under user control. This certification does not violate the provisions of the RODO in the sense that personal data processing operations related to the European Digital Identity Wallet can only be certified under Articles 42 and 43 of the RODO. The regulation emphasizes that any processing of personal data under the regulation should be carried out in full compliance with the RODO, and the regulation introduces specific safeguards for data protection.

Summarizing the above, it can be said that the difference between personal data and identity is important, although the two concepts are related. Personal data is defined in the RODO and should uniquely identify a person. Digital identity is a more complex concept and includes, in addition to data, a set of characteristics, information, attributes that allow a person to be recognized as a unique individual in the digital world. Identity can include personal data, but also other elements that make up the individual character of a person in a social, professional or digital context. Basic differences include: conceptual scope, context, and scope of protection. Personal data is specific information that identifies a person, while digital identity is a broad set of characteristics and information that defines who a person is as a whole. In terms of context, personal data is mainly used to identify and verify identity in formal processes, such as banking, administration, while digital identity can also include social, professional, psychological and digital contexts, creating a complete picture of a person. Finally, personal data is protected primarily under the RODO, due to its sensitivity and potential privacy risks. Identity protection, on the other hand, requires a broader approach, taking into account both the protection of personal data and other aspects of a person's life, such as privacy, digital security. In summary, personal data is a component of digital identity. Digital identity is a more complex concept that encompasses various aspects of a person's life, creating a unique and holistic picture of that person.

3. Digital identity and the right to privacy

The concept of the right to privacy as a protectable personal good is a product of the American "right of privacy" doctrine[1089]. The issue of the right to privacy on the basis of the Polish legal order has for years been the subject of research[1090] and has developed a rich line of jurisprudence. In Poland, A. Kopff was the first to formulate the thesis that the sphere of a person's private life belongs to his personal property and is subject to protection under the law, including the Civil Code. In the author's view, the sphere of private life is a personal property that

1089 S. Warren, L. Brandeis, "The Right to Privacy," *Harvard Law Review* 193 (1890) as cited in S. Kulhari, op. cit. p. 23.

1090 Cf. extensive discussion of the problem: A. Kopff, "The Concept of Rights to Intimacy and to Privacy of Personal Life. Zagadnienia konstrukcyjne", *Studia Cywilistyczne* XX (1972), pp. 32-33; M. Safjan, "Reflections around constitutional conditions for the development of the protection of personal goods", *Private Law Quarterly* 1 (2002), p. 234; J. Sieńczyło-Chlabicz, *Naruszenie prywatności osób publicznych przez prasę. A civil law analysis*, Warsaw 2006.

includes everything "which, due to the individual's legitimate seclusion from the general public, serves him for the development and psychological personality and the preservation of the social position achieved."[1091].

The purpose of the considerations undertaken in this part of the article is to establish the interrelation between the right to privacy and digital identity. In the literature, privacy is defined by indicating the protected spheres, the functions it performs, or formulating a catalog of situations in which the right in question is violated. The scope of the right to privacy can cause disputes and doubts in practice. Helpful in resolving them is the judicial jurisprudence[1092]. It should be emphasized that the right to privacy is one of the fundamental human rights, which is reflected in many legal acts around the world. In the context of digital identity, this right takes on particular importance, as the collection, processing and storage of data about an individual, including personal data by various entities is becoming increasingly common.

Protecting an individual's right to privacy online is primarily about securing such person's personally identifiable information from unauthorized access, modification or deletion. Also very important is the information policy implemented by the entity itself, which disposes of this information, by sharing it (data management policy).

An example of an online privacy violation is identity theft. It is generally recognized that identity theft is the illegal use of someone's personal data or information for individual gain. Identity thieves target information like: names, dates of birth, drivers licenses, credit cards, bank information. Usually they use the stolen information to gain access to existing accounts and open new accounts. Identity theft can have financial consequences for the victim. The cost to the victim depends on when the crime is reported and how it occurred[1093]. Thus, we speak of identity theft when someone unlawfully comes into possession of another person's personal data and uses it against his or her will, impersonating another person, usually for financial gain. The scope of the data and its unlawful use, treated as identity theft, can vary greatly. These can be so-called nicknames, logins, passwords, as

---

1091 A. Kopff, op. cit. p. 33.

1092 See K. Chałubińska-Jentkiewicz, M. Nowikowska, *Bezpieczeństwo, tożsamość, prywatność - aspekty prawne*, Warsaw 2020, p. 11 et seq.

1093 M. Nowikowska, "*Identity theft. Protection of personal data in cyberspace*" in *Human Rights. Digital Well-Being - a concern for the quality of life*, eds. L. Tafaro, I. Laki, I. Florek, Jozefow 2023, p. 149.

well as the full range of data about the individual that is used to defraud, such as ID number, name, image[1094].

The object of protection of identity theft is private and personal data. The principles of protection of privacy have been regulated under Polish law in several legal acts. The fundamental act which stipulates the protection of private life is the Constitution of the Republic of Poland of April 2, 1997[1095]. The right to privacy is a unique legal construct intended to protect the values referred to in Article 47 of the Constitution of the Republic of Poland. The Constitution provides that everyone is entitled to the legal protection of their private life, family life, honor, and reputation, as well as the right to decide on their personal life. In the relevant literature, the individual's right to protect their personal data is called information autonomy[1096].

The crime of identity theft has been expressed in Art. 190 a § 2 of the Penal Code, according to which identity theft is impersonating another person, thereby using his or her image or other personal data to cause him personal or material damage. Identity theft is all actions taken to obtain real data from real people. These data are obtained with the use of various technical and ICT means using social engineering[1097]. In 2023, phishing campaigns, i.e. attacks using social engineering, increased significantly[1098]. NASK's Report on the Activities of CERT Polska shows that in 2023, 95,696 reports of phishing in Polish networks were received. These involved 51,374 URLs with 49,039 domains, which resolved to 3,097 IP addresses[1099]. The most common target of phishing was investment fraud.

In the context of digital identity, technologies such as encryption, multi-component authentication, and access management policies play a special role. Modern regulations, such as the aforementioned RODO, place specific requirements on companies and organizations to protect the individual This includes the need to obtain consent for data processing, the obligation to report data security breaches, and the right for individuals to access and correct their data. Despite existing regulations, the protection of an individual's digital identity, personal data

1094 What is identity theft https://www.bik.pl/poradnik-bik/czym-jest-kradziez-tozsamosci (accessed 26.06.2024).

1095 (Journal of Law No. 78, item 483).

1096 K. Chalubinska-Jentkiewicz, M. Nowikowska, "Artificial Intelligence v. Personal Data," *Polish Political Science Yearbook*, 51(3) (2022), pp. 185.

1097 (Journal of Law 2024, item 17).

1098 Annual Report on the Activities of CERT Poland 2023 https://www.nask.pl/pl/raporty/raporty/5381,RAPORT-CERT-2023.html (accessed 20.06.2024).

1099 Ibid, p. 86.

and privacy faces many challenges. The increasing number of cyber-attacks, the development of big data and artificial intelligence technologies are making data management increasingly difficult[1100]. Identity theft is one of the fastest growing crimes in cyberspace. Cyberspace has become a domain which pertains to many areas of human life[1101].

The future of digital identity and data protection will require not only the further development of security technologies, but also the adaptation of regulations to the rapidly changing digital environment. Raising users' awareness of the importance of protecting their data and developing a culture of security among employees of companies that process data will also be key.

4. Final conclusions

Digital identity and the right to privacy and protection of personal data are inextricably linked to functioning in a modern society. Ensuring the security of personal data requires coordinated action on many levels - from the use of advanced technologies, to compliance with laws and regulations, to user education. This is the only way to effectively protect individual privacy and security in the digital world.

The right to the protection of personal data is categorically associated with the right to privacy, recognizing it as its unique form. Regulation (EU) 2016/679 of the European Parliament and of the Council of April 27, 2016 on the protection of natural persons with regard to the processing of personal data and the free movement of such data, and repealing Directive 95/46/EC (The General Data Protection Regulation) (GDPR), is also of fundamental importance in this regard.

Summarizing the above, it can be said that digital identity is a set of information that allows an individual to be identified in the digital space. It consists of a range of data, including personal data, biometric data, and online activity. Digital identity is essential for using various online services, such as online banking, online shopping, and access to e-government.

1100 M. Nowikowska, "Identity theft...", p. 150.

1101 See more: A. Mukerji, "The Need for an International Convention on Cyberspace," *Horizons: Journal of International Relations and Sustainable Development* 16 (2020), pp. 198-209; D.R. Johnson, D. Post, "Law and Bodrers: the Rise of law in Cyberspace," *Stanford Law Review* 48/5 (1996), pp. 1367-1402; G. Brown, K. Poellet, "The Customary International Law of Cyberspace," *Strategic Studies Quarterly* 6/6 (2012), pp. 126-145.

The considerations carried out showed that personal data and information from private life are part of digital identity. This means that digital identity is a broader concept, including not only personal data, but also other information specific to a person's online activities. In the context of an individual's constitutionally guaranteed right to privacy and the protection of personal data, as a component of digital identity, it is important to consciously manage information about an individual in the virtual world. These behaviors are crucial to the protection of digital identity. Protecting digital identity to the extent that it contains personal data requires the same safeguards required to protect that data.

Bibliography

Aaronson, S.A., "What Kinds of Threats Are Posed by Inadequate Governance of Personal Data?" *Data Is Dangerous: Comparing the Risks That the United States, Canada and Germany See in Data Troves*, Centre for International Governance Innovation 2020.

Brown, G., Poellet, K., "The Customary International Law of Cyberspace," *Strategic Studies Quarterly* 6/6 (2012).

Chałubińska-Jentkiewicz, K., Nowikowska M., *Bezpieczeństwo, tożsamość, prywatność - aspekty prawne*, Warszawa 2020.

Chałubińska-Jentkiewicz, K., Nowikowska, M., *Protection of personal data in cyberspace*, Warsaw 2021.

Chałubińska-Jentkiewicz, M. Nowikowska, "Artificial Intelligence v. Personal Data," *Polish Political Science Yearbook*, 51(3) (2022).

Chase, P.H., *Perspectives on the General Data Protection Regulation Of the European Union*. German Marshall Fund of the United States 2019.

Coomaraswamy, R., "Identity within: Cultural Relativism, Minority Rights and the Empowerment of Women," The George Washington International Law Review 34/3 (2002).

Johnson, D.R., Post, D., "Law and Bodrers: The Rise of Law in Cyberspace," *Stanford Law Review* 48/5 (1996).

Kopff, A., "The concept of rights to intimacy and to privacy of personal life. Constructive issues" *Civil Studies* XX (1972).

Kulhari, S., "Data Protection, Privacy and Identity: A Complex Triad" in S. Kulhari, *Building-Blocks of a Data Protection Revolution: The Uneasy Case for Blockchain Technology to Secure Privacy and Identity*, Nomos Verlagsgesellschaft mbH, 2018.

Mukerji, A., "The Need for an International Convention on Cyberspace," *Horizons: Journal of International Relations and Sustainable Development* 16 (2020).

Nowikowska, M., "*Digital Identity on the Internet - Challenges and Threats*" in *Wielowymiarowość cyberbezpieczeństwa*, ed. J. Żylińska, K. Huczek, K. Borkowski, Warsaw 2024.

Nowikowska, M., "*Identity theft. Protection of personal data in cyberspace*" in *Human Rights. Digital Well-Being - a concern for the quality of life*, eds. L. Tafaro, I. Laki, I. Florek, Jozefow 2023.

Safjan, M., "Reflections on the constitutional conditions for the development of the protection of personal property," *Private Law Quarterly* 1 (2002).

Schwartz, P.M., "Property, Privacy, and Personal Data," *Harvard Law Review* 117/7 (2004), p. 2056.

Sieńczyło-Chlabicz, J., *Naruszenie prywatności osób publicznych przez prasę. Analiza cywilnoprawna*, Warsaw 2006.

Sullivan, C., *Digital Identity: An Emergent Legal Concept*, University of Adelaide Press, 2011.

Taczkowska-Olszewska J., "Concept and types of personal data" in J. Taczkowska-Olszewska, M. Nowikowska, *Right to public information. Classified information. Protection of personal data*, Warsaw 2019.

Warren, S., Brandeis, L., "The Right to Privacy" *Harvard Law Review* 193 (1890) as cited in Kulhari, S., "Data Protection, Privacy and Identity: A Complex Triad" in S. Kulhari, *Building-Blocks of a Data Protection Revolution: The Uneasy Case for Blockchain Technology to Secure Privacy and Identity*, Nomos Verlagsgesellschaft mbH, 2018.

Legal acts

Proposal for a Regulation of the European Parliament and of the Council amending Regulation (EU) No. 910/2014 as regards the establishment of a European framework for digital identity, 3.06.2021. (COM(2021) 281 Final).

Regulation (EU) 2024/1183 of the European Parliament and of the Council of April 11, 2024 amending Regulation (EU) No. 910/2014 with regard to the establishment of a European framework for digital identity with (OJ EU 30.04.2024 L).

Regulation (EU) 2016/679 of the European Parliament and of the Council of April 27, 2016 on the protection of natural persons with regard to the processing of personal data and on the free movement of such data and repealing Directive 95/46/EC (General Data Protection Regulation) (Official Journal of the EU L 119 of 4.05.2016, p. 1.).

List of online sources

Annual Report on the Activities of CERT Poland 2023 https://www.nask.pl/pl/raporty/raporty/5381,RAPORT-CERT-2023.html (accessed 20.06.2024).

European digital identity https:// commission.europa.eu/strategy-and-policy/priorities-2019-2024/europe-fit-digital-age/european-digital-identity (accessed: 16.06.2024).

European Digital Identity Wallet http:// digital-strategy-ec.europa.eu/en/policies/eudi-wallet-implementation (accessed 23.02.2024).

European Digital Identity - Questions and Answers, https://ec.europa.eu (accessed 16.06.2024).

PWN Dictionary of the Polish Language https://sjp.pwn.pl/slowniki/tożsamość.html (accessed: 16.06.2024).

What is identity theft https://www.bik.pl/poradnik-bik/czym-jest-kradziez-tozsamosci (accessed 26.06.2024).

Katarzyna B. Wojtkiewicz[1102]

The role of legal entity identification in modern governance and data management

Abstract: This chapter examines the critical role of legal entity identification systems in shaping modern governance and data management, focusing on the Legal Entity Identifier (LEI). It explores the historical evolution of governance from Ancient Rome to the present, highlighting the impact of technological advancements, data-centric frameworks, and decentralized decision-making processes. The discussion draws from Kornhauser's "Law as an Achievement of Governance" concept,[1103] underscoring how legal norms emerge as dynamic outcomes of effective governance structures in a data-driven world. The chapter emphasizes how LEIs promote transparency, regulatory compliance, and efficiency in global financial and legal transactions. Recommendations for further integration of LEI into national and international legal frameworks are provided, offering pathways for enhancing governance precision, inclusivity, and sustainability in the face of complex global challenges.

Keywords: Legal Entity Identifier (LEI), Modern governance, Data governance, Legal norms, Public administration, Decentralized decision-making, Kornhauser theory

1. Introduction

From the centralized and control-oriented models of Ancient Rome to the technologically driven frameworks of modern times, governance systems have transformed significantly. This evolution reflects changes in the purpose, objectives, and operationalization of governance, driven by technological advancements, shifting societal values, and evolving economic structures.

In Ancient Rome, governance was crucial for maintaining order, implementing laws, and expanding territorial control. The model focused on political stability, military conquest, and consolidating power within the ruling class, designed to ensure the empire's dominance and longevity through robust and centralized authority. According to Loewenstein's analysis,[1104] Rome's political structure evolved through phases like the Republic and the Empire, each with distinct

1102 SWPS University, ORCID: 0000-0003-0630-4139.
1103 L. A. Kornhauser, 'Law as an Achievement of Governance', *Journal of Legal Philosophy*, vol. 47, no. 1, 2022, pp. 1-23.
1104 K. Loewenstein, *The Governance of Rome*, Springer Science & Business Media, 2012.

governance mechanisms. His study highlights Rome's adaptability and ability to integrate various elements of power and administration to maintain the empire's dominance and longevity.[1105] Establishing and enforcing a comprehensive legal framework to maintain social order and resolve conflicts were paramount, setting a strong historical foundation for later European legal systems. This adaptability and the strategic implementation of reforms were key factors in the longevity and success of Roman governance and may serve as mechanisms for the adaptation of governance systems in the Anthropocene to present challenges and rapid technological development. The Roman model of integrating legal, administrative, and military reforms to enhance efficiency and control can offer valuable insights for modern governance, particularly in addressing the complexities and rapid changes characteristic of the Anthropocene era.

Territorial expansion through military conquest and colonization was integral to Rome's strategy for increasing its wealth and influence. Efficient management of resources, including land, labour, and taxes, was crucial to support the state's needs and ensure the empire's prosperity. Power was centralized in the hands of the emperor, the Senate, and a bureaucratic administrative system, allowing for decisive and coordinated governance. The military played a crucial role, both in terms of territorial control and maintaining internal order. Extensive public

1105 During the Republic, the political institutions, such as the Senate, magistrates, and popular assemblies, played key roles in decision-making processes and maintaining a balance of power between the patricians and plebeians. The Republic's governance emphasized the importance of civic duty and collective decision-making, though it was often marred by class struggles and conflicts. The political institutions of the Republic were crucial in providing a system of checks and balances that allowed for a relatively stable and inclusive governance model, despite internal conflicts. With the establishment of the Principate under Augustus, the governance structure shifted towards a more centralized authority, combining elements of monarchy and republicanism. The Augustan reforms were pivotal in creating a stable and enduring governance model that integrated legal, administrative, and military reforms to enhance efficiency and control. Augustus restructured the Senate, created a professional standing army, and introduced reforms that streamlined the administration of justice and provincial governance. The legal framework established during this period laid the foundation for later European legal systems and underscored the Roman emphasis on justice and civic order. The codification of laws and the development of a sophisticated legal system were instrumental in maintaining social order and resolving conflicts. This legal tradition influenced the development of civil law systems in many parts of Europe, demonstrating the lasting impact of Roman governance on Western civilization.

works projects, funded by taxes and tributes from conquered territories, supported infrastructure and public services essential for the economic and social welfare of the empire.

Kettl argues that Modern governance systems maintain order, implement laws, and promote societal well-being, but they have evolved to leverage technology to address the needs of a broader population.[1106] This approach ensures transparency and accountability, although modern governance often caters to influential societal segments. Encouraging citizen engagement through voting, public consultations, and digital platforms is crucial for legitimizing governmental actions and policies. However, the actual level of meaningful participation can be limited, with influential groups and economic elites having disproportionate sway over political decisions.

Implementing mechanisms to ensure government actions are transparent and officials are held accountable builds public trust and prevents corruption.[1107] Promoting economic growth through innovation, technology adoption, and regulatory frameworks that support market efficiency is essential. Enhancing the quality of life by providing healthcare, education, and social security and ensuring environmental sustainability reflects a commitment to equitable and sustainable development. However, the distribution of these benefits can still be unequal.

Power is often decentralized, with significant roles played by local governments, private sector entities, civil society, and international organizations. Decision-making involves multiple stakeholders, reflecting a more collaborative approach, though real influence often remains with the most powerful entities. Technology, such as e-governance platforms, big data analytics, and Blockchain, has revolutionized how governments interact with citizens and manage public affairs.[1108] Systems like the Legal Entity Identifier (LEI) facilitate clear and transparent identification of legal entities involved in financial transactions, enhancing regulatory compliance and reducing systemic risks.

1106 D. F. Kettl, *The Transformation of Governance: Public Administration for the Twenty-First Century*, JHU Press, 2015, pp. 189 and following.

1107 K. B. Wojtkiewicz, 'Applying the Business-Process-Oriented Approach to Data Designs, Governance and Management: Case Study of the EIOPA', in A. Szpaderski, P. Cywiński, W. Karczewski, C. Neck, and K. B. Wojtkiewicz (eds), *Human and Management: Emerging, Contemporary, and Unorthodox Perspectives*, 2022.

1108 H. Song, W. Liu, K. Yu, and M. Han, 'Trusting the Trust Machine: How Does Blockchain-Enabled Governance Configuration Enhance Financing Credibility?', *Technovation*, vol. 135, 2024.

2. The Role of Data in Contemporary Society

As we transition into a data-centric society, the influence of data governance on societal values cannot be overstated. Recognizing the role of data in contemporary society is paramount to navigating the complexities of this new era. Data now occupies a pivotal role in our daily lives, influencing everything from personal decisions to societal trends. It shapes norms and behaviours by providing insights into patterns and preferences that drive human interaction and institutional policies. Effective data governance is crucial as it directly impacts societal values, determining how data is collected, stored, and used. This governance must balance innovation with ethical considerations, ensuring that data benefits society while protecting individual rights. Understanding the significance of data in contemporary society is essential for fostering an environment where data can be leveraged for positive societal impact.

The transition from a predominantly tangible asset-based economy to one dominated by intangible assets marks a significant shift in the valuation of corporate assets. In the 1970s, tangible assets such as property, equipment, and physical infrastructure constituted approximately 90% of a company's total value. However, in the contemporary economy, the value of tangible assets has drastically decreased, now comprising only about 10% of a company's total value. Conversely, intangible assets—such as intellectual property, brand equity, and customer relationships—have become increasingly valuable, making up 90% of a company's value. This shift highlights the growing importance of intangible assets in driving economic value and growth in today's economy. Global corporate intangible value increased by 8% in 2023, after a sharp decline in 2022. The US, Ireland, Denmark, the UK, and France are the most intangible asset-intensive economies. India, Turkey, Indonesia, Mexico, and China rank among the top 20.[1109] Brownsword similarly suggests that questions about emerging technologies should be framed within the broader context of good governance. He argues that good governance must be legitimate, balancing effectiveness with legitimacy, and must begin with respect for the global commons as a primary, non-negotiable criterion.[1110]

1109 Global corporate intangible value increased by 8% in 2023, after a sharp decline in 2022. The US, Ireland, Denmark, the UK, and France are the most intangible asset-intensive economies. India, Türkiye, Indonesia, Mexico, and China rank among the top 20.

1110 R. Brownsword, 'Law, Regulation, and Technology: The Bigger Picture of Good Governance', in *Research Handbook on Law and Technology*, 2023, pp. 12-27.

The rapid evolution of technology has further cemented the importance of data. Advancements in artificial intelligence, big data analytics, and Blockchain technology are transforming industries and societal norms at an unprecedented pace. These technological changes are dynamic, often outpacing existing standards and regulations. As a result, there is a pressing need for adaptable governance frameworks that can respond to these innovations. Ensuring these frameworks are flexible yet robust enough to address technological advancements' ethical and practical implications is critical for maintaining societal trust and progress.

Data governance is inherently a multi-stakeholder endeavour involving a diverse range of participants. Effective data governance frameworks must include the input of government, businesses, civil society, and individuals. Each stakeholder brings a unique perspective and set of priorities, making it essential to create collaborative platforms where these voices can be heard and integrated into policy-making processes. This inclusivity ensures that data governance is comprehensive and responsive to the needs and concerns of all sectors of society. Data flows transcend national borders, creating a globalized data ecosystem. This borderless nature of data presents significant challenges to traditional legal frameworks, which are often based on territorial jurisdiction. Harmonizing norms and standards across different regions is crucial for effectively managing the global data flow. International cooperation and the development of global standards can help address these challenges, ensuring that data governance is consistent and fair globally. As we navigate the complexities of a data-centric society, the importance of recognizing the central role of data cannot be overstated. The rapid technological advancements, diverse range of stakeholders, and global nature of data flows necessitate adaptable and inclusive governance frameworks. By addressing these challenges with a holistic and collaborative approach, we can harness the power of data to drive positive societal change while safeguarding individual rights and ethical standards.

3. Concept of "Legal Norm as an Achievement of Data Governance"

In the context of Kornhauser's concept of "Law as an Achievement of Governance," governance is a multifaceted social phenomenon that warrants detailed investigation. The idea is rooted in the understanding that legal norms are not just static rules but dynamic outcomes of effective governance systems that embody legal values. The concept of legal norms as achievements of data governance formulated herein by the author aligns with Kornhauser's theoretical framework.

Governance, in its complexity, includes various components such as structures, institutions, and functioning systems. It is imperative to distinguish between these elements to achieve clarity and effective implementation. Governance structures refer to the organizational frameworks and hierarchies, while governance institutions denote the formal bodies and agencies involved. Functioning systems pertain to the operational mechanisms and processes that ensure effective governance. Understanding governance requires dissecting its structures, institutions, and functioning systems. This differentiation helps clarify discussions about law and management, which often are ambiguous, particularly regarding whether they refer to governance structures or functioning systems. This lack of clarity can hinder effective communication and implementation of governance principles. The achievement concept in governance derives from an evaluative notion of legality. It identifies functioning governance systems that embody the value of legality, ensuring that legal norms are established, effectively implemented, and adhered to. This perspective emphasizes the operational aspects of governance that support legal and ethical standards, aligning with Kornhauser's view that law is an artefact of governance structures. Understanding global and local governance systems is essential for building a practical legal and information management framework. This effort requires analysing and understanding global and institutional governance systems and establishing adequate technical frameworks to facilitate implementation.

Governance now operates in a global context where data flows across borders, requiring harmonized norms and standards to manage international cooperation and regulatory challenges. Emphasizing sustainability in policymaking to balance economic growth with environmental protection and social equity is paramount. Modern governance systems aim to create resilient and adaptable frameworks that respond to contemporary challenges. The advent of the internet, social media, and mobile communications has democratized access to information and empowered citizens to participate more actively in governance. These technologies enable real-time information sharing, transparency, and public scrutiny of governmental actions, allowing citizens to access governmental data, contribute to public debates, and hold authorities accountable like never before. The fundamental purposes and objectives of governance have remained consistent over time, focusing on order, law, and societal well-being, but the methods and operational strategies have evolved significantly. Modern governance systems, driven by technological advancements, emphasize transparency, accountability, and inclusivity. However, the extent to which these systems are genuinely democratic remains debatable, as influential groups often hold significant sway over political decisions, reflecting a continuity in the power dynamics of governance. The main finding of this research underscores a transformative shift in how legal norms are formulated and extracted in contemporary governance models. Unlike in the past, where norms were positively formulated and dictated by centralized governing bodies, today's legal norms emerge from the operational nature of governance models. This shift necessitates a deep exploration into the operational aspects of governance to ensure that fundamental and cardinal norms serve society and support democracy effectively. Concepts such as 'Law as an Achievement of Governance' highlight the dynamic nature of legal norms, driven by the interactions and operations within governance systems rather than by top-down mandates.[1111] To uphold the principles of democracy, it is essential to scrutinise and understand these operational frameworks, ensuring that the norms they produce align with societal values and democratic ideals. Nieprzecka approaches this from another angle of criminal law, introducing the concept of interconnected norms, distinguishing between sanctioned and sanctioning norms.[1112] She emphasises that the concept of interconnected norms is not only applicable to the norms inferred from the Rome Statute but also enables readers to grasp some normative nuances that often escape academic attention, coming to similar conclusions. Additionally, Sas-Kulczycka et al. describe the governance model of collective investment institutions in Poland, further illustrating the importance of robust governance structures in different contexts.[1113]

As illustrated in Figure 1, the contemporary governance ecosystem reflects the concept of 'Legal Norm as an Achievement of Data Governance,' drawing on the legal theory by Kornhauser in *Law as an Achievement of Governance.*[1114] This ecosystem incorporates key elements such as technology (data management), governance, law (legal system), and entity (decision-making).

1111 L. A. Kornhauser, 'Law as an Achievement of Governance', *Journal of Legal Philosophy*, vol. 47, no. 1, 2022, pp. 1-23.

1112 A. Nieprzecka, 'Theory of Legal Norms', in *Participation in Crime Falling within the Subject-Matter Jurisdiction of the International Criminal Court* (T.M.C. Asser Press, 2024).

1113 K. Sas-Kulczycka, D. Chorylo, J. Król, and Z. Lasota, *Institutions of Common Investment in Poland: Investment and Pension Funds* (WIG-Press, 1998).

1114 See Kornhauser, 'Law as an Achievement of Governance', *Journal of Legal Philosophy.*

Figure 1: Contemporary Governance Ecosystem.

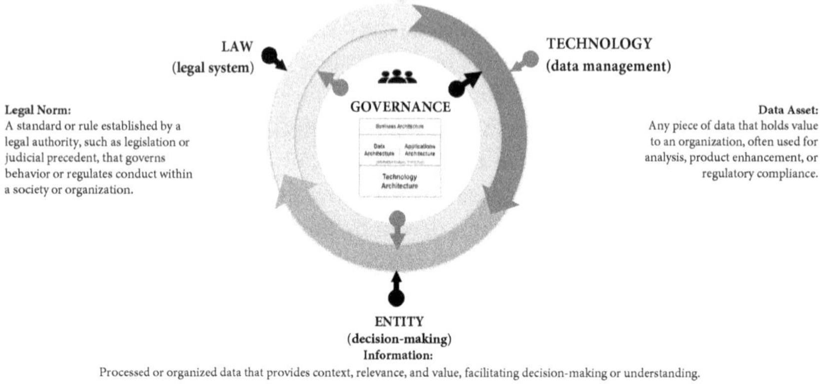

Source: Own elaboration.

Legal norms are standards or rules established by a legal authority, such as legislation or judicial precedent, that govern behaviour or regulate conduct within a society or organization. Data assets refer to any data that holds value to an organization and is often used for analysis, product enhancement, or regulatory compliance. Information is processed or organized data that provides context, relevance, and value, facilitating decision-making or understanding.

In the past, the black arrows reflected the traditional, external-to-internal influence where governance and legal norms were primarily externally driven, focusing on how external legal systems and regulatory requirements shaped internal data governance practices. However, the red arrows indicate a current shift to internal-to-external influence, where internal governance frameworks and data management practices now influence and shape the development and application of legal norms and regulatory standards.

The rapid advancement in technology, especially digital communication, has significantly impacted this shift in influence. Digital communication facilitates instant and widespread dissemination of information, enhances transparency and accountability within organizations, and empowers entities to adapt and innovate governance practices quickly. Advanced data management technologies allow for better data collection, processing, and analysis, enabling organizations to develop robust internal governance frameworks based on real-time data insights.

This technology integration creates a dynamic feedback loop in which internal practices are continuously informed by data, enabling organizations to pre-emptively adapt to potential regulatory changes. This proactive approach influences the development of legal norms and regulations, reflecting the realities and needs of the digital age. Thus, the transformation in governance ecosystems, driven by enhanced digital communication and advanced data management, promotes an internally driven model that shapes the broader legal and regulatory landscape.

Figure 2: Evolution of Governance systems.

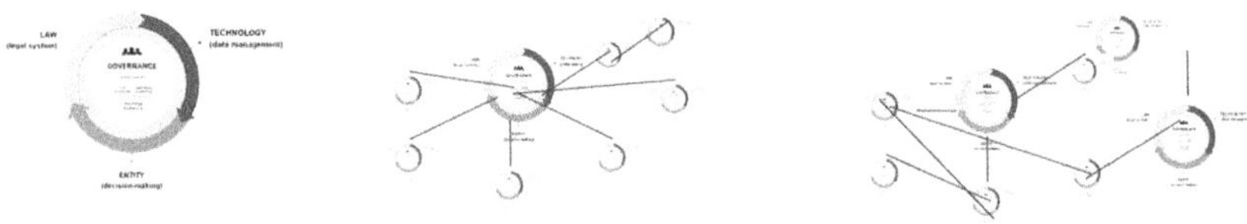

Source: Own elaboration.

As depicted in Figure 2, the evolution of governance systems from ancient times to the present day demonstrates a shift from centralized control to more decentralized and participatory approaches. Historically, governance was characterized by rigid hierarchies and top-down decision-making processes. Modern governance, however, increasingly emphasizes inclusivity, transparency, and adaptability. The contemporary approach to governance highlights the importance of stakeholder engagement, collaboration, and the integration of diverse perspectives.

This evolution underscores the need for flexible and responsive regulatory frameworks that adapt to the rapidly changing technological landscape. Such adaptability is crucial for addressing the challenges posed by emerging technologies like artificial intelligence, Blockchain, and big data analytics. By embracing these changes, governance systems can better meet the needs of contemporary societies and promote sustainable development.

The concept of "Legal Norm as an Achievement of Data Governance" underscores the critical need for a comprehensive and dynamic approach to governance. This approach aligns with Kornhauser's theory, emphasizing the importance of governance structures that embody legal values and support sustainable and prosperous futures.

The role of legal norms within this framework is not merely to dictate behavior but to emerge as the outcome of effective governance systems. This dynamic nature of legal norms, shaped by interactions within governance systems, highlights the necessity of understanding and adapting to contemporary challenges.

4. The Role of Entity Identification in Modern Governance

The evolving landscape of data governance highlights the critical need for clear definitions of each entity, as seen in the "Norm as an Achievement of Data

Governance" framework. Like Kornhauser's dynamic legal norms, data governance norms are shaped by interactions among technological innovations, regulations, and societal values. Precise legal entity definitions in data governance serve crucial purposes. Clear authority and responsibility boundaries are vital in data governance, extending beyond traditional systems to include data-driven mechanisms and global networks.[1115] Ambiguities can cause jurisdictional conflicts, regulatory uncertainties, and accountability issues.

Sharp definitions enhance transparency and accountability, helping stakeholders understand their roles and obligations in sophisticated, multi-stakeholder data governance mechanisms. Transparent definitions facilitate scrutiny of decision-making processes, ensuring adherence to ethical standards, legal requirements, and societal expectations. Precise definitions enable effective regulation and risk management for emerging technologies like AI, Blockchain, and big data analytics. Clear definitions of legal entities involved in data processes help design targeted regulatory measures balancing innovation with privacy, security, and ethics.[1116]

4.1. The Legal Entity Identifier (LEI)

The LEI initiative, established post-2008 financial crisis, enhances transparency and efficiency in global financial transactions. It uniquely identifies legally distinct entities in financial transactions, aiding transparency, reducing counterparty risk, and improving regulatory oversight accuracy and efficiency. Endorsed by the G-20, the LEI initiative began in 2011, launching in 2014 with the Global LEI Foundation (GLEIF) overseeing issuance and maintenance. Financial institutions, regulatory authorities, and stakeholders worldwide have adopted it, with the Regulatory Oversight Committee (ROC) setting standards and monitoring the system.[1117] The LEI supports risk management, regulatory compliance, market surveillance, procurement, and taxation. It ensures legal accountability, aids

---

1115 K. Wojtkiewicz, 'Efektywne Zarządzanie Informacją jako Strategiczny Czynnik Sukcesu Nadzoru Rynku Finansowego', in T. Czerwińska and A. Z. Nowak (eds), *Rynek Kapitałowy – Regulacje i Fundamenty*, Wydawnictwo Naukowe Wydziału Zarządzania Uniwersytetu Warszawskiego, 2019, pp. 25.

1116 K. B. Wojtkiewicz, 'Identification of Legal Entities in Financial Market Infrastructures, ie "Who is Who on the Digitised Market?"', in A. Szpaderski, P. Cywiński, W. Karczewski, C. Neck, and K. B. Wojtkiewicz (eds), *Human and Management: Emerging, Contemporary, and Unorthodox Perspectives*, 2022, pp. 143-163.

1117 Global Legal Entity Identifier Foundation, 'Regulatory Use of the LEI', n.d., https://www.leiroc.org/, accessed 30 June 2024.

regulatory compliance, mitigates misrepresentation and fraud risks, and promotes effective public governance and efficient international transactions.

4.2. LEI in Regulations

Approximately 200 regulations globally reference the LEI, with many requiring active LEIs, highlighting its critical role in data reporting by legal entities. Regulations in major financial markets like the EU, US, and UK mandate LEI use. Robust regulatory advocacy has driven LEI adoption, with over 2.46 million LEIs issued by early 2024, notably increasing in regions like India, Japan, and parts of Europe. This global distribution underscores the LEI's integral role in enhancing transparency and reducing financial and legal transaction risks.[1118]

4.3. LEI in Legal Taxonomies

Integrating the LEI into legal systems is crucial. Legislative frameworks must incorporate the LEI for consistent legal entity identification and maintaining law and regulation application coherence. Regulatory standards should mandate LEI use for accurate reporting and compliance. Contractual agreements benefit from LEIs by clearly identifying parties and reducing disputes. Reporting obligations become more efficient with LEIs, ensuring accurate entity tracking. LEIs ensure accurate identification and monitoring in cross-border transactions, facilitating secure international trade and financial operations. Embedding the LEI within legal systems enhances transparency, accountability, and efficiency in governing legal entities, underscoring its importance in modern legal and regulatory frameworks.

5. Conclusions and Postulates *de lege ferenda*

A comprehensive analysis of the LEI system, its inception, and its global implementation reveals its benefits in promoting transparency, reducing counterparty risk, and enhancing the accuracy of financial reporting and regulatory oversight.

Entity identification streamlines administrative processes and enhances public participation. Unique identifiers empower citizens, facilitate better public service delivery, and promote inclusivity in governance.

By integrating LEI frameworks and embracing the evolving landscape of data governance, modern governance systems can achieve greater precision, transparency, and inclusivity, ultimately fostering a more sustainable and equitable future.

1118 Global Legal Entity Identifier Foundation, 'Global LEI Index', n.d., https://www.gleif.org/en/lei-solutions/regulatory-use-of-the-lei, accessed 30 June 2024.

Effective communication is essential for optimal governance systems. The LEI streamlines communication processes and its transparency by providing a common language for identifying and referencing entities across various stakeholders and jurisdictions. This facilitates seamless information exchange, collaboration, and coordination, ultimately enhancing the efficiency and effectiveness of governance efforts.

The LEI facilitates informed decision-making processes for individuals and registered entities. By accurately identifying these entities, governance systems can assess their contributions to societal well-being, enabling policymakers to make informed decisions that align with broader societal goals and individual preferences. Holistic societal progress requires inclusive decision-making processes that consider the perspectives and interests of all stakeholders. The LEI facilitates inclusivity by providing a universal identification framework for all entities, regardless of their legal status. By incorporating LEI into governance systems, policymakers can ensure that decisions reflect individuals' and registered entities' diverse needs and contributions, fostering a more equitable and participatory society.

In modern governance, precision is paramount in addressing complex societal challenges. The LEI enables precise identification of entities, whether individuals or registered businesses. This precision allows policymakers to tailor governance interventions to specific needs and circumstances, maximizing effectiveness and minimizing unintended consequences.

The concept of law as a "Legal Norm as an Achievement of Data Governance" emphasizes that legal norms are not merely static rules but dynamic outcomes of effective governance systems. Complex interactions between technological innovations, regulatory frameworks, and societal values shape these systems. Within this framework, the Legal Entity Identifier (LEI) system is crucial in enhancing governance and ensuring that legal norms are effectively implemented and adhered to. The following postulates *de lege ferenda* outline how the LEI can be integrated into governance at the European and national levels to achieve these goals.

It is proposed that the European level adopt a robust constitution for decision-making entities based on the Legal Entity Identification System Governance Model established by the Regulatory Oversight Committee (ROC) to enhance governance and decision-making processes. This model should incorporate the following elements:

1. Identification of Entities: Ensure that all entities constituted in business registers are uniquely identified. This clarity in identification is essential for establishing precise and enforceable legal norms.

2. Natural Person Entity Identifiers: Implement interconnections to identifiers for natural persons for ensuring comprehensive coverage. This inclusion enhances transparency and accountability, aligning with the broader data governance goals.
3. Inclusion of Other Entities: Extend the LEI system to cover other entities involved in decision-making processes, such as artificial intelligence and entities acting in various capacities. This extension acknowledges the evolving nature of governance and the need to adapt legal norms to new realities.
4. Monitoring Interconnections: Legislation should act as an umbrella framework requesting LEIs to monitor interconnections between entities. This would enhance transparency and oversight of relationships and dependencies within and across borders, promoting economic stability and reducing systemic risks. Effective monitoring and data-driven insights help shape and refine legal norms, ensuring they are responsive to contemporary challenges.

In Poland, it is recommended that the Legal Entity Identifier (LEI) be initially integrated into the national tax law framework to streamline administrative processes and enhance regulatory compliance. This integration should include:

5. Replacing Multiplied Non-Connected Identifiers:[1119] All entities constituted in business registers should be assigned an LEI to establish the connections with existing identifiers such as KRS, NIP, RFI, RFE, PESEL or REGON, facilitating clear and accurate identification. This unification supports the creation of precise legal norms that are easier to enforce and monitor.

1119 The following identifiers are defined and requested by the Tax Law regulations:

- *Act of 13 October 1995 on the Rules for Registration and Identification of Taxpayers and Payers* [*Ustawa z dnia 13 października 1995 r. o zasadach ewidencji i identyfikacji podatników i płatników*] (Journal of Laws 1995 No. 142, item 702).
- *Act of 20 August 1997 on the National Court Register* [*Ustawa z dnia 20 sierpnia 1997 r. o Krajowym Rejestrze Sądowym*] (Journal of Laws 1997 No. 121, item 769).
- *Act of 29 June 1995 on Public Statistics* [*Ustawa z dnia 29 czerwca 1995 r. o statystyce publicznej*] (Journal of Laws 2015, item 2009).
- *Act of 27 May 2004 on Investment Funds* [*Ustawa z dnia 27 maja 2004 r. o funduszach inwestycyjnych*] (Journal of Laws 2016, item 2188).
- *Act of 28 August 1997 on the Organisation and Functioning of Pension Funds* [*Ustawa z dnia 28 sierpnia 1997 r. o organizacji i funkcjonowaniu funduszy emerytalnych*] (Journal of Laws 1998 No. 69, item 456).
- *Act of 24 September 2010 on Population Records* [*Ustawa z dnia 24 września 2010 r. o ewidencji ludności*] (Journal of Laws 2010 No. 217, item 1427).

Once successfully implemented in the tax legislation, the LEI system should be extended to the entire legal framework in Poland. This broader integration will ensure that all legal and regulatory processes benefit from the enhanced clarity, accountability, and efficiency provided by a unified entity identification system. By incorporating LEIs into the national legal framework, Poland can ensure that its legal norms are reflective of and responsive to the needs of modern governance, aligning with the principles of data governance.

In the context of the concept of law as "Legal Norm as an Achievement of Data Governance," these postulates *de lege ferenda* highlight the critical role of the LEI system in modernizing and enhancing governance frameworks. By ensuring precise identification of entities and monitoring their interconnections, the LEI system helps create legal norms that are dynamic, transparent, and enforceable. This integration supports the broader goals of data governance, promoting economic stability, regulatory compliance, and societal well-being. Through these measures, legal norms can be seen not just as rules to be followed but as achievements of a sophisticated, data-driven governance system.

Bibliography

Brownsword, R., 'Law, Regulation, and Technology: The Bigger Picture of Good Governance', in *Research Handbook on Law and Technology*, 2023, pp. 12-27.

Kornhauser, L. A., 'Law as an Achievement of Governance', *Journal of Legal Philosophy*, vol. 47, no. 1, 2022, pp. 1-23.

Global Legal Entity Identifier Foundation, 'Global LEI Index', n.d., https://www.leiroc.org/, accessed 30 June 2024.

Kettl, D. F., *The Transformation of Governance: Public Administration for the Twenty-First Century*, JHU Press, 2015, pp. 189 and following.

Global Legal Entity Identifier Foundation, 'Regulatory Use of the LEI', n.d., https://www.gleif.org/en/lei-solutions/regulatory-use-of-the-lei, accessed 30 June 2024.

Loewenstein, K., *The Governance of Rome*, Springer Science & Business Media, 2012.

Nieprzecka, A., 'Theory of Legal Norms', in *Participation in Crime Falling within the Subject-Matter Jurisdiction of the International Criminal Court*, T.M.C. Asser Press, The Hague, 2024.

Sas-Kulczycka, K., Choryło, D., Król, J., and Lasota, Z., *Instytucje Wspólnego Inwestowania w Polsce: Fundusze Inwestycyjne i Emerytalne* [Institutions of Common Investment in Poland: Investment and Pension Funds], WIG-Press, 1999.

Song, H., Liu, W., Yu, K., and Han, M., 'Trusting the Trust Machine: How Does Blockchain-Enabled Governance Configuration Enhance Financing Credibility?', *Technovation*, vol. 135, 2024.

Wojtkiewicz, K., 'Efektywne Zarządzanie Informacją jako Strategiczny Czynnik Sukcesu Nadzoru Rynku Finansowego', in Czerwińska, T., and Nowak, A. Z., *Rynek Kapitałowy – Regulacje i Fundamenty*, Wydawnictwo Naukowe Wydziału Zarządzania Uniwersytetu Warszawskiego, 2019, pp. 25.

Wojtkiewicz, K. B., 'Applying the Business-Process-Oriented Approach to Data Designs, Governance and Management: Case Study of the EIOPA', in Szpaderski, A., Cywiński, P., Karczewski, W., Neck, C., and Wojtkiewicz, K. B., *Human and Management: Emerging, Contemporary, and Unorthodox Perspectives*, 2022, pp. 163-167.

Wojtkiewicz, K. B., 'Identification of Legal Entities in Financial Market Infrastructures, ie "Who is Who on the Digitised Market?"', in Szpaderski, A., Cywiński, P., Karczewski, W., Neck, C., and Wojtkiewicz, K. B. (eds), *Human and Management: Emerging, Contemporary, and Unorthodox Perspectives*, 2022, pp. 143-163.

Maciej Pleban[1120]

Abuse of access to public information in a democratic state of law

Abstract: The right on access to public information arises from the civil rights provided under the Constitution of the Republic of Poland. In connection with the threat, it was designed as a provider of tools for the society to control the government. More and more often, there may be confirmed new pathologies that can be found as dangers for the legislator's intention and purpose that has access to other users. Both in jurisprudence and doctrine, there can be acquired trends that leads to limiting the absolute character of this right, that breaches the rules of a democratic state of law. That noticeable phenomenon of abuse of the right to public information, requests for access by unauthorized entities, and finally private *vendettas* against authority. All this means that every day a civil society, grow the pathologies by ourselves. The right to obtain public information does not absolutely assuming the right of everyone to receive any kind of information from state institutions.

Keywords: public information, abuse of rights, court obstructions, administrative courts, abuse of public information

1. General remarks

Abuse of access to public information has become such a dangerous and and moreover undesirable phenomenon in a democratic state of law. It takes various forms, mostly manifesting themselves in rapidly increased numbers of applications that obstructs normal activity of public authorities and administrative courts. Meanwhile provisions of the Act on access to public information[1121] does not contain any safeguards against abusing of the rights granted on its basis, leaving large fields for administrative courts to solve occurred problems. The volume of this paper allows only the highlighting of the most important issues connected with the topic. Therefore I wish to focus on the concept of abuse of a subjective right - the right to public information - by a citizen in relation to state authorities and other public and economic entities that may be the addressee of the application, as well as further repercussions related to the simultaneous abuse of the right to a fair trial in matters of access to public information. The essence

---

1120 SWPS University, ORCID - 0009-0007-5810-4207.

1121 Ustawa z dnia 6 września 2001 r. o dostępie do informacji publicznej (Dz. U. z 2022 r. poz. 902), further as „Act" or „Act on access to public information".

of the study would occur around an attempt to find systemic and *ad hoc* solutions to combat the abuse of this right.

The right on access to public information arises from the human rights provided under the Constitution of the Republic of Poland. In connection with the threat, it was designed for the society to provide them tools to control the government. More and more often, new pathologies can be confirmed and can be found as dangers for the legislator's intention.

2. Objective and subjective scope of public information

Leaving aside the general legal definition based in the Act and moving on to the one created by case law, as a public information – there can be found "any kind of message created or referred to public authorities, also created or referred to other entities performing public functions within the scope of their performance of public authority tasks and management of municipal property or property of the State Treasury"[1122] This definition is established in case law, also widely used and shared. Therefore, this is the type of information about the activities of the state and its authorities which, from the public interest point of view, are important in terms of citizen control over the exercise of power. What should be clear is that not every case or subject that in any way relates to the authority, will have this nature.

Moving on to the group of entitled to submit an application, there should be, under the provisions of Constitution, a Polish citizen, while the rules of the act on access to public information indicates everybody. A purposive and systemic interpretation of those two acts leads to the assumption that this should applied to every Polish citizen and every Polish legal person. Even as it follows from the constitutional provisions, the legislator did not include any restrictions such as possession of polish citizenship, in further provisions of the Constitution referring to obtain information about the environment.[1123] M. Jabłoński, K. Wygoda, correctly points out that "those who will effectively benefit from their rights, even if formally - from the point of view of systemic solutions - do not have the legal capacity to do so"[1124]. Statement above is a consequence of the informalized procedure of filling an application, which – to ask, even to acquire the information,

1122 Judgement of NSA, 25 March 2003, signature II SA 4059/02, all judgments of administrative courts available and published in the Central Database of Administrative Court Judgments at: http://orzeczenia.nsa.gov.pl.

1123 (art. 74 ust. 3 of Constitution of Republic of Poland).

1124 M. Jabłoński, K. Wygoda [w:] *Ustawa o dostępie do informacji publicznej. Komentarz*, red. A. Piskorz-Ryń, M. Sakowska-Baryła, Warszawa 2023, art. 2.

does not require checking the applicant's identity – only indicating his/her name and surname. Similarly, the provisions of the Act on access to public information only in a few cases bind the actions of the authority or parties to the detailed identification of the person and it's other important features, such as full legal capacity.

The problem and conclusion is that basically anyone can ask about totally anything. It must be said that this is not tantamount with a statement that everyone will receive any information requested. Although the legislator has provided few restrictions on making it available – important is the unlimited possibility of asking.

3. The concept of abuse of the right to public information

Moreover in case law and doctrine there are visible trends aimed at limiting the absolute nature of the right to obtain public information, used contrary to the rules of a democratic state of law. As a main threats there are mentioned negative impact of the freedom to apply on the daily operate of obliged entities, bunch of cases solved day by day in administrative courts, and finally the destabilization of authorities and their bodies, as well as attempts to obtain information in an unauthorized manner and inconsistent with applicable law. However, the question remains whether and to what we can extent the rules of law-making and the basic principles of the state system. M. Jaśkowska notices that admissibility of preventing this phenomenon is strongly axiologically conditioned, therefore „mechanisms that are preventing abuse of the law should be assessed in the light of basic, accepted values"[1125] The right to fair trial or the right to information states as fundamental human rights and civil liberties, guaranteed by the provisions of the Constitution. Their restrictions therefore have to fulfil the criteria provided by legislator in art. 61 ust. 3 of Constitution of Republic of Poland. Therefore restrictions are allowed solely for the purpose of protecting the freedoms and rights of other persons and economic entities as defined in statutes, as well as the protection of public order, security or important economic interests of the state.

Deliberation on the topic of abuse of the right to public information shall begin with sharing the opinion, that it may concern both the sphere of public law, when authorities abuse their power over citizens, and vice versa, when a citizen uses it's

1125 M. Jaśkowska, *Nadużycie publicznego prawa podmiotowego jako przesłanka ograniczenia dostępu do sądu w sprawach z zakresu informacji publicznej*, ZNSA 2018, nr 1, p. 31.

right in a manner inconsistent with that act intended purposes[1126]. The concept of abuse of law has not been unified in legal science. This is a blurred legal concept, which means that, as noted by prof. Kmieciak, following prof. Wyrzykowski, "it is subject to interpretation procedures, and finding the correct content of such a vague concept, is nothing more than searching for the goal, so it's the function that the provision or legal norm is to fulfil"[1127]. In addition A. Szpunar states that "the prohibition of abuse of law is therefore a postulate of equitable law."[1128] The literature is dominated by civil concepts, analyzes of concepts that constitute a violation of both procedural law and the abuse of specific procedural instruments or international legal disputes.[1129]

Simultaneously the scientists in doctrine of administrative law also attempt to define the phenomenon for the needs of their branch of law. And although noticeable is "lack of a clear normative clause preventing abuse of law"[1130] then, according to P. Przybysz, "abuse of public subjective right occurs when a specific entity undertakes legally permitted actions to achieve goals other than those provided for by the legislator"[1131]. Furthermore there is easily claimed that "therefore it is an action with legal basis, which are inconsistent with the general assumptions of this law"[1132]. Those above statements should be fully shared.

Going further in this context, to the phenomenon of abuse of the right to public information. As it is cleverly pointed in the studies of administrative law, this phenomenon can be described as "using its institution to achieve a goal other than caring for the public interest known as the right to a transparent state, its structures, compliance with the law by public life entities, transparency of the

---

1126 Similarly points M. Jaśkowska, *Ponowne wykorzystanie informacji publicznej*, [w:] *Dziesięć lat polskich doświadczeń w Unii Europejskiej. Problemy prawnoadministracyjne*, red. J. Sługocki, t. II, Wrocław 2014, p. 275.

1127 Z. Kmieciak, *Nadużycie prawa do środka odwoławczego w postępowaniu sądowoadministracyjnym*, PiP 2011, nr 10, p. 24.

1128 A. Szpunar, *Nadużycie prawa podmiotowego*, Kraków 1947, p. 8.

1129 following: M.G. Plebanek, *Nadużycie praw procesowych w postępowaniu cywilnym*, Warszawa 2012, p. 69.

1130 M. Jaśkowska, *Nadużycie…*, op. cit., p. 32.

1131 P. Przybysz, *Nadużycie prawa w prawie administracyjnym*, [w:] red. H. Izdebski, A. Stępkowski, *Nadużycie prawa. Konferencja Wydziału Prawa i Administracji*, Warszawa 2003, p. 197.

1132 R. Cybulska, *Sprawy prywatne będące przedmiotem wniosku o udostępnienie informacji publicznej. Glosa aprobująca do wyroku Naczelnego Sądu Administracyjnego z 29 kwietnia 2020 r. (I OSK 1561/19)*, Samorząd Terytorialny 12/2023 p. 84.

administration and other bodies"[1133] It is an extension of the concept of contradiction in the use of law with its assumptions. Therefore it must be said, that it should be considered, what kind of purpose the legislator gave to the right granted to citizens to obtain public information. In this matter, it is rightly noted in the jurisprudence that act on access to public information aims at "guaranteeing the citizens the exercise of their constitutional right of access to public information (...) provisions of this act shall be interpreted in the way to provide citizens the widest possible access to public information and therefore in a case of necessary limiting the access due to necessity of securing of the other legally protected interests, there should be an opportunity to learn and understand the grounds for refusing the access to public information and possibility to check that refusal in the courts"[1134]. The act on access to public information was designed as a way to provide the ability to control and insight inside functioning and activity of state authorities. Both in its organization and financial sphere, as well as in external activities – the implementation of public functions – and also the other parties, that are obliged by the rules of the act to share public information. That regulation assumed transparency of state, as well as openness and transparency of activities undertaken by participating entities.[1135]

There should be shared J. Drachal's view that the purpose of the right to public information "is not satisfing or fulfillment of individual needs in the forms of obtaining information, even if it has public nature, but used inter alia for professional or commercial purposes or to disorganise functioning of the state."[1136].

Going through analysis of administrative court jurisprudence state that phenomenon of abusing that law is clearly visible in pointed earlier two aspects: procedural and material. It is a multi-layered activity, often of a complex nature and with deep moral or equitable foundations. As examples of abusing connected with its material character there can be entitled requests for access by unauthorized entities, cases of intellectual theft. On the other hand as examples of abusing connected with its procedural character: filing applications despite having information, asking about trivial matters, abuse of procedural institutions in ongoing

1133 J. Drachal, *Prawo do informacji publicznej w świetle wykładni funkcjonalnej*, [w:] red. J. Góral, R. Hauser, J. Trzciński, *Sądownictwo administracyjne gwarantem wolności i praw obywatelskich 1980–2005 r.*, Warszawa 2005, p. 141 i 147.

1134 Judgement of First instance Administrative Court in Rzeszów, 10 May 2017, signature II SAB/Rz 27/17.

1135 Podobnie: M. Kowalski, *Nadużycie prawa do informacji publicznej*, ZNSA 2016, nr 2, p. 51.

1136 J. Drachal, *Prawo do informacji...*, op. cit., p. 147.

court proceedings in access to public information, and finally private *vendettas* against public administration bodies. It must be said that abuse of legal permission will not apply only when someone uses the right to access public information in a way that paralyzes the normal activity of the authority and the court, but also whenever this request does not actually serve to protect public interests, as well as when the application is justified in terms of the subject matter, but the circumstances of the case confirm the thesis about the applicant's personal *vendetta*, which keeps coming up with new applications.

Unfortunately, all above leads to a statement that every day society grows its own "hydra" that paralyzes authorities and massively engages administrative judiciary. This situation shall be treated as undesirable. It consumes significant public funds and wastes time of civil servants who, instead of carrying out their daily duties, have to examine an applications submitted by one person. This also leads to the extension of the trails and dates of hearing because judges and the court staff have to examine simple cases, that are limited to indicating the provisions breached by authorities – entities obliged to provision of public information, for example in a matter of untimely response. All above harms society, which has to wait for their terms, with cases that are involved in serious legal issue that requires interpretation or intervention from the court regarding the inaction of the authority.

4. Examples of abusing the right of access to public information

During my analyses of the case law and with sharing my professional experience in this part of the resume, there should be mentioned main axes of interest of the applicants and their *modus operandi.*

1. **Politicians**
   - public information is used as an element of a political game, questions arise about access to information related to current events;[1137]
2. **Organizations specializing in obtaining public information**
   - there are many examples of associations, foundations, their statutory activity is usually focused around controlling the transparency of public life, they initiate many proceedings, they often use the services of third parties or attorneys;[1138]

1137 F.e Judgement of Supreme Administrative Court, 3 March 2023, signature III OSK 2330/21.

1138 F.e Judgement of Supreme Administrative Court 10 April 2024, signature III OSK 1632/22.

3. **Law offices**
   - *modus operandi* - submitting a request for public information for the purposes of proceedings conducted by the Law Firm or in the interest of their clients, cases often concern the individual economic interest of a rivals in public procurement proceedings, "Warsaw Decree" cases or even leads to trying to obtain entire files of civil court or even criminal proceedings;[1139]
4. **The world of science**
   - using public information to collect and analyse data, processes, positions;
5. **Journalists**
   - they exercise their right alternatively to "press information" under provisions by another act;[1140]
6. **The so-called "Vexatious litigators"**
   - who are using all possible procedural ways to impede daily activity of public administration and the judiciary in Poland[1141];
7. **Natural persons conducting a private *vendetta***
   - how do they differ from Vexatious litigators? They usually wage war against a specific authority, while the First Instance Administrative Courts and the Supreme Administrative Court "only ricochet" the matter; the matters are often private, very local[1142];
8. **People requesting trivial information:**
   - here I would like to present a few cases in which a trivial request was made:
     1. The complainant submitted numerous applications "demanding various information on the functioning of the employment office, that started after the authority terminated the contract with her mother (represented by the complainant) regarding the reimbursement of the costs of equipping workstations due to failure to comply with the terms of the contract. (…) The complainant's behaviour is characterized by persistence in submitting subsequent applications."[1143]

1139 F.e Judgement of Supreme Administrative Court, 17 November 2023, signature III OSK 6547/21.

1140 F.e Judgement of Supreme Administrative Court, 1 December 2023, signature III OSK 517/23.

1141 F.e Judgement of Supreme Administrative Court, 1 July 2022, signature III OSK 1241/21.

1142 F.e Judgement of First instance Administrative Court in Warsaw, 24 March 2020, signature II SAB/Wa 864/19.

1143 Judgement of First instance Administrative Court in Kielce, 20 March 2019 r., signature II SAB/Ke 6/19.

2. The Supreme Administrative Court pointed out that information about the place of residence of a common court judge is neither information about the activities of public authorities nor information about the activities of persons performing public functions.[1144]
3. The date of birth of a judge or prosecutor as public information.[1145]
4. And my favorite, which I have seen for years, addressed to Public Broadcaster regarding answers to questions from the song that was the intro to a children's program, asking about where the sun is when it sleeps, whether the wolf is always angry and where does the hedgehog go at night?[1146]

Of course, there can not be forgotten that some applications are still submitted in compliance with the provisions of the Act on Access to Public Information, its purpose, and by those whose will is to obtain specific public information without abusing the law.

5. Ways of combat with the abuse of the right to public information

It is necessary to distinguish individual activities depending on the place of prevention of abuse. As points M. Jaśkowska – sharing the opinion of A. Piskorz-Ryń – while "previous supporters of the concept of abuse argued for the necessity to legally regulate it due to existing legal loopholes, they did not associate it with limiting the right to a fair trial."[1147]. In few European countries, the legislator has created specific legal norms "containing general clauses or vague phrases enabling obliged entities to refuse access to information due to the nature of the request, as well as specific regulations".[1148] It must be clearly stated here that the right to obtain public information is not absolute assuming the right of every person to receive any information about the activities of state institutions. It already has its statutory restrictions on disclosure. Therefore, it may be worth considering *de lege ferenda* amendment to both provisions of act of proceedings before administrative

1144 Judgement of Supreme Administrative Court 21 April 2017 r., signature I OSK 1953/15.

1145 Judgement of Supreme Administrative Court, 5 January 2017 r., signature I OSK 2569/15.

1146 https://images.app.goo.gl/J5h4TPvHxKrLU2Xy9 (30.06.2024 r.).

1147 M. Jaśkowska, *Nadużycie…*, op. cit., p. 39.

1148 *Ibidem*.

courts[1149] and provisions of act on access to public information - in accordance with and respecting protected constitutional values, such as ensuring the party's right to a court or the right to information.

Moving forward to possible solutions of counteracts against phenomenon of abusing the right to public information during the administrative judicial proceedings, there should be mentioned that one sufficient seems to be limiting the possibility for the court party, in cases which are consistent with this matter, to ask for exemption or for achieving court-appointed attorney. Furthermore also risen of the court fees could be great idea. It is worth to be said that itself value has not been indexed for years. Since 2003, there are strict, low fees in some cases, and what is hard to believe, even with amount of 200 PLN for the action before administrative court against the act and 100 PLN for the action before administrative court against the inactivity of a state authorities, parties still can apply for exemption from court fees. All above causes yearly enlargement of complaints to the administrative courts.[1150]

There should be mentioned that disabling possibility of asking for exemption from court costs or for achieving court-appointed attorney can be treated as limiting civil liberties. On the other hand this solution can be limited just to disabling possibility of asking for exemption from court costs nor the attorneys, or to limit that right only after the judgement of first instance court is given. In this case, the party still be able to submit legal remedies that requires attorneys.

This kind of changes connected with the limitation or banning possibility of claiming for the judge exclusion could have positive impact on the length of the trail. Both there will be less cases and those that are in conduct, would have been solved faster. Yet to be mentioned that true is that institution of judge exclusion is a guarantee of its impartiality in the process, but this right also can be abused in way designed only for extending terms in process and particularly further extension of the waiting time for the case to be heard.

The question that remains open is how to cope with trivial cases? The concept adopted in the Anglo-Saxon model assumes no protection for this type of "vexatious litigation".[1151] Current legal system allows the Court to dismiss a complaint against a state decision that refuse to provide information due to the trivial nature of the request. Of course there is no provision in the Act on access to public information for that kind of legal structure. In line with the case law, it is noted that

---

1149 ustawa z dnia 30 sierpnia 2002 r. – Prawo o postępowaniu przed sądami administracyjnymi (Dz. U. z 2023 r., poz. 1634, dalej: „p.p.s.a.").

1150 Similary points M. Jaśkowska, *Nadużycie...*, op. cit., p. 27.

1151 M. Jaśkowska, *Nadużycie...*, op. cit., p. 39.

"in the context of abuse of the right to information, the practice of jointly assessing applications addressed to various (dispersed) authorities is even approved - in order to eliminate the so-called salami practice."[1152]

However, all above will not reduce the number of cases, because over the years society has believed that you are allowed to ask everyone about everything. Also, a potential amendment introducing an additional ground for refusal, and therefore resulting as a decision, will result in same amount of cases. The only difference that can be predicted is that they would be shorter and more repeatable. In turn, omitting the decision and granting entities obliged to provide public information the right to decide in the form of a non-decision action – simple response paper – would also cause another increase the number of complaints addressed to administrative courts, but this time for inaction, nor against decisions. The court will be obliged to decide not only whether the information is a public information, but also whether the request is not trivial. However, it seems that the potential arbitrary right of the obliged entity to leave the application unconsidered – without further judicial review – is in contradiction with the previously indicated constitutional principles and would not constitute consequences of the legislator.

6. Concluding remarks

The phenomenon of abusing of access to public information seemed to become serious problem for modern civil societies in democratic state of law. Individuals make use of their granted rights in contrary to rule intended purpose and in way that paralyzes daily conduct and activities of state authorities and courts.

It seems to be reasonable to demand amending act of proceedings before administrative courts in way of limiting some granted procedural rights like ability to apply for judge or division official exclusion or ask for exemption from court fees or for achieving court-appointed attorney. There is an open issue, but it seems to be right that also act of access to public information shall be amended with including it its provision another prerequisite of refusal to obtain information due to its trivial nature or the abuse of rights, that will slightly shorten refusal procedure.

There should be mentioned that lack of any kind of activity, will result in occurring more and more negative consequences in daily state offices and administrative courts activities and efficiency, particularly in the further extension of the time wasted for any case to be heard.

1152 Judgement of Supreme Administrative Court, 26 January 2023 r., signature III OSK 7265/21.

Bibliography

Cybulska R., Sprawy prywatne będące przedmiotem wniosku o udostępnienie informacji publicznej. Glosa aprobująca do wyroku Naczelnego Sądu Administracyjnego z 29 kwietnia 2020 r. (I OSK 1561/19), Samorząd Terytorialny 12/2023.

Drachal J., Prawo do informacji publicznej w świetle wykładni funkcjonalnej, [w:] red. Góral J., Hauser R., Trzciński J., Sądownictwo administracyjne gwarantem wolności i praw obywatelskich 1980–2005 r., Warszawa 2005.

Jabłoński M,, Wygoda K. [w:] Ustawa o dostępie do informacji publicznej. Komentarz, red. Piskorz-Ryń A., Sakowska-Baryła M., Warszawa 2023.

Jaśkowska M., Nadużycie publicznego prawa podmiotowego jako przesłanka ograniczenia dostępu do sądu w sprawach z zakresu informacji publicznej, ZNSA 2018, nr 1.

Jaśkowska M., Ponowne wykorzystanie informacji publicznej, [w:] Dziesięć lat polskich doświadczeń w Unii Europejskiej. Problemy prawnoadministracyjne, red. Sługocki J., t. II, Wrocław 2014.

Kmieciak Z., Nadużycie prawa do środka odwoławczego w postępowaniu sądowoadministracyjnym, PiP 2011, nr 10.

Kowalski M., Nadużycie prawa do informacji publicznej, ZNSA 2016, nr 2.

Plebanek M.G., Nadużycie praw procesowych w postępowaniu cywilnym, Warszawa 2012.

Przybysz P., Nadużycie prawa w prawie administracyjnym, [w:] red. Izdebski H., Stępkowski A., Nadużycie prawa. Konferencja Wydziału Prawa i Administracji, Warszawa 2003.

Szpunar A., Nadużycie prawa podmiotowego, Kraków 1947.

Acts of law

Constitution of Republic of Poland (Dz. U. z 1997 r. nr 78 poz. 483).

Ustawa z dnia 6 września 2001 r. o dostępie do informacji publicznej (Dz. U. z 2022 r. poz. 902).

Ustawa z dnia 30 sierpnia 2002 r. – Prawo o postępowaniu przed sądami administracyjnymi (Dz. U. z 2023 r., poz. 1634).

Case Law

Judgement of NSA, 25 march 2003, signature II SA 4059/02, all judgments of administrative courts available and published in the Central Database of Administrative Court Judgments at: http://orzeczenia.nsa.gov.pl.

Judgement of Supreme Administrative Court, 3 march 2023, signature III OSK 2330/21.

Judgement of First instance Administrative Court in Rzeszów, 10 may 2017, signature II SAB/Rz 27/17.

Judgement of Supreme Administrative Court 10 April 2024, signature III OSK 1632/22.

Judgement of Supreme Administrative Court, 17 November 2023, signature III OSK 6547/21.

Judgement of Supreme Administrative Court, 1 December 2023, signature III OSK 517/23.

Judgement of Supreme Administrative Court, 1 July 2022, signature III OSK 1241/21.

Judgement of First instance Administrative Court in Warsaw, 24 March 2020, signature II SAB/Wa 864/19.

Judgement of First instance Administrative Court in Kielce, 20 March 2019 r., signature II SAB/Ke 6/19.

Judgement of Supreme Administrative Court 21 April 2017 r., signature I OSK 1953/15.

Judgement of Supreme Administrative Court, 5 January 2017 r., signature I OSK 2569/15.

Judgement of Supreme Administrative Court, 26 January 2023 r., signature III OSK 7265/21.

Ius, Lex et Res Publica
Studies in Law, Philosophy and Political Cultures

Edited by
Barbara Janusz-Pohl

Vol. 1 Anna Jaron: Socio-Economic Constitutional Rights in Democratisation Processes. An Account of the Constitutional Dialogue Theory. 2012.

Vol. 2 Stanisław Filipowicz: Democracy – The Power of Illusion. 2013.

Vol. 3 Teresa Dukiet-Nagórska (ed.): The Postulates of Restorative Justice and the Continental Model of Criminal Law. As Illustrated by Polish Criminal Law 2014.

Vol. 4 Agnieszka Kupzok: Enforcement of Patents on Geographically Divisible Inventions. An Inquiry into the Standard of Substantive Patent Law Infringement in Cross-Border Constellations. 2015.

Vol. 5 Alicja Jagielska-Burduk / Wojciech Szafrański: Legal Issues in Cultural Heritage Management. A Polish Perspective. 2016.

Vol. 6 Maciej Mataczyński (ed.): The Takeover of Public Companies as a Mode of Exercising EU Treaty Freedoms. 2017.

Vol. 7 Maciej Barczewski (ed.): Value of Information. Intellectual Property, Privacy and Big Data. 2018.

Vol. 8 Pawel Smoleń, Marcin Burzec: Introduction to Polish Tax Law. 2018.

Vol. 9 Łukasz Pohl, Konrad Burdziak: Judicial Interpretation of the 1997 Criminal Code Provisions on Self-Defence. 2019.

Vol. 10 Adam Szot: Judicial Review of Administrative Discretion. The Influence of Court Decisions on Administrative Actions. 2019.

Vol. 11 Michał Peno / Konrad Burdziak (eds.): The Concept of Modern Law. Polish and Central European Tradition. 2019.

Vol. 12 Leszek Leszczyński / Bartosz Lińewski / Adam Szot (eds.): Potential of Precedent in the Statutory Legal Order. 2019.

Vol. 13 Łukasz Bolesta: In Search of a Model for the Legal Protection of a Whistleblower in the Workplace in Poland. A legal and comparative study. 2020.

Vol. 14 Paweł Chmielnicki / Adam Sulikowski (eds.): New Perspectives on Legislation. A Comparative Approach. 2020.

Vol. 15 Marcin Burzec / Beata Kucia-Guściora / Paweł Smoleś: Agricultural Activity in Poland: A Fiscal and Legal Study. 2020.

Vol. 16 Magdalena Półtorak / Ilona Topa (eds.): Women, Children and (Other) Vulnerable Groups. Standards of Protection and Challenges for International Law. 2021.

Vol. 17 Josef Albert Fox: Die polnische Verfassung vom 3. Mai 1791. Hintergründe der Entstehung und der Außerkraftsetzung. Stellung Polens im Zeitalter der Aufklärung. 2021.

Vol. 18 Barbara Janusz-Pohl (ed.): Juvenile Justice Systems: Poland-Brazil-Portugal. 2021.

Vol. 19 Leszek Leszczyński: General Reference Clauses in the Judicial Process. Context of Legislative Intentions Interpretative Discretion. 2021.

Vol. 20 Francisco J. Campos Zamora: Das Problem der Begründung richterlicher Entscheidungen. Eine Analyse auf der Grundlage der Theorie der juristischen Argumentation. 2021.

Vol. 21 Aneta Skorupa-Wulczyńska: Language Rights of the Citizen of the European Union. 2022.

Vol. 22 Mateusz Osiecki: International Legal Aspects of Aerial Terrorism. Methods of Law Enforcement in Aviation. 2022.

Vol. 23 Vladimír Sharp / Gabriela Blahoudková / Jakub Handrlica (eds.): Law, Pandemics and Ownership Restrictions. 2022.

Vol. 24 Piotr Kasprzyk / Anna Konert: Drones – Future of Aviation Law? Interference of Public Law in Private Law. 2023.

Vol. 25 Szymon Pawelec (ed.): Consensual Mechanisms in Criminal Proceedings – Integrative and Comparative Perspective. 2023.

Vol. 26 Dorota Pudzianowska: Statelessness in Public Law. 2023.

Vol. 27 Boguslaw Przywora / Aleksander Wróbel: Formalised Access to Pre-jurisdictional Free Legal Aid. 2023.

Vol. 28 Ewa Dawidziuk / Patricia Panero / Anny Tarwacka (eds.): Family, Law, and Society: from Roman Law to the Present Day. 2024.

Vol. 29 Marian Grzybowsk / Boguslaw Przywora / Aleksandra Syryt (eds.): Free Legal Aid, Theory, Legal Basis and Practice. European Standards. 2024.

Vol. 30 Karolina Gmerek: Trial as a Social Communication Occurrence. 2024.

Vol. 31 Pawel Wiliński (ed.): Effective Legal Remedies in Criminal Justice System. European Perspective. 2024.

Vol. 32 Jakub Hanc / Olga Sitarz / Anna Jaworska-Wieloch: On the (non)existence of the right to religious freedom of persons deprived of liberty. 2024.

Vol. 33 Marian Grzybowsk / Boguslaw Przywora / Aleksandra Syryt (eds.): Free Legal Aid – A Comparative Approach. 2024.

Vol. 34 Dominik Gajewski (ed.): Functioning of Administrative Judiciary in the Context of Economic Changes. 2024.

Vol. 35 Mikołajczyk, Barbara: Older Migrants – Vulnerable and Excluded. 2024.

Vol. 36 Świder, Maciej: The Exercise of the Right to a Fair Trial in the Era of the COVID-19 Pandemic. 2024.

Vol. 37 Tomasz Barankiewicz / Boguslaw Przywora (eds.): Public and Civil Service in Poland. 2024.

Vol. 38 Daniele Vicoli (ed.): Effective Justice 1. Effective Justice. International and Comparative Approaches. 2025.

Vol. 39 Barbara Janusz-Pohl (ed.): Effective Justice 2. Effective Justice. International and Comparative Approaches. 2025.

Vol. 40 Kinga Anna Gajda / Marta Pietras-Eichberger / Małgorzata Skawińska (eds.): Mediation as an Inclusive and Sustainable Method of Resolving Conflicts. 2025.

Vol. 41 Ewa Dawidziuk / Anna Tarwacka / Sławomir Kursa (eds.): Historical and Contemporary Issues of Democracy, Person and Human Rights. 2025.

www.peterlang.com

www.ingramcontent.com/pod-product-compliance
Ingram Content Group UK Ltd.
Pitfield, Milton Keynes, MK11 3LW, UK
UKHW020833290926
15470UKWH00004B/1325

9 783631 928349